June 6–8, 2016
Shanghai, China

Association for Computing Machinery

Advancing Computing as a Science & Profession

SACMAT'16

Proceedings of the 21st ACM

Symposium on Access Control Models and Technologies

Sponsored by:

ACM SIGSAC

Association for Computing Machinery

Advancing Computing as a Science & Profession

The Association for Computing Machinery
2 Penn Plaza, Suite 701
New York, New York 10121-0701

Notice to Past Authors of ACM-Published Articles
ACM intends to create a complete electronic archive of all articles and/or other material previously published by ACM. If you have written a work that has been previously published by ACM in any journal or conference proceedings prior to 1978, or any SIG Newsletter at any time, and you do NOT want this work to appear in the ACM Digital Library, please inform permissions@acm.org, stating the title of the work, the author(s), and where and when published.

ISBN: 978-1-4503-3802-8 (Digital)

ISBN: 978-1-4503-4598-9 (Print)

Additional copies may be ordered prepaid from:

ACM Order Department
PO Box 30777
New York, NY 10087-0777, USA

Phone: 1-800-342-6626 (USA and Canada)
+1-212-626-0500 (Global)
Fax: +1-212-944-1318
E-mail: acmhelp@acm.org
Hours of Operation: 8:30 am – 4:30 pm ET

Printed in the USA

General Chair and PC Chairs' Welcome

It is our great pleasure to welcome you to the ACM Symposium on Access Control Models and Technologies (SACMAT 2016), taking place in Shanghai, China, on June 6-8, 2016. This is the 21st edition of the symposium series, continuing the tradition of being the premier forum for presentation of research results and experience reports on leading edge issues of access control in terms of models, systems, applications, and theory. The symposium aims to share novel access control solutions that fulfill the needs of heterogeneous applications and environments, and to identify new directions for future research and development. SACMAT provides researchers and practitioners with a unique opportunity to share their perspectives with others interested in the various aspects of access control, aside from visiting the various attractions offered by the big international metropolis Shanghai.

This year, 55 abstracts and papers were submitted from a variety of countries around the world. Submissions were anonymous; each paper has been reviewed by at least three reviewers who are experts in the field. Extensive online discussions took place to make the selections for the symposium. The program committee finally accepted 18 papers as full papers and 3 papers as short ones for presentation at the symposium. The topics covered include network and mobile access control, access control in applications, policy engineering, access control specification and access control enforcement.

In addition to the main research paper sessions, the symposium offers a panel discussion session entitled "Security and privacy in the era of Internet of Things: research opportunities and challenges", and a poster session. Above all, the conference proudly presents three exciting keynote talks by Virgil Gligor of Carnegie Mellon University, Bhavani Thuraisingham of University of Texas at Dallas, and Robert Deng of Singapore Management University, respectively.

Putting together SACTMAT'16 has been a team effort. We wish to thank all the authors who provided the basic content of the symposium program. We are very grateful to the organizers of the symposium, including all the chairs. Special thanks go to the SACMAT Steering Committee Chair Gail-Joon Ahn of Arizona State University for the overall guidance, and the Local Organization Chair Weili Han of Fudan University for the smooth running of the symposium. We also wish to thank the CITS Shanghai staff for providing much of the logistic support, and the Fudan University students who volunteered their time to help out.

We hope that you will find the symposium interesting and thought-provoking. Enjoy SACMAT 2016!

X. Sean Wang
General Chair
Fudan University, China

Lujo Bauer
PC co-Chair
Carnegie Mellon Univ., USA

Florian Kerschbaum
PC co-Chair
SAP, Germany

Table of Contents

Session: Access Control Specification

Session: Access Control Enforcement

SACMAT 2016 Symposium Organization

General Chair:	X. Sean Wang (Fudan University, China)
Program Chairs:	Lujo Bauer (Carnegie Mellon University, USA) Florian Kerschbaum (SAP, Germany)
Panels Chair:	Jianwei Niu (University of Texas at San Antonio, USA)
Proceedings Chair:	Hongxin Hu (Clemson University, USA)
Demonstrations Chair:	Hassan Takabi (University of North Texas, USA)
Poster Chairs:	Adam Lee (University of Pittsburgh, USA) William Garrison (University of Pittsburgh, USA)
Local Arrangements Chair:	Weili Han (Fudan University, China)
Publicity Chair:	Yulong Shen (Xidian University, China)
Web Master:	Dongwan Shin (New Mexico Tech, USA)
Treasurer:	Basit Shafiq (LUMS, Pakistan)
Steering Committee Chair:	Gail-Joon Ahn (Arizona State University, USA)
Steering Committee:	Axel Kern (Beta Systems Software AG, Germany) Barbara Carminati (University of Insubria, Italy) Bhavani Thuraisingham (University of Texas at Dallas, USA) Indrakshi Ray (Colorado State University, USA) James Joshi (University of Pittsburgh, USA) Ninghui Li (Purdue University, USA)
Program Committee:	Adam Aviv (US Naval Academy, USA) Sherman S. M. Chow (Chinese University of Hong Kong, Hong Kong) Jason Crampton (Royal Holloway, University of London, UK) Isao Echizen (National Institute of Informatics, Japan) Philip W. L. Fong (University of Calgary, Canada) Weili Han (Fudan University, China) Hannes Hartenstein (Karlsruhe Institute of Technology, Germany) Urs Hengartner (University of Waterloo, Canada) Trent Jaeger (Pennsylvania State University, USA) Limin Jia (Carnegie Mellon University, USA) Ghassan Karame (NEC Laboratories Europe, Germany) Adam J. Lee (University of Pittsburgh, USA) Ninghui Li (Purdue University, USA)

Sponsor:

State-aware Network Access Management for Software-Defined Networks

Wonkyu Han[†], Hongxin Hu[‡], Ziming Zhao[†], Adam Doupé[†],
Gail-Joon Ahn[†], Kuang-Ching Wang[‡], and Juan Deng[‡]
[†]Arizona State University   [‡]Clemson University
{whan7, zzhao30, doupe, gahn}@asu.edu, {hongxih, kwang, jdeng}@clemson.edu

ABSTRACT

OpenFlow, as the prevailing technique for Software-Defined Networks (SDNs), introduces significant programmability, granularity, and flexibility for many network applications to effectively manage and process network flows. However, because OpenFlow attempts to keep the SDN data plane simple and efficient, it focuses solely on L2/L3 network transport and consequently lacks the fundamental ability of stateful forwarding for the data plane. Also, OpenFlow provides a very limited access to connection-level information in the SDN controller. In particular, for any network access management applications on SDNs that require comprehensive network state information, these inherent limitations of OpenFlow pose significant challenges in supporting network services. To address these challenges, we propose an innovative connection tracking framework called STATEMON that introduces a global state-awareness to provide better access control in SDNs. STATE-MON is based on a lightweight extension of OpenFlow for programming the stateful SDN data plane, while keeping the underlying network devices as simple as possible. To demonstrate the practicality and feasibility of STATEMON, we implement and evaluate a *stateful network firewall* and *port knocking* applications for SDNs, using the APIs provided by STATEMON. Our evaluations show that STATEMON introduces minimal message exchanges for monitoring active connections in SDNs with manageable overhead (3.27% throughput degradation).

1. INTRODUCTION

Over the past few years, Software-Defined Networks (SDNs) have evolved from purely an idea [12, 13, 18] to a new paradigm that several networking vendors are not only embracing, but also pursuing as their model for future enterprise network management. According to a recent report from Google, SDN-based network management helped them run their WAN at close to 100% utilization compared to other state-of-the-art network environments with about 30% to 40% network utilization [22].

As the first widely adopted standard for SDNs, OpenFlow [28] essentially separates the control plane and the data plane of a network device and enables the network control to become directly programmable as well as the underlying infrastructure to be abstracted for network applications. With OpenFlow, only the data plane exists in the network device, and all control decisions are conveyed to the device through a logically-centralized controller. In this way, OpenFlow can tremendously help administrators access and update configurations of network devices in a timely and convenient manner and provide this ease of control to SDN applications as well.

While the abstraction of a logically centralized controller, which is a core principle of SDNs is powerful, a fundamental limitation of OpenFlow is *the lack of capability to enable the maintenance of network connection states inside both the controller and switches*. First, OpenFlow-enabled switches only forward the first packet of a new flow to the controller so that the controller can make a centralized routing decision. Because the controller is unaware of subsequent packets of the flow, including those that change the state of a network connection (e.g., TCP FIN), the controller has no knowledge of the state of the connections in its network. Second, OpenFlow-enabled switches are incapable of monitoring network connection states as well. The "match-action" abstraction of OpenFlow heavily relies on L2/L3 fields (e.g., src_ip and dst_ip) and the limited L4 fields (only src_port and dst_port), yet essential information for identifying and maintaining the state of connections is contained in other L4 fields, such as TCP flags and TCP sequence and acknowledgment numbers.

The lack of knowledge of network connection states in SDNs brings significant challenges in building *state-aware* access control management schemes [30]. In particular, some critical security services, such as stateful network firewalls that perform network-wide access control, cannot be realized in SDNs. A stateful network firewall, which is a key network access control service in a traditional network environment [17, 20, 34] and requires state-awareness, keeps track of the states of connections in the network and makes a decision for its access (e.g., ALLOW or DENY) according to the states of connections in networks. However, it is impossibly hard to realize them in current SDNs due to the inherent limitations of OpenFlow.

Some recent research efforts [29, 30, 14, 36, 11, 6, 10, 37] extended the OpenFlow data plane abstraction to support stateful network applications. They attempted to let individual switches, rather than the controller, track the state of connections. We believe that, not only does this design go against the spirit of SDN (because it brings the control plane back to switches and makes switches manipulate connection states and performs complex actions beyond a simple forwarding operation), these existing approaches are only applicable for designing applications that need only *local states* on a single switch [10]. However, such solutions force SDN applications individually access every single switch to collect entire

SACMAT'16, June 05-08, 2016, Shanghai, China
© 2016 ACM. ISBN 978-1-4503-3802-8/16/06. . . $15.00
DOI: http://dx.doi.org/10.1145/2914642.2914643

network states, consequently network-wide monitoring to detect abnormalities and enforcing network-wide access control of flows become extremely difficult.

To overcome the limitations of existing approaches, we argue that utilizing the SDN controller for *global* tracking connections is more advantageous than existing solutions in terms of its state visibility across SDN applications that is crucial to some security applications such as a stateful network firewall. To bring such a *state-aware* network access management in SDNs, we propose a novel state tracking framework called STATEMON. STATEMON models active connections in SDNs and monitors *global* connection states in the controller with the help of both a *global state table* that records the current state of each active connection and a *state management table* that governs the state transition of new and existing connections. STATEMON also introduces a lightweight extension to OpenFlow, called *OpenConnection*, that programs the data plane to forward the state-changing packets to the controller. At the same time, it retains the simple "match-action" programmable feature of OpenFlow and avoids scalability problems over the communication channel between the controller and switches. In essence, STATEMON follows the general SDN principle of logical-to-physical decoupling and avoids embedding complicated control logic in the physical devices, therefore, keeping the SDN data plane as simple as possible.

In addition, to demonstrate the practicality and feasibility of STATEMON and state-aware network access management applications in SDNs, we design a stateful network firewall based on the APIs provided by STATEMON. Our firewall application provides more in-depth access control than a stateless SDN firewall [21]. It detects and resolves connection disruptions and unauthorized access attempts targeting active connections in SDNs. To demonstrate the generality of STATEMON, we re-implement a prior work (port knocking) based on STATEMON (Section 5.2.3). Our experimental results show that STATEMON and network access management applications (stateful firewall and port knocking) introduce manageable performance overhead to manage network access control.

Contributions: The contributions are summarized as follows:

- We propose a connection tracking framework called STATEMON that enables SDN to support state-aware access control schemes by leveraging global network states. STATEMON keeps the data plane as simple as possible, thus being compliant with the spirit of SDN's design principle.

- We propose the *OpenConnection* protocol, which is a lightweight extension to OpenFlow and retains the simple "match-action" programmable feature of OpenFlow to enable a stateful SDN data plane.

- We implement a prototype of STATEMON using Floodlight [1] and Open vSwitch. Our experiments demonstrate that STATEMON introduces a minimal increase of communication messages with manageable performance overhead (3.27% throughput degradation).

- We design a stateful network firewall application, using the APIs provided by STATEMON. Our experiments show that the stateful firewall provides more control than existing stateless firewalls and it can effectively detect and mitigate certain connection-related attacks (e.g., connection disruptions and unauthorized access) in SDNs.

This paper is organized as follows. We overview the motivating problems in Section 2. Section 3 presents the design of state-

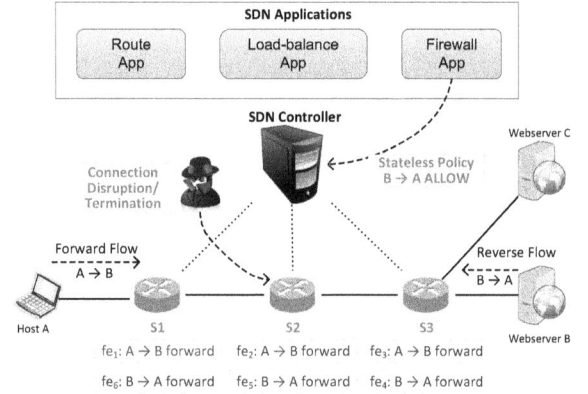

Figure 1: Standard OpenFlow Operation and its Stateless Property.

aware STATEMON. Section 4 describes the design of stateful network firewall supported by STATEMON, and the implementation and evaluation details are in Section 5. Section 6 discusses the related work of this paper, and Section 7 describes several important issues. In Section 8, we conclude this paper.

2. BACKGROUND AND PROBLEM STATEMENT

To understand our proposed solution to adding state-awareness to SDNs, we provide an overview of the current OpenFlow operation. When an OpenFlow-enabled switch receives a packet, it first checks its *flow tables* to find matching rules. If no such rules exist, this means it is the first packet of a new flow. The switch then forwards the packet to the controller, and it is the controller's job to decide how to handle the flow and to install flow table rules in the appropriate switches. Specifically, the packet is encapsulated in an `OFPT_PACKET_IN` message sent to the controller, and the controller then installs corresponding rules called *flow entries* into the switches along the controller's intended path for the flow. Once these flow entries are installed, all subsequent packets of this flow are automatically forwarded by the switches, without sending the packet to the controller.

For example, in Figure 1, host A wants to initiate a TCP connection with web server B. The first packet (TCP SYN) sent by host A is checked by the ingress switch S1 and forwarded to the controller because S1 has no flow table entry for the packet. The controller allows the flow from host A to server B by installing flow entries fe_1, fe_2, and fe_3, into switches S1, S2, and S3, respectively. The flow from host A to server B is called a *forward flow*. Using the same process, the response packet (TCP SYNACK) generated by server B will trigger the controller to install fe_4, fe_5, and fe_6 into S3, S2, and S1, respectively. The flow from server B to host A is called a *reverse flow*.

As can be seen from Figure 1, neither the OpenFlow-enabled switch nor the controller has the ability to track and maintain connection states, which makes it impossible to directly develop stateful access control based on OpenFlow in SDNs. As a result, existing SDN controllers (e.g., Floodlight) only have a stateless firewall application that enforces ACL (Access Control List) rules to monitor all `OFPT_PACKET_IN` behaviors.

Using Figure 1 as an example, these stateless firewall applications can only specify simple rules, such as "packets from server B to host A are allowed." In contrast, a *stateful* firewall is a critical component in traditional systems and networks which provides more control over whether a packet is allowed or denied based on

Table 1: Existing Stateful Inspection and Management Methodologies for SDNs (D = data plane, C = control plane, A = application plane).

Solution	Inspection			Storage			Implementation	Description
	D	C	A	D	C	A		
App-aware [29]	✓			✓			FW, LB	Maintain App-table in a switch; A switch performs handshaking on behalf of servers.
FAST [30]	✓			✓			FW	Controller compiles the state machine and installs it into switches.
FlowTags [14, 15]	✓		✓			✓	Proxy cache	Add tags to in-flight packets for keeping middleboxes' state rather than checking state via switches or the controller.
OpenNF [16]	✓	✓			✓		IDS, Net-Monitor	OpenNF enables dynamic migration of middlebox states from one to another by supporting some operations (e.g., move, copy and share).
UMON [36]	✓			✓			SW Switch	Put UMON tables in the middle of OpenvSwitch pipelines to perform anomaly detection.
P4 [11]	✓			✓	✓		-	A proposal for embedding programmable parser inside of switches to allow administrators to flexibly configure and define the data plane.
Conntrack [6]	✓			✓			SW Switch	Build the conntrack module on top of existing OpenvSwitch implementation to enable stateful tracking of flows.
OpenState [10]	✓			✓			SW Switch	Perform state checking using the state table in conjunction with an extended finite state machine that is directly programmable by the controller.
SDPA [37]	✓			✓			FW, HW Switch	Insert the forwarding processor in packet processing pipeline to enable stateful forwarding scheme; It also includes hardware-based design.
STATEMON	✓	✓			✓		FW, Port-Knock	Using OpenConnection protocol, the controller centrally manages network states and provides them to SDN applications via APIs.

connection state information. For example, a stateful firewall rule could specify "packets from server B to host A are allowed, if and only if host A initiates the connection to server B." These stateful rules are incredibly useful for security purposes, for instance to specify that a web server should be able to accept incoming connections but never initiate an outgoing connection. However, despite the great security benefit of these stateful policies, it is challenging to build a stateful firewall in SDNs without the full support of stateful packet inspection [21], which is critical to provide effective network access control management.

In addition to the development of a stateful firewall application, the knowledge of connection states in SDNs can also help maintain the network's availability. The SDN controller and applications can install, update, or delete flow entries for their own purposes. However, *these actions may interrupt established connections*, which may consequently damage the availability of services in the network. Consider the case of a load balancer application, which switches flows between two web servers (Servers B and C in Figure 1). If the flows are changed while a network connection is still in progress, the availability of the service would be affected. Also, attackers, who are able to perform a man-in-the-middle attack on OpenFlow-enabled switches [9], can also disrupt existing connections in the network by intentionally updating flow entries. The root cause of these issues is that the controller and the SDN applications have no knowledge of the connection states, which results in creating potential chances of unauthorized access into existing connections by attackers. We argue that a critical functionality of OpenFlow or any other SDN implementation is that the controller should be able to identify the conflicts between active connections and any pending flow entry update and provide network administrators with an early warning before a conflicting flow entry takes effect. Existing verification tools [23, 24, 25, 27] cannot detect and address such conflicts, *because they are unaware of connection states in the network.* By tracking global connection states in the network, the controller will be able to deal with such conflicts and help maintain the availability of the services in the network.

We summarize existing solutions in Table 1 that are mostly applicable only for designing applications that need states locally. Among those solutions, only OpenNF [16] and P4 [11] attempt to utilize the control plane of SDNs for state checking and consolidating network states. OpenNF focuses on collecting states of network middleboxes (e.g., IDS, Net-Monitor) to support dynamic middlebox migration, and P4 is a proposal for next generation of OpenFlow to support state inspections. However, the former is not applicable for collecting generic network states (e.g., connection state), and the latter does not include a workable implementation. Thus, we argue that a global connection monitoring framework, which can be aggregated by the controller, is imperative for network-wide connection monitoring and access management. Such a global connection awareness not only enables stateful firewall applications to detect *indirect* policy violations considering *dynamic packet modi-*

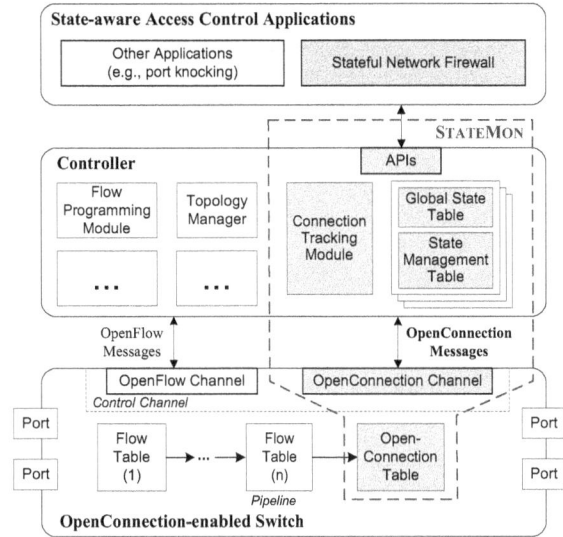

Figure 2: STATEMON Architecture Overview

fication in SDNs, but also helps identify connection disruptions and unauthorized access occurred in existing connections.

3. STATEMON DESIGN

In this section, we first present the key design goals of our STATEMON framework. Then, we illustrate the overall architecture and working modules of STATEMON and further show how they meet our design goals.

3.1 Design Goals

To enable stateful access management applications and overcome the limitations of existing approaches, we propose a novel state-aware connection tracking framework called STATEMON to support building stateful network firewall for SDNs. STATEMON is designed with the following goals in mind:

- **Centralization**: STATEMON should, in adhering to the principles of SDN, manage a global view of all network connection states in a centralized manner at the control plane.

- **Generalization**: STATEMON should support any state-based protocols and provide state information to SDN applications.

- **High Scalability**: STATEMON should minimize message exchanges between the controller and switches so that the control channel will not be the performance bottleneck when monitoring all network connection states.

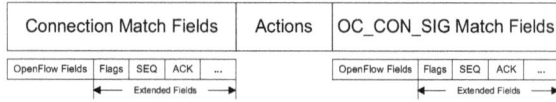

Figure 3: Structure of An Entry in An OpenConnection Table.

3.2 STATEMON Architecture Overview

Figure 2 shows an overview of the STATEMON architecture, which adds new modules in both the control plane (controller) and the data plane (switches) of the OpenFlow system architecture.

To achieve the centralization goal, STATEMON modules in switches use only the match-action abstraction to perform packet lookups, forwarding, and other actions based on the *OpenConnection* table (Section 3.3), whereas modules in the controller track a global view of states (Section 3.4). A controller uses the *OpenConnection* protocol to program *OpenConnection* tables, which are added to the OpenFlow processing pipeline by introducing a "Goto OpenConnection Table" instruction (Goto-OCT) in OpenFlow action set.

To achieve the generality goal, STATEMON maintains a pair of global state table and state management table for each state-aware application. A state-aware application initializes those tables and registers callback functions using the APIs provided by STATEMON. The global state table records network-wide connection state information. Each entry in this table represents an active connection by specifying the flow entries that govern the active connection (e.g., $fe_1, \cdots, fe_6$ in Figure 1) and its connection state (e.g., ESTABLISHED in TCP). The state management table keeps state transition rules and actions that should be performed on each state (e.g., send an OpenConnection message to the controller).

STATEMON uses three methods to minimize the communication overhead between the controller and switches to meet the high scalability design goal. First, STATEMON leverages existing OpenFlow protocols such as OFPT_PACKET_IN message for monitoring connection states. For example, the first packet of a new flow delivered by OFPT_PACKET_IN message would not trigger a separate OpenConnection message. Second, STATEMON identifies ingress and egress switches for each connection and only installs necessary OpenConnection entries into those switches to perform a state-based inspection. Thus, STATEMON minimizes the increase of additional table entries and avoids the potential overhead that can be generated by other intermediate switches on the path. Third, the OpenConnection protocol sends only expected state-changing packets from switches to the controller.

3.3 OpenConnection Protocol

On receipt of a packet, an OpenConnection-enabled switch starts with the OpenFlow-based packet process. For any new flow, the first packet of this flow is forwarded to the controller via an OFPT_PACKET_IN message. Then, the controller determines whether that packet should be sent. If so, the controller will install new flow entries into corresponding switches to handle future packets of the same flow. STATEMON also listens to the OFPT_PACKET_IN message. If this message carries a packet that any state-aware application wants to monitor (Section 3.5), STATEMON will install OpenConnection entries in OpenConnection tables (Section 3.3.1) of corresponding switches using OpenConnection messages (Section 3.3.2) and add a Goto-OCT instruction in the flow entries to start OpenConnection processing pipeline.

3.3.1 OpenConnection Table

Before illustrating how OpenConnection-enabled switches process packets, we first explain the structure of the OpenConnection

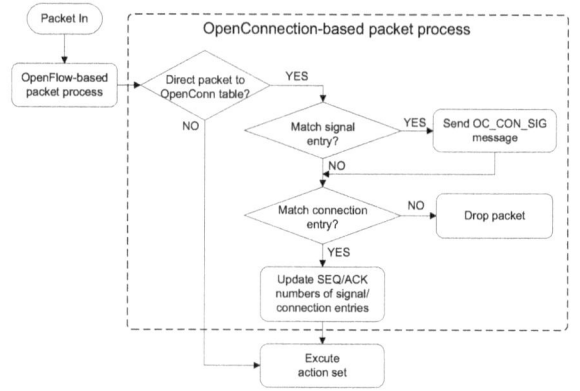

Figure 4: Flowchart for OpenConnection Packet Processing.

Table 2: OpenConnection Messages (C: controller, S: switch)

Message Name	Direction	Description
OC_CON_SIG	S→C	Encapsulate entire packet (including payload) and forward it to connection tracking module
OC_ADD	C→S	Install a new entry in an OpenConnection table
OC_UPDATE	C→S	Update an OpenConnection entry
OC_REMOVE	C→S	Remove an OpenConnection entry

table. An OpenConnection entry, which is shown in Figure 3, has (1) connection match fields, (2) actions for a decision of forward, drop, and update fields, etc., and (3) OC_CON_SIG match fields that triggers switches to send OC_CON_SIG message when matched. To achieve generality, both connection and OC_CON_SIG match fields are directly programmable by state-aware SDN applications (Section 3.5).

If and only if a packet matches connection match fields, the packet will be processed by both the OpenFlow and OpenConnection pipeline as shown in Figure 4. In case the packet also matches the OC_CON_SIG match fields, which means the packet is a state changing packet, such as FIN in TCP, it will be encapsulated in an OC_CON_SIG message and forwarded to the connection tracking module of STATEMON in the controller. The connection tracking module will maintain the state and manage associated switches accordingly. Upon completion of these OpenConnection-based packet process, the action set that includes the rest of the OpenFlow actions will be executed.

The design of the OpenConnection table is aligned in spirit to the design of the flow table, so that the data plane can process packets using the simple "match-action" paradigm. However, OpenConnection tables are more scalable than OpenFlow tables, because OpenConnection table entries are only installed in the OpenConnection tables of the two *endpoint* switches that directly connect the initiating host and the receiving host of a connection. In contrast, using OpenFlow for each new flow, corresponding flow entries must be installed in *all* flow tables of switches that the flow traverses.

3.3.2 OpenConnection Message Exchanging Format

We define four OpenConnection messages to enable state-based connection monitoring. OpenConnection messages help the connection tracking module of STATEMON monitor the overall process of connection establishment and tear-down behaviors occurring in the data plane. Table 2 summarizes the four OpenConnection messages with a brief description of each.

The OC_CON_SIG message is used to encapsulate the state-changing packet and conveying it to the controller (switch-to-controller direction). The main difference from OpenFlow OFPT_PACKET_IN

Table 3: State Management Table Example for TCP connection. (A (or B) refers a pair of ⟨IP, port⟩.)

State	Transition Conditions			Next State	OpenConnection Events			Timeout
	Message Type	Source	Match Fields		Message Type	Destination	OC_CON_SIG Match Fields	
INIT	OFPT_PACKET_IN	Ingress	A→B, TCP, Flag=SYN	SYN_SENT	OC_ADD	Ingress	A→B, TCP, Flag=ACK	∞
SYN_SENT	OFPT_PACKET_IN	Egress	B→A, TCP, Flag=SYNACK	SYNACK_SENT	OC_ADD	Egress	B→A, TCP, Flag=FIN	5
SYNACK_SENT	OC_CON_SIG	Ingress	A→B, TCP, Flag=ACK	ESTABLISHED	OC_UPDATE	Ingress	A→B, TCP, Flag=FIN	5
ESTABLISHED	OC_CON_SIG	Ingress	A→B, TCP, Flag=FIN	FIN_WAIT				1800
		Egress	B→A, TCP, Flag=FIN					
FIN_WAIT	OC_CON_SIG	Egress	B→A, TCP, Flag=FIN	CLOSED				60
		Ingress	A→B, TCP, Flag=FIN					
CLOSED	-	-	-	INIT	OC_REMOVE	Ingress		0
					OC_REMOVE	Egress		

is that the OC_CON_SIG message is only for STATEMON (so that it will not be effective to other SDN applications), and it also contains a randomly generated unique identifier for the connection to distinguish the affiliation of the message. The other messages are sent from the controller to the switches to program an Open-Connection table. The connection tracking module generates an OC_ADD message to install a new entry in an OpenConnection table. For instance, to monitor a TCP connection, it installs an entry to match TCP ACK packet at its ingress switch of the flow path. OC_UPDATE is used for updating an OpenConnection table entry. If a connection is terminated (or by timeout mechanism), the connection tracking module sends an OC_REMOVE message to remove all associated entries. Compared with OpenFlow, which exchanges messages between the controller and multiple switches, OpenConnection introduces only a constant number of message exchanges between the controller and two endpoint switches for handling a specific state-based connection. Using TCP as an example, Open-Connection uses eight messages in total for a TCP connection (see Table 5): (1) three OC_CON_SIG messages, (2) two OC_ADD messages, (3) one OC_UPDATE message, and (4) two OC_REMOVE messages.

3.4 Tracking Connection States

For generality, STATEMON maintains a pair of global state table and state management table for each state-aware application. The connection tracking module listens to OFPT_PACKET_IN messages to initialize an entry in the global state table for a connection and listens to OC_CON_SIG messages to update the states of the connection based on state transition rules in the *state management table* provided by the application.

3.4.1 Global State Table

The global state table records network-wide connection state information. However, simply extracting a connection's state from a specific switch is not sufficient to account for the overall global state of a connection. Because OpenFlow-enabled switches are able to rewrite packets' headers at any point using the Set-Field action, a packet's header may look different at its ingress and egress switches. This poses a challenge for the controller to identify which packets belong to the same connection. To solve this problem, STATEMON bonds a connection's state (e.g., ESTABLISHED) with its associated network rules (i.e.,the forward and reverse flow entries) to effectively monitor and track an active connection.

We design the entry in the global state table as a 5-tuple entry denoted $\langle C_I, C_E, \sigma_F, \sigma_R, S_a \rangle$. Connection information at the ingress switch (C_I) contains a set of packet header fields along with its incoming physical switch port, p_i. Connection information at the egress switch (C_E) contains the same elements, except p_o which refers to the outgoing physical switch port. For instance, C_I for a TCP connection can be defined as ⟨src_ip, src_port, dst_ip, dst_port, network_protocol, p_i⟩. Note that some fields in C_I and C_E (e.g., $src\_ip, src\_port, dst\_ip, dst\_port$) might not be identical

due to dynamic packet modification (Set-Field action) in SDNs. σ_F is a series of identifiers of flow entries that enable the forward flow, and σ_R is also a series of identifiers for the reverse flow. For example, the forward flow and the reverse flow in Figure 1 would be $\sigma_F = \langle fe_1, fe_2, fe_3 \rangle$ and $\sigma_R = \langle fe_4, fe_5, fe_6 \rangle$, respectively. The last element, S_a, denotes the state of a connection and it will be further elaborated in Section 3.4.2.

The elements in a global state table entry have several properties. The relation between C_I and C_E is to be determined by σ_F or σ_R such that $C_I \xrightarrow{\sigma_F} C_E$ and $C_E^{-1} \xrightarrow{\sigma_R} C_I^{-1}$. C_I^{-1} and C_E^{-1} are directly derived from C_I and C_E by replacing the source with the destination and changing the incoming port (p_i) to the outgoing port (p_o). For example, if $C_I =$⟨src_ip: 10.0.0.1, src_port: 3333, dst_ip: 10.0.0.2, dst_port: 80, network_protocol: tcp, p_i: 2⟩ then $C_I^{-1} =$⟨src_ip: 10.0.0.2, src_port: 80, dst_ip: 10.0.0.1, dst_port: 3333, network_protocol: tcp, p_o: 2⟩.

3.4.2 State Management Table

An entry in the state management table is a 5-tuple denoted as ⟨*State, Transition Conditions, Next State, OpenConnection Events, Timeout*⟩. When an OFPT_PACKET_IN or OC_CON_SIG message is received, the connection tracking module compares its originated location and header of the encapsulated packet with the *Source* and *Match Fields* of the current state in the state management table. If the packet meets the *Transition Conditions* of the current state, the state will be updated to the *Next State* and *OpenConnection Events* will be triggered. OpenConnection events instruct the connection tracking module to send OC_ADD, OC_UPDATE, or OC_REMOVE to corresponding switches. The *Match Fields* in *OpenConnection Events* will configure the OpenConnection table entries in corresponding switches to initialize connection and OC_CON_SIG match fields. *Timeout* allows STATEMON to automatically close a connection.

Table 3 shows how a state-aware application can use the state management table for the TCP state transitions. A TCP connection starts with INIT state that transitions to SYN_SENT when it receives an OFPT_PACKET_IN message that contains a TCP SYN flag. STATEMON identifies the location of the ingress switch (I) from the message, and it sends an OC_ADD message back to I with its match fields. STATEMON locates the egress switch (E) as well by listening for the second OFPT_PACKET_IN message. OC_CON_SIG messages collected from I or E are then used to update the connection states. CLOSED is a temporary state only used for sending OC_REMOVE messages and removing the associated entries. Note that one state can transition to multiple Next States based on matching conditions and generate a variety of actions as defined by SDN applications.

3.5 STATEMON APIs

STATEMON provides three types of application programming interfaces (APIs) for SDN applications so that the applications only need to implement their business logic. The APIs can be used (1)

Table 4: STATEMON APIs

Category	API Name	Key Parameters	Description
Type I	InitGST()	Match fields in C_I and/or C_E	Initialize the global state table
	InitSMT()	5-tuple of state management table	Initialize the state management table
	SetInterest()	Range of match fields with wildcard	
Type II	SearchEntry()	Raw packet or ConnectionID	Search an associated global state entry
	GetConnState()	ConnectionID	Obtain current state of a connection
	DeleteEntry()	ConnectionID	Delete a connection
Type III	ConnAttempt()	Type of message and raw packet	Callback function: return one of actions (allow or drop)
	StateChange()	ConnectionID and next state	

to configure both the global state table and the state management table (Type I), (2) to retrieve state information from the global state table (Type II), and (3) to register callback functions in STATEMON to subscribe specific state-based events (Type III). The APIs are summarized as follows:

- Type I is used to configure the two state-specific tables in STATEMON: the global state table and the state management table. To customize the global state table, SDN applications can specify match fields for C_I or C_E (e.g., IP and port number) to distinguish one connection from another. Applications can also define a state set for the connection along with its transition rules for the state management table.

- Type II APIs are built for sending queries (applications to STATEMON) to retrieve network states, which SDN applications are interested in. Because all connection information is recorded in the global state table, those queries are directly conveyed to the global state table.

- Type III APIs are used to register callback functions in STATEMON. For example, when a global state entry is updated, STATEMON can call this function to subscribing applications to allow them to execute their own business logic.

4. STATEFUL FIREWALL DESIGN

In this section, to demonstrate the practicality and feasibility of STATEMON and state-aware network access management applications in SDNs, we illustrate how a stateful firewall can take advantage of STATEMON to implement its state-aware access control logic in SDNs.

The stateful firewall application first calls Type I APIs to initialize its global state table and state management table. We focus on TCP connections as a state-based protocol for this application. To enforce a stateful firewall policy such as "host B can communicate with host A if and only if host A initiates the connection," our firewall uses the state management table shown in Table 3. Then, STATEMON calls the registered callback function (Type III) when a state changing event occurs. The application only needs to implement the logic in the callback function: (1) a packet (or flow) heading from host B to host A should be denied when its state is in INIT or SYNACK_SENT and (2) a packet (or flow) heading from host B to host A should be allowed when its state is in SYN_SENT or ESTABLISHED. Thus, the connection attempt (e.g., TCP SYN) initiated from host B cannot be made whereas the attempt from host A will pass.

To show some benefits of our stateful firewall, we focus on following features: (1) state-aware firewall policy enforcement, (2)

Algorithm 1: Obtaining Affected Entry Set (AES)

Input: New (or Updated) flow entry (nf) and existing flow entries ($FE = \{e_1, e_2, ...\}$) at the same switch.
Output: Affected entry set $AES = \{a_1, a_2, ...\}$ such that $a_i \in FE$.
/* First, append the new flow entry (nf) to AES */
$AES.append(nf)$;
/* FE_t: a set of flow entries installed in table t */
$FE_t \longleftarrow retrieveEntries(nf.getSwitchID, nf.getTableID)$;
foreach $e \in FE_t$ **do**
  /* Check if nf has higher priority than e and is dependent with e */
  if $nf.priority \geq e.priority$ and $nf.match \cap e.match \neq \emptyset$ **then**
    $AES.append(e)$;
    /* Recursively perform identical operation if e has Goto-OCT instruction */
    if $e.getInstruction$ contains $GotoTable$ **then**
      $temp\_e.match \longleftarrow e.applyActions()$;
      $temp\_e.setTableID(e.getInstruction.getTableID)$;
      $AES\_child = self.(temp\_e, E)$;
      $AES.append(AES\_child)$;

return AES;

---

connection disruption prevention, and (3) unauthorized access prevention against active connections.

4.1 State-aware Firewall Policy Enforcement

Since STATEMON provides global network states to the firewall, our firewall application utilizes the state information for the following scenarios: (1) a host attempts to establish a new connection, (2) the state of an active connection has been updated, and (3) the firewall application updates the firewall policy.

First, when host A attempts to open a new connection to host B, both host A and host B exchange initiating signal packets to establish the connection. As soon as STATEMON receives these attempts, the firewall would get relevant information via the Type III callback function defined when it called ConnAttempt(). If this attempt violates the pre-defined stateful firewall policy, the initiating packet is immediately denied and the firewall stops the controller from executing the rest of the OFPT_PACKET_IN handling process so that no flow entry is sent to the switches.

Second, if a global state entry is updated, the stateful firewall will also be notified via Type III callback function, StateChange(). Our firewall application performs pair-wise comparison, the current state of the connection against existing stateful firewall policies. The firewall searches the associated global state entry by calling SearchEntry() and acquires the connection information from the entry. To consider Set-Field actions, it retrieves *tracked* space denoted $T(I, E)$, getting $\langle src\_ip, src\_port \rangle$ from I and $\langle dst\_ip, dst\_port \rangle$ from E. By putting them together, we obtain $T(I, E) = \langle I.src\_ip, I.src\_port, E.dst\_ip, E.dst\_port \rangle$. Using the combination of $T(I, E)$ and its current state, the firewall checks for rule compliance with firewall policies. If the update of the state is not allowed by the policy, the application raises an alarm to network administrators and the update is denied by setting the return value of StateChange() to drop. In case the stateful firewall application wants to remove the connection, it may invoke DeleteEntry() function to remove the associated entries from the OpenConnection and flow tables.

The final scenario deals with the case of updating firewall policies. When the firewall application updates a stateful rule in its policy set, all active connections are examined against the new rule to identify potential violations. Because each firewall policy has a priority, computing dependency relations of firewall rules after the

6

Table 5: Additional State Management Table Entries for Unauthorized Access Prevention

State	Transition Conditions			Next State	OpenConnection Events			Timeout
	Message Type	Source	Match Fields		Message Type	Destination	OC_CON_SIG Match Fields	
SYNACK_SENT	OC_CON_SIG	Ingress	A→B, TCP, Flag=ACK	ESTABLISHED	OC_ADD	Egress	A→B, TCP, Flag=FIN	5
SYNACK_SENT	OC_CON_SIG	Ingress	A→B, TCP, Flag=ACK	ESTABLISHED	OC_ADD	Ingress	B→A, TCP, Flag=FIN	5
ESTABLISHED	OC_CON_SIG	Egress	A→B, TCP, Flag=FIN	**DETECTED**				1800
ESTABLISHED	OC_CON_SIG	Ingress	B→A, TCP, Flag=FIN	**DETECTED**				1800
DETECTED	-	-	-	ESTABLISHED				0

updates are vital for identifying overlaps between rules. All violating connections are to be deleted from the network by calling the API DeleteEntry(). As a result, the associated OpenConnection and flow entries will be flushed from the OpenConnection tables and flow tables.

4.2 Connection Disruption Prevention

A malicious SDN application can manipulate existing flow entries or install new flow entries to disrupt active connections that consequently damage the availability of services in the network. To prevent this type of attack, detecting these attempts before they take effect in the network is mandatory, so our firewall application proactively analyzes the expected impact of updates on active connections. To this end, the application computes the Affected Entry Set (AES) as described in Algorithm 1. When a new flow entry is to be inserted into the network or an existing flow entry is about to be updated, the application computes its dependencies with existing flow entries in the same switch. To this end, it first retrieves all flow entries FE from a specific switch and computes affected flow entries by new (or updated) flow entry nf. The application next selects the exact flow table affected by nf and builds FE_t which is a subset of FE. Then, it compares the priority and matching conditions between e and nf, to decide whether e is affected. If nf is dependent on e and has higher priority than e, the application adds e into AES. If e has a goto instruction, the application further visits the specified flow table to find AES_{child}. Considering Set-Field actions e may have, the actions will be applied first in advance before pipelining to another flow table. The firewall makes use of AES to detect the connection disruption attacks.

Detection of connection disruption attacks: Newly installed (or updated) flow entry nf triggers the application to compute AES and check AES against active connections obtained from STATE-MON. The application then compares AES with σ_F and σ_R of each of active connections and invokes the connection tracking module to re-calculate σ'_F and σ'_R. The updated σ'_F may change the relation between C_I and C_E i.e., $C_I \xrightarrow{\sigma'_F} C'_E$. If $C_E \neq C'_E$, the firewall concludes that the candidate flow entry nf will disrupt an active connection. nf may also disrupt the reverse flow of the connection. If $C_E^{-1} \xrightarrow{\sigma'_R} C'^{-1}_I$ and $C_I^{-1} \neq C'^{-1}_I$, the firewall also concludes nf will disrupt an active connection.

Countermeasure: When the controller receives the request of installation of a new flow entry nf which may cause a connection disruption or interruption, STATEMON treats it as a candidate flow entry and holds it until STATEMON evaluates its impact on the network. Upon completion of computing AES and σ'_F (or σ'_R), if the firewall detects any error such as $C_E \neq C'_E$ or $C_I^{-1} \neq C'^{-1}_I$, it raises an alarm to the administrator about the attempt. The administrator can decide whether it is legitimate and an intended request. If it turns out nf is valid, STATEMON allows it to be installed in the network. Otherwise, the firewall rejects the installation of nf.

4.3 Unauthorized Access Prevention

An attacker can attempt unauthorized access into an active connection by performing a man-in-the-middle attack such as TCP se-

quence inference attack to spoof packets. TCP protocol is inherently vulnerable to sequence inference attacks [33, 32]. We do not fundamentally solve these known vulnerabilities but can partially prevent specific types of unauthorized access to an active connection (e.g., TCP termination attacks). If an attacker successively infers the sequence number of the next packet, he/she will be able to create a spoofed termination packet by setting the TCP flags with FIN (i.e., man-in-the middle attack [9]). Our firewall can leverage STATEMON to detect such an attack by customizing the state management table and adding OpenConnection entries.

Detection of connection termination attacks: The key idea of the detection mechanism is to add additional checking logic in the egress switch for the forward flow (or the ingress switch for the reverse flow) by installing new OpenConnection entries. In addition to the state management table described in Table 3, the firewall adds additional transition rules (Table 5) to install OpenConnection entries and detect connection termination attacks. The firewall first creates a new *OpenConnection Events* (the first line in Table 5) for the SYNACK_SENT state that instructs the egress switch to install a new OpenConnection entry that matches the forward flow. OC_CON_SIG match fields of this entry will match the TCP FIN packet that belongs to the forward flow. Benign TCP FIN requests sent from the initiating host will be checked at its ingress switch by Table 3, so STATEMON transitions the state of the connection to the ESTABLISHED state. Hence, OC_CON_SIG fields of the third entry in Table 5 will not match the packet. However, attacking packet which is forged by an attacker in the middle of the flow path will match the OC_CON_SIG conditions of the third entry at the egress switch which results the state to be DETECTED. DETECTED state defined in the fifth line in Table 5 is a temporary state that is used to inform the existence of a TCP termination attack to the firewall. In the case of the reverse flow, the firewall leverages the second and the fourth entry for detecting connection termination attacks. In such a way, the firewall can capture this type of attack with the help of STATEMON.

Countermeasure: To protect the network from the aforementioned unauthorized access (e.g., TCP termination attack), the firewall can take two countermeasures: (1) return *actions* in the Type III callback function with drop to drop the spoofed packet and (2) rollback the connection state (DETECTED to ESTABLISHED) to maintain the connectivity between end hosts. In addition, the firewall may add complementary business logic in a Type III callback function to implement post processing behaviors such as sending warning messages to the network administrator.

5. IMPLEMENTATION AND EVALUATION

5.1 Implementation

To implement STATEMON, we chose a widely used controller, Floodlight, and a reference OpenFlow software switch implementation, Open vSwitch (ovswitch). The routing module and link discovery modules in Floodlight are used to provide network topology information to the connection tracking module. To track existing flow entries in the network and build its reachability graph, we used header space analysis [24] which translates each flow entry into a transition function that consists of a set of binaries, 0, 1, and x (for wildcard), to represent its matching conditions and actions. We also added `OFPT_PACKET_IN` listener within the controller along with an OpenConnection message handler to receive the state changing packets and program OpenConnection tables. Each global state entry has a unique identifier to distinguish it from other entries for ease of maintenance. The connection tracking module leverages the `OFPT_FLOW_MOD` OpenFlow message to construct controller-to-switch OpenConnection messages.

In the data plane, we implemented the OpenConnection table along with OpenConnection message handler. Because current versions of ovswitch can only support OpenFlow up to version 1.3.0, which cannot inspect TCP flags and sequence/acknowledgment numbers, we implemented a parsing module to additionally retrieve TCP flags and sequence/acknowledgment numbers. Then, we modified the legacy OpenFlow pipelining logic to enable OpenConnection-based packet processing. In total, less than 500 lines of C code were added to the ovswitch code base.

To implement the stateful firewall we leveraged a built-in firewall application in Floodlight to add a stateful checking module. A stateful checking module in the firewall is able to access the global state table by using STATEMON APIs for checking and enforcing its stateful firewall policy. We added the `state` parameter to REST interface methods provided by the built-in firewall so that users can define a stateful policy using REST requests. To prevent connection disruption and unauthorized access, we added a listener in the *Static Flow Pusher* module in Floodlight, so the application is able to intercept potentially malicious or accidentally harmful flow entry update requests and analyze their impacts on active connections before they become effective.

5.2 Evaluation

To manage the state of a connection, existing solutions add the transition logic of the connection in the data plane (Table 3). The fundamental question, therefore, is how many additional messages and/or performance overhead are introduced to achieve the same goal in STATEMON. To this end, we conducted experiments using three virtual machines, each of which had a quad-core CPU and 8GB memory and ran a Linux operating system (Ubuntu). One virtual machine was used to run the Floodlight controller and each of another ran Mininet [3] to simulate two networks. After we built two separated networks, we connected them using a GRE tunnel to flexibly add new hosts and links in one network without impacting the other network. We also modified the size of the network by changing the number of intermediaries (i.e., network switches).

5.2.1 STATEMON

To measure the worst-case performance of STATEMON, it was configured to monitor every connection in the network. However, in a real-world deployment, STATEMON only needs to monitor connections specified by state-aware applications, which will only improve the performance.

We first conducted experiments on an OpenConnection-enabled switch to test the overhead created by STATEMON in the data plane. OpenConnection enabled-switch spent less than 1μ for checking the affiliation of incoming traffic in an OpenConnection table when the table is set to have 100 entries. Creating and updating the corresponding entries in the OpenConnection table have been completed within $2\mu s$ on average.

In the controller side, the connection tracking module is in charge of installing/deleting an entry in the global state table and computing next state using the state management table. This module spent less than $3\mu s$ on average to complete those two tasks when there

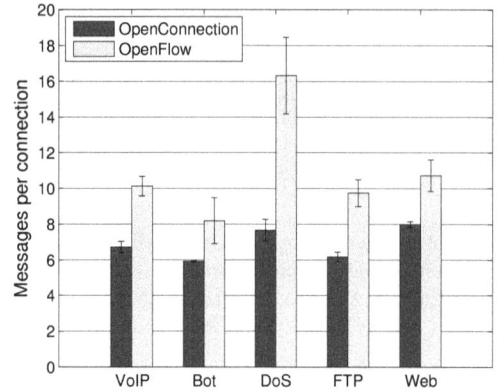

(a) Messages per connection of each PCAP file.

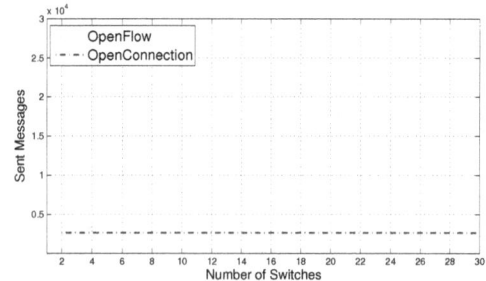

(b) Message exchanges with different number of switches.

Figure 5: Message Exchanges in STATEMON

exist 100 connections in the network. To evaluate how much of the delay can be attributed to network latency, we compared the numbers of message exchanges generated by both OpenFlow protocol and OpenConnection protocol. We collected real network traffics (five PCAP files) from different sources (available at [4, 7]) to generate real network traffic. Our testing framework (1) automatically identifies source and destination IP addresses of each packet in a PCAP file, (2) dynamically generates hosts for those IP addresses in a network, and (3) sends the packet through their network interfaces. Figure 5(a) shows the number of message exchanges. The first traffic is collected from VoIP traffic and consists of 32 connection attempts and 29 successful establishments. Network traffic generated by this file caused the controller to generate 324 OpenFlow messages along with 215 OpenConnection messages, which mean 10 OpenFlow messages and 7 OpenConnection Messages per connection on average. For counting OpenFlow messages, we excluded unrelated messages, such as `OFPT_HELLO`, `OFPT_ECHO_REQUEST`, and `FEATURE_REPLY`, and filtered out unrelated `OFPT_PACKET_IN` messages used to handle connectionless packets, such as LLDP, ARP, and DNS. Therefore, OpenConnection protocol actually generated much fewer messages than OpenFlow protocol. To account for theoretical number of OpenFlow messages, we develop the equation (1). For one way flow, we need one `OFPT_PACKET_IN` message and n number of `OFPT_FLOW_MOD` messages where n is the number of switches on the path. Because a connection requires bi-directional flows, it is computed by $2 * (1 + n)$.

$$B_{OF}(n) = 2 * (1 + n) \quad (1)$$

However, the number of OpenConnection messages does not depend on n. Because STATEMON requires eight messages for monitoring a connection, every PCAP type in Figure 5(a) creates ≤ 8

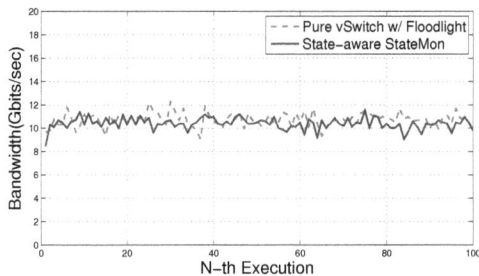

Figure 6: Throughput between End Hosts

OpenConnection messages per connection. Considering the third traffic that contains DoS attacks, it has generated a large number of OpenFlow messages due to substantial connection attempts, while the count of OpenConnection messages remained unchanged. This results clearly show STATEMON creates minimal message exchanges under any circumstances. Figure 5(b) shows how STATEMON scales with respect to increasing the number of switches in the network. To stress an overhead, we maintained 300 connections when measuring Figure 5(b). As expected, OpenFlow message count was linearly increased in accordance with the growing number of switches while STATEMON maintains a constant number of message exchanges no matter how many switches exist in the network.

To discover overall overhead of STATEMON including network latency, we first measured the time for establishing a connection using a TCP handshake with and without STATEMON. As defined in Table 3, STATEMON exchanges 4 messages to monitor a TCP handshake. While a TCP handshake took $3.356ms$ on average without STATEMON, it took $3.651ms$ on average with STATEMON. This means STATEMON only introduced a $0.295ms$ delay, which is 8.79% overhead for a TCP handshake. To evaluate the overall performance degradation caused by STATEMON, we used the throughput between hosts as another metric. We used Iperf [2] for this experiment. Iperf client (host in network A) initiated a new connection with Iperf server (host in network B) and exchanged a set of packets to measure the throughput. In an Open vSwitch and Floodlight setting without STATEMON, the throughput scored an average of 10.74 Gbits/sec (100 runs). With STATEMON enabled, the throughput scored 10.40 Gbits/sec on average, with only 3.27% throughput degradation.

5.2.2 Stateful Network Firewall

We configured the number of firewall policies to be 1k and fixed the size of global state entries with 10k to measure the overhead of our stateful firewall.

For performing state-aware firewall policy enforcement, the firewall spent $1.02ms$ on average. When a host attempts to establish a new connection, it took $0.83ms$ to complete the searches with existing firewall policies, and the attempt was immediately denied in real-time ($0.01ms$). Whenever a global state entry is updated, the firewall performed a pair-wise comparison of the update with existing state-based rules within $1.16ms$, and it took $0.26ms$ to delete the violating connection from the network. In case of firewall policy updates, the firewall finished its dependency checking mostly within $0.5ms$, and spent a similar time ($0.31ms$) for deleting the conflicting connection from the network.

Preventing connection disruptions in the network is another key feature in our firewall. To this end, the firewall computes the Affected Entry Set (AES), and generating AES took less than $0.35ms$ on average. In addition to AES, the firewall computes updated flow entries, namely σ'_F or σ'_R, to further compute C'_E and C'_I, respectively. By comparing the relation the old C_E and the updated C'_E,

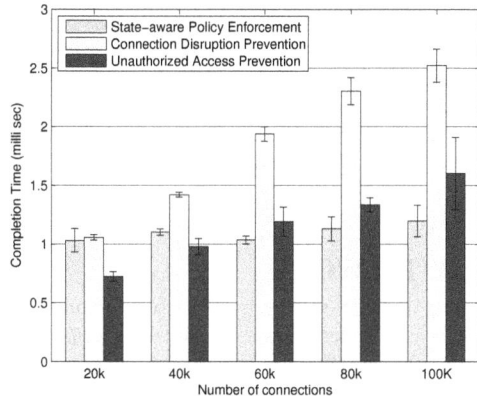

Figure 7: Scalability Analysis of Stateful Firewall

the firewall draw a conclusion of potential connection disruption iff $C_E \neq C'_E$. All these tasks were completed in $0.49ms$ on average.

To detect/prevent unauthorized access into active connections, the firewall manipulates the state management table as described in Section 4.3. As shown in Table 5, the firewall proactively installs necessary rules in the state management table. Once a connection has successfully been established between two end hosts, the firewall asks STATEMON to install an additional OpenConnection entry to monitor the terminating packet at its egress switch. Since the firewall will be directly notified by STATEMON when a connection termination attack is detected, the firewall only implements a logic to drop the attack packet. The firewall drops this packet and recovers the connection's state to its previous one, ESTABLISHED. Duration time for handling this type of unauthorized access took around $0.44ms$ in total.

We also checked the scalability of the stateful firewall application by measuring the duration time for completing three types of strategies. We gradually increased the number of existing connections from 20k to 100k. As shown in Figure 7, state-aware policy enforcement took almost constant time ($\approx 1ms$) no matter how many connections exist in the network. The firewall spent more time in preventing connection disruptions than that of unauthorized access prevention due to the computation overhead incurred by Algorithm 1. However, overall duration time for both cases linearly increased with respect to increasing number of connections and took less than 3 milliseconds at 100k connections, which is manageable.

5.2.3 Other Application: Port Knocking

Even though we mainly focused on TCP connection in this paper, a key design goal is that STATEMON can support different state-based protocols, such as port knocking. Port knocking is a method to open a *closed* port by checking a unique *knock sequence*, a series of connection attempts destined to different ports [26]. Thus, we developed this application to demonstrate how other network access management schemes can be also implemented using STATEMON in SDNs.

For example, an application may want to allow a connection iff a series of requests matches a specific *port* order of A, B, C, and D. By modifying the state management table in STATEMON, the application can receive state-changing packets by listening OFPT_PACKET_IN messages. In other words, the initial state can transition to the first *knock* state (e.g., PORT_KNOCK1) when the packet is destined to port A, waiting for the subsequent knocking sequence (port B). Such a way, the application *opens* the *closed* port of a server if the state becomes the OPEN state.

To evaluate the overhead incurred by STATEMON-based application, we re-implemented the port knocking that has been demonstrated in prior work [26], which performs the same functions but locally maintains the state in the switch. We installed the state transition rules for the port knocking in the switch. To complete the knocking sequence, it took $104.96ms$ without STATEMON, and STATEMON-based application spent $113.83ms$ in total (8.45% overhead).

6. RELATED WORK

As explained in Table 3, majority of existing solutions are focused on performing stateful inspection in the data plane [29, 30, 14, 36, 11, 6, 10, 37]. There is some debate as to whether this design goes against the spirit of SDN's control and data plane separation. In addition, none of these approaches give much attention on how to leverage the *logically centralized controller* for providing a *global* state visibility of the network to applications. In contrast, the unique contribution of STATEMON comes from its consolidated state checking mechanism enabled by OpenConnection protocol and the connection tracking module. Specifically, STATEMON can provide *global* state-based connection information to SDN applications along with several APIs that allows them to define application-specific states. Even though OpenNF [16] attempts to achieve a similar state sharing, it mainly collects a state of middleboxes (e.g., firewall, proxy, and load-balancer), not generic network states.

A number of verification tools [31, 21, 27, 25, 23, 24] for checking network invariants and policy correctness in SDNs have been recently proposed. FortNOX [31] was proposed as a software extension to provide security constraint enforcement for OpenFlow-based controllers. However, the conflict detection algorithm provided by FortNOX is incapable of analyzing *stateful* security policies. FlowGuard [21] was recently introduced to facilitate not only an accurate detection but also a flexible resolution of firewall policy violations in dynamic OpenFlow-based networks. However, the design of FlowGuard fully relies on flow-based rules in the data plane and is only capable of building a *stateless* firewall application for SDNs. Anteater [27] is indeed an offline system and cannot be applied for a real-time flow tracking. VeriFlow [25] and NetPlumber [23] are able to check the compliance of network updates with specified invariants in real time. VeriFlow uses graph search techniques to verify network-wide invariants and deals with dynamic changes. NetPlumber utilizes Header Space Analysis [24] in an incremental manner to ensure real-time response for checking network policies through building a dependency graph. Nevertheless, none of those tools are capable of checking *stateful* network properties in SDNs.

7. DISCUSSIONS

The OpenFlow protocol is evolving continuously, and the latest version (v1.5.0) has been recently released [8]. The newest version of OpenFlow attempts to add *TCP flags* for the extended matching criteria to address the problem of insufficient L4 header inspection capability as we have discussed.

However, the newest version of OpenFlow could not answer critical questions related to the maintenance and manipulation of network connection states. Especially, it does not articulate how to leverage *TCP flags* to monitor states in both the switch and controller. We expect that our design of OpenConnection in STATEMON could provide an inspirational solution for OpenFlow to build and enable its future stateful inspection scheme.

While we took great efforts to realize state-aware applications for SDNs, the deployment of STATEMON to real-world production networks requires additional considerations in terms of network security. For example, defense mechanisms against DDoS attacks discussed in [35] may need to be considered in STATEMON. In addition, the current design and implementation of STATEMON utilize OpenFlow-based controller and switch modules, hence it only works in the context of an OpenFlow-based environment. However, the main idea of STATEMON, which is to provide state tracking framework for various network applications, can be also realized in other network paradigms, such as Network Function Virtualization (NFV) [5, 19] .

8. CONCLUSION

In this paper, we have articulated network access control issues in SDNs and presented a state-aware connection tracking framework called STATEMON that facilitates the control and data planes of SDN to enable stateful inspection schemes. In the control plane, we have designed a novel connection tracking mechanism using a global state table and a state management table to track active connections. To enable a state-aware data plane, we have introduced a new OpenConnection protocol, which defines four message formats and a state-aware OpenConnection table. We have implemented STATEMON using Floodlight and Open vSwitch along with two access management applications (i.e., a stateful network firewall application and a port knocking application) for SDNs, to demonstrate the flexibility of STATEMON. Our experimental results have demonstrated that STATEMON and two state-aware network access management applications showed manageable performance overhead to enable critical state-aware protection of SDNs.

Acknowledgments

This work was partially supported by grants from National Science Foundation (NSF-IIS-1527421, NSF-CNS-1537924 and NSF-CNS-1531127), Intel corporation and Center for Cybersecurity and Digital Forensics at Arizona State University.

9. REFERENCES

[1] Floodlight: Open SDN Controller. http://www.projectfloodlight.org.

[2] Iperf. https://iperf.fr/.

[3] Mininet: An Instant Virtual Network on Your Laptop. http://mininet.org.

[4] Public PCAP Files for download. http://www.netresec.com/?page=PcapFiles.

[5] Service Function Chaining (SFC) Architecture. https://tools.ietf.org/html/draft-ietf-sfc-architecture-02.

[6] Stateful Connection Tracking & Stateful NAT. http://openvswitch.org/support/ovscon2014/17/1030-conntrack_nat.pdf.

[7] The Internet Traffic Archive. http://ita.ee.lbl.gov/.

[8] OpenFlow Switch Specification Version 1.5.1 (Protocol version 0x06), December, 2014. https://www.opennetworking.org/images/stories/downloads/sdn-resources/onf-specifications/openflow/openflow-switch-v1.5.1.pdf.

[9] K. Benton, L. J. Camp, and C. Small. Openflow vulnerability assessment (poster). In *Proceedings of ACM SIGCOMM workshop on Hot topics in software defined networking (HotSDN'13)*, pages 151–152. ACM, 2013.

[10] G. Bianchi, M. Bonola, A. Capone, and C. Cascone. Openstate: programming platform-independent stateful

openflow applications inside the switch. *ACM SIGCOMM Computer Communication Review*, 44(2):44–51, 2014.

[11] P. Bosshart, D. Daly, G. Gibb, M. Izzard, N. McKeown, J. Rexford, C. Schlesinger, D. Talayco, A. Vahdat, G. Varghese, et al. P4: Programming protocol-independent packet processors. *ACM SIGCOMM Computer Communication Review*, 44(3):87–95, 2014.

[12] M. Casado, M. J. Freedman, J. Pettit, J. Luo, N. McKeown, and S. Shenker. Ethane: Taking control of the enterprise. In *Proceedings of the ACM SIGCOMM 2007 conference*. ACM, 2007.

[13] M. Casado, T. Garfinkel, A. Akella, M. J. Freedman, D. Boneh, N. McKeown, and S. Shenker. Sane: a protection architecture for enterprise networks. In *Proceedings of the 15th conference on USENIX Security Symposium*. USENIX Association, 2006.

[14] S. Fayazbakhsh, V. Sekar, M. Yu, and J. Mogul. Flowtags: Enforcing network-wide policies in the presence of dynamic middlebox actions. In *Proceedings of ACM SIGCOMM Workshop on Hot Topics in Software Defined Networking (HotSDN'13)*, August 2013.

[15] S. K. Fayazbakhsh, L. Chiang, V. Sekar, M. Yu, and J. C. Mogul. Enforcing network-wide policies in the presence of dynamic middlebox actions using flowtags. In *Proceedings of the 11th USENIX Conference on Networked Systems Design and Implementation*, pages 533–546. USENIX Association, 2014.

[16] A. Gember-Jacobson, R. Viswanathan, C. Prakash, R. Grandl, J. Khalid, S. Das, and A. Akella. Opennf: Enabling innovation in network function control. In *Proceedings of the 2014 ACM Conference on SIGCOMM*, pages 163–174. ACM, 2014.

[17] M. G. Gouda and A. X. Liu. A Model of Stateful Firewalls and its Properties. In *International Conference on Dependable Systems and Networks (DSN)*, pages 128–137. IEEE, 2005.

[18] A. Greenberg, G. Hjalmtysson, D. A. Maltz, A. Myers, J. Rexford, G. Xie, H. Yan, J. Zhan, and H. Zhang. A clean slate 4d approach to network control and management. *ACM SIGCOMM Computer Communication Review*, 35(5):41–54, 2005.

[19] R. Guerzoni et al. Network functions virtualisation: an introduction, benefits, enablers, challenges and call for action, introductory white paper. In *SDN and OpenFlow World Congress*, 2012.

[20] D. Hartmeier and A. Systor. Design and Performance of the OpenBSD Stateful Packet Filter (pf). In *USENIX Annual Technical Conference, FREENIX Track*, pages 171–180, 2002.

[21] H. Hu, W. Han, G.-J. Ahn, and Z. Zhao. Flowguard: building robust firewalls for software-defined networks. In *Proceedings of ACM SIGCOMM Workshop on Hot Topics in Software Defined Networking (HotSDN'14)*, pages 97–102. ACM, 2014.

[22] S. Jain, A. Kumar, S. Mandal, J. Ong, L. Poutievski, A. Singh, S. Venkata, J. Wanderer, J. Zhou, M. Zhu, et al. B4: Experience with a globally-deployed software defined wan. In *ACM SIGCOMM Computer Communication Review*, volume 43, pages 3–14. ACM, 2013.

[23] P. Kazemian, M. Chang, H. Zeng, G. Varghese, N. McKeown, and S. Whyte. Real time network policy checking using header space analysis. In *Proceedings of the 10th USENIX conference on Networked Systems Design and Implementation*, pages 99–112. USENIX Association, 2013.

[24] P. Kazemian, G. Varghese, and N. McKeown. Header space analysis: static checking for networks. In *Proceedings of the 9th USENIX conference on Networked Systems Design and Implementation*. USENIX Association, 2012.

[25] A. Khurshid, X. Zou, W. Zhou, M. Caesar, and P. B. Godfrey. Veriflow: verifying network-wide invariants in real time. In *Proceedings of the 10th USENIX conference on Networked Systems Design and Implementation*, pages 15–28. USENIX Association, 2013.

[26] M. Krzywinski. Port knocking from the inside out. *SysAdmin Magazine*, 12(6):12–17, 2003.

[27] H. Mai, A. Khurshid, R. Agarwal, M. Caesar, P. Godfrey, and S. T. King. Debugging the data plane with anteater. In *Proceedings of the ACM SIGCOMM 2011 conference*, pages 290–301, 2011.

[28] N. McKeown, T. Anderson, H. Balakrishnan, G. Parulkar, L. Peterson, J. Rexford, S. Shenker, and J. Turner. Openflow: enabling innovation in campus networks. *ACM SIGCOMM Computer Communication Review*, 38(2):69–74, 2008.

[29] H. Mekky, F. Hao, S. Mukherjee, Z.-L. Zhang, and T. Lakshman. Application-aware data plane processing in sdn. In *Proceedings of ACM SIGCOMM Workshop on Hot Topics in Software Defined Networking (HotSDN'14)*, pages 13–18. ACM, 2014.

[30] M. Moshref, A. Bhargava, A. Gupta, M. Yu, and R. Govindan. Flow-level state transition as a new switch primitive for sdn. In *Proceedings of ACM SIGCOMM Workshop on Hot Topics in Software Defined Networking (HotSDN'14)*, pages 61–66. ACM, 2014.

[31] P. Porras, S. Shin, V. Yegneswaran, M. Fong, M. Tyson, and G. Gu. A security enforcement kernel for openflow networks. In *Proceedings of ACM SIGCOMM Workshop on Hot Topics in Software Defined Networking (HotSDN'12)*, August 2012.

[32] Z. Qian and Z. M. Mao. Off-path tcp sequence number inference attack-how firewall middleboxes reduce security. In *Security and Privacy (SP), 2012 IEEE Symposium on*, pages 347–361. IEEE, 2012.

[33] Z. Qian, Z. M. Mao, and Y. Xie. Collaborative tcp sequence number inference attack: how to crack sequence number under a second. In *Proceedings of the 2012 ACM conference on Computer and communications security*, pages 593–604. ACM, 2012.

[34] C. Roeckl and C. M. Director. Stateful inspection firewalls. *Juniper Networks White Paper*, 2004.

[35] S. Shin, V. Yegneswaran, P. Porras, and G. Gu. Avant-guard: scalable and vigilant switch flow management in software-defined networks. In *Proceedings of the 20th ACM conference on Computer and communications security (CCS'13)*, pages 413–424. ACM, 2013.

[36] A. Wang, Y. Guo, F. Hao, T. Lakshman, and S. Chen. Umon: Flexible and fine grained traffic monitoring in open vswitch. In *Proceedings of the 11th International Conference on emerging Networking EXperiments and Technologies (CoNEXT'15)*, December 2015.

[37] S. Zhu, J. Bi, C. Sun, C. Wu, and H. Hu. Sdpa: Enhancing stateful forwarding for software-defined networking. In *Proceedings of the 23rd IEEE International Conference on Network Protocols (ICNP 2015)*, pages 10–13.

An Empirical Study on User Access Control in Online Social Networks

Minyue Ni
Software School
Shanghai Key Laboratory of Data Science
Fudan University
myni14@fudan.edu.cn

Weili Han
Software School
Shanghai Key Laboratory of Data Science
Fudan University
wlhan@fudan.edu.cn

Yang Zhang
Faculty of Science, Technology and
Communication
University of Luxembourg
yang.zhang@uni.lu

Jun Pang
Faculty of Science, Technology and
Communication
University of Luxembourg
jun.pang@uni.lu

ABSTRACT

In recent years, access control in online social networks has attracted academia a considerable amount of attention. Previously, researchers mainly studied this topic from a formal perspective. On the other hand, how users actually use access control in their daily social network life is left largely unexplored. This paper presents the first large-scale empirical study on users' access control usage on Twitter and Instagram. Based on the data of 150k users on Twitter and 280k users on Instagram collected consecutively during three months in New York, we have conducted both static and dynamic analysis on users' access control usage. Our findings include: female users, young users and Asian users are more concerned about their privacy; users who enable access control setting are less active and have smaller online social circles; global events and important festivals can influence users to change their access control setting. Furthermore, we exploit machine learning classifiers to perform an access control setting prediction. Through experiments, the predictor achieves a fair performance with the AUC equals to 0.70, indicating whether a user enables her access control setting or not can be predicted to a certain extent.

Keywords

Online social networks; access control; empirical analysis; data mining

1. INTRODUCTION

Online social networks (OSNs) have gained a huge success in the past decade. Leading players in the business including Facebook, Twitter and Instagram have attracted a huge number of users. Nowadays, OSNs have become a primary way for people to connect, communicate and share life moments. For instance, every day, 500M tweets are shared on Twitter, and Instagram users publish 60M photos[1]. OSNs have brought a lot of convenience to our life, users' privacy, on the other hand, has become a major concern due to the large amount of personal data shared online. Previously, researchers showed that a user's personal information can be inferred through statuses [18] and locations [25] that she shared in OSNs.

To mitigate users' privacy concern, major OSNs have deployed access control schemes to delegate the power to users themselves to control who can view their information. For example, Facebook provides a fine-grained access control scheme which enables users to apply different policies on each post they publish. Twitter and Instagram, on the other hand, provide a much simpler scheme. A Twitter or Instagram user could enable her access control setting such that strangers cannot have access to all detailed contents in her account, except for her profile picture, number of friends and number of online posts. To study and further improve access control in OSNs, academia have conducted many research, most of which take either formal or logical approaches. For instance, researchers have modeled access control with hybrid logic [11] and semantic web technology [3]. On the other hand, understanding how users exploit access control in their daily life is essential to improve access control in OSNs. Much to our surprise, this is left largely unexplored.

In this paper, we perform a large-scale empirical study on access control usage of Twitter and Instagram users in New York. To the best of our knowledge, this is the first work on analyzing users' access control on Twitter and Instagram. We collect data of 150k Twitter users and 280k Instagram users continuously within three months and study their access control usage from both static and dynamic point of view. Especially, the dynamic analysis is conducted on a daily base instead of a yearly base as done in previous works [8, 21]. This allows us to understand in depth how users exploit access control in their daily OSN life. Our contributions in this paper can be summarized as follows.

- We perform a static analysis on New York users' access control usage and find that female users and young

SACMAT'16, June 05-08, 2016, Shanghai, China
© 2016 ACM. ISBN 978-1-4503-3802-8/16/06. . . $15.00
DOI: http://dx.doi.org/10.1145/2914642.2914644

---

[1]http://bit.ly/1Fij4er

users are more likely to enable their access control setting. Moreover, users who enable their access control setting tend to have smaller online social circles, but are more willing to conduct social activities in the offline world represented by location check-ins.

- We conduct a dynamic analysis on users' access control usage based on the three-month consecutive data. We find that a considerable amount of users change their access control setting frequently and there are more users (especially female users and young users) enabling their access control setting than disabling it. When users disable the access control setting, they tend to become less active online and delete some of their followers. Interestingly, we also find that important festivals and events cause more users to disable access control setting.

- We apply machine learning techniques to conduct a prediction on whether a user would enable her access control setting or not. By combining users' online behavior such as the number of followers, together with user demographics, our prediction experiments achieve a fair result in which the AUC (area under the ROC curve) equals to 0.70. This indicates a user's access control setting can be predicted to a certain degree.

The rest of the paper is organized as follows. Section 2 introduces background information of Twitter and Instagram's access control schemes as well as the dataset used for our study. Section 3 and Section 4 present static and dynamic analysis on users' access control usage, respectively. Section 5 performs an access control setting prediction using machine learning techniques. Section 6 discusses limitations of this paper. Section 7 summarises related work and Section 8 concludes the paper with some future works.

2. BACKGROUND AND DATASET

2.1 Access Control in OSNs

Facebook, Twitter and Instagram are among the most popular OSNs at the moment. By September 2015, Facebook has around 1.5 billion monthly active users with 83.5% of its users are outside the US and Canada[2], while Twitter and Instagram have 316 million and 400 million monthly active users respectively. Besides the difference in size, the three OSNs are also appealing to different demographics and usage. Facebook is a general purpose OSN[3] with users distributed more evenly to diverse ages, races and genders; Twitter on the other hand is largely treated as a news source, also its percentage of users with high education and income is higher than those of the other two OSNs; Instagram is a platform for users to share their life styles and its users are more skewed to young people.

Access control schemes on these three OSNs are different as well. Facebook deploys a fine-grained access control scheme for users to control who can view their resources. This scheme is on a per-resource base, i.e., a user can define a specific access control policy for each of her photos and statuses. In addition, Facebook also introduces a function, namely friend list to help users categorize their friends

into different lists, e.g., colleagues and family, and the organized friend lists can then be directly used in a user's access control policy which improves its access control scheme's usability. Different from Facebook, Twitter[4] and Instagram[5] provide users with a much simpler access control scheme. On Twitter and Instagram, users can only choose whether to enable their access control setting, i.e., protect their account or not. Once a user enables her access control setting, others who are not the user's approved followers cannot view any of her information except for her profile photo, number of followers/followees and number of posts. In the following analysis, we refer users who enable their access control setting as *private users* while others as *public users*.

To improve access control in OSNs, one important perspective is to understand how users apply their access control in their OSN life. Several previous works [12, 8, 21, 13] have focused on the access control usage on Facebook. However, to the best of our knowledge, there do not exist works focusing on Twitter and Instagram. As discussed above, these two OSNs deploy different access control schemes from Facebook. Therefore, it is important and meaningful to understand how users apply their access control setting on Twitter and Instagram to protect their privacy.

2.2 The Dataset

In this paper, we collect the access control usage data of New York users on Twitter and Instagram. Even though the dataset of New York users is not a random sample of the global population, due to the diversity of New York users [8], we believe that our analysis should be indicative enough to reflect users' access control usage in general.

To identify users in New York, we leverage check-ins (user-shared location information) on the two OSNs. Nowadays, many people use their OSN services on mobile devices, e.g., 80% of Twitter's active users are on mobile[6]. To adapt to this trend, major OSNs add new functionalities to their mobile versions, one of which is location sharing, namely check-in, through mobiles' GPS sensors. It is quite common for users to share a photo together with the location where the photo is taken. By exploiting check-ins to identify users in New York, we can ensure accurate results from our analysis. Moreover, it allows us to compare public and private users' mobility behaviors as well (see Section 3).

To obtain users' check-ins, we first define a geo-coordinate bounding box covering New York region and then exploit Twitter [16] streaming API[7] and Instagram REST API[8] to collect users' check-ins respectively. To make sure that the users are locals in New York rather than visitors, we only keep those users with more than 10 check-ins. Figure 1 depicts a sample of check-ins in New York on Instagram.

After identifying the users in New York, we use Twitter REST API[9] and Instagram REST API to extract users' access control setting together with some general information such as number of followers/followees and number of posts, on a daily basis for nearly three months, from October 15th, 2015 until January 12th, 2016. We regard accounts with more than 2,000 followers as celebrities and those whose fol-

[2]http://newsroom.fb.com/company-info/
[3]http://bit.ly/1OPYYwN

[4]https://support.twitter.com/articles/14016
[5]https://help.instagram.com/116024195217477/
[6]https://about.twitter.com/company
[7]https://dev.twitter.com/streaming/overview
[8]https://www.instagram.com/developer/endpoints/
[9]https://dev.twitter.com/rest/public

Table 1: Summary of the conducted analysis on Twitter and Instagram.

	Static analysis			Dynamic analysis			Prediction
	Demographics	Online	Offline	Demographics	Online	Global events	
Twitter	✓	✓	✓	✓	✓	✓	✓
Instagram			✓	✓		✓	

Figure 1: Check-ins in New York on Instagram.

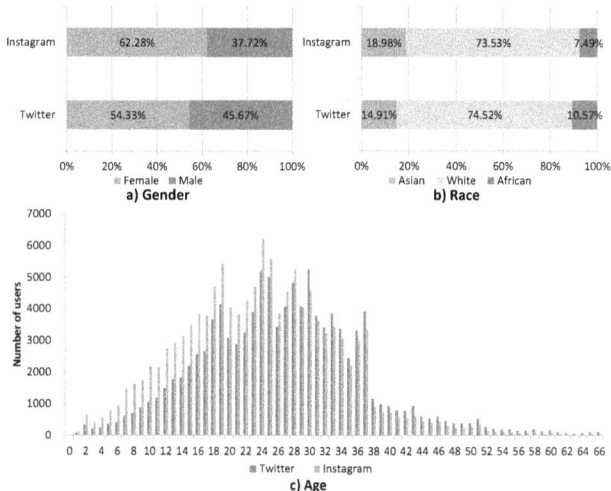

Figure 2: Gender, race and age distributions of New York users on Twitter and Instagram.

lowers are 1,000 more than followees as business accounts, and remove them from the dataset.

For static analysis, we focus on the data collected on November 12th with 175,202 users for Twitter and 292,406 users for Instagram[10]. For dynamic analysis, we focus on users that appear in our dataset everyday. In the end, we get 155,387 Twitter users and 282,066 Instagram users[11].

Note that when we exploit API to extract a private user's information, Twitter allows us to access the user's profile photo, number of followers/followees, and number of posts while Instagram forbids all the access. Since we get users' demographics through analyzing their profile photos, and quantify their online behavior through their numbers of followers/followees, and numbers of posts, we cannot conduct analysis related to those information on Instagram users. Table 1 lists the analysis we perform on the two OSNs.

Users' demographic information is another important aspect of our analysis. To get users' demographics, we resort to Face++[12], a state-of-the-art facial recognition service that detects a user's gender, race (Asian, White, African American) and age information from her profile photo. Face++ is based on deep learning techniques and has won several international competitions, it has also been exploited in other works for detecting users' demographics, such as [20, 19]. Figure 2 depicts gender, race and age distributions of our users on Twitter and Instagram. As we can see, there are more female users than male users on Twitter and Instagram in New York, and the proportion of female is much higher on Instagram. In addition, as mentioned before that

Instagram attracts more young users than Twitter, thus its users' age distribution is skewed to younger ages than that of Twitter users.

3. STATIC ANALYSIS

In this section, we perform static analysis on users' access control usage. We start by checking the percentage of private users in our dataset, then analyze the relation between users' demographics and their access control usage. Users' online and offline behavior is discussed in the end. Here, a user's online behavior is quantified by her number of posts and followers/followees in OSNs, while offline behaviors are quantified by her mobility, i.e., check-ins. As mentioned in Section 2, we have no access to the demographic information and online bahaviors of private users on Instagram, thus we cannot perform static analysis on Instagram users' demographics and online behaviors.

3.1 General Statistic

As shown in Table 2, the general percentages of private users in our dataset are 5.22% for Twitter and 11.92% for Instagram. This indicates that Instagram users pay more attention to their privacy than Twitter users. The reason could be the different purposes of using the two OSNs (see Section 2): Twitter is treated as a news spreading medium, thus its users are less likely to share personal sensitive information; Instagram, on the other hand, is a photo-sharing OSN and photos can contain personal sensitive information.

So far there does not exist official data from Twitter and Instagram on their private users' percentages. Cha et al. [5] claim that the percentage of private Twitter users is more

---

[10]We have analyzed data collected on other dates and the analysis results are similar.

[11]Some users might delete their accounts or get suspended during the three months, thus the number of users for dynamic analysis is slightly smaller than the number of users used for static analysis.

[12]http://www.faceplusplus.com/

Table 2: Statistics of public and private users.

		General	With _Demo	Without _Demo
Twitter	Private	9,145 (5.22%)	6,066 (5.65%)	3,079 (4.54%)
	Public	166,057 (94.78%)	101,347 (94.35%)	64,710 (95.46%)
Instagram	Private	34,844 (11.92%)	-	-
	Public	257,562 (88.08%)	-	-

than 7% which is close to our observation. The slight difference can be due to the sampling methodologies. The dataset in [5] is sampled through randomly picking user ids, while our dataset focuses on users in New York. On the other hand, the percentage of private users on Instagram is unclear from the literature. We emphasize that the focus of this paper is to understand how users exploit their access control in real life, the general percentages of private users on Twitter and Instagram are certainly interesting but left as future work.

3.2 Demographics

OBSERVATION 1: *Access control usage is different among users with different genders, races and ages. Female users, young users and Asian users are more likely to enable their access control setting than others.*

Gender. We calculate private users' percentages of male and female users respectively, and find out that more female users enable their access control setting than male users. As we can see from Figure 3, 4.15% of male Twitter users enable their access control setting while the corresponding rate of female users is 6.91%.

Race. Among people of three races in New York (see Figure 3), the private users' percentage of Asian users is the highest (6.20%) followed by White users (5.60%). African American users, on the other hand, have the lowest percentage (5.22%). One possible explanation could be the culture difference: Asian people are considered more conservative than White and African American people in general[13].

Age. Figure 3 shows that for all Twitter users who are older than 10, the percentages of private users are decreasing when the age grows. This trend is especially notable for users aged from 20 to 40, which indicates younger people are more concerned about their privacy than people of other ages. Interestingly, the private users' percentages of users under 10 years old (children) are high as well. Since children under 10 are less likely to be frequent Twitter users, we conjecture that these users use children's photos in their profiles.

We further analyze users under 10 through their race and gender. Compared with Figure 3, Figure 4 shows that the percentages of private users have increased for both genders and all races. The percentage of female private users increases 1.33 percents to 8.24%, while that of male users increases 1.84 percents to 5.99%. Furthermore, Asian users remain to have the most private users, with the percentage of private users increases about 2.1 percents to 8.3%.

---

[13] http://pewrsr.ch/1ccm9EL

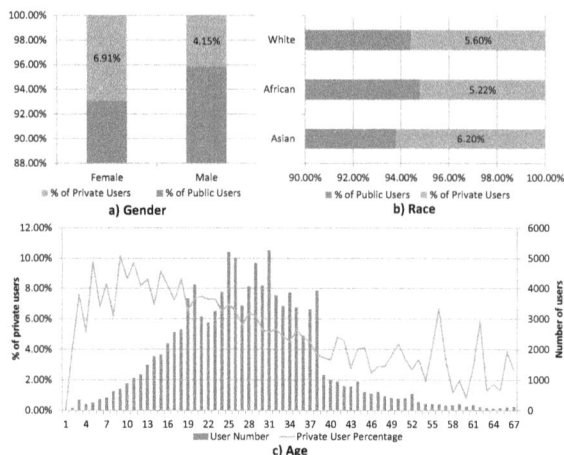

Figure 3: Demographic distributions of Twitter users.

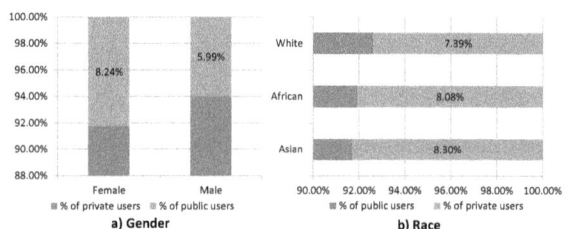

Figure 4: Demographic distributions of all users and users whose ages are below 10 on Twitter.

Those two results coincide with the results in our analysis above that female users and Asian users are more concerned about their privacy. More importantly, we can see that users who use children's photos in their profiles tend to be more privacy-aware.

Profile pictures. As introduced in Section 2.2, we extract a user's demographic information through recognizing her profile photo with Face++. Therefore, if a user uses non-human pictures, such as a cat, in the profile, we cannot get her demographics[14]. Private users' percentages of Twitter users with and without demographics are listed in Table 2. Among 107,413 users with demographics, 6,066 (5.65%) users are private, while for 67,789 users without demographics, only 3,079 (4.54%) of them are private. This indicates that users without demographics (not using human photos) on Twitter care less about their privacy than those who use human pictures. The reason might be that using fake profile pictures makes users feel secure.

3.3 Online Behavior

OBSERVATION 2: *Private users share more contents but have smaller online social circles than public users.*

Four metrics are exploited to quantify a Twitter user's online behavior, including the number of posted tweets, the number of favorites, the number of followers and the number of followees. The former two metrics can be used to evaluate the active level of each user on Twitter, while the latter two

---

[14] By manually checking 100 users without demographics in our dataset, we find that more than 90% of these users use non-human pictures in their profiles.

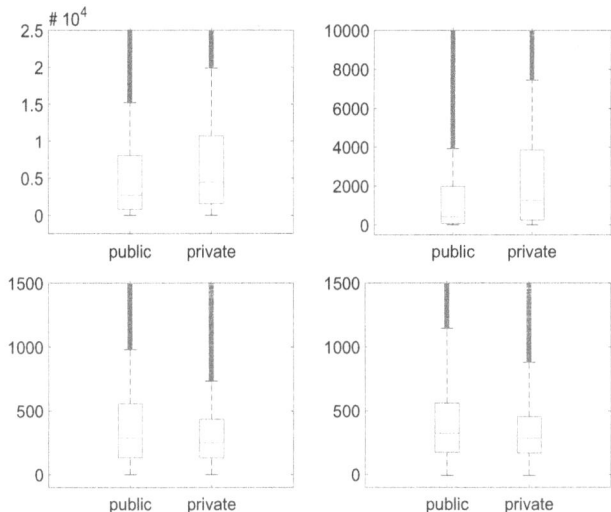

Figure 5: Users' distributions of posted tweets (top-left), favored tweets (top-right), followers (bottom-left) and followees (bottom-right).

represent the size of each user's social circle.

We use box plots [23] to visualize the distributions of four metrics for private and public users respectively (see Figure 5). Box plot, i.e., box and whisker diagram, is a standardized way of displaying data distribution based on the five number summary: minimum, first quartile (25%), median, third quartile (75%), and maximum.

From Figure 5, we observe that, compared with public users, private users have published and favored more tweets. On average, private users have posted 8,864.07 tweets and favored 3,380.43 tweets, while public users posted 7,550.96 tweets and favored 2,277.58 tweets. There are two possible explanations for this result:

- Private users publish more tweets, i.e., to express themselves, since they are aware that their privacy is guaranteed to a certain extent;

- Users who have used Twitter for a longer period of time are more likely to become private since they are more aware of the privacy threats. Meanwhile, their longer Twitter-ages result in more tweets.

In Section 4, we perform further analysis on this from a dynamic point of view.

Public users have more followers and followees than private users (see Figure 5). On average, public users have 423.26 followers and 431.73 followees, while private users have 329.37 followers and 355.17 followees. This indicates that private users have much smaller social circles. Fewer followers may due to Twitter's access control scheme since private users have to give approvals to their followers. On the other hand, private users following less people is an interesting observation. This suggests that private users tend to filter not only their followers, but also followees to ensure their social circles to be less chaos.

3.4 Offline Behavior

OBSERVATION 3: *Private users are more socially active than public users in the offline world.*

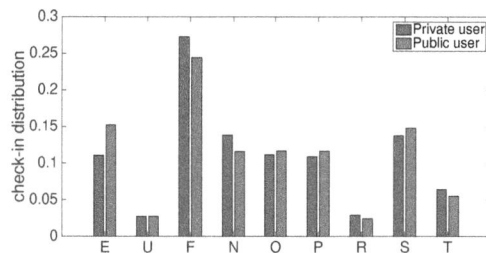

Figure 7: Check-in distributions over location categories on Instagram, each category is represented by its first letter, e.g., F stands for food.

The mobility data we get from Twitter and Instagram can be a good reflection of New York users' offline life. Our mobility dataset is composed of users' check-ins, and each check-in of a user tells us when and where the user is. In the following, we conduct our analysis from these two aspects.

Time. Figure 6 depicts the distributions of users' check-in time on a daily base on Twitter and Instagram. Despite the different distribution curves (Twitter users are more active at late night and early morning), we can observe an agreement between the two OSNs: compared to public users, private users are more active at night. As most offline social activities happen at night rather than working hours, this indicates that private users are more socially active in the offline world.

Locations. Due to the different designs of the two OSNs' APIs, we can extract the category information of each location for Instagram while not for Twitter. Here, location category information on Instagram is from Foursquare, a popular location-based social network, in which different location categories are organized into a tree structure[15]. In this paper, we take the first layer of the category tree (nine categories) to label each location, including entertainment, university, food, nightlife, outdoor, professional, residence, store and transportation.

Figure 7 depicts distributions of public and private users' check-ins over different location categories. It shows that private users have more check-ins at food and nightlife places. Since many offline social activities happen at these two types of places, this further confirms that private users are more active in the offline world.

3.5 Summary

Our static analysis focuses on three aspects including demographics, online behavior and offline behavior. We have observed that:

- Female users, young users and Asian users are more concerned about their privacy than others;

- Private users publish more posts than public users, but have smaller online social circles;

- In the offline world, private users are more socially active than public users.

---

[15]https://developer.foursquare.com/categorytree

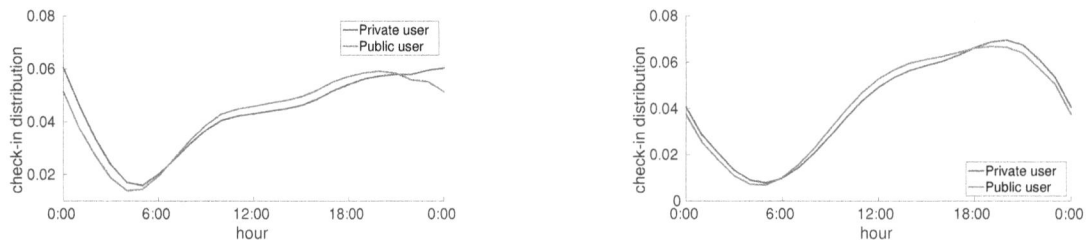

Figure 6: Check-in distribution over time on Twitter (left) and Instagram (right).

4. DYNAMIC ANALYSIS

After the static analysis, in this section we study New York users' access control usage from a dynamic perspective. Questions we attempt to answer include: how many users have changed their access control setting; what is the changing trend; who are these users; what is the correlation between users' changing of access control and other factors such as online behavior and global events?

We start by checking the general statistics of users who change access control setting, then focus on these users' demographics. Next, the correlation between access control changes and users' online behavior is analyzed. In the end, we study the influence from global events and festivals on users' decisions of changing access control.

4.1 General Statistics

OBSERVATION 4: *A considerable amount of users' access control usage is dynamic, i.e., they change their access control setting from time to time. There are more users changing their access control setting from public to private than from private to public.*

Changing frequency. A considerable amount of users in our dataset have changed their access control setting during the three months. On Twitter, 7,590 (5.21% of total Twitter users) users have changed their access control setting, while the proportion on Instagram is much higher (19.95% of 56,261 users).

Table 3 further presents the statistics of times that users have changed their access control setting. Among all the Twitter users who have changed their access control, 54.44% of users have changed more than once. On the other hand, Instagram users seem to be more indeterminate on access control usage: 69.09% of them have changed more than once during the three months. Moreover, 553 Instagram users have even changed more than 15 times.

Changing trend. From the dataset, we have observed an increasing trend of users enabling their access control setting during the three months, i.e., more users change from public to private than changing from private to public. On October 14th 2015, 4.89% of Twitter users and 9.36% of Instagram users in our dataset are private, while on January 12th 2016, the percentages have increased to 5.62% on Twitter and 14.20% on Instagram. This result indicates that users' privacy concerns are increasing day by day. Note that similar reslts are obtained for New York [8] and Pittsburgh [21] users on Facebook.

4.2 Demographics

OBSERVATION 5: *Female users and young users change access control setting more frequently and have a faster chang-*

Table 3: Statistics of users' changing frequency.

Times Changed	Twitter User	% of Users	Instagram User	% of Users
1	3,458	45.56%	17,390	30.91%
2	2,494	32.86%	15,252	27.11%
3	473	6.23%	4,397	7.82%
4	506	6.67%	5,179	9.21%
5	171	2.25%	2,121	3.77%
6	153	2.02%	2,597	4.62%
7	83	1.09%	1,220	2.17%
8	59	0.78%	1,470	2.61%
9	44	0.58%	849	1.51%
10	39	0.51%	955	1.70%
11	20	0.26%	552	0.98%
12	23	0.30%	721	1.28%
13	11	0.14%	455	0.81%
14	12	0.16%	493	0.88%
15	5	0.07%	267	0.47%
>15	28	0.51%	553	4.16%
Total	7,590		56,261	

ing trend from public to private than others. White users change access control setting least frequently and their changing trend from public to private remains the slowest.

Changing frequency and demographics. The statistics of both Twitter and Instagram[16] users' changing frequency w.r.t. demographics is presented in Table 4, 6.52% of female users and 3.66% of male users on Twitter, and 19.20% of female users and 13.92% of male users on Instagram have changed their access control setting. In addition, female users change access control more frequently than male users. Especially on Instagram, the average changing times for female users is 3.60, while it is 2.93 for male users.

On Twitter, Asian users have the highest proportion of access control changing (6.11%), while African American users have the most frequent changing times, i.e., 2.40 times on average. On the other hand, 20.63% of African American users have changed their access control setting on Instagram, but Asian users have the most changing times, 3.84 on average. On both Twitter and Instagram, White users are the most determinate about their access control setting.

We discretize age into four bins and study users' changing frequency w.r.t. each age bin. On both Twitter and

---

[16]As some public users with demographics on Instagram change their access control setting to private during the three months, we can still study Instagram users' changing frequency and trend w.r.t. demographics here.

Table 4: Statistics of users' changing frequency on Twitter and Instagram w.r.t. demographics.

		General	Gender		Race			Age			
			F	M	Asia	Africa	White	0-10	11-30	31-45	>46
Twitter	users changed (%)		6.52	3.66	6.11	5.16	5.04	7.72	5.95	3.29	2.41
	average changed times	2.29	2.37	2.09	2.37	2.40	2.25	2.52	2.28	2.23	2.07
	users changed once (%)	45.59	43.77	49.44	42.28	42.14	46.89	41.15	44.77	51.23	48.45
Instagram	users changed (%)		19.20	13.92	19.33	20.63	16.32	20.19	18.09	13.14	11.34
	average changed times	3.40	3.60	2.93	3.84	3.78	3.22	3.74	3.47	2.82	2.90
	users changed once (%)	34.85	31.68	42.08	27.79	30.53	37.55	32.26	33.26	43.63	46.71

Instagram, younger users change their access control setting more frequently. For instance, 18.09% Instagram users between 11 and 30 years old have changed at least once and the average changing times is 3.74. While for users between 31 and 45 years old, the two number is 13.14% and 2.82 respectively. In addition, users under 10 is the group with the highest number of users who change their access control setting freqently, this is consistent with our previous analysis that users under 10, i.e., users using children's photos in their profiles are more concerned about their privacy.

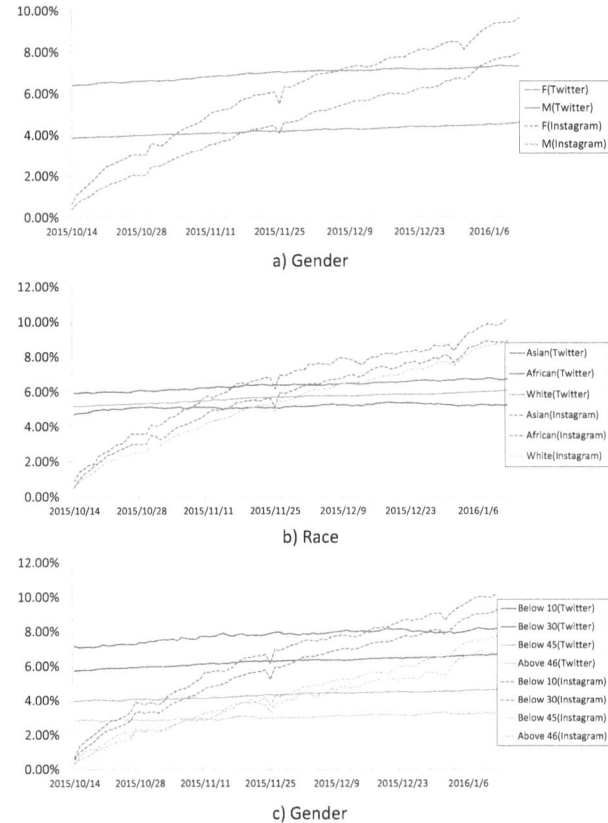

a) Gender

b) Race

c) Gender

Figure 8: Changing trends of proportions of private users based on their demographics in our dataset. As we cannot get private users' demographics from Instagram in the beginning, thus the beginning proportion for Instagram users w.r.t. different demographics is approaching 0.

Changing trend and demographics. We further study the changing trend of users w.r.t. demographics. As shown in Figure 8a), female private users' percentage grows faster than that of male users. On Twitter, the percentage of private female users increases 0.94%, while that of private male users is 0.72%. This trend is more obvious on Instagram, private female users' percentage increases nearly 10% while private male users' percentage increases about 8%.

Trends of enabling access control setting by users of different races are exhibited in Fig. 8b). On Twitter, the proportion of private African American users increases the slowest, while on Instagram, it becomes the fastest. We believe it is caused by the different purposes of the two OSNs.

The changing trend for users of different age (bin) is plotted in Fig. 8c). On both Twitter and Instagram, the private users' percentage of younger users increases faster than older users. This accords with the result in Section 3 that young users are more concerned about their privacy.

4.3 Online Behavior

OBSERVATION 6: *In general, users being private through all the three months and users changing from public to private tend to be less active in publishing new contents. Besides, these users barely establish new relationships with others, and their followers become fewer. Moreover, topics of users' posts on both OSNs are more (less) personal/sensitive when changing from public (private) to private (public).*

Statistics of online behavior. We first refer users staying private (public) within the three month as *constantly-private* (*constantly-public*) users, users who have changed their access control setting are named *inconstant users*. Based on users' online behavior presented in Section 3, we design four metrics to evaluate users' dynamic online behavior, including 1) new tweets; 2) new favorites; 3) new followers; and 4) new followees, added daily[17].

The comparisons between the constantly-public users and constantly-private users w.r.t. four metrics of dynamic online behavior are shown in Figure 9. Recall the observation in Section 3 that private users have more tweets (and favored tweets) than public users in general. Here, we find that, on the contrary, constantly-private users have less new and favored tweets everyday than constantly-public users on average. In Figure 9a), both curves representing constantly-private users are below the ones for constantly-public users. In Section 3, the two explanations why private users having more tweets than public users include: users are more

---

[17]Different from demographics, users' online behaviors are dynamic, for instance, number of followers may vary everyday. Thus, we cannot apply the same method for demographics to analyze Instagram users' dynamic online behavior in this section.

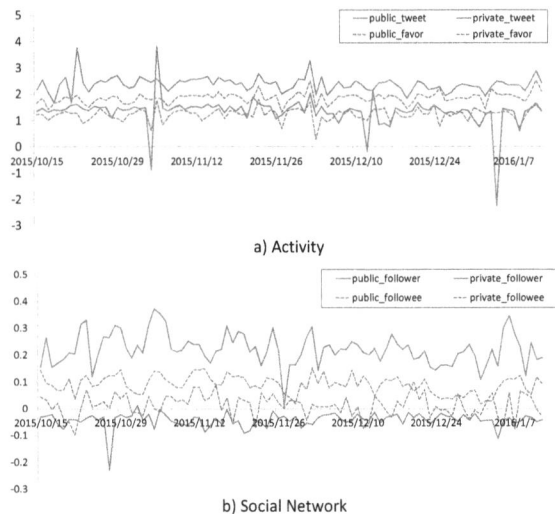

Figure 9: Constantly-public and constantly-private users daily added new tweets, favored tweets, followers and followees.

comfortable to express themselves in the private context; private users have longer Twitter-ages, thus having more tweets. The result in Figure 9a) gives a strong support for the second explanation, i.e., longer Twitter-age is the reason why private users have more Tweets than public users.

We also find that constantly-private users barely establish new links with others, i.e., their average amount of daily new followers and followees are very close to 0, while constantly-public users often have new followers and followees every day. This suggests that private users are more careful on choosing their followers and followees (similar to the summary in Section 3).

Inconstant users' dynamic online behavior statistics are presented in Table 5. It appears that users changing from public to private have fewer newly posted and favored tweets than those changing from private to public. Moreover, inconstant users changing from public to private are reducing their followers and followees. In addition, more followers are deleted than followees (-0.15 vs. -0.04), which indicates that users' one purpose of enabling access control is, to some extent, to protect themselves from being viewed by someone from whom they are hiding sensitive information. In another way, users are more concerned about privacy leakage through who follows them than who they follow. This result reflects some fundamental differences between follower and followee relations on Twitter.

Table 5: Statistics of inconstant users' dynamic online behaviors.

	Public to private	Private to public
Tweets	3.12	5.64
Favorites	4.35	4.67
Followers	-0.15	0.25
Followees	-0.04	0.14

User topics. Next, we analyze posts (tweets for Twitter and captions of photos for Instagram) that users publish

Table 6: Topics of users' posts one day before and after changing their access control settings.

Twitter	Public to private		Private to public	
	before	after	before	after
Topic 1	happy years new	woman get never	just one time	can party still
Topic 2	music nothing three	family made truth	person every crying	one just kids
Topic 3	nice looking needs	like boys text	bitch whole one	team really win

Instagram	Public to private		Private to public	
	before	after	before	after
Topic 1	follow keep coming	thankful already missing	good morning feeling	god person remember
Topic 2	go let strong	feels puppy wake	come show true	inspiration goodnight sleep
Topic 3	can't wait next	get also link	family friends lit	art music yesterday

before and after they change access control setting and check whether topics of users' posts have changed.

We exploit a classical topic modeling algorithm in the natural language processing field, namely Latent Dirichlet Allocation (LDA) [1] to detect topics from users' posts. We start to query each inconstant user's posts through the corresponding API one day before and after she changed her access control setting, then aggregate posts of each user together as one document. Punctuations and stop words are filtered out during the process. We then organize all the documents into a corpus, and remove words that appear in less than 20 documents and more than 70% of the documents [24]. Note that for users who change from public to private, we cannot get their published posts on both Twitter and Instagram. However, as users frequently change their access control setting and some private users become public on the day we collect their published posts (January 21, 2016), we are able to extract topics from their posts when they change from public to private.

Table 6 lists the top 3 topics for Twitter and Instagram when users change their access control setting. We observe that when users are public, their topics are not privacy-sensitive, for instance, "happy, years, new" published during the New Year on Twitter and "follow, keep, coming" representing the popular hashtags on Instagram. On the other hand, when users enable their access control setting, their topics become more private, such as "family" on Twitter and "missing" on Instagram.

4.4 Global Events and Festivals

OBSERVATION 7: *Global events and festivals cause more users to change access control setting from private to public.*

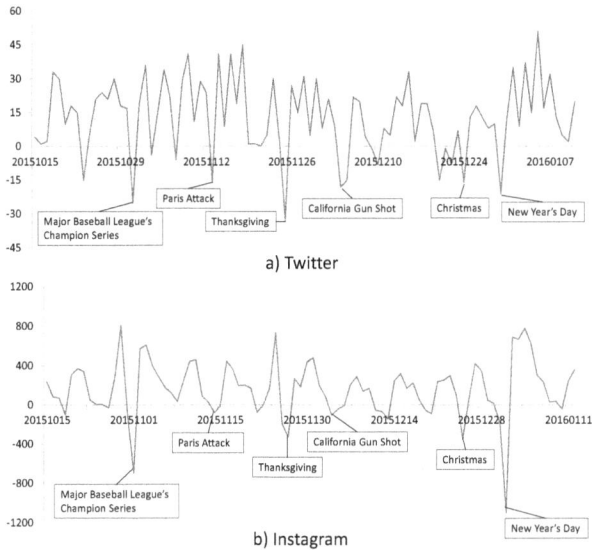

Figure 10: Differences between daily new private users and daily new public users.

As stated before, the trend for users to enable their access control setting is increasing, thus there should be more users changing from public to private than from private to public every day. However, when plotting the difference between daily new private users and public users (the number of new private user subtracts the number of new public users), we have found several interesting dates on which many more users changed from private to public than from public to private (see Figure 10).

On three important festivals in the US, i.e., Thanksgiving (November 26th, 2015), Christmas (December 25th, 2015) and New Year's Day (January 1st, 2016), more users disable their access control setting on both Twitter and Instagram. This indicates that on holidays, users are more open and less concerned about their privacy for the purpose of meeting new people and expressing gratitude.

In addition, we find that some global events might cause more people to become public in OSNs as well. For instance, more users become public on November 13, 2015 (Paris terrorist attack) and on December 3rd, 2015 (California gun shot case). This is probably because users are more willing to express their opinions when such events take place.

There also exists an obvious drop on November 1, 2015 on both OSNs, we believe this is due to the final match of the Major Baseball League's champion series between New York Mets and Kansas City Royals held in New York. Even though New York Mets lost the championship on that day, there are still New York users becoming public to communicate with other baseball fans on Twitter and Instagram.

4.5 Summary

In this section, we study dynamic usage of users' access control in OSNs and have observed the following.

- Many users change their access control setting from time to time. Instagram users change more often than Twitter users. More users change from public to private, showing that users become more concerned about their privacy day by day.

- Female users and young users change their access control setting more frequently and their changing trend from public to private is faster than others. Asian and African American users behave differently on Twitter and Instagram, while White users' changing behavior is the least active on both OSNs.

- Constantly-private users are less active than constantly-public users in terms of published posts and new followers/followees. When users change from public to private, they publish less tweets than users changing from private to public, and delete their followers, their posts' topics are more privacy-sensitive than before.

- Global events and festivals cause more users to change access control setting from private to public.

5. ACCESS CONTROL PREDICTION

After analyzing users' access control usage, in this section we investigate whether it is possible to predict a user's access control setting. Being able to predict a user's access control setting opens up opportunities for appealing applications. For instance, OSNs can automatically assign access control setting to their users for better privacy protection; government can develop a privacy advisor to remind users of their privacy leakage. Our prediction is based on users' static information, by only using a user's information listed on the OSN page, we aim to predict whether the user should enable access control setting or not.

We model access control prediction as a binary classification problem, and intend to solve the problem with machine learning classifiers. We label private users as positive cases while public users as negative cases. For features used in classification, two models are constructed, namely Model1 and Model2. Model1 exploits users' static online behavior including number of followers/followees, number of tweets and number of favorites as features for classification. Model2 combines the features of Model1 with demographics. In demographics, there are two categorical variables including gender and race, we change them into dummy variables for classification. Three machine learning classifiers, i.e., logistic regression, random forest and gradient boosting, have been used to conduct prediction. ROC (Receiver operating characteristic) curve and AUC (area under the ROC curve) are used as evaluation metrics.

Table 7: AUC of prediction.

	Model1	Model2
logistic regression	0.59	0.62
random forest	0.61	0.64
gradient boosting	0.69	0.70

Table 7 lists the AUC for two models under each classifier. Our best prediction result (gradient boosting and Model2) is fair, the AUC equals to 0.70[18], which indicates that users' access control setting can be predicted to a certain extent. Model2 achieves a better result than Model1 indicating demographics' usefulness on separating public and private users. Figure 11 further depicts the ROC curves for Model1 and Model2, respectively.

[18]AUC is not sensitive to label imbalance problem and AUC for random guessing is around 0.5.

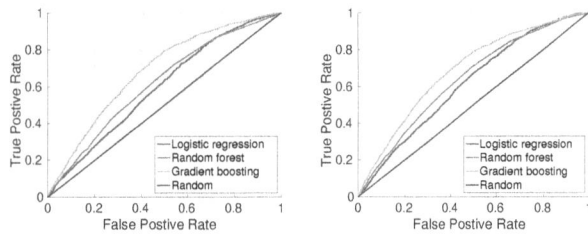

Figure 11: ROC curves for Model1 (left) and Model2 (right) w.r.t. different classifiers.

As we cannot get private users' demographics and online behavior information from Instagram's API (see Section 2), we only focus on Twitter users for access control prediction.

6. LIMITATIONS

In this section, we discuss a few limitations in our study.

Dataset. The current work focus on New York users' access control usage. Even though the user sample is large (more than 150k users for Twitter and and more than 280k users for Instagram), there still exist some region bias in our analysis. Meanwhile, knowing users being in New York allows us to conduct some more interesting analysis, such as users' offline behaviors (see Section 3) as well as a base ball match's influences on users' access control changing (see Section 4).

Social relation and access control. Section 4 concludes that when a user changes her access control setting from public to private, the user is more likely to reduce her number of followers. However, we haven't conducted the detailed analysis on who are these users being deleted. One obstacle for this analysis is the restriction of the API: Twitter allows much less access to their users' social networks[19], while Instagram provides only a small number of followers/followees of a user each time[20].

7. RELATED WORK

Access control in OSNs has attracted academia a considerable amount of attention during the past decade. Many researchers have focused on modeling access control schemes in OSNs from a formal or logical perspective. Carminati et al. [4] propose three regulations for access control scheme in OSNs, including social relation, distance in social network as well as trust level. The authors of [10] describe a two-stage access control where, to access a resource of a certain user, one has to be able to reach that user in the social network and then requests the access. Besides modeling access control schemes, researchers have also proposed methods to precisely define access control policies. In [3], access control policies are defined by semantic web technologies. The authors of in [9, 2] propose to use hybrid logic as the policy language, this logic has been demonstrated quite powerful and later be used in several works including [22, 7, 14, 17, 6, 15].

Compared to the formal perspective, not many works focus on the empirical perspective of access control in OSNs. Existing works include [12, 8, 21, 13]. Compared to these works, this paper has the following advantages:

- We perform dynamic analysis on users' access control usage within three consecutive months, which allows us to study users' change from a daily perspective and provide with more insightful conclusion on users daily online activities. On the other hand, the dynamic analysis in [8, 21] is yearly-based, which can only provide a general trend of access control usage. For instance, the authors of [21] study users' access control setting once a year from 2005 to 2011 and discover that more and more Facebook users in Pittsburgh enable their access control setting every year.

- This paper conducts a much more comprehensive study than previous ones ranging from users' demographics to online behavior. Besides, we are the first to analyze the relation between access control and users' offline behaviors (mobility information), topics of published texts and global events.

- This paper is the first to show that it is possible to use users' information to predict their access control setting to a certain extent. This result can potentially lead to promising applications such as automatic access control enforcement and privacy advisor.

- Our user sample is bigger than most of the previous works. We have more than 150k users for Twitter and more than 280k users for Instagram while the dataset in [12] focuses on 200 users and the one in [21, 13] has around 1,000 users. On the other hand, the authors of [8] use a bigger sample than us (1.4 million New York users on Facebook).

Besides the above advantages, all of [12, 8, 21, 13] only focus on Facebook while, to the best of our knowledge, this is the first work to analyze users' access control usage on Twitter and Instagram. As stated in Section 2, Twitter and Instagram have different types of users and functions compared to Facebook, thus it is very interesting and meaningful to study their users' access control usage.

8. CONCLUSION AND FUTURE WORK

We have conducted the first large-scale empirical study on users' access control usage on Twitter and Instagram. Our analysis focused on both static and dynamic perspectives. We further demonstrated that users' access control setting can be predicted to a certain extent.

For the future work, we plan to conduct analysis on other cities to check whether culture differences play a role in users' access control usage. Our access control prediction is only based on users' static information, we plan to explore users' dynamic information to predict whether a user will change her access control setting on a certain day by using more sophisticated features in machine learning classifiers.

Acknowledgement

Minyue Ni and Weili Han are supported by NSFC (Grant No. 61572136). We thank anonymous reviewers for their comments.

References

[1] D. Blei, A. Ng, and M. Jordan. Latent dirichlet allocation. *Journal of Machine Learning Research*, 3:993–1022, 2003.

---

[19]https://dev.twitter.com/rest/public/rate-limiting
[20]https://www.instagram.com/developer/endpoints/relationships/

[2] G. Bruns, P. W. L. Fong, I. Siahaan, and M. Huth. Relationship-based access control: its expression and enforcement through hybrid logic. In *Proc. 2nd ACM Conference on Data and Application Security and Privacy (CODASPY)*, pages 117–124. ACM, 2012.

[3] B. Carminati, E. Ferrari, R. Heatherly, M. Kantarcioglu, and B. Thuraisingham. A semantic web based framework for social network access control. In *Proc. 14th ACM Symposium on Access Control Models and Technologies (SACMAT)*, pages 177–186. ACM, 2009.

[4] B. Carminati, E. Ferrari, and A. Perego. Rule-based access control for social networks. In *Proc. IFIP WG 2.12 and 2.14 Semantic Web Workshop (OTM)*, volume 4278 of *LNCS*, pages 1734–1744. Springer, 2006.

[5] M. Cha, H. Haddadi, and F. B. K. P. Gummadi. Measuring user influence in Twitter: The million follower fallacy. In *Proc. 4th AAAI Conference on Weblogs and Social Media (ICWSM)*, pages 10–17. The AAAI Press, 2010.

[6] M. Cramer, J. Pang, and Y. Zhang. A logical approach to restricting access in online social networks. In *Proc. 20th ACM Symposium on Access Control Models and Technologies (SACMAT)*, pages 75–86. ACM, 2015.

[7] J. Crampton and J. Sellwood. Path conditions and principal matching: a new approach to access control. In *Proc. 19th ACM Symposium on Access Control Models and Technologies (SACMAT)*, pages 187–198. ACM, 2014.

[8] R. Dey, Z. Jelveh, and K. Ross. Facebook users have become much more private: A large-scale study. In *Proc. 2012 IEEE International Conference on Pervasive Computing and Communications Workshops*, pages 346–352. IEEE, 2012.

[9] P. W. L. Fong. Preventing sybil attacks by privilege attenuation: a design principle for social network systems. In *Proc. 32nd IEEE Symposium on Security and Privacy (S&P)*, pages 263–278. IEEE CS, 2011.

[10] P. W. L. Fong, M. M. Anwar, and Z. Zhao. A privacy preservation model for Facebook-style social network systems. In *Proc. 14th European Symposium on Research in Computer Security (ESORICS)*, volume 5789 of *LNCS*, pages 303–320. Springer, 2009.

[11] P. W. L. Fong and I. Siahaan. Relationship-based access control policies and their policy languages. In *Proc. 16th ACM Symposium on Access Control Models and Technologies (SACMAT)*, pages 51–60. ACM, 2011.

[12] Y. Liu, K. P. Gummadi, B. Krishnamurthy, and A. Mislove. Analyzing Facebook privacy settings: user expectations vs. reality. In *Proc. 2011 ACM SIGCOMM conference on Internet measurement conference (IMC)*, pages 61–70. ACM, 2011.

[13] M. Mondal, Y. Liu, B. Viswanath, K. P. Gummadi, and A. Mislove. Understanding and specifying social access control lists. In *Proc. 10th Symposium on Usable Privacy and Security (SOUPS)*, pages 271–283. USENIX Association, 2012.

[14] J. Pang and Y. Zhang. A new access control scheme for Facebook-style social networks. In *Proc. 9th Conference on Availability, Reliability and Security (ARES)*, pages 1–10. IEEE CS, 2014.

[15] J. Pang and Y. Zhang. Cryptographic protocols for enforcing relationship-based access control policies. In *Proc. 39th Annual IEEE Computers, Software & Applications Conference (COMPSAC)*, pages 484–493. IEEE CS, 2015.

[16] J. Pang and Y. Zhang. Location prediction: communities speak louder than friends. In *Proc. 3rd ACM on Conference on Online Social Networks (COSN)*, pages 161–171. ACM, 2015.

[17] J. Pang and Y. Zhang. A new access control scheme for Facebook-style social networks. *Computers & Security*, 54:44–59, 2015.

[18] M. J. Paul and M. Dredze. You are what you tweet: Analyzing twitter for public health. In *Proc. 5th AAAI Conference on Weblogs and Social Media (ICWSM)*, pages 265–272. The AAAI Press, 2011.

[19] M. Redi, D. Quercia, L. Graham, and S. Gosling. Like partying? your face says it all. Predicting the ambiance of places with profile pictures. In *Proc. 9th AAAI Conference on Weblogs and Social Media (ICWSM)*, pages 347–356. The AAAI Press, 2015.

[20] F. Souza, D. de Las Casas, V. Flores, S. Youn, M. Cha, D. Quercia, and V. Almeida. Dawn of the selfie era: The whos, wheres, and hows of selfies on Instagram. In *Proc. 3rd ACM on Conference on Online Social Networks (COSN)*, pages 221–231. ACM, 2015.

[21] F. Stutzman, R. Gross, and A. Acquisti. Silent listeners: The evolution of privacy and disclosure on Facebook. *Journal of Privacy and Confidentiality*, 4(2):2, 2013.

[22] E. Tarameshloo, P. W. L. Fong, and P. Mohassel. On protection in federated social computing systems. In *Proc. 4th ACM Conference on Data and Application Security and Privacy (CODASPY)*, pages 75–86. ACM, 2014.

[23] J. W. Tukey. *Exploratory Data Analysis*. Pearson, 1977.

[24] W. X. Zhao, J. Jiang, J. Weng, J. He, E.-P. Lim, H. Yan, and X. Li. Comparing Twitter and traditional media using topic models. In *Proc. 33rd European Conference on IR Research (ECIR)*, volume 6611 of *LNCS*, pages 338–349. Springer, 2011.

[25] Y. Zhong, N. J. Yuan, W. Zhong, F. Zhang, and X. Xie. You are where you go: Inferring demographic attributes from location check-ins. In *Proc. 8th ACM International Conference on Web Search and Data Mining (WSDM)*, pages 295–304. ACM, 2015.

An Application Restriction System for Bring-Your-Own-Device Scenarios

Oyindamola Oluwatimi
Department of Computer Science
Purdue University
West Lafayette, IN, USA
ooluwati@purdue.edu

Elisa Bertino
Department of Computer Science
Purdue University
West Lafayette, IN, USA
bertino@purdue.edu

ABSTRACT

Different containerization techniques have been developed to ensure the separation of enterprise content and personal data on an end-user's device. Although the enterprise manages the environment in which work-related activities are conducted, referred to as a work persona, third-party applications installed on the mobile devices may make the enterprise content vulnerable to misuse or exfiltration. It is thus critical that enterprises be given the ability to restrict the capabilities of third-party applications that reside in the work persona. In mobile systems, applications typically request to use a list of capabilities on the device prior to being installed on the device, and *all* capabilities must be granted in order for the applications to be installed. Our approach, that we refer to as DroidARM, focuses on post-installation application restriction policies. Such policies dynamically restrict the capabilities of mobile applications at run-time. An application restriction policy is configured through our Application Restriction Manager (ARM) Policy Manager that allows one to set different restrictions for each installed application. Adhering to the policy, our ARM system limits the capabilities of an application by restricting access to data and system resources contained within the work persona. Data shadowing is a data and system resource protection technique we have chosen to leverage. We have implemented DroidARM and integrated it into the Android operating system. Our experimental results show that our approach is efficient and effective.

Keywords

Access Control; Android; BYOD; Containerization; EMM

1. INTRODUCTION

In bring-your-own-device (BYOD) scenarios, an enterprise end-user, such as an employee, uses the same device for both personal and business purposes. Regardless of whether the device is supplied by the enterprise or independently acquired by the employee, the device stores both enterprise and personal data, and has the ability to remotely access secure enterprise networks. However, the security implications of such a dual use must be considered. The risk of breaches for sensitive enterprise data increases [15], as adversaries, whether human or software, with malicious intent may attempt to access, read, modify, and/or covertly exfiltrate data from a user's device. An employee can surreptitiously steal enterprise data by copying it to a cloud service via a mobile application such as Dropbox [11]. End-user devices may be vulnerable to malware that exploit mobile platforms' design flaws or architectural weaknesses [21], which potentially leads to unauthorized access to enterprise resources. To support such a dual use, various mobile device containerization techniques were developed to secure accessible enterprise content as well as the privacy of employees [13]. In a broad sense, containerization primarily aims to secure a portion of a device's resources (e.g., application, storage, or network access) from other applications and systems running on the same device.

In order to administer/manage secure containers to/on end-users' devices, enterprises use Enterprise Mobility Management (EMM) systems. Existing EMM systems operate at either the application or platform level. The level at which these systems operate determines the types of containerization technologies they are able to leverage to isolate content. Application-level EMM systems create an application-level container supported by a non-native application-layer (EMM) framework (Figure 1a) that allow an application, or a set of trusted applications, to isolate itself and its data from other untrusted applications. Platform-level EMM systems, supported by a native EMM framework (Figure 1b), create multiple environments referred to as "personas" to isolate content so that trusted applications do not execute in a persona in which untrusted applications also reside. Independently of whether the container is implemented at the application or platform level, enterprises are able to configure policies for the container that modify the behavior of the applications (e.g., accessing data and system resources).

EMM systems address BYOD scenarios by assuming that enterprises *only* desire to control and manage the capabilities of an end-user and his/her container and, more importantly, that all entities within a container are trusted. Enterprises thus have full control of the applications within a container, but as a negative consequence, also have the burden to vet all applications that are uploaded into the container. Such assumptions lead to two significant problems with respect to the policies that EMM systems allow enterprises to configure for containers [1]. First, the policies are usually

SACMAT'16, June 05-08, 2016, Shanghai, China

© 2016 ACM. ISBN 978-1-4503-3802-8/16/06...$15.00

DOI: http://dx.doi.org/10.1145/2914642.2914645

too broad to be applied on a per-application basis. For example, most often, an enterprise can disable GPS services for *all* applications within the container rather than for a selected subset of applications. Second, the policies contain too few, if any at all, configuration options for restricting an application's access to a device's data and system resources. For example, most EMM systems that allow multiple applications to reside within a container cannot prevent a specific member of that container from reading the device's contacts list.

Previously, such broad policies were considered adequate as they satisfied most enterprises' desired functionality in early BYOD scenarios. However, the proliferation and ever-increasing advancement in mobile applications, especially those focusing on end-user productivity, have made these applications critical for enterprises that thus need to include them in the enterprises' containers. A new BYOD scenario is introduced in which an enterprise needs to introduce *not fully trusted* third-party applications within a secured container. This reintroduces the problem of managing trusted and not fully trusted applications in the same environment that containerization initially addressed. Therefore, enterprises may encounter security risks such as enterprise data exfiltration through Bluetooth services or covert audio recording and exfiltration of information about end-user's business meetings acquired by the device's microphone. Such risks can be mitigated by configuring the container's policies to restrict access to Bluetooth or audio recording services, for example, but those policies, in most cases, will also apply to trusted members of the container. The all-or-nothing principle in policy configuration and the very few options for restricting data and system resources, or simply, *device content*, in such policies of modern EMM systems cannot address the requirements of such new BYOD scenarios without hindering the functionality of the enterprise container and its trusted members. Given such a BYOD scenario, a management facility to restrict applications' capabilities on a per-application basis should be provided to enterprises. Current EMM systems lack such a facility.

The design of a solution to support such BYOD scenarios must address three main issues. First, we must consider which restrictions must be supported and configurable, and to which level of granularity. The restrictions should be associated with devices' content that an enterprise may deem sensitive and require protection. A second issue is whether restrictions should also specify configurable responses or return values that will be used at the time of content access. Restrictions and the level of granularity with respect to which they are configurable in turn require addressing how to ensure the continuity of application operations if access to device content is denied. Applications may behave erratically [19] because applications assume they have unfettered access to content since they cannot be installed on the device unless the end-user grants full privileges to the set of requested device content and resources (explained further in Section 2). The third issue is at which level of the software stack the solution has to be implemented at (i.e., application or platform level). Answers to such issue require considering various aspects of ease-of-adoption of the solution. For example, implementing a solution solely at the application level will involve utilizing application-level containerization techniques. A burden is thus placed on enterprises to utilize an external tool such as a Software Developer Kit (SDK)

that must be created to integrate application restriction facilities. On the other hand, a more passive approach would be using platform-level containerization that can support application restriction transparently.

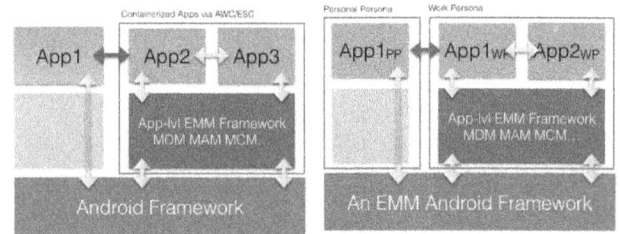

(a) Application-level Container.   (b) Platform-level Container

Figure 1: **The interactions between two containerized applications and an untrusted application that exists outside of the secure area. The gray and red arrows represent permitted and non-permitted communication channels, respectfully.**

Given such considerations, the design of an application restriction management solution should fulfill the following requirements:

1. Policy restrictions should be applicable to all applications within a container.

2. Policy restrictions should be fully customizable per application to give enterprises complete flexibility in granting/blocking access to device content.

3. Applications should not be able to bypass restrictions enforced by the solution.

4. When attempting to access device content, if blocked, an application should not crash.

5. The solution should not require application developers to modify source code, or impose any additional requirements on existing EMM systems.

6. The solution should not cause significant delays in the device functionality that could negatively impact the system performance.

7. An enterprise should be able to transmit a policy to a designated administrative application executing on an employee's mobile device.

In this paper, we propose an approach that addresses the above requirements. Our approach utilizes an application restriction manager that dynamically restricts or hinders an application's access to device content at run-time. To achieve this, the manager leverages the device content protection techniques implemented as part of IdentiDroid [19]. IdentiDroid supports permission revocation and data shadowing. Permission revocation denies an application the use of a permission at run-time. However, the experimental results in [19] demonstrate that revoking permission dynamically caused 29% of the tested applications operating on IdentiDroid to crash, which is too high for practical use. Therefore, we solely rely on data shadowing techniques, that is, obfuscating device content from selected applications.

Once one such application requests access to protected device content, the call is intercepted and the returned data is randomized for the purpose of concealing the content.

We implemented our approach in a platform called Droid Application Restriction Manager (DroidARM). We chose to build our custom Android platform on top of Lollipop because Lollipop is the first Android operating system (OS) to natively support standard user-based containerization techniques for smartphone devices. DroidARM integrates two main components into the Android OS: ARM Policy Manager (PM) and ARM System (ARMS). The PM is an application layer tool for creating, configuring, and deploying ARM policies, each consisting of a set of applications and their respective device content access restrictions. In addition, ARM policies can specify *global* configurable response actions or return data in the event that returning randomized data is insufficient. These policies are exclusively configurable by the controller of the persona, that is, either an enterprise IT admin or an enterprise end-user. Policies can be generated via a device's PM, a designated enterprise device admin application, or through our ARM policy configuration web server. The ARMS sits at the OS-level acting as a reference monitor restricting applications' capabilities by protecting device content from applications attempting to access such content. The ARMS secures device content by enforcing the ARM policies provided by the PM. We utilize a native Android component as a secure communication service to allow the ARMS, as well as any authorized entities, to query the database in which the PM stores its policies.

The DroidARM platform provides an enterprise member the means to limit application capabilities. Using our approach, access to device content by installed applications can be controlled. Therefore, if an untrusted third-party application is introduced within a container, the capabilities of such application can be restricted *post-installation* to maintain the security of the container.

This paper is organized as follows. Section 2 introduces various containerization techniques, the basic Android concepts, and IdentiDroid. Section 3 introduces the architecture and underlying components of our approach followed by the implementation and technical details in Section 4. We next report the results of our experiments and provide an analysis in Section 5 and Section 6. We briefly discuss related works in Section 7. Section 8 concludes the article by discussing improvements to DroidARM based on our experimental results.

2. BACKGROUND

2.1 Containerization

Implementation and application of containerization can occur at different levels: application-level, device-level, and OS-level [13].

Application-level containerization is an application-centric approach that involves end-users' devices having *one* environment which consists of both trusted and untrusted applications operating side-by-side. Two main techniques at the application level are usually employed in order to protect an application and the sensitive contents it operates on: Encrypted Space Container (ESC) and Application Wrapping Container (AWC). Both techniques create an encrypted container to isolate enterprise applications and data. However the former allows multiple applications to reside within

the container increasing data reusability. It also makes it possible to achieve consistent security for all resident applications. Last, it is possible for ESC to have either custom container- or application-specific policies allowing broad or granular policy configuration, as opposed to AWC only having application-specific policies.

Platform-level containerization encompasses techniques implemented at the user-, OS-, and system level. The main difference between the three techniques is which layers of the mobile software stack are shared. These containerization strategies are built directly into the OS, and they all share one key characteristic: they focus on environments where all data and applications in each environment are grouped together. In the EMM community, these environments are referred to as "personas". The aforementioned application-centric strategies led to the development of application-level frameworks by which mutually trusted applications can communicate with each other in a secure manner. Instead of isolating groups of mutually trusted applications, these platform-level strategies are able isolate and/or protect environments from one another. In other words, instead of having *one* persona, there could be separate personas for personal and work activities. It is assumed that any entity in one persona is equally trusted or as sensitive as any other entity in that same persona. Generally the two persona-type containerization techniques are Multi-User Container (MUC) and Mobile Virtual Container (MVC).

2.2 Android Overview

Android is a Linux-based, mobile phone platform designed with a multi-layered security infrastructure [7]. Loaded on top of the Linux kernel are the System Libraries, Android Runtime, and Application Framework software layers (Figure 2). Each application, which is assigned a unique user ID (UID), is given a dedicated part of the file system for its own data, and executes in a separate Dalvik Virtual Machine, thus creating an application sandbox. Along with Linux's discretionary access control mechanism, Android includes a fine-grained permission system that determines the set of device resources an application has access to. An application's permissions, which can be extracted from its AndroidManifest.xml file, are also associated with its UID. At the time of an application installation, users have to either grant all the requested permissions to proceed with the installation of the APK, or cancel the installation completely. As of Lollipop (API 22 v5.1), there are currently over 120 permissions.

An *Intent* is an Android messaging facility to support inter-component communication. A component (i.e., Android activity, service, content provider, or broadcast receiver) sends an Intent message to the OS, which basically specifies the intent of starting, accessing, or requesting information from a particular component, including ones from another application.

Android For Work

Android for Work (AFW), which is integrated into Android Lollipop, is an EMM system operating at the platform-level. It introduces the ability for a device to have multiple Android environments. That is, it utilizes the MUC technique to create user profiles (i.e., personas) to isolate content for different device users. A device owner, via the stock Settings application, can create up to a preset limit of personas for his/her device. A newly created persona is provided with its own clean userspace that includes all the applications from the device owner's persona. These applications do not retain any application data from the original profile, and therefore, once activated, execute as if they were just installed. Each persona is assigned a UID that is different from the application UID previously mentioned. From this point forward, we call this *persona ID* to distinguish between the two.

Through an *application-level* EMM system, an enterprise can create and manage AFW personas, deploy personas to end-user devices, and perform application management and distribution. The technical means for persona-deployment is through using Android's Device Administration APIs to create an enterprise-built custom, admin application that is deployed to employees' devices by the EMM system. Using an EMM system in conjunction with a custom admin application has security benefits such as ensuring a single point of entry to modify the behavior of end-users' devices.

Although it is not intended to protect a persona's contents (because all entities within a persona are assumed trusted), AFW provides a facility to restrict an application's capabilities via the *RestrictionsManager* class. This is only achievable if the application developer makes the capabilities configurable option; for example, configuring an application to only use Wifi instead of cellular data. However, this facility is not sufficient as it can only act on voluntary application-dependent configurations.

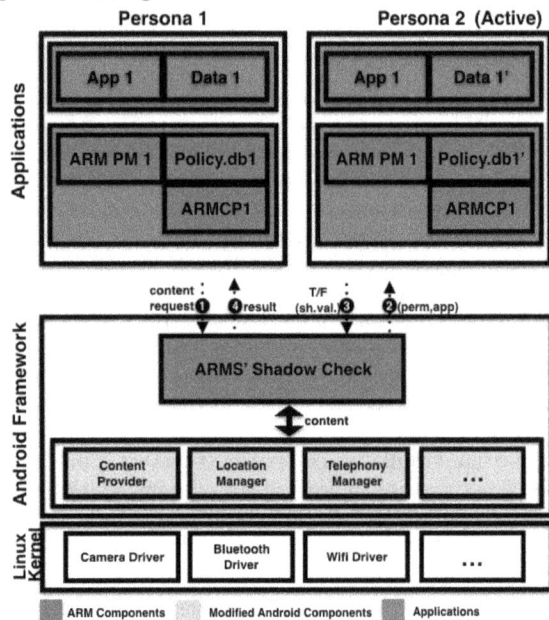

Figure 2: **System diagram displaying the steps the DroidARM platform performs once an application request sensitive content. The dash arrows show that the sensitive content and the ARM Policy are dependent on the active persona. The ARMS will return a global shadow value (*sh.val*) as the *result* if an enterprise member has configured it.**

2.3 IdentiDroid

IdentiDroid is a tool for protecting users' privacy at the application level on the Android platform as network anonymizers, like Tor and Hotspot Shield, are only able to assure the anonymity of IP addresses and not of data exchanged at the application level.

For the purposes of IdentiDroid, sensitive (device) content residing on Android is categorized into four groups, according to the method used for accessing the data.

- **System Data:** It consists of all the data concerning the system state and identity. Such data is typically accessed by calling value-returning methods for each data entity.

- **User Data:** It consists of common data generated by the user, such as contacts and SMSs. Such data is typically accessed by calling methods that return a *Cursor* to the requested databases.

- **System Resources:** It consists of resources provided by the device, such as camera and GPS. Resources are typically accessed by calling their corresponding *Activity* or *Service*.

- **Application Data:** It consists of the data stored and managed autonomously by the applications. This data represents the application data storage and can be only accessed by the application itself.

In order to help the devices' users in preserving their anonymity under anonymous networks, IdentiDroid (based on Android JellyBean API 17) was created to specifically limit and restrict the access capabilities of programs executing at the application layer. IdentiDroid is therefore a solution integrated into Android OS that acts as a reference monitor (within the application framework layer). IdentiDroid hinders applications when attempts to access identifying data occur. IdentiDroid consists of three main components: Data Shadowing Manager, Sensitive Permission Manager, and IdentiDroidProfile Manager.

The **data shadowing manager** enables the user to choose which information needs to be hidden from each application that might access it. The design of this solution was achieved by understanding all possible ways and methods by which an application can access sensitive content. As an example of multiple methods accessing a resource, applications can use the *Camera* resource either through an *Intent* call or through the *Camera* class. The manager shadows each category according to its access method. Shadowing *device information* returns a fake value for the requested information to any application configured to be shadowed. The returned value is randomized upon each data request so that different applications (or the same application) receive different device information. Shadowing *user databases* means returning an empty list of database records to any application trying to access protected data. Shadowing *device resources* consist of either: (a) not providing access to the resource by intercepting the application request; (b) returning modified or fake information, and sometimes no information. Whether an application uses an intent call to an Activity with that resource or the resource is associated with a set of class methods for accessing the resource itself determines how the device resource will be shadowed.

The **sensitive permission manager** controls the applications' access to sensitive permissions at run-time. Even though Android applications are granted all their required permissions at installation time, the manager can dynamically block permissions when these permissions are required at run-time by applications. For example, if an application like "Skype" requests to load the contacts address book saved on the device, the Android OS will check at run-time if this application has been granted the permission READ_CONTACTS. However, if "Skype" has been configured through the IdentiDroid Profile Manager not to have access to the contacts list, the permission call is dynamically intercepted and denied at run-time, thus blocking the application access to such list. As part of our previous work [19] we have identified 41 permissions as sensitive.

Preventing applications from accessing sensitive content via permission revocation is achieved by returning the PackageManager.PERMISSION_DENIED value at run-time. However, a security exception is thrown when such constant is returned and this usually causes problems for applications. The reason is that developers usually do not expect their applications to be revoked a permission they requested because users must grant all permissions in order to install the applications. Therefore, when a permission that was initially granted is revoked, applications have the likely chance of crashing, with the OS subsequently force-closing it.

The **profile manager** is an Android application that hosts customizable configurations represented as profiles. Each profile has the ability to configure settings for the shadow manager and the permission manager. Each of the aforementioned settings is unique per profile, giving users the ability to tailor different profiles for protecting various aspects of their identity against a subset of user-installed applications. The manager populates a list of currently-installed user applications and allow users to choose which applications they desire to deny access to sensitive data and resources. One profile, the anonymity profile, is designated to be used in conjunction with the user's connection to an anonymous network.

3. ARCHITECTURE

In this section, we describe our DroidARM platform (Figure 2). Application-level containerization is achieved through our Application Restriction Management (ARM) PM. It provides a means to configure *application restrictions* post-installation. It is the responsibility of the ARMS to enforce the restrictions presented by the PM. We leverage the MUC technique introduced in Lollipop to create personas, so each persona has only one active ARM policy.

3.1 Personas on DroidARM

The operations of the DroidARM platform are centered around personas (i.e., user profiles) and the specific enterprise members that deploy those personas. We define an *enterprise member* as the entity which deploys, controls, and manages a persona. An enterprise member assumes, exclusively, one of two roles. In most BYOD scenarios, the enterprise member is the IT admin (of a business/corporation) which has the responsibility of managing a large number of employees' mobile devices. In other BYOD scenarios, the enterprise member is simply an end-user, possibly self-employed, that has the responsibility of managing only his/her own mobile device. Regardless of the assumed role, the enterprise member desires to limit the capabilities of applications residing within the deployed persona.

We leverage Android facilities to deploy personas on our platform. Suppose the enterprise member is an IT admin, then the persona deployment is achieved through the development of a custom (device) admin application built using Android's Device Administration APIs. Use of such APIs increases DroidARM's ease of adoption as current enterprises' IT admins may have already built an admin application to control their employees' devices running AFW, which DroidARM is built upon. Once the admin application is downloaded to an employee's device, the admin application creates a new persona dedicated to work-related activities. On the other hand, suppose the enterprise member is a self-employed end-user, then a new work persona can be manually deployed through Android's Settings application's user interface (UI). Regardless of the persona deployment method, a clean userspace containing the same list of applications as the default persona (i.e., *Persona 1* in Figure 2), including the PM, will be instantiated. The enterprise member has full authority on which applications are uploaded to or removed from the persona once the deployment process is complete. At this time, the default ARM policy becomes active. Because the default ARM policy initially contains no application restrictions, the ARMS does not hinder any application from accessing sensitive content. The persona's policy, however, can be updated manually or remotely depending on the role the enterprise member assumed, which we further explain later in this section.

3.2 ARM Policy

An ARM policy contains application restrictions. Specifically, it consists of a set of applications and their respective sensitive content access restrictions. When creating or updating an ARM policy, the enterprise member can specify two restrictions types, per-application restrictions and/or global restrictions, which are both based on data shadowing. Below, we provide a brief description of each restriction type; further details of how they are utilized are provided in Section 4.

3.2.1 Per-Application Restrictions

Per-application restrictions specify the sensitive content that an application no longer has the privilege to access. We also refer to these reductions in privileges as revoked permissions. We have identified 40 sensitive Android permissions in Lollipop in which each permission, in essence, specifies which device content the application may potentially use. However, each sensitive permission could be related to several API functions that control or access various information about the associated content. Configuring that many permissions for just a single application can be daunting, and quite confusing for anyone attempting to configure an ARM policy [9]. We have thus abstracted these permissions into 13 generic sensitive permission categories (left side of Figure 3) that are more intuitive to understand. These categories along with their access decisions instruct the ARMS by default to return a randomized return value (i.e., shadow value) on a per-application basis at the time of an API call.

3.2.2 Global Restrictions

Global restrictions apply to all applications that cannot access device content. Under certain conditions, if an enterprise member revokes a permission category to an application, when that application attempts to access the content, DroidARM returns a *specific* shadow value set by the enterprise member. Global restrictions are used to only shadow simple value-returning APIs which mostly consist of APIs to retrieve *System Data*, as opposed to per-application restrictions that also shadow complex resources.

Package Name	Permission Category	Access
com.androidillusion.cameraillusion	CAMERA	true
com.facebook.katana	LOCATION	true
com.estrongs.android.pop	DEVICE_INFO	true
com.skype.raider	SOCIAL_INFO	true
com.instagram.android	DEVICE_INFO	true

Table 1: **The package names for several popular Android applications which are denied access to various device content via data shadowing.**

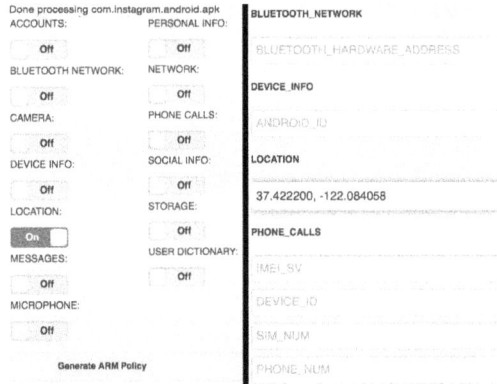

Figure 3: **The web server's user interfaces once the Instagram APK has been uploaded. It displays our defined abstracted permission categories (based on the processed APK) on the left, and global restrictions that can be shadowed on the right.**

3.3 ARM Policy Manager

The ARM PM is located at the application layer, and its main task is to store an ARM policy. The policy specifies application restrictions for the active persona on an end-user's device. The PM allows only one policy to exist at any one time within a persona, and this policy is always active. By default, applications within a persona have unfettered access to sensitive content. An enterprise member's assumed role dictate the method by which ARM policies are deployed and the mode the PM operates under.

3.3.1 Deploying Policies

The PM also allows the end-user to locally configure a policy through a simple UI, but only in BYOD scenarios in which an end-user is self-managing the device. Other BYOD scenarios require that policies cannot be configurable by an end-user and must be deployed in a remote manner from a source external to the end-user's device. That is, scenarios in which the enterprise IT admin is managing employees' devices. We take advantage of various technologies and other communication platforms so that policy dissemination is easily scalable. First, we leverage Android's *Content Provider* APIs to integrate a means to query or update current ARM policies, and we ensure that read/write access is only granted to authorized external applications or processes on the device. Second, we adopt the approach in AFW to use an admin application to provide *remote* control of an end-user's device. Besides a persona's PM, we only allow a designated admin application to update the ARM policy ensuring the security of the policy. Third, we also implemented a remote server that aids enterprises in creating an ARM policy, and configuring the per-application restrictions and global restrictions within it. Because admin applications are au-

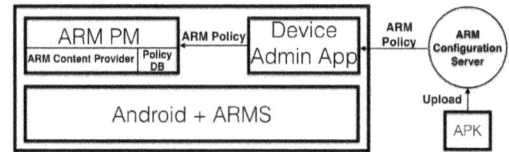

Figure 4: **The diagram displays the method by which an ARM policy can be configured on an employee's device remotely by an enterprise admin.**

thorized to communicate policies to our content provider, enterprises can easily and securely configure ARM policies for employees' devices in a remote manner.

3.3.2 ARM Operation Modes

The ARM PM operates under only *one* of two modes: *master* or *slave*. These modes determine what the end-user is able to accomplish via the PM's UI. Initially, when a persona is newly created, the PM will be in master mode. When in master mode, the end-user is allowed to configure the ARM policies. If it is operating under slave mode, then policy configuration is disallowed completely by disabling the PM's UI, otherwise policy violations will occur.

To illustrate the circumstances in which a PM, and therefore the persona it resides in, becomes a master or slave, we describe two generic BYOD scenarios that our system handles. In the first scenario, a controller entity desires to limit the capabilities of applications residing in a controllee's persona. For example, the IT admin of an enterprise would act as the controller while an employee acts as the controllee. The setup of the persona container in this instance is executed as follows. The admin application creates a new persona, and therefore the newly instantiated PM will automatically be set to master mode. We first assume that the IT admin has access to all APKs stored within the persona since the IT admin has full control of which applications are permitted in the persona (Section 2). Once the admin application retrieves the policy generated by our web server (Figure 4), the admin application will send those policies to our content provider. The received ARM policy will be set as the active policy and the slave operation mode will be activated. Now as it is an enslaved persona, the persona cannot revert back to master mode nor can the employee modify the policy.

In the second scenario, the controller and the controllee are essentially the same party. For example, an independent business owner that has full control over his/her device is concerned with the capabilities of his/her own applications, and thus desires to limit them. In this persona-creation instance, the owner creates a new persona for business purposes. Similarly, the PM in the new persona is also set to master mode. The owner can freely modify the ARM policy at anytime because the PM will never be set to slave mode.

3.4 Application Restriction Manager System

The ARMS is our reference monitor that is integrated into the Android OS. It specifically resides within the application framework layer and partially in the Android Runtime environment acting as an intermediary entity that intercepts every request for device content associated with our permission categories. Normally, if an application has been granted a sensitive permission at installation time, the application has full access to the associated sensitive content. However, if the application has been configured through our PM to be denied the associated permission category, then at runtime, the sensitive content is dynamically shadowed. As previously stated, we do not dynamically revoke Android permissions as a technique to hinder access to sensitive content because security exceptions are thrown that will most likely cause the application to crash [19].

4. IMPLEMENTATION

4.1 ARM Policy

We make use of Android's key-value database facilities to create ARM policies. When a per-application restriction is configured for an application, we store within the database the application's package name, the permission category, and a Boolean value indicating whether the restriction is active (see Table 1 for an example). Although a UID is a unique identifier for an application, the same application most likely will not have the same identifier on another device when considering the support of remote policy configuration via our web server for many employees using different devices that was explained in Section 3. Therefore, we use an application's package name as it is a unique global identifier for all published applications submitted to Google. Global restrictions are also stored within the database using the specific name of the device content along with the enterprise-specified shadow value.

4.2 ARM Content Provider

It is the responsibility of the ARMS to ensure that restrictions comply with the ARM policies presented by the PM. Therefore, we need to provide the ARMS a means to communicate with the PM in order for the ARMS to make run-time decisions on whether an application has legitimate access to sensitive content. As such, we implemented our *ARMContentProvider* Android component within the PM that allows the ARMS to access application restrictions. The ARMS needs only to send three parameters to the content provider: the application package name, the sensitive permission category, and the device content name that the application is attempting to utilize. These parameters are passed via the ContentProvider's *call (Uri uri, String method, String arg, Bundle extras)* method.

We do not need to also pass the *persona ID* as a parameter for the active persona because the policy stored by the PM is intrinsically attached to the persona. This is the result of a new application data space being created for each application, including the PM, whenever a new persona is created. Thus the system will automatically apply the correct policy even though multiple personas may exist on that device. Leveraging Lollipop's MUC implementation in such a way gives DroidARM an advantage over other persona-type EMM systems because most systems only allow up to two maximum work-related personas to be created, while persona-creation on DroidARM is only limited by the availability of device resources such as disk space.

4.3 ARMS

The ARMS utilizes and supplements the implementation of the data shadowing facilities in IdentiDroid. In order to dynamically shadow data, we modify the set of Android classes utilized by developers to access sensitive content, according to the sensitive data classification discussed in Sec-

Data	Method	Permission Category
System Data		
Android_ID	Settings.System.getString(Android_ID)	DEVICE_INFO
IMEI or CDM or ESN	TelephonyManager.getDeviceId()	DEVICE_INFO
Current Cell Location	TelephonyManager.getCellLocation()	DEVICE_INFO
Phone Number	TelephonyManager.getLine1Number()	DEVICE_INFO
IP Address	WifiInfo.getIpAddress()	NETWORK
User Data		
Contacts	ContentResolver.Query()	SOCIAL_INFO
Photo Albums	ContentResolver.Query()	CAMERA
SMS	ContentResolver.Query()	MESSAGES
Bookmarks/History	ContentResolver.Query()	PERSONA_INFO
System Resources		
Camera	Camera.open()	CAMERA
Location	LocationManager.getLastLocation()	LOCATION
WiFi MAC Address	WifiInfo.getMacAddress()	NETWORK

Table 2: **Some of the sensitive content considered, with access method and related permission category.**

tion 2. At the time of an API call, the ARMS intercepts the request and delegates it to our ARMContentProvider's *revokeResourceAccess()* function. The ARMContentProvider requires the application's package name, the abstracted category of the permission, and the specific name of the requested device content. We derive the package name of the application using the UID of the application that performed the API call. The UID is retrieved using one of Android's hidden management facilities, *UserHandle.myUid()*. Next, we derive the permission category. Many of the classes associated with sensitive content contain special functions that control access to the requested content. These access control functions rely on Android's *ActivityManagerService* class, which is natively tasked with verifying that a particular application attempting to access device content has the appropriate Android permissions. The verification process involves invoking the method *checkComponentPermission(String permission, int pid, int uid,...)* where the "permission" parameter is the permission associated with the device content that is requested. We manually inspected each access control function to determine the specific permission that is submitted to the *ActivityManagerService*, and translated the Android permission to one of our defined permission categories. Once we derive and send the necessary parameters, our content provider returns a *Bundle* object. Android's Bundle class allows one to store various types of data simultaneously. The ARMContentProvider utilizes this data structure by storing a Boolean access decision. In the event that the access decision is false, that is, access is denied, the ARMContentProvider also stores within the bundle the shadow value that must be returned to the application. If the enterprise member has not set a global restriction for that specific content, then a randomized shadow value is returned. Otherwise, if the access decision is true, the normal process to access the content is resumed.

Table 2 lists some of the classes we modified. *System Data* is obfuscated by replacing returned values with random ones (e.g., return the string ABCDEF1234 as the device's ID). *User Databases* are obfuscated by returning a *Null Cursor* object instead of the expected Cursor object in *ContentResolver.query()*. The *Null Cursor* represents an empty dataset. Additionally, obfuscating the querying function minimizes the number of places where source code has to be modified as that function is a single point of entry to access any of Android's relational databases. *System Resources* are obfuscated by either returning fake values or by ignoring the requests made by applications (e.g., intercepting and dropping an *Intent* object designated for the *Camera* Activity).

Data	Stock System	ARMS Shadowing
System Data		
IMEI/MEID/ESN	353850932165477	1234567890ABCDE
Phone Number	111-111-1111	123-456-7890
WiFi MAC Address	10:BF:48:F2:7E:EB	Null via null WiFiInfo
Android ID	A23BF6FD34	ABCDEF1234
User Data		
Contacts	Access to Contacts	Empty List of Contacts
Photo Albums	Access to Photo Albums	Empty List of Photos
SMS	Access to SMS	Empty List of SMS Messages
Calendar	Access to Calendar	Empty List of Events
Account Manager	Access to User Accounts	Empty List of Accounts
System Resources		
Camera	Access to Camera	Unable to open to camera via intent
Location	41.103807, -85.399449	37.428434, -122.072382
Microphone	Access to Record Audio	Unable to open Audio Recorder
Network	Access to Network	Believes there is no active Network

Table 3: **DroidARM's effect on some of the sensitive data.**

4.4 ARM Web Server

The server presents an online form by which an enterprise member can submit a physical copy of an application's APK to be introduced into an employee's work persona. The server then processes the application by extracting the Android permissions within the Android.xml and translating any existing sensitive permissions into our defined permission categories. Next, the server presents a configuration wizard to allow the IT admin to revoke any of these permission categories for this particular application. At this point, an ARM policy can be generated, and it is left to the enterprise to disseminate the policy to all the admin applications on each of the employees' devices.

The web server also supports the configuration of global restrictions. The form presents for each permission category a list of form fields by which an IT admin can specify preferred shadow values for sensitive content that can be accessed via value-returning Android APIs. In the event that the IT admin does not fill in a subset of the form fields, unauthorized applications will retrieve randomized shadow values at each access. Global shadow restrictions can be configured subsequent to configuring per-application restrictions, and therefore be included at the time of policy generation. Allowing enterprises to specify shadow values for sensitive content provides them even higher granularity in application restrictions that are not present in other EMM systems.

For example, suppose an enterprise allows the Instagram application within the work persona; however, the enterprise does not desire that the application be able to retrieve the device's genuine GPS coordinates. Instead, thus the IT admin, through our web server, can first revoke the LOCATION permission category and then specify dummy GPS coordinates. Figure 3 displays the UIs for per-application restrictions (left) and global restrictions (right) once the IT admin has uploaded the Instagram APK.

5. EXPERIMENTAL RESULTS

Our experiments were performed on Google's Nexus 4 smartphone device running Android 5.1.1. We acquired 100 applications from the Google Play Store. Although only a subset, all of the applications that were used in our experiments were also used in IdentiDroid. The selected applications were known to use functions that are dependent on Android sensitive resources, and thus we also utilize for our experiments to test dynamic restrictions to said resources. The Android Debug Bridge (ADB) utility for logging system and application events was utilized in each of the experiments.

Experiment 1: Testing DroidARM on Applications - Expected Behavior Validation. The focus of this experiment is to validate that sensitive content is indeed being shadowed, and observe any visual indication within tested applications' Activities. We tested the system against 100 applications based on the sensitive data categories listed in Section 2. We excluded *Application Data* because, in an BYOD context, enterprises should not be concerned with data that applications manage autonomously. An application may very well need to store various data within its own application directory in order to provide its essential service, otherwise, the application should not be installed within the persona because it will be inoperable.

Table 3 displays our experimental results showing some of the values returned to these applications and the actions taken by DroidARM. For demonstration purposes, the shadowed values displayed are of the general form $1234567890AB$ $CDEF$, as sensitive APIs are supposed to return random values whenever an application accesses such data explicitly when global restrictions do not exist.

Experiment 1 shows that the network resource is one sensitive content that is unique amongst the rest. The shadowing implementation relies on the APIs that the stock Android platform currently provides to application developers for accessing sensitive content, which includes APIs from both the Android application framework layer and core Java libraries. The former provides APIs to interrogate the state of the network, whether it is Wifi or cellular based. We shadow those APIs returning false for *WifiManager.isEnabled()* or *TelephonyManager.DISABLED* for *TelephonyManager.getState()*, for example. In addition to obfuscating network connectivity information in Android APIs, we also had to modify the *Socket* and *URL* classes in core Java libraries, which exist in the Android Runtime environment. Good application developers would test the state of the network prior to using the network resource; however, during the experiment, we observed that some applications attempted to connect even though they were alerted that the network was unavailable. In very few cases, applications were able to access the network. 4% of applications in the *Network* permission category exhibited this behavior. Figure 5 displays an application that is denied access to the INTERNET category, and although it states that it cannot load images, it is still able to load some metadata in various Activities such as profile names, number of "likes", and comments. A security analysis of such behaviour is discussed in Section 6.

Experiment 2: Overhead Performance of DroidARM. In this experiment, we evaluate the performance of our modified Android platform. We measured the overhead of execution times for only one method. This method is transparently called when applications attempt to access sensitive content. Specifically, we measure the elapsed time immediately prior to calling our ARMContentProvider's *revokeResourceAccess()* function and up to after returning a *Boolean* value. Although we made minor modifications throughout the Android framework, most of these modifications simply entail invoking *revokeResourceAccess()* and then proceeding with executing an uncomplicated appropriate reaction to the Boolean value (i.e., return randomized data or drop an intent). Each measurement was taken 9 times then averaged.

Table 4 reports in milli-seconds (ms) the time overhead for invoking our ARMContentProvider. Our results demon-

Figure 5: **Instagram is denied access to INTERNET resources, and consequently cannot load images. It, however, is able to load metadata for those images such as profile name, number of likes, and comments.**

Method	Overhead
ACP.revokeResourceAccess()	3.23

Table 4: **Time overhead (in ms) for the core methods that are called very often in DroidARM**

strate that DroidARM has a small impact on system performance. Shadowing content in our system incurs $3.23ms$ overhead. Given such a small overhead, we determined that users of the DroidARM platform will not be able to perceive any performance impact.

Experiment 3: Impact of Data Shadowing on Applications. The goal of this experiment is to evaluate the impact of data shadowing by the ARMS. That is, we performed stress tests on 100 applications and observed the impact of denying these applications access to *all* sensitive content (excluding *Application Data*). It is necessary to understand the overall effect of data shadowing on Android applications because enterprises assuring application operational continuity under various combinations of application restrictions within ARM policies is critical.

The evaluation of each application was carried as follows. For every application, we first used Android's Settings application to determine the list of Android permissions that an installed application contains within its AndroidManifest.xml file. We then used the PM, through the UI, to deny the application access to all the sensitive content that it may potentially attempt to access based on the permissions acquired from the Settings application. Next, we manually interacted with the application of interest forcing it to use all of its functionalities to ensure that access to sensitive content is requested. We examine the ADB log output in real-time to determine which content were accessed. We observed and then noted whether an application crashed (i.e., force-closed) after being denied access to the sensitive content.

Results in Figure 6 show that the ARMS is effective in denying applications access to sensitive content while maintaining application operational continuity. Only 1% of applications crashed operating on the DroidARM platform. One application, CameraIllusion, crashed when the Camera resource was shadowed. It occurred when *Camera.open()* function was called. In the stock Android OS, such func-

tion is supposed to return *null* when a camera is either not present or, if present, may be in current use by another application running on the platform. When the camera resource is shadowed, we return null. The application lacked proper error handling when getting a null; however, such circumstance is understandable. First, the application's AndroidManifest.xml file contains the XML tags "uses-feature" that enforces three different restrictions in regards to camera: the camera itself, autofocus, and camera flash. If a user's device does not contain such hardware or hardware capabilities, the application cannot be installed on the user's device. Second, if multiple applications are using the camera resource, higher priority to the resource is granted to the application in the immediate foreground. That is, background applications are evicted from using the resource and thus returning null should not occur.

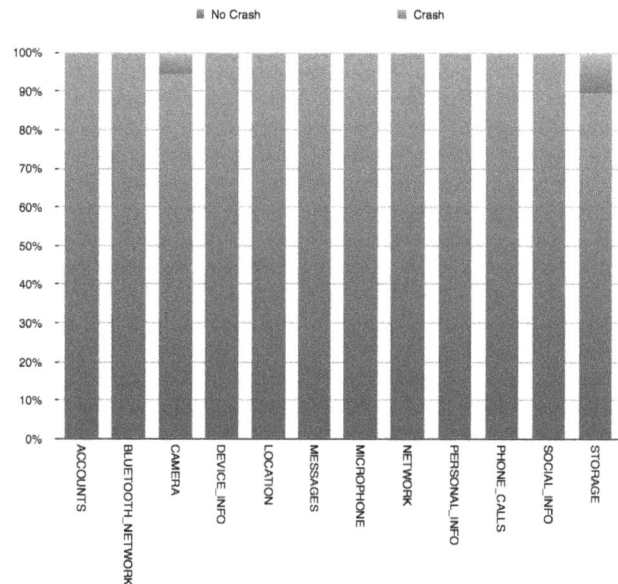

Figure 6: **Impact of data shadowing on 100 applications**

6. SECURITY ANALYSIS

In this section, we present a security analysis of our DroidARM platform to analyze possible threats of circumventing ARMS's application restriction policies or violating the integrity of the ARM policies stored by the ARM PM. Below, we provide various attack vectors that could be used for circumvention and, subsequently, a means to mitigate the threat or minimize the attack vector surface.

6.1 Native Development Kit

We briefly mentioned in the experimental results section that 4% of the applications were able to access the network resource even though those same applications were denied access to it in the ARM policies. Such an ability is the result of a native feature that Android supports. Low level resources (Figure 2) that the Linux kernel provides (e.g., camera, WiFi, bluetooth, location, network, etc.) are usually accessed by application layer Java APIs. However, low level resources can also be accessed via Android's Native Development Kit (NDK). Android's NDK is a toolset that allows Android developers to build portions of their applications in native code or port existing libraries written in

C and C++. Even though developers usually refer to Java code when calling higher-level functionalities in the Android system, they may prefer to write lower-level system calls using C/C++. In particular, by using an external standard C library, developers can call functions such as *connect()*, *read()*, *socket()*, *write()*, etc.

Attempts to utilize the NDK does not circumvent Android's stock upper layer permission verification process because the application sandbox does not depend on the technology used to build the application. The Linux kernel adds another level of defense by also restricting access to these resources. An application is added to the low level list of processes (i.e. a resource group) that are able to access a resource at the time of installation if the application has the associated upper layer Android permission. If an application uses a C/C++ class to access a low level resource, the Linux kernel checks its own access control list to verify whether the application is part of the associated group and subsequently grants or revokes access to that resource. Herein lies the problem. ARMS is unable to block application access to a resource once the Linux kernel grants access to the resource since the Linux kernel and the ARMS reside at lower levels and upper levels of the platform, respectively. That is, the ARMS cannot deny the access via *shadowing*. This is a special case in application restriction management: sensitive content that cannot be denied via data shadowing because the data or resource may exist outside of the application layer framework. We now provide an example of an access to low level resources.

Suppose that an application that has the Android INTERNET permission uses *socket()* to access the network. The Linux kernel then checks its own access control list to verify whether the application is part of the network group and subsequently grants or denies access to the resource. The inability to completely deny access at the upper layers of the software stack to the network resource, which may possibly be the most sensitive resource in all the resource categories, results in the risk of content exfiltration. In addition, it can be used as a means to acquire other sensitive content. For example, the device's IP address or course-/fine- grained location could be determined [18]. To mitigate this problem, the INTERNET permission could be revoked within the *checkComponentPermission(...)* function, but that would result in a thrown security exception with a high probability of force-closing the application. Another approach that would ensure the continued safe execution of the application, would be to insert data shadowing capabilities to the lower levels of platform. Therefore, if lower-level system calls were issued, network resources would be blocked.

6.2 Android Application UID

In Android, each application is assigned a UID that the system uses to refer to an application. If two applications are created and signed by the same developer, the system will give both applications the same UID, which gives these applications the ability to share the same sandbox. Consequently, this grants applications much power. Executing within the same sandbox allows each application to access each other's private application data directory and form a conglomerate of permissions. Accumulation of permissions is classified as type of privilege escalation in which an application at run-time is able to access sensitive content that it would not otherwise have [6]. Thus, permission-verification

in the stock Android OS applies its security policies not based on the application label or its package name, but rather on the process UID.

In our modifications of the OS, we obtain all the names of the packages associated with the UID of the application that is performing an action by calling the PackageManager's *getPackagesForUid(int uid)*, and store them into an array. Our PM must use applications' package names because they are global identifiers across all end-users' devices unlike UIDs. We always select the first element in the array and pass it as one of the parameters to the *revokeResourceAccess()* function for our content provider. The ARMContentProvider correctly returns access control decisions regarding all applications associated with the given package name as a result of how the PM stores ARM policies during configuration. Once an application restriction is configured for a particular application, the PM will subsequently retrieve the UID of the application using its package name. The PM then uses *getPackagesForUid(int uid)* to retrieve all associated package names for that UID. Lastly, it stores the configured application restriction for each one of those package names. Therefore, applications that exist in the same sandbox will not be able to circumvent the ARMS in this manner.

6.3 Accessing ARM Policies

We make use of Android's key-value database facilities to create ARM policies. These policies are automatically stored within the data directory of the application utilizing such facilities. Such directories can only be accessed by the processes operating within a designated sandbox. Specifically, Android uses the Linux kernel to provide access control for file directories only allowing processes with a specific UID to access the application data directory associated with that UID. Therefore, the integrity of ARM policies is assured.

Android's content provider component acts as a global instance so that all applications on the device can use it to store or retrieve data belonging to the owner application. The only two entities that should be allowed to write/update ARM policies are the PM and the device admin application. The PM naturally has unfettered access to the PM, but to ensure that the admin application is the only other entity with such privilege, we call Android's *DevicePolicyManager.getActiveAdmins()* function. It returns a list of all admin applications, but only one should exist as the enterprise controls the list of applications that exist within the work persona. Prior to the updating of the policies, we verify that the package name of the entity attempting to update policies is authorised to do so.

7. RELATED WORK

Limiting mobile applications' capabilities on the Android platform is not novel. Approaches have been proposed to support the restriction of device content access, but not in the context of BYOD scenarios [20]. Apex [12], AppFence [10], TISSA [22], MockDroid [4], and YAASE [17] have developed modifications to the Android OS in order to limit data leakage and restrict application permissions. In addition, EMM-related functionalities are not provided such as the ability for a remote entity to configure policies for a client device. The (popular and commercial) systems that do aim at solving the problem in BYOD scenarios – such as Android For Work and Samsung KNOX – usually approach it by removing the need to restrict access. They mostly rely on broader techniques to isolate trusted and untrusted applications, and the data they operate on, altogether. Therefore, *all applications in an isolated environment are trusted*, which leads to the assumption that there is no need to restrict the applications within that environment. However, there are circumstances in which not fully trusted applications must be uploaded into the environment. Current systems do not provide sufficient facilities to limit the privileges of those applications in said circumstances. Below, we describe systems that come close to achieving finer granularity in application restriction in BYOD scenarios.

IdentiDroid can be considered a platform-level EMM system. The configuration profiles are analogous to personas. Unlike other platform-level systems, IdentiDroid also contain facilities for application-level containerization through the integration of the data shadowing and the permission manager. IdentiDroid lacks high granularity in policy configurations as it does not allow the customization of returned shadow values. A containerization-like feature is supported by IdentiDroid by relocating *Application Data* when an anonymous profile is de/activated. On the other hand, DroidARM utilizes multi-user containerization offered by Android to isolate applications and data, and therefore, it is more robust against changes in the Android platform going forward as it relies on native facilities rather than custom solutions. Lastly, IdentiDroid was not implemented in the context of BYOD scenarios, and therefore does not offer application-level EMM integration or remote policy configuration.

Android Marshmallow (API 23 v6.0) was recently released which has updated Android's permission model for the first time since the original release of the platform. It includes the ability for users to configure permissions post-installation. However, this new permission model directly affects the stability of applications running on Marshmallow. Google has placed a burden on application developers to insert permission checking code prior to calling APIs that are associated with permissions in all of their applications, existing and new. With thousands of mappings between API calls and Android permissions to utilize sensitive resources, it may be difficult for developers to port the code under this new model [2]. Unlike Marshmallow, DroidARM does not require application developers to modify application source code to run on the system as per our requirement mentioned in Section 1.

Several other platform-level EMM systems exist that integrate various level of granularity for application-level restriction [1, 16]. Moses [16] is a custom Android OS that isolates sensitive content from different personas by tainting data [8] at the OS level with the name of the persona the data is associated with. Moses offers very fine-grained restriction policies at lower levels of the OS not present in other solutions, such as the ability to revoke access to specific network addresses from a subset of applications. However, it has very limited upper-layer access control such as restricting applications from system resources (e.g., Camera or Bluetooth). Samsung KNOX 2.0, the system AFW actually adopted its MUC approach from, incorporates significantly more hardware and platform security than any other platform-level EMM system, thus providing stronger guarantees of preventing root attacks. It, however, suffers the same lack of granular application restrictions as AFW does.

Application-level EMM systems [1] are able to support application restriction policies on a per-app basis, but the restrictions themselves are limited. For example, Bluetooth and Camera are the only two resources that such systems can restrict access to. In addition, the methods by which restrictions are enforced require that enterprise must utilize either application-wrapping or a custom SDK, and therefore violating our requirement that enterprise applications must not be modified.

In general, a multi-partition technique as provided by existing EMM solutions *cannot* solve the BYOD scenario addressed in this paper. That is, a scenario in which enterprises desire to introduce highly advanced third-party productivity applications, such as Microsoft Word, into their *trusted* containers of end-users' mobile environments. The purpose of a container is to isolate applications *and* data from other containers. Therefore, an end-user cannot create multiple trusted containers and expect them to communicate properly as that is in direct opposition to the objectives of containers. For example, enterprises will be unable to place Microsoft Word in a less trustworthy container and allow it to operate on enterprise data that exist in a fully trusted container. An application restriction mechanism must also be considered which we address in this paper.

8. CONCLUSION AND FUTURE WORK

In this paper, we presented our DroidARM platform. We extend Android Lollipop, which uses standard user-based containerization techniques to create multiple personas, with application restriction management facilities to dynamically deny an application's access to data and resources residing on the device in which it is executing on. Based on the experimental results presented in [19], we selected data shadowing as the data and resource protecting technique which obfuscates the protected content in various ways. We provide enterprise members, which assume the roles of either enterprise IT admin or self-employed end-users, the means to configure specific shadow values if randomized values are not sufficient within ARM policies. ARM policies can be configured locally (on the device) or remotely via our ARM Policy Manger or ARM policy configuration web server, respectively, depending on the role the enterprise member assumes. The experimental results show the effectiveness our approach as 99% of the applications, on average, operating on our DroidARM platform did not crash. However since we obfuscate the sensitive content, application behavior may be unpredictable (see Figure 5). In addition, some of our experiments involved a long and an extensive process that could not be fully automated, and required manual user intervention on an application to application basis. Therefore our results are only based on 100 applications selected from the set tested against the IdentiDroid platform. In future work, we plan to perform a thorough analysis against a significant set of applications to provide a more in-depth evaluation of DroidARM's impact on applications in the Google Play Store.

We plan to extend DroidARM to improve on EMM-related functionality. It is easier to deny access to data and resources within the application level framework and less intrusive in terms of minimizing custom modifications to the Android platform. However our experimental analysis has shown that also the lower levels of the platform must be modified in order to prevent applications from accessing special resources that cannot be fully denied at the application layer. Specifically, we plan to add shadowing capabilities to the Android NDK APIs.

Next, we will focus on various aspects surrounding ARM policies. First, extending our policies with even more granular restrictive options, which would involve investigating various policy types suited for mobile environments [3]. Second, we will introduce more security measures to protect such policies. As stated, KNOX is the only platform-level system that provides strong protection against root attacks. The policies that are stored on the DroidARM platform will be susceptible to attack if the device becomes rooted. To ensure the integrity of the policies, we will investigate how to leverage the secure element of smartphones to protect policies at rest via encryption [5, 14].

9. REFERENCES

[1] Enterprise mobility management smackdown. http://www.pqr.com/ enterprise-mobility-management-smackdown.

[2] K. W. Y. Au, Y. F. Zhou, Z. Huang, and D. Lie. Pscout: analyzing the android permission specification. In *Proceedings of the 2012 ACM conference on Computer and communications security*, pages 217–228. ACM, 2012.

[3] G. Bai, L. Gu, T. Feng, Y. Guo, and X. Chen. Context-aware usage control for android. In S. Jajodia and J. Zhou, editors, *Security and Privacy in Communication Networks*, volume 50 of *Lecture Notes of the Institute for Computer Sciences, Social Informatics and Telecommunications Engineering*, pages 326–343. Springer Berlin Heidelberg, 2010.

[4] A. R. Beresford, A. Rice, N. Skehin, and R. Sohan. Mockdroid: trading privacy for application functionality on smartphones. In *Proceedings of the 12th Workshop on Mobile Computing Systems and Applications*, HotMobile '11, pages 49–54, New York, NY, USA, 2011. ACM.

[5] B. Choudhary and J. Risikko. Mobile device security element. *Key Findings from Technical Analysis*, 1:1–8, 2005.

[6] L. Davi, A. Dmitrienko, A.-R. Sadeghi, and M. Winandy. Privilege escalation attacks on android. In M. Burmester, G. Tsudik, S. Magliveras, and I. Ili?, editors, *Information Security*, volume 6531 of *Lecture Notes in Computer Science*, pages 346–360. Springer Berlin Heidelberg, 2011.

[7] N. Elenkov. *Android Security Internals: An In-depth Guide to Android's Security Architecture*. No Starch Press, 2014.

[8] W. Enck, P. Gilbert, S. Han, V. Tendulkar, B.-G. Chun, L. P. Cox, J. Jung, P. McDaniel, and A. N. Sheth. Taintdroid: an information-flow tracking system for realtime privacy monitoring on smartphones. *ACM Transactions on Computer Systems (TOCS)*, 32(2):5, 2014.

[9] S. Furnell, A. Jusoh, and D. Katsabas. The challenges of understanding and using security: A survey of end-users. *Computers and Security*, 25(1):27 – 35, 2006.

[10] P. Hornyack, S. Han, J. Jung, S. Schechter, and D. Wetherall. These aren't the droids you're looking for: retrofitting android to protect data from imperious applications. In *Proceedings of the 18th ACM conference on Computer and communications security*, CCS '11, NY, USA, 2011.

[11] B. Morrow. Byod security challenges: control and protect your most sensitive data. *Network Security*, 2012(12):5–8, 2012.

[12] M. Nauman, S. Khan, and X. Zhang. Apex: extending android permission model and enforcement with user-defined runtime constraints. In *Proceedings of the 5th ACM Symposium on Information, Computer and Communications Security*, ASIACCS '10, pages 328–332, New York, NY, USA, 2010. ACM.

[13] O. Oluwatimi, D. Midi, and E. Bertino. Overview of mobile containerization approaches and open research directions. *Under submission*, 2016.

[14] M. Reveilhac and M. Pasquet. Promising secure element alternatives for nfc technology. In *Near Field Communication, 2009. NFC'09. First International Workshop on*, pages 75–80. IEEE, 2009.

[15] H. Romer. Best practices for byod security. *Computer Fraud & Security*, 2014(1):13–15, 2014.

[16] G. Russello, M. Conti, B. Crispo, and E. Fernandes. Moses: supporting operation modes on smartphones. In *Proceedings of the 17th ACM symposium on Access Control Models and Technologies*, pages 3–12. ACM, 2012.

[17] G. Russello, B. Crispo, E. Fernandes, and Y. Zhauniarovich. Yaase: Yet another android security extension. In *Privacy, Security, Risk and Trust (PASSAT) and 2011 IEEE Third Inernational Conference on Social Computing (SocialCom), 2011 IEEE Third International Conference on*, pages 1033–1040. IEEE, 2011.

[18] B. Shebaro, O. Oluwatimi, and E. Bertino. Context-based access control systems for mobile devices. *Dependable and Secure Computing, IEEE Transactions on*, 12(2):150–163, 2015.

[19] B. Shebaro, O. Oluwatimi, D. Midi, and E. Bertino. Identidroid: Android can finally wear its anonymous suit. *Trans. Data Privacy*, 7(1):27–50, Apr. 2014.

[20] C. Stach and B. Mitschang. Privacy management for mobile platforms–a review of concepts and approaches. In *Mobile Data Management (MDM), 2013 IEEE 14th International Conference on*, volume 1, pages 305–313. IEEE, 2013.

[21] T. Vidas, D. Votipka, and N. Christin. All your droid are belong to us: A survey of current android attacks. In *Proceedings of the 5th USENIX Conference on Offensive Technologies*, WOOT'11, pages 10–10, Berkeley, CA, USA, 2011. USENIX Association.

[22] Y. Zhou, X. Zhang, X. Jiang, and V. W. Freeh. Taming information-stealing smartphone applications (on android). In *Proceedings of the 4th international conference on Trust and trustworthy computing*, TRUST'11, pages 93–107, Berlin, Heidelberg, 2011. Springer-Verlag.

Tri-Modularization of Firewall Policies

Haining Chen, Omar Chowdhury,
Ninghui Li, Warut Khern-am-nuai
Purdue University
{chen623, ochowdhu, ninghui,
wkhernam}@purdue.edu

Suresh Chari, Ian Molloy,
Youngja Park
IBM T. J. Watson Research Center
{schari, molloyim,
young_park}@us.ibm.com

ABSTRACT

Firewall policies are notorious for having misconfiguration errors which can defeat its intended purpose of protecting hosts in the network from malicious users. We believe this is because today's firewall policies are mostly monolithic. Inspired by ideas from *modular programming* and *code refactoring*, in this work we introduce three kinds of modules: *primary*, *auxiliary*, and *template*, which facilitate the refactoring of a firewall policy into smaller, reusable, comprehensible, and more manageable components. We present algorithms for generating each of the three modules for a given legacy firewall policy. We also develop ModFP, an automated tool for converting legacy firewall policies represented in access control list to their modularized format. With the help of ModFP, when examining several real-world policies with sizes ranging from dozens to hundreds of rules, we were able to identify subtle errors.

CCS Concepts

•Security and privacy → Access control; Firewalls;

Keywords

Firewall policies; Modularization; Firewall tool

1 Introduction

A *firewall* is among the first lines of defenses for protecting a network (or, a host) from malicious users. A firewall intercepts network packets, and based on a specific *firewall policy*, decides whether to *allow* or *deny* certain packets to pass through it. As firewalls are developed by many vendors (*e.g.*, Cisco, Check Point), the syntaxes and semantics of firewall policy languages vary. However, at its core, most of the packet filtering rules expressed in these specification languages can be translated into an *access control list* (*ACL*) representation. An ACL firewall policy is specified as an *ordered list of rules*. Each rule has the form "target→action", in which target specifies a set of packets to which this rule is applicable, and action states what should be done with the packet. In an ACL, multiple rules can be applicable to a single packet and the decision of the first rule that is applicable to the packet is imposed on the packet. This is known as the "*first match semantics*".

SACMAT'16, June 05-08, 2016, Shanghai, China
© 2016 ACM. ISBN 978-1-4503-3802-8/16/06. . . $15.00
DOI: http://dx.doi.org/10.1145/2914642.2914646

Due to the dynamic nature of a network and its surrounding environment (*e.g.*, addition of new services, discovery of new attacks, a host becoming compromised), the firewall policies must evolve over time, in order to maintain a robust defense against malicious users while allowing legitimate traffic. Hence, it is necessary for firewall policies to be *intellectually manageable*, a term used in the context of programming by Edsger W. Dijkstra in his 1972 ACM Turing Lecture [16]. That is, administrators should be able to understand existing policies, possibly designed by other administrators. They should be able to modify a policy to achieve some intended objectives, mentally assess what the policy does, and "debug" the policy when problems arise.

Regrettably, many firewall policies are not intellectually manageable. For instance, it has been observed that most firewalls on the Internet are poorly designed and have many configuration errors in their rules [38, 39]. As firewalls can only be as effective as their configuration, misconfigurations of firewalls undermine their intended purpose of protecting the networks in question, causing firewalls to offer only a false sense of security.

One characteristic of firewall ACL languages is that two ACL rules may be in *conflict* with each other if they have different decisions (*e.g.*, one allows the packet to pass, and the other drops the packet) but their applicable sets of packets overlap. This means that the semantic of one rule may be changed by other rules that are in conflict with it. Because of this, writing firewall policies has been compared with writing programs with extensive use of goto statements. (See, *e.g.*, [18].) However, as policy rules often have exceptions, more often than not using conflicts is the most succinct way of expressing actual policies.

We argue that (1) the potential for conflicts is only one of three factors causing the difficulty. The other two are (2) policies expressed in ACL-based languages are monolithic; and (3) complex policies require a large number of rules. A monolithic policy can only be understood as a whole. This becomes infeasible as the policy gets large, since most people are unable to put a large amount of information in the working memory.

Since we cannot change the fact that many policies are inherently complex and that conflicts are useful, the only factor we can affect is the monolithic nature of current firewall policies. A notion of modular firewall policy was introduced in [5], where a firewall policy is considered modular if the policy is partitioned into multiple policy components $M_1, \ldots, M_r$ such that each packet is accepted by at most one component. This approach is still inherently monolithic, since one still potentially needs to examine all components when trying to understand what is the decision for one packet.

The goal of our work is to elevate firewall policies from monolithic to modular. The contributions of this paper are as follows.

First, we recognize five requirements for a successful modularization approach (*i.e.*, logical partitioning, isolation among modules, flexible partitioning structure, human-computable policy slicing, and readily deployability), and analyze existing approaches using these requirements to identify their shortcomings.

Second, we introduce our approach of modularizing firewall policies. This includes the concept of a *primary attribute*, which is either the source IP, the destination IP, or the service. The optimal choice of the primary attribute is policy dependent, although for the several dozens of policies we have observed, most of them benefit more from choosing the destination IP as the primary attribute. A policy is partitioned into three kinds of modules: *primary*, *auxiliary*, and *template*. Beyond making policies more modular and easier to understand, our approach also supports policy refactoring, either by distilling templates from recurring patterns, or by breaking up a large module into multiple smaller ones, each covering a subset of the IP range.

Third, to support legacy firewall policies, we have defined a 5-step process and introduced algorithms for converting them into their modularized form. We have also implemented an automated tool called ModFP for this purpose. By utilizing ModFP, we have converted several real-world firewall policies into their modularized form, and found that the process consistently improved the understanding of a policy, and the benefit is much more significant when the policy is large and/or when it has substantial usage of both permit and deny rules. For majority of the real-world firewall policies, their modularized version—translated with ModFP—enjoys a significant number of rule reduction (*i.e.*, 25.3%-68.7%) compared to the original ACL policy. Additionally, the translation from ACL to the modularized version takes a matter of seconds (*i.e.*, 0.26-19.35 seconds). For every large policy we have examined, we have found clear errors (such as redundant rules) as well as irregularities that we conjecture to be errors. For one such policy deployed in a corporate setting, we were able to contact the administrators and confirm that most of our findings are indeed policy errors.

2 Background and Related Work

In this section, we review the ACL representation of firewall policies, and then discuss related work.

2.1 Background on Firewall

A *firewall* typically operates at the gateway of a network to protect the network. The firewall determines whether to allow (resp., deny) certain packets based on some configurable *firewall policy*. Such a policy considers the following fields of a packet while matching it against the rules' target: source IP address (denoted by sIP), source port (denoted by sPort), destination IP address (denoted by dIP), destination port (denoted by dPort), and protocol/service (denoted by protocol). A firewall policy consists of rules, where each rule has the form "target → action", where the four actions in Table 1 are possible.

action	**Effect of** action
allow	allow the matched packet to pass
deny	drop the matched packet
chain Y	for matched packet, go use chain "Y"
return	resume calling chain

Table 1: Four actions in firewall rules.

Most firewall languages use a *simple list model* where each rule's action (or, decision) is either allow or deny. Linux netfilter uses a *complex chain model*, where a policy consists of multiple chains and all four actions can be used. The chain Y action directs the evaluation to another chain Y, which should include rules using the return action. Similar to a subroutine, the chain Y can be invoked from multiple places.

In a policy, more than one rules may match a packet, and their decisions may conflict. Firewall rule lists use the "*first match semantics*". Hence, the order in which the rules are organized is important in making the decision about whether a packet should be accepted or denied. Most policies have a "catch-all" rule as the last rule, which will match all packets and provide a default decision for any packet that is not matched by any earlier rules. In most cases, this "catch-all" rule has "deny" as the decision.

2.2 Related Work

Wool [38, 39] studied errors in real-world Firewall policies. They define certain characteristics as configuration errors and found that the number of errors in a policy is correlated with the number of rules in a policy. 36 such characteristics are used in [39], including "to any address allow any service" rules, outbound "any" service rules, inbound or outbound instance messaging rules, and so on. While our experience also shows that firewall policies contain many errors, we point out that most of these "configuration errors" as defined in [39] are really irregularities. They may indicate an error, but could also be intended by administrators for some specific reasons. This indicates a fundamental challenge in dealing with firewall configuration errors. Without knowing the original intention of the administrators, it is often impossible to tell whether something in a policy is a feature or a bug.

Analysis and Testing Tools. One line of research aims to identify anomalies in firewall policies [8–11, 13, 24, 40], either in a single policy, or in multiple policies placed on a network. Algorithms and tools were developed to detect anomalies and recommend how they can be fixed. Such techniques resemble static analysis tools for detecting bugs in software programs. They can detect errors manifested as anomalies, but not logical bugs where the policy does not implement what the administrators intend to enforce.

Another approach to deal with firewall policy errors is to develop debugging tools. Some tools generate and send testing packets and check whether they can go through firewalls. Other tools model firewalls using some formal modeling tools (often decision diagrams) and allow administrators to query the policy model [19–21,26,27,29,34,37]. For example, one can issue queries such as *"Which hosts can access the web server at 10.10.2.3?"*. With these techniques, administrators need to come up with appropriate queries that provide sufficient coverage and expected answers for these queries.

Several other interesting approaches have been proposed. One is change-impact analysis [23], which takes as input a firewall policy and a proposed change, and outputs the impact of applying the change, such as what packets will have their decisions reversed. Another is classifying the hosts of a network into equivalence classes [28]. Two hosts are equivalent if after changing a packet's source (similarly for destination) IP address from one to the other, the decision remains the same. Techniques to automatically correct errors in firewall policies, when a number of test cases (i.e., packets and the corresponding correct decisions) are given as input, were developed in [15].

Like the case of software development, static analysis and debugging tools are valuable; however, they cannot fully mitigate the problem caused by a primitive programming language lacking support for abstractions and modularization. The work we present in this paper aims at introducing such support.

Automatic policy generation. Instead of specifying firewall policies, in [17], a method is proposed to discover firewall policy rules by first mining the network traffic log using association rule mining, then aggregating the resulting rules, and finally detecting and removing anomalies in the policy using techniques in [11]. In [31], an architecture is proposed for automatically generating conflict-free firewall rules with alert information from network and system logs in multiple-firewall scenarios.

Policy representation. A method to convert an ACL rule list to a textual representation was proposed in [12]. The method first aggregates rules that are similar (*e.g.*, they differ only in one field) together, and then translate them into text. For example, it may produce a rule that reads: "accept all TCP traffic from address 140.192.37.* and {to port 80 or to port 21}". A similar approach was proposed by Tongaonkar *et al.* [33], in which given a firewall policy, they first flatten the policy rules into non-overlapping ones using Directed Acyclic Graph (DAG), so that the order of the rules does not affect the policy semantic. Then they merge similar rules to make compound rules such that a complexity metric is minimized. This kind of methods are beneficial to represent legacy policies in a more compact and understandable flavor.

Bartal *et al.* [14] develop a workflow for specifying firewall policies which proceeds in three stages: (i) abstract policy specification, (ii) policy instantiation, and (iii) automatic rule generation. They also develop a rule illustrator that visualizes which traffic between any two hosts are allowed. Their workflow is suitable for a new organization which is setting up their network instead of improving the manageability of legacy firewall policy.

Most commercial firewall policy languages or tools provide similar textual or graphical-based interface, as well as the ability of defining objects that can group multiple hosts into a group, and use these groups in a policy. This provides the functionality of macros at the level of individual fields in firewall policies.

Several efforts exist to specify firewall policies over packet flows between two ranges of IP addresses (which can be implemented by multiple firewalls that are in between the source and destination networks). One example is a firewall specification language for Linux netfilter introduced in [6].

In summary, the languages discussed above provide three kinds of abstractions: (1) named objects that group related IP addresses or port numbers together, similar to macros; (2) defining policies in a global network view instead of the view of a single firewall; and (3) syntactic sugars, *e.g.*, making the rules more like a natural language description. These are orthogonal to the kinds of abstractions we introduce for modularization.

An alternate way of representing firewall policies is by firewall decision diagram (FDD) [18, 25]. An FDD is a decision diagram where nodes are divided into levels, with each level corresponding to one field in a packet. This method is, of course, drastically different from using ACLs. It is unclear whether a policy specified in this form is easier to understand or modify for an administrator.

Policy chains/subroutines. The concepts of policy chains and subroutines exist in firewall products such as Linux netfilter [3] and SRX series firewalls by Juniper [2]. A sequence of rules can be organized into a subroutine and can be invoked from multiple places. This can improve the understandability of policies, especially when the same requirements are repeatedly applied, *e.g.*, the same sequence of rules are applied to multiple hosts.

This, however, does not provide the full advantage of modularization. There is no isolation among subroutines and the full policy, or among different chains specifically in netfilter. Policy chains and subroutines provide the mechanical support for modularization, without the methodology on how to modularize a policy. If one simply divides a long sequence of rules into multiple smaller ones that are chained together, that does not make the policy easier to understand.

Only-one-accept modules. In [5], a notion of modular firewall policy was introduced, where a policy is considered modular if it can be partitioned into multiple policy components $M_1, \ldots, M_r$ such that each packet is accepted by at most one component. In such an approach, a packet is accepted by the overall policy only if it is accepted by one component, and is denied otherwise. This approach is still inherently monolithic because of interactions among different components. As conflicts are still allowed, for example, one module may reject a packet whereas another module may allow it, when trying to understand the decision for a packet, one may still need to examine all components of a policy. There is also no logical basis for partitioning a policy into different modules. Finally, determining the slice of a policy, with respect to a specific packet or packet space, is not easier than in ACL.

3 Tri-Modularization Design Philosophy

In the context of software engineering, modularization signifies the concept of breaking up large, monolithic software source code and organizing them into smaller, reusable units based on the specific tasks these units implement. Modularization hence reduces the size of a program due to reusability, and makes a program easier to understand and debug, making it less error-prone and more reliable. Although the concept of modularization in firewall policies is very appealing, it is not obvious how to most effectively achieve this.

3.1 Requirements

In the context of firewall policies, a modularization approach would divide a policy into smaller pieces, which we call *modules*. To be able to analyze the effectiveness of different approaches of introducing modularization into policies, we identify the following requirements for a successful modularization approach.

Isolation among modules. The modules should be (at least partially) isolated. By isolation, we mean that the interactions among modules are limited and well defined. Only with adequate isolation, would it be possible to understand what each module achieves, without requiring to keep the details of other modules in one's mind. This also makes it possible to make local changes without unintended global side effects.

Logical partitioning. The criteria of partitioning should be simple and logical. That is, it should be easy to identify modules that are relevant to a particular situation. This and the isolation requirements together enable one to first have a global and high-level view of a policy, without understanding each module in depth, and then gradually refine the understanding by understanding the modules one by one.

Flexible partitioning structure. The partitioning should be flexible enough so that when a module becomes too large, one can break it up. This requirement is motivated by the dynamic nature of policies and aims at supporting *policy refactoring*. A policy often needs to evolve over time resulting in large modules which should then be broken up.

Human-computable policy slicing. To help understand policies, it is necessary to support mental policy slicing. In computer programming, *program slicing* [36] is the computation of the set of program statements (*i.e.*, the program slice) that may affect the values at some point of interest. In the context of a firewall policy, slicing can be done not only for a single packet, but also for some natural subspace of the whole space of possible packets. For intellectual manageability of policies, it is desirable that administrators can mentally calculate relevant slices of a policy with respect to a given packet or packet space.

Deployability. If an approach can only be deployed with a new firewall product that provides specialized support for it, then the benefit of modularization can be exploited by that product's customers alone. On the contrary, if modularization can be adopted by someone who understands the approach when writing a policy with existing products, then it can be adopted widely.

3.2 Two Extremes of Expressing Policies

Our tri-modularization design is the result of our investigation of many real-world firewall policies and the analysis of how to express them in a succinct and intellectually manageable way. However, it is natural to ask what is the philosophy behind tri-modularization and why such a design is useful in practice.

Effectively expressing a function. Abstractly, a firewall policy is a function that maps a tuple of several input attribute values (*e.g.*, IP address, port) to a binary decision (*i.e.*, allow or deny). Our problem is similar to that of how to most effectively represent boolean functions. Standard ways of expressing boolean functions include truth tables, boolean formulas, and circuits. Firewall policies differ in that the input attributes are not boolean. Some of these attributes (such as IP addresses) can take a very broad range of values hence using truth tables for our purpose is infeasible.

The typical approach of using a rule list (or, ACL representation) is close in spirit to using a formula to express a function. The problem is that when the number of rules is large, the formula becomes complicated and difficult to understand.

Another approach that has been proposed is the *firewall decision diagram* (FDD) which partitions the whole packet space, attribute by attribute [18, 25]. This is similar to using a circuit. The problem is that the circuits can become large, as it requires a large number of redundancies. In the case of FDD, partitioning is performed using all policy attributes.

Table 2 gives a running example policy. It is an abridged version of an actual policy used in a large-scale US-based IT organization. The complete policy is given in Table 6 in Appendix B and has 209 rules. To fix a misconfiguration error in the policy that we have found and the administrator has confirmed, two rules need to be added, resulting in a 211-rule policy. The added rules are rules 15 and 51 in Table 2.

The FDDs to represent the 211-rule policy have sizes varying from $2, 500$ nodes to roughly $22, 000$ nodes, depending on the order of the attributes. With the optimal attribute order, the FDD for the given policy has more than $2, 500$ nodes. Even though an FDD representation of a firewall policy can contain many more rules than its ACL counterpart due to the partition of the packet space, it has the innate advantage that the following query can easily be calculated by a human user: *Is a particular packet allowed by the firewall policy?* However, neither ACL nor FDD enables a human user to have a global understanding of what the policy achieves. This is highly relevant to the incremental management of firewall policies.

3.3 Tri-Modularization Design

Our tri-modualization approach lies in the middle of the two extremes (*i.e.*, ACL and FDD) discussed above. It combines the advantage of partitioning the packet space by FDD and the advantage of succinctness enjoyed by ACL due to allowing conflicts in the policy. We will use the policy in Table 3–which is equivalent to that in Table 2—as an example when explaining our design. The first column in the table contains the rule numbers, to allow us to refer to them in our discussion whereas the last column contains explanations of rules or modules. We ignore the columns containing sPort and protocol as all rules in the policy have a value of "*" (*i.e.*, wildcard character) in these two fields. In the rest of this Section, when we say lines XX, we refer to Table 3.

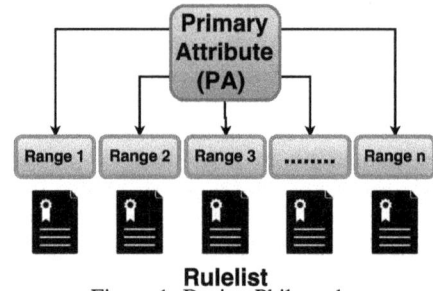

Rulelist
Figure 1: Design Philosophy

Primary attribute and primary modules. One natural approach to achieve isolation and logical partitioning is to require each module to cover a disjoint subset of the possible packets. Each packet is decided by one and only one such module. To ensure that a logical global structure exists and that it is straightforward to figure out which module a packet belongs to, we introduce the concept of *primary attribute*. In our approach, one can choose either sIP or dIP as the "primary attribute", and a policy is divided into modules in such a way that each module covers a *disjoint range* for the primary attribute. We call such modules *primary modules*. This is similar to partitioning in FDD but we restrict ourselves to partition along the primary attribute only (see Figure 1).

Choice of primary attribute. Through analyzing real-world policies, we have found that firewall policies essentially have three logical attributes: sIP, dIP, and service. The service is typically defined by the protocol information (*e.g.*, TCP, UDP, or ICMP) along with dPort. The sPort of most rules is essentially "don't care" (contains "*"). Using service as the primary attribute, however, does not support a flexible partitioning structure, because even if one limits to a single service, there are often too many rules to make one primary module difficult to understand. We have further observed that the ideal primary attribute for most policies is dIP, but some policies benefit more from using sIP as the primary attribute.

Representing primary modules. Once the policy is partitioned into disjoint ranges of the primary attribute value, our design exploits the succinctness of ACL due to conflicts in the rules. There are 4 primary modules in Table 3, each of which covers one of the disjoint ranges. PM1 (lines 11-13), PM2 (line 19) and PM3 (lines 20-22) cover single IPs "207.89.182.41", "207.89.182.248" and "207.89.182.57", respectively. PM4 covers a range "71.121.90.128/26", so it has rules relevant to "71.121.90.128/26" and "71.121.90.154" in the primary attribute. Moreover, a primary module may consist of one or more *primary* rules (primary rules cannot have "*" in the primary attribute field) or *instantiation* rules (instantiation rules are relevant to calling template or auxiliary modules). For example, line 13 is an instantiation rule for calling the template module TM1.

Auxiliary modules. One may desire a firewall policy to be fully partitioned into primary modules. For example, a policy may be divided into modules each of which covers a particular range for dIP. While this provides modularization, it can be undesirable, because there are often "*global*" rules that apply across all values in the primary attribute. For example, one often wants to blacklist certain hosts, or block specific ports, etc. When forcing all policies into primary modules, we have to duplicate these global policies in each module. When these rules need to change, one has to make changes to every copy of them. We call these rules that do not

No.	sIP	dIP	dPort	decision
1	71.100.64.0/19	*	*	deny
2	71.240.50.0/26	*	*	deny
3	71.206.182.0/24	*	*	deny
4	71.121.88.84	207.89.182.41	25	allow
5	71.121.92.96	207.89.182.41	25	allow
6	*	*	25	deny
7	*	*	137	deny
8	*	*	445	deny
9	*	*	135	deny
10	*	*	138	deny
11	71.14.116.1	71.121.90.184	1953-1954	allow
12	71.14.116.1	71.121.90.191	1953-1954	allow
13	71.14.116.1	207.89.176.60	1953-1954	allow
14	71.14.116.1	207.89.182.41	1953-1954	allow
15	71.14.116.1	207.89.182.248	1953-1954	allow
16	71.14.116.1	207.89.182.57	1953-1954	allow
17	71.14.116.1	71.121.90.128/26	1953-1954	allow
18	71.87.147.117	71.121.90.184	1950-1951	allow
19	71.87.147.117	71.121.90.191	1950-1951	allow
20	71.87.147.117	207.89.182.41	1950-1951	allow
21	71.87.147.117	207.89.182.248	1950-1951	allow
22	71.87.147.117	207.89.182.57	1950-1951	allow
23	71.87.147.117	71.121.90.128/26	1950-1951	allow
24	71.87.147.117	71.121.90.184	1960	allow
25	71.87.147.117	71.121.90.191	1960	allow
26	71.87.147.117	207.89.182.41	1960	allow
27	71.87.147.117	207.89.182.248	1960	allow
28	71.87.147.117	207.89.182.57	1960	allow
29	71.87.147.117	71.121.90.128/26	1960	allow
30	71.67.95.202	71.121.90.184	1960	allow
31	71.67.95.202	71.121.90.191	1960	allow
32	71.67.95.202	207.89.182.41	1960	allow
33	71.67.95.202	207.89.182.248	1960	allow
34	71.67.95.202	207.89.182.57	1960	allow
35	71.67.95.202	71.121.90.128/26	1960	allow
36	*	71.121.90.184	1953-1954	deny
37	*	71.121.90.191	1953-1954	deny
38	*	207.89.182.41	1953-1954	deny
39	*	207.89.182.248	1953-1954	deny
40	*	207.89.182.57	1953-1954	deny
41	*	71.121.90.128/26	1953-1954	deny
42	*	71.121.90.184	1950	deny
43	*	71.121.90.191	1950	deny
44	*	207.89.182.41	1950	deny
45	*	207.89.182.248	1950	deny
46	*	207.89.182.57	1950	deny
47	*	71.121.90.128/26	1950	deny
48	*	71.121.90.184	1960	deny
49	*	71.121.90.191	1960	deny
50	*	207.89.182.41	1960	deny
51	*	207.89.182.248	1960	deny
52	*	207.89.182.57	1960	deny
53	*	71.121.90.128/26	1960	deny
54	71.0.0.0/8	71.121.90.154	22	allow
55	71.0.0.0/8	71.121.90.154	80	allow
56	71.0.0.0/8	71.121.90.154	443	allow
57	71.0.0.0/8	71.121.90.154	5800-5809	allow
58	71.0.0.0/8	71.121.90.154	5900-5909	allow
59	71.0.0.0/8	71.121.90.154	3690	allow
60	*	71.121.90.154	*	deny
61	71.0.0.0/8	*	*	allow
62	71.67.94.12	207.89.182.27	55555	allow
63	71.121.92.53	207.89.182.179	52311	allow
64	207.89.182.142	207.89.182.57	179	allow
65	207.89.182.143	207.89.182.57	179	allow
66	71.0.0.0/8	*	80	allow
67	71.121.88.50	207.89.182.17	52311	allow
68	71.121.59.54	207.89.182.17	52311	allow
69	*	*	*	deny

Table 2: The original policy in ACL

	Subroutine				
	sIP	dIP	dPort	decision	Annotation
1	71.14.116.1	$	1953-1954	allow	**TM1**
2	71.87.147.117	$	1950-1951	allow	
3	71.87.147.117	$	1960	allow	
4	71.67.95.202	$	1960	allow	
5	*	$	1953-1954	deny	
6	*	$	1950	deny	
7	*	$	1960	deny	
-	*	$	*	return	

	Main policy				
	sIP	dIP	dPort	decision	Annotation
8	71.100.64.0/19	*	*	deny	**AM1**
9	71.240.50.0/26	*	*	deny	
10	71.206.182.0/24	*	*	deny	
11	71.121.88.84	207.89.182.41	25	allow	**PM1** with IP
12	71.121.92.96	207.89.182.41	25	allow	207.89.182.41
13	*	207.89.182.41	*		**TM1**
14	*	*	25	deny	**AM2**
15	*	*	137	deny	
16	*	*	445	deny	
17	*	*	135	deny	
18	*	*	138	deny	
19	*	207.89.182.248	*		**TM1** — **PM2** with IP 207.89.182.248
20	*	207.89.182.57	*		**TM1** — **PM3** with IP
21	207.89.182.142	207.89.182.57	179	allow	207.89.182.57
22	207.89.182.143	207.89.182.57	179	allow	
23	*	71.121.90.128/26	*		**TM1** — **PM4** with range
24	71.0.0.0/8	71.121.90.154	22	allow	71.121.90.128/26
25	71.0.0.0/8	71.121.90.154	80	allow	
26	71.0.0.0/8	71.121.90.154	443	allow	
27	71.0.0.0/8	71.121.90.154	5800-5809	allow	
28	71.0.0.0/8	71.121.90.154	5900-5909	allow	
29	71.0.0.0/8	71.121.90.154	3690	allow	
30	*	71.121.90.154	*	deny	
31	71.0.0.0/8	*	*	allow	**AM3**
32	*	*	*	deny	**AM4**

Table 3: The modularized version of the example policy in Table 2

into exactly which subnets are blacklisted only when necessary. We encourage policy authors to move auxiliary rules of the same type to be adjacent as much as possible, to reduce the number of auxiliary modules as much as possible. Lines 8-10, 14-18, 31, and 32 are examples of auxiliary modules.

Template modules. In many large policies, a sequence of rules may apply to many different IP addresses (*e.g.*, applicable to all webservers). To enable reuse, we allow a third kind of module dubbed *template modules*. A template module consists of one or more template rules that may be applied to many different IP addresses. For example, lines 1-7 form a template module, with "*TM1*" as its name. This template module is invoked in lines 13, 19, 20, and 23 for IP addresses 207.89.182.41, 207.89.182.248, 207.89.182.57, and 71.121.90.128/26, respectively. Template rules have their primary attribute field being "$", indicating that this is a *formal argument* and can be instantiated when this template module is invoked. We use "$" instead of "*" to differentiate template rules from auxiliary rules.

Putting it all together. As our modularization approach uses three kinds of modules, we call it a tri-modularization design. The high-level idea of our approach is illustrated in Figure 1. The primary attribute is partitioned into disjoint ranges each of which is covered by one primary module. Each primary module is essentially an ACL, and may call auxiliary modules and template modules. Both auxiliary modules and template modules are reusable, and they can be called by multiple primary modules.

In Table 3, there are 4 primary modules, 4 auxiliary modules, and 1 template module. There are no interactions among primary modules, while there are some limited interactions between primary modules and auxiliary/template modules. To evaluate a packet, one only needs to look at the primary module that matches the

belong to any primary module "*auxiliary rules*"; they can be easily identified because their primary attribute field contains "*".

We propose to group these auxiliary rules into what we call *auxiliary modules* based on the types of the rules. For example, all adjacent rules that block all traffic from some subnet are considered to be in one auxiliary module. This enables one to abstract the meaning of this module as "*some source IPs are blacklisted here*", when trying to form a global understanding of the policy, and dig packet, template modules called by the primary module, and auxiliary modules, safely ignoring other primary modules. For example, for a packet matching PM3, one may only check the following modules in sequence: AM1, AM2, TM1, PM3, AM3, and AM4. The evaluation will stop whenever the packet's fate can be determined. Thus, a relevant slice of a policy can be easily computable by a human in our design.

3.4 Deployability of Tri-Modularization

The next aspect of tri-modularization we investigate is its deployability. The relevant questions in this regards are: *How deployable the tri-modularization approach is? Can existing firewall products support it?* We observe that some existing products supporting chains/subroutines, such as Linux netfilter/iptables can be used to implement the modules we proposed, especially the reusable auxiliary modules and template modules.

In netfilter, a rule's *target* can be a user-defined chain. When a packet matches a rule whose target is a user-defined chain, the rules in the chain will be evaluated against the packet. If the chain does not deny or allow the packet after the traversal of the chain is done, the next rule in the current chain will be evaluated. Therefore, users can define a new chain for either an auxiliary module or a template module, and then write normal ACL rules whose target is this chain and whose matching conditions are the input arguments when calling the chain. In Table 3, we use similar syntax of chains in netfilter. TM1 can be viewed as a new user-defined chain. There are multiple places where this chain will be jumped to, such as in PM1, PM2, PM3 and PM4. Take PM1 as an example, when the matching condition in line 13 is satisfied, we will jump to TM1 and the rules there will be evaluated.

4 Tri-Modularization of Legacy Policies

Although network administrators can easily use the concept of tri-modularization when writing a new firewall policy, one of the main challenges of tri-modularization's adaptability is the legacy policies. To convert legacy policies to their tri-modularized form and hence enable adaptability, we present an automatic translation procedure, which at a high level has the following steps.

1. **Determining primary attribute**: decide which field (*e.g.*, sIP, dIP) is used as the primary attribute (PA).
2. **Removing redundancies**: identify and remove redundant rules. Removing redundant rules in ACL is straightforward and due to space limitations we do not describe it here.
3. **Creating auxiliary modules**: reorder the rules and assemble auxiliary rules of the same type together.
4. **Creating primary modules**: generate a set of disjoint ranges of PA, each of which will be covered by a primary module; reorder the rules and try to sort primary rules based on the PA values, and then create suitable primary modules.
5. **Creating template modules**: identify frequent rule patterns in the policy and use them to create template modules.

We have developed a tool dubbed ModFP which can help administrators perform the above steps automatically. In the rest of the section, we describe the above steps and the key algorithms.

4.1 Choosing the primary address

The main heuristic in choosing the primary attribute is that we want fewer rules where the primary attribute value is a "*" so that there are fewer auxiliary rules. As primary rules are partitioned into modules that are disjoint, they can be understood independently. As a result, a policy that has many primary rules is not necessarily much more difficult to understand. However, as auxiliary rules apply to all following primary rules (resp., modules), trying to decrease the number of auxiliary rules (resp., modules) can increase the intellectual manageability of a policy significantly. Examining the policy in Table 2, we can see 25 rules have "*" in the sIP field whereas only 11 rules have "*" in the dIP field. We thus choose dIP as the primary attribute. We have observed that—for a dozen or so real-world policies we have converted to their modularized format—dIP turns out to be a better choice as the primary attribute, likely because most of the rules are controlling traffic from outside the network to hosts inside the network, and thus are better grouped by dIP. We also point out that one can always try to modularize a policy first with dIP as primary attribute, then with sIP or some other fields as primary attribute, and compare the results.

4.2 Creating Auxiliary Modules

Recall that in a policy there may be "*global*" rules that do not belong to any specific primary module and instead can apply across primary modules following them. We want to assemble such auxiliary rules of the same type together to form auxiliary modules. This will reduce the number of auxiliary modules, and also make auxiliary modules more manageable. For this purpose, we need to move rules around without changing the policy semantics. We also want to move primary rules that are about the same IP addresses (or the same prefix) together as much as possible to create primary modules, as described in the next section. Therefore, we now introduce how to reorder rules.

4.2.1 Rule reordering

We first introduce the notion of what it means for a rule to be *switchable* with another rule.

Definition 1 (Switchable rules). *For a given policy, we say that rules r_i and r_j are switchable iff r_i and r_j are adjacent rules and switching their order has no impact on the semantics of the policy.*

Two rules r_i and r_j are switchable if and only if either they have the same decision or their sets of applicable packets are disjoint. When two rules have different decisions and their sets of applicable packets overlap, if these two rules are the first two rules in a policy, switching their order will change the decisions on packets that they both are applicable to.

To determine whether certain rules can be moved to be adjacent, we need to know to what extent these rules can be moved around without changing the policy semantics. Given a policy expressed as a list of rules $\mathcal{R}$ where each rule has an index, we use $\mathsf{pre}(r_j)$ to denote the set of rules that should come before the rule r_j, the rule with index j, when we move the rules around. This set can be computed as follows. Going up from r_j, ignore any rule that is switchable with r_j. When we reach the first rule r_i that is not switchable with r_j, if we want to further move r_j up, we need to move r_i together with r_j, we thus add r_i to our set and now check whether they can be moved up together. We can similarly define

---

Algorithm 1: Creating auxiliary modules in $\mathcal{R}$

Input: A rule set $\mathcal{R}$

1 **foreach** $r_i \in \mathcal{R}$ **do**
2   **if** r_i *is an auxiliary rule* **then**
3   Create an auxiliary module am with r_i only
4   **foreach** r_j *after* r_i **do**
5   **if** r_j *is an auxiliary rule* $\wedge r_i.type = r_j.type$ **then**
6   **if** $\mathsf{post}(\mathsf{am}) \cap \mathsf{pre}(r_j) = \emptyset$ **then**
7   Merge r_j into am

$\mathsf{post}(r_j)$, which is the set of rules that appear after r_j such that

r_j cannot be moved past them without changing the policy semantics. $\mathsf{pre}(r_j)$ and $\mathsf{post}(r_j)$ can be calculated using Algorithms 3 and 4, respectively (see Appendix A). For instance, according to the policy in Table 2, $\mathsf{pre}(r_3) = \emptyset$ (r_3 refers to the rule in line 3), $\mathsf{pre}(r_6) = \{r_4, r_5\}$, and $\mathsf{post}(r_{66}) = \{r_{69}\}$. The definitions of $\mathsf{pre}(\cdot)$ and $\mathsf{post}(\cdot)$ for a rule can be generalized to a sequence to rules. Given a sequence of rules $\mathcal{R}$, $\mathsf{pre}(\mathcal{R})$ denotes the set of rules that should come before all the rules in $\mathcal{R}$, and $\mathsf{post}(\mathcal{R})$ denotes the set of rules that should come after all the rules in $\mathcal{R}$.

Lemma 1. *Given two sequences of rules $\mathcal{R}_1$ and $\mathcal{R}_2$, where $\mathcal{R}_1$ appears earlier than $\mathcal{R}_2$, they can be merged together if there is no rule that belongs both to $\mathsf{post}(r_i)$ for some $r_i \in S_1$ and to $\mathsf{pre}(r_j)$ for some $r_j \in S_2$, i.e., $\mathsf{post}(\mathcal{R}_1) \cap \mathsf{pre}(\mathcal{R}_2) = \emptyset$.*

4.2.2 Merging Auxiliary Rules

According to the primary attribute chosen by users, primary rules and auxiliary rules can be distinguished. Recall that rules with the value of "*" in the primary attribute are auxiliary rules. Further, auxiliary rules can be categorized into different types after the primary attribute is set, see Table 4. "*" means that an auxiliary rule can take any values in the field, while "Specific" means that an auxiliary rule has a specific value in that field, such as a specific IP address, subnet, or service. Algorithm 1 can be applied to generate auxiliary modules based on their types. For each auxiliary rule, we try to merge it with other auxiliary rules with the same type.

4.3 Creating Primary Modules

The objective of creating primary modules is to partition the policy into disjoint sections such that each of the sections can be understood and managed independently with little to no interaction with other portions of the policy. Each primary module contains rules that cover a specific range of primary attribute values. The main challenge is to determine what these disjoint ranges of primary attribute values are. Once such ranges are generated, the next challenge is to group rules that falls into a specific interval together.

4.3.1 Range Generation

Threshold of primary module size. The size of each primary module should not become too large. For example, an administrator may want to have primary modules each of which includes no more than δ rules (*e.g.*, 20). Therefore, users are required to set a threshold δ for how many rules can be in a primary module. If a primary module covering a range has rules more than δ, it means that the range should be further divided. However, in case a range covers a single IP address and cannot be further divided, the above approach is not applicable. In this case, the value of δ should be increased to solve the problem. Therefore, the value of δ needs to be adjusted to the maximal size of primary modules covering single IP addresses, if needed.

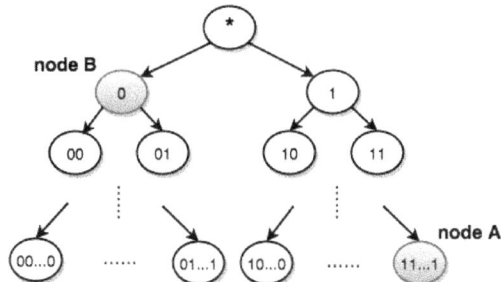

Figure 2: The binary tree structure used for generating ranges

Generating ranges. Algorithm 2 is used to generated a set of disjoint ranges for a rule set with auxiliary modules generated already.

The initial input is a rule set and an empty string meaning "*" (*i.e.*, the whole range in the primary attribute). This algorithm uses a tree structure, as show in Figure 2. The left child of a node is obtained by appending one more bit "0" to the node, and the right child by appending "1" to the node. A node in the tree represents either a single value or a range in the primary attribute. In Figure 2, since the primary attribute is dIP, node A represents a single IP (32 one's, *i.e.*, 255.255.255.255). Node B is "0" meaning that the first bit of the total 32 bits is 0 and the other 31 bits can be anything. This node hence represents a range [0, 2147483647]. Algorithm 2 uses the following cost function as a utility function.

Given a rule set $\mathcal{R}$ and a range I, the cost function $\mathsf{cost\_func}(\mathcal{R}, I)$ outputs the number of primary modules that are needed to cover the range I. $\mathsf{cost\_func}(\mathcal{R}, I)$ returns ∞ if one of the primary modules is required to have more than δ number of rules while creating primary modules to cover the range I. $\mathsf{cost\_func}(\mathcal{R}, I)$ returns $n \in \mathbb{N}$, otherwise.

Algorithm 2: $getRanges(\mathcal{R}, root)$

Input: A rule set $\mathcal{R}$ with auxiliary modules generated already, and a root range $root$
Output: A set of disjoint ranges $ranges$

1   $list = \emptyset$
2   **if** $root.length > num\_of\_bits\_in\_primary\_attr$ **then**
3 | Return $list$
4   $cost = cost\_func(\mathcal{R}, root)$
5   **if** $cost < \infty$ **then**
6 | **if** $cost > 0$ **then**
7 | | **if** *left child's cost equals to root's cost* **then**
8 | | | $list = list + getRanges(\mathcal{R}, root + \text{"0"})$
9 | | **else if** *right child's cost equals to root's cost* **then**
10 | | | $list = list + getRanges(\mathcal{R}, root + \text{"1"})$
11 | | **else**
12 | | | Add $root$ to $list$
13 | Return list
14   **else**
15 | $list = list + getRanges(\mathcal{R}, root + \text{"0"})$
16 | $list = list + getRanges(\mathcal{R}, root + \text{"1"})$
17   Return $list$

4.3.2 Merging Primary Rules

After a set of disjoint ranges are obtained, we can create primary modules by merging together primary rules overlapping with the same range. For each of the ranges, when the first primary rule that is overlapping with the range is found, a primary module is created having only this rule in it. After that, any primary rules that overlap with the range will be appended to this primary module. When trying to move a primary rule into the primary module, there may be primary rules, primary modules, and auxiliary modules lying between them. We can safely ignore those primary rules and primary modules because of the benefit of having disjoint ranges. For auxiliary modules that are switchable with the primary rule to be inserted, we can safely ignore them as well. For other auxiliary modules, however, we need to create instantiation rules for calling those auxiliary modules, put the instantiation rules before the primary rule, and then append them together to the primary module.

A primary rule is overlapping with a range, if the primary rule (1) equals to the range, (2) is a subset of the range, (3) is a super set of the range, or (4) intersects with the range. For the first 2 cases, we just simply append the primary rule to the appropriate primary module. For the last 2 cases, we only add the intersecting parts of the primary rule to the appropriate primary module. In addition to

43

that, we need to duplicate the rule for the non-intersecting parts of the rule, and keep the duplicate rule(s) in the original rule's place.

4.4 Creating Template Modules

In a policy, some rules may appear multiple times in a primary module or different primary modules with distinct primary attribute values. We want to create templates for those rules and form template modules so that they can be reused. The problem of creating template modules has similarities with the role mining problem [22, 30, 32, 35].

4.4.1 Frequent Rule Pattern Mining Problem

A list of *similar* primary rules may appear in multiple primary modules in a firewall policy, or even appear in a primary module multiple times. We call such a list of rules a *rule pattern* or just *pattern*. Note that *primary* rules that differ only in the primary attribute are regarded as similar rules w.r.t. a pattern. Template modules can be instantiated by invoking it with different values/ranges in the primary attribute field. The notion of template module is similar to the concept of subroutines in programming. Instantiation of a template module is similar to subroutine invocation. We now state the frequent rule pattern mining problem.

Definition 2 (Frequent rule pattern mining problem). *Given a list of primary modules and an argument Ψ_{min} that specifies the minimum number of occurrences of a rule pattern, the frequent rule pattern mining problem is to find all rule patterns whose support (i.e., the number of occurrences) is at least Ψ_{min} from those primary modules. Such patterns are called* frequent rule patterns.

Frequent itemset mining algorithms like Apriori [7] can be applied for mining rule patterns from primary modules. Each primary module is translated to a transaction, and each rule in a primary module is an item. Again, primary rules that differ only in the primary attribute field are regarded as the same rule. In this way, we obtain the input for our modified Apriori algorithm.

We modify the Apriori algorithm from the following two aspects. Firstly, items in an itemset are order-insensitive in the original Apriori algorithm. However, rules in a pattern are order-sensitive, and there may be other rules in between those rules in the pattern. In our modified Apriori algorithm, whenever a potential frequent itemset (*i.e.*, a pattern) is found, we need to go back to the primary modules where the pattern appears and check if the pattern can actually occur in those primary modules. For example, when a candidate itemset $\{a, b, c\}$ is found, we need to go back to a primary module where it appears to check if its support should be increased. Assume that the primary module includes rules $\{A, B, X, Y, C\}$ ($a - A$, $b - B$, and $c - C$ are similar rules). The pattern $\{a, b, c\}$ appearing in the primary module as rules $\{A, B, C\}$. If rules $\{X, Y\}$ in between the pattern can be moved away, the support for the pattern will be increased; otherwise, the support will not be increased.

Secondly, in the original Apriori algorithm, an itemset in a transaction will be counted only once even if it appears more than once in the transaction. Since a pattern may appear in a primary module multiple times, and if a template module is created using this pattern, the primary module should call the template module using an instantiation rule whenever the pattern appears. For this purpose, in our modified Apriori algorithm, all occurrences of an itemset in a transaction will contribute to its support. For example, assume that a candidate itemset is $\{a, b, c\}$, and a primary module where it appears consists of rules $\{A, B, C, A', B', C'\}$. This candidate appears twice, so its support should be increased by 2 instead of 1.

The value of Ψ_{min} can be specified by users. For example, if the value is set to 3, it means that a frequent itemset should appear at least 3 times (in different transactions and/or within the same transaction). The value of Ψ_{min} should not be too small or too large. If it is too small, too many frequent itemset will be generated; if it is too large, perhaps no frequent itemsets will be found. We modify the Apriori implementation in SPFM [4] for our purpose.

4.4.2 Template Module Assignment Problem

Given the result of our modified Apriori algorithm which is a list of patterns with lengths from 1 to k, where k is the length of the longest pattern(s) found, we want to find a subset of these patterns optimizing the number of rules reduced by creating template modules for them. We first define the assignment problem.

Definition 3 (Template module assignment problem). *Variables x_i^j is created for each pair of a pattern P_i and a primary module PM_j where the pattern appears. The assignment problem is to assign either 0 or 1 to each of these variables, with 1 meaning that the pattern should be used in the primary module and 0 meaning that it should not, so that the total number of rules reduced by using the patterns assigned with 1's will be maximal.*

The number of rules reduced by using a given pattern P_i can be calculated using the following formula: $|P_i| * sup_i - |P_i| - sup_i$, where $|P_i|$ is length of the pattern, and sup_i is the number of occurrences of P_i. The intuition behind the formula is that $|P_i| * sup_i$ rules can be saved, but some penalties also need to be deducted since an extra template module with $|P_i|$ rules and sup_i instantiation rules are created.

Using the longest pattern(s) will not always yield the optimal result. For example, suppose that the longest pattern is $P_1 = \{a, b, c, d, e, f\}$ with $sup_1 = 3$. However, there are 2 shorter patterns $P_2 = \{a, b, c, d\}$ with $sup_2 = 5$ and $P_3 = \{e, f\}$ with $sup_3 = 4$. Using patterns P_2 and P_3 together is better than using P_1 only, since the number of rules reduced is $(4 * 5 - 4 - 5) + (2 * 4 - 2 - 4) = 13$ in the former case instead of only $6 * 3 - 6 - 3 = 9$ in the latter case. Finding an optimal solution among the patterns found by our modified Apriori algorithm is not trivial. We model the assignment problem as an integer programming problem, and use IBM CPLEX optimizer [1] to solve the problem.

Suppose that m patterns (*i.e.*, potential template modules to be created) are found. In Figure 4 in Appendix A, we show an optimizer model with 4 patterns and 3 primary modules. Each pattern is used by one or more primary modules. This information is obtained by the modified Apriori algorithm mentioned above. Note that the support of a pattern may be different from the number of primary modules where it occurs, since it may appear more than once within a primary module. Each edge between a pattern and a primary module where it appears is represented by a variable $x_i^j \in \{0, 1\}$. $x_i^j = 1$ when pattern P_i will be eventually used by primary module PM_j, and $x_i^j = 0$ otherwise. The goal of the optimizer is to find the assignments of those binary variables to optimize our objective function described in Figure 3.

There are several constraints during the optimization. **(1)** n_i is the actual number of occurrences of the pattern P_i, and it should satisfy $0 \leq n_i \leq sup_i$, where sup_i is the support (*i.e.*, the total number of occurrence) of P_i. If all values of x_i^j ($j = 1 \ldots k$, where k is the number of primary modules where P_i appears) is assigned to be 1, then $n_i = sup_i$. If all x_i^j is assigned to be 0, then $n_i = 0$. **(2)** $h(n_i)$ is a function to decide whether a template module should be created for pattern P_i. When $n_i = 0$, it means that pattern P_i will not be used by any primary modules where it appears, $h(n_i) = 0$ so no template module will be created for this pattern; otherwise $h(n_i) = 1$ so one template module will be created. **(3)** A primary module can not simultaneously use patterns that are overlapping. Therefore, for each primary module PM_j, the

$$\text{maximize} \quad \sum_{i=1}^{m} n_i \times |P_i| - h(n_i) \times |P_i| - n_i$$

$$\text{subject to} \quad n_i = \sum_{j=1}^{k} sup_i^j \times x_i^j, \text{ where } x_i^j \in \{0, 1\}$$

$$0 \le n_i \le sup_i$$

$$h(n_i) = \begin{cases} 0 & \text{if } n_i = 0 \\ 1 & \text{otherwise} \end{cases}$$

$$0 \le x_s^j + x_t^j \le 1 \text{ for any pair of patterns that are}$$
$$\text{overlapping and co-exist in the same } PM_j$$

Figure 3: Formulation of template module assignment problem

constraint $0 \le x_s^j + x_t^j \le 1$ should be satisfied, which means that at most one of the overlapping patterns P_s and P_t can be eventually used by PM_j.

4.4.3 Generating Template Modules

A template module is created for each pattern P_i that is used by at least one primary module (*i.e.*, at least one variable x_i^j for some j is assigned to be 1) such that the pattern inside every primary module where it appears and for which the corresponding x value is 1 will be replaced by an instantiation rule. Moreover, a pattern may appear in a primary module multiple times, so each occurrence of the pattern will be replaced by an instantiation rule accordingly.

5 Evaluation

Using the tri-modualization approach, we implemented ModFP in Java, and used it to examine a dozen or so real-world policies with sizes from dozens to hundreds. We show the results of the 4 largest policies in Table 5, among which *Policy 3* is the complete and corrected version of the policy we presented in Table 2. Three of these policies belong to an academic institution and have been used in prior work on firewall policies. The remaining policy (*i.e., Policy 3*) belongs to a large-scale US-based IT company.

5.1 Effect on Number of Rules

By utilizing ModFP to convert *Policy 1*, *Policy 3*, and *Policy 4* to their modularized format, the number of rules is reduced by 64.3%, 68.7%, and 25.3%, respectively. For *Policy 2*, the number of rules is increased by 1. For all policies, ModFP only take seconds to convert them into the modularized form. For *Policy 2*, the number of rules increases from 87 to 88 after the conversion because of the following reasons. First, there is only 1 redundant rule in the policy, so removing redundancies does not decrease the number of rules much. Second, by creating a template module for a pattern with a length of 2 and a support of 3, only 1 ($= 2 \times 3 - 2 - 3$) rule is reduced. Third, 3 instantiation rules are created when some rules are merged into the primary module they belong, since there are 3 auxiliary modules that are not switchable. Therefore, eventually the number of rules is increased by 1.

For *Policy 4*, the number of rules does not decrease dramatically like in the cases of *Policy 1* and *Policy 3*. After removing redundancies, the number of rules decreases from 661 to 572. After creating primary modules 24 rules are added, since a destination subnet overlaps with multiple disjoint ranges, and the set of rules related to this subnet needs to be duplicated. And then the number of rules decreases by 102 by using template modules. Therefore, the number of rules decreases by 167 (*i.e.*, 25.3%) in total.

Our tri-modualization approach enjoys additional advantages on top of reducing the number of ACL rules.

5.2 Additional Advantages

Enabling a global understanding of a policy. Several design features of our tri-modualization approach aims at enabling a global understanding of a policy. Primary modules force one to group related rules together. Auxiliary modules group rules of the same type together. With a policy in its modularized form, one can mentally partition a potentially very large number of rules into meaningful modules, to have a global mental picture of the overall policy. One can hence provide a verbal summary of what the policy means and attempts to reason about it.

For example, for the policy in Table 2, we came up with the summary below based on its modularized form in Table 3. First, a list of source IPs are blacklisted. Then for the host 107.89.182.41, beyond "TM1", it also has port 25 open to two other hosts. "TM1" allows traffics to ports 1950-1951, 1953-1954, and 1960 from some specific IPs, and otherwise blocks traffic to ports 1950, 1953-1954, and 1960. Next "AM2" blocks ports 25, 135, 137, 138, and 445. Then the template "TM1" is applied to 3 other IP addresses and subnets. For the host 207.89.182.248, only "TM1" is applied. For the host 207.89.182.57, it has port 179 open to two hosts beyond "TM1". Primary Module "PM4" covers the range "71.121.90.128/26" , so subnet 71.121.90.128/26 and host 71.121.90.154 are covered by this range. "TM1" applies to subnet 71.121.90.128/26. Host 71.121.90.154 is most special: traffics from 71.0.0.0/8 to ports 22, 80, 443, 3690, 5800-5809, and 5900-5909 are allowed, and everything else is blocked. Finally, everything from 71.0.0.0/8 is allowed, and everything else is blocked.

We do not think it is feasible to come up with a similar description from the policy in its original form.

Making policy errors easier to identify. The modular nature of policies make policy configuration errors manifest themselves.

We have converted a dozen or so real-world firewall policies into their modularized form using ModFP. For every large policy we have examined, we have found clear errors as well as strange features that we conjecture to be errors. For the issues we have found with the complete version of the policy in Table 2 (see Table 6 in Appendix B for the complete policy), we have checked with the system administrator, and include the responses here as well.

There are a number of redundancies. For example, lines 202-203 and 206-208 are shadowed by line 201. Line 41 can be removed, as any packet it accepts will reach line 201 and is accepted. Further, since IP addresses 71.121.90.184 and 71.121.90.191 are in the subnet of 71.121.90.128/26, lines 27 and 28 can be removed because of line 50, and 12 other rules are in the same situation. The system administrator's comment on this is that *"The overshadowing is likely due to the number of different people who have access to the firewall policies."*

Less obvious issues can be found as well. Lines 27-193 in Table 6 correspond to a template module. We found that we could not apply the template module to host 207.89.182.248 because two rules (line 1 and line 7 in Table 3) are missing. That is, while lines 1-7 apply to 20+ other IP addresses, only lines 2-6 apply to 207.89.182.248. We found this rather strange, since there is a rule blocking ports 1953-1954 for all traffic, but no rule allowing the ports for certain specific source hosts. And there is a rule allowing port 1960 for certain specific source hosts, but no rule blocking it for all traffic. The system administrator confirms that this IP does not seem to be an active device in the DMZ anymore, and this is likely the result of incomplete cleanup processes.

Another issue is with the template module itself. Overall the

Source IP	Service	Decision
*	Specific	allow
*	Specific	deny
Specific	*	allow
Specific	*	deny
Specific	Specific	allow
Specific	Specific	deny
*	*	allow
*	*	deny

Table 4: Types of auxiliary rules (when dIP is the primary attribute)

Policy	ACL Rules	Modularized Policy				Translation time in seconds				
		PMs	AMs	TMs	Rules	Removing Redundancy	Creating AMs	Creating PMs	Creating TMs	Total
1	42	4	3	1	15	0.046	0.005	0.084	0.121	0.256
2	87	8	6	1	88	0.183	0.017	0.120	0.138	0.458
3	211	17	4	1	66	0.294	0.048	0.226	1.356	1.924
4	661	20	3	10	494	0.551	0.089	0.251	18.460	19.351

Table 5: Experimental Results

intention seems to be that for ports 1950, 1951, 1953, 1954, and 1960, only traffic from a specific host is allowed, and traffic from all other hosts is denied. However, Line 2 in Table 3 allows port 1950-1951 traffic from one specific host, but line 6 blocks only port 1950, and not 1951. A further piece of evidence is that if this is indeed intended, then rule 2 needs to mention only 1950, since as it is, port 1951 will be opened to all hosts in the $71.0.0.0/8$ subnet according to Line 31. Missing 1951 in line 6 was also confirmed to be an oversight. Some of the other comments we have received from the system administrator are:

We don't expend any effort to make the firewall rules easy to read or understand, and in fact we don't generally look at the entire set at all.

If we had software that made it easier to view the rule sets, and make changes to them efficiently, then we would probably have a cleaner set of firewall rules.

Enabling piece-by-piece understanding of a policy. As primary modules cover disjoint ranges, at most one primary module is applicable to each packet. Thus for each packet, one can consider only the auxiliary and template modules (if any), and at most one primary module. To understand the behavior of certain packets, one can quickly decide which primary modules would be applicable and ignore the rest of the primary modules.

Enabling policy refactoring. Our approach enables policy refactoring in two ways. First, template modules enable the definition of reusable templates that can be applied multiple times, similar to reusable subroutines in programming. Second, when a primary module becomes too large and complicated, one can divide it into multiple primary modules, each covering a smaller range.

6 Conclusion

Utilizing the idea of modular programming and code refactoring, we have introduced the tri-modularization design of firewall policies, which consist of three types of modules (*i.e.*, primary, auxiliary, and template). Our approach provides helpful abstraction and makes the policy more understandable and manageable. It also naturally supports policy refactoring in the authoring process. It can significantly reduce the number of rules in a policy and can also make configuration errors stand out and easier to identify. We present algorithms for converting legacy firewall policies in ACL to their tri-modular form, and also present a tool ModFP that automates the conversion. We have shown that using our approach one can understand complex real-world policies as well as identifying subtle errors, which are confirmed by the system administrator.

7 Acknowledgments

This work was supported by the Science of Security Lablet Program of National Security Agency under Grant No. H98230-14-C-0139, and by a gift grant from IBM Research. We also thank Prof. Alex Liu for providing us with some firewall policies.

8 References

[1] IBM CPLEX optimizer. http://www-01.ibm.com/software/commerce/optimization/cplex-optimizer/.

[2] Juniper. http://www.juniper.net/.

[3] Netfilter. http://www.netfilter.org/.

[4] SPMF: An Open-Source Data Mining Library. http://www.philippe-fournier-viger.com/spmf/.

[5] H. B. Acharya, A. Joshi, and M. G. Gouda. Firewall modules and modular firewalls. In *ICNP'10*, pages 174–182, 2010.

[6] P. Adão, C. Bozzato, G. Dei Rossi, R. Focardi, and F. Luccio. Mignis: A semantic based tool for firewall configuration. In *CSF'14*, pages 351–365, 2014.

[7] R. Agrawal and R. Srikant. Fast algorithms for mining association rules in large databases. In *VLDB '94*, pages 487–499, 1994.

[8] E. Al-Shaer and H. Hamed. Firewall policy advisor for anomaly detection and rule editing. In *IM'03*, pages 17–30, 2003.

[9] E. Al-Shaer and H. Hamed. Discovery of policy anomalies in distributed firewalls. In *INFOCOM'04*, 2004.

[10] E. Al-Shaer and H. Hamed. Modeling and management of firewall policies. *IEEE TNSM*, 1-1, 2004.

[11] E. Al-Shaer, H. Hamed, R. Boutaba, and M. Hasan. Conflict classification and analysis of distributed firewall policies. *IEEE JSAC*, 23(10), 2005.

[12] E. S. Al-shaer and H. H. Hamed. Design and implementation of firewall policy advisor tools. Technical report, 2002. http://citeseerx.ist.psu.edu/viewdoc/summary?doi=10.1.1.134.3344.

[13] F. Baboescu and G. Varghese. Fast and scalable conflict detection for packet classifiers. *Comput. Netw.*, 42(6):717–735, 2003.

[14] Y. Bartal, A. Mayer, K. Nissim, and A. Wool. Firmato: A novel firewall management toolkit. *ACM TOCS*, 22(4):381–420, 2004.

[15] F. Chen, A. X. Liu, J. Hwang, and T. Xie. First step towards automatic correction of firewall policy faults. *ACM TAAS*, 7(2):27:1–27:24, 2012.

[16] E. W. Dijkstra. The humble programmer. *Commun. ACM*, 15(10):859–866, 1972.

[17] K. Golnabi, R. K. Min, L. Khan, and E. Al-Shaer. Analysis of firewall policy rules using data mining techniques. In *NOMS'06*, pages 305–315, 2006.

[18] M. G. Gouda and A. X. Liu. Structured firewall design. *Comput. Netw.*, 51(4):1106–1120, 2007.

[19] J. D. Guttman. Filtering postures: Local enforcement for global policies. In *IEEE S&P'97*, pages 120–129, 1997.

[20] J. D. Guttman and A. L. Herzog. Rigorous automated network security management. *Int. J. Inf. Sec.*, 4(1-2):29–48, 2005.

[21] J. Hwang, T. Xie, F. Chen, and A. X. Liu. Systematic structural testing of firewall policies. *IEEE TNSM*, 9(1):1–11, 2012.

[22] M. Kuhlmann, D. Shohat, and G. Schimpf. Role mining - revealing business roles for security administration using data mining technology. In *SACMAT '03*, pages 179–186, 2003.

[23] A. X. Liu. Firewall policy change-impact analysis. *ACM Trans. Internet Technol.*, 11(4):15:1–15:24, 2008.

[24] A. X. Liu and M. G. Gouda. Complete redundancy detection in firewalls. In *DBSec'05*, pages 193–206, 2005.

[25] A. X. Liu and M. G. Gouda. Diverse firewall design. *IEEE TPDS*, 19(9):1237–1251, 2008.

[26] A. X. Liu and M. G. Gouda. Firewall policy queries. *IEEE TPDS*, 20(6):766–777, 2009.

[27] R. Marmorstein and P. Kearns. A tool for automated iptables firewall analysis. In *USENIX ATC'05*, pages 71–81, 2005.

[28] R. Marmorstein and P. Kearns. Firewall analysis with policy-based host classification. In *LISA '06*, pages 41–51, 2006.

[29] A. Mayer, A. Wool, and E. Ziskind. Fang: A firewall analysis engine. IEEE S&P'00, pages 177–187, 2000.

[30] I. Molloy, H. Chen, T. Li, Q. Wang, N. Li, E. Bertino, S. Calo, and J. Lobo. Mining roles with semantic meanings. In *SACMAT'08*, pages 21–30, 2008.

[31] A. D. Santis, A. Castiglione, U. Fiore, and F. Palmieri. An intelligent security architecture for distributed firewalling environments. *JAIHC*, 4(2):223–234, 2013.

[32] J. Schlegelmilch and U. Steffens. Role mining with ORCA. In *SACMAT'05*, pages 168–176, 2005.

[33] A. Tongaonkar, N. Inamdar, and R. Sekar. Inferring higher level policies from firewall rules. In *LISA'07*, pages 17–26, 2007.

[34] T. E. Uribe and S. Cheung. Automatic analysis of firewall and network intrusion detection system configurations. *Journal of Computer Security*, 15(6):691–715, 2007.

[35] J. Vaidya, V. Atluri, and Q. Guo. The role mining problem: Finding a minimal descriptive set of roles. In *SACMAT'07*, pages 175–184, 2007.

[36] M. Weiser. Program slicing. In *ICSE'81*, pages 439–449, 1981.

[37] A. Wool. Architecting the lumeta firewall analyzer. In *SSYM'01*, 2001.

[38] A. Wool. A quantitative study of firewall configuration errors. *Computer*, 37(6):62–67, June 2004.

[39] A. Wool. Trends in firewall configuration errors: Measuring the holes in swiss cheese. *IEEE Internet Computing*, 14(4):58–65, July 2010.

[40] L. Yuan, J. Mai, Z. Su, H. Chen, C.-N. Chuah, and P. Mohapatra. Fireman: A toolkit for firewall modeling and analysis. In *IEEE S&P'06*, pages 199–213, 2006.

APPENDIX

A Algorithms of ModFP

Algorithms 3 and 4 show how to calculate $\text{pre}(r_j)$ and $\text{post}(r_j)$, respectively.

Algorithm 3: Calculate $\text{pre}(r_j)$

Input: A rule r_j

1 $s = \{r_j\}$
2 **for** $i \leftarrow j - 1$ **to** 0 **do**
3   **if** r_i *is not switchable with some rule in* s **then**
4 | Add r_i to s
5 $\text{pre}(r_j) = s \setminus \{r_j\}$

Algorithm 4: Calculate $\text{post}(rule_j)$

Input: A rule r_j

1 $s = \{r_j\}$
2 **for** $i \leftarrow j + 1$ **to** $|\mathcal{R}| - 1$ **do**
3   **if** r_i *is not switchable with some rule in* s **then**
4 | Add r_i to s
5 $post(r_j) = s \setminus \{r_j\}$

Figure 4 shows an optimizer model with 4 patterns and 3 primary modules.

B Complete Version of The Example Policy

In Table 6, we show the complete version of the policy in Table 2.

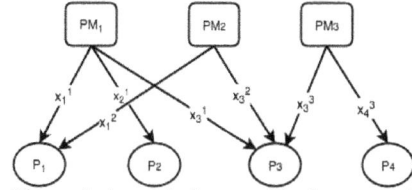

Figure 4: An optimizer model when $m = 4$

No.	sIP	dIP	dPort	decision
1	71.100.64.0/19	*	*	deny
2	71.240.50.0/26	*	*	deny
3	71.206.182.0/24	*	*	deny
4	71.206.190.0/23	*	*	deny
5	71.206.188.0/24	*	*	deny
6	71.206.91.0/24	*	*	deny
7	71.206.88.0/23	*	*	deny
8	71.196.181.0/24	*	*	deny
9	71.196.56.0/22	*	*	deny
10	71.128.0.0/13	*	*	deny
11	71.59.128.0/17	*	*	deny
12	71.59.32.0/19	*	*	deny
13	71.59.11.0/24	*	*	deny
14	71.59.8.0/23	*	*	deny
15	71.59.12.0/22	*	*	deny
16	71.59.16.0/20	*	*	deny
17	71.59.64.0/18	*	*	deny
18	71.121.88.84	207.89.182.61	25	allow
19	71.121.88.84	207.89.182.41	25	allow
20	71.121.92.96	207.89.182.61	25	allow
21	71.121.92.96	207.89.182.41	25	allow
22	*	*	25	deny
23	*	*	137	deny
24	*	*	445	deny
25	*	*	135	deny
26	*	*	138	deny
27	71.14.116.1	71.121.90.184	1953-1954	allow
28	71.14.116.1	71.121.90.191	1953-1954	allow
29	71.14.116.1	207.89.182.61	1953-1954	allow
30	71.14.116.1	207.89.176.14	1953-1954	allow
31	71.14.116.1	207.89.182.57	1953-1954	allow
32	71.14.116.1	207.89.182.61	1953-1954	allow
33	71.14.116.1	207.89.182.41	1953-1954	allow
34	71.14.116.1	207.89.182.27	1953-1954	allow
35	71.14.116.1	207.89.182.26	1953-1954	allow
36	71.14.116.1	207.89.171.57	1953-1954	allow
37	71.14.116.1	207.89.182.251	1953-1954	allow
38	71.14.116.1	207.89.182.250	1953-1954	allow
39	71.14.116.1	207.89.170.190	1953-1954	allow
40	71.14.116.1	207.89.174.60	1953-1954	allow
41	71.14.116.1	207.89.176.60	1953-1954	allow
42	71.14.116.1	207.89.179.185	1953-1954	allow
43	71.14.116.1	207.89.182.107	1953-1954	allow
44	71.14.116.1	207.89.182.179	1953-1954	allow
45	71.14.116.1	207.89.182.198	1953-1954	allow
46	71.14.116.1	207.89.182.50	1953-1954	allow
47	71.14.116.1	207.89.182.143	1953-1954	allow
48	71.14.116.1	207.89.182.142	1953-1954	allow
49	71.14.116.1	207.89.182.17	1953-1954	allow
50	71.14.116.1	71.121.90.128/26	1953-1954	allow
51	71.87.147.117	71.121.90.184	1950-1951	allow
52	71.87.147.117	71.121.90.191	1950-1951	allow
53	71.87.147.117	207.89.182.37	1950-1951	allow
54	71.87.147.117	207.89.176.14	1950-1951	allow
55	71.87.147.117	207.89.182.57	1950-1951	allow
56	71.87.147.117	207.89.182.61	1950-1951	allow
57	71.87.147.117	207.89.182.41	1950-1951	allow
58	71.87.147.117	207.89.182.27	1950-1951	allow
59	71.87.147.117	207.89.182.26	1950-1951	allow
60	71.87.147.117	207.89.171.57	1950-1951	allow
61	71.87.147.117	207.89.182.251	1950-1951	allow
62	71.87.147.117	207.89.182.250	1950-1951	allow
63	71.87.147.117	207.89.170.190	1950-1951	allow
64	71.87.147.117	207.89.174.60	1950-1951	allow
65	71.87.147.117	207.89.179.185	1950-1951	allow
66	71.87.147.117	207.89.182.248	1950-1951	allow
67	71.87.147.117	207.89.182.107	1950-1951	allow
68	71.87.147.117	207.89.182.179	1950-1951	allow
69	71.87.147.117	207.89.182.198	1950-1951	allow
70	71.87.147.117	207.89.182.50	1950-1951	allow

No.	sIP	dIP	dPort	decision
71	71.87.147.117	207.89.182.143	1950-1951	allow
72	71.87.147.117	207.89.182.142	1950-1951	allow
73	71.87.147.117	207.89.182.17	1950-1951	allow
74	71.87.147.117	71.121.90.128/26	1950-1951	allow
75	71.87.147.117	71.121.90.184	1960	allow
76	71.87.147.117	71.121.90.191	1960	allow
77	71.87.147.117	207.89.182.37	1960	allow
78	71.87.147.117	207.89.176.14	1960	allow
79	71.87.147.117	207.89.182.57	1960	allow
80	71.87.147.117	207.89.182.61	1960	allow
81	71.87.147.117	207.89.182.41	1960	allow
82	71.87.147.117	207.89.182.27	1960	allow
83	71.87.147.117	207.89.182.26	1960	allow
84	71.87.147.117	207.89.171.57	1960	allow
85	71.87.147.117	207.89.182.251	1960	allow
86	71.87.147.117	207.89.182.250	1960	allow
87	71.87.147.117	207.89.170.190	1960	allow
88	71.87.147.117	207.89.174.60	1960	allow
89	71.87.147.117	207.89.179.185	1960	allow
90	71.87.147.117	207.89.182.248	1960	allow
91	71.87.147.117	207.89.182.107	1960	allow
92	71.87.147.117	207.89.182.179	1960	allow
93	71.87.147.117	207.89.182.198	1960	allow
94	71.87.147.117	207.89.182.50	1960	allow
95	71.87.147.117	207.89.182.143	1960	allow
96	71.87.147.117	207.89.182.142	1960	allow
97	71.87.147.117	207.89.182.17	1960	allow
98	71.87.147.117	71.121.90.128/26	1960	allow
99	71.67.95.202	71.121.90.184	1960	allow
100	71.67.95.202	71.121.90.191	1960	allow
101	71.67.95.202	207.89.182.37	1960	allow
102	71.67.95.202	207.89.176.14	1960	allow
103	71.67.95.202	207.89.182.57	1960	allow
104	71.67.95.202	207.89.182.61	1960	allow
105	71.67.95.202	207.89.182.41	1960	allow
106	71.67.95.202	207.89.182.27	1960	allow
107	71.67.95.202	207.89.182.26	1960	allow
108	71.67.95.202	207.89.171.57	1960	allow
109	71.67.95.202	207.89.182.251	1960	allow
110	71.67.95.202	207.89.182.250	1960	allow
111	71.67.95.202	207.89.170.190	1960	allow
112	71.67.95.202	207.89.174.60	1960	allow
113	71.67.95.202	207.89.179.185	1960	allow
114	71.67.95.202	207.89.182.248	1960	allow
115	71.67.95.202	207.89.182.107	1960	allow
116	71.67.95.202	207.89.182.179	1960	allow
117	71.67.95.202	207.89.182.198	1960	allow
118	71.67.95.202	207.89.182.50	1960	allow
119	71.67.95.202	207.89.182.143	1960	allow
120	71.67.95.202	207.89.182.142	1960	allow
121	71.67.95.202	207.89.182.17	1960	allow
122	71.67.95.202	71.121.90.128/26	1960	allow
123	*	71.121.90.184	1953-1954	deny
124	*	71.121.90.191	1953-1954	deny
125	*	207.89.182.37	1953-1954	deny
126	*	207.89.176.14	1953-1954	deny
127	*	207.89.182.57	1953-1954	deny
128	*	207.89.182.61	1953-1954	deny
129	*	207.89.182.41	1953-1954	deny
130	*	207.89.182.27	1953-1954	deny
131	*	207.89.182.26	1953-1954	deny
132	*	207.89.171.57	1953-1954	deny
133	*	207.89.182.251	1953-1954	deny
134	*	207.89.182.250	1953-1954	deny
135	*	207.89.170.190	1953-1954	deny
136	*	207.89.174.60	1953-1954	deny
137	*	207.89.179.185	1953-1954	deny
138	*	207.89.182.248	1953-1954	deny
139	*	207.89.182.107	1953-1954	deny
140	*	207.89.182.179	1953-1954	deny
141	*	207.89.182.198	1953-1954	deny
142	*	207.89.182.50	1953-1954	deny
143	*	207.89.182.143	1953-1954	deny
144	*	207.89.182.142	1953-1954	deny
145	*	207.89.182.17	1953-1954	deny
146	*	71.121.90.128/26	1953-1954	deny
147	*	71.121.90.184	1950	deny
148	*	71.121.90.191	1950	deny
149	*	207.89.182.37	1950	deny
150	*	207.89.176.14	1950	deny
151	*	207.89.182.57	1950	deny
152	*	207.89.182.61	1950	deny
153	*	207.89.182.41	1950	deny
154	*	207.89.182.27	1950	deny
155	*	207.89.182.26	1950	deny
156	*	207.89.171.57	1950	deny
157	*	207.89.182.251	1950	deny
158	*	207.89.182.250	1950	deny
159	*	207.89.170.190	1950	deny
160	*	207.89.174.60	1950	deny
161	*	207.89.179.185	1950	deny
162	*	207.89.182.248	1950	deny
163	*	207.89.182.107	1950	deny
164	*	207.89.182.179	1950	deny
165	*	207.89.182.198	1950	deny
166	*	207.89.182.50	1950	deny
167	*	207.89.182.143	1950	deny
168	*	207.89.182.142	1950	deny
169	*	207.89.182.17	1950	deny
170	*	71.121.90.128/26	1950	deny
171	*	71.121.90.184	1960	deny
172	*	71.121.90.191	1960	deny
173	*	207.89.182.37	1960	deny
174	*	207.89.176.14	1960	deny
175	*	207.89.182.57	1960	deny
176	*	207.89.182.61	1960	deny
177	*	207.89.182.41	1960	deny
178	*	207.89.182.27	1960	deny
179	*	207.89.182.26	1960	deny
180	*	207.89.171.57	1960	deny
181	*	207.89.182.251	1960	deny
182	*	207.89.182.250	1960	deny
183	*	207.89.170.190	1960	deny
184	*	207.89.174.60	1960	deny
185	*	207.89.179.185	1960	deny
186	*	207.89.182.107	1960	deny
187	*	207.89.182.179	1960	deny
188	*	207.89.182.198	1960	deny
189	*	207.89.182.50	1960	deny
190	*	207.89.182.143	1960	deny
191	*	207.89.182.142	1960	deny
192	*	207.89.182.17	1960	deny
193	*	71.121.90.128/26	1960	deny
194	71.0.0.0/8	71.121.90.154	22	allow
195	71.0.0.0/8	71.121.90.154	80	allow
196	71.0.0.0/8	71.121.90.154	443	allow
197	71.0.0.0/8	71.121.90.154	5800-5809	allow
198	71.0.0.0/8	71.121.90.154	5900-5909	allow
199	71.0.0.0/8	71.121.90.154	3690	allow
200	*	71.121.90.154	*	deny
201	71.0.0.0/8	*	*	allow
202	71.67.94.12	207.89.182.27	55555	allow
203	71.121.92.53	207.89.182.179	52311	allow
204	207.89.182.142	207.89.182.57	179	allow
205	207.89.182.143	207.89.182.57	179	allow
206	71.0.0.0/8	*	80	allow
207	71.121.88.50	207.89.182.17	52311	allow
208	71.121.59.54	207.89.182.17	52311	allow
209	*	*	*	deny

Table 6: The complete version of the policy in Table 2

Panel
Security and Privacy in the Age of Internet of Things: Opportunities and Challenges

Jianwei Niu
moderator
University of Texas at San Antonio
jianwei.niu@utsa.edu

Yier Jin
University of Central Florida
yier.jin@eecs.ucf.edu

Adam J. Lee
University of Pittsburgh
adamlee@cs.pitt.edu

Ravi Sandhu
University of Texas at San Antonio
ravi.sandhu@utsa.edu

Wenyuan Xu
University of South Carolina
wyxu@cse.sc.edu

Xiaoguang Zhang
Morgan Stanley
xiaoguang.zhang@morganstanley.com

ABSTRACT

In response to the new security and privacy concerns raised by emerging Internet of Things (IoT) technology, this panel discusses the current efforts and challenges to secure the IoT devices and to protect the integrity and privacy of users' data.

Keywords

Internet of Things; Security; Privacy

1. PANEL SUMMARY

The Internet of Things (IoT) connects the world. Everyday devices, including home automation systems, vehicles, medical devices, cameras, watches, and phones, are increasingly equipped with sensors and Internet connectivity for remote sensing and control. Experts predict there will be 50 billion smart entities by 2020. Such a huge number of interconnected devices along with a significant amount of available data open up new opportunities for services across many different domains such as electronic healthcare and assisted living, smart city service, environmental monitoring, smart vehicles, among many others [2]. Though they may seem harmless, these smart entities can actually track, collect, and relay consumers' data that could include confidential and sensitive personal information. This data can be sent to remote locations for further analysis, processing, or retention on a variety of application and service platforms (e.g, cloud services). Every single device and platform in the IoT space might present a potential risk or threat [3–5, 7] that could be exploited to harm consumers by (1) enabling unauthorized access and misuse of personal information; (2)

facilitating attacks on other systems; and (3) creating risks to personal safety [1].

In response to the new security and privacy challenges posed by emerging IoT technology [6], the panelists will discuss the current efforts and concerns in regard to putting measures in place to protect the confidentiality, integrity, and privacy of massive data as well as to secure the devices. First, we will pose the question of the possibility and effects of compromising such IoT devices. Concentrating on the design flow of IoT and wearable devices, we will discuss some common design practices and their implications on security and privacy. Multiple commercial smart/IoT devices will be selected as examples of how the industry's current practice of security as an afterthought or an add-on affects the resulting devices and the potential consequences to the end users' security and privacy. We will then discuss design flow enhancements, through which security mechanisms can efficiently be added to a device, vastly differing from traditional practices. Second, as a mass amount of data will be generated by devices and retained by service providers, we will present how organizations implement consistent, comprehensive, and proactive identity and access management platforms to manage the technology and information related risks. Third, since securing the IoT space remains challenging, we will discuss what is missing in regard to security of the IoT as well as what scalable access control techniques are needed to prevent unauthorized access to a single device which can subsequently open up access to the whole network of hundreds of thousands of devices and platforms.

2. PANELIST

Yier Jin is currently an assistant professor in the EECS Department at the University of Central Florida. He received his PhD degree in Electrical Engineering in 2012 from Yale University after he got the B.S. and M.S. degrees in Electrical Engineering from Zhejiang University, China, in 2005 and 2007, respectively. His research focuses on the areas of trusted embedded systems, trusted hardware intellectual property (IP) cores and hardware-software co-protection on computer systems. He proposed various approaches in the area of hardware security, including the hardware Trojan detection methodology relying on local side-

SACMAT'16 June 05-08, 2016, Shanghai, China

© 2016 Copyright held by the owner/author(s).

ACM ISBN 978-1-4503-3802-8/16/06.

DOI: http://dx.doi.org/10.1145/2914642.2927920

channel information, the post-deployment hardware trust assessment framework, and the proof-carrying hardware IP protection scheme. He is also interested in the security analysis on Internet of Things (IoT) and wearable devices with particular emphasis on information integrity and privacy protection in the IoT era. He is the best paper award recipient of the 52nd Design Automation Conference in 2015 and the 21st Asia and South Pacific Design Automation Conference in 2016. He serves and has served on the Organizing Committees and Technical Program Committees of many Conferences and Workshops such as DAC, ICCAD, ASP-DAC, HOST, ISVLSI, ICCD, etc.

Adam J. Lee is currently an Associate Professor of Computer Science at the University of Pittsburgh, where he previously held the position of Assistant Professor (2008-2014). Prior to joining the University of Pittsburgh, he received the MS (2005) and PhD (2008) degrees in Computer Science from the University of Illinois at Urbana-Champaign, and received his BS in Computer Science from Cornell University (2003). His research interests lie at the intersection of the computer security, privacy, and distributed systems fields. Dr. Lee's research has been supported by the NSF and DARPA, and he is an NSF CAREER award recipient (2012). For more information, please see http://www.cs.pitt.edu/~adamlee.

Ravi Sandhu is Executive Director of the Institute for Cyber Security at the University of Texas at San Antonio, where he holds the Lutcher Brown Endowed Chair in Cyber Security. Previously he served on the faculty at George Mason University (1989-2007) and Ohio State University (1982-1989). He holds BTech and MTech degrees from IIT Bombay and Delhi, and MS and PhD degrees from Rutgers University. He is a Fellow of IEEE, ACM and AAAS, and has received awards from IEEE, ACM, NSA and NIST. A prolific and highly cited author, his research has been funded by NSF, NSA, NIST, DARPA, AFOSR, ONR, AFRL and private industry. His seminal papers on role-based access control established it as the dominant form of access control in practical systems. His numerous other models and mechanisms have also had considerable real-world impact. He served as Editor-in-Chief of the IEEE Transactions on Dependable and Secure Computing, and previously as founding Editor-in-Chief of ACM Transactions on Information and System Security. He was Chairman of ACM SIGSAC, and founded the ACM Conference on Computer and Communications Security, the ACM Symposium on Access Control Models and Technologies and the ACM Conference on Data and Application Security and Privacy. He has served as General Chair, Steering Committee Chair, Program Chair and Committee Member for numerous security conferences. He has consulted for leading industry and government organizations, and has lectured all over the world. He is an inventor on 30 security technology patents and has accumulated over 31,000 Google Scholar citations for his papers. At the Institute for Cyber Security his research projects include attribute-based access control, secure cloud computing, secure information sharing, social computing security, and secure data provenance. His web site is at http://www.profsandhu.com.

Wenyuan Xu is currently a professor in the College of Electrical Engineering at Zhejiang University. She received her B.S. degree in Electrical Engineering with the highest honor from Zhejiang University in 1998, an M.S. degree in Computer Science and Engineering from Zhejiang University in 2001, and the Ph.D. degree in Electrical and Computer Engineering from Rutgers University in 2007. Her research interests include wireless networking, network security, and IoT security. Dr. Xu received the NSF Career Award in 2009, and was selected as a young professional of the thousand talents plan in China in 2012. She was granted tenure (an associated professor) in the Department of Computer Science and Engineering at the University of South Carolina in the U.S. She has served on the technical program committees for several IEEE/ACM conferences on wireless networking and security, and she is an associated editor of EURASIP Journal on Information Security.

Xiaoguang Zhang is an Executive Director of Technology & Info Risk Department and responsible for Access Management Technology. Since joining Morgan Stanley in 2010, Xiaoguang Zhang has have devoted himself as a Developer manager and Architect in to a number of critical access management projects. He also led the team to set up the first Morgan Stanley Innovation Center of Computing on Financial Services in collaboration with Shanghai Jiao-Tong University since March 2011. Prior to Morgan Stanley, Xiaoguang Zhang served at SAP Sybase between 1998 and 2004 as a Developer Manager on PowerDesigner, which has the No. 1 market share worldwide of Data Modeling Tooling. He also worked in BenQ mobility between 1998 to and 2004, where he specialized in the first generation of GSM mobile phone. In 2000, Xiaoguang received his Ph.D degree from Shanghai JiaoTong University. His research results were published in EI/SCI Indexed IEEE conference and Journals. His recent research interests are mainly focused on Identify and Access Management, Data Analysis, and Behavior Based Monitoring.

3. REFERENCES

[1] Internet of things: Privacy & security in a connected world, FTC staff report, 2015.

[2] E. Borgia. The internet of things vision: Key features, applications and open issues. *Computer Communications*, 54:1–31, 2014.

[3] M. Henze, L. Hermerschmidt, D. Kerpen, R. Häußling, B. Rumpe, and K. Wehrle. User-driven privacy enforcement for cloud-based services in the internet of things. In *International Conference on Future Internet of Things and Cloud*, pages 191–196. IEEE, 2014.

[4] R. Roman, J. Zhou, and J. Lopez. On the features and challenges of security and privacy in distributed internet of things. *Computer Network*, 57(10):2266–2279, 2013.

[5] S. Sicari, A. Rizzardi, L. Grieco, and A. Coen-Porisini. Security, privacy and trust in internet of things: The road ahead. *Computer Networks*, 76:146–164, 2015.

[6] R. H. Weber. Internet of things – new security and privacy challenges. *Computer Law & Security Review*, 26(1):23 – 30, 2010.

[7] J. H. Ziegeldorf, O. G. Morchon, and K. Wehrle. Privacy in the internet of things: threats and challenges. *Security and Communication Networks*, 7(12):2728–2742, 2014.

Enabling Dynamic Access Control for Controller Applications in Software-Defined Networks

Hitesh Padekar
San Jose State University
hitesh.padekar@sjsu.edu

Younghee Park*
San Jose State University
younghee.park@sjsu.edu

Hongxin Hu
Clemson University
hongxih@clemson.edu

Sang-Yoon Chang
Advanced Digital Sciences
Center
sychg@adsc.com.sg

ABSTRACT

Recent findings have shown that network and system attacks in Software-Defined Networks (SDNs) have been caused by malicious network applications that misuse APIs in an SDN controller. Such attacks can both crash the controller and change the internal data structure in the controller, causing serious damage to the infrastructure of SDN-based networks. To address this critical security issue, we introduce a security framework called AEGIS to prevent controller APIs from being misused by malicious network applications. Through the run-time verification of API calls, AEGIS performs a fine-grained access control for important controller APIs that can be misused by malicious applications. The usage of API calls is verified in real time by sophisticated security access rules that are defined based on the relationships between applications and data in the SDN controller. We also present a prototypical implementation of AEGIS and demonstrate its effectiveness and efficiency by performing six different controller attacks including new attacks we have recently discovered.

Keywords

Software-defined networks, access control, API misuse, network attacks, security

1. INTRODUCTION

Software-Defined Networking (SDN) is an emerging network architecture that provides unprecedented programmability, automation, and network control by decoupling the control plane and the data plane. The SDN architecture abstracts the underlying network infrastructure for network applications with logically centralized control [15, 7, 11]. Due

---

*The first two authors contributed equally to this work. Younghee Park is the corresponding author.

SACMAT'16, June 05-08, 2016, Shanghai, China
© 2016 ACM. ISBN 978-1-4503-3802-8/16/06... $15.00
DOI: http://dx.doi.org/10.1145/2914642.2914647

to its centralized feature, the SDN controller plays an important role in programmability and management, and allows programmers to create various network applications running on top of its core services. Therefore, it is crucial to protect the SDN controller from potential attacks.

In spite of many favorable characteristics and benefits of SDN, the SDN controller is most susceptible to attacks [18]. Any vulnerability in the controller would prompt a near seizing-up of the network. Furthermore, due to the lack of adequate security protection, malicious applications can easily launch attacks on the controller, wreaking havoc on the entire SDN network. Recently, various methods have been proposed to defend against specific attacks in SDN networks. AvantGuard proposed a connection migration solution against saturation attacks in the data plane [19]. The Rosemary controller was developed using network application containment to provide an isolated environment for running SDN applications [18]. VeriFlow provided a validation technique to check flow modification messages [13]. TopoGuard developed a topology checker to validate updates of network topology against network topology poisoning attacks [12]. FortNOX provided role-based authorization and security constraint enforcement in the controller kernel [4].

However, those existing solutions have either addressed *specific* attacks or proposed *specific* defense methods. They often overlooked a fundamental requirement for verifying the usage of API calls, which specify how SDN applications interact with the SDN controller. In fact, most of discovered attacks in SDN networks were caused by the misuse of controller APIs. In addition, many undiscovered vulnerabilities in the SDN controller still remain that can be leveraged by attackers to continue threatening the controller. Furthermore, as discussed in [12] [18], the most promising security solution for SDN is to have a robust SDN controller that can withstand misleading applications from vulnerable APIs. Therefore, there is a critical need to design a *general* security solution that can defense against various vulnerabilities in the SDN controller and protect the controller from a wide range of misuse of controller APIs.

To this end, we propose a novel security framework, AEGIS, to protect the SDN controller from various attacks by generating and enforcing security access rules. AEGIS aims to provide a dynamic access control mechanism for the usage of APIs and for the validation of data in the controller whenever controller applications utilize any controller service. In particular, AEGIS monitors SDN applications running on top of the controller's core modules, and intercepts the execution flow of applications through *API hooking*. It validates a service request by inspecting the pre-defined rules and by verifying input/output parameters in captured APIs. In essence, AEGIS dynamically validates the legitimacy of a service request by checking whether the associated application follows security access rules, and then it makes a decision to either block or allow the service request.

We design three core components for AEGIS: a data generator, a security rule generator, and a decision engine. The data generator identifies a list of important APIs along with internal data in the controller that must be protected from potential attacks. Our system can automatically extract invariant or variant data, the values of which need to be checked syntactically or semantically at runtime. The security rule generator in AEGIS defines a set of security access rules based on extracted information from the data generator. Invariant data is defined as syntactic information consistent throughout all services. By contrast, variant data is defined as semantic information needed for updates during the service. The security rule generator defines rules that describe the relationships among applications, APIs, and their inputs and outputs. Moreover, to validate service requests from applications, the decision engine intercepts APIs in real time and checks the input/output data of each API based on security access rules. We implement AEGIS based on *API hooking* in SDN controllers. To evaluate our system, we generate six different controller attacks, including new attacks we recently discovered, to illustrate the effectiveness and efficiency of our system. Our experimental results show that our system can detect various malicious SDN applications and dynamically control access of controller APIs on the fly.

This paper makes the following contributions:

- We propose a general security framework called AEGIS that enables dynamic access control for SDN controller applications. AEGIS can identify important relationships between SDN applications and critical data in the SDN controller, and generate security access rules for protecting the SDN controller.

- We propose a runtime verification technique, which verifies the legitimacy of services in the dynamic context of API calls, to control access of controller APIs.

- We implement a prototype of AEGIS based on Floodlight [4], an open source SDN controller, and evaluate the effectiveness and performance of AEGIS using a number of typical controller attacks.

This paper is organized as follows. In Section 2, we address our motivation through the discussion of various attacks that misuse controller APIs. Section 3 presents the design of AEGIS. The implementation and evaluation of our system are described in Section 4. Section 5 addresses the related work, and Section 6 discusses several important issues. In Section 7, we conclude this paper.

2. PROBLEM STATEMENT

Many network applications provide network services through calling core APIs, which are common interfaces to develop network applications, in the SDN controller. Since the applications are vulnerable to software bugs due to the lack of

authentication and access control [19, 12], they can misuse APIs to launch serious attacks in SDN networks. Specifically, they can exhaust system resources, shut down the controller, and change important internal data, such as network topology information [19, 12], in the controller. Since it is challenging to write bug-free controller code, it is more desirable to handle such misuse cases in real time before any attack is launched.

To make a robust SDN controller, the controller's APIs and its data structure should be protected against application bugs and network attacks. The first step to achieve this is to validate API usage called by the network applications. Before allowing any service to be used, the legitimacy of service requests need to be checked by investigating the relationships between the caller and callee of the APIs, and their input and output in the controller.

We next introduce several attack cases that result from misusing core APIs through network applications in the SDN controller. Most open-source controllers contain a set of core modules that define the controllers' major functionalities. The proposed attack model targets these core modules and causes the misuse of these controllers' core APIs. We will readdress some attacks, which have been studied in previous research. We will also discuss several new attack cases that we newly discovered. We target core APIs that are related to the five main functionalities: *topology manager*, *device manager*, *statistics manager*, *host tracker*, and *switch manager*. These core modules provide major network services through common APIs in most of popular SDN controllers. Table 1 summarizes attack cases that could cause serious damage with respect to three popular SDN controllers: Floodlight, OpenDaylight [6], and ONOS [5]. We can divide these attacks into two categories: *system resource attacks* and *internal data attacks*. We found a set of misused API lists based on both known attacks and newly discovered attacks. We discuss those attacks in the following subsections, mainly explaining in detail two new attack cases we recently discovered: *Network Saturation Attack* and *Bypassing Device Authorization*.

2.1 System Resource Attacks

[Attack 1] System Crashing Attack: In this attack, the unprivileged applications can call *System.exit()* function to shut down the controller completely [19], thus affecting controller robustness.

[Attack 2] Memory Resource Consumption Attack: The malicious applications can launch a memory leakage attack, causing memory to run out if they use enough resources [19].

[Attack 3] Network Saturation Attack: In addition to above two known attacks, we newly discovered that the controller is vulnerable to many resource consumption attacks, such as bandwidth exhaustion attacks and flooding attacks, due to misused APIs. For example, the forwarding modules in Floodlight are responsible for making packet forward decisions, such as FORWARD_OR_FLOOD, FORWARD, MULTICAST, DROP or taking no action. *createMatchFromPacket()* in the forwarding modules of Floodlight constructs a specific match based on the deserialized *OFPacketIn()* payload. It uses the source MAC address, destination MAC address, and other IP and TCP header fields to create a match for the received packet. However, it does not take into consideration the switch *inPort()* or the TCP packet type while making a forwarding decision. Hence,

Table 1: Misused controller APIs.

Attacks	Module	Floodlight	OpenDaylight	ONOS
Crashing SDN controller	System	System.exit()	System.exit()	System.exit()
Data attacks	Link discovery manager	rowsDeleted	rowsDeleted	removeLinks or removeLink
Resources consumption attacks	Memory	java.util.LinkedList.add	java.util.LinkedList.add	java.util.LinkedList.add
Network saturation attacks	Forwarding	handleMessage processPacketInMessage createMatchFromPacket	receiveDataPacket	processPacket
Bypassing device authorization	Device manager	learnDeviceByEntity	learnDeviceByEntity	networkConfigService.getConfig
Host location hijacking attacks	Host tracking service	isEntityAllowed switchPortChanged	isEntityAllowed updateNodeConnector	validateHost BasicHostConfig.isAllowed()

any spoofed messages matching existing flow rules can be forwarded to the target host due to no validation of the same-origin security policy. Even though resource saturation attacks are known problems, we discovered a new way to launch such attacks through investigating other API calls.

In particular, as shown in Figure 1, we examine the controller code to understand the process through the execution flow for the flooding attack. Figure 1 shows various subsystems that are involved during the flooding attack, the API sequence of actions, and the relationships between them. The top and bottom dotted lines represent boundaries created by northbound and southbound APIs, respectively. The provider is responsible for interacting with the network environment and OpenFlow (OF) protocol. The OF Channel Handler and OF Connection communicate with the OpenFlow protocol. The OF Connection then invokes the provider to transmit a sensing event to the OF Switch Handler via Provider Service *messageReceived()* API. The control plane contains core components for manager services and it exposes several interfaces that are communicating with northbound and southbound APIs. The OF Switch Handler processes this *packetIn* event and identifies the switch object **sw** associated with this communication. The OF Switch Manager maintains the context for this communication and provides an OFPacketIn message to the forwarding module. The forwarding module follows routing decisions from the controller and performs the forwarding actions.

To perform each of these forwarding actions, the OF Switch Manager invokes *createMatchFromPacket()* API, which does not take into consideration the TCP packet type header. In other words, the controller does not validate that the TCP SYN packet is derived from the same source inside the *createMatchFromPacket()* API. Any spoofed traffic can create a bottleneck between the control and the data plane. Eventually, the flooding attack creates multiple flow rules, and thus such flooding attacks cause control plane saturation and bandwidth exhaustion. Validating the behavior of the *createMatchFromPacket()* API requires to avoid this vulnerability in the controller.

2.2 Internal Data Attacks

The controller has a lot of important data, such as topology information, device information, and link information inside the controller. We discuss various attack cases to compromise the internal data in the controller by misusing APIs.

[Attack 4] Compromised Link Data: Applications can call controller APIs to manipulate internal link information. One such study on Rosemary [18] showed that network link

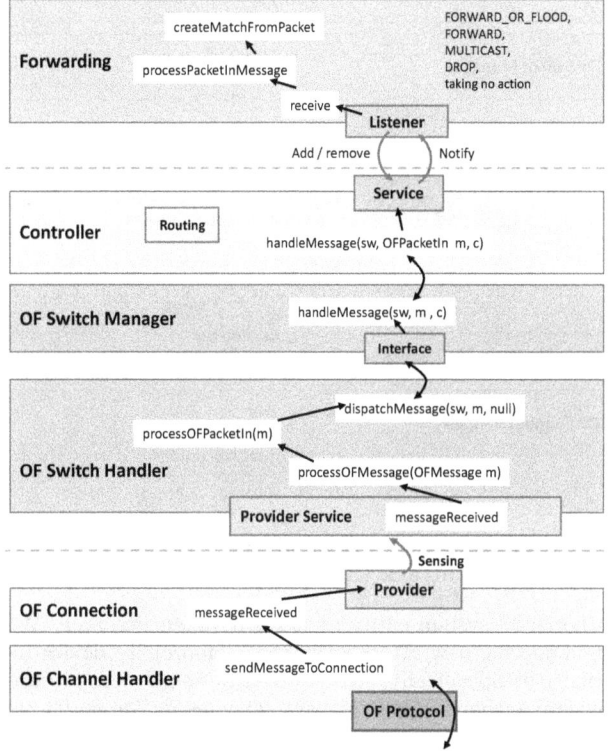

Figure 1: Execution flow of the flooding attack (Attack 3).

information can be modified or deleted using a simple test application. In this attack scenario, a vulnerable application can change the controller's network link information. Even though the previous research did not give a clear attack case inside code, we particularly identified the misuse case of two APIs: *addOrUpdateLink()* and *deleteLinks()* in the Floodlight's link discovery module.

[Attack 5] Host Location Hijacking Attack: Attackers exploit the host tracking service in the controller, as described in [12]. They can tamper with the host location information of the controller to break the security and impersonate the target host. All traffic on the target host is routed to the attacker's host. For example, *isEntityAllowed()* in Floodlight and Opendaylight allows any device to join the current network without any validation.

[Attack 6] Bypassing Device Authorization: The device manager controls device entities in a database based on MAC addresses and network addresses mapped to the devices and their locations in networks. The device manager

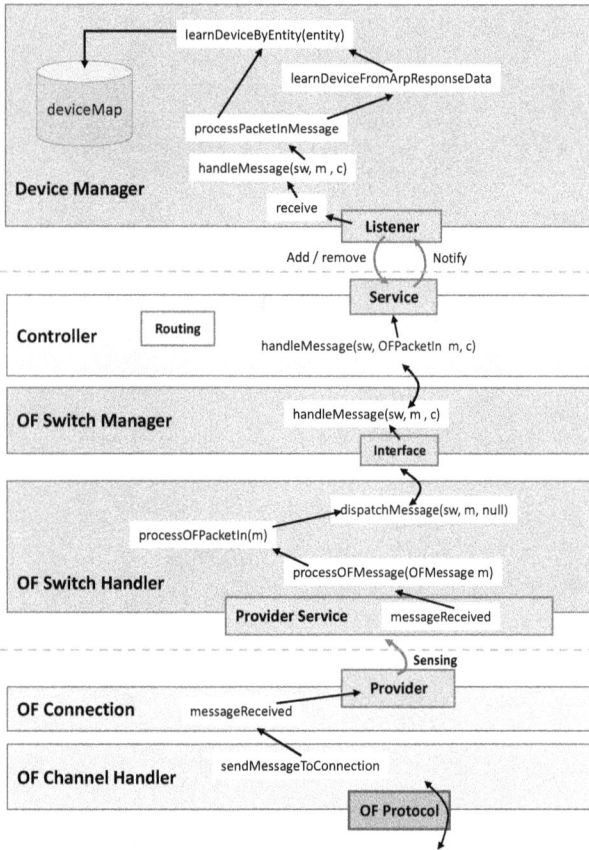

Figure 2: Execution flow of the bypassing device authorization attack (Attack 6).

authorizes a system entity to access a system resource. We found specific new attack cases that compromise device information. Specifically, *getSourceEntityFromPacket()* in the device manager in Opendaylight retrieves device entity information from the incoming packet. *learnDeviceByEntity()* in Floodlight looks up entity information in the database based on the device key, a host's MAC address.

For example, in the Floodlight controller's device manager, *getSourceEntityFromPacket* method retrieves device entity information from the packet. Based on this, the *learnDeviceByEntity* method does a lookup in the device entity database of the device manager module. The lookup is based on a device key, which is created using the host's MAC address. However, for a spoofed ICMP request with a wrong MAC address, this lookup matches an existing entity. We implemented this attack case by using ARP spoofing attacks. We assume that attackers were aware of IP addresses of victims and compromised hosts in a local network. The attack utilizes a gratuitous ARP request to probe the compromised host's MAC address. Then, it generates the spoofed ICMP message towards the compromised host and uses the victim as its destination. The spoofed ICMP requests with the spoofed MAC address bypass the lookup for the entity database. Due to the misuse of these APIs, the device manager can accidentally grant the spoofed entity access to controller resources.

In particular, Figure 2 demonstrates the Bypassing Device Authorization attack by examining the execution flow of APIs. Before the controller receives an OF packet, the API flow is the same as explained earlier. The controller exposes an OF service that is used by the Device Manager module. Upon receiving the *packetIn* event message, the Device Manager computes the source entity from the Ethernet packet based on the MAC address, VLAN ID, IPv4 address, IPv6 address, switch DPID, OF port and current timestamp. It then does a lookup in the *deviceMap database* using *deviceKey*, which is formed using the MAC address, VLAN ID, IPv4 address, IPv6 address, switch DPID and OF port. However, this lookup does not take into consideration the switch ingress port for the devices. When an attacker impersonates another host and generates spoofed ICMP packets, this lookup matches the existing entity in the *deviceMap* database. Thus, without installing new flow rules and using existing flow rules, attackers' spoofed ICMP packets get forwarded to the compromised host and the victim. Validating the *learnDeviceByEntity* API and failing to respond in the case of spoofed requests will prevent such attacks through our proposed system.

3. SYSTEM DESIGN

This paper aims to design a general security framework for investigating API usage and to define a set of security access rules for monitoring API calls in the controller at runtime. The following design goals should be achieved to address the aforementioned challenges.

1. *No Controller Code Change.* The deployment of the proposed system must be streamlined. Without changing the current code, the system should monitor applications running on the controller. For example, OpenDaylight has more than 20 open-source applications and many proprietary applications. Changing all the applications and the controller code may not feasible or practical. Any code modification would introduce extra bugs in the controller and might also lead to other serious issues. With the extracted data described in the subsection 3.1 and the API hooking, the proposed system can provide security functionalities without changing the internal controller code.

2. *Realtime Behavior Control and Monitoring.* The proposed system must continuously monitor applications and control their behaviors. To do so, it must intercept and control any API call on the fly since the APIs include all runtime behaviors. It must dynamically check the legitimacy of API calls based on pre-defined security access rules. Through intensive API inspection using the rules, the system must validate execution behaviors in real time before providing services. It must block or allow services according to the results of evaluating pre-defined security access rules.

3. *Realtime Security Access Rules Adjustment.* The proposed system pre-defines security access rules that can be applied to any new code release. It must add or delete the rules dynamically in real time. Even though applications can be often updated, the controller code might be intact. The proposed system should dynamically update the rules for new applications and new APIs in the controller.

4. *Semi-automatic Data and Rules Extraction.* Due to the huge amount of code, a complete manual inspection is error-prone and time-consuming. The proposed

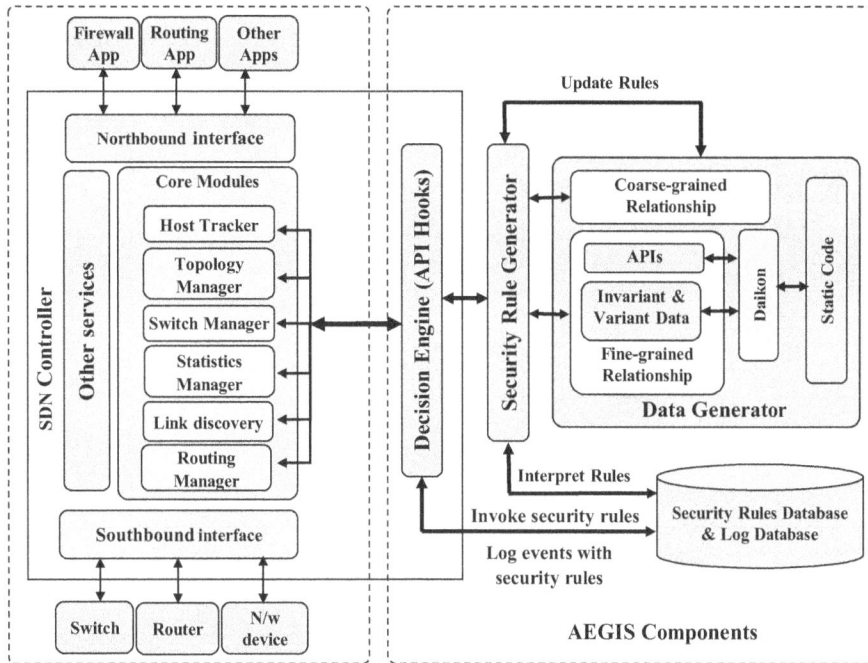

Figure 3: Overview of AEGIS architecture.

system should identify syntactic or semantic data automatically while the security access rules can be generated manually.

We propose AEGIS, a general security framework, to monitor the usage of APIs in SDN controllers whenever applications access APIs to get network services. Figure 3 shows an overview of AEGIS architecture. AEGIS contains three core components: *data generator, security rule generator,* and *decision engine*. We explain each component in detail as follows.

3.1 Data Generator

An SDN controller has APIs, data, and databases to store information related to SDN networks and systems. We identify the important data and relationships by using Daikon [3], which allows us to achieve automatic inspection of controller code.

Table 2 summarizes various applications and databases after code inspection for three popular open-source SDN controllers: Floodlight, ONOS, and OpenDaylight. In AEGIS, among important data in the controller, we first identify applications running in the controller and databases to store information related to the SDN controller. A database is closely related to each important module. Specifically, the statistics manager module has a statistics database. The topology manager module has topology information. In addition, we automatically identify important APIs along with invariant or variant data from runtime execution. Invariant data is defined as syntactic information that is consistent across all services, such as IP addresses and device information. By contrast, variant data is defined as semantic information that would be verified during the service due to update or modification operations.

We leverage Daikon in order to automatically generate important information from the controller code. Daikon dynamically detects program invariants using a static con-

troller code. We run the Floodlight controller inside Daikon Chicory Java front end. It executes the Java Floodlight controller, creates data trace files, and runs Daikon on them to detect invariants. The data traces include the results after running the controller code, such as variables and their values. If the value for each variable does not change during runtime, it is invariant data. Our tool also creates program points in declaration files with vectors for an API call and its input/output parameters. Using this method, the data generator automatically generates the controllers' APIs and input/output parameter values, and detects the program invariant and variant data.

Once the APIs and their input/output parameters are identified and the invariants are detected, we extract the important APIs and controller data from the Daikon results. Table 3 shows partial results applying Daikon to inspect Floodlight. It is a summary of sample important data structures for Floodlight's Device Manager, Link Discovery Manager and Topology Manager, classified into invariant data and variant data.

More specifically, from the results of Daikon, *deviceMap*, *primaryIndex* and *secondaryIndexMap* are invariants whenever a new device is attached to the network. For example, Device Manager maintains a master device map that maps device IDs to device objects within its execution in *deviceMap* database and adds new devices to this when they are discovered in the network. It also uses *primaryIndex* snd *secondaryIndexMap* to maintain primary and secondary indices over the fields in the devices. During the security check, our system validates whether these values are correct or not. However, *DeviceEvent* and *syncStroreWriteIntervalMs* are invariant data due to fixed values for each. *DeviceEvent* is the finite set of events (only add or remove a device with device ID), and *syncStoreWriteIntervalMs* is an interval within certain boundary limit, such as *debugCounters* and *deviceKeyCounter*, which are also classified as invariant data.

Table 2: Security directives (D) for applications in Floodlight, ONOS, and OpenDaylight controllers.(r = read, w = write, d = delete, (-) = no access required).

Controller	Applications	Flow Rules	Device Manager	Topology Manager	Link Manager	Configuration
Floodlight	Static Flow Entry Pusher	r, w, d	r	-	r	r
	Forwarding	r, w, d	r	r	r	r
	Firewall	r, w, d	r	-	r	r
	Circuit Pusher	r, w, d	r, w	r, w	r, w, d	r
ONOS	Flow Analyzer	r	-	r	r	-
	BGP Router	r, w, d	r	r	r	r
	ACL Service	r, w, d	r	-	-	-
	DHCP	-	r	r	-	r
OpenDaylight	Reservation	r, w, d	r	r,w	r,w, d	r,w,d
	Group Based Policy	r, w, d	r	r	r	r, w
	Network Internet Composition	r, w, d	r	-	-	r, w
	Device Identification and Driver Management	r, w	r	-	-	r

Table 3: Summary of Daikon results for Floodlight.

Modules	Device Manager	Link Discovery Manager	Topology Manager
Invariant Data	debugCounters deviceKeyCounter entityCleanupTask DeviceEvent syncStoreWriteIntervalMs	LLDP_STANDARD_DST_MAC_STRING LINK_LOCAL_MASK EVENT_HISTORY_SIZE LLDP_BSN_DST_MAC_STRING TLV_DIRECTION_TYPE forwardTLV, reverseTLV DISCOVERY_TASK_INTERVAL LINK_TIMEOUT LLDP_TO_ALL_INTERVAL LLDP_TO_KNOWN_INTERVAL tunnelPorts, externalPortsMap	CONTEXT_TUNNEL_ENABLED currentInstance currentInstance numTunnelPorts TOPOLOGY_COMPUTE_INTERVAL_MS
Variant Data	deviceMap primaryIndex secondaryIndexMap apComparator	controllerTLV, links, switchLinks portLinks linkDiscoveryAware suppressLinkDiscovery	switchPorts, switchPortLinks tunnelPortsa, directLinks portBroadcastDomainLinks externalPortsMap

3.2 Security Rule Generator

The rule generator defines a set of security access rules from the output of the data generator. The rules consist of two levels of regulations: directives and specific instructions. A security directive indicates a coarse-grained relationship between an application and a database, such as read, write, and delete as shown in Tables 2. A security instruction displays a fine-grained relationship between an API and data from the data generator. It describes more specific detailed instructions between calling APIs and input/output data.

Table 4 presents the basic primitives for our security access rule, which are based on a tuple, $< P, SD, A, SI, I, O >$, where P is a set of applications running on the controller, SD is a set of security directives showing the access relationships between applications and core data in the controller, A is a set of the core APIs in the controller, on which we focus, SI is a set of security instructions to verify the input data passing through calling APIs (depending on the input data and the output data, security instructions can check the data syntactically and semantically), I is a set of inputs, and O is a set of outputs for the calling APIs, which can

be any network and system information, such as existing IP addresses, existing MAC addresses, and existing devices.

Table 2 show coarse-grain relationships for security directives. For example, in Floodlight, the Circuit Pusher [9] creates a bidirectional circuit based on IP addresses and priorities. It can *read/write/delete* flow rules in the controller. In addition, a stateless Firewall applies ACL (Access Control List) rules for OpenFlow switches using flow rules and by monitoring ingress traffic. It can *read/write/delete* flow rules. However, it can only *read* other modules in the controller. Similar in OpenDaylight, the DIDM (device identification and driver management) can *read* and *write* a database of flow rules; however, it can only *read* the device databases and cannot access the topology and link databases. If this application tries to update topology information, it will cause a security violation due to security access rules. Futuremore, the security instructions for fine-grained relationships can verify the input/output data on each API call.

For instance, a security access rule is defined as, $< Main, write, main, null, System.exit(), null, null >$ which states that a Main module can only write (i.e. execute) the *System.exit()*. Except of the controller *main()* function, applications cannot

Table 4: Basic primitives for security access rules for AEGIS.

Lanuage	Description
$P = p_1, p_2, ...$	P is a finite set of the applications of the controller.
$D ::= < read\|write\|delete >$	A security directive is one of read, write, and delete.
$DB = < db_1, db_2, ... >$	DB is a set of different database storing data related to networks and systems.
$A = a_1, a_2, ...$	A is a finite set of all controller APIs for all $A(i) \subseteq$ controller APIs
$SI = s_1, s_2, ...$	SI is a set of instructions applicable to the calling APIs
$I :: = < IP\|Port\|...\|Devices >$	I is a set of input for the calling API.
	It can be all the network and systems information,
	such as IP addresses, port numbers, MAC addresses, and device, and so on.
$O ::= < IP\|Port\|...\|Devices >$	O is a set of output for the calling API.
$R ::= < P, SD, A, SI, I, O >$	R is a security rule.
	A rule defines a set of the directive SD applicable for the application P,
	the calling API A with its input parameters I, and output parameters O.

call this *exit()* function. It prevents the controller system from crashing. Another example is $< DeviceManager, read\|write, deviceMap, learnDeviceByEntity, entity, device >$, which means that the application *DeviceManager* can only read or write *deviceMap* through *learnDeviceByEntity()* with the device entity instance. It returns device information or updates it in the device entity database. It syntactically checks the device information in the *deviceMap*. Therefore, it protects the *deviceMap* from being accessed or modified by any controller module other than the DeviceManager.

The security access rules are saved into a rules database which contains controller APIs, variant/invariant data, and security directives and instructions. It is maintained in a hash table and uses an API name as the key to fetch entries from the hash table. The rules cover all the possible cases to prevent APIs from be misused into three categories: syntactic, semantic, and communication information. Syntactic information is related to invariant data. Semantic information indicates variant data that needs to data values checked. Lastly, communication information is related to network behavior. This violation will cause a DoS attack and a problem between two modules or interfaces. The hooked APIs will maintain the state of the communication for verification.

Static information related to existing data such as an IP address, a port number, or a switch interface number are the parameters that qualify as syntactic information. Dynamically changing address range and flow entry are semantic information. For example, when a new device is added to the network, the new device's IP address is within the expected range of IP addresses. In addition, depending on the services, we need to check the range of port numbers. Communication information is used to verify whether any of the parameters violate the execution of the flow of the protocol. For example, if any part of the network link is migrated from one switch port to the other switch port without proper shutdown of the link, this is considered to be a violation of the communication. APIs that handle link-level information, flow rules, and host tracking are categorized as communication information.

3.3 Decision Engine

We propose a state machine to make a decision for the legitimacy of API calls while monitoring API calls from applications. The notation we use for the state machine is a 6-tuple $<Q, q_0, R, \sum, f, o>$, where:

- Q is a finite set of states,
- $q_0 \in Q$ is the start (initial) state,
- R is a set of accepting rules,
- $\sum$ is the input accepted,
- f is a state-transition function $f: Q \times \sum \times R \longrightarrow Q$,
- o is an output function.

The input $\sum$ has a set of data extracted from the data generator. The data includes APIs, invariant and variant data passing through the API call. Q has two states: *True* or *False*. R is a set of security access rules from r_0 to r_n. The decision engine invokes a state-transition function f whenever an application requests a service and uses core APIs in the controller. If the engine is in a state q and reads input a with a rule r in R, it moves *True* (allow) or *False* (block) state depending on the access rules. It will *allow* or *block* a specific request while investigating APIs with input/output data.

The decision engine utilizes *API hooking* to intercept the behaviors of applications in the controller. It intercepts the function calls and their parameters at runtime. It gains control over the controller APIs, validates the parameters passed to the APIs, and validates the rules related to the applications and the API calls. When an application requests a service in the controller, it hooks the API calls and checks the security access rules. The decision engine retrieves security access rules from the rules database and applies the rules to the API parameter. If any rule is violated, the request is dropped or a negative response is returned.

4. IMPLEMENTATION AND EVALUATION

4.1 Implementation

We implemented our proposed system using Floodlight master version along with Daikon and hooking techniques. Because all code changed is in API hooks and AEGIS plugs, which are separate modules from the controller, our system does not need to change the controller code.

To generate interesting data, we analyzed the controller code using Daikon offline. We implemented hooking by using AspectJ [1] supported by Spring [8]. AspectJ is a seamless aspect-oriented extension to Java. We created a new

Table 5: Security access rules for evaluating the validation latency.

Number	API	Security Rule (R)
1	System.exit()	< Main, write, null, System.exit() CallerModule == Main, null, null>
2	learnDeviceByEntity	< DeviceManager, read | write, deviceMap, learnDeviceByEntity, entity.sw_port ∉ entitydatabase entity, device >
3	isEntityAllowed	< DeviceManager, read, deviceMap, primaryIndex, isEntityAllowed, entity.sw_port ∉ entitydatabase && entity.state == validShutdown , entity, EntityClass, boolean >
4	LinkedList.add	< ALL MODULES, write, null, LinkedList.add, resourceRequested < reserved , object, boolean>
5	addOrUpdateLink	< LinkDiscovery, write, links, addOrUpdateLink, CallerModule == LinkDiscovery Link, LinkInfo, boolean >
6	deleteLinks	< LinkDiscovery, delete, links, switchLinks, portLinks, deleteLinks, CallerModule == LinkDiscovery Links, reason, updateList , boolean >
7	switchPortChanged	< OFSwitchManager, write, switchLinks, portLinks, links , switchPortChanged , CallerModule == OFSwitchManager , switchId, port, type, null >

AspectJ library in the Floodlight controller written in Java. It allows us to hook the controller APIs at run-time and to check the security access rules for applications. Our system checks the hooked APIs for each of the input and output parameters against the security access rules.

The testbed to emulate attacks consists of three hosts, one Floodlight controller, and one switch. To evaluate system performance, we used *c*bench [2], a performance benchmark tool, on the controller host to measure the memory usage, execution time, latency, and effectiveness of our system. After making a number of runs, we computed an average for each experiment.

4.2 Evaluation

Startup Time of AEGIS in Floodlight: We measured boot-up time for the Floodlight controller with and without AEGIS implementation for various numbers of security access rules. The timer started when the controller entered the *main()* function and ended when it loaded all modules of the Floodlight controller with or without AEGIS including all necessary modules, such as REST APIs and AspectJ. We computed an average boot-up time for the fixed number of security access rules. The evaluated boot-up time also included additional time required for looking up and fetching the right security access rules.

As in Figure 4, the overhead of Floodlight with AEGIS was an average of 2.5%. Floodlight spent an average of 1.85 seconds for booting time. However, Floodlight with AEGIS expended an average of 2.19 seconds. This was 0.34 seconds more than the original controller. The boot-up time slightly increased as we added more security access rules to AEGIS. The original Floodlight showed consistent costs and AEGIS increased the cost only very slightly depending on the number of security access rules added, except for an initial spike time. For AEGIS, the beginning of the boot-up showed a spike time because of loading other Java libraries, such as AspectJ and Spring. After the spike time, it showed a stable cost regardless of the number of security access rules. Therefore, the performance overhead for the booting time caused only a very slight increase in the number of the rules except for the first spike time.

Memory Consumption: The controller loads all modules's jar files into the memory. To estimate memory usage, we utilized the *c*bench tool. Figure 5 demonstrates that the memory size used by the controller remained constant regardless of the number of switches. Both Floodlight and AEGIS consumed around 6.5MB. The difference between them was only 52 bytes in memory. Therefore, the additional libraries to the controller caused a negligible amount of overhead to memory usage regardless of the number of switches. However, while the number of switches did not have much effect on memory, the number of API calls did, which affected memory usage with additional runtime java libraries.

Table 6: The processing time of Daikon with Floodlight.

Module Name	data processing time (sec)	(in)variant generation time (sec)
Link discovery	111	72
Device manager	386	262
Topology manager	24	20

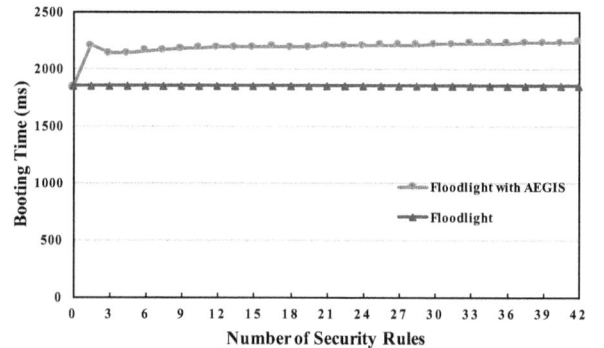

Figure 4: Booting time according to the number of security access rules.

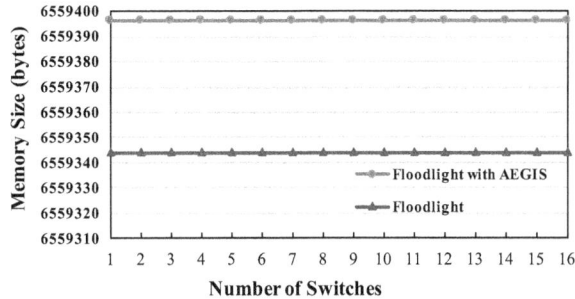

Figure 5: Memory consumption according to the number of switches added in an SDN network.

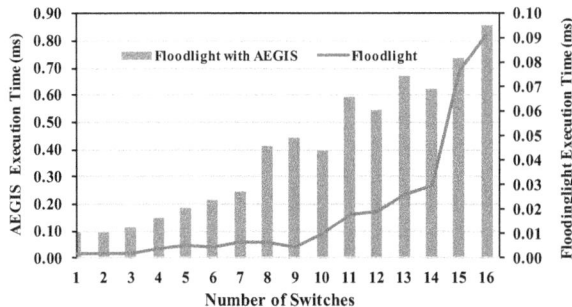

Figure 6: Average execution time of AEGIS according to the number of switches added into a SDN network.

Execution Time: We evaluated the execution time of our proposed system with *c*bench [2]. The *c*bench creates a number of OpenFlow switches, connects to the controller, creates 1000 unique source MAC addresses per switch, and measures average execution time for the number of flow rules installed per second. As already discussed, we targeted a security rule related to a *learnDeviceByEntity()* API that we implemented in AEGIS. When this API was invoked by adding a new host to the network, a *packetIn* event was received from the OpenFlow switch. We estimated the execution time of the security rule with different numbers of switches added into the network.

As shown in Figure 6, the average execution time of the APIs varied depending on the number of switches. When we added one switch, the execution time of AEGIS was 0.0933 ms and the original Floodlight took 0.0018 ms. As each switch was added into the network, the execution time of AEGIS increased. When the switches were added, the original Floodlight showed an average execution time of 0.0037 ms, but our system had an average execution time of 0.1571. After seven switches were added, the execution time increased slightly with AEGIS until ten switches were added. However, once eleven switches were added and thereafter, execution time with AEGIS increased dramatically while less dramatically increasing the execution time for the original Floodlight. The reason for increased execution time with AEGIS is that AspectJ implementation to support API hooking in Java inflates overhead of the API execution. This overhead is proportional to the controller's API usage based on the number of switches.

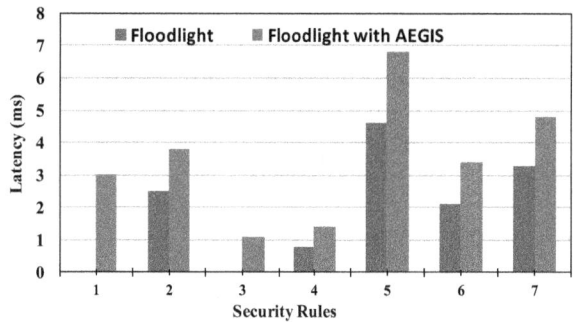

Figure 7: Average latency of AEGIS to check each security rule against each attack case, as shown in Table 5. Note that each number in x-axis is corresponding to the number in Table 5.

Latency for Security Rule Validation: Figure 7 shows the overhead needed by our system to verify the security access rules against each attack scenario described in Section 2. We evaluated the latency of API execution to check our security access rules against each attack with or without AEGIS. Table 5 [1] shows a list of our attack cases with specific security access rules that need to be verified. Based on these security access rules, as shown in Figures 1 and 2, AEGIS inspected all successive API calls before allowing the services. A comparison of the amount of overhead needed for different attacks shows that, on average, our system requires around 30% more latency with AEGIS than without AEGIS in order to validate the security access rules. For a few of the unimplemented APIs, such as the *isEntityAllowed()* API, the latency is high because this API has not in fact been implemented.

AEGIS protects APIs by implementing security access rules, which add overhead. The latency is affected by the amount of data and the number of other API calls. The reason that the overhead is high is that we examine all data, including all input and output parameters passing through the APIs. To reduce this overhead, we can apply a heuristic method by profiling common application behaviors. For example, based on the log information, the same application with the same security rule can be checked very quickly.

Effectiveness: We evaluated a detection rate to measure the effectiveness of our system with the six attack cases shown in Table 1 and the security access rules shown in Table 5. We ran the Floodlight with AEGIS implementation and randomly generated various attack test scenarios under the active legitimate traffic for the controller. Among sixty test cases by randomly selecting the cases in sixty times, the proposed system failed to detect only 2 test cases. It showed 96% detection rate to identify attack cases. Our experimental results demonstrated the effectiveness of our proposed system, and we can achieve 100% detection rates through increasing the number of security access rules.

---

[1]Note that P is any application that uses any core module in the controller. Since there are many applications in the controller, we do not specify a particular application. For example, Device Manager can indicate a group of applications that use the Device Manager module in the controller. These rules are closely related to our current implementation for AEGIS.

Lastly, we evaluated the processing time of Daikon with Floodlight and there are two parts: data trace and invariant/variant generation. The data generation obtains data trace files related to API calls and variables. Table 6 shows the results of processing time for each core module. It requires much time to analyze invariants and variants. However, it is an one-time cost to obtain the data.

5. RELATED WORK

Several approaches have been proposed to protect the SDN controller from application bugs and exploitation cases. Many of these approaches focus on generating new attack scenarios and implementing a defense mechanism for preventing each of them.

Attacks in SDNs: Many prior research efforts have identified *specific* application misuse scenarios and provided corresponding defense mechanisms. The Rosemary controller implemented a network application containment and resilience strategy to defend against system crash and data compromise attacks [18]. TopoGuard identified a few of misused APIs and generated new attack scenarios such as host location hijacking attack [12]. However, this approach does not address a way to protect the controller from misusing other APIs. Avant-Guard demonstrated the control plane saturation attack, which disrupts the network operation, and proposed a connection migration mechanism in which they altered the data plane to proxy the TCP handshake and only completed handshakes are moved to the control plane [19]. However, such an approach needs the control plane as well as the data plane to accommodate the new design. FLOVER implemented a dynamic controlled protection mechanism for the flow rules and a model checking framework, which verifies the flow policies instantiated within an OpenFlow Network [20]. In this paper, we identify additional misused APIs through comprehensive code analysis. Based on sophisticated security access rules, we present a promising solution to protect the controller from other APIs misuse scenarios.

Policy Based Approaches in SDNs: As discussed in [14], an access control and policy-based scheme for the SDN controller may help in securing the northbound APIs. In particular, a controller needs to be protected from various network attacks. SE-Floodlight implemented security features using trust model and policy mediation logic for the SDN applications [16]. They addressed many security issues with an authentication service, role-based authorization, a permission model for mediating configuration changes and detecting conflicting flow rules. Such an implementation requires rigorous validation and testing for the controllers' existing behaviors for the trustworthy operations. AEGIS focuses on protecting core controller APIs and does not involve changes in existing logic of the controller to solves such issues, thus, securing the controller from future attack scenarios as well. OperationCheckpoint presented an approach to secure the northbound interfaces by introducing a permission system that ensures that controller operations are available to trusted applications only [17]. This is also an attempt to make northbound APIs secure and define the permissions for applications for using these APIs. However, this research work does not attempt to secure the controller core modules from network attacks. In [21], researchers implemented *read*, *notification*, *write* and *system access* permissions for OpenFlow applications and they isolated the

controller and apps in thread containers. They also introduced an access control layer between the applications and the operating system. Although this gives an idea about providing access policies for applications, the proposed design does not provide a method to dynamically control access for the OpenFlow applications. Frenetic [10] is a specific northbound API designed to resolve policy conflicts. Our study focuses on protecting the controller core modules from malicious applications as well as network attacks. This unique approach can be used for protecting both northbound and southbound interfaces, and securing controller from future attack scenarios.

6. DISCUSSION

The new security framework, AEGIS, not only intensifies the SDN controller by enforcing intensive security checks, but also protects the controller from malicious behaviors that could launch network and system attacks. In this section, we discuss our proposed work in various respects and also compare it with current open source security services.

Code-based Security Framework: Most access control frameworks have been based on external observed behaviors and user-centric approaches. More specifically, users usually define security access rules based on their network activities and patterns. For example, users only allow incoming SSH connections to a system. However, in our work, security access rules are defined based on the internal code specification because most of discovered attacks in SDN networks have given risen to specific internal code.

Performance Overhead: We cannot avoid performance overhead in order to achieve trustworthy and dependable SDN controllers. The booting time is an one-time cost that will not affect the controllers during runtime. However, the execution time of AEGIS is proportional to the number of controller APIs as the number of switches added to the network increases. To address this problem, we can only focus on investigating important APIs instead of the entire list of APIs. Then, the performance overhead of AEGIS could be reduced significantly.

Semi-automated Security Access Rules Generation: In general, security access rules can be manually defined through observation and analysis, but we achieved semi-automation for the rule generation in AEGIS. We manually defined our security directives after examining applications and databases in the controller. By using the Daikon function, we were able to automatically identify significant relationships in variant or invariant data for security instructions, and then automatically set up the rules related to these extracted data along with the extracted APIs.

Comparisons with Current Controller Security: ONOS implemented AppGuard, which has a general secure mode and a non-secure mode of operations. Upon enabling Secure Mode ONOS (SM-ONOS), AppGuard aids performing API-level permission checking. It checks whether the caller has the required permissions, and uses Java's security module *AccessController* for access control operations and decision making, which can protect critical system resources and decides on access based on current security policies in effect. It also marks the code as being 'privileged', thus affecting subsequent access determinations. In addition, it obtains a snapshot of the current calling context to make access control decisions from a different context. However, Floodlight and OpenDaylight controllers do not allow the implementation of such a security model. AppGuard implementation only checks for access permissions for APIs, does not carry out any semantic or syntactic validation of API input parameters, and does not validate the flow of executing controller APIs.

7. CONCLUSION

In this paper, we have presented AEGIS, a security framework, to detect the misuse of APIs called by SDN controller applications. AEGIS provides three core functions including data generation, security rule generation, and decision making to protect controller APIs. AEGIS hooks various SDN controller APIs at runtime and validates pre-defined relationships for all available data. In particular, AEGIS identifies sophisticated relationships among diverse data, such as applications, APIs and their input/output data, invariant/variant data, and databases in the controller using a combination of Daikon tool and manual inspection. From these complicated relationships, AEGIS defines a set of precise security access rules in order to control application behaviors. At runtime, AEGIS automatically checks applications' behaviors when they call APIs, and prevents controller APIs from being misused. Experimental results have shown that AEGIS is able to prevent various network attacks and inadvertent use of controller APIs. In addition, AEGIS can generate standard security access rules, which could help in preventing any potential *new* attack scenarios.

Acknowledgments

This work was partially supported by grants from National Science Foundation (NSF-IIS-1527421, NSF-CNS-1537924 and NSF-CNS-1531127).

8. REFERENCES

[1] AspectJ: A seamless aspect-oriented extension to the Java programming language. https://www.eclipse.org/aspectj/.
[2] cbench: Performance benchmarking tool for the controller. https://www.github.com/andi-bigswitch/oflops/tree/master/cbench.
[3] The daikon invariant detector. http://plse.cs.washington.edu/daikon/.
[4] Floodlight: Open SDN Controller. http://www.projectfloodlight.org.
[5] ONOS: Open Networking Operation System. http://onosproject.org/.
[6] OpenDaylight Platform. https://www.opendaylight.org/.
[7] SDN. http://www.sdncentral.com/flow/sdn-software-defined-networking/.
[8] Spring: Platform with inbuilt AspecJ libraries for JVM-based systems. https://www.spring.io/.
[9] Project Foodlight. Circuit Pusher. http://www.projectfloodlight.org/circuit-pusher/.
[10] Nate Foster, Rob Harrison, Michael J Freedman, Christopher Monsanto, Jennifer Rexford, Alec Story, and David Walker. Frenetic: A network programming language. In *ACM SIGPLAN Notices*, volume 46, pages 279–291. ACM, 2011.
[11] Open Networking Fundation. Software-defined networking: The new norm for networks. *ONF White Paper*, 2012.
[12] Sungmin Hong, Lei Xu, Haopei Wang, and Guofei Gu. Poisoning network visibility in software-defined networks: New attacks and countermeasures. In *Proceedings of the 22nd Annual Network and Distributed System Security Symposium (NDSS'15)*, February 2015.
[13] Ahmed Khurshid, Wenxuan Zhou, Matthew Caesar, and P Godfrey. Veriflow: verifying network-wide invariants in real time. *ACM SIGCOMM Computer Communication Review*, 42(4):467–472, 2012.
[14] Felix Klaedtke, Ghassan O Karame, Roberto Bifulco, and Heng Cui. Access control for sdn controllers. In *Proceedings of the third workshop on Hot topics in software defined networking*, pages 219–220. ACM, 2014.
[15] Nick McKeown, Tom Anderson, Hari Balakrishnan, Guru Parulkar, Larry Peterson, Jennifer Rexford, Scott Shenker, and Jonathan Turner. Openflow: enabling innovation in campus networks. *ACM SIGCOMM Computer Communication Review*, 38(2):69–74, 2008.
[16] Phillip Porras, Steven Cheung, Martin Fong, Keith Skinner, and Vinod Yegneswaran. Securing the software-defined network control layer. In *Proceedings of the 2015 Network and Distributed System Security Symposium (NDSS), San Diego, California*, 2015.
[17] Sandra Scott-Hayward, Christopher Kane, and Sakir Sezer. Operationcheckpoint: Sdn application control. In *Network Protocols (ICNP), 2014 IEEE 22nd International Conference on*, pages 618–623. IEEE, 2014.
[18] Seungwon Shin, Yongjoo Song, Taekyung Lee, Sangho Lee, Jaewoong Chung, Phillip Porras, Vinod Yegneswaran, Jiseong Noh, and Brent Byunghoon Kang. Rosemary: A robust, secure, and high-performance network operating system. In *Proceedings of the 2014 ACM SIGSAC Conference on Computer and Communications Security*, pages 78–89. ACM, 2014.
[19] Seungwon Shin, Vinod Yegneswaran, Phillip Porras, and Guofei Gu. Avant-guard: Scalable and vigilant switch flow management in software-defined networks. In *Proceedings of the 2013 ACM SIGSAC Conference on Computer and Communications Security*, pages 413–424. ACM, 2013.
[20] S. Son, Seungwon Shin, V. Yegneswaran, P. Porras, and Guofei Gu. Model checking invariant security properties in OpenFlow. In *Communications (ICC), 2013 IEEE International Conference on*, pages 1974–1979, June 2013.
[21] Xitao Wen, Yan Chen, Chengchen Hu, Chao Shi, and Yi Wang. Towards a secure controller platform for openflow applications. In *Proceedings of the second ACM SIGCOMM workshop on Hot topics in software defined networking*, pages 171–172. ACM, 2013.

A Context-Aware System to Secure Enterprise Content

Oyindamola Oluwatimi
Department of Computer
Science
Purdue University
West Lafayette, IN, USA
ooluwati@purdue.edu

Daniele Midi
Department of Computer
Science
Purdue University
West Lafayette, IN, USA
dmidi@purdue.edu

Elisa Bertino
Department of Computer
Science
Purdue University
West Lafayette, IN, USA
bertino@purdue.edu

ABSTRACT

In this paper, we present an architecture and implementation of a secure, automated, proximity-based access control that we refer to as Context-Aware System to Secure Enterprise Content (CASSEC). Using the pervasive WiFi and Bluetooth wireless devices as components in our underlying positioning infrastructure, CASSEC addresses two proximity-based scenarios often encountered in enterprise environments: Separation of Duty and Absence of Other Users. The first scenario is achieved by using Bluetooth MAC addresses of nearby occupants as authentication tokens. The second scenario exploits the interference of WiFi received signal strength when an occupant crosses the line of sight (LOS). Regardless of the scenario, information about the occupancy of a particular location is periodically extracted to support continuous authentication. To the best of our knowledge, our approach is the first to incorporate WiFi signal interference caused by occupants as part of proximity-based access control system. Our results demonstrate that it is feasible to achieve great accuracy in localization of occupants in a monitored room.

Categories and Subject Descriptors

D.4.6 [**Operating Systems**]: Security and Protection—*Access Control*; K.6.5 [**Management of Computing and Information Systems**]: Security and Protection; H.4 [**Information Systems Applications**]: Miscellaneous

Keywords

Access Control Security; Mobility; Context awareness

1. INTRODUCTION

The proliferation and technological advancement of wireless networking and sensor technologies – such as WiFi, Bluetooth, and GPS – enable portable mobile devices to be used in context-aware systems. Such systems operate in pervasive computing environments in which certain applications require contextual information in order to provide a service or resource. The term *context* is used to characterize any information (i.e., identity, activity, and state) associated with the situation of an entity (i.e., users or objects). In terms of access control, such systems aim to secure access to sensitive resources by adapting their access authorizations to the current context *without* explicit user intervention. Consider an enterprise organization in which an employee is allowed to access a confidential financial document, but only if the access is executed within the supervisor's office. To enforce such a policy, the office's location would have to be submitted to a context-aware system as a contextual parameter in this access authorization process.

Proximity-based access control (PrBAC) addresses scenarios in which relative proximity constraints are required [21]. Under such an access control model, a policy could specify restrictions regarding either the presence or the absence of *other users* in the same physical space as the requesting user. Following the previous enterprise scenario, an example of a PrBAC policy would be to require also the presence of the supervisor, in the supervisor's office, for the employee to be able to view the confidential document. Location-based context-aware systems, like the well known GEO-RBAC [9], cannot support such a policy because they do not factor in contextual information associated with proximity.

The design of a solution to support PrBAC must consider two main issues. First, we must address whether users within a monitored space should be trusted to report information regarding their location and their proximity to other users. Users may attempt to circumvent the access control process by not reporting their location or by providing false location data. The second issue is how to address the *occupancy detection problem* [16], that is, *who is* and/or *how many* people are in a given space. Solutions to such issues require investigating the most suitable type of wireless technology and techniques to utilize in order to automatically retrieve spatial information associated with occupancy. Answers to such issues also require considering various aspects concerning the feasibility, practicality, and ease-of-adoption of the solution. For example, enterprises may be concerned with the financial expenditure of adopting a context-aware access control system, and some existing PrBAC systems are costly to deploy in that they require specialized, expensive hardware [22, 23]. We observe, however, that enterprise environments already have several characteristics that can be leveraged to our advantage. For example, we observe that wireless devices are pervasive in

SACMAT'16, June 05-08, 2016, Shanghai, China
© 2016 ACM. ISBN 978-1-4503-3802-8/16/06. . . $15.00
DOI: http://dx.doi.org/10.1145/2914642.2914648

enterprise environments. First, many modern mobile smart-phone devices are Bluetooth-enabled, and corporate-owned, personally-enabled (COPE) and bring-your-own-device (BYOD) scenarios allow an enterprise end-user to use a smartphone for enterprise purposes. Second, many modern office buildings are already equipped with WiFi-capable devices, such as routers, workstations, and laptops.

Given such considerations, the design of a context-aware PrBAC solution should fulfill the following requirements:

1. Proximity-based detection should not require user intervention.

2. Users should not be able to bypass access restrictions enforced by the solution.

3. As users are assumed to be mobile, any authorized access to resources should be monitored and changed as location and proximity information are updated.

4. The solution should not cause significant delays when authorized users attempt to access resources.

5. The solution should not impose significant costs to enterprises to deploy.

In this paper, we present the architecture and implementation of a secure, automated proximity-based access control that we refer to as Context-Aware System to Secure Enterprise Content (CASSEC). The proposed architecture supports access control decisions based on the location of the user requesting access and the proximity of other users in a monitored area, so that the appropriate privileges to access enterprise content are *automatically* granted. CASSEC specifically addresses two proximity-based scenarios often encountered in enterprise environments: Separation of Duty (SoD) and Absence of Other Users (AOU). To address such access control scenarios, CASSEC takes a wireless, infrastructure-based approach for localizing occupants within a monitored space. At a high-level, our design incorporates four main components: a client, an enterprise content server (ECS), an authorization server, and a proximity module. A client is a device operated by a user to access enterprise content. The ECS component delivers enterprise resources to users requesting access. The authorization server authenticates and authorizes users of the system that request access to resources from the ECS. The proximity module collects and analyzes contextual information from the environment in order to detect physical proximity.

While our system is agnostic with respect to the technological choices in detecting physical proximity, we demonstrate the feasibility of our approach by providing a simple implementation of the complete CASSEC architecture. We leverage wireless devices widely used in enterprise environments to implement an example proximity module. In the paper, we then first show how to enforce SoD by using Bluetooth MAC addresses of the mobile devices of nearby occupants as proof-of-location. That is, we extract the MAC address from these devices to determine *who* is in a given space. Second, we show how to enforce AOU by exploiting the degradation of WiFi received signal strength as a result of human-induced interference when people are near access points. That is, we utilize the WiFi-capable devices to determine *how many* people are in a given space. With such information, spatial proximity-based constraints can be specified in RBAC policies, and therefore allowing CASSEC to restrict access to enterprise content depending on the presence, or lack thereof, of users. Our experimental results show that our approach is efficient and effective.

The paper is organized as follows. Section 2 introduces proximity-based scenarios and specific examples that motivate this work. We then briefly discuss related work on proximity-based access controls and some implemented systems in Section 3. In addition, we provide background information on wireless techniques and technologies. We provide in Section 4 a PrBAC policy specification in CASSEC. Section 5 introduces the architecture and underlying components of our approach followed by the implementation and technical details in Section 6. We next report the results of our experiments in Section 7. We analyze the security of our approach in Section 8. Next, we discuss relevant work in Section 9. Section 10 concludes the paper by discussing improvements to CASSEC based on our experimental results.

2. MOTIVATING SCENARIOS

Pervasive computing has enabled context-aware systems to be leveraged in a variety of settings, including mobile cloud services, hospitals, enterprises, and military organizations [14,17,29,31]. In what follows we present scenarios motivating the need for context-aware systems in which access to sensitive resources must be controlled based on proximity parameters.

Consider a military organization with monitored government facilities such as restricted military bases or buildings. Military personnel are assigned roles that reflect ranking and privileges. The roles *General* and *Private* are assigned to the highest- and lowest-ranking personnel in the army, respectively. In terms of accessing restricted facilities or resources, the former is granted many privileges, while the latter has very few. Consider also the role *Civilian*, which indicates an individual operating outside of the military organization, and who is granted no privileges. Suppose that three military personnel, two *Generals* and one *Private*, are granted access to documents classified up to the level of *top secret* and *restricted*, respectively, according to a multi-level security model.

Separation of Duty Scenario. *A document classified as top secret is highly sensitive, and requires that **at least** two personnel with the role General be present in order for it to be accessed. The document is accessed via desktop terminal and is stored within a designated, but restricted office in which only Generals are allowed to enter.*
This scenario reflects the security principle SoD. That is, two or more people are responsible for cooperatively completing a task. In addition, the circumstances requires that said document must be accessed at a specific location.

Absence of Other Users Scenario. *A document classified as restricted, but with the additional caveat "**for your eyes only**", requires that a specific Private can access it via smartphone mobile, however, only if no other individuals are present at the time of access.*
Such an absence-based restriction not only includes military personnel of various rankings, but also people that assume the role of Civilian. Civilians are often temporarily recruited to work on military projects, but are highly monitored and usually given only the set of privileges needed to complete the project and nothing more. We note that, unlike the SoD scenario, in this AOU scenario the document can be accessed via the Private's smartphone device in any location includ-

ing locations that Civilians may have access to. Therefore, less infrastructure is required as it is not necessary to know the identity of every person in the Private's vicinity.

3. BACKGROUND

3.1 Proximity-Based Access Control

The role-based access control (RBAC) model is mainly used in enterprise settings to facilitate administration of access control polices [15]. In such settings, users are assigned different roles whereby each role is granted predefined access privileges to enterprise resources. Various access control models and systems have been proposed that use RBAC as a foundational paradigm, and some augment the model so that privileges associated with a role can only be exercised if contextual parameters are adhered to. The most common extension is the inclusion of spatial constraints. GEO-RBAC is a spatially-aware RBAC model that defines the concept of spatial roles which allow an authorized user to assume a role (i.e., role enabling) and exercise its associated privileges (i.e., role activation) only if the user is at or within a designated location specified by physical coordinates [9]. LoT-RBAC and STARBAC are other augmented RBAC models that incorporates spatio-temporal constraints for role enabling and role activation [2, 12]. Such models however are not implemented and therefore no enforcement mechanism has been developed to support these models.

Proximity-based Access Control (PBAC) [18] is an access control model developed specifically for Smart-Emergency Environments that takes into account the user's proximity to a resource (e.g., a computer). Prox-RBAC, which extends GEO-RBAC, is a formal authorization model based on a notion of proximity [22]. That is, access control decisions are not solely based on the requesting user's location, but also on the location of other users in the physical space. Prox-RBAC incorporates elements of the $UCON_{ABC}$ usage control model [28]. Prox-RBAC has been further extended to incorporate a large variety of proximity constraints in addition to the spatial ones, namely attribute-based, social, cyber, and temporal proximity constraints [17].

3.2 Occupancy Detection

There is a variety of technologies that address the localization problem, that is, to determine and retrieve a user's location. Generally, each positioning system has at least two separate hardware components, a transmitter and a receiver to send and receive signals, respectively [32]. The receiver analyzes one of three characteristics of the received signal which are: angle-of-arrival (AoA), received-signal strength (RSS), and time of arrival (ToA). For example, the most widely used technology in context-aware applications is the Global Position System (GPS). It is a positioning tool which uses the propagation time of signals (i.e., ToA) from satellites to compute the position of a receiver anywhere on Earth. Other positioning techniques with different technologies include Infrared (IR), Radio Frequency (RF), Radio Frequency Identification (RFID) [23], magnetic field [24], ultrasound [29], Bluetooth [11], and WiFi [5, 10, 20, 30, 31].

The proposed positioning systems vary with respect to many parameters, such as the techniques utilized, technologies on which they are based on, security, privacy, precision level of positional data, and therefore have their inherent advantages and disadvantages. Relevant to our work are radio-based localization technologies. Such technologies can potentially provide an accuracy as high as 10 cm using ranging techniques such as ToA [38]. However, objects of various size, shape, and material (e.g., humans or other radio signals) in the environment can obstruct the propagation path of radio signals, thus diminishing the accuracy [4, 20]. For example, the work in [10] demonstrates the effect of human interference with the propagation path of radio signals, and leverages this effect as a technique to determine the location of a user in a residential area. Careful consideration must be given in selecting a particular system for a given use case scenario. The design our solution considers the advantages and shortcomings of the described techniques, architectures, and systems.

4. POLICY SPECIFICATION

Much work has been done in the design of policy languages [3, 9, 15, 22, 25, 28]. In this section we introduce a simple, yet expressive policy specification (Table 1) that leverages existing policy languages. We adopt the syntactical structure of XACML, which is an XML-based language for access control, and apply it in defining proximity-based RBAC policies for CASSEC. The terms in quotes ' ' represent static tokens. The terms in italics indicate functions.

As it is standard in RBAC policies, a **role** is a job function that represents a set of privileges to perform actions on objects. An **object** is a data construct that is acted upon by a subject that has assumed a role. An **action** is an appropriate operation that can be applied to an object. We assume that users of our system may be mobile, and therefore, we incorporate usage controls regarding continuity of access [28]. An *obligation* specifies that certain constraints must be satisfied *prior* to or *while* accessing an object. A *topology* indicates a relation between the role and the **location** within the spatial domain. Often in enterprise environments, access to restricted resources is contingent on not only the presence (or absence) of other people, but the relation towards the individual requesting access. A **role-predicate** specifies a specific role or relational function that takes the role of the requesting user and outputs a ranking relative to that role (i.e., superior(roleOfRequestingUser)). Figure 1 provides two examples of access control policies to specify the restrictions in SoD scenario and AOU scenario.

```
<Policies>                              <Policies>
  <policy-list>                           <policy-list>
    <policy>                                <policy>
      <role> General</role>                   <role> Private</role>
      <object>TopSecretDocument</object>      <object>RestrictedDocument</object>
      <action>Read</action>                   <action>Read</action>
      <context>                               <context>
        <obligation>ongoing</obligation>        <obligation>ongoing</obligation>
        <location-constraint>                   <location-constraint>
          <topology> in </topology>               <topology> in </topology>
          <location> GeneralsRoom</location>      <location> Room105</location>
        </location-constraint>                  </location-constraint>
        <proximity-constraints>                 <proximity-constraints>
          <proximity-constraint>                  <proximity-constraint>
            <cardinality>at_least</cardinality>     <cardinality>at_most</cardinality>
            <digit>2</digit>                        <digit>0</digit>
            <role> General</role>                   <role>empty </role>
            <location> GeneralsRoom </location>     <location> room105</location>
          </proximity-constraint>                 </proximity-constraint>
        </proximity-constraints>                </proximity-constraints>
      </context>                              </policy>
    </policy>                                </context>
  </policy-list>                           </policy-list>
</Policies>                              </Policies>
```

Figure 1: The policy on the left refers to the SoD scenario: at least two Generals must be present in order to access the TopSecretDocument. The policy on the right refers to the AOU scenario: the Private can access the ResctrictedDocument only if no one else is around.

Table 1: PrBAC POLICY LANGUAGE

```
<Policies> ::= 'Begin' <policy-list> 'End'
<policy-list> ::= <policy> <policy-list> | <policy>
<policy> ::= <role> <object> <action> (<context>)
<action> ::= read | write | delete ...
<context> ::= <obligation> <location-constraint>
| <obligation> <location-constraint> <proximity-
constraints>
<obligation> ::= previous | ongoing
<location-constraint> ::= <topology> <location>
<topology> ::= in | out | adjacent ...
<proximity-constraints> ::= <proximity-constraint>
<proximity-constraints> | <proximity-constraint>
<proximity-constraint> ::= <cardinality> <digit>
<role-predicate><location-constraint>
<cardinality> ::= at_least | at_most
<role-predicate> ::= <role> | <ranking>
<ranking> ::= equal | inferior | superior
<digit> ::= ['0'-'9']
```

5. SYSTEM DESIGN

In this section, we describe our CASSEC platform that securely supports the SoD Scenario and the AOU scenario described in Section 2. We first discuss our design goals, and define our interpretation of the term *proximity*. We then provide an overview of the architectural components of CASSEC and how it relates to our access control framework.

5.1 Design Goals

Generalized Architecture: In our design, we aim to make our system model as general as possible. A simple, abstracted model allows each component in our system to be clearly defined with distinct designated responsibilities. Such separation of responsibilities is influenced by widely-adopted enterprise authorization frameworks [19, 26]. Each component, except the client, acts as a remote, independent server with wireless networking capabilities, allowing one to easily provide different implementations for the component.

Automation: In some context-aware access control systems, in order for a user to acquire access to a resource, the user must manually report such contextual information. We strive, however, to make a user's access to remote enterprise content as fluid as possible. We completely automate the access control process through eliminating the need for the user to report contextual information.

Security: Another one of our design goals is to assume the least amount of trusted parties possible in the system. The design of our architecture allows the system to be truly context-aware [6] by proactively monitoring and collecting information about the environment in lieu of manual intervention by entities within that environment. Specifically, we do not rely on users, possibly malicious, to manually report their location. Therefore, we choose a infrastructure-based approach that uses wireless hardware to achieve the localization of occupants within a monitored space.

Maximize efficiency: The dynamic nature of enterprise environments requires that context-aware systems should be readily updated when context changes. We aim to minimize the steps in the communication process between the architectural components while not impacting system performance.

5.2 Proximity Zone

We rely on geographical proximity, which indicates that two entities are located within a certain distance in the physical space [17]. That is, in our work, *proximity* of a user is defined by a region of space monitored by a proximity module that a user must be within in order for that user to gain access. We refer to this region of monitored space as a *proximity zone*. The level of precision in determining the location of a user and the proximity of other users is application dependent [10, 16].

5.3 Components

Client: A Client is a device used to request access to a resource by a user. If the request is granted, a user can view the data on the device (e.g., desktop terminal or mobile smartphone).

Enterprise Content Server (ECS): The ECS, which acts as the Policy Enforcer Point (PEP), delivers enterprise resources to users who request access. By designing this component as a server, a heterogeneous network of end-users' devices can be serviced. Therefore, access to resources can be requested from desktop terminals or mobile devices.

Authorization Server (AS): The AS hosts the access control decision-making engine of the authorization framework. After a user has been authenticated by the AS via login credentials, it returns an authentication token to the Client device. The token, which is submitted to the ECS by the Client, is used to associate an authenticated user with authorized roles. The AS itself is composed of two sub-components: Policy Decision Point (PDP) and Policy Information Point (PIP). We discuss in more detail the construction of the authentication token and AS's sub-components later in Section 5.4.

Proximity Module (PM): The role of the PM is to collect and analyze contextual information in order to detect the proximity of users in the system. This detection process occurs periodically, and proximity-related information is sent to the AS. Although a PM is the set of physical devices that determines proximity, we consider it as independent of the PIP as the PIP is the entity that directly communicates with the PDP.

Our architectural components as well as the relationships between them are shown in Figure 2. We do not discuss cryptographic schemes to protect network communication between the entities in our system model. We assume that an underlying secure network infrastructure is in place, as usual in enterprise environments. Although the figure only shows one PM and consequently only one proximity zone, in practice an enterprise building will have multiple PMs, possibly one for each room.

5.4 Access Control Framework

The **PDP** is the specific entity that is delegated to make access decisions. It maintains a database of PrBAC policies. Given these policies, the PDP first verifies if someone is a user of the system. The PDP then retrieves the latest information regarding the user's location and the presence of other users from the PIP. Such information allows the PDP to determine the set of authorized geo-spatial roles if proximity constraints are satisfied. Next, the PDP constructs and returns to the Client an authentication token. The token, at minimum, contains a generated temporary ID. It may also contain an expiration date. As such, the token is

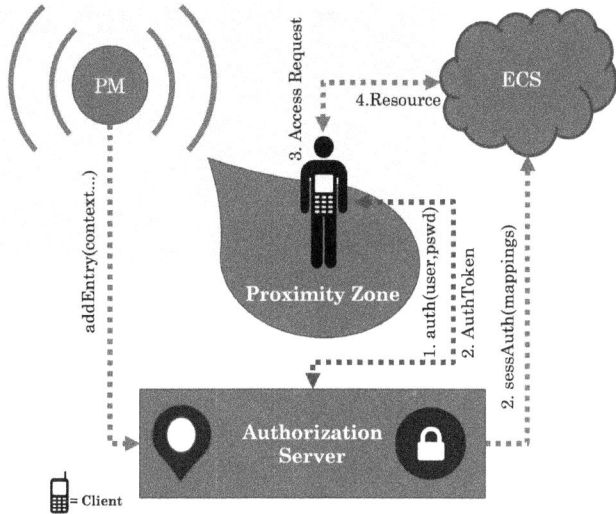

Figure 2: CASSEC's Proximity-based access control architecture. Arrows indicate wireless network communication.

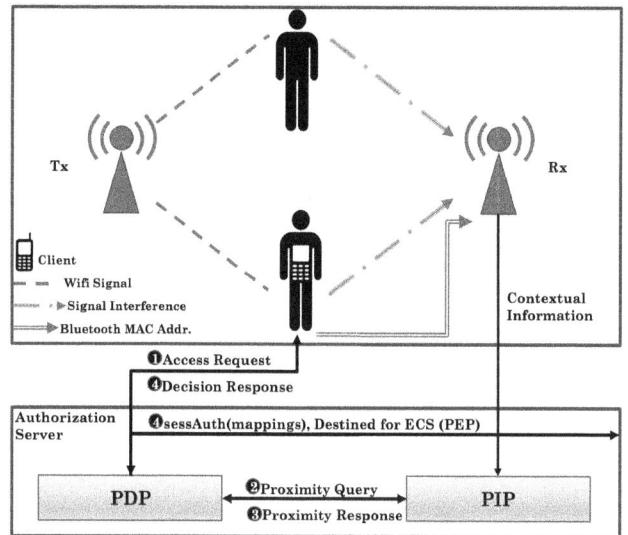

Figure 3: CASSEC's access control framework communicating with our prototype proximity module.

utilized as a session identifier. Last, the PDP maintains a database mapping of session IDs to the set of active authorized geo-spatial roles for each user. This mapping is *also* sent to the PEP each time a role is authorized.

The **PEP**'s role, implemented as part of the ECS, is to enforce proximity restrictions for enterprise content. During a request, a Client submits an authentication token to the ECS. The PEP extracts the temporary session ID from the token. Like the PDP, the PEP maintains a database mapping of session IDs to a set of active authorized geo-spatial roles. First, the mapping enables it to enforce access restrictions according to the roles associated with that ID. Second, it also enables it to service multiple Client devices simultaneously. Third, this design anonymizes users as the PEP does not have any information that identifies users such as locations and credentials.

The **PIP**'s role is to store and maintain contextual information about an enterprise's proximity zones. Each PM is required to transmit four pieces of information to the PIP: a proximity zone identifier, the number of people detected, a list of captured UIDs, and a timestamp. We assume that each user of the system has at least one identifier unique to that user. The PIP then publishes the collected data into its context database. Instead of the PIP polling the PM for information, we minimize communication by requiring that the PM updates the AS only when characteristics of the proximity zone changes. In addition, this clear designation of duties also minimizes overhead in both the PM and AS. Considering the dynamic nature of the environment, the PIP must update the PDP as frequently as the occurrences of updates to the context database. Such updates allow the PDP to continuously check for any instance of proximity-based violations by users. At the time of violation, the PDP invalidates the relevant session ID mappings by associating existing session IDs with newly recomputed *authorized* geo-spatial roles, if any, according to PrBAC policies. The PDP then remotely informs the PEP of invalid mappings while providing new authorized ones. The PDP can also alert the enterprise's administrators to take appropriate action. Such

a design makes the system completely automated by only requiring users to be authenticated once by the AS.

6. PROTOTYPE IMPLEMENTATION

6.1 The ECS

The ECS was implemented in PHP and hosted on a remote commercial server. The resources that it could serve to Clients were simple text files. We implemented user interfaces (UI) in order for Clients to request access to specific files. The ECS provides a function that can be remotely invoked via URL: *sessAuth(mappings)*. The function is invoked by the AS to update the ECS regarding the active geo-spatial roles for Clients in the event that location updates reflect proximity violations.

6.2 The AS

The AS was also implemented in PHP and hosted on the same server as the ECS. We implemented the UI in order for Clients to pass in authentication credentials via a login page. The AS provides two functions that can be remotely invoked via URLs: *auth(user,psswd)* and *addEntry(pzoneID,numOfPpl, UIDs, time)*. The first function is invoked by a Client via the UI and the second is invoked by the PM to update proximity information within the context database.

6.3 The PM

As in any basic positioning system, a PM incorporates a transmitter and a receiver. We define a transmitter as a wireless-enabled device that is a source of contextual information regarding the occupants within a proximity zone. A receiver is a wireless-enabled device that acts as a sink for such contextual information.

We utilize Bluetooth-enabled smartphones and WiFi access points (APs) as transmitters. In regards to smartphones, these devices periodically broadcast their 48-bit Bluetooth MAC addresses (with a less than 10 meter range) when Bluetooth is enabled. We require that users of the system permanently enable their smartphones' Bluetooth. Such a requirement can be easily enforced by Enterprise Mobility Management services [27]. WiFi APs transmit data over signals that can be measured. However, such signals are significantly influenced by the environment. We rely on the interference of signals as a result of human activity to determine the number of occupants in a proximity zone. In our system, the precise location of the user is not needed, rather the information needed is that a user is in a specific proximity zone (i.e., a room).

The PM's receiver was implemented on a laptop using Python running Linux. The PM was charged with periodically scanning signals produced by Bluetooth and WiFi devices every 10 seconds, which is the amount of time needed for the Linux command-line Bluetooth scanner function *hcitool* to fully execute. The PM extracts the MAC addresses of broadcast packets from nearby occupants' smartphones. The MAC addresses are used as proof-of-location which determines *who* is in a given space. It also measures the received signal strength from a designated WiFi AP. The receiver processes the measured RSS value and determines *how many* occupants are in a given space. Last, the receiver publishes the MAC addresses (i.e, UIDs) and the number of occupants to the authorization server only when previously collected contextual information changes.

We note that the various components of the CASSEC's system architecture can be integrated into the same physical component when implemented. For example, a smartphone mobile device can act both as *Client* and transmitter because the same device used to request access to a resource is the same device that periodically broadcasts its Bluetooth MAC address. Similarly, a desktop terminal can act both as *Client* and receiver because it can also be used to scan and process WiFi and Bluetooth contextual information.

7. EXPERIMENTAL RESULTS

7.1 Deployment

In this section, we report experimental results of our prototype system of CASSEC. We deployed our hardware and tested our prototype system in a two bedroom apartment whose layout is shown in Figure 4. We now briefly describe the hardware utilized in our platform.

The Wireless-N (802.11n) WiFi AP transmitter was a Motorola SURFBoard SBG6580, indicated in blue, that supports two frequency bands which are 2.5GHz and 5.0GHz. We chose the higher-frequency band to take advantage of additional channels that are less prone to interference than 2.4GHz. The receiver was a Dell Latitude E6430, indicated in green, equipped with a BCM4313 802.11bgn wireless network adapter and a Dell Wireless 380 Bluetooth 4.0. The transmitter and the receiver were placed 3 meters apart and were elevated 1 meter above the floor. The Bluetooth-enabled transmitters used in our experiments were Samsung S3 GT-i9300 and a Nexus Android-based smartphone devices.

7.2 Experiments

Experiment 1: Selecting Frequency Channel. Given a wireless link between a transmitter and a receiver, an individual crossing the line of sight between the two communicating wireless sensors affects the RSS measured by the receiver. However, the change in RSS depends on the fre-

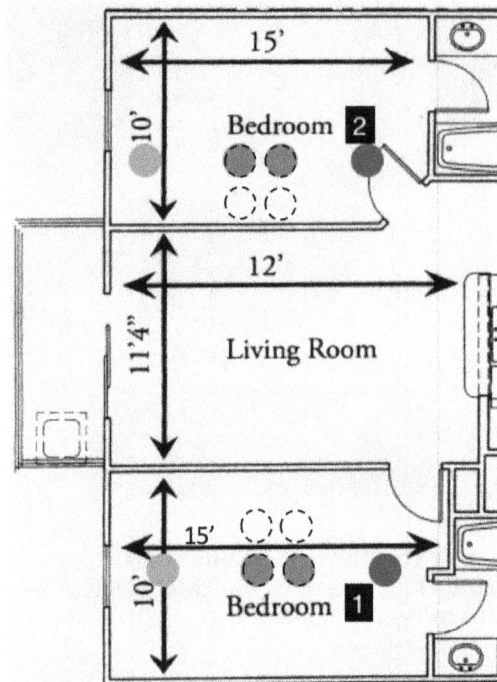

Figure 4: The blueprint of a two-bedroom apartment in which the prototype system had been deployed. The blue markers and green markers indicate the positions of WiFi access points and laptops, respectively. The dotted lines indicate the two possible positions for each human, and transitions simply require moving two steps without changing body orientation. The red dots represent the current positions of the humans standing still while facing the laptop.

quency channel [10]. The goal of this experiment is to determine which channel is the best for detecting human activity based on our particularly WiFi-enabled devices. We test 2 non-overlapping 40MHz channels: Channel A (5180MHz) and Channel B (5220MHz). The experiment setup is as follows. Throughout the complete test, we continuously measure the RSS value sampling twice per second. Every 30 seconds we change the number of individuals obstructing the LOS by 1 starting from zero to two, and then in a decreasing fashion. The occupants were situated equidistant from each receiver. A Python script was written to automatically begin the test. The tests were conducted in Bedroom 1.

The results in Figure 5 demonstrate that there is not a significant difference in measurement variation in human-induced interference in RSS signals between Channel A and Channel B. At first, Channel A appears to be more consistent as the level of signal interference in samples 60 - 120 aligns with values in samples 180 - 240 when the number of individuals increases from zero to one and two to one, respectively. This is not observed in Channel B during that period. However, the values for Channel A appear to indicate the presence of a number of individuals different from the number of individuals actually present from samples 330 onward. This fluctuation is not observed in Channel B. Although Figure 5 shows the results of only one complete experiment,

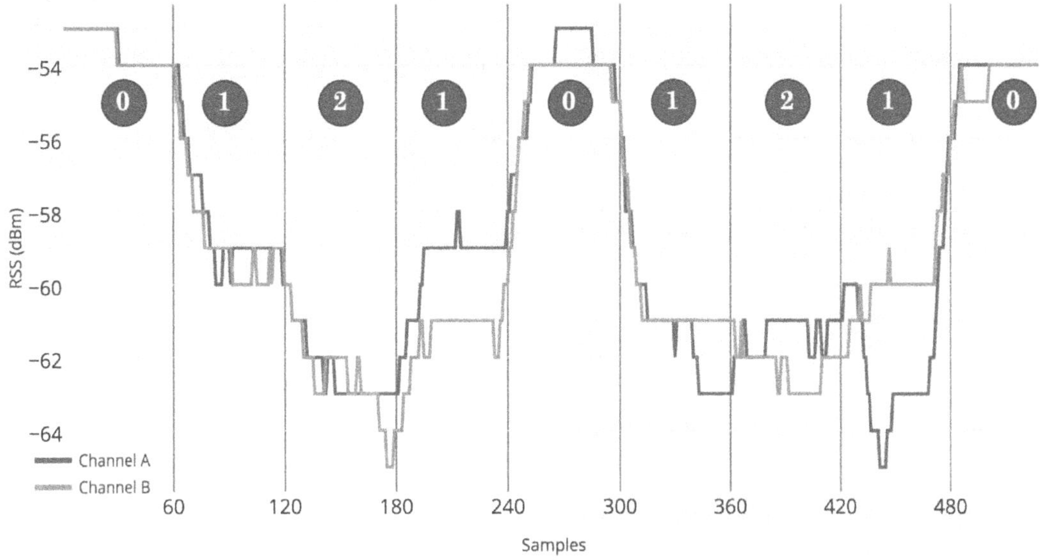

Figure 5: RSS measurements of wireless links on different frequency bands when human bodies obstruct the line of sight (LOS). The blue circles indicate the number of humans in the LOS within each 60-sample period (i.e., every 30 seconds).

we performed this experiment 3 times and observed similar changes in values. Given these observations, we select Channel B as a means for testing in other experiments.

We also make some general observations about human-induced RSS changes. We observed distinct variances in signal strength almost every 30 seconds (multiple of 60 units in Figure 5). First, by initiating the experiment with no individuals obstructing the LOS, we were able to establish a baseline for the signal strength between the transmitter and receiver. The RSS value remained always constant within that time period up until to two seconds after the 30 second mark. That is, using our existing hardware, we were able to determine that once we increase the number of individuals by one, the individuals must remain in the LOS for *at least* one second for the receiver to observe some interference from human activity. Such phenomena was also observed at the beginning or end of each period. Second, regardless of the selected channel, when the LOS is obstructed by an individual the RSS on average decreases. In addition, distinct dBm drop ranges exist depending on the number of individuals. Therefore we can infer the presence or absence of humans based on RSS' ranges. For example, in Channel A, we consistently observed a drop range of 6-8 dBm between 30-60, 90-120, 150-180, and 210-240 seconds. We note that our observations are likely to change using different WiFi-enabled hardware.

Experiment 2: Detection Accuracy. The goal of this experiment is to test the WiFi localization component of our PM. Specifically, we implemented a simple algorithm to detect the number of people within the LOS based on our observations of human-induced RSS changes from Experiment 1. The setup to this experiment is similar to the setup for Experiment 1, except that we perform the experiment in *both* Bedrooms 1 and 2. We conduct the experiment on Channel B.

Table 2 displays the results of this experiment. The system was able to detect with strong accuracy (89%) the number of occupants obstructing the line of sight in Bedroom 1. At certain points, sporadic fluctuations occurred that caused the system to return an incorrect number. On the other hand, the system was only able to detect occupancy with 44% accuracy in Bedroom 2. After further analysis (by performing Experiment 1 in Bedroom 2), we observed the human-induced interference was slightly different in RSS levels. Although the physical layouts of Bedroom 1 and 2 are identical, there may be other (unseen) environmental factors that also influenced the RSS levels to slightly differ between the two rooms. For example, such factors may include overlapping wireless networks (possibly using the same channel) from neighboring apartments, appliances and electronics emitting radio frequency interference, and simply walls and floors blocking wireless signals in different ways depending on the location of access points [4]. We leave further analysis of WiFi signal interference caused by various environmental factors for future work.

Bedroom1	89%
Bedroom2	43%

Table 2: We leverage the human-induced signal interference in WiFi received signal strength (RSS) to detect occupancy within a monitored room. 89% **and** 48% **accuracy was achieved for Bedroom 1 and 2, respectively. We believe that detection accuracy in the latter case were low because our technique was based on data acquired in Experiment 1 which analyzed signal interference from Bedroom 1. Specifically, we believe that there were *other* unseen environmental factors that influenced the RSS values of human activity in Bedroom 2.**

8. SECURITY ANALYSIS

In this section, we present a security analysis of our CASSEC platform to analyze attacks aiming at circumventing its PrBAC restrictions. Below, we provide various attack vectors that could be used and, subsequently, a means to mitigate the threat or minimize the attack vector surface.

8.1 Bluetooth Manipulation

The PIP maintains a database of a one-to-one relationship between a Bluetooth MAC address and a particular user of the system. When a PM publishes a MAC address to the PIP, it attests that a specific individual user is at a specific proximity zone. A malicious user may attempt to root his/her device and modify the MAC address in order to impersonate another user of the system. In our tests, we utilized a Samsung Galaxy device. Samsung provides Samsung KNOX 2.0 which is a custom Android OS intended for enterprise environments [27]. KNOX 2.0 provides significantly strong guarantees against root attacks, as Samsung's platform includes hardware and software mechanisms to enhance security. It has a low-level feature that leaves the device inoperable once it detects a root attack, which is a sufficient mechanism to defend against malicious modification of the MAC address.

One attack that malicious users may attempt is masking their smartphones' MAC addresses by either disabling the Bluetooth or simply leaving the device in another room. Although we require that Bluetooth be permanently enabled on users' devices, we do not incorporate an enforcement mechanism within the phone to meet such requirement. However, our system is able to detect if the violation of such requirement occurs. The WiFi localization technique is able to determine the number of occupants in the room. If the number of occupants and the number of MAC addresses, which are published to the PIP, for a given room do not match, the PDP will infer such malicious behaviour and subsequently revoke access to resources. In addition, appropriate actions can be taken by the system administrator.

Another attack vector involves an unauthorized individual obtaining an authorized user's phone, whether by theft or voluntary provision. If such an attack occurs, then the unauthorized individual can gain access to restricted resources. Therefore, our system must incorporate a mechanism that is able to determine biometric signatures for every user in the system. The work presented in [34], for example, explores biometric signatures using WiFi-based techniques, but it requires one receiver and one transmitter for *every* user in order to distinguish multiple subjects at a time, which is not practical for enterprise environments. In reality, this sort of attack exploits social engineering and/or insider threats that are usually already covered as part of an enterprise's global security efforts. Nevertheless, we leave the investigation of practical solutions to this issue for future work so that unauthorized users will not be able to bypass security by using someone else's device.

A malicious user may attempt a Denial-of-Service (DoS) attack by acquiring a high-powered Bluetooth-enabled device [8, 13, 37]. Specifically, the user first adjusts the special device to mimic his original (or another user's) smartphone's MAC address, and then boosts the signal strength. As a consequence, receivers in different rooms within a certain radius may incorrectly publish the proof-of-location. Therefore, the PDP will believe that multiple violations are occurring. Several methods could be employed to counteract this attack. For example, a temporal localization analysis could determine if multiple receivers have published the same MAC address within a time-based threshold.

8.2 WiFi Manipulation

We leverage the WiFi signal interference caused by human activity to determine the number of occupants in a given room. A malicious user could attempt a DoS by disrupting WiFi signals. That is, an attacker could acquire a special device that would, for example, completely nullify WiFi signals [8, 13, 37]. Another means to circumvent the system would be to obstruct the LOS with something other than a human body such as a chair. Therefore, in either case, when the receiver processes the signal interference, it may publish an incorrect number of users within that room. However, the authorization server will detect violations because inconsistencies will exist within the PIP.

Regardless of whether Bluetooth or WiFi manipulation is employed, the scenarios that we address make it more difficult to circumvent CASSEC. That is, in both the SoD Scenario and the AOU scenario, multiple users with mutual interests must collude and agree in order to attempt bypassing the system.

9. RELATED WORK

Prox-RBAC was implemented using near-field communication (NFC) allowing a NFC phone to transmit signals to a NFC reader to lock and unlock a door, and although it provides high-integrity proof of location, it requires user intervention. On the other hand, PBAC was implemented using ultra-wide band RFID which calculated AoA and ToA to support automated access access control. Although the system did not require user intervention, active tags (worn by users) and mounted receivers had to be deployed to determine the tags position. Many systems, including Prox-RBAC and PBAC, inherently assume that every individual within a monitored space is trusted. Systems that are solely based on location tracking devices worn or held by users can be easily circumvented through collusion. Consider the two motivating scenarios discussed in Section 2 on which our work is based. In the SoD scenario, which assumes top secret documents to be stored within a protected office, one of the Generals that has a high security clearance will unlock the door with his/her tracking device (e.g., NFC), but a Private can easily follow immediately behind prior to the door locking. By not initiating contact between the transmitter and the receiver, the system would be tricked into believing that no unauthorized personnel is occupying the protected office. The AOU scenario requires that an eyes-only, restricted document to be accessible by a Private only when no other individuals are in the vicinity. However, a Civilian, assuming he/she was given a tracking device, can simply remove the device (e.g., active tag) so as to not be tracked. In addition, costs for deployment and management of these systems, and others used in similar architectures, remain significant and limit the widespread adoption of these systems.

XACML is a standardized access control policy language and an abstract enforcement model. In our work, we leverage the syntactical structure of XACML policies (specified in XML) as well as the main components in its enforcement mechanism. Specifically, our policy specification is written in XML (Section 4), and our underlying PrBAC reference architecture is the same as the one of XACML. However, the communication model as well as the duties of each architectural component differ in CASSEC as our objective is to provide an abstract context-aware system architecture to support an automated access control system.

10. CONCLUSIONS

Enterprise organizations have adopted proximity-based context-aware systems that leverage role-based access control to mitigate threats of information leakage. In this paper, we describe a secure, automated proximity-based access control architecture and prototype system that we refer to as Context-Aware System to Secure Enterprise Content (CASSEC). CASSEC addresses two proximity-based scenarios often encountered in enterprise environments: Separation of Duty and Absence of Other Users. To address such access control scenarios, CASSEC takes a wireless, infrastructure-based approach to achieve the localization of occupants within a monitored space which enables geo-spatial RBAC. A wireless, infrastructure-based approach makes the system more resilient to malicious attacks. In addition, access control is automated, and therefore, does not require user intervention. While our system is agnostic with respect to the technological choices for detecting physical proximity, we demonstrate the feasibility of our approach by providing a simple implementation of the complete CASSEC architecture. No additional hardware is needed to deploy our system as we utilized Bluetooth and WiFi devices, which are widely used in enterprise environments. The localization technique utilized has a detection accuracy up to 89%. The technique has, however, some limitations. Occupants were required to stand in the line of sight (between a wireless transmitter and receiver) for at least one second to detect human activity and subsequently the number of occupants within a room. We leave the investigation of other localization techniques with higher accuracy and more robust detection for future work [1, 7, 10, 23, 24, 29, 33, 35, 36]. In addition, we will also investigate secure device fingerprinting techniques to protect against forgery and context-manipulating adversaries [8, 13, 37].

Acknowledgement
The work reported in this paper has been partially funded by NSF under grant CNS-1111512.

11. REFERENCES
[1] F. Adib and D. Katabi. *See through walls with wifi!*, volume 43. ACM, 2013.

[2] S. Aich, S. Sural, and A. K. Majumdar. Starbac: Spatiotemporal role based access control. In *On the Move to Meaningful Internet Systems 2007: CoopIS, DOA, ODBASE, GADA, and IS*, pages 1567–1582. Springer, 2007.

[3] A. Anderson. Xacml profile for role based access control (rbac). *OASIS Access Control TC committee draft*, 1:13, 2004.

[4] N. Baccour, A. Koubâa, L. Mottola, M. A. Zúñiga, H. Youssef, C. A. Boano, and M. Alves. Radio link quality estimation in wireless sensor networks: a survey. *ACM Transactions on Sensor Networks (TOSN)*, 8(4):34, 2012.

[5] B. Balaji, J. Xu, A. Nwokafor, R. Gupta, and Y. Agarwal. Sentinel: occupancy based hvac actuation using existing wifi infrastructure within commercial buildings. In *Proceedings of the 11th ACM Conference on Embedded Networked Sensor Systems*, page 17. ACM, 2013.

[6] M. Baldauf, S. Dustdar, and F. Rosenberg. A survey on context-aware systems. *International Journal of Ad Hoc and Ubiquitous Computing*, 2(4):263–277, 2007.

[7] A. Banerjee, D. Maas, M. Bocca, N. Patwari, and S. Kasera. Violating privacy through walls by passive monitoring of radio windows. In *Proceedings of the 2014 ACM conference on Security and privacy in wireless & mobile networks*, pages 69–80. ACM, 2014.

[8] S. Banerjee and V. Brik. Wireless device fingerprinting. In *Encyclopedia of Cryptography and Security*, pages 1388–1390. Springer, 2011.

[9] E. Bertino, B. Catania, M. L. Damiani, and P. Perlasca. Geo-rbac: a spatially aware rbac. In *Proceedings of the tenth ACM symposium on Access control models and technologies*, pages 29–37. ACM, 2005.

[10] M. Bocca, O. Kaltiokallio, and N. Patwari. Radio tomographic imaging for ambient assisted living. In *Evaluating AAL Systems Through Competitive Benchmarking*, pages 108–130. Springer, 2012.

[11] R. Bruno and F. Delmastro. *Personal Wireless Communications: IFIP-TC6 8th International Conference, PWC 2003, Venice, Italy, September 23-25, 2003. Proceedings*, chapter Design and Analysis of a Bluetooth-Based Indoor Localization System, pages 711–725. Springer Berlin Heidelberg, Berlin, Heidelberg, 2003.

[12] S. M. Chandran and J. B. Joshi. Lot-rbac: a location and time-based rbac model. In *Web Information Systems Engineering–WISE 2005*, pages 361–375. Springer, 2005.

[13] L. C. C. Desmond, C. C. Yuan, T. C. Pheng, and R. S. Lee. Identifying unique devices through wireless fingerprinting. In *Proceedings of the first ACM conference on Wireless network security*, pages 46–55. ACM, 2008.

[14] J. El-Sobhy, S. Zickau, and A. Kupper. Proximity-based services in mobile cloud scenarios using extended communication models. In *Cloud Networking (CloudNet), 2015 IEEE 4th International Conference on*, pages 125–131. IEEE, 2015.

[15] D. Ferraiolo, D. R. Kuhn, and R. Chandramouli. *Role-based access control*. Artech House, 2003.

[16] S. K. Ghai, L. V. Thanayankizil, D. P. Seetharam, and D. Chakraborty. Occupancy detection in commercial buildings using opportunistic context sources. In *Pervasive Computing and Communications Workshops (PERCOM Workshops), 2012 IEEE International Conference on*, pages 463–466. IEEE, 2012.

[17] A. Gupta, M. S. Kirkpatrick, and E. Bertino. A formal proximity model for rbac systems. *Computers & Security*, 41:52–67, 2014.

[18] S. K. Gupta, T. Mukheriee, K. Venkatasubramanian, and T. Taylor. Proximity based access control in smart-emergency departments. In *Pervasive Computing and Communications Workshops, 2006.*

PerCom Workshops 2006. Fourth Annual IEEE International Conference on, pages 5–pp. IEEE, 2006.

[19] D. Hardt. The oauth 2.0 authorization framework. 2012.

[20] Y. Jiang, X. Pan, K. Li, Q. Lv, R. P. Dick, M. Hannigan, and L. Shang. Ariel: Automatic wi-fi based room fingerprinting for indoor localization. In *Proceedings of the 2012 ACM Conference on Ubiquitous Computing*, pages 441–450. ACM, 2012.

[21] M. S. Kirkpatrick and E. Bertino. Enforcing spatial constraints for mobile rbac systems. In *Proceedings of the 15th ACM symposium on Access control models and technologies*, pages 99–108. ACM, 2010.

[22] M. S. Kirkpatrick, M. L. Damiani, and E. Bertino. Prox-rbac: a proximity-based spatially aware rbac. In *Proceedings of the 19th ACM SIGSPATIAL International Conference on Advances in Geographic Information Systems*, pages 339–348. ACM, 2011.

[23] A. Larchikov, S. Panasenko, A. V. Pimenov, and P. Timofeev. Combining rfid-based physical access control systems with digital signature systems to increase their security. In *Software, Telecommunications and Computer Networks (SoftCOM), 2014 22nd International Conference on*, pages 100–103. IEEE, 2014.

[24] M. Moreno, J. L. Hernandez, and A. F. Skarmeta. A new location-aware authorization mechanism for indoor environments. In *Advanced Information Networking and Applications Workshops (WAINA), 2014 28th International Conference on*, pages 791–796. IEEE, 2014.

[25] T. Moses et al. Extensible access control markup language (xacml) version 2.0. *Oasis Standard*, 200502, 2005.

[26] B. C. Neuman and T. Ts' O. Kerberos: An authentication service for computer networks. *Communications Magazine, IEEE*, 32(9):33–38, 1994.

[27] O. Oluwatimi, D. Midi, and E. Bertino. Overview of mobile containerization approaches and open research directions. *Under submission*, 2016.

[28] J. Park and R. Sandhu. The ucon abc usage control model. *ACM Transactions on Information and System Security (TISSEC)*, 7(1):128–174, 2004.

[29] K. B. Rasmussen, C. Castelluccia, T. S. Heydt-Benjamin, and S. Capkun. Proximity-based access control for implantable medical devices. In *Proceedings of the 16th ACM conference on Computer and communications security*, pages 410–419. ACM, 2009.

[30] T. Saelim, P. Chumchu, and T. Mayteevarunyoo. Design and performance evaluation of novel location-based access control algorithm using ieee 802.11 r. *Journal of Convergence Information Technology*, 10(4):33, 2015.

[31] B. Shebaro, O. Oluwatimi, and E. Bertino. Context-based access control systems for mobile devices. *Dependable and Secure Computing, IEEE Transactions on*, 12(2):150–163, 2015.

[32] M. Vossiek, L. Wiebking, P. Gulden, J. Wieghardt, C. Hoffmann, and P. Heide. Wireless local positioning. *Microwave Magazine, IEEE*, 4(4):77–86, 2003.

[33] G. Wang, Y. Zou, Z. Zhou, K. Wu, and L. M. Ni. We can hear you with wi-fi! In *Proceedings of the 20th annual international conference on Mobile computing and networking*, pages 593–604. ACM, 2014.

[34] W. Wang, A. X. Liu, M. Shahzad, K. Ling, and S. Lu. Understanding and modeling of wifi signal based human activity recognition. In *Proceedings of the 21st Annual International Conference on Mobile Computing and Networking*, pages 65–76. ACM, 2015.

[35] W. Wang, A. X. Liu, M. Shahzad, K. Ling, and S. Lu. Understanding and modeling of wifi signal based human activity recognition. In *Proceedings of the 21st Annual International Conference on Mobile Computing and Networking*, pages 65–76. ACM, 2015.

[36] Y. Wang, J. Liu, Y. Chen, M. Gruteser, J. Yang, and H. Liu. E-eyes: device-free location-oriented activity identification using fine-grained wifi signatures. In *Proceedings of the 20th annual international conference on Mobile computing and networking*, pages 617–628. ACM, 2014.

[37] Q. Xu, R. Zheng, W. Saad, and Z. Han. Device fingerprinting in wireless networks: Challenges and opportunities. 2015.

[38] F. Zafari, I. Papapanagiotou, and K. Christidis. Micro-location for internet of things equipped smart buildings. 2015.

Detecting Privilege Escalation Attacks through Instrumenting Web Application Source Code

Jun Zhu, Bill Chu, Heather Lipford
University of North Carolina at Charlotte
Charlotte, NC 28223, USA
zhujunfirst1@gmail.com, {billchu, Heather.Lipford}@uncc.edu

ABSTRACT

Privilege Escalation is a common and serious type of security attack. Although experience shows that many applications are vulnerable to such attacks, attackers rarely succeed upon first trial. Their initial probing attempts often fail before a successful breach of access control is achieved. This paper presents an approach to automatically instrument application source code to report events of failed access attempts that may indicate privilege escalation attacks to a run time application protection mechanism. The focus of this paper is primarily on the problem of instrumenting web application source code to detect access control attack events. We evaluated false positives and negatives of our approach using two open source web applications.

Categories and Subject Descriptors

D.4.6 [**Security and Protection**]

General Terms

Security

Keywords

Unauthorized access; privilege escalation; application sensors; security.

1. INTRODUCTION

Violation of access control policies is a core computer security problem. A great deal of effort by the access control research community has focused on designing and implementing the right access control policies. However, this is a difficult challenge both for developers and for tools. We believe more research is needed on run-time protection against access control attacks. Experience based attack models, such as the kill chain model [14], show that a successful attack is preceded by a number of failed probing attempts. In this paper, we propose a method to instrument web application source code to detect attacks on access control so an attack kill chain can be stopped before it completes successfully.

Consider a fund transfer function of an online banking application illustrated in Listing 1. If the condition highlighted in italics failed, it means a user is attempting to transfer funds out of an account he/she does not own. For most online banking applications, this is strong evidence of an attack because it is unlikely caused by an innocent user. Such a user should not be allowed to interact with the application as he/she may successfully exploit unknown access control vulnerabilities. We describe an approach that automatically instruments the application code as illustrated in Listing 2, where the function call in bold reports this privilege escalation event to a run time protection mechanism. We refer to added code as *reporting code*, as it reports to an external agent.

```
public Response fundTransfer () {
if (owns([$_SESSION['user'], $_SESSION['accountNo']]) {
// make the transfer
              }
else {
 // rejection transfer
}
```

Listing 1. An application event that signals unauthorized access.

```
public Response fundTransfer () {
if (owns([$_SESSION['user'], $_SESSION['accountNo']]){
// make the transfer
              }
else {
sensor();
// rejection transfer
}
```

Listing 2. Instrument application to report access control attacks.

A good example of a run time application protection mechanism is the open source AppSensor project [13] which aims to detect possible attacking agents based on application specific information as illustrated in Figure 1. It is modeled after network intrusion detection/prevention frameworks, but using application as opposed to network events. A number of mechanisms are available for AppSensor to stop attackers, including blocking the attacker's IP address and suspending the attacker's access credentials.

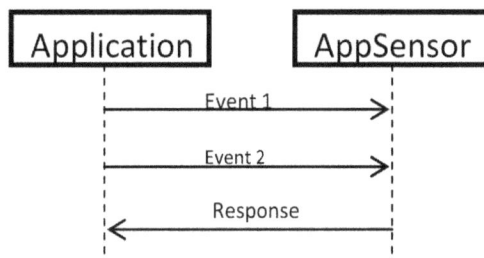

Figure 1. Using AppSensor to protect applications against attacks

AppSensor may make the determination that an application is under attack by correlating multiple events from a given

SACMAT'16, June 5-8, 2016, Shanghai, China.
© 2016 ACM. ISBN 978-1-4503-3802-8/16/06…$15.00
DOI: http://dx.doi.org/10.1145/2914642.2914661

application or events from multiple applications as well as with reports from network sensors.

Relying on developers to manually insert reporting code as shown in Listing 2 is unlikely to lead to wide adoption. First, inserting such code is extra effort that is not part of the application specification and that will add to developer work load, both in terms of programming and testing to make sure the added reporting code does not change the application's business logic. Second, as part of normal application maintenance, reporting code must be updated and tested to make sure they are in sync with relevant application logic. We believe that developers should be focused on developing applications (and practice secure programming!). Instrumenting code to report access control attacks should be (a) done in an automated way, (b) without changing the intended functions of the application, and (c) having minimal performance impact. Furthermore, instrumented code could be added as part of code deployment so the developer will not have to be aware of added reporting code.

For the rest of the paper we describe an approach that automatically instruments a web-based application to detect likely privilege escalation attack events. This is accomplished in two steps. First we describe an approach to identify candidate web pages to insert code to detect failed attempts to access sensitive information. Second, we present a model on how to automatically insert reporting code without impacting application logic. We report our evaluation results based on two open source web applications.

2. FORCED BROWSING DETECTION

In the context of web applications, privilege escalation often takes the form of forced browsing [6] where an attacker seeks to gain access by directly invoking a particular web page. Our approach is to instrument web application source code to report failed forced browsing attempts. However, not all access failures reliably signal forced browsing attacks.

In a web-based application a typical user navigates application functions by following links and menu items. For example, a micro blog application may require a user to login before writing comments. However, a comment link is always available on web pages even if the user has not logged in (for example see Twitter's web interface where the reply button is always visible). Clicking on the comment link may lead to an access control failure but it is not indicative of a forced browsing attack.

Forced browsing is defined as an action where a subject visits a web page without following available links and menu items. There are, however, scenarios where an innocent user may exhibit forced browsing behavior. The most common case is a user refreshing a protected page after session expiration. False alarms can be minimized by considering context information. For example malicious forced browsing differs from innocent cases in that an attacker often attempts forced browsing on multiple pages over a short period of time. Such context-based decisions can be made by the AppSensor. For example, it may suspend the user after multiple forced browsing attempts on different pages within five minutes, much like suspending user account after repeated failed login in attempts. We are not going to explore possible decision rules for the AppSensor in this paper. Instead, our focus is on automatic code instrumentation to report possible forced browsing events.

The road map for forced browsing detection is as follows. First we discuss how to identify code that implements access control in web-applications. Second we extract a sitemap of a web application as a graph where each node is a web page and edges represent URL links between pages. Third, we identify those web pages that are protected by access control logic, that is, links to such pages are only shown when access privileges are checked. We will insert code to report access control failures in such protected pages as forced browsing attempts.

2.1 Identify Access Control Checks

There is a significant body of research on identifying access control logic in applications. Approaches range from automatic detection using code mining [3,4,5,6,7,8,9] to interactive annotation by soliciting input from developers [1,2,12,16,17]. For our discussions here, we assume one can identify access control logic in the application source with reasonable amount of effort using such techniques. For empirical evaluation of our approach, we chose two open source web applications that have been used by other researchers to show that access control logic can be identified from source code. Specifically we assume the following elements are identified.

Security Sensitive Operation (SSO). Identifying SSOs is an important step in a secure software development lifecycle (SSDLC) [10] because knowing which data elements have security implications is critical for threat modeling [11].We consider SSOs as database operations (e.g. SELECT, INSERT, UPDATE, DELETE on specific database tables) for our work. This can be extended easily to include other operations such as file access.

Code implementing access control check. An access control check for a given SSO must satisfy several requirements: (1) it must be on the execution path from the program entry point to the SSO; (2) it must have the option of changing the execution path to deny access to the SSO. This can be accomplished by either (2.a) a set of Boolean expressions in a branch/conditional statement that lead to altering the execution path leading to the SSO involved, or (2.b) method invocations that could either throw exceptions or terminate the execution. Listing 3 shows a snippet of code from an application. Code that implements access control is shown in *italics*. Here function *require_login()* throws an exception if the user is not logged in and access to the SSO will be denied. Function *print_error* will never return after printing a message, again denying access to the SSO.

```
require_login($course, false, $cm);
if(isguestuser()){print_error('noguests','chat');}
if (!$chat_sid = chat_login_user($chat->id, 'sockets', $groupid, $course)) {
print_error('cantlogin');}
```

Listing 3. Example code snippet, access control checks are shown in *italics*.

2.2 Determine Candidate Webpages to Report Forced Browsing

Our first step is to construct a sitemap. Figure 2 shows part of a sitemap for Wheatblog, an open source PHP application. A sitemap shows possible navigation paths by following links inside web pages. It is a directed graph where each node is a web page. A link between node A and B indicates page A has an URL link pointing to page B. We distinguish two types of links. A link from page C to D is a *conditional* link if this link is displayed on page C pointing to D only if certain access control checks are satisfied. They are shown as dashed links in Figure 2. Conditional links are often found in an index page where links pointing to pages accessing sensitive information are displayed after the user has been authorized. In other words web applications often "hide" links to pages accessing sensitive information until the access level of the user is determined.

For example in Figure 2 links to blog administration functions (nodes inside the dashed box) are displayed only if the user logged in is an administrator. Because web applications are multi-entrant, access control checks must be repeated in every page accessing sensitive information to prevent forced browsing attacks. For example, in Figure 2 any of the administrative web pages must implement access control checks to make sure the user is an admin. A common access control vulnerability is that one of the pages for an admin function did not contain proper access control check and therefore can be subject privilege escalation attacks.

An *unconditional* link from page A to page B means there is a web link displayed in page A referring to page B without the need to satisfy access control checks. They are shown as solid links in Figure 2.

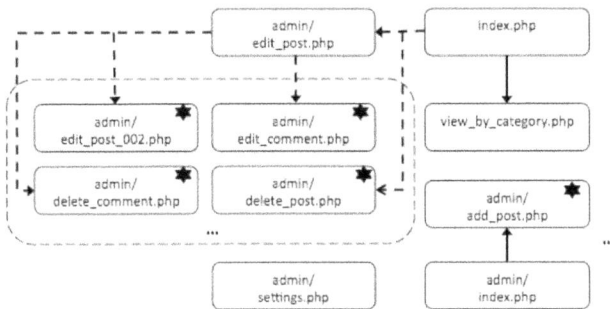

Figure 2. Part of the sitemap of Wheatblog (some pages are omitted as ellipsis due to page limit)

Web applications are built with intended execution paths. Intended starting pages (typically files named index.php in various directories) are assumed to be provided as input to constructing the sitemap. For example, in Figure 2, index.php and admin/settings.php are entry pages. The dashed box in Figure 2 contains a set of pages that are candidates for inserting code to report forced browsing events. This is because each page in that box has at least one SSO and it cannot be reached from an entry point via a path consisting of unconditioned links. That is to say, links to pages in the dashed box are protected by access control logic. We will describe how to identify conditional links in the next subsection. Failed access attempts reported by pages in the dashed box in Figure 2 are good indications of forced browsing.

2.2.1 Rough Sitemap Construction
The process of identifying candidate pages starts with building a rough site map by extracting links from the source files. We call it a 'rough' sitemap because the graph at this stage does not distinguish conditional vs. unconditional links. Input to this process is all web page source files (PHP files).

A PHP file refers to a file with a .php extension. A PHP file may contain function definitions as well as PHP executable programs. Some PHP files contain only function definitions. Such files serve as a function library. A PHP web page is a PHP file with a PHP

executable program that is not part of any function definition. Execution of a PHP web page starts with the first statement in the file that is not part of a function definition.

The challenge to build a rough sitemap is to extract links out of web pages as links can be dynamically generated by PHP programs. For example, PHP API calls such as "echo" and "print" are often used to render links. Listing 3 and 4 show example code snippets displaying web links. For both cases, regular expressions can be used to match and locate HTML anchor, form, frame tags, etc. Listing 4 represents a static link, pointing to editsession.php. Listing 5 represents a dynamic link, because $lang is a string variable. Identifying its target involves resolving string variable $lang. Sun et. al. described a comprehensive approach for extracting links from PHP web pages [3], including extraction of most dynamic links. We use their method to identify the rough site map. For this paper, we take a somewhat simplified approach by only looking at static links. The rest of the algorithm for constructing the rough site map follows a fairly standard graph building process. It should be noted that the rough sitemap is represented as a multi-graph as it is possible to have parallel links from one page pointing to another page.

```
print "<a href='editsession.php'>(edit)</a>";
```
Listing 4. Static link example from SCARF

```
print "<a href=".$lang.".php>Anchor</a>";
```
Listing 5. Dynamic link example

We use an example adapted from Wheatblog shown in Figure 2 to illustrate the algorithm. The first step of the rough sitemap construction is to put all known entry pages into a worklist queue. Then we pick a node from the worklist queue, suppose it is index.php. If the node has not been processed before, we extract all links from this PHP webpage. This process will return tuples, for example (index.php, admin/edit_post.php) and (index.php, admin/delete_post.php), indicating that index.php points to both admin/edit_post.php and admin/delete_post.php. For page nodes with no links identified on it, tuples (nodes, _) will be returned. Tuples representing links to web pages outside the application are discarded. Identified tuples will be added to the rough sitemap. Nodes admin/edit_post.php and admin/delete_post.php will be added to the worklist. We remove index.php from the worklist and add it to the visited set to prevent processing it again. This process continues until the worklist is empty. The resulting set of tuples is the rough sitemap.

2.2.2 Identify Conditional Links
Listing 6 shows an example of a conditional link to web page editsession.php. This link is shown on the screen if the user has admin rights. Identifying a link that is displayed conditionally is straightforward. Either the link is rendered as part of a branch statement (as indicated in Listing 6), or the rendering of the link is preceded by a function call that may not return due to either an exception or abort statement in the function. When considering exceptions, all subclasses of the PHP class Exception must be considered. The challenge is to determine whether such a condition in rendering the link is related to access control.

```
if (is_admin()) {
print " <a href='editsession.php'>(edit)</a>";
}
```
Listing 6. Rendering a link upon condition in SCARF

As mentioned in Section 3.1, we assume the code implementing access control checks has been identified. As part of one of the author's dissertation research [15], six open source PHP applications were studied for their implementation of access control. We discovered that many conditional links involve checking global variables (e.g. values associated with the web session) that are known to be involved in making access control decisions.

This observation has a reasonable explanation. Access control decisions often involve database queries. A common pattern to implement access control is to extract a given user's access privilege information from the database and store them in the web session and use session variables to perform both access control checks as well as determining what links should be displayed to a given user. We want to test how well this heuristic works in identifying conditional links in PHP web applications.

We use the term *critical global variable* to refer to trusted global variables that determine the course of an execution path. A global variable is trusted if it has never been assigned a value from an untrusted source in its data flow chain. In this paper we consider critical global variables as either part of a Boolean expression that are involved in a branch statement (if-then-else, or switch), or from functions that do not return due to exceptions or abort statements. We collectively refer to functions that may not return as function calls with abnormal returns. A third type of program construct, not considered in this work, may also be involved in determining execution outcome. That is conditions may be part of the WHERE clause in SQL statements. Monshizadeh et al. [9] have developed an approach to work with conditional logic in SQL statements. Our definition of critical global variables can be expanded to include these cases in the future.

Critical global variables can be directly extracted from Boolean expressions and switch statements because global variables can be easily identified directly or through dataflow analysis. We leverage open source software that constructs abstract syntax trees (AST) for PHP programs and perform data flow and control flow analyses using AST structures. For function calls with abnormal return we extract those global variables that cause the function to not return normally. We construct a function call graph and determine those global variables that are part of the decision to determine whether the function returns. We illustrate the process of critical global variable extraction using two examples from SCARF.

```
function require_admin(){
if(!is_admin())
        die("You don't have access to view it");
}
function is_admin() {
        if ($_SESSION['privilege'] == 'admin') return TRUE;
        else return FALSE;
}
```

Listing 7. Illustrative example from SCARF for security critical variable extraction

The first example concerns with extracting critical global variables from a function with abnormal return. Function *require_admin()* in Listing 7 returns if the user is an administrator. It aborts if the user is not an administrator by making the *die()* system call. Function *is_admin()* is called by

function *require_admin()* to determine whether a user is an administrator. Definitions of both functions are shown in Listing 7. In order to extract critical variables associated with function *require_admin()* we construct a function call graph consisting of *require_admin()* invoking *is_admin()*. Global variables involved in making decisions whether *require_admin()* returns involves $_SESSION['privilege']. This variable is not tainted because it does not come from the user. Thus, the critical variable extracted from *require_admin()* is $_SESSION['privilege'].

```
$action = $_GET['action'];
$user_level = $_SESSION['user_level']; //data from global variables
if($user_level == 'Admin' && $action =='deleteAll') //annotated check
query("DELETE FROM sensitive_table "); //SSO
```

Listing 8. Example of Boolean expression as access control check

Listing 8 is another example from SCARF to illustrate the extraction of critical global variables from Boolean expressions. Consider the Boolean expression *$user_level == 'Admin' && $action =='deleteAll'*. First, a set of variables {*$user_level, $action* } is identified in the Boolean expression. We then perform dataflow analysis. One finds *$user_level* depends on global variable $_SESSION['user_level'], so it is added to the set of variables identified. Variable *$action* depends on global variable $_GET['action'], so it too is added to the set of variables identified. To obtain critical global variables, we remove variables that are not global, so variables *$user_level* and *$action* are removed. We further remove global variables that may contain untrusted data. In this example, because $_GET['action'] contains data from user input and it is widely regarded as a tainted source, $_GET['action'] is removed. Then the obtained set of critical variables is {$_SESSION['user_level']};

We define a *security critical global variable* as a critical global variable that is known to be involved in access control decisions. Recall that one of our assumptions is that we are given a set of annotated access control checks for security sensitive operations. Critical global variables extracted from these checks are security critical global variables. For example both the Boolean expression in Listing 8 and function *require_admin()* are identified access control checks. So the set of security critical variables associated with them is {$_SESSION['privilege'], $_SESSION['user_level']}.

A link is considered to be a *candidate for conditional link* if it is displayed as part of a branch statement (if-then-else statement or switch statement), or proceeded in the execution path by a function call that may not return.

We use the following steps to determine whether the link is a conditional link.

1. Extract a set of security critical global variables from the set of identified access control checks for SSOs, referred to as SCV_ssos.

2. For each link l in the rough sitemap that is a candidate for conditional link

a. Extract a set of critical global variables for displaying l, referred to as CV_link_l.

b. Compare CV_link_l with the set of security critical global variables for SSOs SCV_ssos, if the two sets share one or more elements (variables), then the link is regarded as a conditional link.

We illustrate this process using the SCARF example in Listing 6. The if-branch *if(is_admin())* determines whether the link displaying code will be executed, so this link is a candidate for conditional links. Critical global variables are extracted for function call *is_admin()* which is defined in Listing 7. From our earlier description, we know the critical global variable for *is_admin()* is {$_SESSION['privilege']}. Since security critical global variables for application SCARF includes {$_SESSION['privilege'], $_SESSION['user_level']}, this link to *editsession.php* is a conditional link.

2.2.3 Identify Candidate Pages

Based on the rough sitemap constructed using steps described in Section 3.2.1 and the set of conditional links identified using steps described in Section 3.2.2, a candidate web page for inserting forced browsing events is a web page satisfying the following conditions: (1) the page has at least one SSO, and (2) there does not exist any navigation paths from any entry page to it with only unconditional links. In Figure 2, all page nodes with a star on their top right are pages with SSOs; six pages in the dashed box are identified as candidate pages.

2.3 Automatic Code Insertion

One of the authors studied six open source PHP applications as part of his dissertation research [blind ref]. Based on analysis of these empirical results, we created a model for automatic insertion of code to report forced browsing events.

When reporting a forced browsing event, application context information could be captured by calling APIs or retrieving from global variables. For example, in PHP, a session id could be obtained by calling API *session_id()*, host IP address could be obtained by retrieving from global variable *$_SERVER*. One could also provide a serialized object for session content along with time and date stamps. Insertion of code to report forced browsing must be done in such a way that does not impact the normal application flow. Throughout this paper, we use the function call **sensor()** to denote reporting code that is instrumented into the application.

Since **sensor()** is used to capture failure events of access control checks, it should be placed on all execution paths other than the path leading to execution of the SSO. As described earlier, access control checks could be a Boolean expression or a function calls with abnormal return. We did not observe any access control checks involving loops. We first describe code instrumentation for Boolean expression access control checks, followed by code instrumentation for function calls with abnormal returns.

2.3.1 Code Instrumentation for Boolean Expression Access Control Checks

We illustrate code insertion through examples. The left side of each listing is the code before inserting **sensor()**. Access control checks are shown in *italics*. The right side shows after code instrumentation. Newly inserted code is shown in **bold**.

In Listing 9, SSO is executed if *condition* is true. Forced browsing will be reported if *condition* fails, or access is denied. Function **sensor()** will be called right after the if statement containing the access control check.

```
if (condition){          if (condition){
    SSO;                     SSO;
}                        }
                         sensor();
```

Listing 9. If-then statement

Listing 10 shows an if-then-else statement where the SSO is executed if *condition_a* succeeds. Reporting code must be added in the else block before code indicated by "//some logic", as that logic may contain an exception.

```
if (condition_a){        if (condition_a){
    SSO;                     SSO;
} else {                 } else {
    //some logic             sensor();
}                            //some logic
                         }
```

Listing 10. If-then-else statement

List 11 shows a switch statement where the SSO is one of the cases. In this case instrumented code must be inserted into all other cases of the switch statement.

```
switch (expr) {          switch (expr) {
    case label1:             case label1:
    SSO;                     SSO;
    break;                   break;
    case label2:             case label2:
    break;                   sensor();
}                            break;

                         default:
                         sensor();
                         break;
                         }
```

Listing 12. Switch branch

2.3.2 Code Insertion for Function Call Access Control Checks

We illustrate code insertion for function calls with abnormal returns through an example adapted from SCARF (Listing 13). The top part of the listing shows the access control check (function *require_logggedin()*) and the SSO. The bottom part shows the definition of function *require_loggedin()* which aborts if the user's identify (email) is unknown. Since access control check *require_loggedin()* dominates the path flowing to the SSO, access control fails when *require_loggedin()* fails. Thus reporting code should be inserted in *require_login()* right before the abortion of normal execution, as shown on the right half of Listing 13. There may exist multiple abnormal returns, each needs to be instrumented with a call to **sensor()**. Function *require_login()* may invoke another function that contains abnormal return. If that is the case, that function needs to be analyzed using the same process describe in this section.

```
require_loggedin();                    require_loggedin();
query("INSERT        INTO            query("INSERT        INTO
comment ...); //SSO                    comment ...); //SSO


function require_loggedin() {        function require_loggedin() {
if (getEmail() === FALSE) {          if (getEmail() === FALSE) {
die ("You must be logged in");         sensor();
//abnormal return                      die ("You must be logged in");
}}                                     //abnormal return
                                       }}
```

Listing 13. Function call with abnormal return

3. EVALUATION

We performed a proof-of-concept evaluation using two PHP open source projects Wheatblog and SCARF that were used in previous research on access control implementations [6,7], [9,10,11,12]. We choose these applications in part because it has been shown that access control logic can be identified from their source code. Wheatblog is a blogging application with over 4000 lines of code. SCARF is a conference paper discussion forum with over 1300 lines of code. We seek to answer the following questions: (a) what is the likelihood that instrumented code will generate false positive forced browsing reports: i.e. a forced browsing event is incorrectly detected; and (b) false negatives: a forced browsing event is not reported.

Table 3 and Table 4 lists all the PHP web pages in Wheatblog and SCARF respectively, each page is assigned a number which will be referenced in subsequent discussions. For example, in row three of Table 3 is Wheatblog's page admin/add_post.php. Pages that are identified as targets for forced browsing are listed in *italics* in Tables 3 and 4. This page is subsequently referred to as page 3 of Wheatblog. Tables 5 and 6 summarize the sitemap for Wheatblog and SCARF respectively. Each row in these tables represents a page, e.g. in table 5 the web page in row 3, Wheatblog's admin/add_post.php, has one SSO; Wheatblog's page 17 has an unconditional link pointing to Wheatblog's page 3. Wheatblog's pages 10-14 and 18 have conditional links pointing to Wheatblog's page 3. Pages that are not pointed to by any other pages are regarded as entry pages as these pages may be published in public web pages as entry points to the application.

Pages identified as a candidate for reporting forced browsing are underlined. Figure 3 shows a part of the constructed sitemap. Dashed links represent conditional links, solid links for unconditional links, and dashed box represents pages with SSO. In Figure 3, page admin/add_link.php is a candidate page, because one can only navigate to it via conditioned links.

Table 3. Wheatblog web pages, italics represent forced browsing targets

No.	PHP executable file
1	*admin/add_category.php*
2	*admin/add_link.php*
3	*admin/add_post.php*
4	*admin/delete_category.php*
5	*admin/delete_comment.php*
6	*admin/delete_link.php*
7	*admin/delete_post.php*
8	*admin/edit_categories.php*
9	*admin/edit_comment.php*
10	admin/edit_post.php
11	*admin/edit_post_002.php*
12	admin/manage_categories
13	admin/manage_links.php
14	*admin/manage_links_002.php*
15	admin/manage_posts.php
16	admin/manage_users.php
17	admin/index.php
18	includes/header.php
19	index.php
20	add_comment.php
21	view_by_permalink.php
22	view_by_category.php
23	view_by_archive.php
24	view_by_title.php
25	archive.php
26	update_archive.php
27	list_category.php
28	registration.php
29	view_links.php
30	admin/settings.php

Table 4. SCARF web pages, italics reprent forced browsing targets.

No	PHP executable file
1	*editpaper.php*
2	*addsession.php*
3	*editsession.php*
4	useroptions.php
5	comments.php
6	*generaloptions.php*
7	header.php
8	showpaper.php
9	showsessions.php
10	index.php
11	fogot.php
12	login.php
13	install.php
14	register.php

Table 5. Wheatblog sitemap (Candidate pages underlined)

No.	SSOs	Pages having unconditional links to it	Pages having conditional links to it

1	1		12
2	1		13
3	1	17	10-14, 18
4	1		12
5	2		10
6	1		13
7	1		15,19
8	1		12
9	1		10
10	0		5,15,19
11	1		10
12	0	17	4,8,10-14,18
13	0	17	2,6,10-14,18
14	1		13
15	0	17	7,9-14,18
16	3	17	10-14,18
17	0	Entry page	Entry page
18	0	3,5,10,11,17,19-25,27-29	12-16,26,30
19	0	Entry page	Entry page
20	2	21	
21	0	19,20,22-24	
22	0	18,19,21,23,24,27	15
23	0	25	26
24	0	18	
25	0		26
26	0	Entry page	Entry page
27	0	Entry page	Entry page
28	0	18	
29	0	Entry page	Entry page
30	1	Entry page	Entry page

Table 6. SCARF sitemap (Candidate pages underlined)

No	SSOs	Pages having unconditional links to it	Pages having conditional links to it
1	8		7-9
2	1		7
3	6		9
4	3	7	5
5	3	8	7
6	3		7
7	0	1-6,8-14	
8	0	9	1,3
9	0	3,10	7
10	0	Entry page	Entry page
11	0	12	
12	0	5,7	
13	0	10	
14	0	7,10,12	

The accuracy of the algorithm described in section 3 is evaluated based on false positives and false negatives. A false positive is when the algorithm miss-identifies a page as only reachable by conditioned links. False positives could occur due to inaccuracy of our approach to identify conditioned links (section 3.22). We examined all candidate pages in Tables 5 and 6 by source code review and did not find any false positive cases. False positives are certainly possible. We have at least two places to address potential false positives. First the heuristics we used in section 3.2.2 can be refined. Second, decision rules in AppSensor may be tuned to seek multiple sources of evidence before taking preventive measures.

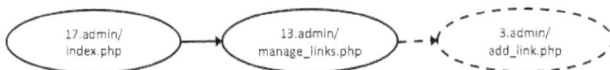

Figure 3. Admin/add_link.php is a candidate page.

Wheatblog's page 3, admin/add_post.php, on row 3 in Table 5, on the other hand is not a candidate page because it is pointed to by entry pages admin/index.php (page 17). This means an unauthorized user could access admin/add_post.php by clicking a visible link on page admin/index.php.

Among 30 Wheatblog pages, 10 pages are considered as candidate pages for reporting forced browsing events. Results for SCARF are similarly reported in Table 6, with 4 candidate pages out of 14 web pages. All candidate pages require administrative privileges and are "hidden" behind administrative login pages.

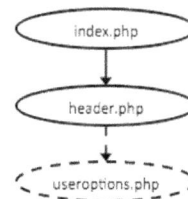

Figure 4. A false negative case

A false negative refers to a situation where a forced browsing event would be missed. We examined every page in both Wheatblog and SCARF. Based on intended application functions we determine whether a forced browsing attack could occur on each page. We found one false negative case in SCARF as illustrated in Figure 4. SCARF is a public discussion forum for published conference papers. All papers are publicly available for discussions. However, in order to participate in discussions, one must be logged in. The false negative case involves the link between page 7 and 4. Page useroptions.php, containing user options, should be displayed for authenticated users only thus viewing it without first logged in could indicate a forced browsing attack.

Close examination shows that SCARF uses condition isset($_SESSION['email']) to check whether a link to page 4 should be displayed. The critical global variable for displaying this link is $_SESSION['email']. However this global variable is not involved in any access control checks to access database resources. Therefore our algorithm did not regard this link as a conditional link. We found that global variable $_SESSION['priviledge'] was used to check for authenticated users in the application logic for access control. There is a relationship between $_SESSION['priviledge'] and $_SESSION['email'] in that they were assigned values from the source, namely a logged in user. It may be possible to mitigate such false negative situations by performing more sophisticated data flow analysis on dependencies of session variables to discover that certain groups of variables are "equivalent" because they are fed from the same source. We plan to investigate this in future research.

4. CONCLUSION AND FUTURE WORK

Our research aims at providing run time protection against privilege escalation attacks by automatically instrumenting application source code to report possible forced browsing attacks. The main technical contribution of this paper is to outline a method to automatically identify web pages that may be the target of forced browsing attacks. Our method is based on an observed pattern of how developers implement access control in PHP web applications. The work presented in this paper is the first step in our research plan: providing a proof of concept evaluation and prototyping to establish the feasibility of this approach. We evaluated our method using two open source PHP web applications and found this approach promising. No false positives were found. There was one false negative and we discussed how this might be mitigated through more in-depth data flow analysis of dependencies among global variables.

Our future research plan includes (a) more empirical evaluation of applications of different types and complexity, (b) looking at other heuristics to detect unauthorized access attempts, (c) more rigorous description of the algorithm for identifying unconditional links, including fully considering conditions in SQL statements, with the purpose of making sure all possible cases are thoroughly considered, (d) more thorough analysis of the correctness of inserted reporting code and its impact on performance, and (e) examining strategies for decision making rules for AppSensor to detect unauthorized accesses.

5. ACKNOWLEDGMENTS

NSF grants: 1129190, 1318854.

6. REFERENCES

[1] Zhu, J. Xie, J. Lipford, H., Chu, B. December 2013. Support Secure Programming In Web Applications through Interactive Static Analysis. Journal of Advanced Research. Elsevier.

[2] Xie, J., Chu, B., Lipford, H.R., Melton, J.T., 2011. ASIDE: IDE support for web application security. In Proceedings of the 27th Annual Computer Security Applications Conference ACM, 267-276.

[3] Sun, F., Xu, L., Su, Z. (2011, August). Static Detection of Access Control Vulnerabilities in Web Applications. In USENIX Security Symposium.

[4] Son, S., Shmatikov, V., 2011. SAFERPHP: Finding semantic vulnerabilities in PHP applications. In Proceedings of the ACM SIGPLAN 6th Workshop on Programming Languages and Analysis for Security, ACM.

[5] Tan, L., Zhang, X., Ma, X., Xiong, W., Zhou, Y., 2008. AutoISES: Automatically Inferring Security Specification and Detecting Violations. In USENIX Security Symposium, 379-394.

[6] Dalton, M., Christos K., Nickolai Z.. "Nemesis: Preventing Authentication & Access Control Vulnerabilities in Web Applications." USENIX Security Symposium. 2009.

[7] Son, S., Mckinley, K.S., Shmatikov, V., 2011. Rolecast: finding missing security checks when you do not know what checks are. In ACM SIGPLAN Notices, ACM, 1069-1084.

[8] Gauthier, F., Lavoie, T., Merlo, E. (2013, December). Uncovering access control weaknesses and flaws with security-discordant software clones. In Proceedings of the 29th Annual Computer Security Applications Conference (pp. 209-218).

[9] Monshizadeh, M., Prasad N., Venkatakrishnan V. N., 2014. "Mace: Detecting privilege escalation vulnerabilities in web applications." In Proceedings of the 2014 ACM SIGSAC Conference on Computer and Communications Security. ACM, 2014.

[10] Howard, M., Lipner, S. (2006) The Security Development Lifecycle. Microsoft Press.

[11] Shostack, A. Threat Modeling, Design for Security. 2014. John Wiley & Sons Inc.

[12] Zhu, J., Chu, B., Lipford, H., Thomas, T. "Mitigate Access Control Vulnerabilities through Interactive Static Analysis", in *Proceedings of the 20th ACM Symposium on Access Control Models and Technologies (SACMAT). ACM, 2015.*

[13] Watson, C., Groves, D. and Melton, J., *AppSensor* OWASP Foundation, 2014.

[14] Hutchins, E., Clopper, M., and Amin, R. "Intelligence Driven Computer Network Defense Informed by Analysis of Adversary Campaigns and Intrusion kill Chains", White paper Lockheed Marin Corporation, http://www.lockheedmartin.com/content/dam/lockheed/data/corporate/documents/LM-White-Paper-Intel-Driven-Defense.pdf

[15] Zhu, J. *Interactive Static Analysis for Application Security* Ph.D. Dissertation, UNC Charlotte June, 2015.

[16] Tomas, T., Smith, J., Murphy-Hills, E., Chu, B., and Lipford, H. "A study of Interactive Code Annotation For Access Control Vulnerabilities" in *Proceedings of the IEEE Symposium on Visual Languages and Human-Centric Computing (VL/HCC15)* Oct. 2015.

[17] Smith, J. Johnson, B. Murphy-Hill, E., Chu, B. Lipford, H. "Questions Developers Ask While Diagnosing Potential Security Vulnerabilities with Static Analysis" in *ACM SIGSOF FSE*, Oct 2015.

Data-Centric Access Control for Cloud Computing

Thomas Pasquier, Jean Bacon
Jatinder Singh
University of Cambridge
firstname.lastname@cl.cam.ac.uk

David Eyers
University of Otago
dme@cs.otago.ac.nz

ABSTRACT

The usual approach to security for cloud-hosted applications is strong separation. However, it is often the case that the same data is used by different applications, particularly given the increase in data-driven ('big data' and IoT) applications. We argue that access control for the cloud should no longer be application-specific but should be data-centric, associated with the data that can flow between applications. Indeed, the data may originate outside cloud services from diverse sources such as medical monitoring, environmental sensing etc. Information Flow Control (IFC) potentially offers data-centric, system-wide data access control. It has been shown that IFC can be provided at operating system level as part of a PaaS offering, with an acceptable overhead.

In this paper we consider how IFC can be integrated with application-specific access control, transparently from application developers, while building from simple IFC primitives, access control policies that align with the data management obligations of cloud providers and tenants.

Keywords

Information Flow Control, Cloud Computing, Data Protection

1. INTRODUCTION

Given the shared nature of cloud infrastructure, and security concerns holding back its uptake, a key focus has been on isolating tenants (data and processing) in order to prevent interference and information leakage. The goal of isolation is to segregate tenants, protecting their data and computation, and to limit a tenant's (direct) knowledge of others. A common approach involves containing tenants by allocating them their own virtual machines (VMs), each VM maintaining its own operating system (OS). Containers [34] have enabled strong isolation of tenants over a shared OS, and more recently Unikernels [16] have made library OSs practical, allowing applications' software stacks to be compiled down to run directly over the hypervisor.

SACMAT'16, June 05-08, 2016, Shanghai, China
© 2016 ACM. ISBN 978-1-4503-3802-8/16/06. . . $15.00
DOI: http://dx.doi.org/10.1145/2914642.2914662

Though strong isolation of tenants is important, many applications and services will require data sharing across and outside isolation boundaries. For example, government or a medical institution may provide several related services, the data for which may correspond to the same people, whose data has to be recorded separately for every service. Data originating outside the cloud, such as that gathered from medical or environmental sensors, may pass through several different cloud services before being stored in cloud-hosted databases, and subsequently used for various purposes. We see a requirement for both isolation and controlled sharing for cloud-hosted data, particularly when cloud services form part of wider 'big data' and Internet of Things (IoT) architectures [31].

Guidance, regulations and laws exist regarding the protection of data, particularly personal data. For example, EU directives aim to restrict the circumstances in which personal data may leave the EU's geographical boundaries [6]. Another example is the need to anonymise/pseudonymise medical data when used for research [35]. Both cloud providers and tenants are subject to data management obligations, many of which concern the flow of information.

Access control mechanisms currently in place in the cloud do not entirely meet the requirements of highly regulated sectors. These mechanisms typically address access to data by principals, and do not implement any further control once the data has been accessed. Further, these mechanisms are often principal-centric, application dependent and heterogeneous in their implementation. In practice, this means that as some data flows through a complex multi-component system, it may fall under different access control regimes, with varying granularity (e.g. a front-end application authenticating individual users versus a back-end database authenticating entire applications for whole-table access).

While the above mechanisms contribute towards data security, they are insufficient to meet entirely the complex requirements of today's software systems. None of them can control the proper usage of data once "out of the hands" of the data owner, i.e. beyond their direct control. Each mechanism has its place, and we propose to complement them with a means to express and enforce data usage requirements throughout a multi-component system. We argue that access control for the cloud should no longer solely be application-specific but should be data-centric, controlling data flows between applications. *Information Flow Control* (IFC) provides such a mechanism.

An outstanding challenge for IFC in cloud computing is to integrate IFC with data-specific access control requirements to enable continuous, data-centric, system-wide control. Work on IFC to date has focussed on steady-state operation, rather than on how IFC is set up as part of (dynamic) application lifecycles, particularly when applications may need to collaborate—considerations that are especially relevant to cloud computing. Further, there is potential for IFC to enable the data management obligations of cloud tenants, cloud providers and third parties to be clearly defined, and when combined with audit, to help demonstrate that obligations have been met.

The contributions of this paper are in detailing how an IFC system can best be designed and engineered to meet such concerns. The IFC mechanism provider, e.g. a cloud PaaS provider where IFC is enforced at OS level, can be expected to provide a correct enforcement mechanism, but cannot take responsibility for the correct definition of application policies. Those with data management responsibilities are usually the cloud tenants/application managers. They should be able to specify data-centric policies that operate independently of provider specifics and across application instances running on behalf of end users. Ideally, application developers should not need to be aware of policies; policy-related behaviour should be separated from the application. This improves general security and allows applications to run unmodified within different policy domains, e.g. organisational or jurisdictional. Again, policy should be data-centric, rather than principal or application-centric.

Application managers (cloud tenants) therefore need to be able to set up an IFC framework, often on behalf of individual end users, within which application instances are governed by the IFC regime. In simple cases, application instances may be isolated, in which case IFC ensures that data is not deliberately or inadvertently leaked due to bugs or misconfigurations. More generally, applications may be required to collaborate and share data, sometimes as part of an umbrella organisation or as unrelated applications running on behalf of the same user. We address how this can be achieved, especially the support the IFC system can provide to application managers, including a novel approach to dynamically interpose security transformation services to meet policy requirements and data management obligations, in a manner transparent to application instances.

2. BACKGROUND

We first outline current approaches to achieve application and principal-specific access control, as background for addressing IFC integration. We argued in §1 that access control should be data centric for a cloud-service model, and that IFC provides such an approach. We therefore define the basic model and mechanisms of IFC.

2.1 Current access control mechanisms

Access controls (AC), comprising authentication and authorisation, are the main means to control the dissemination of information. Typically, a principal is authenticated, and perhaps associated with various roles. Authorisation to access data is then carried out at policy enforcement points in the application to grant or deny access to system objects by principals (in roles). Once access to data is granted, generally no further control is applied to ensure the data is handled properly; the application is trusted not to leak the data. This has been seen as a shortcoming of AC systems as discussed in §5.2, but is typical of cloud implementations.

This application-specific approach is insufficient when it is important to remain in control of data after access. For example, in an IoT scenario, personal medical data gathered by sensors, monitoring a patient at home, may flow into cloud services and databases. In such a scenario, IFC allows the patient's policy on how the data can be used throughout its lifetime to be attached to the data. For example, a tag *medical-research* on data ensures that it can flow only to those conducting medical research, who also have this tag.

2.2 Information Flow Control (IFC)

It is vital for computer systems to control how information flows through them. IFC tracks and constrains the flow of information continuously throughout whole systems and ensures that data is handled according to the associated policy. Research on IFC dates back to the 1970's [5] in the context of centralised military systems. Here, data was classified system-wide as *public, confidential, secret* and *top-secret*. Later, decentralised IFC was proposed [21], and has formed the basis of subsequent IFC research and implementations, including our work on CamFlow [27].[1] When implemented at the OS level, IFC can be described as a data-centric, continuous, Mandatory Access Control (MAC) enforcement mechanism.

IFC relates to two data properties: its *secrecy* and its *integrity*; respectively, where the data is allowed to flow to (as defined by Bell and LaPadula) and where it can flow from (as defined by Biba). These concerns are represented by associating with an entity A, two security labels $S(A)$ for secrecy and $I(A)$ for integrity; *active* (e.g. processes) and *passive* (e.g. data) entities are labelled. Many IFC models use labels that comprise a set of tags, each tag representing a particular security concern (e.g. $S = \{medical\}$, $I = \{validated\}$). Tags are defined as required in order to represent policy, for example, relating to how personal medical data can flow. The **security context** of an entity is defined as the state of its two labels, S and I. The flow of data between entities composing the systems is only allowed towards equally or more constrained entities in order to guarantee for example, the proper usage of data.

These requirements are captured in the following constraints, which are applied on every data flow from an entity A to an entity B:

$$A \rightarrow B, \text{ iff } \{S(A) \subseteq S(B) \wedge I(B) \subseteq I(A)\}$$

Creation flows. If an entity *creates* an entity (active or passive), the created entity inherits the labels of its parents. In a context of OS-level IFC enforcement, examples of entity creation include a process creating a file, and a process forking a child process.

Privileges for label change. In addition to their S and I labels, certain entites may have privileges to add and/or remove tags from these labels. If an active entity A has a privilege to add t to its secrecy label, we denote this $t \in P_S^+(A)$, and to remove t from its secrecy label: $t \in P_S^-(A)$ (and similarly $P_I^+(A)$ and $P_I^-(A)$ are the privileges for integrity). An active entity may therefore have four privilege sets in addition to its security context. Though a created entity inherits the labels (security context) of its creator, privileges are not inherited and have to be passed explicitly. Application managers will typically set up application instances in security

---

[1] http://camflow.org/

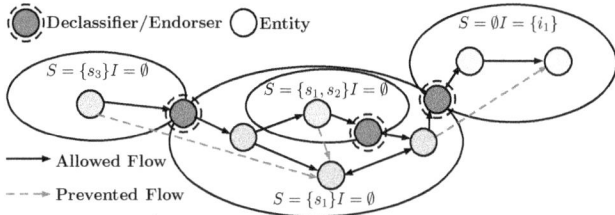

Figure 1: Declassification and endorsement.

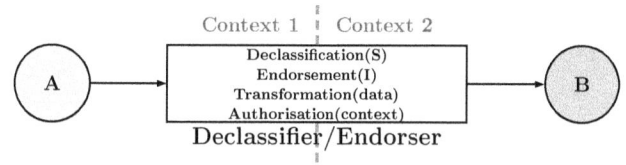

Figure 2: Declassifier/Endorser services as security context transformers.

contexts, without the privileges to change them, see §4.

Tag Ownership. In some IFC models [20], the concept of tag ownership is used to assign privileges to an entity. Privileges must be passed on with care, especially a privilege to remove a tag from a label, see §2.3 and §5.3.

Trust. If IFC is enforced at OS level, the applications running above the OS are obliged to run under the policy constraints expressed by the IFC labels' tags. They do not need to be trusted not to leak data [12]. In a cloud context, we believe that it is a reasonable assumption that the cloud service provider is more trusted and trustworthy than the many tenants' applications.[2] This means that when parties need to collaborate they do not need mutual trust, but only a shared trust in the underlying IFC enforcement mechanism.

Audit. Enforcement of IFC can provide the opportunity for recording flow decisions to build a provenance-like audit graph [26]. This can be analysed to understand where, how, why and by whom the data was manipulated within the system. This audit data, captured during IFC enforcement, can help to demonstrate compliance with regulations [24] by providing tangible traces, showing how the data was handled.

2.3 Security context domains

As described, the security context of an entity is its pair of labels, S and I. A security context domain comprises entities with the same labels. The flow of data can therefore be within a security context domain or into a more constrained domain. Once data has flowed into a more constrained domain further flows are confined to that domain or into increasingly constrained domains. For example, as shown in Fig. 1, data tagged as s_1 can flow to an entity tagged with $S = \{s_1, s_2\}$ but then can only flow within the $S = \{s_1, s_2\}$ domain. Generally, building a system with increasing constraints can lead to situations of "label creep".

In practice, perhaps after a certain time has elapsed, secret data may need to be made publicly available, or when data has gone through an encryption or anonymisation process it is allowed to flow more freely. To achieve these things, an IFC system needs to support more complex flow policies. We now discuss how these are provided within the IFC model. The rest of this paper is concerned with how such processes can be provided as part of an IFC system deployment, to ease adoption of IFC by cloud tenants.

Certain entities within an IFC system are given the capability to modify their labels in order to transfer information across security contexts; these are the four privilege sets defined in §2.2. For entity A, a label transformation is denoted:

$$A[S, I] \rightsquigarrow A[S', I']$$

An entity that performs such security context modification is called a *declassifier* when it modifies secrecy constraints, and an *endorser* when it modifies integrity constraints. Endorsers and declassifiers can therefore be seen as trusted gateways between security context domains, where the overall IFC constraints would prohibit a direct flow. Fig. 1 shows how trusted gateways allow information to flow across security domains when IFC constraints would disallow the flows. Such gateways can help ensure that regulation is enforced, e.g., medical data might only flow to a research domain if it has gone through a declassifier that applies a specified anonymisation algorithm. Therefore, a *transformation* of the data might also be needed, as well as checks, such as the time the data is authorised to be released.

Fig. 2 shows the basic behaviour of a declassifier/endorser. The main purpose, from an IFC perspective, is to apply a function to transform the S and/or I labels. For example, applying the transformation:

$$A[S, I] \rightsquigarrow A[S \setminus \{medical\}, I]$$

that indicates declassification over *medical*.

We aim to minimise the extent to which application developers need to be aware of IFC specifics. In §4.2 we show that declassification and endorsement can be offered as services by the IFC system, sometimes associated with transforming the data, i.e., tailored to the required policies of each application domain.

We now discuss how policies can be expressed in terms of IFC labels and consider how security context changes can be incorporated transparently into system design.

3. EXPRESSING POLICY IN IFC

In §2 we introduced IFC as a data-centric continuous MAC scheme. In this section, we discuss how complex policy can emerge from simple IFC constraints.

3.1 Simple applications

We envisage that some simple applications will be able to run in the same security context throughout their lifetimes. In this case, they can be set up as IFC-unaware application instances by an IFC-aware application manager, see §4.1. An example is an application instance, with no cross-application data sharing requirements, that is set up for an authenticated user. IFC isolates this user's instance and generated data from those of other users, by enforcing the non-interference principle between security contexts.

Consider the EU directive that aims to restrict when per-

---

[2] The major cloud providers tend to have more technical expertise than most tenants, and are more visible to regulators. The transfer of data from cloud providers to government agencies is a different problem, particularly where there is a legal requirement relating to "national interest". Because of this, mechanisms have been proposed to constrain data within geographical boundaries [10], or to encrypt data to prevent government surveillance [14]. These issues are beyond the scope of this paper.

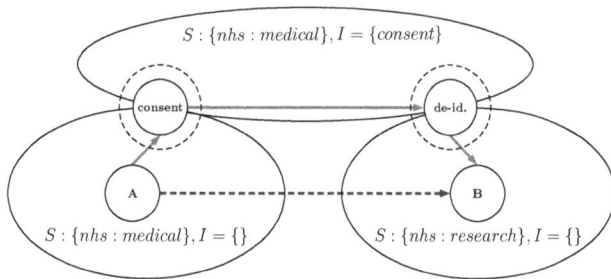

Figure 3: IFC enforcement of the medical data sharing policy, as described in Listing 1.

sonal data can leave EU's geographical boundaries [6]. We can envisage a security context domain where a tag EU is used within entities' security labels to authorise flows within the EU and to prevent flows outside, to entities without the EU tag. Such tags can be bound to hardware guarantees such as the mechanism presented in [10], that allows the geo-location of a server to be verified.

3.2 Building complex policies

Two examples show the need for security context changes:

1. Medical data must only be stored in encrypted form [7].

2. Medical data can be used for research purposes only if the consent of the owner is obtained and the data is anonymised [35], as illustrated by the policy described in Listing 1.[3]

We have seen that the IFC model, via declassification and endorsement, supports the required security context changes (§2.3). To achieve (1) we assume the database labels are set up so that only appropriately labelled data, e.g. *encrypted*, can flow into it. An encryption function must be applied to the data together with an endorser to add *encrypted* to its integrity label.

To achieve (2), as shown in Fig. 3,[4] the data owner's consent must be established and indicated with the data, an approved anonymising function must be applied to the data (e.g. simple deidentification for internal research), and a declassifier must transform its labels. The data is therefore constrained to flow between related applications in a (potentially) large-scale *medical* domain, in accordance with the obligations of the organisation, and demonstrably so. The assurance that such policies are expressible and enforceable, with adherence demonstrable makes cloud deployment of application domains that handle sensitive data more feasible.

We have argued that the provider of the IFC mechanism cannot be aware of the need for these data and label transformations, which therefore must be the responsibility of, in this case, "the managers of medical applications". We believe there is scope to provide system support for these transformations (§4.2). In some cases, data transformations are not needed, but only label transformation, such as when

secret data can be released publicly after a specified time has elapsed.

Another policy could relate to data usage by third parties. The French National Data Protection Agency (NDPA) presents a set of recommendations when the manipulation of customer data is concerned, in an electricity smart metering context.[5] Data can be shared between parties, if it aligns with providing the services the customer registered for. Here we envisage that data is labelled, e.g. $S = \{ownerID\}$ and the service instances to which that user's data can flow are similarly labelled.

Another French NDPA recommendation is that the collected data can be used for marketing purposes only when anonymised, for example through aggregation. Here we see the need for an anonymising aggregation process and a security context change so that the output of the aggregation process can flow to the appropriately labelled marketing study.

The specification of IFC constraints and declassifiers/endorsers can ensure that such constraints are respected.

4. IMPLEMENTING POLICY USING IFC

We now discuss how the simple and complex policies defined above can be implemented in an IFC system.

4.1 Initialising application instances for users

Many application instances run in an unchanging security context throughout their lifetimes, subject to simple policies as described in §3.1. Application instances must be set up in the appropriate security context, according to the application and the principal on behalf the instance is acting.

In decentralised IFC, sets of tags can be created by any applications without a need for a central authority. Consider an application domain such as "UK National Health Service (NHS)" where a number of related applications operate on behalf of registered users, each user having an *nhs-id*. For authentication and authorisation, we assume the credentials of an NHS user are checked, say, against a registration database. A similar scenario arises if a set of local government applications run on behalf of registered citizens, for example, local tax collection, social services, electoral roll management, etc.

In an IFC context, we assume an application manager is given a framework in which application instances, for authenticated and authorised users (e.g. through RBAC policy), can be set up with appropriate domain-specific sets of tags in their S and I labels. In addition, we assume that each user's application instance is set up with their personal *nhs-id* tag in their S label. Such tags can be stored with users' entries in the domain registration database, for example using an IFC-aware database [29]. Simple application instances do not require privileges because they need no context changes during their lifetimes.

Unrelated applications that run on behalf of the same user may also share data if the user so desires. The applications may be offered by different cloud tenants, and current isolation mechanisms may make sharing difficult. If the same tag can be agreed for a given user by different applications, data can potentially flow between them. For example, if

---

[3]Often regulations relating to data privacy can be represented as constraints over the flow of data associated with some authorisation and/or transformation. Note that, though beyond the scope of this paper, translating law into a machine understandable set of rules is an active area of research of the computational law community [15].

[4]The NHS is the UK National Health Service.

[5]http://www.cnil.fr/fileadmin/documents/Vos_responsabilites/Packs/Compteurs/Pack_de_Conformite_COMPTEURS_COMMUNICANTS.pdf.

```
1  [S={nhs:medical}, I={}]->[S={nhs:medical}, I={nhs:consent}]:<consent_checker>
2  [S={nhs:medical}, I={nhs:consent}]->[S={nhs:research}, I={}]:<de-identification>
3  [S={nhs:medical}, I={nhs:consent}]->[S={harvard:research}, I={}]:<anonymisation>
4  [S={nhs:medical}, I={nhs:consent}]->[S={UN:research}, I={}]:<aggregation>
```

Listing 1: Policy concerning the release of medical data.

IFC is provided in a container-based cloud service, IFC tags potentially allow cross-container flows on behalf of a given user. A negotiation is therefore needed between the cloud tenants, prior to such applications being set up. This would involve a means to bestow the capability to use a specific tag, for example by means of a message from one application to another (see [17]). The details of how this can be achieved are left for future work.

4.2 Supporting dynamic security contexts

From a system design perspective we must consider how label transformations (by declassification and endorsement), sometimes associated with authorisation checks and transformations of the data, are provided to applications. For conciseness, we refer to DETA (Declassify, Endorse, Transform, Authorise) functions carrying out DETA policies. This is in order to effect the complex policies described in §3.2.

Our aim is that an application does not need to know about security context, nor about the gateways between security contexts, but simply attempts to send data to another entity within the system. This will breach IFC policy if it represents a transfer of data across incompatible security contexts. When such a breach is detected, the underlying platform should check the DETA policies specified by the relevant tag owners, indicating that a declassifier/endorser (or a combination) would allow the data to be transferred. Such declassifiers/endorsers are then invoked by the platform, the data flows through them, authorisations, transformations and label modifications are applied, as appropriate to enable the data to reach its specified destination. The interposition of these DETA functions is likely to occur during the establishment of a connection between two parties.

Fig. 3 illustrates such a scenario. The flow of information from A in the *nhs:medical* security context to B in the *nhs:research* security context would have been prevented through IFC policy (as $S(A) \not\subset S(B)$). However, following the policy described in Listing 1, an endorser and a declassifier are interposed on the path between A and B, by the platform. In addition to security context modifications, the endorser verifies that consent has been given for the use of data in a research context, and only allows the endorsement to occur in this case. The deidentification declassifier performs the transformation of data before it can be transferred into a different security context.

Authorisation for transforming labels and data could potentially be based on a property of the sender (e.g. does the sender have the appropriate role to send data across the two security contexts), attributes of the data or its structure, akin to an attribute-based access control decision [11], or based on the provenance of the data in a manner akin to a provenance-based access control decision [22].[6] While IFC policies themselves are relatively simple (solely based on subset relationships), DETA functions and their composition can implement policy as complex as required.

Transformations are applied to data either to decrease its sensitivity or to increase its trustworthiness. Transformation examples include encryption, deidentification, anonymisation, etc. Further examples of transformations are as follows:

Unit conversion: In an IoT environment a database may receive data from a vast range of sensors. Some of the sensors may provide values in International Standard (SI) Units, while others may use the Imperial system or US Customary Units. In order to maintain the integrity of the database its input software is labelled with $I=\{SI\}$, to accept only SI units. An application involving persistent storage of sensor data may specify a policy that automatically converts Imperial and US units to their SI equivalent before input into the database. The process would be totally transparent for both the sensors and the cloud application, as the conversion would be handled through interposition of a declassifier/endorser service. Similarly, an application displaying the values to the end users, may specify automatic transformation to meet user preferences on output.

Sanitisation: In order to guarantee its integrity, an application may set its security context such that it accepts only sanitised data as input (i.e. specifying in its integrity label the requirement for the presence of a *sanitised* tag). Properly specified IFC policy can ensure that the data flows through a sanitisation endorser service before reaching its destination.

Declassification: After a certain period of time, the data is no longer considered sensitive and therefore can flow freely outside of the security context. Here the authorisation of the security context change is simply that sufficient time has elapsed.

As DETA policy is separated from application logic, the same application code can run under different policy regimes. The same base application can, for example, be constrained to comply with the requirements of different organisations, departments or jurisdictions, such as the EU and the US. Further, when collaborating with other parties, the policy being applied is independent from the application and defined in terms of the IFC tags by the tags' owner. This means that no trust is required in third parties, as long as proper interposition of DETA functions is guaranteed by the cloud provider (see Footnote 2).

4.3 Representing policies as graphs

We now describe how to specify the interposition of DETA services. Policy, such as that described in Listing 1, can be understood and represented as (potentially disjoint) directed graphs. The nodes in the graph represent a security context. The edges represent the specification of a DETA service, which provides a gateway from a source security context to a destination security context. The DETA specification must take account of how interactions between entities are implemented. For example, if a messaging middleware is used, the permitted message type might be part of a DETA specification. The service to interpose and other parameters as required, are also included.

---

[6]Provenance data can easily be captured during enforcement of IFC, see [26]

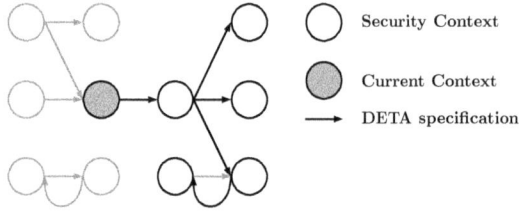

Figure 4: Policy subgraph to be considered.

In Fig. 4, the current context could be $[S = \{nhs : medical\}, I = \{\}]$, the edges originating from this node the consent checker, and the destination the context $[S = \{nhs : medical\}, I = \{nhs : consent\}]$. When IFC constraints would prevent the flow, there is a query for an appropriate path from the current security context to the destination security context. The DETA service(s) are then interposed between the relevant source and destination entities.

The concept of interposition was presented in Fig. 3, to effect a particular DETA policy. To find an applicable policy on an IFC flow failure, there is no need to query the whole set of graphs representing the whole set of policies applying to the platform. Only the subgraph which originates from the sending entity's security context, see Fig. 4 need be queried. When a new instance of an application, running in a particular security context, is created, the associated policy subgraph can be loaded. Given such caching, nodes must be informed of any changes to the global graph.

The syntax to express DETA services placement policy could be as follows (see Listing 1 for an example):
placement::= **security_context** '->' **security_context** ':' ⟨ DETA reference ⟩
security_context::= '[' **S** '=' **label** ';' '**I**' '=' **label** ']'
label::= '{' ⟨ **tag** ⟩ (',' ⟨ **tag** ⟩)* '}' | ∅
tag::= owner':'concern

The cloud provider is solely concerned with enabling the enforcement of application-provided DETA policies via the placement of DETA functions on disclosure paths. The policy being enforced is beyond its understanding or concern.

4.4 DETA services

It is important that the DETA services operate in a self-contained, standalone manner. This is in order to enable the requisite DETA functions to be interposed, when and as necessary, across various applications and runtime contexts.

Given the power of DETA services, in practice such services should be rigorously validated and verified. Any erroneous declassification or endorsement service, where dynamically interposed, has the potential to impact a range of applications, in possibly unforeseen ways. Further, it will be useful to ensure that DETA processes are audited, which is useful for both detecting errors and demonstrating policy adherence, see §5.4.

Our approach is agnostic to the method by which DETA services are effected. Some services may be long-running and well-known. However, we anticipate that in many cases, DETA services should be instantiated 'just-in-time,' to execute a particular transform or perform some authorisation verification. In a traditional cloud context, this might entail invoking a particular service within a cloud VM. Unikernels offer much potential in this space, by enabling small, very lightweight and (more easily) verifiable images that could encapsulate (only) a single DETA instance, and be rapidly instantiated and executed on demand [16].

5. RELATED WORK

5.1 Comparison with sticky policies

IFC is a simple, low-level mechanism. At a higher level, *sticky policies* have been proposed to achieve end-to-end control over data [4, 28] In sticky policy systems, data is encrypted along with the policy to be applied to that data. To obtain the decryption key from a Trusted Authority (TA), a party must agree to enforce the policy. This agreement may be considered part of forming a contractual link between the data owner and the party decrypting the data.

Sticky policies provide no means to ensure the proper usage of data once decrypted. A malicious service could be black-listed by the TA, but only if and when a breach of agreement is detected. The system builds on the trust established between the data owner, the TAs and services interacting with the data. Our IFC approach builds only upon the trust between the data owner and the cloud provider.

5.2 Usage Control

Usage Control (UCON) [23] proposes to formalise a model that extends access control beyond server-side authorisation, to encompass obligations, conditions, continuity and mutability. The aim is a unified model, incorporating traditional access control, digital rights and trust management. Access decisions are made based on pre-, post- and ongoing-properties relating to mutable subject and object attributes, traditional authorisation, obligations that the subject must meet before or during an access to the object, and conditions that represents the environmental or system status. Purpose-based policy, or usage control in relation to privacy, has been demonstrated to be feasible using IFC [13].

IFC can be integrated into a distributed system environment [38], and can run on a variety of devices including cars [2], while the trust in the enforcement mechanism can be assured through the use of 'trusted hardware' [25].

The advantages of IFC compared with UCON and sticky policies are its conciseness of expression and the speed of an OS-level enforcement mechanism. IFC constraints, coupled with effective interposition of DETA services allow complex policy to be expressed and enforced.

5.3 IFC

Since 1997, most research on IFC has followed the decentralised IFC model proposed in [21], including CamFlow [27].

IFC in systems has been investigated via clean slate OS implementations [37] before moving towards a more practical implementation for standard OSs [12]. SELinux [33], the most well known example of a MAC implementation for Linux (via a Linux Security Module), provides (centralised) IFC, albeit only over the secrecy dimension.

An individual machine enforcing IFC can be connected through an IFC-aware communication mechanism to form a distributed system respecting IFC constraints [38]. From this, it is possible to build underlying IFC enforcement for a cloud environment [1, 27]. An IFC-aware communication mechanism can take the form of fully-featured communication middleware [27, 30]. In CamFlow, IFC constraints are checked on the establishment of a connection between two entities via the communication middleware. The validity of the connection is re-evaluated when/if any entity modifies its security context.

In general, IFC research has focussed on steady state operation, and the labelling of simple web-applications e.g. [12, 37, 38]. Here, for the first time, we show how decentralised IFC can operate for cloud tenant applications.

5.4 Assisting compliance

The uptake of public cloud services by regulated sectors, such as healthcare, finance, etc. is comparatively low. To leverage the public cloud, it is necessary for such sectors to demonstrate compliance with their obligations, when cloud-hosted. Awareness of law and regulation relating to cloud computing is increasing [18] and there is ongoing research on technical mechanisms towards this.[7]

As stated by a US NIST member [9], *"monitoring and addressing security and privacy issues remain in the purview of the [tenant]"*, and further that mechanisms need to be provided not only when data is at rest or in transit, but also while in use. This is especially true in regulated sectors where financial consequences of data mishandling can be severe. Techniques such as "colouring" [8] or tainting [19] of data and resources have been proposed as a means to protect data in use. These approaches are similar to IFC, but do not provide the continuous aspect of enforcement, as colour or taint are only verified and acted upon at well defined parts ("sink points") of the system. When providing the same tracking granularity as IFC, colour/taint propagation is as costly as performing the simple subset verification of IFC.

IFC as a means to assist with adhering to regulations in a cloud computing context has been explored [32], and later extended to provide tangible proof of compliance [24, 26]. Other work, such as Cloudopsy [36], has focused on the tracking of information flow to provide such tangible proof, but without addressing enforcement issues. More generally, the tracking and recording of information flow is an active area of research, often under the umbrella of provenance [3]. The continuous enforcement of IFC, that can easily be combined with such data flow tracking, makes it an appealing technology, when evidence supporting compliance (or non-compliance) needs to be obtained.

6. CONCLUSION

Access control alone is not sufficient for current and emerging cloud-based systems. Personal data may originate from a wide range of sensors and flow to various cloud services. There is a clear need to control its flow, as it moves between systems and/or administrative domains. We see IFC as a key technology to augment traditional access control with end-to-end, lifelong data flow control.

We have focussed here on cloud-based IFC implementation, but we have begun to work on extending IFC for IoT architectures that include cloud services. A basic assumption of IoT is that data will flow widely, to a variety of services, and may come to be used for originally unforeseen purposes [31]. It is important that application logic is separate from policy to achieve such flexible application composition, while adhering to data owners' policies.

We have shown how an authenticated and authorised user can be set up in a security context with labels appropriate to the application domain and their personal identification, see §3.1. We envisage application domains such as health services, emergency services, education, smart cities, etc.

A user initiating an application in such a context inherits the tags of the umbrella domain, and the user's tag as data owner is deployed as appropriate.

Work on IFC to date has focussed on steady state systems, rather than on how IFC is set up as part of (dynamic) application lifecycles, particularly when related applications may need to collaborate—considerations that are particularly relevant to cloud computing. Regarding the allocation of responsibilities: the IFC provider can have no responsibility for applications' policies but only to provide a trustworthy IFC mechanism and associated services. An application need not be written with IFC-awareness and we have shown how this can be achieved for simple policies in §3.1 and §4.1. Those responsible for data can specify data-centric management policy that will be respected system-wide, without understanding application or service specifics.

Complying with complex policies that require data transformation and security context change needs to be supported. We propose interposable label and data transformation services to achieve this, separating application logic from IFC policy enforcement, see §4. Thus, the same application code can run under different policy regimes, including different organisations, departments or jurisdictions, such as the EU and the US.

There is potential for IFC to enable the data management obligations of cloud tenants, cloud providers and third parties to be clearly defined, and when combined with audit, to demonstrate that obligations have been met. It is often stated that security concerns hinder cloud adoption. In particular, the uptake of cloud services by highly regulated sectors has lagged behind other sectors. We believe that IFC could help to facilitate adoption in such sectors.

Through automating the interposition of declassifiers and endorsers, as required for data to flow according to policy, we showed how the burden on application developers of being IFC-aware could be alleviated. This decoupling of policy specification and enforcement from application code has wide-ranging possibilities for current and future distributed systems.

7. ACKNOWLEDGEMENTS

This work was supported by UK EPSRC grant EP/K011510 CloudSafetyNet. We acknowledge the support of Microsoft through the Microsoft Cloud Computing Research Centre.

8. REFERENCES

[1] J. Bacon, D. Eyers, T. Pasquier, J. Singh, I. Papagiannis, and P. Pietzuch. Information Flow Control for Secure Cloud Computing. *Transactions on Network and System Management SI Cloud Service Management*, 11(1):76–89, 2014.

[2] A. Bouard, B. Weyl, and C. Eckert. Practical information-flow aware middleware for in-car communication. In *Workshop on Security, privacy & dependability for cyber vehicles*, pages 3–8. ACM, 2013.

[3] L. Carata, S. Akoush, N. Balakrishnan, T. Bytheway, R. Sohan, M. Selter, and A. Hopper. A primer on provenance. *Communications of the ACM*, 57(5):52–60, 2014.

[4] D. W. Chadwick and S. F. Lievens. Enforcing sticky security policies throughout a distributed application. In *Workshop on Middleware Security*, pages 1–6. ACM, 2008.

---

[7]See IEEE Cloud, SI on Legal Clouds, 2015 and IEEE Workshop on Legal and Technical Issues in Cloud Computing.

[5] D. E. Denning. A lattice model of secure information flow. *Communications of the ACM*, 19(5):236–243, 1976.

[6] European Commission. Proposal for a General Data Protection Regulation, 2012/0011(COD), C7-0025/12, Brussels COM(2012) 11 final, 2012.

[7] J. C. Garner. Final HIPAA security regulations: a review. *Aspen Publishers, Managed care quarterly*, 11(3):15–27, 2003.

[8] K. Hwang and D. Li. Trusted cloud computing with secure resources and data coloring. *Internet Computing, IEEE*, 14(5):14–22, 2010.

[9] W. A. Jansen. Cloud hooks: Security and privacy issues in cloud computing. In *44th Hawaii International Conference on System Sciences (HICSS)*, pages 1–10. IEEE, 2011.

[10] K. R. Jayaram, D. Safford, U. Sharma, V. Naik, D. Pendarakis, and S. Tao. Trustworthy Geographically Fenced Hybrid Clouds. In *ACM/IFIP/USENIX Middleware*. ACM, 2014.

[11] X. Jin, R. Krishnan, and R. S. Sandhu. A Unified Attribute-Based Access Control Model Covering DAC, MAC and RBAC. *DBSec*, 12:41–55, 2012.

[12] M. Krohn, A. Yip, M. Brodsky, N. Cliffer, M. F. Kaashoek, E. Kohler, and R. Morris. Information Flow Control for Standard OS Abstractions. In *Symposium on Operating Systems Principles*, pages 321–334. ACM, 2007.

[13] N. Kumar and R. Shyamasundar. Realizing Purpose-Based Privacy Policies Succinctly via Information-Flow Labels. In *Big Data and Cloud Computing (BDCloud'14)*, pages 753–760. IEEE, 2014.

[14] T. Loruenser, A. Happe, and D. Slamanig. ARCHISTAR: Towards Secure and Robust Cloud Based Data Sharing. In *International Conference on Cloud Computing Technology and Science (CloudCom'15)*. IEEE, 2015.

[15] N. Love and M. Genesereth. Computational law. In *10th International Conference on Artificial Intelligence and Law*, pages 205–209. ACM, 2005.

[16] A. Madhavapeddy, T. Leonard, M. Skjegstad, T. Gazagnaire, D. Sheets, D. Scott, R. Mortier, A. Chaudhry, B. Singh, J. Ludlam, et al. Jitsu: Just-in-time summoning of unikernels. In *Symposium on Networked Systems Design and Implementation (NSDI 15)*, pages 559–573. USENIX, 2015.

[17] M. Migliavacca, I. Papagiannis, D. M. Eyers, B. Shand, J. Bacon, and P. Pietzuch. DEFCon: High-performance event processing with information security. In *USENIX Annual Technical Conference*, Boston, MA, USA, 2010.

[18] C. J. Millard, editor. *Cloud Computing Law*. Oxford University Press, 2013.

[19] D. Muthukumaran, D. O'Keeffe, C. Priebe, D. Eyers, B. Shand, and P. Pietzuch. FlowWatcher: Defending against data disclosure vulnerabilities in web applications. In *22nd ACM SIGSAC Conference on Computer and Communications Security*, pages 603–615. ACM, 2015.

[20] A. C. Myers. JFlow: Practical Mostly-static Information Flow Control. In *26th SIGPLAN SIGACT POPL'99*, pages 228–241. ACM, 1999.

[21] A. C. Myers and B. Liskov. A Decentralized Model for Information Flow Control. In *Symposium on Operating Systems Principles (SOSP)*, pages 129–142. ACM, 1997.

[22] J. Park, D. Nguyen, and R. Sandhu. A provenance-based access control model. In *Annual International Conference on Privacy, Security and Trust*, pages 137–144. IEEE, 2012.

[23] J. Park and R. Sandhu. The UCON ABC usage control model. *Transactions on Information and System Security (TISSEC)*, 7(1):128–174, 2004.

[24] T. Pasquier and D. Eyers. Information Flow Audit for Transparency and Compliance in the Handling of Personal Data. In *IC2E International Workshop on Legal and Technical Issues in Cloud Computing (CLaw'16)*. IEEE, 2016.

[25] T. Pasquier, J. Singh, and J. Bacon. Clouds of Things need Information Flow Control with Hardware Roots of Trust. In *International Conference on Cloud Computing Technology and Science (CloudCom'15)*. IEEE, 2015.

[26] T. Pasquier, J. Singh, J. Bacon, and D. Eyers. Information Flow Audit for PaaS clouds. In *International Conference on Cloud Engineering (IC2E)*. IEEE, 2016.

[27] T. Pasquier, J. Singh, D. Eyers, and J. Bacon. CamFlow: Managed Data-Sharing for Cloud Services. *IEEE Transactions on Cloud Computing*, 2015.

[28] S. Pearson and M. Casassa-Mont. Sticky Policies: An Approach for Managing Privacy across Multiple Parties. *Computer*, 44, July 2011.

[29] D. Schultz and B. Liskov. IFDB: Decentralized Information Flow Control for Databases. In *European Conference on Computer Systems (Eurosys'13)*, pages 43–56. ACM, 2013.

[30] J. Singh, T. Pasquier, J. Bacon, and D. Eyers. Integrating Middleware and Information Flow Control. In *International Conference on Cloud Engineering (IC2E)*, pages 54–59. IEEE, 2015.

[31] J. Singh, T. Pasquier, J. Bacon, H. Ko, and D. Eyers. Twenty security considerations for cloud-supported Internet of Things. *IEEE IoT Journal*, 2015.

[32] J. Singh, J. Powles, T. Pasquier, and J. Bacon. Data flow management and compliance in cloud computing. *Cloud Computing, IEEE*, 2(4):24–32, July 2015.

[33] S. Smalley, C. Vance, and W. Salamon. Implementing SELinux as a Linux Security Module. *NAI Labs Report*, 1:43, 2001.

[34] S. Soltesz, H. Pötzl, M. E. Fiuczynski, A. Bavier, and L. Peterson. Container-based operating system virtualization: a scalable, high-performance alternative to hypervisors. In *SIGOPS Operating Systems Review*, volume 41, pages 275–287. ACM, 2007.

[35] UK Medical Research Council. Obtaining data from the Health and Social Care Information Centre for health research - a guide for researchers, 2015.

[36] A. Zavou, V. Pappas, V. P. Kemerlis, M. Polychronakis, G. Portokalidis, and A. D. Keromytis. Cloudopsy: An autopsy of data flows in the cloud. In *Human Aspects of Information Security, Privacy, and Trust*, pages 366–375. Springer, 2013.

[37] N. Zeldovich, S. Boyd-Wickizer, E. Kohler, and D. Mazières. Making information flow explicit in HiStar. In *Proc. 7th USENIX OSDI '06*, pages 19–19, 2006.

[38] N. Zeldovich, S. Boyd-Wickizer, and D. Mazières. Securing Distributed Systems with Information Flow Control. In *5th Symposium on Networked System Design and Implementation (NSDI 08)*, pages 293–308. USENIX, 2008.

Modular Synthesis of Enforcement Mechanisms for the Workflow Satisfiability Problem: Scalability and Reusability*

Daniel R. dos Santos
Fondazione Bruno Kessler
SAP Labs France
University of Trento
dossantos@fbk.eu

Serena Elisa Ponta
SAP Labs France
serena.ponta@sap.com

Silvio Ranise
Fondazione Bruno Kessler
ranise@fbk.eu

ABSTRACT

Modularity is an important concept in the design and enactment of workflows. However, supporting the specification and enforcement of authorization in this setting is not straightforward. In this paper, we introduce a notion of component and a combination mechanism for security-sensitive workflows. These are business processes in which execution constraints on the tasks are complemented with authorization constraints (e.g., Separation of Duty) and authorization policies (specifying which users can execute which tasks). We show how authorization constraints can also be imposed across components and demonstrate the usefulness of our notion of component by showing (i) the scalability of a technique for the synthesis of run-time monitors for security-sensitive workflows; and (ii) the design of a plug-in for the reuse of workflows and related run-time monitors inside an editor for security-sensitive workflows.

Categories and Subject Descriptors

D.4.6 [**Operating Systems**]: Security and Protection; K.6.5 [**Management of Computing and Information Systems**]: Security and Protection

Keywords

Business Process, Modularity, Workflow Satisfiability

1. INTRODUCTION

Business process designers constantly strive to adapt to rapidly evolving markets under continuous pressure of regulatory and technological changes. In this respect, a frequent problem faced by companies is the lack of automation when trying to incorporate new requirements into existing processes. A traditional approach to business process modeling frequently results in large models that are difficult to change and maintain. This makes it critical that business process models be modular and flexible, not only for increased modeling agility at design-time but also for greater robustness and flexibility of enacting at run-time (see, e.g., [18] for a discussion about this and related problems).

The situation is further complicated when considering the class of security-sensitive workflows [2], i.e. when tasks in processes are executed under the responsibility of humans or software agents acting on their behalf. This means that, besides the usual execution constraints (specified by causal relations among tasks), there are authorization policies and constraints, i.e. the conditions under which users can execute tasks. Authorization policies are usually specified by using some variant of the Role Based Access Control (RBAC) model (see, e.g., [30]), while authorization constraints restrict which users can execute some set of tasks in a given workflow instance; an example is the Separation of Duty (SoD) constraint requiring two tasks to be executed by distinct users.

Since authorization policies and constraints may prevent the successful termination of the workflow, it is crucial to be able to establish if all tasks in the workflow can be executed satisfying the authorization policy without violating any authorization constraint, which is known as the Workflow Satisfiability Problem (WSP) [7]. In case of large and complex workflow specifications with expressive access control policies, detecting user assignments that may prevent the termination of a workflow becomes a computationally heavy task; the WSP is known to be NP-hard already in presence of one SoD constraint [31]. At run-time, the situation poses even more constraints on performance since at each new user request to execute a task, it is necessary to solve a new instance of the WSP by taking into account the history of the execution so far, i.e. which users have executed which tasks up to that instant (see, e.g., [3, 4]). Many of the available solutions to the WSP (such as [31, 3, 10, 17, 9]) do not provide practical tools capable of enabling designers of business processes to compose satisfiable workflows with authorization requirements. This ultimately prevents the development of efficient enactment mechanisms for security-sensitive workflows.

The modular design of business processes has been advocated for a long time in academia because of its support to reuse at design-time and scalability at run-time [21, 22]. In industry, it is more and more common to find solutions allowing

*This work has been partly supported by the EU under grant 317387 SECENTIS (FP7-PEOPLE-2012-ITN).

the reuse of (parts of) workflows to realize complex business processes. For instance, SAP Operational Process Intelligence[1] supports the creation of end-to-end business processes spanning multiple workflows. Such (template) workflows can be created once and stored to be then operated in different contexts. As an example, a *Purchase Order* workflow with tasks *Create Purchase Order* and *Create Invoice* would be part of any end-to-end business process selling goods, whereas a *Warehouse Management* workflow composed of tasks *Locate Product* and *Send Product* would be included only in cases where physical goods are involved.

Although techniques for modular specification and enactment of workflows and their impact have been extensively studied in the literature (see, e.g., [21, 22, 15]), the same is not true for security-sensitive workflows. In this special class of workflows, not only the control-flow spans several modules, but even authorization constraints may be defined across different components. Given the difficulties in specifying and enforcing execution and authorization constraints in this context, it is not surprising that vulnerabilities can be exploited by malicious users. For example, recently, the incorrect handling of authorization constraints between a *Purchase Order* and a *Warehouse Management* workflow allowed an Amazon employee to pay for cheap products and deliver expensive electronics to himself[2]. This kind of fraud could be avoided by specifying at design-time and enforcing at run-time a SoD constraint between tasks *Create Purchase Order* and *Send Product*.

To summarize, the modular specification and enactment of security-sensitive workflows is complicated by the lack of adequate answers to the following questions:

(i) how to specify authorization constraints that span multiple modules (inter-module constraints)?

(ii) how to enforce such constraints?

(iii) how to scale the enforcement mechanism and handle large workflows?

(iv) how to reuse already specified modules across processes?

In this paper, we introduce an approach capable of answering the questions above by making the following **contributions**:

- the definition of security-sensitive workflow components equipped with interfaces that allow to glue components together and define constraints between them (Section 3), to answer question (i);

- an automated technique, extending previous work [4], to synthesize run-time monitors from workflow components ensuring that all tasks can be executed without violating the policy or the constraints (Section 3.2), to answer question (ii);

- an experimental evaluation of our approach that clearly shows its viability and scalability (Section 4.1), to answer question (iii); and

- a description of a prototype implementing the reuse of workflow modules and monitors that can be integrated with industrial BPM systems (Section 4.2), to answer question (iv).

Section 2 presents the required background and an overview of the technique, while Section 5 discusses related work, a promising future direction of research, and concludes the paper.

---

[1] https://help.sap.com/hana-opint
[2] https://goo.gl/1bySZH

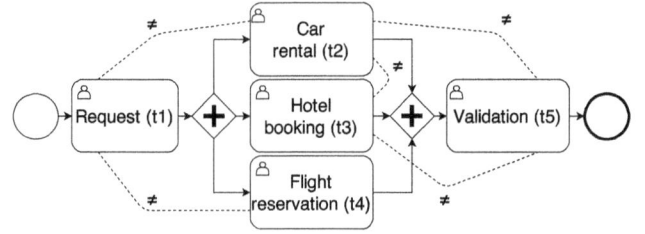

Figure 1: TRW in extended BPM notation

2. OVERVIEW

Our goal is to support the modular design and enactment of security-sensitive workflows and the synthesis of run-time monitors solving the WSP for these workflows. To introduce our approach, in this section we first recall the (non-modular) workflow specification and monitor synthesis technique from [4] (Section 2.1), and then we show the main intuitions and examples on how to extend the technique to support modular workflows (Section 2.2).

2.1 Workflow Specification and Monitor Synthesis

We illustrate our technique [4] for synthesizing a run-time monitor to solve the WSP by means of a simple example.

Example 2.1. The workflow shown in Figure 1 represents the Trip Request Workflow (TRW), whose goal is requesting trips for employees in an organization. It is composed of five tasks: Request ($t1$), Car rental ($t2$), Hotel booking ($t3$), Flight reservation ($t4$), and Validation ($t5$). Five SoD constraints must be enforced, i.e. the tasks in the pairs ($t1, t2$), ($t1, t4$), ($t2, t3$), ($t2, t5$), and ($t3, t5$) must be executed by distinct users in any sequence of task executions of the TRW.

The workflow is specified in extended BPM Notation (BPMN) [20]. It contains two circles, the one on the left represents the start event (triggering the execution of the workflow), whereas that on the right the end event (terminating the execution of the workflow), tasks are depicted by labeled boxes, the constraints on the execution of tasks are shown as solid arrows (for sequence flows) and diamonds labeled by + (for parallel flows), the fact that a task must be executed under the responsibility of a user is indicated by the man icon inside a box, and SoD constraints as dashed lines labeled by $\neq$.

A simple situation in which the TRW can be deployed is a tiny organization with a set $U = \{a, b, c\}$ of three users and the following authorization policy $TA = \{(a, t1), (b, t1), (a, t2), (b, t2), (c, t2), (a, t3), (b, t3), (c, t3), (a, t4), (a, t5), (b, t5), (c, t5)\}$, where $(u, t) \in TA$ means that user u is entitled to execute task t. The organization would then like to know if there is a concrete execution that allows the process to terminate. Indeed, this is possible as shown by the following sequence of task-user pairs: $\eta = t1(b), t3(c), t4(a), t2(a), t5(b)$ where $t(u)$ means that user u has executed task t and the position in the sequence corresponds to the order in which the tasks have been executed (i.e. $t1$ has been executed first, $t5$ last, $t3$ after $t1$ but before $t4$, $t2$, and $t5$, etc). It is easy to check that the tasks in η are executed so that the ordering constraints on task execution are satisfied, each user u in each pair $t(u)$ of η is authorized to execute t since $(u, t) \in TA$, and each SoD constraint is

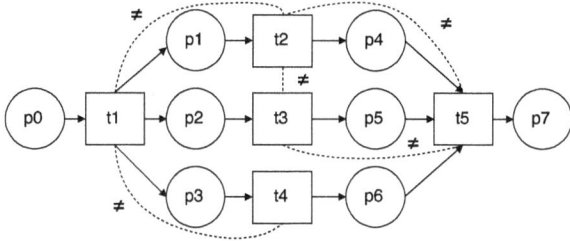

id	enabled		action	
	CF	Auth	CF	Auth
$t1(u)$	$p0 \wedge \neg d_{t1}$	$a_{t1}(u)$	$p0,p1,p2,p3,d_{t1}$ $:= F,T,T,T,T$	$h_{t1}(u)$ $:= T$
$t2(u)$	$p1 \wedge \neg d_{t2}$	$a_{t2}(u) \wedge \neg h_{t3}(u)$ $\wedge \neg h_{t1}(u)$	$p1,p4,d_{t2}$ $:= F,T,T$	$h_{t2}(u)$ $:= T$
$t3(u)$	$p2 \wedge \neg d_{t3}$	$a_{t3}(u) \wedge \neg h_{t2}(u)$	$p2,p5,d_{t3}$ $:= F,T,T$	$h_{t3}(u)$ $:= T$
$t4(u)$	$p3 \wedge \neg d_{t4}$	$a_{t4}(u) \wedge \neg h_{t1}(u)$	$p3,p6,d_{t4}$ $:= F,T,T$	$h_{t4}(u)$ $:= T$
$t5(u)$	$p4 \wedge p5 \wedge$ $p6 \wedge \neg d_{t5}$	$a_{t5}(u) \wedge \neg h_{t3}(u)$ $\wedge \neg h_{t2}(u)$	$p4,p5,p6,p7,d_{t5}$ $:= F,F,F,T,T$	$h_{t5}(u)$ $:= T$

Figure 2: TRW as an extended Petri net (top) and as a transition system (bottom)

satisfied (e.g., tasks $t1$ and $t2$ are executed by the distinct users b and a, respectively).

Workflows can be represented at different levels of abstraction: in a modeling language like BPMN, which is suited for process designers but abstracts details of the semantics of the systems; as transition systems, which are amenable to formal analysis, but require descriptions much more detailed than what is usually provided by designers; and as Petri nets, which are often not familiar to designers, but have a formal semantics and are more intuitive than transition systems. The translation between these levels of abstraction can be done automatically (see, e.g., [28]), i.e. workflow designers can work at the BPMN level (e.g., the TRW in Figure 1) and a procedure, that is transparent to end-users, can translate them to Petri nets (e.g., top of Figure 2 for the Petri net corresponding to the BPMN in Figure 1) and then to transition systems (bottom of Figure 2 for the transition system corresponding to the Petri net at the top of the same figure), which are amenable to formal analysis.

We now briefly recall the technique in [4] to synthesize run-time monitors solving the WSP (i.e. enforcement mechanisms capable of finding a solution to the WSP). It takes as input the specification of a security-sensitive workflow (e.g., the BPMN in Figure 1 for the TRW) with the specification of an authorization policy TA and consists of two steps.

Off-line step.

Let $S = (V, Tr)$ be the (symbolic) transition system [26] derived from a security-sensitive workflow composed of a finite set T of tasks, a finite set U of users, and a finite set C of authorization constraints where V is the (finite) set of state variables and Tr is the (finite) set of transitions. The authorization policy TA is not taken into consideration in this step as we are able to synthesize a monitor for the WSP which can accommodate any such policy.

Example 2.2. To illustrate, let us consider the transition system at the bottom of Figure 2. The set V of state variables contains the (Boolean) control-flow variables p_i and d_{ti}, where p_i represents the existence of a token in the place pi of

the Petri net at the top of the same figure and d_{ti} represents the fact that transition ti of the Petri net at the top of the same figure has been executed. Additionally, V contains the authorization variables a_{ti} and h_{ti} that are (Boolean) arrays such that $a_{ti}(u)$ means that user u is entitled to execute task ti and $h_{ti}(u)$ means that user u has executed task ti.

The transitions in Tr are listed in the table at the bottom of Figure 2 and are composed of three parts: an id(entifier), an enabling condition, and an effect. To illustrate, consider the second line of the table: the id indicates that user u executes task $t2$, the enabling condition is composed of two parts CF, which stands for control-flow, and $Auth$, which stands for authorization. The enabling condition CF is the conjunction of predicates $p1$ and $\neg d_{t2}$ indicating that, for this event to be enabled, there must be a token in place $p1$ of the Petri net (at the top of the same figure) and task $t2$ has not been executed yet. The enabling condition $Auth$ is the conjunction of predicates $a_{t2}(u)$, indicating that the user requesting to execute this task must be authorized to do so by the authorization policy (i.e. $(u, t) \in TA$), $\neg h_{t3}(u)$, indicating that the user requesting to execute this task should not have executed task $t3$ (notice that $t2$ and $t3$ can be executed in parallel, due to the gateway), and $\neg h_{t1}(u)$, indicating that the user requesting to execute this task should not have executed task $t1$ (notice that the SoD constraint between $t2$ and $t5$ is not present in $t2(u)$ because $t5$ is always executed after $t2$). The effect is also divided in a CF and an $Auth$ part. The effect of executing $t2$ at the control flow level (CF) is to remove a token from place $p1$ and put a token in place $p4$ (formally, this is done by setting $p1$ to $False$ and $p4$ to $True$, as well as recording the execution of $t2$ by setting d_{t2} to $True$). The effect of executing $t2$ at the authorization level $(Auth)$ is to update the history function h_{t2} to record the fact that $t2$ has been executed by user u (formally, $h_{t2}(u) := T$).

The transition system S is used to compute a *(symbolic) reachability graph* RG, i.e. a directed graph whose edges are labeled by task-user pairs in which users are symbolically represented by variables (called *user variables*) and whose nodes are labeled by a symbolic representation (namely, a formula of first-order logic) of the set of states from which it is possible to reach a state in which the workflow successfully terminates (for the TRW, this is the set of states in which all five tasks have been executed). A sequence $\eta_s = t_1(v_{j_1}), ..., t_n(v_{j_n})$ of task-user pairs is a *symbolic execution* where v_{j_i} is a user variable with $1 \leq j_i \leq n$ and $i = 1, ..., n$. A *well-formed* path in RG is a path starting with a node without an incoming edge and ending with a node without an outgoing edge. The crucial property of RG is that the symbolic execution $\eta_s = t_1(v_{j_1}), ..., t_n(v_{j_n})$ collected while traversing one of its well-formed paths corresponds to an eligible (i.e. not violating any constraint in C) concrete execution $\eta_c = t_1(\mu(v_{j_1})), ..., t_n(\mu(v_{j_n}))$ for μ an injective function from the set $\Upsilon = \{v_{j_1}, ..., v_{j_n}\}$ of user variables (also called *symbolic users*) to the given set U of users (since μ is injective, distinct user variables are never mapped to the same user).

Example 2.3. An excerpt of the symbolic reachability graph for the TRW is depicted in Figure 3. The formulae labeling the nodes are not shown in the figure for the sake of simplicity. As an example, we show formula β_3, attached to node 3 of

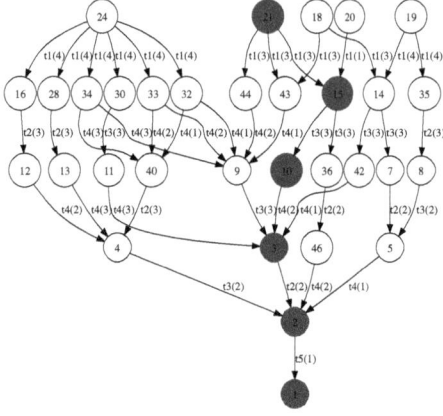

Figure 3: An excerpt of the symbolic reachability graph for the TRW

the graph, from which it is possible to execute $t2$:

$$\neg p0 \wedge p1 \wedge \neg p2 \wedge \neg p3 \wedge \neg p4 \wedge p5 \wedge p6 \wedge$$
$$d_{t1} \wedge \neg d_{t2} \wedge d_{t3} \wedge d_{t4} \wedge \neg d_{t5} \wedge$$
$$a_{t2}(v2) \wedge \neg h_{t1}(v2) \wedge \neg h_{t3}(v2) \wedge$$
$$a_{t5}(v1) \wedge \neg h_{t3}(v1) \wedge \neg h_{t2}(v1) \wedge v1 \neq v2$$

Formula β_3 encodes the fact that, in order for a user $v2$ to be allowed to execute $t2$, the system must be in a state where there are tokens in places $p1$, $p5$, and $p6$ while there are no tokens in places $p0$, $p2$, $p3$, and $p4$ (first line), tasks $t1$, $t3$, and $t4$ have been already executed while tasks $t2$ and $t5$ have not been executed (second line), user $v2$ should be authorized to perform $t2$ and should not have executed neither $t1$ nor $t3$ (third line), and there should exist a user $v1$ (distinct from $v2$) authorized to execute $t5$ who should have executed neither $t1$ nor $t3$ (last line).

Concerning the labels on the edges of the symbolic reachability graph, in Figure 3, a task-user pair $t(v_k)$ labeling an edge is abbreviated by $t(k)$ for the sake of compactness. So, for instance, the symbolic execution $\eta_s = t1(v_3), t3(v_3), t4(v_2), t2(v_2), t5(v_1)$ (cf. the well-formed path identified by the blue nodes in Figure 3) represents all those executions in which a symbolic user identified by v_3 first performs task $t1$ followed by $t3$, then a symbolic user identified by v_2 performs $t4$ and $t2$ in this order, and finally a symbolic user identified by v_1 executes $t5$. If we apply an injective function μ from the set $\Upsilon = \{v_1, v_2, v_3\}$ of user variables to any finite set U of users (of cardinality at least three), the corresponding execution $\eta_c = \mu(\eta_s)$ is eligible according to the set C of SoD constraints shown in Figure 1.

The final action of the off-line step is to derive a non-recursive Datalog program M (with negation) from the symbolic reachability graph RG by generating a clause of the form $can\_do(v, t) \leftarrow \beta_v$ for each node v in the graph RG.

Example 2.4. To illustrate, consider again node 3 in the graph as done in Example 2.3. Then, the Datalog program M will contain the following clause:

$$can\_do(t2, v2) \leftarrow \quad \neg p0, p1, \neg p2, \neg p3, \neg p4, p5, p6,$$
$$d_{t1}, \neg d_{t2}, d_{t3}, d_{t4}, \neg d_{t5},$$
$$a_{t2}(v2), \neg h_{t1}(v2), \neg h_{t3}(v2),$$
$$a_{t5}(v1), \neg h_{t3}(v1), \neg h_{t2}(v1), v1 \neq v2.$$

where the comma stands for logical conjunction.

On-line step. To build a run-time monitor for the WSP, we explain how to combine the Datalog program M obtained in the off-line step with the authorization policy TA. For this, the following observation is crucial. As shown in Example 2.4, the formula β_v contains invocations to the binary predicates a_{ti} and h_{ti}. The former is the interface to the authorization policy and it is such that $a(u, t)$ holds iff $(u, t) \in TA$ while the latter keeps track of which user has executed which task, i.e. $h(t, u)$ means that t has been executed by u. Following an established tradition (see, e.g., [16]) claiming that (variants of) Datalog are adequate to express a wide range of access control policy idioms, we assume a to be defined by a Datalog program P. The predicate h is dynamic and defined by a set H of (ground) facts which is updated after each task execution. Thus, if the query $can\_do(u, t)$ can be derived from M, P, H (in symbols, $M, P, H \vdash can\_do(u, t)$), user u can execute task t and the workflow can terminate while satisfying the authorization policy and the authorization constraints.

Example 2.5. For the TRW, let us consider the relation TA presented after Example 2.1, which can be specified after the RBAC model [25] by the Datalog program P:

$$ua(a, r1). \; ua(a, r2). \; ua(a, r3). \; ua(b, r2). \; ua(b, r3). \; ua(c, r2).$$
$$pa(r_3, t1). \; pa(r_2, t2). \; pa(r_2, t3). \; pa(r_1, t4). \; pa(r_2, t5).$$
$$a(v, \tau) \leftarrow ua(v, \rho), \; pa(\rho, \tau).$$

where $r1$, $r2$, and $r3$ are roles, ua is the user-role assignment (cf. first line of facts), pa is the role-task assignment (cf. second line of facts), v is a user variable, τ is a variable ranging over tasks, and a is defined as the join of the relations ua and pa (cf. Datalog clause in the last line). Notice that $P \vdash a(u, t)$ iff $(u, t) \in TA$ for user u and task t.

An example run of the monitor derived from the symbolic reachability graph in Figure 3 combined with the RBAC policy above is shown in Table 1: column 'History' shows which facts are added to the set H and column 'Answer' reports grant (deny, respectively) when the query in column 'Query' can (cannot, respectively) be derived from M, P, H. For instance, there are two denied requests: in line 0, user a requests to execute task $t1$ but this is not possible since a is the only user authorized to execute $t4$, and if a executes $t1$, he/she will no more be allowed to execute $t4$ because of the SoD constraint between $t1$ and $t4$ (see Figure 1); in line 4, user b requests to execute task $t2$ but again this is not possible since b has already executed task $t1$ and this would violate the SoD constraint between $t1$ and $t2$. All other requests are granted, as they violate neither task execution nor authorization constraints. The execution resulting from this run of the monitor is $t1(b), t3(c), t4(a), t2(a), t5(b)$, which is derived from the

Table 1: A run of the monitor program for the TRW

#	History	Query	Answer
0	$\emptyset$	$can\_do(a, t1)$	deny
1	-	$can\_do(b, t1)$	grant
2	$h(t1, b)$	$can\_do(c, t3)$	grant
3	$h(t3, c)$	$can\_do(a, t4)$	grant
4	$h(t4, a)$	$can\_do(b, t2)$	deny
5	-	$can\_do(a, t2)$	grant
6	$h(t2, a)$	$can\_do(b, t5)$	grant
7	$h(t5, b)$	-	-

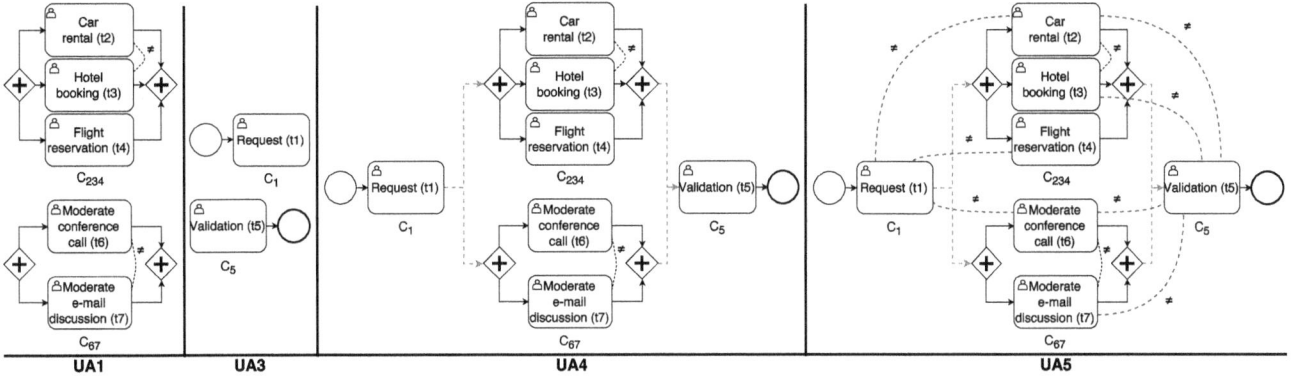

Figure 4: User actions necessary to specify and compose modules representing the TRW and MDW

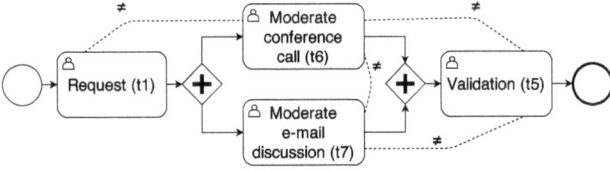

Figure 5: MDW in extended BPM notation

symbolic execution $t1(v_1), t3(v_3), t4(v_2), t2(v_2), t5(v_1)$ in the graph of Figure 3 (cf. the path with the blue nodes; see also Example 2.3) by applying the injective function μ mapping v_1 to b, v_2 to a, and v_3 to c.

As described so far, our technique to synthesize run-time monitors for the WSP is based on representing each workflow with a single transition system. In [4], it is shown that monitor synthesis done this way is not scalable due to state space explosion. Additionally, the technique offers no support to the reuse and composition of (selected parts of) workflow specifications in larger workflows. We now explain how to extend this technique to handle a composition of (modular) workflows, making the approach scalable while fostering workflow reuse.

2.2 Modular Design and Enactment

We introduce our approach for the modular design and enactment of security-sensitive workflows by combining the previously introduced TRW with another example workflow.

Example 2.6. Figure 5 shows the Moderate Discussion Workflow (MDW) whose goal is to organize a discussion and voting process in an organization. It is composed of four tasks: Request ($t1$), Moderate Conference Call ($t6$), Moderate e-mail Discussion ($t7$), and Validation ($t5$). Four SoD constraints must be enforced: ($t1, t6$), ($t6, t5$), ($t6, t7$), and ($t7, t5$). Again, each task is executed under the responsibility of a user who is entitled to do so according to some authorization policy, which we leave unspecified for the sake of brevity and because the synthesis technique that we use generates a monitor that can accommodate any authorization policy (see Section 3.2 for details).

Notice that tasks $t1$ and $t5$ in Figures 1 and 5 are the same in both TRW and MDW. The notion of security-sensitive component introduced in this paper allows to reuse the specification of tasks $t1$ and $t5$ in different systems so that only

the specification of the parallel execution of tasks $t2$, $t3$, and $t4$ for the TRW and $t6$ and $t7$ for the MDW must be developed from scratch.

By using the approach in this paper, a process designer can model both TRW and MDW by executing the following user actions, that are also depicted in Figure 4 (where the elements in black represent the internal specification of components, the red dashed arrows represent inter-component execution (control-flow) constraints and the blue dashed lines represent inter-component authorization constraints):

UA1 specify the parallel execution of tasks $t2$, $t3$, and $t4$ as a new component $\mathcal{C}_{234}$ for the TRW and of $t6$ and $t7$ as $\mathcal{C}_{67}$ for the MDW together with their authorization constraints, i.e. SoD between $t2$ and $t3$ for TRW and between $t6$ and $t7$ for MDW;

UA2 synthesize run-time monitors for the new components $\mathcal{C}_{234}$ and $\mathcal{C}_{67}$ to be stored (together with the monitors) in a repository for future use;

UA3 import, from the available workflow repository, the security-sensitive components containing tasks $t1$ and $t5$ in Figures 1 and 5, called $\mathcal{C}_1$ and $\mathcal{C}_5$, respectively;

UA4 define the control-flow among components; and

UA5 define inter-component authorization constraints.

As we will see, together with security-sensitive component specifications, in the workflow repository it is also possible to store the associated run-time monitors solving the run-time version of the WSP. To enact the modularly designed business processes TRW and MDW, the designer can simply add an authorization policy and deploy the process to the run-time environment. Behind the scenes, the monitors of the various components are automatically combined to build one for the composed processes, namely TRW and MDW. This combination is done by using a set G of "gluing assertions," which are logical assertions connecting the components, i.e. transferring control-flow and constraining the execution of tasks in the next components.

The main result of this paper (Theorem 3.1) shows that the combination of monitors M_1, M_{234}, and M_5 synthesized for components $\mathcal{C}_1$, $\mathcal{C}_{234}$ and $\mathcal{C}_5$, respectively, with their Datalog authorization policies P_1, P_{234}, P_5 and their execution histories H_1, H_{234}, H_5, and using the assertions in G, answers to user requests in the same way as a monitor M computed for the TRW as a single component. Formally, $M_1, M_{234}, M_5, G, P_1, P_{234}, P_5, H_1, H_{234}, H_5 \vdash can\_do(u, t)$ iff $M, P, H \vdash can\_do(u, t)$. Therefore, a similar run as the one shown in Table 1 for M can be obtained with M_1, M_{234}, M_5.

Indeed, the simplicity of the TRW and MDW spoils the advantages of a modular approach; the small dimension of the workflows allows us to keep the paper to a reasonable size. However, for large workflows—as we will see in Section 4—the advantages are substantial. To give an intuition of this, imagine replacing the tasks reused in both workflows, i.e. $t1$ and $t5$, with complex workflows: reusing their specifications and synthesized run-time monitors in larger workflows in which they are plugged, becomes much more interesting.

Each of the aforementioned user actions is based on the approach and notions introduced in the rest of the paper: **UA1** and **UA3** in Section 3; **UA4** and **UA5** in Section 3.1; and **UA2** in Section 3.2.

3. SECURITY-SENSITIVE WORKFLOW COMPONENTS

The goal of this Section is to identify a refinement of the notion of security-sensitive workflow, introduced in Section 2.1, that can be modularly composed with others through an appropriate interface. Technically, this is done by extending and partitioning the state variables of the transition system representing a security-sensitive workflow and then adding an appropriate notion of interface to support composition. The resulting notion is called a security-sensitive component. Below, we provide the key ideas underlying our techniques while omitting some of the formal details, which are available in a technical report [13].

Example 3.1. Preliminarily, we give some intuitions about the notion of security-sensitive component by considering the modular specification of both the TRW and MDW. Figure 6 shows the four components $\mathcal{C}_1$, $\mathcal{C}_{234}$, $\mathcal{C}_{67}$, and $\mathcal{C}_5$ whose composition gives both TRW and MDW. Each component is represented as a Petri net that is automatically derived from the BPMN model of Figure 4 (in a way similar to the one discussed in Section 2.1 to derive the Petri net at the top of Figure 2 from the BPMN model in Figure 1). The left side of the figure shows the extended Petri nets representing the four components: circles represent places, rectangles with a man icon transitions to be executed under the responsibility of users, rectangles without the icon transitions not needing human intervention, (black) dashed lines represent SoD constraints between tasks belonging to the same component, and (black) solid arrows the control flow in the same component. The right side of the figure shows how to connect these components in order to obtain the TRW and the MDW: (blue) dashed lines represent SoD constraints between tasks belonging to distinct components and (red) dashed arrows the control flow between two components.

The control flow between two components is outside of the semantics of extended Petri nets. For example, a token in place $p0$ of $\mathcal{C}_1$ goes to $p1$ of $\mathcal{C}_1$ after the execution of $t1$ and, at the same time a token is put in place $p1$ of $\mathcal{C}_{234}$ because of the (red) dashed arrow from $p1$ in $\mathcal{C}_1$ to $p0$ in $\mathcal{C}_{234}$ representing an inter-component execution constraint. When the token is in $p0$, the system executes the split transition s in C_{234} that removes the token from $p0$ and puts one in $p1$, $p2$, and $p3$ so that $t2$, $t3$, and $t4$ in $\mathcal{C}_{234}$ become enabled. Notice that the execution of $t2$ is constrained by a SoD constraint from task $t1$ in component C_1 (dashed arrow between $t1$ in C_1 and $t2$ in $\mathcal{C}_{234}$): this means that the user who has executed $t1$ in $\mathcal{C}_1$ cannot execute also $t2$ in $\mathcal{C}_{234}$.

Refined transition systems. Recall the description of

the transition system $S = (V, Tr)$ associated to the TRW and derived from the Petri net at the top of Figure 2 given in Example 2.2. The state variables V can be partitioned in the following (disjoint) sets: P containing the Boolean variables pi's encoding the fact that a token is in place pi of the Petri net or not, D containing the Boolean variables d_{ti}'s encoding the fact that the task ti has been executed or not, A containing the Boolean arrays a_{ti}'s encoding the fact that a certain user is entitled to execute task ti or not, and H containing the Boolean arrays h_{ti}'s encoding the fact that a certain user has executed or not task ti. To support the definition of authorization constraints across components, we add a set C of Boolean arrays c_{ti}'s to the state variables of the transition system in order to represent SoD or BoD constraints (involving task ti) together with a set B of (so-called) *always constraints* fixing the values of the variables in C as Boolean combinations of the (history) variables in H. Formally, we assume B to contain a formula of the form $\forall u.v(u) \Leftrightarrow hst$, where v is in C, u is a variable ranging over users, and hst is a Boolean combination of atoms of the form $w(u)$ with $w \in H$. A *(refined) transition system* is a tuple of the form $((P, D, A, H, C), Tr, B)$ where the P, D, A, H, and C are sets of state variables, Tr is the set of transitions, and B is the set of always constraints.

Example 3.2. We refine the transition system $S = (V, Tr)$ in Example 2.2 as the tuple $((P, D, A, H, C), Tr', B)$ introduced above. The sets of state variables are defined as $P = \{p0, ..., p7\}$, $D = \{d_{t1}, ..., d_{t5}\}$, $A = \{a_{t1}, ..., a_{t5}\}$, $H = \{h_{t1}, ..., h_{t5}\}$, and $C = \{c_{t1}, ..., c_{t5}\}$. The set B of always constraints contains the formulae: $\forall v.c_{t1}(v) \Leftrightarrow T$, $\forall v.c_{t2}(v) \Leftrightarrow \neg h_{t1}(v) \wedge \neg h_{t3}(v)$, $\forall v.c_{t3}(v) \Leftrightarrow \neg h_{t2}(v)$, $\forall v.c_{t4}(v) \Leftrightarrow \neg h_{t1}(v)$, and $\forall v.c_{t5}(v) \Leftrightarrow \neg h_{t1}(v) \wedge \neg h_{t3}(v)$. The set Tr' contains the transitions shown in Table 2. The table at the bottom of Figure 2 can be derived from Table 2 by simply replacing each occurrence of the c_{ti}'s with the formula hst in the corresponding always constraint in B. While in this case the c_{ti}'s play the simple role of abbreviations, they are crucial to support the specification of authorization constraints spanning across components. This will be clear in Example 3.3 and Section 3.1 below, when considering the specification of the TRW as a composition of sub-modules.

The last observation above indeed holds in general: given a refined transition system $((P, D, A, H, C), Tr', B)$, it is always possible to build a transition system (V, Tr) by taking V as the union of P, D, A, H, C, and Tr to contain the transitions obtained by replacing each c_{ti} in Tr' with the corresponding hst in B. In this way, the classical interleaving semantics

Table 2: Refined transitions

id	enabled		action	
	CF	Auth	CF	Auth
$t1(u)$	$p0 \wedge \neg d_{t1}$	$a_{t1}(u) \wedge c_{t1}(u)$	$p0, p1, p2, p3, d_{t1}$:= F, T, T, T, T	$h_{t1}(u)$:= T
$t2(u)$	$p1 \wedge \neg d_{t2}$	$a_{t2}(u) \wedge c_{t2}(u)$	$p1, p4, d_{t2}$:= F, T, T	$h_{t2}(u)$:= T
$t3(u)$	$p2 \wedge \neg d_{t3}$	$a_{t3}(u) \wedge c_{t3}(u)$	$p2, p5, d_{t3}$:= F, T, T	$h_{t3}(u)$:= T
$t4(u)$	$p3 \wedge \neg d_{t4}$	$a_{t4}(u) \wedge c_{t4}(u)$	$p3, p6, d_{t4}$:= F, T, T	$h_{t4}(u)$:= T
$t5(u)$	$p4 \wedge p5 \wedge p6 \wedge \neg d_{t5}$	$a_{t5}(u) \wedge c_{t5}(u)$	$p4, p5, p6, p7, d_{t5}$:= F, F, F, T, T	$h_{t5}(u)$:= T

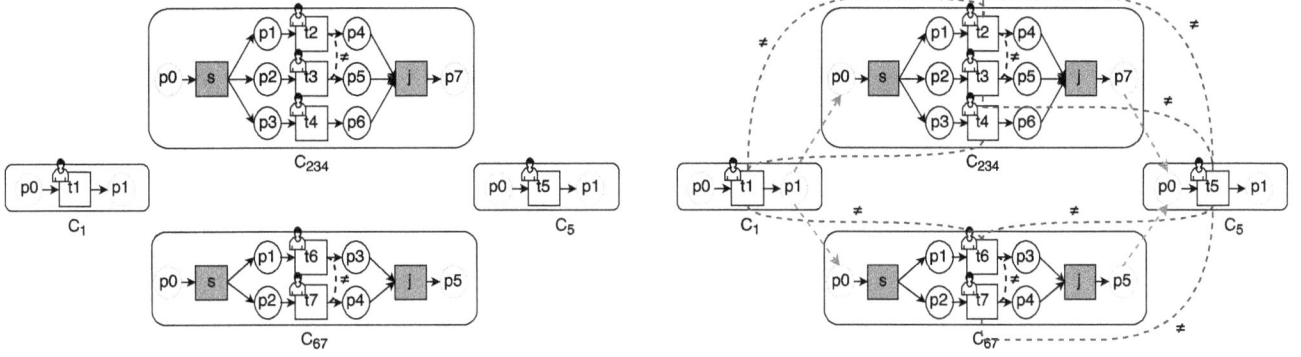

Figure 6: Security-sensitive components (left) and how to glue them together (right)

defined for (V, Tr) in [4] can also be adopted for the refined transition system $((P, D, A, H, C), Tr', B)$.

Adding the interface. A *security-sensitive (workflow) component* is a pair (S, Int) where $S = ((P, D, A, H, C), Tr, B)$ is a refined transition system and Int is its interface. Intuitively, Int identifies the variables of S whose values can be set by another component (called input variables, indicated by the super-script i) and those that are set by the component itself (called output variables, indicated by the super-script o). Formally, Int is a tuple of the form (A, P^i, P^o, H^o, C^i) where

- $P^i \subseteq P$ and each $p^i \in P^i$ is such that $p^i := T$ does not occur in the parallel assignments of an event in Tr,
- $P^o \subseteq P$ and each $p^o \in P^o$ is such that $p^o := T$ occurs in the parallel assignments of an event in Tr whereas $p^o := F$ does not,
- $H^o \subseteq H$, $C^i \subseteq C$, and
- only the variables in $(C \setminus C^i) \cup H^o$ can occur in a symbolic always constraint of B.

A is included in Int as the values of its variables are induced by the authorization policy TA specifying which users are entitled to perform which task. When P^i, P^o, H^o, and C^i are all empty, the security-sensitive component (S, Int) can only be interfaced with an authorization policy via the interface variables in A. The state variables in D are only used internally, to indicate that a task has been or has not been executed; thus, none of them is exposed in the interface Int. The variables in P, H, and C are local to S but some of them can be exposed in the interface in order to enable the combination of S with other components in a way which will be described in Section 3.1. The requirement that variables in P^i are not assigned the value T(rue) by any transition of the component allows their values to be determined by those in another component. Dually, the requirement that variables in P^o can only be assigned the value T(rue) by any transition of the component allows them to determine the values of variables in another component. Similarly to the values of the variables in P^i, those of the variables in C^i are fixed when combining the module with another; this is the reason for which only the variables in $C \setminus C^i$ can occur in the always constraints of the component.

Example 3.3. We now specify the interface of the components presented in Example 3.1. For components $\mathcal{C}_1$ and $\mathcal{C}_5$ (supporting **UA3**) we set $P^i_y := \{p0_y\}$, $P^o_y := \{p1_y\}$, $H^o_y := \{h_{ty}\}$ (for $y = 1, 5$), $C^i_1 := \emptyset$, and $C^i_5 := \{c^i_{t5}\}$ The

interface of each component is the following: $p0_y$ is the input place, $p1_y$ is the output place, and the history variable h_{ty} can be used to constrain the execution of tasks in other components (for instance of $t2$ in the TRW as $t1$ and $t2$ are involved in a SoD). Notice that the execution of task $t1$ cannot be constrained by the execution of tasks in other components (thus $C^i_1 := \emptyset$) since $t1$ is always executed before all other tasks and cannot possibly be influenced by their execution. Contrarily, $C^i_5 := \{c^i_{t5}\}$, since $t5$ is always executed after all other tasks. In particular, c^i_{t5} will be defined so as to satisfy the SoD constraints between $t5$ and $t2$ or $t3$ for TRW and $t6$ or $t7$ for MDW. For component $\mathcal{C}_{234}$ (supporting **UA1**) we set $P^i_{234} := \{p0_{234}\}$, $P^o_{234} := \{p7_{234}\}$, $H^o_{234} := \{h_{t2}, h_{t3}\}$, and $C^i_{234} := \{c^i_{t2}, c^i_{t4}\}$. The interface of $\mathcal{C}_{67}$ is similar to that of $\mathcal{C}_{234}$. Section 3.1 below explains how components $\mathcal{C}_1$, $\mathcal{C}_{234}$, $\mathcal{C}_{67}$, and $\mathcal{C}_5$ can be "glued together" to build TRW and MDW.

3.1 Gluing Together Security-Sensitive Components

We now show how components can be combined together in order to build other, more complex, components. In the same way as the transition systems and interfaces presented above are derived from the internal elements of workflow components specified in BPMN, also the elements used to compose them (gluing assertions) are derived automatically from a high-level specification (e.g., the red arrows and blue lines in Figures 4 and 6).

Formally, for $l = 1, 2$, let (S_l, Int_l) be a security-sensitive component where $Int_l = (A, P^i_l, P^o_l, H^o_l, C^i_l)$ and $S_l = ((P_l, D_l, A_l, H_l, C_l), Tr_l, B_l)$ is such that P_1 and P_2, D_1 and D_2, A_1 and A_2, H_1 and H_2, C_1 and C_2 are pairwise disjoint sets. Furthermore, let $G = G_{EC} \cup G_{Auth}$ be a set of *gluing assertions* over Int_1 and Int_2, where G_{EC} is a set of formulae of the form $p^i \Leftrightarrow p^o$ for $p^i \in P^i_k$ and $p^o \in P^o_j$, called *inter execution constraints*; and G_{Auth} is a set of always constraints in which only the variables in $C^i_k \cup H^o_j$ may occur, for $k, j = 1, 2$ and $k \neq j$. Intuitively, the gluing assertions in G specify inter component constraints; those in G_{EC} specify how the control flow is passed from one component to another, whereas those in G_{Auth} specify authorization constraints across components, i.e. how the fact that a task in a component is executed by a certain user constrains the execution of a task in another component by a sub-set of the users entitled to do so.

The *security-sensitive component (S, Int) obtained by*

95

gluing (S_1, Int_1) *and* (S_2, Int_2) *together with* G, in symbols $(S, Int) = (S_1, Int_1) \oplus_G (S_2, Int_2)$, is defined as $S = ((P, D, A, H, C), Tr, B)$ and $Int = (A, P^i, P^o, H^o, C^i)$, where

- $P = P_1 \cup P_2$, $D = D_1 \cup D_2$, $A = A_1 \cup A_2$, $H = H_1 \cup H_2$, $C = C_1 \cup C_2$,
- $Tr := [Tr_1]_{G_{EC}} \cup [Tr_2]_{G_{EC}}$ where $[Tr_j]_{G_{EC}} := \{[tr_j]_{G_{EC}} | tr_j \in Tr_j\}$,
- $B = B_1 \cup B_2 \cup G_{Auth}$,
- $P^i = \{p \in (P_1^i \cup P_2^i) | p \text{ does not occur in } G_{EC}\}$,
- $P^o = \{p \in (P_1^o \cup P_2^o) | p \text{ does not occur in } G_{EC}\}$,
- $H^o = H_1^o \cup H_2^o$,
- $C^i = \{c \in (C_1^i \cup C_2^i) | c \text{ does not occur in } G_{Auth}\}$,

and $[tr_j]_{G_{EC}}$ is obtained from tr_j by adding the assignment $p^i := b$ if p^i is in P_j^i, there exists an inter execution constraint of the form $p^i \Leftrightarrow p^o$ in G_{EC}, p^o is in P_k^o, and $p^o := b$ is among the parallel assignments of tr_j; otherwise, tr_j is returned unchanged, for $j, k = 1, 2$ and $j \neq k$.

The definition is well formed since S is obviously a security-sensitive transition system and Int satisfies all the structural constraints defined above.

Example 3.4. Let us consider components $\mathcal{C}_1$ and $\mathcal{C}_{234}$ of previous examples. We glue them together by using the following set $G = G_{EC} \cup G_{Auth}$ of gluing assertions where $G_{EC} := \{p1_1 \Leftrightarrow p0_{234}\}$ and $G_{Auth} := \{\forall u. c_{t2}^i(u) \Leftrightarrow \neg h_{t1}(u), \forall u. c_{t4}^i(u) \Leftrightarrow \neg h_{t1}(u)\}$. G_{EC} and G_{Auth} support **UA4** and **UA5**, respectively (see Figure 4). The inter execution constraint in G_{EC} corresponds to the dashed arrow connecting $p1$ in component $\mathcal{C}_1$ ($p1_1$) to $p0$ in component $\mathcal{C}_{234}$ ($p0_{234}$) in Figure 6. The always constraints in G_{Auth} formalize the dashed lines linking task $t1$ of component $\mathcal{C}_1$ to tasks $t2$ and $t4$ of component $\mathcal{C}_{234}$. Notice that $\mathcal{C}_1 \oplus_G \mathcal{C}_{234}$ can be combined with $\mathcal{C}_5$ to form a component corresponding to the TRW in Figure 1. This is possible by considering the following set $G' = G'_{EC} \cup G'_{Auth}$ of gluing assertions where $G'_{EC} := \{p7_{234} \Leftrightarrow p0_5\}$ and $G'_{Auth} := \{\forall u. c_{t5}^i(u) \Leftrightarrow \neg h_{t2}(u) \wedge \neg h_{t3}(u)\}$.

The operator $\oplus_G$ is both commutative and associative. This implies the desirable property that the result of combining components does not depend on the order in which these are imported (provided the execution and authorization constraints are unchanged).

3.2 Modular Synthesis of Run-time Monitors

Section 2.1 illustrates the methodology to automatically derive a monitor capable of solving the run-time version of the WSP for security-sensitive workflow systems. As argued above, the notions of security-sensitive workflow component and that of security-sensitive workflow system are equivalent. Below, let $\mathcal{M}$ be the function taking as input a security-sensitive component $S_C = ((P, D, A, H, C), Tr', B)$ and returning a security-sensitive transition system $S = (V, Tr)$ as explained at the end of Example 3.2. Based on this observation, we show how to turn the monolithic synthesis methodology of Section 2.1 into a modular one.

Let $\mathcal{RM}$ be the function taking as input a security-sensitive transition system $S = (V, Tr)$ and returning a Datalog program $\mathcal{RM}(S)$ defining a predicate $can\_do(u, t)$ such that user u can execute task t and the workflow S can successfully terminate. We define the function $\mathcal{RM}_c$ that takes as input a security-sensitive component $S_C = ((P, D, A, H, C), Tr, B)$ as follows: $\mathcal{RM}_c(S_C) = \mathcal{RM}(\mathcal{M}(S_c))$, i.e. first it transforms the security-sensitive component into a security-sensitive

transition system and then applies the synthesis procedure of Section 2.1.

We now show how to reuse $\mathcal{RM}_c$ for the modular construction of run-time monitors for the WSP, i.e. we build a monitor for a composite component by combining those for their constituent components. Let $G = G_{EC} \cup G_{Auth}$ be a set of gluing assertions where G_{EC} is a set of inter execution constraints and G_{Auth} a set of always constraints over an interface (A, P^i, P^o, H^o, C^i), then $\langle G \rangle := \langle G_{EC} \rangle \cup \langle G_{Auth} \rangle$, where $\langle G_{EC} \rangle := \{p^i \leftarrow p^o | p^i \Leftrightarrow p^o \in G_{EC}\}$ and $\langle G_{Auth} \rangle := \{c^i(u) \leftarrow hst^i(u) | \forall u. c^i(u) \Leftrightarrow hst^i(u) \in G_{Auth}\}$. Intuitively, the shape of the Datalog clauses in $\langle G_{EC} \rangle$ models how the execution flow is transferred from a component (that with an output place) to the other (that with an input place), while $\langle G_{Auth} \rangle$ models how the execution of tasks in one component constrains the set of users who can execute tasks in another. Recall that, in Figures 4 and 6, the Datalog clauses in $\langle G_{EC} \rangle$ are shown as dashed red arrows and those in $\langle G_{Auth} \rangle$ as dashed blue lines.

Theorem 3.1. *Let* (S_k, Int_k) *be a security-sensitive component,* $S_k = ((P_k, D_k, A_k, H_k, C_k), Tr_k, B_k)$, $\mathcal{H}_k$ *is a set of (history) facts over* H_k, *and* $\mathcal{P}_k$ *a Datalog program (for the authorization policy) over* A_k, *for* $k = 1, 2$. *If* G *is a set of gluing assertions over* Int_1 *and* Int_2, *then* $\mathcal{RM}(S), \mathcal{H}_1, \mathcal{H}_2, \mathcal{P}_1, \mathcal{P}_2 \vdash can\_do(u, t)$ *iff* $\mathcal{RM}(S_1), \mathcal{H}_1, \mathcal{P}_1, \langle G \rangle, \mathcal{RM}(S_2), \mathcal{H}_2, \mathcal{P}_2 \vdash can\_do(u, t)$, *where* $(S, Int) = (S_1, Int_1) \oplus_G (S_2, Int_2)$.

The idea underlying the proof is that the monitors for the components are computed by considering all possible values for the variables in their interfaces. The additional constraints in the gluing assertions simply consider a sub-set of all these values by specifying how the execution flow goes from one component to the other and how the authorization constraints across components further constrain the possible executions of a component depending on which users have executed certain tasks in the other.

Theorem 3.1 supports action **UA2** in Section 2; additional applications are investigated in the section below.

4. APPLICATIONS

We have performed experiments focusing on two aspects: the scalability of the technique for the synthesis of run-time monitors for security-sensitive workflows (Section 4.1); and the design of a plug-in for the reuse of workflows and related run-time monitors inside an editor for security-sensitive workflows (Section 4.2).

4.1 Scalability

To show the practical scalability of our approach, we have performed a set of experiments with the random workflow generator from [4], which is capable of generating random security-sensitive workflows with an arbitrary number of tasks and composing them sequentially. For the experiments, we have generated components with a fixed size of 5 tasks and a varying number of constraints. The number of constraints is specified as a percentage (5%, 10% and 20%) of the number of tasks in each component for intra-component constraints and as a percentage of the total number of tasks for inter-component constraints[3]. Thus, in the configurations

---

[3]These configurations are taken from the experimental setup in [11], since the random generator was also based on the same work.

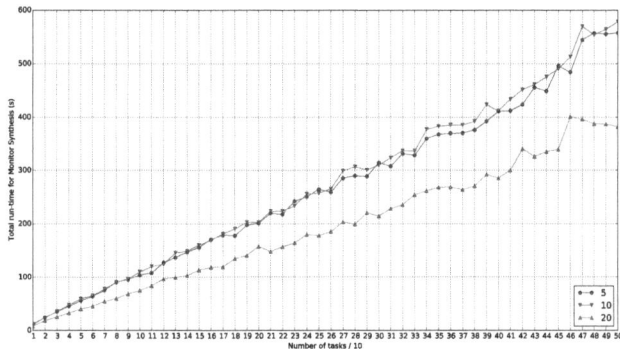

Figure 7: Time taken to synthesize a monitor varying with the number of tasks

5% and 10% there are no intra-component constraints, while in the configuration 20% there is one for each component; e.g., for a workflow with 100 tasks, there are 5 inter-component constraints in the configuration 5%, 10 in the configuration 10% and 20 in the configuration 20%. The experiments have been conducted on a MacBook Air 2014 with a 1.3GHz dual-core Intel Core i5 processor and 8GB of RAM running MAC OS X 10.10.2. The results are shown in Figure 7, in which the x-axis contains the total number of tasks in a workflow divided by 10 (the total number of components is the number in the x-axis times 2) and the y-axis shows the total time in seconds taken by the monitor synthesis procedure $\mathcal{RM}_c$ described above. Each data point is taken as the average of running $\mathcal{RM}_c$ 5 times for each configuration. Figure 7 suggests a linear (instead of the expected exponential!) behavior with respect to the number of tasks on this set of synthetic benchmarks. Indeed, without a modular approach the monitor synthesis technique is limited to only a few tasks, due to state space explosion.

We do not provide detailed timings for the on-line phase (i.e. how long does it take to answer authorization queries by the synthesized monitors) as these are under a second for workflows with (up to) 300 tasks and under 2 seconds for workflows (up to) 500 tasks. In case of multiple instances of the same workflows, we run a distinct (and independent) instance of the synthesized monitor; thus, the timings are similar to those of considering just one instance.

4.2 Reuse

It is possible to use the result of Theorem 3.1 to generate monitors for workflows specified as composed components and to reuse the monitor across different business processes (e.g., **UA3** in Section 2).

We have implemented the modular monitor synthesis technique as a tool composed of a single back-end developed in Python (ca. 3000 lines of code) and a series of front-ends which integrate with different BPM systems. The back-end takes as input specifications of modular workflows in the form of BPMN files (in XML), extended with support for authorization constraints. It derives a transition system for each component, the set of gluing assertions, and subsequently generates the corresponding run-time monitors, as described in Section 3.2. The front-end is responsible for calling the back-end and integrating with a workflow and monitor repository to store and retrieve the results of the back-end.

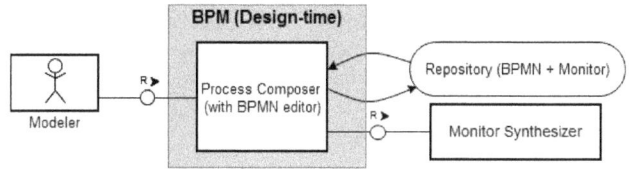

Figure 8: Architecture of a BPM design tool with a repository of models and monitors

To use the tool, process designers only have to input the graphical specification of the workflow and the constraints. The whole process of translating from BPMN to transition systems, applying the monitor synthesis procedure, storing, combining and retrieving monitors and workflows is automatic and happens behind the scenes. Thus, the tool does not require any knowledge besides BPMN modeling to be used.

The monitors that are stored in the repository are parametric wrt the user-task authorization relation, i.e. a synthesized monitor can accommodate several specifications of authorization policy (cf. Section 3.2). This allows secure enactment to be handled by simply composing together individual monitors.

An example front-end, integrated with the SAP HANA Workflow (HWF) engine was described in [6]. At design-time, execution constraints are modeled in BPMN and authorization constraints are input as part of the documentation of tasks, then HWF translates BPMN models into executable SQL procedures that are stored in the integrated HANA repository. The monitor synthesizer is invoked when a user calls the HWF compiler and it generates an SQL view[4] that is queried at run-time by the HWF execution engine. The monitor views are also stored in the HANA repository. Workflows and monitors can therefore be read from the repository and reused across deployments. At run-time, a synthesized monitor is invoked whenever a user tries to execute a task from the graphical user interface.

Our approach can be easily integrated into other existing BPM systems offering editors and repositories of business processes as outlined in the high-level architecture of Figure 8, where rectangles represent components, ovals represent storage systems, R-labeled links represent request/response communication between components and arrows represent access to storage. The *BPM* component represents existing solutions including a modeling environment for business processes, where the *Process Composer* sub-component contains a BPMN editor. The *Monitor Synthesizer* component implements the procedure described in Section 3.2 to compute (modular) monitors for workflow components and their composition modeled in the process composer. The *Repository* component represents a storage system for workflow models and synthesized monitors. Note that such repository may be part of the BPM solution or remotely located (e.g., Apromore [24]). The *modeler* interacts with the process composer with a request/response relation. The same relation exists between the process composer and the monitor synthesizer to request the synthesis of a run-time monitor for the BPMN model under specification. The process composer can store/retrieve BPMN models together with the synthesized

---

[4]Aggregation-free SQL and non-recursive Datalog are equivalent [1] and this translation is straightforward

monitors to/from the repository. The business process modeling and repository components in the proposed architecture are part of common reference architectures, e.g., [32].

5. CONCLUSIONS

The main contributions of the paper are (i) a modular approach to the synthesis of run-time monitors for (reusable) security-sensitive workflow components, (ii) the demonstration of the scalability of modular monitor synthesis by means of experiments, and (iii) a description of a tool integrating an editor with a repository of business processes (capable of storing run-time monitors) for business reuse. We regard these findings as the first significant step towards the development of efficient and practical enactment mechanisms for security-sensitive workflows, which go beyond the more theoretically oriented solutions to the WSP available in the literature.

5.1 Related and Future Work

Solutions to the WSP. Wang and Li [31] proposed a reduction of the WSP to SAT, which allows the use of off-the-shelf SAT solvers. The authors also showed that, with only equality and inequality relations, the WSP is fixed-parameter tractable (FPT) in the number of tasks. Later, Crampton et al. [10] improved the complexity bound for the WSP and extended the types of constraints for which it remains FPT. There are many works that take advantage of the FPT complexity result and design algorithms to solve the WSP with different kinds of constraints. The works in [8, 5] experimentally compare the results of FPT algorithms against those of a SAT solver on workflows of up to 30 tasks and conclude that FPT algorithms are better than those based on the SAT solver (the latter runs out of memory). [11] employs model checking on a fragment of LTL and experiments with workflows of up to 220 tasks.

On the practical side, our experiments show the scalability of our approach on workflows larger (up to 500 tasks) than those of the work above. On the theoretical side, the algorithms based on the use of SAT solving cannot cope with arbitrary authorization policies, while those based on FPT results must be invoked from scratch on "similar" instances of the WSP (a new instance is obtained from the previous one by asserting that a certain user has executed a given task at the previous step). Instead, our approach is capable of synthesizing a monitor for arbitrary authorization policies in the on-line phase and needs to keep track of which user has executed which tasks according to a given authorization policy at run-time, thereby significantly reducing the time to answer authorization requests, which—as pointed out in Section 4.1—remains under 2 seconds for workflows with 500 tasks. Even if algorithms based on SAT or FPT can be faster on smaller instances than our approach because the off-line phase requires to pre-compute all possible execution paths, our monitor synthesis approach offers the advantage of doing this just once and reuse the resulting monitors with arbitrary authorization policies while it is unclear (if possible at all) how this can be done with SAT- or FPT-based algorithms.

Resiliency. Workflow resiliency relates to the unavailability of users during the execution of a workflow instance. Mace et al. [17] discussed *quantitative* workflow resiliency, i.e. how likely a workflow is to terminate with an associated authorization policy and user availability model. Their solution uses Markov Decision Processes and exploits the off-line generation of an assignment tree, which shows all the possible executions of the workflow with different user assignments. The main difference between their assignment tree and our reachability graph is the fact that we use symbolic users, which allows us to accommodate different authorization policies at run-time. Crampton et al. [9] also considered a version of the problem called Valued WSP, where costs are associated to the violation of policies and constraints. A solution to the Valued WSP is an assignment of users to tasks with minimal cost and this problem was also shown to be FPT with user-independent constraints. It would be interesting to extend our approach to cope with resiliency or consider the costs of satisfying certain authorization constraints and synthesize risk-based monitors for the WSP. This is left as future work.

Modularity and reuse of workflow patterns. Reuse in Business Process Management has been an intense topic of research and industrial application; see, e.g., [14, 12]. Several works in the field of Petri nets have investigated modularity; see, e.g., [19]. None of these works addresses security issues as we do here. We observe that Theorem 3.1 may be used together with available techniques for decomposing large business processes; see, e.g., [23]. This would enable the synthesis of monitors that would be otherwise impossible to derive when considering monolithic processes because of the state-space explosion problem. Moreover, since workflows are built from basic control-flow patterns, see, e.g., [29, 15], a corollary of Theorem 3.1 is that it is possible to compute reachability graphs once for each basic security-sensitive workflow model, store the result, and modularly combine it with others along the lines of Section 3.2. In the following, we elaborate a bit on this idea according to which a workflow is seen as a combination of basic components (e.g., sequential, alternative and exclusive execution) that can be expressed by the gluing operator $\oplus$ introduced in Section 3.1.

For the sake of simplicity, we consider the *sequential, parallel*, and *alternative* composition of just two security-sensitive workflow components (S_1, Int_1) and (S_2, Int_2) (the generalization to n components is straightforward). We also assume that there is just one input and just one output place in both components (this is satisfied for the important class of workflow nets; see, e.g., [27]).

Sequential composition. It is sufficient to consider a set $G = G_{\text{EC}} \cup G_{\text{Auth}}$ of gluing assertions over Int_1 and Int_2 such that $G_{\text{EC}} = \{p_2^i \Leftrightarrow p_1^o\}$. Notice that $(S_1, Int_1) \oplus_G (S_2, Int_2) = (S_2, Int_2) \oplus_G (S_1, Int_1)$ but because the gluing assertion in G_{EC} is $p_2^i \Leftrightarrow p_1^o$, and not $p_2^o \Leftrightarrow p_1^i$, the process specified by component (S_1, Int_1) will always be executed before that specified by (S_2, Int_2).

Parallel composition. We need to preliminarily introduce two other components, each containing a single transition, one for splitting (and *s*plit) and one for joining (and *j*oin) the execution flow. The transitions are as follows:

$$Tr_{as} := \{p0_{as} \wedge \neg d_{as} \rightarrow p0_{as}, p1_{as}, p2_s, d_{as} := F, T, T, T\}$$
$$Tr_{aj} := \{q0_{aj} \wedge q1_{aj} \wedge \neg d_{aj} \rightarrow$$
$$q0_{aj}, q1_{aj}, q2_{aj}, d_{aj} := F, F, T, T\}$$

Then, it is sufficient to consider a set $G = G_{\text{EC}} \cup G_{\text{Auth}}$ of gluing assertions over Int_1, Int_2, Int_{as}, and Int_{aj} (recall that the gluing operator is associative) such that $G_{\text{EC}} = \{p1_{as} \Leftrightarrow p_1^i, p2_{as} \Leftrightarrow p_2^i, p_1^o \Leftrightarrow q0_{aj}, p_2^o \Leftrightarrow q1_{aj}\}$.

Alternative composition. Similarly to parallel composition, we need to introduce two other components, each containing two non-deterministic transitions (*or s*plit and *or* join) to route the execution flow in one of the two components (S_1, Int_1) or (S_2, Int_2). The transitions are

$$Tr_{os} \quad := \quad \left\{ \begin{array}{l} p0_{os} \wedge \neg d_{os} \rightarrow \\ \quad p0_{os}, p1_{os}, p2_s, d_{os} := F, T, F, T, \\ p0_{os} \wedge \neg d_{os} \rightarrow \\ \quad p0_{os}, p1_{os}, p2_s, d_{os} := F, F, T, T \end{array} \right\}$$

$$Tr_{oj} \quad := \quad \left\{ \begin{array}{l} q0_{oj} \wedge \neg d_{oj} \rightarrow q0_{oj}, q2_{oj}, d_{oj} := F, T, T, \\ q1_{oj} \wedge \neg d_{oj} \rightarrow q1_{oj}, q2_{oj}, d_{oj} := F, T, T \end{array} \right\}$$

Then, it is sufficient to consider a set $G = G_{EC} \cup G_{Auth}$ of gluing assertions over Int_1, Int_2, Int_{os}, and Int_{oj} such that $G_{EC} = \{p1_{os} \Leftrightarrow p_1^i, p2_{os} \Leftrightarrow p_2^i, p_1^o \Leftrightarrow q0_{oj}, p_2^o \Leftrightarrow q1_{oj}\}$.

Tool development. We plan to integrate our prototype with other front-ends and perform extensive experiments concerning modularity and reuse of business processes available in repositories and libraries, such as the SAP Business Process Repository.[5]

6. ACKNOWLEDGMENTS

The authors would like to thank the constructive criticisms of anonymous reviewers and Charles Morisset.

7. REFERENCES

[1] S. Abiteboul, R. Hull, and V. Vianu. *Foundations of Databases.* Addison-Wesley, Boston, 1995.

[2] A. Armando and S. E. Ponta. Model Checking of Security-sensitive Business Processes. In *Proc. of FAST*, 2009.

[3] D. Basin, S. J. Burri, and G. Karjoth. Dynamic enforcement of abstract separation of duty constraints. *TISSEC*, 15(3):13:1–13:30, Nov. 2012.

[4] C. Bertolissi, D. R. dos Santos, and S. Ranise. Automated synthesis of run-time monitors to enforce authorization policies in business processes. In *Proc. of ASIACCS*, 2015.

[5] D. Cohen, J. Crampton, A. V. Gagarin, G. Gutin, and M. Jones. Algorithms for the workflow satisfiability problem engineered for counting constraints. *CoRR*, abs/1504.02420, 2015.

[6] L. Compagna, D. R. dos Santos, S. E. Ponta, and S. Ranise. Cerberus: Automated synthesis of monitors for security-sensitive business processes. In *Proc. of TACAS*, 2016.

[7] J. Crampton. A reference monitor for workflow systems with constrained task execution. In *Proc. of SACMAT*, 2005.

[8] J. Crampton, A. V. Gagarin, G. Gutin, and M. Jones. On the workflow satisfiability problem with class-independent constraints. In *Proc. of IPEC*, 2015.

[9] J. Crampton, G. Gutin, and D. Karapetyan. Valued workflow satisfiability problem. In *Proc. of SACMAT*, 2015.

[10] J. Crampton, G. Gutin, and A. Yeo. On the parameterized complexity and kernelization of the workflow satisfiability problem. *TISSEC*, 16(1):4:1–4:31, June 2013.

[11] J. Crampton, M. Huth, and J. Kuo. Authorized workflow schemas: deciding realizability through LTL(F) model checking. *STTT*, 16(1):31–48, 2014.

[12] J. de Freitas. Model business processes for flexibility and re-use: A component-oriented approach. Technical report, IBM, 2009.

[13] D. R. dos Santos, S. Ranise, and S. E. Ponta. Modularity for Security-Sensitive Workflows. Technical report, arXiv, 2015. Available at http://arxiv.org/abs/1507.07479.

[14] A. Koschmider, M. Fellmann, A. Schoknecht, and A. Oberweis. Analysis of process model reuse: Where are we now, where should we go from here? *Decision Support Systems*, 66(0):9–19, 2014.

[15] C. Leuxner, W. Sitou, and B. Spanfelner. A formal model for work flows. In *Proc. of SEFM*, 2010.

[16] N. Li and J. C. Mitchell. Datalog with constraints: a foundation for trust management languages. In *Proc. of PADL*, 2003.

[17] J. C. Mace, C. Morisset, and A. Moorsel. Quantitative workflow resiliency. In *Proc. of ESORICS*, 2014.

[18] I. Markovic and A. C. Pereira. Towards a formal framework for reuse in business process modeling. In *Proc. of BPM*, 2008.

[19] O. Oanea. *Verification of Soundness and Other Properties of Business Processes.* PhD thesis, TU Eindhoven, 2007.

[20] OMG. Business Process Model and Notation, v2.0. Technical report, Object Management Group, 2011.

[21] H. Reijers and J. Mendling. Modularity in process models: Review and effects. In *Proc. of BPM*, 2008.

[22] H. Reijers, J. Mendling, and R. Dijkman. On the usefulness of subprocesses in business process models. Technical report, BPM Center, 2010.

[23] H. Reijers, J. Mendling, and R. Dijkman. Human and automatic modularizations of process models to enhance their comprehension. *Inf. Syst.*, 36(5):881 – 897, 2011.

[24] M. L. Rosa, H. Reijers, W. van der Aalst, R. Dijkman, J. Mendling, M. Dumas, and L. Garca-Banuelos. Apromore: An advanced process model repository. *Expert Syst. Appl.*, 38(6):7029–7040, 2011.

[25] R. Sandhu, E. Coyne, H. Feinstein, and C. Youmann. Role-Based Access Control Models. *IEEE Computer*, 2(29):38–47, 1996.

[26] A. U. Shankar. An Introduction to Assertional Reasoning for Concurrent Systems. *ACM Comput. Surv.*, 25(3):225–262, Sept. 1993.

[27] W. van der Aalst. Workflow verification: Finding control-flow errors using petri-net-based techniques. In *Proc. of BPM*, 2000.

[28] W. van der Aalst and A. ter Hofstede. Yawl: Yet another workflow language. *Inf. Syst.*, 30:245–275, 2003.

[29] W. van der Aalst, A. ter Hofstede, B. Kiepuszewski, and A. Barros. Workflow patterns. *Distrib. Parallel Databases*, 14(1):5–51, July 2003.

[30] J. Wainer, A. Kumar, and P. Barthelmess. Dw-rbac: A formal security model of delegation and revocation in workflow systems. *Inf. Syst.*, 32(3):365–384, May 2007.

[31] Q. Wang and N. Li. Satisfiability and resiliency in workflow authorization systems. *TISSEC*, 13:40:1–40:35, December 2010.

[32] M. Weske. *Business Process Management: Concepts, Languages, Architectures.* Springer, Secaucus, 2007.

---

[5] https://implementationcontent.sap.com/bpr

Resiliency Policies in Access Control Revisited

Jason Crampton
Royal Holloway
University of London
Egham, TW20 9QY
United Kingdom
jason.crampton@rhul.ac.uk

Gregory Gutin
Royal Holloway
University of London
Egham, TW20 9QY
United Kingdom
gutin@cs.rhul.ac.uk

Rémi Watrigant
Royal Holloway
University of London
Egham, TW20 9QY
United Kingdom
remi.watrigant@rhul.ac.uk

ABSTRACT

Resiliency is a relatively new topic in the context of access control. Informally, it refers to the extent to which a multi-user computer system, subject to an authorization policy, is able to continue functioning if a number of authorized users are unavailable. Several interesting problems connected to resiliency were introduced by Li, Wang and Tripunitara [13], many of which were found to be intractable. In this paper, we show that these resiliency problems have unexpected connections with the workflow satisfiability problem (WSP). In particular, we show that an instance of the resiliency checking problem (RCP) may be reduced to an instance of WSP. We then demonstrate that recent advances in our understanding of WSP enable us to develop fixed-parameter tractable algorithms for RCP. Moreover, these algorithms are likely to be useful in practice, given recent experimental work demonstrating the advantages of bespoke algorithms to solve WSP. We also generalize RCP in several different ways, showing in each case how to adapt the reduction to WSP. Li *et al.* also showed that the coexistence of resiliency policies and static separation-of-duty policies gives rise to further interesting questions. We show how our reduction of RCP to WSP may be extended to solve these problems as well and establish that they are also fixed-parameter tractable.

CCS Concepts

•**Security and privacy** → **Access control**; *Security requirements;* •**Theory of computation** → **Fixed parameter tractability**;

Keywords

access control; resiliency; workflow satisfiability; computational complexity; fixed-parameter tractability

SACMAT'16, June 05-08, 2016, Shanghai, China
© 2016 ACM. ISBN 978-1-4503-3802-8/16/06. . . $15.00
DOI: http://dx.doi.org/10.1145/2914642.2914650

1. INTRODUCTION

Access control is a fundamental aspect of the security of any multi-user computing system, and is typically based on the idea of specifying and enforcing an authorization policy. Such a policy identifies which interactions between users and resources are to be allowed by the system.

Over the last twenty years, authorization policies have become more complex, not least because of the introduction of constraints, which further refine an authorization policy. A separation-of-duty constraint (also known as the "two-man rule" or "four-eyes policy") may, for example, require that no single user is authorized for some particularly sensitive group of resources. Such a constraint is typically used to prevent misuse of the system by a single user.

In the context of workflow systems, such constraints may mean that it is impossible to complete all the steps in a workflow, while simultaneously ensuring that each step is executed by an authorized user and all constraints are satisfied. Hence, there has been considerable interest in analyzing workflow specifications to determine whether they are "satisfiable" or not [3, 4, 9, 11, 15]. Here, the intent of the analysis is to confirm that a system satisfies functional or operational requirements, in the presence of security policies and constraints.

More recently, we have seen the introduction of *resiliency policies*, whose satisfaction indicates a system will continue to function as intended in the absence of some number of authorized users [13, 15]. The purpose of specifying such policies is again to determine whether or not a system satisfies certain operational requirements. Li, Wang and Tripunitara's seminal work on resiliency in access control [13] introduces a number of problems associated with the simultaneous satisfaction of separation-of-duty constraints and resiliency policies. They established that many of these problems were intractable, although certain special cases did admit polynomial-time algorithms. It is these problems that are the focus of this paper.

One interesting aspect of the work by Li *et al.* is the relative sizes of the parameters. In particular, it may be assumed for practical purposes that certain parameters are significantly smaller than others. With this in mind, we exploit the theory of fixed-parameter tractability to investigate the problems introduced by Li *et al.* [13]. Informally, we develop algorithms whose running time is polynomial in the large parameters but may be exponential in the small parameters. Such algorithms can be very useful, particularly if the assumptions underlying the relative sizes of the parameters hold in practice.

The fundamental contribution of this paper is to exhibit a polynomial-time construction to transform an instance of the resiliency checking problem (RCP) to an instance of the workflow satisfiability problem (WSP). Recent advances in the understanding of WSP enable us to characterize the complexity of RCP, in order to obtain efficient algorithms. Moreover, we are able to exploit particular characteristics of the WSP instances obtained from RCP to specialize existing algorithms for solving WSP. In particular:

- we establish that RCP is fixed-parameter tractable for parameters which are likely to take small values in practice;

- we adapt the *Pattern Backtracking* algorithm for WSP [3] to solve transformed instances of RCP;

- we generalize RCP to model additional situations that may be of practical interest, and establish that the reduction to WSP also holds in these cases.

We then consider several problems arising from the interaction of resiliency policies and static separation-of-duty policies. We use a similar reduction to the workflow satisfiability problem to establish that these problems are also fixed-parameter tractable.

In the next section, we introduce relevant concepts from the literature, including resiliency policies, WSP and fixed-parameter tractability. In Section 3, we show how to reduce RCP to WSP, and adapt a known algorithm in order to obtain a better running time. We also consider several generalizations of the problem which are likely to be of practical interest. In Section 4, we extend our approach to find a fixed-parameter tractable algorithm for the policy consistency checking problem. In doing so, we introduce a simpler variant of this problem, called the *mixed policy checking problem*, that is of independent interest. We conclude the paper with a summary of our contributions and some suggestions for future work.

Due to the page limits, the proofs of Theorem 2 and Lemma 2 are given in the appendix.

2. BACKGROUND

In this section, we recall relevant material on resiliency policies, workflow satisfiability and fixed-parameter tractability. We assume there exists a set of resources R, access to which must be controlled, by specifying and enforcing authorization policies for a set of users U. These resources may, for example, be data objects, permissions (typically modeled as an object-action pair, as in RBAC96 [14]), or steps in a workflow [2]. We follow existing work on resiliency policies by assuming an authorization policy is specified as a user-resource relation $UR \subseteq U \times R$, where $(u, r) \in UR$ means that user u is authorized to access resource r.[1]

For a user $u \in U$, we write $N(u)$ to denote $\{r \in R : (u, r) \in UR\}$; that is, $N(u)$ is the set of resources for which u is authorized, and is called the *neighborhood*[2] of u. We extend this notation so that $N(V)$, for any $V \subseteq U$, denotes $\bigcup_{u \in V} N(u)$; that is, $N(V)$, called the *neighborhood*

of V, is the set of resources for which users in V, collectively, are authorized. For any integer $q \in \mathbb{N}$, we will write $[q]$ to denote $\{1, \ldots, q\}$.

2.1 Resiliency policies

Informally, resiliency in the context of access control is related to fault tolerance. It refers to the ability of a multi-user system, governed by some access policy, to continue functioning if authorized users are unavailable. In order to formalize the notion of resiliency and to study its properties, Li, Wang and Tripunitara [13] introduce the concept of a *resiliency policy*, which has the form $\mathsf{res}(P, s, d, t)$, where P is a subset of R, and s, d and t are integers such that $s \geqslant 0$, $d \geqslant 1$ and $t \geqslant 1$. The satisfaction of policy $\mathsf{res}(P, s, d, t)$ is determined in the context of a user-resource authorization relation UR.

DEFINITION 1. *An authorization relation UR satisfies $\mathsf{res}(P, s, d, t)$ if and only if upon removal of any set of s users, there exist d mutually disjoint sets of users $V_1, \ldots, V_d$ such that $N(V_i) \supseteq P$ and $|V_i| \leqslant t$. We call such a set $\{V_1, \ldots, V_d\}$ a solution/set of teams.*

Informally, the resiliency policy $\mathsf{res}(P, s, d, t)$ specifies a requirement that the access control state UR should be able to tolerate the absence of at most s users and still have sufficient users authorized for some critical task (associated with the resources in P). In the most general version, the critical task requires d teams of users, each of size at most t, such that each team independently has all authorizations for resources in P. Li *et al.* then define the following decision problem [13, Definition 2].

DEFINITION 2. *Given a user-resource relation UR and a resiliency policy $\mathsf{res}(P, s, d, t)$, the RESILIENCY CHECKING PROBLEM (RCP) asks whether UR satisfies $\mathsf{res}(P, s, d, t)$.*

Li *et al.* introduce bracket notation $\mathrm{RCP}\langle\rangle$ to denote some restrictions of the problem, in which one or more parameters (among s, d and t) are fixed: s and d can respectively be set to 0 and/or 1 (or other fixed positive values), while t can be set to infinity (∞), meaning that there is no constraint on the size of the sets. Note that setting $t = \infty$ is equivalent to setting $t = |P|$, as the size of any suitable team contains at most $|P|$ authorized users. Henceforth, we write p to denote $|P|$.

As Li *et al.* [13] point out, $\mathrm{RCP}\langle\rangle$ and its special cases are connected to several well-known combinatorial problems such as the SET COVER and DOMATIC PARTITION problems. They were thus able to establish several, mainly negative, results concerning the computational complexity of $\mathrm{RCP}\langle\rangle$, summarized by the following result [13, Theorem 1].

THEOREM 1. *We have the following:*

- $\mathrm{RCP}\langle\rangle$, $\mathrm{RCP}\langle d = 1\rangle$ *and* $\mathrm{RCP}\langle t = \infty\rangle$ *are NP-hard and are in* $\mathrm{coNP^{NP}}$.

- $\mathrm{RCP}\langle s = 0, d = 1\rangle$, $\mathrm{RCP}\langle s = 0, t = \infty\rangle$ *and* $\mathrm{RCP}\langle s = 0\rangle$ *are NP-complete.*

- $\mathrm{RCP}\langle d = 1, t = \infty\rangle$ *can be solved in linear time.*

In practice, it seems reasonable to assume that s will be much smaller than the total number of users. This amounts

---

[1]Clearly, more complex policies may be specified, but invariably such policies may be reduced to such a relation in polynomial time.

[2]We use the term neighborhood as we view UR as a bipartite graph; this view may help the reader, too.

to saying that at any given time only a very small percentage of users will be unavailable. Similarly, in many settings, it seems reasonable to assume that d will also be much smaller than the total number of users. Indeed, in many settings, the case $d = 1$ will be the only one of interest.

Given the relative sizes of the parameters, in particular the sharp disparity between the number of users and the other parameters, it is worth investigating the extent to which the complexity of $\text{RCP}\langle\rangle$ is influenced by each of the parameters. For this reason, we will analyze $\text{RCP}\langle\rangle$ using the techniques from parameterized complexity, also called multivariate complexity analysis [7].

2.2 Workflow satisfiability

A workflow is a collection of steps that must be executed by some users in order to achieve an objective. The order in which those steps should be executed is usually given, as well as constraints and authorization policies, restricting the users that can be assigned to steps [2, 15].

More formally, a *workflow specification* is defined by a directed, acyclic graph $G = (S, E)$, where S is a set of steps and $E \subseteq S \times S$. Given a workflow specification (S, E) and a set of users U, an *authorization policy* for a workflow specification is a relation $A \subseteq S \times U$; we say user u is *authorized* to perform step t if $(t, u) \in A$. A *workflow constraint* has the form (T, Θ), where $T \subseteq S$ and Θ is a family of functions with domain T and range U; we say T is the *scope* of the constraint (T, Θ). (Informally, Θ defines the set of authorized mappings from steps in T to users in U. Generally speaking, the elements of Θ are not explicitly enumerated; we discuss this in more detail below.) Then a *constrained workflow authorization schema* is a pair $((S, E), U, A, C)$, where (S, E) is a workflow specification, U is a set of users, A is an authorization policy, and C is a set of workflow constraints.

Once a constrained workflow authorization schema has been defined, the goal is to assign a user to each step, so that all constraints and the authorization policy are satisfied. More formally, a (partial) *plan* is a function $\pi : T \to U$, where $T \subseteq S$. A plan π is *complete* if $T = S$. Given a plan $\pi : T \to U$ and $T' \subseteq T$, we write $\pi|_{T'} : T' \to U$ to denote the plan such that $\pi|_{T'}(t) = \pi(t)$ for all $t \in T'$. We say a plan $\pi : S' \to U$ *satisfies* a workflow constraint (T, Θ) if $T \nsubseteq S'$ or $\pi|_T \in \Theta$. (Informally, if the range of π includes the scope of a constraint, then the restriction of π to T must be one of the authorized mappings.) Finally, we say a plan $\pi : S \to U$ is *valid* if it satisfies every constraint in C and, for all $t \in S$, $(t, \pi(t)) \in A$. The combination of authorization policy and constraints may mean that no valid plan exists, motivating the following problem.

DEFINITION 3. *Given a constrained workflow authorization schema* $W = ((S, E), U, A, C)$, *the* WORKFLOW SATISFIABILITY PROBLEM *(WSP) asks whether there exists a valid plan for* W.

In practice, we do not define constraints by enumerating all possible elements of Θ. Instead, we define different families of constraints that have "compact" descriptions. For instance, two simple constraints we will use in this paper are the atleast and atmost constraints. Both have two arguments: the scope $P \subseteq S$ to which they apply, and an integer $\ell \leq |U|$. Then, a plan $\pi : S \to U$ satisfies atleast(P, ℓ) (resp. atmost(P, ℓ)) if and only if $|\pi(P)| \geq \ell$ (resp. $|\pi(P)| \leq \ell$),

that is, if the steps in P are assigned to at least (resp. at most) ℓ users.

There now exists a substantial body of work on constraints in workflow systems, beginning with the seminal work of Bertino, Ferrari and Atluri [2]. In particular, separation/binding of duty constraints and cardinality constraints are recognized as being important and have been widely studied. Informally, atleast constraints generalize separation of duty constraints, and are analogous to the ssod constraints studied by Li *et al.* [13], while atmost constraints generalize binding-of-duty constraints. In particular, atleast$(\{t, t'\}, 2)$ requires that steps t and t' are performed by separate users, while atmost$(\{t, t'\}, 1)$ requires that steps t and t' are performed by the same user.

User-independent constraints generalize all these forms of constraints [3]. Informally, such a constraint limits the execution of steps in a workflow, but is indifferent to the particular users that execute the steps. More formally, a constraint (T, Θ) is user-independent if whenever $\theta \in \Theta$ and $\psi : U \to U$ is a permutation then $\psi \circ \theta \in \Theta$ (where $\circ$ denotes function composition). A separation of duty constraint, on two steps for example, simply requires that two *different* users execute the steps, not that, say, Alice and Bob must execute them. Similarly, a binding of duty constraint on two steps only requires that the *same* user executes the steps. More generally, atleast and atmost constraints are user-independent. It appears most constraints that are useful in practice are user-independent: all constraints defined in the ANSI-RBAC standard [1], for example, are user-independent.

2.3 Fixed-parameter tractability

It is generally assumed that no polynomial-time algorithm exists to solve an NP-hard decision problem. In other words, the running-time of any algorithm for solving such a problem is exponential in the size of the input to the problem. However, many decision problems have multiple parameters and the relative magnitude of the values taken by those parameters might be quite different in most, if not all, conceivable practical instances of the problem. Hence, it is worth considering whether there are algorithms whose running-time is exponential in the parameters expected to take small values (and polynomial in the size of the input). It is this approach we will adopt in the study of this paper.

Formally, we say that a decision problem is *fixed-parameter tractable* (FPT) if there exists an algorithm that decides if an instance is positive in $O(f(k)p(n)) = O^*(f(k))$ time[3] for some computable function f and some polynomial p, where n denotes the size of an instance, and is k a parameter (or a combination of several parameters) of the instance. Accordingly, we will call such an algorithm an *FPT algorithm*. Multivariate analysis of the complexity of a problem may identify an FPT algorithm whose running time is exponential in specific parameters that are known to be small in practice, leading to the development of efficient algorithms for problem instances of practical interest. For more details about parameterized complexity, we refer the reader to the monograph of Downey and Fellows [7].

In the particular case of WSP, a naive algorithm to solve the problem considers every possible plan in turn. Assum-

---

[3]We will follow the convention adopted in the literature on FPT algorithms [7] by using the $O^*(.)$ notation, which omits polynomial terms and factors.

ing we can test whether a plan is valid in time polynomial in $n = |U|$ and $k = |S|$, the algorithm has running time $O^*(n^k)$. Wang and Li [15] were the first to observe that the number of users n is typically an order of magnitude larger than the number of steps k. They used this observation to show that WSP is FPT when k is the parameter and all constraints are separation-of-duty or binding-of-duty constraints [15]. Recent work has significantly extended Wang and Li's results, in terms of the running times for FPT algorithms and the range of constraints that can be included in the workflow specification. The most powerful theoretical results relate to user-independent constraints [3] and extensive experimental work has shown that implementations of the resulting FPT algorithms have practical value [3, 11].

3. THE RESILIENCY CHECKING PROBLEM

We first argue that the main interest in designing efficient algorithms for RCP⟨⟩, either from the practical or theoretical point of view, lies in the case where $s = 0$. Notice that all the following ideas also apply to the variant RCP⟨$t = \infty$⟩ (mainly because, as we saw previously, we may assume that $t = p$).

We first review the method used by Li *et al.* [13] to solve RCP⟨⟩ (and RCP⟨$t = \infty$⟩). Given a resiliency policy $\mathsf{res}(P, s, d, t)$ and a relation UR, their initial idea is to enumerate all subsets of at most s users, and, for each such subset V, to test whether the resiliency policy $\mathsf{res}(P, 0, d, t)$ is satisfied by the instance obtained by removing the users in V from U (and deleting the corresponding elements from UR accordingly). Then, using a domination argument, they observe that the exhaustive enumeration of all such subsets can be avoided, and define two kinds of pruning strategies. The satisfaction of the resulting instance (in which $s = 0$) is then determined by translating the problem into a SAT instance and using SAT4J, an off-the-shelf SAT solver, to solve it. In their experiments, they observe that their *static pruning* strategy is quite efficient, and that the bottleneck of their algorithm seems to be the satisfiability test for the $\mathsf{res}(P, 0, d, t)$ policy on the reduced instance. From this observation, it makes sense to focus on the resolution of RCP⟨$s = 0$⟩ only.

Another argument for this approach is the parameterized complexity of RCP⟨⟩. As we mentioned earlier, it makes sense to analyse the performance of our algorithms for RCP⟨⟩ and its variants using parameters such as $p = |P|$, s, d and t. The following result asserts that RCP⟨⟩ can be tackled by solving $2^{s \log(dt)}$ instances of RCP⟨$s = 0$⟩.[4] This result will let us focus on the development of an efficient algorithm for RCP⟨$s = 0$⟩, and more precisely of a fixed-parameter tractable algorithm parameterized by (p, d) (Theorem 3). Combining these two results, we will be able to show that RCP⟨⟩ is itself fixed-parameter tractable parameterized by (p, s, d, t).

THEOREM 2. *Suppose that there is an algorithm for* RCP⟨$s = 0$⟩ *which returns a set of teams in case of a satisfiable instance (and answers no in case of an unsatisfiable one) in time $O^*(f(p, d, t))$ for some computable function f. Then* RCP⟨⟩ *can be solved in $O^*(2^{s \log(dt)} f(p, d, t))$ time.*

---

[4] All logarithms used in this paper are in base 2, unless otherwise stated.

In summary, using RCP⟨$s = 0$⟩ as a black box for solving the more general case makes sense both from a practical and theoretical point of view. In the remainder of this section, we thus focus on RCP⟨$s = 0$⟩ only, and show how the workflow satisfiability problem can be used to solve the problem as well as several generalizations of it which might be of practical interest.

3.1 RCP as a workflow satisfiability problem

We first discuss how an instance of RCP⟨$s = 0$⟩ may be transformed into an instance of WSP with user-independent constraints. We then show that it is possible to define several interesting generalizations of RCP⟨⟩ and to use a similar transformation to WSP to solve these problems.

3.1.1 Reduction

The intuition behind our reduction from RCP⟨⟩ to WSP lies in the observation that RCP⟨⟩ asks for a mapping from d copies of a resource to d different authorized users, while WSP asks whether there exists a mapping from steps to authorized users, subject to some constraints. Hence, we translate the set of resources in RCP⟨⟩ into an appropriate set of steps and the constraints imposed on the structure of the teams by a resiliency policy to user-independent workflow constraints.

CONSTRUCTION 1. *Given $UR \subseteq U \times R$ and $\mathsf{res}(P, 0, d, t)$ with $P \subseteq R$, we construct a constrained workflow authorization scheme W in which $E = \emptyset$ and S comprises d copies of P. We write these distinct sets as $P^1, \dots, P^d$ and, for $r \in P$, we write r^i to denote the copy of r in set P^i. Then we define:*

$$A = \bigcup_{i=1}^{d} \{(u, r^i) : (u, r) \in UR\};$$

$$C = \{\mathsf{atleast}(\{r^i, s^j\}, 2) : r, s \in P, 1 \le i < j \le d\} \cup$$
$$\{\mathsf{atmost}(P^i, t) : i \in [d]\}.$$

LEMMA 1. $\mathsf{res}(P, 0, d, t)$ *is satisfied by UR if and only if W is satisfiable.*

PROOF. Suppose that UR satisfies $\mathsf{res}(P, 0, d, t)$, *i.e.* there exists a set of teams $\{V_1, \dots, V_d\}$. Since $N(V_i) \supseteq P$ for all $i \in [d]$, and since all teams are pairwise disjoint, for every $r \in P$ there exists $(u_1^r, \dots, u_d^r) \in V_1 \times \dots \times V_d$ such that $(u_i, r) \in UR$ for all $i \in [d]$. By definition of A, observe that we can construct a plan $\pi : P^1 \cup \dots \cup P^d \to U$, by setting, for all $i \in [d]$ and all $r \in P^i$, $\pi(r) = u_i^{r^i}$. This plan will not violate any $\mathsf{atleast}$ constraint by definition, and will not violate any atmost constraint since $|V_i| \le t$ for all $i \in [d]$.

Conversely, suppose that W is satisfiable, *i.e.* there exists a valid plan $\pi : P^1 \cup \dots \cup P^d \to U$. For all $i \in [d]$, we define $\pi_i : P^i \to U$ by $\pi_i(r) = \pi(r)$ for all $r \in P^i$, and let $V_i = \pi_i(P^i)$. Since π is a valid plan, the atmost constraints ensure that $|V_i| \le t$ while the $\mathsf{atleast}$ constraints ensure that all V_i are pairwise disjoint. Finally, by construction we have $N(V_i) \supseteq P$, which proves that $\mathsf{res}(P, 0, d, t)$ is satisfied. $\square$

Note that if $d = 1$ (meaning we require a single team of authorized users), then we have a simple instance of WSP, where the set of steps corresponds exactly to P. Note also that if $t = \infty$ (or indeed $t = p$), then we do not require any atmost constraints.

3.1.2 Algorithm

There has been a considerable amount of research into FPT algorithms for WSP in recent years. In particular, recent work by Cohen *et al.* [3] and Karapetyan *et al.* [11] has led to optimized and demonstrably efficient algorithms for WSP (in the case that k is considerably smaller than n).

The instances of WSP obtained from instances of $\text{RCP}\langle\rangle$ have a particular form, because of the specific constraints a resiliency policy imposes. In this section, we improve the running-time $O^*(2^{k\log(k)}) = O^*(2^{dp\log(dp)})$ of the Pattern Backtracking algorithm [11], exploiting the particular nature of the WSP instances obtained from $\text{RCP}\langle\rangle$.

THEOREM 3. $\text{RCP}\langle s = 0\rangle$ *can be solved in* $O^*(2^{dp\log(p)})$.

PROOF. As described in Construction 1, we are given a set S of steps composed of d pairwise disjoint sets $P^1, \ldots, P^d$, each containing p steps, an authorization policy A, and a set of atleast and atmost constraints. In particular, the scope of each atleast constraint lies in two different sets P^i and P^j, while the scope of each atmost constraint lies in a unique set P^i.

Given a plan $\pi : S' \to U$, where $S' \subseteq S$, the *pattern* $Pat(\pi)$ of π is the partition $\{\pi^{-1}(u) : u \in U, \ \pi^{-1}(u) \neq \emptyset\}$ of S' into non-empty sets. We say that two plans π and π' are *equivalent* if they have the same pattern. A pattern is said to be *complete* if $S' = S$. We say that a pattern $T = \{V_1, \ldots, V_{|T|}\}$ is *valid* if there exists a valid plan $\pi : S \to U$ such that $Pat(\pi) = T$. Observe that given a pattern $T = \{V_1, \ldots, V_{|T|}\}$ of S, we can, in polynomial time, decide whether it is valid pattern, and to find in that case a valid plan, by finding a perfect matching in an appropriate bipartite graph (namely, with partite sets $\{1, \ldots, |T|\}$ and U, and an edge between $i \in \{1, \ldots, |T|\}$ and $u \in U$ whenever there exists $r \in V_i$ such that $(u, r) \in A$). Hence, the algorithm is a procedure for finding a valid pattern.

A naive upper bound on the number of all possible patterns of S is the number of all partitions of S into non-empty sets; that is, the $|S|$-th Bell number, $B_{|S|} = O(2^{dp\log(dp)})$. However, it can be seen that in our case, any pattern T containing V such that $V \cap P^i \neq \emptyset$ and $V \cap P^j \neq \emptyset$ for $i \neq j$, cannot be valid, as otherwise it would violate at least one atleast constraint. Thus, the number of valid patterns can actually be reduced to $(B_p)^d = O(2^{dp\log(p)})$, which proves the claimed running time. $\square$

Combining Theorems 2 and 3, we obtain the following result:

THEOREM 4. $\text{RCP}\langle\rangle$ *(and* $\text{RCP}\langle t = \infty\rangle$*) is fixed-parameter tractable parameterized by* (p, s, d, t).

3.1.3 Discussion

The Pattern Backtracking algorithm for WSP has obtained good results in practice [11]. The experiments conducted by Karapetyan *et al.* used values of k between 10 and 65, together with varying numbers of (atleast and atmost) constraints, and defined $n = 10k$. The performance of the Pattern Backtracking algorithm was compared to that of SAT4J, a state-of-the-art off-the-shelf SAT solver, running on WSP instances transformed into pseudo-Boolean SAT instances [11, 15]. The Pattern Backtracking algorithm was able to solve all WSP instances containing less than 60 steps, in contrast to the SAT solver, which was rarely able to find solutions for instances containing more than 25 steps.

The small parameter in WSP is the number k of workflow steps and in the reduction from $\text{RCP}\langle\rangle$ to WSP, the number of workflow steps is dp. The running-time of our algorithm is exponential in $dp\log p$, so we require this parameter to be relatively small for this reduction to be of practical use. In the case $d = 1$, we expect to solve instances of RCP in which P is relatively large (up to 60). If $d > 1$, we will obviously need a corresponding reduction in the size of p.

Hence, we believe that our reduction to WSP and use of the Pattern Backtracking algorithm is of practical value, and will signicantly extend the size of the RCP instances that can currently be solved [13]. With the above observations in mind, we recall the experimental results presented by Li *et al.* [13, Figure 3]. In their experiments, the parameters $s = 3$ and $p = 10$ were fixed, while d varied between 2 and 7, and n varied between 40 and 100. Their approach involved two steps: the first reduced an instance of $\text{RCP}\langle s = 3\rangle$ to multiple instances of $\text{RCP}\langle s = 0\rangle$; the second solved the instance of $\text{RCP}\langle s = 0\rangle$ by translating it to an instance of SAT and solving the SAT instance using SAT4J. The static pruning technique used to perform the first step meant that SAT4J had to solve approximately the same number of instances of RCP for a given value of s (independent of the number of users n) [13, Table I]. This means, that the difference in running times on instances of $\text{RCP}\langle s = 3\rangle$ for a given n is largely determined by d (since p is fixed). Li *et al.* noted that the performance of the SAT solver (on instances of $\text{RCP}\langle s = 0\rangle$) began to degrade significantly as d increased, and do not report results for d larger than 7. We believe that using the Pattern Backtracking algorithm in step two would mean that far larger instances of RCP could be solved. In particular, we could significantly increase the number of users (up to several hundred). Moreover, we could solve a wider range of instances: we could, for example, solve instances in which $d > 7$, provided there was a corresponding reduction in p.

Our multivariate analysis of RCP suggests that instances of $\text{RCP}\langle s = 0\rangle$ can be solved in a reasonable amount of time, provided $dp\log p$ is relatively small. Moreover, as we will see in the next section, our approach to solving RCP is rather flexible, in the sense that we can impose additional requirements on the solution to RCP and, with very simple modifications to Construction 1, translate the problem to an instance of WSP. This is unlikely to be the case for the methods used by Li *et al.* to solve RCP, which involved creating a specific SAT encoding for RCP and the use of a SAT solver; different versions of RCP will require new encodings.

3.2 Generalizing resiliency policies

We now describe how the model of resiliency of Li *et al.* [13] can be generalized in order to capture some other situations that might occur in practice. For each of these cases, we demonstrate that a simple adaptation of Construction 1 enables us to model the problem as an instance of WSP: generally speaking, it is simply a matter of adjusting the set of constraints. As we saw in the beginning of Section 3, it makes sense to focus on the problem of testing the satisfaction of the given property only (the case $s = 0$), rather than its "resiliency" part. That is why only this subcase will be considered in the following sub-sections.

3.2.1 Adding counting constraints

The original definition of a resiliency policy imposes constraints on the composition of the teams, by insisting on disjointness and that each team has at most t users. It is debatable whether disjointness is a property that would be important in practice, and we relax this assumption in Section 3.2.2. However, we first consider, two, perhaps more obvious, constraints on the composition of the teams, and show that we can modify Construction 1 to produce an instance of WSP.

First, we might consider imposing another "local" constraint on team composition, requiring that at least ℓ users belong to each team. Such a requirement might be imposed in the interests of separation of duty or to ensure a reasonably fair division of labor. In particular, we might set $\ell = t$, in which case every team would have exactly t users. Of course, in the context of Construction 1, this simply means including the following (additional) constraints:

$$\left\{ \mathsf{atleast}(P^i, \ell) : i \in [d] \right\}.$$

A further possibility is to impose different constraints on the size of each team. (This simply requires a different value ℓ_i to be associated with each P^i in the atleast constraints.)

Second, we might consider imposing "global" constraints. The effect of insisting that each team has at most t users is that the total number of users is no greater than dt. However, we may wish to impose a global upper bound $L_{\max}$ (less than dt) on the total number of users in the d teams. We can achieve this simply including the constraint $\mathsf{atmost}(S, L_{\max})$ in the WSP formulation. Similarly, we can impose a global lower bound $L_{\min}$ on the total number of users, which we can achieve by including the constraint $\mathsf{atleast}(S, L_{\min})$ in the WSP formulation.

The most important observation to make here is that all of these constraints on team composition are *user-independent* constraints in the WSP instance.

3.2.2 Allowing team overlaps

In their definition of $\mathsf{res}(P, s, d, t)$, Li *et al.* [13] insist on the disjointness of the d teams. We may relax this condition and consider the possibility of allowing teams to overlap. (In the context of workflow systems, this would mean that a user could participate in the execution of more than one workflow instance.) Hence, we introduce an extended form of resiliency policy $\mathsf{xres}(P, s, d, d', t)$, with $d' \leqslant d$. Such a policy is satisfied if, for all subsets V of size s in U, there exist d sets $V_1, \ldots, V_d$ of users such that for all $i \in [d]$ and all $u \in U$: (i) $V_i \cap V = \emptyset$; (ii) u belongs to at most d' of $V_1, \ldots, V_d$; (iii) $|V_i| \leqslant t$; (iv) $N(V_i) \supseteq P$. The condition that u belongs to at most d' teams seeks to limit the workload of each user. Note that setting $d' = d$ imposes no upper limit on the number of teams to which any one user can belong, while $d' = 1$ corresponds to the "standard" resiliency policy $\mathsf{res}(P, s, d, t)$, and thus the satisfaction of this new policy generalizes the one of Definition 1.

We now focus on the problem of testing the satisfaction of a dynamic resiliency policy $\mathsf{xres}(P, 0, d, d', t)$ (*i.e.* with $s = 0$). As noted previously, similar arguments as for $\mathsf{RCP}\langle\rangle$ can be made for this new problem, and the case $s = 0$ can be used as a black-box to solve the more general one.

We introduce a construction to transform the satisfaction of $\mathsf{xres}(P, 0, d, d', t)$ into an instance of WSP. We no longer require that a user belonging to a "team" executing steps in one workflow instance cannot belong to a team executing a different instance. Hence, we no longer require the atleast constraint that we used in Construction 1. Instead, we have to impose constraints on the total number of steps to which any one user is assigned. As in Construction 1, the set of steps will be defined by $S = P^1 \cup \ldots P^d$, where P^i is a copy of P, for all $i \in [d]$, and the authorization policy is defined to be $A = \bigcup_{i=1}^{d} \{(u, r^i) : (u, r) \in UR\}$ (recall that r^i denotes the copy of r in P^i, for all $r \in P$ and $i \in [d]$). Then, we have to ensure that for any set of $(d' + 1)$ steps, each chosen in a different P^i, the number of users assigned to these steps is at least 2. Accordingly, we define

$$\zeta(S) = \{X \subseteq S : |X| = d' + 1, |P^i \cap X| \leq 1, i \in [d]\}.$$

Finally, determining the satisfaction of an $\mathsf{xres}(P, 0, d, d', t)$ policy can be done by replacing the set of constraints of Construction 1 by

$$C = \{\mathsf{atleast}(X, 2) : X \in \zeta(S)\} \cup \{\mathsf{atmost}(P^i, t) : i \in [d]\}$$

and solving the resulting instance of WSP, using *e.g.* the Pattern Backtracking algorithm of [11] (note that the optimization of the algorithm provided in Theorem 3 can no longer be applied to the WSP instance obtained in this particular case).

Note, however, that the WSP instance we now solve contains a number of constraints exponential in d and p, implying an additional computational cost when solving this new problem, as one could expect. Observe that there are exactly $|\zeta(S)| + d$ constraints, and that

$$|\zeta(S)| = O\left(\binom{d}{d'+1} p^{d'+1}\right) = O\left(2^{(d'+1)(\log(d)+\log(p))}\right),$$

since for each $I \subseteq \{1, \ldots, d\}$ of size $d' + 1$, there are at most $p^{d'+1}$ subsets of S intersecting P^i in exactly one element, for all $i \in I$.

It is worth noting that the set of constraints obtained from translating an instance of $\mathsf{RCP}\langle\rangle$ in which $d' = d$ (that is, when we impose no upper limit on the number of teams to which a user can belong) is simply

$$C = \{\mathsf{atmost}(P^i, t) : i \in [d]\}.$$

In other words, if we are not concerned with individual workloads, the WSP instance for the version of RCP in which teams need not be disjoint is actually easier than the original version of $\mathsf{RCP}\langle\rangle$.

Table 1 summarizes the possible requirements for team composition in the context of resiliency and associates those requirements with the corresponding constraints in a WSP instance. Selecting requirements 1 and 2, for example, corresponds to the standard resiliency policies of Li *et al.* Selecting requirements 1, 2 and 3 would insist that all teams have exactly t members and every team is disjoint. In the next two subsections, we consider further possibilities for generalizing RCP.

3.2.3 Independent teams

In the definition of $\mathsf{RCP}\langle\rangle$, all d teams are required to be of size at most t, and are allocated to the same set of resources $P \subseteq R$. A natural generalization is to allow each team to have a different size, and to be associated with a different set of resources.

Resiliency requirement	Constraint(s) in WSP
1. Teams should have no more than t users	$\{\mathsf{atmost}(P^i, t) : i \in [d]\}$
2. Teams should be disjoint	$\{\mathsf{atleast}(\{r^i, s^j\}, 2) : r, s \in P, 1 \le i < j \le d\}$
3. Teams should have at least ℓ users	$\{\mathsf{atleast}(P^i, \ell) : i \in [d]\}$
4. Teams should contain no more than $L_{\max}$ users in total	$\{\mathsf{atmost}(P^1 \cup \cdots \cup P^d, L_{\max})\}$
5. Teams should contain at least $L_{\min}$ users in total	$\{\mathsf{atleast}(P^1 \cup \cdots \cup P^d, L_{\min})\}$
6. Each user should belong to no more than d' teams	$\{\mathsf{atleast}(X, d') : X \subseteq S, |X| = d' + 1, |P^i \cap X| \le 1, i \in [d]\}$

Table 1: Summary of possible resiliency policies

First, we define a *team-independent* constraint $\mathsf{t\text{-}ind}(P, t)$, which is satisfied by $UR \subseteq U \times R$ if and only if there exists a set containing no more than t users who are collectively authorized for P. Then, a *team-independent resiliency* constraint is given by $\mathsf{ti\text{-}res}(s, P_1, t_1, \ldots, P_d, t_d)$, and is satisfied by $UR \subseteq U \times R$ if and only if on removal of any set of s users, the team-independent constraints $\mathsf{t\text{-}ind}(P_1, t_1), \ldots, \mathsf{t\text{-}ind}(P_d, t_d)$ are all satisfied by disjoint sets of users.

In particular, $\mathsf{res}(P, s, d, t)$ (in the sense of Definition 1) is a team-independent resiliency constraint in which the scope and team size of each $\mathsf{t\text{-}ind}(P_i, t_i)$ constraint are P and t, respectively. Hence, this new problem is also a generalization of RCP$\langle\rangle$.

Here again, we modify Construction 1 in order to test the satisfaction of $\mathsf{ti\text{-}res}(0, P_1, t_1, \ldots, P_d, t_d)$. We define the set of steps to be $S = P^1 \cup \cdots \cup P^d$, where P^i is a copy of P_i for all $i \in [d]$. Again, for all $r \in R$, we denote by r^i its copy in P^i, in the case where $r \in P_i$. Then the authorization policy remains $A = \bigcup_{i=1}^{d}\{(u, r^i) : (u, r) \in UR \text{ and } r \in P_i\}$. Finally, we define the set of constraints $C = C_1 \cup C_2$, with:

$C_1 = \{\mathsf{atmost}(P^i, t_i) : i \in [d]\}$;

$C_2 = \{\mathsf{atleast}(\{r^i, s^j\}, 2) : r \in P^i, s \in P^j, 1 \le i < j \le d\}$.

Here again, the Pattern Backtracking algorithm of Theorem 3 can be used to solve the obtained instance of WSP. Thus, the problem of testing whether an authorization policy satisfies $\mathsf{ti\text{-}res}(s, P_1, t_1, \ldots, P_d, t_d)$ is FPT parameterized by $|\bigcup_{i=1}^{d} P_i|$, s, d, and $\max_{i=1\ldots d} t_i$.

Naturally, we can also define an extended version of a team-independent resiliency constraint, in which we relax the condition that the teams be disjoint (as in Section 3.2.2). Again, we may distinguish between the case when there is an upper limit on the number of teams to which a user may belong ($d' < d$), where we will require a large number of additional constraints, and the case where no such limit is imposed ($d' = d$), and the number of constraints is actually reduced.

3.2.4 Weighted resiliency

In Section 3.2.1, we considered the possibility of imposing a global upper limit on the total number of users in the teams. In practice, it might be the case that different users "cost" a different amount. We might imagine, for example, departments charging out the use of its employees by other departments, and that more senior staff cost more than junior staff. In other words, as well as imposing an upper limit on the total number of users, we might consider associating each user with a cost and imposing an upper limit – a budget B – on the total cost of the users. Accordingly, we introduce a cost function defined over the set of users $c : U \to \mathbb{Z}$. This

weighted variant of RCP$\langle\rangle$ then asks for teams $V_1, \ldots, V_d$ such that $|V_i| \le t$ for all $i \in [d]$ and

$$\sum_{i=1}^{d} \sum_{u \in V_i} c(u)$$

is minimum over all possible sets of teams.

In order to deal with this variant, we use a recent generalization of WSP to a weighted version [4], called VALUED-WORKFLOW SATISFACTION PROBLEM (V-WSP). This problem allows us to define, for each set of steps $T \subseteq S$ and user $u \in U$, a weight $w(T, u)$ representing the cost of assigning u to steps in T. The goal is then to find a valid plan $\pi : S \to U$ such that

$$w_A(\pi) = \sum_{u \in U} w(\pi^{-1}(u), u)$$

is minimum over all valid plans[5]. Hence, we use once again Construction 1, and set, for every $u \in U$ and all $T \subseteq P^i$ for all $i \in [d]$:

$$w(T, u) = \begin{cases} c(u) & \text{if } T \subseteq N(u), \\ \infty & \text{otherwise.} \end{cases}$$

Using similar ideas as in the proof of Lemma 1, the algorithm for V-WSP will output d plans $\pi_i : P^i \to U$, $i \in [d]$, defining the teams $V_1, \ldots, V_d$. As explained earlier, this plan will be such that

$$\sum_{i=1}^{d} \sum_{u \in V_i} w(\pi^{-1}(u), u) = \sum_{i=1}^{d} \sum_{u \in V_i} c(u)$$

is minimum, over all plans not violating any constraint. It is worth pointing out that the algorithm for V-WSP of [4] can also be improved in the same way as described in the proof of Theorem 3.

Furthermore, still using the particular structure of the obtained V-WSP instance, it is also possible to change the algorithm so that it outputs a set of teams $V_1, \ldots, V_d$ such that $\sum_{u \in V_i} c(u) \le W_i$ for some given bounds $W_1, \ldots, W_d$, if such a set exists. In other words, we now ask in this variant that each team *independently* respect its own upper bound. A possible application of this variant might be as follows: suppose that the set of users contains a subset U_s of special users, and the task that needs to be achieved (by having

---

[5]Notice that in the definition of V-WSP of [4], a weight function over the constraints w_C is also defined, and the goal is actually to find a plan which minimizes $w_A(\pi) + w_C(\pi)$. However, assigning an infinite cost to each constraint simply forbids the violation of any constraint and forces an optimal solution to minimize $w_A(\pi)$ over all plans with a finite constraint weight, as desired here.

access to all resources in P) necessarily requires the presence of at least one special user. For instance, one might think of the special users as managers, or team leaders. This problem can simply be solved using the aforementioned method by setting $c(u) = -t + 1$ for all $u \in U_s$, $c(u) = 1$ for all $u \in U \setminus U_s$, and setting $W_i = 0$ for all $i \in [d]$.

4. STATIC SEPARATION-OF-DUTY AND RESILIENCY

A *static separation of duty* (SSoD) *policy* has the form $\mathsf{ssod}(P, t)$, where P is a subset of the set of resources R and t is an integer such that $1 < t \leqslant |P|$ [13]. Satisfaction of this constraint is determined by considering the authorization policy UR (and we ensure continuing satisfaction of the constraint by controlling updates to UR). More formally, the SSoD policy $\mathsf{ssod}(P, t)$ is *satisfied* by $UR \subseteq U \times R$ if and only if for all subsets V of U such that $|V| < t$, $P \not\subseteq N(V)$. So, for example, the static separation-of-duty constraint $\mathsf{ssod}(\{p_1, p_2\}, 2)$, requires that two particular resources are not assigned to the same user.

Equivalently, $\mathsf{ssod}(P, t)$ is *violated* if there exists a set of at most $t - 1$ users V such that $N(V) \supseteq P$. A naive algorithm for testing the satisfiability of an $\mathsf{ssod}(P, t)$ policy would be to check if the neighborhood of some subset of at most $t - 1$ users contains P. However, such an algorithm would necessarily be of complexity $O^*(n^{t-1})$, which would be inefficient in practice. Thus, our goal is to obtain an FPT algorithm parameterized by some smaller parameters, like $p = |P|$. To do so, we now explain how the problem of determining whether a static separation-of-duty policy is satisfied may be converted into an instance of WSP.

CONSTRUCTION 2. *Given $UR \subseteq U \times R$ and $\mathsf{ssod}(P, \ell)$, we construct a workflow specification W in which $S = P$, $E = \emptyset$, $A = UR \cap (U \times P)$, and $C = \{\mathsf{atmost}(P, t - 1)\}$.*

LEMMA 2. $\mathsf{ssod}(P, t)$ *is satisfied if and only if W is unsatisfiable.*

Note that $\mathsf{atmost}(P, t)$ is a user-independent constraint, and that the number of steps in the obtained WSP instance is $p = |P|$. Thus, here again the Pattern Backtracking algorithm for WSP [11] gives a practical algorithm to test whether a static separation-of-duty constraint is satisfied by an authorization policy, in a worst-case $O^*(2^{p \log(p)})$ time and polynomial space. In addition, as Li *et al.* [13] notice, the complement of this problem is actually equivalent to the SET COVER problem[6]. Known positive [8] and negative [6] results for SET COVER lead to the following.

THEOREM 5. *Testing whether a static separation-of-duty $\mathsf{ssod}(P, t)$ is satisfied by an authorization policy UR can be done in $O^*(2^p)$ time, while a $O^*(2^{o(p)})$ algorithm would violate Exponential Time Hypothesis[7].*

Notice that the $O^*(2^p)$ algorithm of [8] relies on a dynamic programming approach, thus using exponential space.

---

[6]In the SET COVER problem, we are given a set $\mathcal{S}$ of subsets of a set U, and an integer k, and the aim is to find at most k elements of $\mathcal{S}$ whose union is U.

[7]The Exponential Time Hypothesis is the assumption that 3-SAT cannot be solved in time $O^*(2^{o(n)})$, where n is the number of variables in the CNF formula [10].

Hence, we strongly believe that applying the Pattern Backtracking algorithm on the instance obtained by Construction 2 is likely to be more efficient in practice, although having a worse theoretical running time ($O^*(2^{p \log(p)})$).

4.1 Policy checking problems

The work of Li *et al.* [13] considers the interaction between *static* separation-of-duty constraints and resiliency policies. In this section, we reevaluate the problems they studied using the tools from fixed-parameter tractability, and extend the analysis to include user-independent constraints.

Before doing so, we note there are two types of constraints that can be defined. One type, which we will call *existential* constraints, are satisfied if some condition "guarded" by an existential quantifier holds. A resiliency policy $\mathsf{res}(P, s, d, t)$, for example, is an existential policy (since we need only find one allocation of users to teams). The other type, which we will call *universal* constraints, are satisfied if some condition "guarded" by a universal quantifier holds. A static separation-of-duty constraint $\mathsf{ssod}(Q, t)$ is a universal policy (since every subset of cardinality less than or equal to t must satisfy a particular condition).

A satisfiable instance of WSP indicates the existence of a plan. Informally, then, WSP can be used to determine the satisfaction (or otherwise) of an existential constraint (as we have seen with resiliency policies). Conversely, WSP can be used to determine the violation (or otherwise) of a universal constraint (as we have seen with static separation-of-duty policies).

Clearly, there is some "tension" between resiliency and SSoD policies: informally, resiliency policies require "over-provisioning" in the authorization policy, while SSoD policies require "minimal" provisioning. This leads naturally to the following definition and problem.

DEFINITION 4. *The MIXED POLICY CHECKING PROBLEM is the problem of determining whether a set of resiliency and SSoD policies is satisfied by a given user-resource relation UR.*

Note the MIXED POLICY CHECKING PROBLEM is not considered as a problem in its own right in the work of Li *et al.* [13]. However, it turns out that an algorithm to solve the MIXED POLICY CHECKING PROBLEM can be used as a sub-routine to solve the POLICY CONSISTENCY CHECKING PROBLEM problem defined later. Now, the MIXED POLICY CHECKING PROBLEM can be solved by first asking whether every resiliency policy is satisfied (using Construction 1) and then asking whether any one of the static separation-of-duty policies is violated (using Construction 2). (We have to perform these checks separately because resiliency policies are existential constraints and separation-of-duty policies are universal.) Recall the input to MPCP includes a set F of resiliency and SSoD policies. We denote by s_M, d_M, t_M the maximum values of s, d, t, respectively, in any resiliency policy $\mathsf{res}(P, s, d, t) \in F$, and by p_M the size of the largest scope of any resiliency or SSoD policy of F. Given that testing the satisfiability of an SSoD policy $\mathsf{ssod}(P, t)$ is FPT parameterized by p, and that testing the satisfiability of a resiliency policy $\mathsf{res}(P, s, d, t)$ is FPT parameterized by (p, s, d, t), we obtain the following result:

THEOREM 6. MIXED POLICY CHECKING PROBLEM *is FPT parameterized by (p_M, s_M, d_M, t_M).*

A set of policies comprising resiliency and SSoD policies is said to be *consistent* if and only if there exists an authorization relation UR such that every policy is satisfied [13]. This definition leads naturally to the following decision problem.

DEFINITION 5. *The* POLICY CONSISTENCY CHECKING PROBLEM *consists in deciding whether there exists a user-resource relation UR that satisfies a given set of SSoD and resiliency policies.*

Li *et al.* [13] show that POLICY CONSISTENCY CHECKING PROBLEM is a computationally hard problem: it is in general in $\mathrm{NP^{NP}}$, and the two restrictions where there is only one resiliency policy, and only one SSoD policy are NP-hard and coNP-hard, respectively. On the other hand, there exists a naive algorithm to solve the POLICY CONSISTENCY CHECKING PROBLEM using an algorithm for MIXED POLICY CHECKING PROBLEM as a sub-routine: first enumerate all possible authorization policies, and for each of them, construct an instance of MIXED POLICY CHECKING PROBLEM in order to test whether it satisfies the policies. The obvious question with this strategy is whether the algorithm will terminate, since the number of all possible authorization policies is, *a priori*, not bounded. In the following result, we show that this user set can actually be bounded by a function of the maximum size of the scopes of the input policies, implying an FPT algorithm with this parameter. Let $\mathsf{ssod}(P_1, t_1), \ldots, \mathsf{ssod}(P_{q_1}, t_{q_1})$ and $\mathsf{res}(P_{q_1+1}, 0, 1, t_{q_1+1}), \ldots, \mathsf{res}(P_{q_2}, 0, 1, t_{q_2})$ be the policies in the input of POLICY CONSISTENCY CHECKING PROBLEM (as Li *et al.* [13] note, we may suppose that $s = 0$ and $d = 1$ for all resiliency policies $\mathsf{res}(P, s, d, t)$). We note $P = \bigcup_{i=1}^{q_2} P_i$, and, as before, $p = |P|$.

THEOREM 7. POLICY CONSISTENCY CHECKING PROBLEM *is FPT parameterized by p.*

PROOF. First observe that for any set U and $UR \subseteq U \times R$ such that UR satisfies all policies, removing from UR all elements (u, r) such that $r \notin P$ does not violate any of the constraints. Then, we may also assume that for all $u \in U$, $N(u) \subseteq P$. Now we show that we may also delete every user u having a *twin*, *i.e.* a user u' such that $u \neq u'$ and $N(u) = N(u')$. Indeed, let u, u' be two twins, $U' = U \setminus \{u'\}$, and $UR' = UR|_{U'}$. First assume that UR satisfies two policies $\mathsf{ssod}(P, \ell)$ and $\mathsf{res}(P', 0, 1, t)$. Then, clearly UR' also satisfies $\mathsf{ssod}(P, \ell)$, since every subset V of U' of size at most $\ell - 1$ is also a subset of U of the same size, and thus $N(V) \subsetneq P$. Then, UR' satisfies $\mathsf{res}(P', 0, 1, t)$, since $N(V) = N((V \setminus \{u'\}) \cup \{u\})$ for all $V \subseteq U$ such that $u' \in V$.

Conversely, if UR' satisfies $\mathsf{ssod}(P, \ell)$ and $\mathsf{res}(P', 0, 1, t)$, then the same holds for UR, since, here again, $N(V) = N((V \setminus \{u'\}) \cup \{u\})$ for all $V \subseteq U$ such that $u' \in V$. Hence, we showed that for all U and $UR \subseteq U \times R$ such that UR satisfies all policies, we can iteratively delete all twins without violating any constraint, thus obtaining a solution U' and UR' with $|U'| \leq 2^p$. Hence, instead of enumerating all authorization policies, it is actually sufficient to enumerate all subsets of a user set $\mathcal{U}$ containing 2^p users, namely one user per subset of P, which represent the resources (s)he is authorized for. Then, for each such authorization policy, it remains to test the satisfaction of the separation-of-duty and resiliency policies (*e.g.*, using the algorithm of Theorems 3 and 5). One can observe that the total running time of this algorithm is $O^*(2^{p \log(p) + 2^p})$. □

4.2 Minimizing the number of needed users

The final problem that Li *et al.* [13] consider is the special case that the resiliency policy $\mathsf{res}(P, s, 1, \infty)$ and static separation-of-duty policy $\mathsf{ssod}(P, k, s)$ are defined over the same set of resources $P \subseteq R$. Given enough users, it will clearly be possible to find an authorization relation that simultaneously satisfies both policies. The interesting question is what the minimum number of users is. More formally, Li *et al.* define the following problem.

DEFINITION 6. *Given a set of resources R and $\mathsf{res}(P, s, 1, \infty)$, $\mathsf{ssod}(P, k, s)$, with $P \subseteq R$, $s, k \in \mathbb{N}$, MIN-USERS PCCP SATISFIABILITY (MUPS) consists of determining the smallest integer m_0 for which there exist U, $UR \subseteq U \times R$ such that $|U| \leq m_0$ and UR satisfies $\mathsf{res}(P, s, 1, \infty)$ and $\mathsf{ssod}(P, k, s)$.*

Li *et al.* [13] were not able to settle the complexity of MIN-USERS PCCP SATISFIABILITY. However, they were able to obtain upper and lower bounds for m_0, these bounds being $p(s+1)$ and $k+s$, respectively; moreover, they showed that the lower bound is tight whenever $p \geq \binom{k+s}{s+1}$.

While the general complexity of MUPS remains open, we can establish that it is FPT. In particular, the algorithm discussed in the proof of Theorem 7 can be modified to determine whether a set of resiliency and SSoD policies are satisfied by an authorization policy defined on a set of at most m users, where m is an additional input of the problem. Indeed, one just need to restrict the enumeration of all subsets of $\mathcal{U}$ to those of size at most m. We thus have the following result.

THEOREM 8. MUPS *is FPT parameterized by p.*

5. CONCLUDING REMARKS

The specification and enforcement of policies and constraints is perhaps the most common way of implementing access control requirements in computer systems. These policies and constraints may be mutually incompatible to some extent, in the sense that authorization policies that satisfy one constraint may lead to the violation of another. In particular, static separation-of-duty and resiliency policies may be incompatible in this sense.

Hence, it is important to be able to analyze whether a given authorization policy simultaneously satisfies mutually incompatible constraints. Prior work in this area has established that such analyses are generally intractable [13]. In this paper, we make important contributions to the understanding of the RESILIENCY CHECKING PROBLEM and the POLICY CONSISTENCY CHECKING PROBLEM from the perspective of fixed-parameter tractability.

First, we exhibit a transformation from the RESILIENCY CHECKING PROBLEM to the WORKFLOW SATISFIABILITY PROBLEM, by which a resiliency policy is translated into **atmost** and **atleast** constraints. This enables us to re-use and adapt known results for WSP, leading to new results establishing that RESILIENCY CHECKING PROBLEM is FPT. In addition, the existence of optimized algorithms to solve WSP suggests that it will be possible to solve much larger instances of the RESILIENCY CHECKING PROBLEM than has been possible up to now. Moreover, the fact that WSP is FPT for all user-independent constraints means we can introduce potentially useful generalization of and variations on the Resiliency Checking Problem. Second, we introduce the Mixed Policy Checking Problem, an intermediate problem that can be solved using methods similar to those for the Resiliency Checking Problem (ie, by translating to a WSP instance), and as a basis for solving the Policy Consistency Checking Problem. We show that the Mixed Policy Checking Problem is FPT and how an algorithm to solve the Mixed Policy Checking Problem can be used to solve the Policy Consistency Checking Problem. The method we use introduces a way of bounding the number of users that need to be considered, thus making the Policy Consistency Checking Problem FPT. This method may be of independent interest in the context of workflow satisfiability and is something we intend to explore in future work. We also note that we have recently extended the work in this paper to provide an exhaustive multi-variate analysis of the complexity of the Resiliency Checking Problem [5].

It is perhaps worth mentioning in conclusion that WSP cannot be used directly to solve problems related to *workflow resiliency* [15]. In the case of resiliency in access control systems, the Resiliency Checking Problem asks whether it is possible to allocate users to teams even if up to s users are unavailable. Here the assumption seems to be that the set of (available) users will not change once the users have been allocated to teams. In the case of resiliency in workflow systems, however, three different models of user availability have been proposed [15], based on the assumption that workflow instances may run for a relatively long period of time, and users that were available when the workflow was instantiated may no longer be available when the workflow instance is partially complete. This leads to three distinct definitions of workflow resiliency: static, incremental and dynamic. The work on resiliency in access control essentially corresponds to static resiliency and questions of static resiliency can, presumably, be answered by reducing the problem to (multiple instances of) WSP. In future work, we plan to investigate incremental and dynamic workflow resiliency, using techniques for Valued WSP [4] (since we can use weights to model availability of users).

Finally, we note Khan and Fong's work on *workflow feasibility* [12] in the context of a constrained workflow authorization schema that also includes rules for updating the authorization relation *UR*. A workflow is feasible if there exists a "reachable" authorization relation (by application of the update rules) such that the resulting constrained workflow authorization schema is satisfiable. Khan and Fong's work was set in the specific context of relationship-based access control, where updates to the authorization relation are controlled in particular ways. Workflow feasibility is obviously related to the Policy Consistency Checking Problem and can presumably be modeled as multiple instances of WSP. In future work we hope to consider workflow feasibility in the context of role-based access control (RBAC) together with a suitable administrative model for RBAC to update the user-role and role-step relationships (from which the authorization relation may be derived).

Acknowledgements

This research was partially supported by EPSRC grant EP/K005162/1. Gregory Gutin's research was also supported by Royal Society Wolfson Research Merit Award.

6. REFERENCES

[1] American National Standards Institute. *ANSI INCITS 359-2004 for Role Based Access Control*, 2004.

[2] Bertino, E., Ferrari, E., and Atluri, V. The specification and enforcement of authorization constraints in workflow management systems. *ACM Trans. Inf. Syst. Secur. 2*, 1 (1999), 65–104.

[3] Cohen, D., Crampton, J., Gagarin, A., Gutin, G., and Jones, M. Iterative plan construction for the workflow satisfiability problem. *J. Artif. Intell. Res. (JAIR) 51* (2014), 555–577.

[4] Crampton, J., Gutin, G., and Karapetyan, D. Valued workflow satisfiability problem. In *Proceedings of the 20th ACM Symposium on Access Control Models and Technologies, Vienna, Austria, June 1-3, 2015* (2015), E. R. Weippl, F. Kerschbaum, and A. J. Lee, Eds., ACM, pp. 3–13.

[5] Crampton, J., Gutin, G., and Watrigant, R. A multivariate approach for checking resiliency in access control. *CoRR 1604.01550* (2016).

[6] Cygan, M., Dell, H., Lokshtanov, D., Marx, D., Nederlof, J., Okamoto, Y., Paturi, R., Saurabh, S., and Wahlstrom, M. On problems as hard as CNF-SAT. In *Proceedings of the 2012 IEEE Conference on Computational Complexity (CCC)* (Washington, DC, USA, 2012), CCC '12, IEEE Computer Society, pp. 74–84.

[7] Downey, R. G., and Fellows, M. R. *Fundamentals of Parameterized Complexity*. Texts in Computer Science. Springer, 2013.

[8] Fomin, F. V., Grandoni, F., and Kratsch, D. Measure and conquer: Domination - a case study. In *Automata, Languages and Programming*, L. Caires, G. Italiano, L. Monteiro, C. Palamidessi, and M. Yung, Eds., vol. 3580 of *Lecture Notes in Computer Science*. Springer Berlin Heidelberg, 2005, pp. 191–203.

[9] Gutin, G., Kratsch, S., and Wahlström, M. Polynomial kernels and user reductions for the workflow satisfiability problem. In *Parameterized and Exact Computation - 9th International Symposium, IPEC 2014, Wroclaw, Poland, September 10-12, 2014. Revised Selected Papers* (2014), pp. 208–220.

[10] Impagliazzo, R., Paturi, R., and Zane, F. Which problems have strongly exponential complexity? *J. Comput. Syst. Sci. 63*, 4 (2001), 512–530.

[11] Karapetyan, D., Gagarin, A. V., and Gutin, G. Pattern backtracking algorithm for the workflow satisfiability problem with user-independent constraints. In *Frontiers in Algorithmics - 9th International Workshop, FAW 2015, Guilin, China, July 3-5, 2015, Proceedings* (2015), J. Wang and C. Yap, Eds., vol. 9130 of *Lecture Notes in Computer Science*, Springer, pp. 138–149.

[12] Khan, A. A., and Fong, P. W. L. Satisfiability and feasibility in a relationship-based workflow authorization model. In *Computer Security - ESORICS 2012 - 17th European Symposium on Research in Computer Security, Pisa, Italy, September 10-12, 2012. Proceedings* (2012), S. Foresti, M. Yung,

and F. Martinelli, Eds., vol. 7459 of *Lecture Notes in Computer Science*, Springer, pp. 109–126.

[13] LI, N., WANG, Q., AND TRIPUNITARA, M. V. Resiliency policies in access control. *ACM Trans. Inf. Syst. Secur. 12*, 4 (2009).

[14] SANDHU, R. S., COYNE, E. J., FEINSTEIN, H. L., AND YOUMAN, C. E. Role-based access control models. *IEEE Computer 29*, 2 (1996), 38–47.

[15] WANG, Q., AND LI, N. Satisfiability and resiliency in workflow authorization systems. *ACM Trans. Inf. Syst. Secur. 13*, 4 (2010), 40.

APPENDIX

A. PROOFS

PROOF OF THEOREM 2. Given an instance $(U, R, UR, \mathsf{res}(P, s, d, t))$ of RCP$\langle\rangle$, and $U' \subseteq U$, we define $UR|_{U'} = \{(u, r) \in UR : u \in U'\}$, the restriction of UR to users which belong to U'. By Definition 1, if UR does not satisfy $\mathsf{res}(P, s, d, t)$ then there is a set $V \subseteq U$ of cardinality s, called a *blocker set*, such that for any d mutually disjoint sets of users $V_1, \ldots, V_d$ such that $N(V_i) \supseteq P$ and $|V_i| \leqslant t$, $V_1 \cup \cdots \cup V_d \cap V \neq \emptyset$.

Now, consider the complement of RCP$\langle\rangle$, co-RCP$\langle\rangle$, where we wish to find a blocker set $V \subseteq U$ of size at most s (*i.e.* such that $UR|_{U\setminus V}$ does not satisfy $\mathsf{res}(P, 0, d, t)$). We design an algorithm for a more general version of this problem, which we call co-RCP WITH ADVICE, where the input comes together with a set $V \subseteq U$, and the goal is to find a set $V^* \subseteq U$, such that $V^* \supseteq V$, $|V^*| \leq s$, and $UR|_{U\setminus V^*}$ does not satisfy $\mathsf{res}(P, 0, d, t)$. By the foregoing, solving co-RCP WITH ADVICE with $V = \emptyset$ clearly solves RCP$\langle\rangle$. Recall that a negative answer for co-RCP WITH ADVICE means that the RCP$\langle\rangle$ instance is positive, and conversely. In the following, we will only focus on solving co-RCP WITH ADVICE. Let us denote by $\mathcal{A}$ the algorithm described in the statement.

We are thus given $(U, R, UR, \mathsf{res}(P, 0, d, t))$ and $V \subseteq U$. If $|V| > s$, then we can clearly answer *no* for co-RCP WITH ADVICE. We thus assume in the following that $|V| \leq s$. Using algorithm $\mathcal{A}$, we determine whether $\mathsf{res}(P, 0, d, t)$ is satisfied by $UR|_{U\setminus V}$. In the negative case, then $V^* = V$ is a blocker set for co-RCP WITH ADVICE, and we answer *yes*. Otherwise, $\mathcal{A}$ outputs a set of teams $V_1, \ldots, V_d$, with $V_i \subseteq U \setminus V$ for all $i \in [d]$. For all $u \in V_1 \cup \cdots \cup V_d$, we make a recursive call to our algorithm with input $(U, R, UR, \mathsf{res}(0, d, t))$ and $V \cup \{u\}$, and return *yes* if and only if one of these sub-instances returns *yes*. If the instance is a positive one for co-RCP WITH ADVICE, then observe that any blocker set V^* must intersect $V_1 \cup \cdots \cup V_d$, and thus one of the recursive calls must return *yes*. If the instance is a negative one, then clearly all these recursive calls will return *no* as well, proving the correctness of the algorithm. Finally, observe that we branch on at most dt sub-instances of co-RCP WITH ADVICE, each of them having its input V increased by one element. Since the algorithm stops whenever $|V| > s$, the number of calls to the algorithm is at most $O^*((dt)^s) = O^*(2^{s\log(dt)})$. Since in every execution we make at most one call to algorithm $\mathcal{A}$, the total running time of the algorithm is $O^*(2^{s\log(dt)}f(p, d, t))$. $\square$

PROOF OF LEMMA 2. If W is satisfiable, then there exists a valid plan $\pi : P \to U$. In particular, $|\pi(P)| \leq t - 1$, which means that there exists a set of at most $t - 1$ users which, altogether, have access to all resources in P, thus violating the policy.

Conversely, assume that $\mathsf{ssod}(P, t)$ is violated, which means that there exists a set V of at most $t - 1$ users such that $N(V) \supseteq P$, *i.e.* for all $r \in P$, there exists $u_r \in V$ such that $(u_r, r) \in UR$. Thus, the plan $\pi : P \to U$ defined by $\pi(r) = u_r$ for all $r \in S$ is a valid plan for W. $\square$

Start Here: Engineering Scalable Access Control Systems

Aaron Elliott
Royal Military College of Canada
Kingston, Ontario
Aaron.Elliott@rmc.ca

Scott Knight
Royal Military College of Canada
Kingston, Ontario
Scott.Knight@rmc.ca

ABSTRACT

Role-based Access Control (RBAC) is a popular solution for implementing information security however there is no pervasive methodology used to produce scalable access control systems for large organizations with hundreds or thousands of employees. As a result ten engineers will likely arrive at ten different solutions to the same problem where there is no right or wrong answer but there is both an immediate and long term cost. Moreover, they would have difficulty communicating the important aspects of their design implementations to each other. This is an interesting deficiency because despite their diversity, large organizations are built upon two key concepts, roles and responsibilities, where a role like Departmental Chair is identified and assigned responsibilities. In this paper, our objective is to introduce ORGODEX, a new model and practical methodology for engineering scalable RBAC systems in large organizations where employees require access to information on a need to know basis. First, we motivate the requirement for a new RBAC dichotomy, distinguishing between roles and responsibilities. Next, we introduce our new model for describing and reasoning about RBAC systems with this new dichotomy. Finally, we produce a new iterative methodology for engineering scalable access control systems.

CCS Concepts

•Security and privacy → Formal security models; *Security requirements;* Software security engineering;

Keywords

Role-based access control; Organizational structure; Scalability; Complexity; Least privilege

SACMAT'16, June 05-08, 2016, Shanghai, China
© 2016 ACM. ISBN 978-1-4503-3802-8/16/06. . . $15.00
DOI: http://dx.doi.org/10.1145/2914642.2914651

1. INTRODUCTION

The use of Role-based Access Control (RBAC) for information security has experienced a global proliferation due to the administrative savings afforded by the RBAC model [3][9][28]. However, the administration of large-scale RBAC systems like Dresdner Bank [29], with 40,000 users and 1300 roles, is a challenging open problem [19]. RBAC is an open, generic technology that permits several solutions to the same access control requirements and for this reason, large banking organizations like Dresdner may have similar access control requirements and vastly different RBAC systems. This is an interesting deficiency because despite their diversity, large organizations are built upon two key concepts, roles and responsibilities, where a role like Departmental Chair is identified and assigned responsibilities. It is surprising that the business model of large organizations is often loosely coupled with its RBAC systems, merging the notions of role and responsibility into simplistic, inflexible subject-role-permission relationships. Perhaps this is directly linked to the classic RBAC example where all bank tellers share the same role and have the same permissions. Unfortunately, this example oversimplifies RBAC, making it difficult to understand the challenges inherent when implementing RBAC in large dynamic organizations with highly diversified workforces.

Kuijper and Ermolaev have proposed bi-sorted role-based access control (RBÄC) for existing RBAC implementations [18]. Unlike previous extensions to the classic RBAC model [28], RBÄC revisits first principles, extending the traditional subject-role-permission, or *triangular model*, with a second role to form the subject-role-role-permission *square model*. Although communication with the business side of an organization does not appear to be a primary motivation for RBÄC, we suggest the introduction of this additional layer is an important evolutionary concept.

In business management a roles and responsibility matrix may be used to clarify who is responsible for what. Instead of using the terminology proper role and demarcation as described in RBÄC, using the terminology role and responsibility is a practical approach for implementing RBAC, permitting engineers to more easily communicate the important aspects of their design implementations to each other and the business side of an organization. This is an important concern since role engineering has been determined to be the most expensive aspect of deploying RBAC [22].

Our objective in this work is to extend RBÄC, introducing ORGODEX, a new model and practical methodology for engineering scalable RBAC systems in organizations where hundreds or thousands of employees require access to information on a need to know basis. We make the following contributions:

- We motivate the requirement for a new RBAC dichotomy, distinguishing between roles and responsibilities. We introduce the notion of role evolution.

- We introduce a new model for describing and reasoning about RBAC systems in business terminology, extending previous models with the notion of constraints

- We propose a new iterative methodology for engineering scalable RBAC systems, validating its utility with a real-world case study at a large North-American university

2. BACKGROUND

Access to information systems is controlled by layers of security. The authorization layer specifies who has access to what. The who is a set of subjects (S) and the what is a set of permissions (P) that have been assigned to the subject. This results in the access relation SP $\subseteq$ S $\times$ P, specifying who is authorized to do what in the information system. In this work we assume a subject has successfully authenticated to an information system, for instance by correctly entering their user name and password. After the subject has gained entry to the information system, they are only permitted to read or write information as authorized. We are concerned with the administration of RBAC, where relations between subjects and permissions are explicitly defined and maintained.

RBAC is a popular framework for implementing the authorization layer or who is authorized to do what [28]. Unlike the concept of groups, which only specify group membership, roles identify a set of subjects and a related set of permissions. The administration of RBAC is multi-faceted. Creating user-role, role-role and permission-role relationships are distinct actions that bring subjects and permissions together. For large-scale RBAC systems, thousands of access control relationships must be maintained, a formidable task that is often highly centralized in a small team of security administrators [24]. Several models have been proposed for maintaining access control implementations. Proofs for the utility of these models are typically restricted to contrived examples that fail to reflect the complexity of medium to large organizations [29]. In the following subsection we review related work, observing scalability concerns for each model.

3. RELATED WORK

To our knowledge the term *role explosion* has not been formally defined by the research community [17][14][11]. Instead it would seem there is a belief, notion or sense that some threshold ratio of roles to subjects indicates bad RBAC design. We suggest that the term role explosion be replaced by the notion of **role evolution**, arising from the concepts described by leading researchers more than a decade ago [26][23][24][5][16]. Role evolution does not aim to prevent role explosion, instead it presumes the number of roles will scale uncontrollably in large organizations or controllably using a prescribed methodology. In this work, we prescribe a methodology for controlled growth.

A literature review for the administration of RBAC typically begins with the administrative role-based access control (ARBAC) family of models including ARBAC97, AR-BAC99 and ARBAC02 [26][27][24]. ARBAC97 describes the decentralized administration of subject-role enrollment, role-role grants and permission-role assignment with reference to the RBAC96 model [28]. In their introduction to ARBAC97 the authors presume that *in large enterprise-wide systems, the number of roles can be in the hundreds or thousands, and subjects in the tens of hundreds or thousands* suggesting that the ratio of roles to subjects is 10%.

The belief, notion or sense that the number of subjects far exceeds the roles found in enterprise systems is repeated in each extension to the ARBAC97 model as is the example of a Director overseeing two projects with a Project Lead, Production Engineer, Quality Engineer and a (Junior) Engineer. When we conceptually scale this model up to hundreds of projects in a society where the demand for skilled workers is not being met [15], we wonder whether Junior Engineers are allocated in quantity to single or multiple projects.

Administrative enterprise role-based access control (A-ERBAC), describes the model employed in a commercial enterprise security management software solution [16]. Kern et al. suggest that Enterprise Roles are increasingly used by medium to large organizations as the basis for security management across different systems. A-ERBAC uses the concept of *scopes* to control the authority of administrators on a Target System. We observe that the example with functional and business roles depicted in this work identifies a scenario where eight roles are defined for five subjects.

It is not clear whether the classic subject-role-permission model remains dominant in medium to large organizations with highly skilled workforces. Over a decade and a half ago, the A-ERBAC model described a second layer of roles between subjects and permissions without expressly highlighting the fact that this implies subjects will always hold a minimum of two roles (i.e. subject-role-role-permission). We understand that these roles are meant to be shared but we believe there has been a fundamental shift in the way RBAC systems are implemented and maintained over the past decade. In our analysis we are unable to determine if the research community introduced the notion of at least two roles for each subject [23] or whether this was an organic by-product of real-world implementations [29] or both.

Kuijper and Ermolaev have proposed bi-sorted role-based access control (RBÄC) for existing RBAC implementations, the perceived added value lies within the conceptual boundaries it introduces, decoupling subject and permission management, thus introducing a higher administrative level for access control [18]. For practitioners, this decoupling implies that modeling (1) subjects and (2) permissions is broken into independent activities. With these two aspects maintained by suitable teams, security officers may configure access control rules at an appropriate level of abstraction.

Coyne suggests that the definition of roles is essentially a requirements engineering process [4]. Unlike traditional top-down or bottom-up approaches for role engineering [20], RBÄC proposes an additional layer of abstraction such that permissions are never assigned to subjects in the traditional triangular subject-role-permission model. Instead, permissions are **always** assigned indirectly using a square subject-role-role-permission model, thereby facilitating organizational scalability. Consequently, the problem of determining the

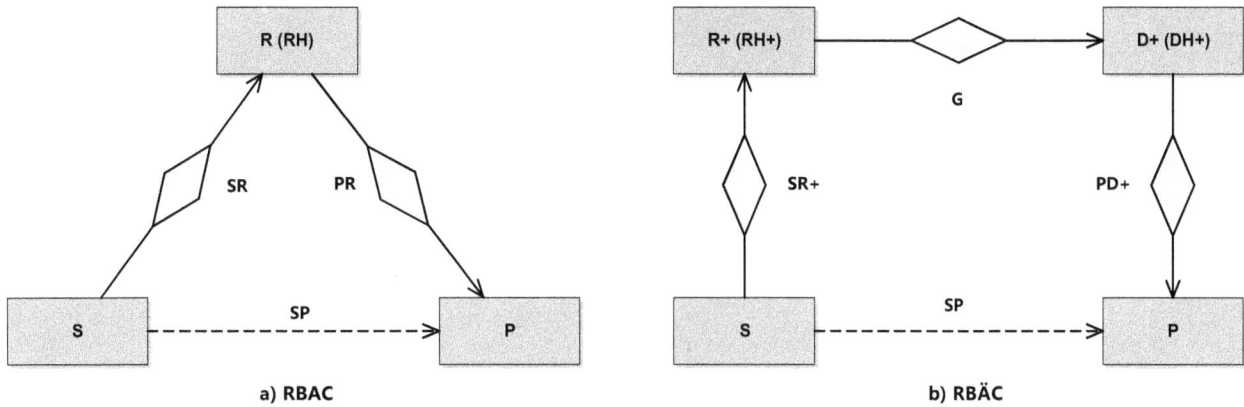

Figure 1: RBÄC proposes a new conceptual boundary between subjects and permissions. Adapted from [18].

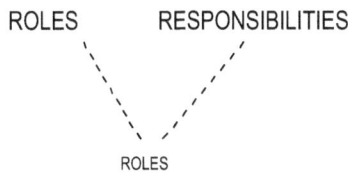

Figure 2: Role Evolution proposes a phylogenetic divergence between Roles and Responsibilities.

optimal set of roles for an RBAC system, referred to as the Role Mining Problem (RMP) is fundamentally redefined in the context of a square model, where finding the minimal set of roles (e.g. Basic-RMP) is not a primary concern [31].

In this work we focus on the added benefit of *dovetailing* role and requirements engineering efforts when designing system functions and user interfaces [4]. Similar to the methodology described by Coyne, we identify a responsibility by determining activities that may be stated as a verb/information pair (e.g. Approve Final Grades). We also identify candidate roles as nouns, describing a group of subjects (e.g. Departmental Chairs) before identifying role-centric constraints (e.g. Departmental Chair #1 and #2).

Peisert and Bishop suggest that traditional access controls have evolved from being static and coarse-grained to being dynamic and very fine-grained [25]. If role explosion is a normal occurrence and previous models for the administration of RBAC consider role explosion a design problem this should motivate a return to first principles [8][13][7].

In the following section, we review the work of Kuijper and Ermolaev in more detail as their model formalizes the conceptual boundaries described in A-ERBAC, suggesting that subjects must **always** have at least two roles. We strongly support this formalized approach and consider it the basis for our new dichotomy, advocating on behalf of **role evolution**.

4. A NEW DICHOTOMY

The Merriam-Webster dictionary defines a **role** as *a part*

that someone or something has in a particular activity or situation and a **responsibility** as *a duty or task that you are required or expected to do*. A dichotomy partitions its membership into two distinct subsets where everything must decidedly belong to one set or the other. In this section, we motivate the requirement for a new RBAC dichotomy, partitioning roles and responsibilities into distinct subsets. In large RBAC systems with hundreds or thousands of roles, the phylogeny of roles is an important evolutionary concern. It is no longer sufficient to think simply in terms of roles. RBAC has evolved. It is time for an evolutionary divergence, separating roles from responsibilities. In Figure 2, we present a new phylogenetic representation for RBAC systems where responsibilities have semantically diverged from roles. This is an important evolutionary concept because there is considerable misunderstanding among information security practitioners, where access control is often performed irregularly and considered a secondary duty [2].

Unlike previous extensions to the classic RBAC model [28], RBÄC revisits first principles with the hypothesis that organizational scalability is facilitated when permissions are managed independently from subjects. RBÄC is presented as a *fragment* of RBAC, a conceptual shift, from the *triangular* RBAC model to the *desirable square* model of RBÄC. In Figure 1a), we see that RBAC introduced the role as a layer of indirection between subjects and permissions. SP is the implicit result of assigning permissions to a role (PR) and then enrolling subjects into this role (SR). To achieve the square of RBÄC in Figure 1b), another layer of indirection is introduced with roles being categorized as either a proper role (R+) or a demarcation (D+) . Permissions are assigned to demarcations (PD+) and subjects are enrolled into proper roles (SR+). Permissions are never assigned to proper roles directly. Instead all subjects obtain permissions indirectly through the grant relation (G) where proper roles and demarcations are *linked up*. Figure 1 slightly adapts the work of Kuijper and Ermolaev, adding directional arrows to depict the explicit role hierarchy that exists between subjects and permissions.

Definition 1. RBÄC retains the principal semantic domains underlying RBAC (i.e. S and P) and defines the following syntax:

- Let S be a set of subjects

- Let P be a set of permissions

- Let R+ be a set of proper roles

- Let D+ be a set of demarcations [1]

- Let SR+ $\subseteq$ S $\times$ R+ be a subject-proper-role assignment relation

- Let PD+ $\subseteq$ P $\times$ D+ be a permission-demarcation assignment relation

- Let RH+ $\subseteq$ R+ $\times$ R+ be a proper-role-hierarchy relation, RH+ is required to be acyclic

- Let DH+ $\subseteq$ D+ $\times$ D+ be a demarcation-hierarchy relation, DH+ is required to be acyclic

- Let G $\subseteq$ R+ $\times$ D+ be a grant relation

Definition 2. The semantics of RBÄC identify the access relations SP $\subseteq$ S $\times$ P such that (s,p) $\in$ SP iff there exists roles r, r' $\in$ R^{+} and demarcations d, d' $\in$ D^{+} and the following conditions hold:

1. (s,r) $\in$ SR^{+}, i.e.: subject s is a member of proper role r.

2. r $\geq_r^+$ r', i.e.: r = r' or r is a senior role of r' [2]

3. (r',d') $\in$ G, i.e.: proper role r' is granted access to demarcation d'

4. d' $\geq_r^+$ d, i.e.: d = d' or d is a sub-demarcation of d'. [3]

5. (p,d) $\in$ PD^{+}, i.e. permission p is part of demarcation d

For small organizations where the number of roles remain relatively few, classic RBAC is often an adequate solution. However, for large organizations where there is an ongoing requirement to support employee turnover, policy changes and reorganization, RBÄC is a logical evolution. Despite the advantages of RBAC, the administrative degrees of freedom become limited when practitioners utilize a triangular RBAC model (Figure 1a) where there are four basic mutations:

1. Enroll a subject s $\in$ S to role r $\in$ R, i.e.: add (s,r) to SR

2. Disenroll a subject s $\in$ S from role r $\in$ R, i.e.: remove (s,r) from SR

3. Assign a permission p $\in$ P to role r $\in$ R, i.e.: add (p,r) to PR

4. Unssign a permission p $\in$ P from role r $\in$ R, i.e.: remove (p,r) from PR

The effect of an atomic RBAC mutation on SP is always one-to-many or many-to-one and never many-to-many. This is referred to as the administrative micro-stepping problem

---

[1] R+ and D+ are disjoint sets
[2] $\geq_r^+$ defines the transitive reflexive closure of RH^{+}
[3] $\geq_d^+$ defines the transitive reflexive closure of DH^{+}

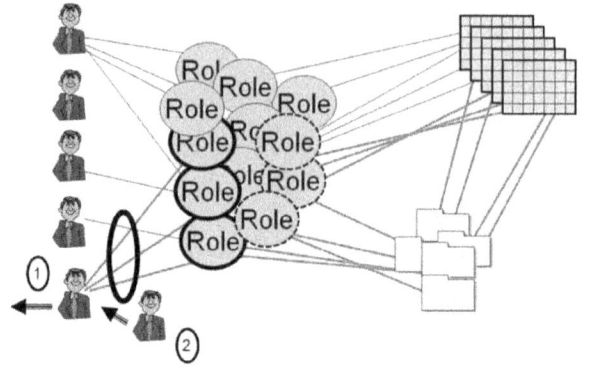

Figure 3: Subject-role relationships may be lost due to employee turnover.

[18]. With RBÄC the intent is to *break away* from the classic triangular example of RBAC, enforcing another degree of freedom and facilitating many-to-many mutations for SP. For practitioners this additional layer of abstraction permits administrative degrees of freedom not enjoyed under the classic triangular RBAC model.

RBÄC is not a new idea. Kuijper and Ermolaev cite Oh and Park as the first researchers proposing permissions be grouped independently into *task-based roles* [23]. Next, the work of Kern et al. [16], on enterprise role-based access control (ERBAC) is provided as an example, clearly demonstrating the practicality of maintaining two distinct role hierarchies. Finally, the work of Nyanchama and Osborn [21] is referenced as further evidence that a *dichotomy* exists between subject and permission management. The important difference to consider with RBÄC is the assertion subjects and permissions are never linked by a single role. Instead, there is **always** *at least two roles* between a subject and a permission.

Theorem 1. There exists a linear translation from RBAC to RBÄC and, vice versa, there exists a linear translation from RBÄC back to RBAC [18].

In terms of complexity, under the most natural formalization of a labeled transition system for the RBÄC scheme it would seem that RBÄC is less expressive (in the strict Tripunitara and Li sense [30]) than RBAC, while under a more liberal formalization based on Theorem 1 it would turn out to be equivalent.

In business management a roles and responsibility matrix may be used to clarify who is responsible for what [10]. Not only does RBÄC improve organizational scalability it improves comprehension by separating proper roles (i.e. roles) from demarcations (i.e. responsibilities). Although communication with the business side of an organization does not appear to be a primary motivation for RBÄC, we suggest the introduction of responsibilities is an important evolutionary concept that facilitates communication in addition to addressing scalability issues. Using organizational structure as the security framework provides clear focus for business analysts charged with eliciting requirements. Unlike Feltus et al. [8], we do not believe responsibilities should ever be directly assigned to subjects. Our argument against

116

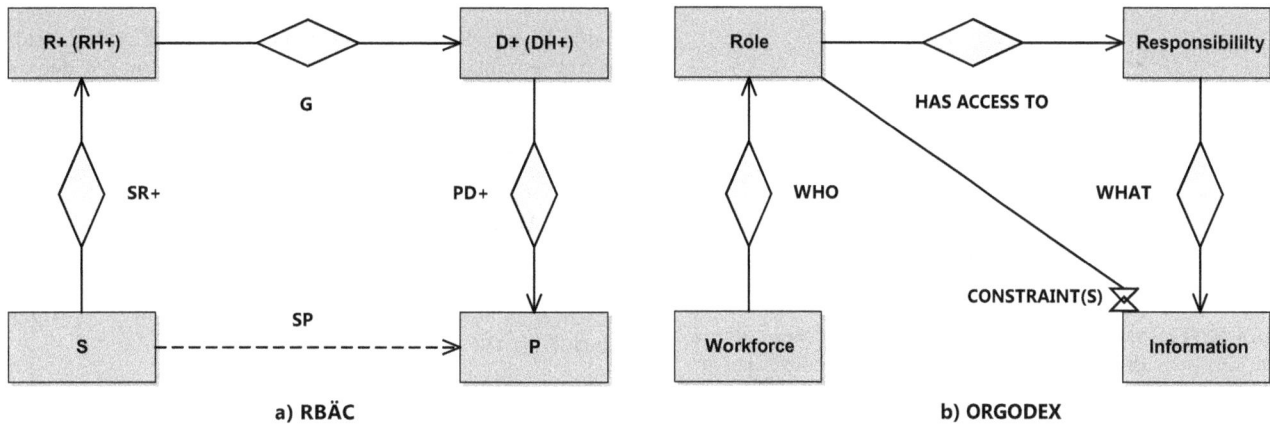

Figure 4: ORGODEX introduces business terminology and supports role-centric contraints

direct atomic responsibility assignment relates to employee turnover.

In large organizations with highly skilled workforces, an employee (i.e. subject) may acquire several responsibilities directly, resulting in the loss of important subject-role relationships when an employee leaves the organization. In Figure 3, we observe that if employee #1 leaves the organization three subject-role relationships may be lost before they are assigned to employee #2. Like the authors of RBÄC, we believe a *conceptual split right down the middle* of RBAC improves scalability, eradicating inflexible subject-role-permission *triangles* from large organizations. Furthermore, we have observed how this conceptual split facilitates information management security in practice, insulating systems against ongoing employee turnover, policy changes and reorganization.

In the following section, we introduce ORGODEX, validating its utility with a real-world case study at ACME university, located in North America. While the institution name is contrived for anonymity, the information that follows is based upon an existing RBAC system, supporting more than 700 employees. In our scenario of interest, we use ORGODEX to analyze an existing RBAC system, re-engineering the information security requirements for Departmental Chairs, who require constrained access to approve final grades for students.

5. ORGODEX

In this section we introduce ORGODEX, a new model and practical methodology for engineering scalable RBAC systems in large organizations where employees require access to information on a need to know basis, validating its utility with an example from a real-world student information system (SIS). ORGODEX is based upon the ISO/IEC 27001 standard for specifying information security management systems, adopting the well-known plan-do-check-act (PDCA) cycle for continuous improvement [12].

In previous work, we describe the addition of role-centric constraints as an extension to RBÄC [7]. In Figure 4, we introduce our new model for describing and reasoning about RBAC systems using terminology that facilitates communication with the business side of an organization. Figure 4a is

an intentional repetition of Figure 1b meant to highlight the similarities and differences between RBÄC and ORGODEX as follows:

- ORGODEX discards the implicit SP relation

- S is renamed **Workforce**

- SR+ is renamed **WHO**

- R+(RH+) is renamed **Role**

- G is renamed **HAS ACCESS TO**

- D+(DH+) is renamed **Responsibility**

- PD+ is renamed **WHAT**

- P is renamed **Information**

- ORGODEX introduces **CONSTRAINT(S)**

The ORGODEX methodology facilitates communication, providing a practical framework for consistent access control solutions through iterative analyze, realize and publicize cycles (Figure 5). In the following subsections, we use our ORGODEX methodology to analyze the business, realize a system and publicize the results of a real-world information management security architecture.

5.1 Analyze

The Plan-Do-Check-Act cycle begins with the Plan phase. With ORGODEX we begin the Analyze Phase with the simple premise that we are interested in the ongoing discovery of WHO - HAS ACCESS TO - WHAT. This process may be completed by a Business Analyst (BA) as follows:

1. Analyze the Roles

2. Produce Role Analysis Document

3. Analyze the Information

4. Produce Information Analysis Document

5. Analyze the Responsibilities

6. Produce Responsibilities Analysis Document

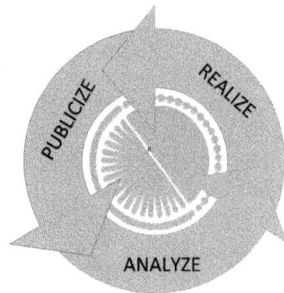

Figure 5: The ORGODEX methodology facilitates communication, providing a practical framework for consistent access control solutions through iterative analyze, realize and publicize cycles.

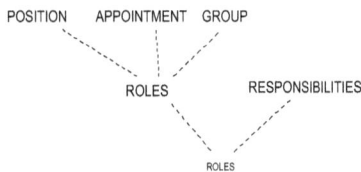

Figure 6: At ACME university, Role Evolution diverges beyond Roles and Responsibilities.

7. Analyze the Constraints

8. Produce Roles and Responsibilities Document

To build one's instance of ORGODEX, an analysis begins by identifying WHO the information management system and its security will support, analyzing the roles to better understand the workforce. At ACME university, fourteen Departmental Chairs report to one of three Deans. In Table 1 we produce a small sampling of our role analysis document, highlighting our fictitious workforce of interest; George Scott and Allan Williams, fulfilling two different Departmental Chair (DC) roles.

Role typing is an important aspect of the role analysis process. In Figure 6, we illustrate how roles have diverged beyond roles and responsibilities at ACME university. Besides appointments, position and group roles are also identified, providing further evidence of an organic role phylogeny that is occurring in real-world RBAC systems.

Like Crook et al. [6], we believe that roles must be typed. In terms of semantics, not all roles are equivalent. In the context of ACME university, an appointment is a role that one fulfills for a specified (or unspecified) period of time above and beyond the responsibilities of a staffing position. For instance, the Dean of Arts is appointed for a 5 year term by the Principal based upon recommendations from an ad-hoc committee. A position role is typically held by an individual employed on an indeterminate, term or casual basis. A position is associated with a number and a job description in the Human Resources Management System (HRMS), for example, position number #123456, Information Systems Manager. A group role describes a logical set of the workforce that are grouped because they share similar responsibilities. It is often the case that while responsibili-

Table 1: A Role Analysis Document identifies WHO, establishing a relationship between the Workforce and a defined Role.

Workforce	Role
George Scott	Departmental Chair (DC)
Allan Williams	Departmental Chair (DC)

Table 2: A Role Analysis Document Provides Type Information for the Roles Identified

Role	Type
Departmental Chair (DC)	Group
DC#1	Appointment
DC#2	Appointment

ties may be similar, scope is different, for example, Departmental Chair #1 and #2 share similar responsibilities but require access to different sets of information (Table 2).

Next, a BA must identify WHAT information management concepts exist, determining the protection levels associated with these information assets. In Table 3 we produce a small sampling of our information analysis document, highlighting concepts of interest such as Course and Student. The rationale for determining the protection levels early in the analysis process is twofold. First, we must establish a balance between security and practicality from the onset. Information deemed to require additional protection levels must be further considered upstream (i.e. Responsibility Analysis). Second, we observed that personnel at ACME university were often unsure of the protection level for the information that they were responsible for, often unknowingly compromising security protocols. To this end, we are not suggesting that our methodology will necessarily fix this problem, however, we do believe that the last phase of our methodology, publicize, should link back to these protection levels, advertising information security on a regular basis, ideally strengthening the posture of an organization.

Next, a BA must analyze responsibilities independently from those charged with the completion of these tasks. Our experience with this activity suggests it is non-trivial and somewhat irregular to think of responsibilities absent those charged with their completion. Nevertheless, we contend that the Responsibility Analysis document may in fact be one of the most important work products established within our methodology. We suggest this based on years observing enterprise organizations where responsibilities dynamically shift on a daily, weekly, monthly and yearly basis. From an information management security viewpoint, we contend

Table 3: An Information Analysis Document Provides Protection Levels for the Concepts Identified

Information	Protection
Course	Public
Student	Protected

Table 4: A Responsibility Analysis Document further identifies WHAT, establishing a relationship between Information and a defined Responsiblity.

Information	Responsibility
Student	Approve Final Grades (AFG)

Table 5: A Roles and Responsibilities Document identifies WHO - HAS ACCESS TO - WHAT

Role	Responsibility	Constraint
DC#1	AFG	#1
DC#2	AFG	#2

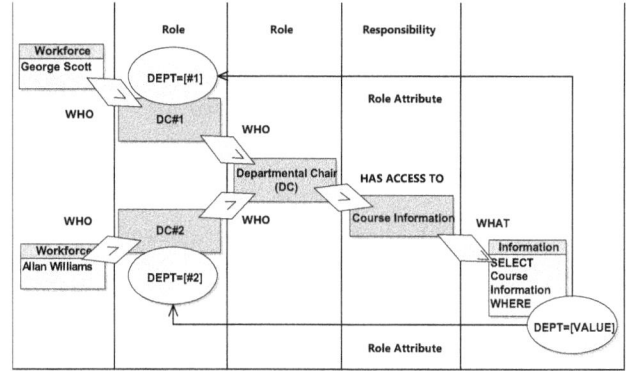

Figure 7: Constraining Information. The List of Courses that may be selected by Departmental Chairs #1 and #2.

that this is the fundamental difference with our model. In Table 4 we produce one record of interest from our responsibility analysis document, indicating the information related to the responsibility.

Finally, the BA must analyze the constraints or scope for each responsibility. Although this is all very abstract and listed sequentially, it is assumed that these activities and their related work products will be carried out simultaneously using various requirements elicitation techniques, perhaps interview questions similar to those described by Jaferian [13].

The roles and responsibilities for a Departmental Chair has been a subject of interest within the research community [1]. At ACME university, each and every Departmental Chair shared similar if not identical permissions but were responsible for different information sets. During our constraints analysis, we observed that each Departmental Chair is responsible for approving final grades for students taking a course delivered within their respective curriculum. Grades are entered by instructors who teach an academic course to students, set up an evaluation scheme and grade the student. In Table 5 we highlight the roles and responsibilities of interest for this work, indicating that DC#1 is only responsible for approving final grades for courses offered by department #1 (AFG#1). Similarly, DC#2 is only responsible for approving final grades for courses offered by department #2 (AFG#2)

In the following subsection, we describe how the Business Analyst's work products, listed in this section, are directly leveraged by information management system architects during the realize phase.

5.2 Realize

The Plan-Do-Check-Act cycle continues with the Do and Check phases. With ORGODEX, the realization of WHO - HAS ACCESS TO - WHAT is achieved through iterative design, implementation and testing of the roles and responsibilities discovered in the previous phase. In this section we present our methodology for realizing information security. We elaborate upon our scenario of interest from the previous subsection where DC#1 and DC#2 are responsible for approving final grades (AFG#1 and AFG#2) at the end of each academic term. Then we describe our role-centric methodology for dynamically constraining access to information.

The realization of WHO - HAS ACCESS TO - WHAT may be completed by an Information Management Security Architect (SA) as follows:

1. Design Information Security

2. Produce Hierarchical Diagram

3. Implement Information Security

4. Test Information Security

In Figure 7 we use our hierarchical diagramming notation to better visualize the directional hierarchy of workforce-role, role-responsibility and responsibility-information grants [7]. The elements of our diagram can be reconfigured to look like the *desirable square (or rectangle)* however, we feel that the notion of hierarchy is an important aspect not well represented in Figure 4. Instead, we use *swim lanes* to depict the conceptual boundaries between the workforce, roles, responsibilities and information. To better comprehend real-world RBAC systems it is important to visualize the directionality of enroll, grant and assign relationships, *visualizing* the depth at which one actually obtains permissions to do something. In our scenario of interest there is a cascade of diamond shaped relationships between entities (i.e. rectangles) ultimately linking the workforce and information together. We use arrows within the diamonds to indicate directionality. There are three roles explicitly defined between George Scott and the permission to select Course information. This hierarchical diagramming technique is also meant to facilitate our notion of role-centric constraints.

At this juncture, the reader may be curious why ACME University has chosen to implement an RBAC system where two roles and one responsibility exist between George Scott and the permission required to view the courses he is responsible for. At ACME University, roles are used to directly influence the records returned in permissions, for example, SELECT information from COURSE. We learned that a role like DC#1, was assigned the role attribute, or (name, value) pair (Department, #1). Then when applicable queries were performed the WHERE clause used this role attribute to determine what records should be returned. This was derived directly from the roles held by the subject. When George Scott, DC#1, accessed the SIS his role attributes were used to determine whether or not courses may be viewed. Figure 7 depicts the *match* condition used to restrict the List of Courses for DC#1 when approving final grades.

Definition 3. ORGODEX constraints are defined for roles (R) as follows:

- Let A be a set of attributes with the form (name,value)
- Let C ⊆ R × A be a role constraint relation

Example 1. Departmental Chairs #1 and #2 are responsible for Approving Final Grades (AFG) within their respective department. For example, DC#1 may only SELECT course information WHERE the DEPT=[#1] (Figure 7)

- C = {(DC#1, (DEPT,#1))}
- C = {(DC#2, (DEPT,#2))}

Although we did not initially see the advantages of such an RBAC system, questioning the excessive number of roles, we began to appreciate the simplicity of workforce-role relations found *on the surface* as we tunneled deeper into the SIS design. Additional examples may be found in the Appendix.

Unlike ARBAC which describes constraints on subject-role enrollments and permission-role assignments [26], ORGODEX constrains permissions already assigned to one or more roles. Unlike RABAC whose intent is to dynamically constrain the set of permissions available to users [14], our intent is to dynamically constrain the information returned by static responsibility-information grants.

With the analysis and design phases completed, the SA is responsible for relating the workforce to their roles and responsibilities which are in turn related to the information. For our scenario of interest the following Structured Query Language (SQL)[1] commands might be used:

- CREATE ROLE Departmental Chair (DC)
- CREATE ROLE DC#1
- CREATE ROLE Approve Final Grades
- INSERT DC#1, (Department,#1) INTO role attributes
- CREATE or REPLACE VIEW course AS (SELECT * FROM course information WHERE dept=value) [2]
- GRANT SELECT ON course TO Approve Final Grades
- GRANT Departmental Chair (DC) to DC#1
- GRANT Approve Final Grades to Departmental Chair
- GRANT DC#1 to George Scott

After implementing as above, the SA must test the records returned by the *VIEW course* for George Scott. If the view returns only the courses from Department #1 then the SA can claim success. After completing the commands listed above, DC#2 is granted access to Department #2 courses with only a few more commands as follows:

---

[1]Relational Databases like Oracle® use a standard language to both store and retrieve information

[2]value is dynamically retrieved from role attributes for DC#1, for instance

- CREATE ROLE DC#2
- INSERT DC#2, (Department,#2) INTO role attributes
- GRANT Departmental Chair (DC) to DC#2
- GRANT DC#2 to Allan Williams

Following these commands, the SA must test the records returned by the *VIEW course* for both Allan Williams and George Scott. If the view returns only the expected courses for each Departmental Chair then the SA can claim success.

5.3 Publicize

The Plan-Do-Check-Act cycle completes with the Check and Act phases. With ORGODEX, the publication of WHO - HAS ACCESS TO - WHAT is achieved by regularly reporting information security aspects implemented during the realize phase. In this section we present our methodology for publishing information security for privileged members of the workforce responsible for validations. One might argue that this is the most important phase of our methodology, providing ongoing validation for the information security architecture.

With ORGODEX, reports are published at regular intervals (e.g weekly) or produced on-demand. At a minimum, an instance of ORGODEX must be able to produce the following reports:

- A Role Analysis Report lists the roles defined by the information system and their type (e.g. DC#1, Appointment)
- An Information Analysis Report lists the concepts identified and their corresponding protection level (e.g. Student, Protected)
- A Responsibility Analysis Report lists the information acted upon while executing a responsibility (e.g. Student, AFG)
- A Roles and Responsibilities Report lists WHO - HAS ACCESS TO - WHAT (e.g. DC#1, AFG#1)

To complete one iteration of our methodology, these reports must match the corresponding documents from the Analyze phase. More importantly, the security architecture must be regularly reported to privileged members of the workforce responsible for validations. Although we do not focus upon the notion of *Insider Threat* in this work [12], we believe ORGODEX inherently addresses this concern, delivering a model and methodology based upon the ISO/IEC 27001 standard where provisioning information on a *need-to-know* basis is a primary concern for access control systems.

Communication with the business side of an organization is a primary motivation for ORGODEX. We believe that the Roles and Responsibilities Report in particular is an interesting solution to the challenging problem of entitlements review [13]. If the Roles and Responsibilities Report directly reflects the work produced by the BA, we believe a communication language that crosses from the business world to the information security world has been achieved. One could envision a software application whereby managers regularly review an interactive Roles and Responsibilities report for their employees as defined by a BA and implemented in ORGODEX as follows:

- The report is an inclusive matrix listing viewable roles and their assigned responsibilities.

- The report resembles a job description for individual roles

In the following section, we discuss how ORGODEX controls growth using our new RBAC dichotomy and the notion of role evolution to *insulate* RBAC systems against ongoing employee turnover, policy changes and reorganization.

6. DISCUSSION

To our knowledge the term *role explosion* has not been formally defined by the research community. We acknowledge that *responsibilities explosion* may be a concern for our model. However, we believe the optimization work found in the role engineering literature could be leveraged to refine the number of responsibilities defined by an information management system [20]. In particular, bottom up role mining might be an interesting means of addressing this concern [31].

Responsibilities explosion is a natural occurrence emerging organically over the lifetime of an information security system, as measured in months and years. A simple example would be a poorly named responsibility that is duplicated when an Information Management Security Architect (SA) does not realize a suitable role for their requirement already exists. With role mining, responsibility duplication could be reported, addressed and controlled. In addition, ORGODEX controls explosion through the use of role-centric constraints, permitting the reuse of responsibilities by different roles. Our *Approve Final Grade* example from Table 5 describes how the constraints of ORGODEX permit an SA to statically define a responsibility with one set of permissions that is shared by roles requiring access to different information sets.

ORGODEX supports controlled role evolution by introducing a dichotomy whereby roles hold no permissions. As a result, orphaned roles no longer needed by an organization may be dropped inconsequentially. However, orphaned responsibilities, holding permissions to perform application functionality, must be more carefully considered and only removed on confirmation from the business side of an organization. With the controls in place to *semantically* check and act upon the population of roles and responsibilities, entitlement review might equate to addressing *alerts* raised by ORGODEX instead of monthly or bi-annually attempting to review reports where business terminology is not being used.

Role evolution does not aim to prevent role explosion, instead it presumes the number of roles will scale uncontrollably in large organizations or controllably using a prescribed methodology. In this work, we prescribe a methodology for controlled growth where the optimal set of roles is a secondary concern. Our primary concern is communication with the business side of an organization. We are motivated to better align role and requirements engineering using a methodology that facilitates communication, using roles and responsibilities to describe and reason about RBAC systems with business terminology.

However, we do acknowledge that it is non-trivial and somewhat irregular to think of responsibilities absent those charged with their completion. Nevertheless, we contend that the highly iterative responsibility analysis and its associated documentation may in fact be one of the most important work products established within our methodology. We suggest this based on years observing enterprise organizations where responsibilities dynamically shift on a daily, weekly, monthly and yearly basis. From an information management security viewpoint, we contend that this is the fundamental difference with our model.

During our analysis at ACME university, we observed that the SA had aggregated permissions into responsibilities and assigned them to Appointment, Position or Group roles in a role hierarchy to avoid losing important security relationships when employees left the organization (Figure 3). In large organizations with highly skilled workforces, an employee (i.e. subject) may acquire several responsibilities directly, resulting in the loss of important subject-role relationships when an employee leaves the organization.

Furthermore, we have observed how this conceptual split facilitates requirements engineering for information security. Like RBÄC, ORGODEX inherently facilitates many-to-many administrative mutations and ultimately leads to more organizational scalability. The speculation being that such an approach might prove beneficial when considering the following:

- workforce-role management may be automated as appropriate in organizations, reducing administrative overhead.

- application architects can focus on mapping the permissions associated with functional requirements to responsibilities

- access control may be delegated and managed in a roles and responsibilities matrix

Further studies are needed to validate the effectiveness of this approach. Rather than producing metrics aimed at optimal role sets, we believe that the degree of automation for roles is of interest. At ACME university, we observed that the enrollment of employees into Appointment roles was automated as part of existing business processes. Unlike Appointment roles, the enrollment of subjects into Positional roles was not automated. We understood this automation would be introduced at a future date.

We also believe the degree of delegation for responsibilities is an interesting metric. The SA is generally not authorized to assign responsibilities absent the confirmation of an approving authority. Developing RBAC systems that facilitate entitlements review and permit managers to directly assign responsibilities to roles has the potential to impact the perception of access control. Rather than being viewed as a necessary burden, access control has the potential to be a well understood, enabling technology.

At this juncture, we believe it is appropriate to acknowledge that both dynamic and static separation of duties are not addressed in this work. The implementation of mutually exclusive roles both statically and dynamically is left for future work but we suggest that our new dichotomy might facilitate these conversations, providing the flexibility to define and implement additional constraints as needed.

In future work we intend to publish the results of additional ORGODEX instances, further validating our model and methodology. More specifically, we are currently engaged in engineering a new RBAC system, using our OR-GODEX model and methodology to communicate with stakeholders, structure the project and iteratively analyze, realize and publicize a new information management system. Our candidate organization is also a higher education institution located in North America. During our initial analysis, we have discovered additional benefits associated with our approach. We are already observing the advantages of *templates* during the requirements engineering phase. Large organizations with comparable objectives, for example higher education institutions, have similar roles and responsibilities, such that one ORGODEX instance may be used as the basis for another and customized as applicable.

7. CONCLUSION

In this paper, our objective is to introduce ORGODEX, a new model and practical methodology for engineering scalable RBAC systems in organizations where hundreds or thousands of employees require access to information on a need to know basis. First, we motivate the requirement for a new RBAC dichotomy, distinguishing between roles and responsibilities. Next, we introduce our new model for describing and reasoning about RBAC systems with this new dichotomy. Finally, we produce a new iterative methodology for engineering scalable access control systems.

We make the following contributions:

- We motivate the requirement for a new RBAC dichotomy, distinguishing between roles and responsibilities. We introduce the notion of role evolution.

- We introduce a new model for describing and reasoning about RBAC systems in business terminology, extending previous models with the notion of constraints

- We propose a new iterative methodology for engineering scalable RBAC systems, validating its utility with a real-world case study at a large North-American university

Despite their diversity, large organizations are built upon two key concepts, roles and responsibilities, where a role like Departmental Chair is identified and assigned responsibilities. It is surprising that the business model of large organizations is often loosely coupled with its RBAC systems, merging the notions of role and responsibility into simplistic, inflexible, triangular subject-role-permission relationships. We believe that an RBAC system that is tightly coupled with the business model, clearly separating roles and responsibilities, inherently improves communication between the business and its Information Management Security Architect(s).

In future work, we intend to continue using the ORGODEX model and methodology to analyze, realize and publicize the information management security architecture for other organizations. This research has the potential to impact the perception of access control. Rather than being viewed as a necessary burden, access control has the potential to be a well understood, enabling technology, directly informed by the business model, a scaffolding for maintaining information systems, where the individual parts are simple but the flexibility and utility achieved through summing its parts provides a framework for scalable access control systems.

Acknowledgement

We would like to thank Florian Schaub for generously performing several thoughtful reviews of this work. We also appreciate the helpful guidance of the anonymous reviewers whose constructive suggestions have been addressed, strengthening the final version of this paper.

8. REFERENCES

[1] I. Berdrow. King among kings: Understanding the role and responsibilities of the department chair in higher education. *Educational Management Administration & Leadership*, 38(4):499–514, 2010.

[2] K. Beznosov, P. Inglesant, J. Lobo, R. Reeder, and M. Zurko. Usability meets access control: challenges and research opportunities. pages 3–4, 2009.

[3] A. Colantonio, R. Di Pietro, and A. Ocello. A cost-driven approach to role engineering. *Proceedings of the 2008 ACM symposium on Applied computing - SAC '08*, page 2129, 2008.

[4] E. J. Coyne. Role engineering. *Proceedings of the first ACM Workshop on Rolebased access control RBAC 95*, (4):4–es, 1996.

[5] J. Crampton and G. Loizou. Administrative scope. *ACM Transactions on Information and System Security*, 6(2):201–231, may 2003.

[6] R. Crook, D. Ince, and B. Nuseibeh. Modelling access policies using roles in requirements engineering. *Information and Software Technology*, 45(14):979–991, nov 2003.

[7] A. Elliott and S. Knight. Towards Managed Role Explosion. In *Proceedings of the New Security Paradigms Workshop*, number 1, pages 100–111, New York, New York, USA, 2015. ACM Press.

[8] C. Feltus, M. Petit, and M. Sloman. Enhancement of Business IT Alignment by Including Responsibility Components in RBAC. *Proceedings of the CAiSE 2010 Workshop Business/IT Alignment and Interoperability*, pages 61–75, 2010.

[9] D. F. Ferraiolo and R. Kuhn. Role-based access controls. *Proc. of 15th NIST-NSA National Computer Security Conference*, 1992.

[10] M. Goold, A. Strategic, M. Centre, A. Campbell, A. Strategic, and M. Centre. Work : Creating Clarity on Unit Roles and Responsibility. 21(3):351–363, 2003.

[11] V. C. Hu, D. Ferraiolo, R. Kuhn, A. Schnitzer, K. Sandlin, R. Miller, and K. Scarfone. Guide to Attribute Based Access Control (ABAC) Definition and Considerations. Technical report, National Institute of Standards and Technology, Gaithersburg, MD, jan 2014.

[12] E. Humphreys. Information security management standards: Compliance, governance and risk management. *Information Security Technical Report*, 13(4):247–255, 2008.

[13] P. Jaferian and K. Beznosov. Poster : Helping users review and make sense of access policies in organizations. In *SOUPS '14: Proceedings of the Tenth Symposium On Usable Privacy and Security*, pages 301–320, 2014.

[14] X. Jin, R. Sandhu, and R. Krishnan. RABAC: Role-centric attribute-based access control. *Lecture*

Notes in Computer Science (including subseries
Lecture Notes in Artificial Intelligence and Lecture
Notes in Bioinformatics), 7531 LNCS:84–96, 2012.

[15] L. Katz and R. Margo. Technical Change and the
Relative Demand for Skilled Labor: The United States
in Historical Perspective. Technical Report January,
National Bureau of Economic Research, Cambridge,
MA, feb 2013.

[16] A. Kern, A. Schaad, and J. Moffett. An
administration concept for the enterprise role-based
access control model. Proceedings of the eighth ACM
symposium on Access control models and technologies -
SACMAT '03, page 3, 2003.

[17] D. R. Kuhn, E. J. Coyne, and T. R. Weil. Adding
attributes to role-based access control. Computer,
43(6):79–81, 2010.

[18] W. Kuijper and V. Ermolaev. Sorting out role based
access control. Proceedings of the 19th ACM
symposium on Access control models and technologies -
SACMAT '14, pages 63–74, 2014.

[19] N. Li and Z. Mao. Administration in role-based access
control. Proceedings of the 2nd ACM symposium on
Information, computer and communications security -
ASIACCS '07, page 127, 2007.

[20] B. Mitra, S. Sural, J. Vaidya, and V. Atluri. A Survey
of Role Mining. ACM Computing Surveys, 48(4):1–37,
2016.

[21] M. Nyanchama and S. Osborn. The role graph model
and conflict of interest. ACM Transactions on
Information and System Security, 2(1):3–33, feb 1999.

[22] A. O'Connor and R. Loomis. 2010 Economic Analysis
of Role-Based Access Control. Technical Report
0211876, NIST, 2010.

[23] S. Oh and S. Park. Task-role based access control
(T-RBAC): An improved access control model for
enterprise environment. Database and Expert Systems
Applications, pages 264–273, 2000.

[24] S. Oh and R. Sandhu. A model for role administration
using organization structure. Proceedings of the
seventh ACM symposium on Access control models
and technologies - SACMAT '02, page 155, 2002.

[25] S. Peisert and M. Bishop. Dynamic, Flexible, and
Optimistic Access Control. Technical report, UC
Davis CS Technical Report CSE-2013-76, 2013.

[26] R. Sandhu, V. Bhamidipati, and Q. Munawer. The
ARBAC97 model for role-based administration of
roles. ACM Transactions on Information and System
Security, 2(1):105–135, feb 1999.

[27] R. Sandhu and Q. Munawer. The ARBAC99 model
for administration of roles. In Proceedings 15th Annual
Computer Security Applications Conference
(ACSAC'99), pages 229–238. IEEE Comput. Soc,
1999.

[28] R. S. Sandhu, E. J. Coyne, H. L. Feinstein, and C. E.
Youman. Role-based access control models. Computer,
29(2):38–47, 1996.

[29] A. Schaad, J. Moffett, and J. Jacob. The role-based
access control system of a European bank. In
Proceedings of the sixth ACM symposium on Access
control models and technologies - SACMAT '01, pages
3–9, New York, New York, USA, 2001. ACM Press.

[30] M. V. Tripunitara and N. Li. Comparing the
expressive power of access control models. ACM
Conference on Computer and Communications
Security, pages 62–71, 2004.

[31] J. Vaidya, V. Atluri, J. Warner, and Q. Guo. Role
engineering via prioritized subset enumeration. IEEE
Transactions on Dependable and Secure Computing,
7(3):300–314, 2010.

APPENDIX

A. ADDITIONAL EXAMPLES

Organizational scalability is enhanced at ACME university by decoupling subject and permission management. In Figure 8 one can visualize how ACME university uses the flexibility and scalability of Structured Query Language (SQL) to reuse the same permission for various user groups, providing consistent, context aware information to a variety of employees at the university.

Security practitioners at ACME University had discovered that who has access to what is difficult to maintain in an environment with constant employee turnover. By aggregating permissions into responsibilities and assigning them to Appointment, Position or Group roles in a role hierarchy they could avoid losing important security relationships when employees left the organization (Figure 3).

Example 2. The Associate Registrar Undergraduate (UG) is responsible for maintaining UG Course Information. The Associate Registrar Undergraduate may only SELECT course information WHERE the CATALOG=[UG] (Figure 8)

- C = {(Associate Registrar Undergraduate, (Catalog,UG))}

Example 3. The Associate Registrar Postgraduate (PG) is responsible for maintaining PG Course Information. The Associate Registrar Postgraduate may only SELECT course information WHERE the CATALOG=[PG] (Figure 8)

- C = {(Associate Registrar Postgraduate, (Catalog,PG))}

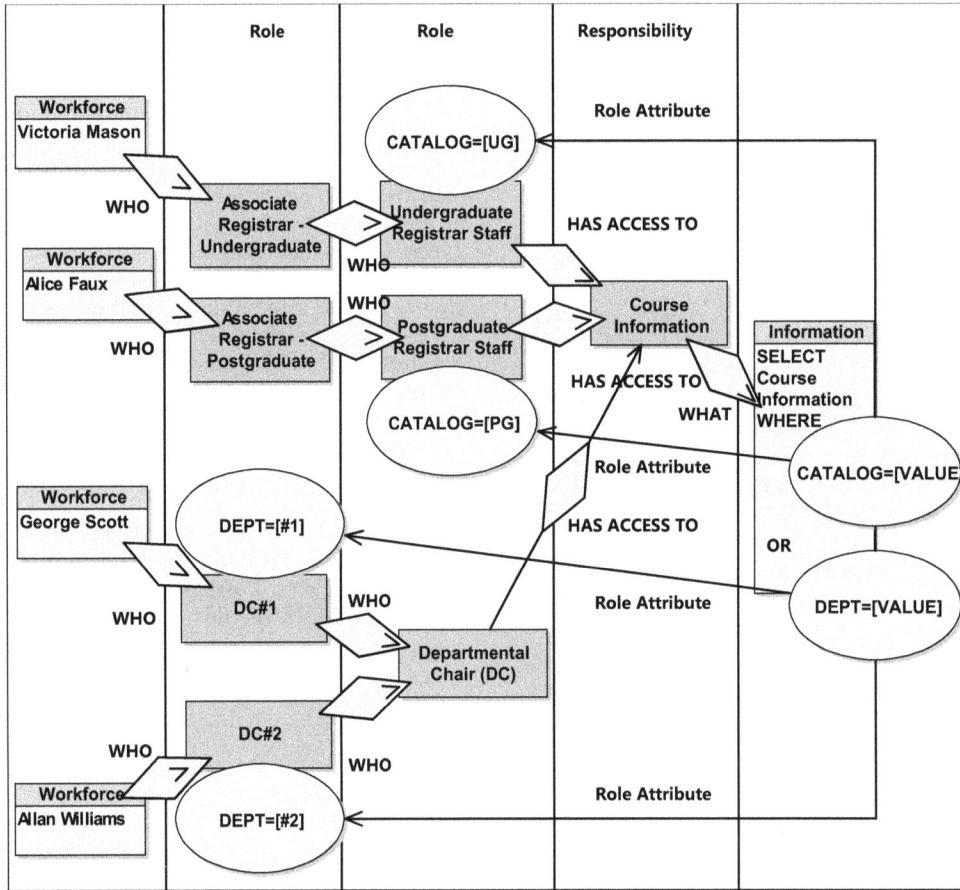

Figure 8: Determining the List of Courses that may be selected by a various members of the Workforce.

Policy Negotiation for Co-owned Resources in Relationship-Based Access Control

Pooya Mehregan and Philip W. L. Fong
Department of Computer Science
University of Calgary
Calgary, Alberta, Canada

ABSTRACT

The collaborative nature of content development has given rise to the novel problem of multiple ownership in access control, such that a shared resource is administrated simultaneously by co-owners who may have conflicting privacy preferences and/or sharing needs. Prior work has focused on the design of unsupervised conflict resolution mechanisms.

Driven by the need for human consent in organizational settings, this paper explores interactive policy negotiation, an approach complementary to that of prior work. Specifically, we propose an extension of Relationship-Based Access Control (ReBAC) to support multiple ownership, in which a policy negotiation protocol is in place for co-owners to come up with and give consent to an access control policy in a structured manner. During negotiation, the draft policy is assessed by formally defined availability criteria: policy satisfiability, resiliency and feasibility, which all belong to the second level of the polynomial hierarchy. We devised two algorithms for verifying policy satisfiability, both employing a modern SAT solver for solving subproblems. The performance is found to be adequate for mid-sized organizations.

Keywords

Multiple Ownership; ReBAC; Negotiation; Availability.

1. INTRODUCTION

One of the most interesting recent developments in the area of Access Control is the study of *multiple ownership*. Specifically, the many and diverse scenarios of resource sharing in social computing applications have brought about a fundamental change in our understanding of Discretionary Access Control (DAC). In the classical formulations of DAC (e.g., the Graham-Denning model [11, 19]), every object has a primary administrator known as its *owner*. Ownership, in the context of Access Control, is about administrative rights and not property rights. The owner is the user who has full administrative privilege to determine the access control policy of the object. While partial administrative privileges can be delegated, the delegatees are considered acting on behalf of the owner, and thus fully trusted. This classical view, however, has been significantly revised due to the emergence of new access control requirements in social computing.

Social computing applications provide support for collaborative authoring of contents. Contents that are originally created by one user are enriched and annotated by other users. Examples of such features include liking, tagging and commenting. Some contents are even co-authored by multiple users. An example is the befriending operation, which creates a joint declaration of two users' relationship. An object of this kind has privacy bearing on multiple parties, and thus they all want to have a say on the access control policy of that object. These parties, who are called *co-owners* in this work, may have different or even conflicting privacy and availability preferences. In other words, co-owned objects are not the ones *accessed/shared* by multiple parties, but the ones that are *administered* by multiple parties. The study of multiple ownership involves the design and analysis of schemes for supporting co-owners in administrating access control policies in a collaborative manner.

There is now a significant and growing body of literature on multiple ownership [23, 26, 30, 24, 12, 13, 14, 15, 25, 21], most notable of which are the seminal work of Squicciarini *et al* [23, 24] and that of Hu *et al.* [12, 13, 14, 15]. A common theme in their works is to devise unsupervised conflict resolution mechanisms for reconciling the potentially conflicting privacy preferences and sharing needs of the various co-owners. These mechanisms are usually blackboxes in the sense that they are mathematically complex enough to escape comprehension by typical end-users [21].

In this work, we venture away from mainstream social media (Facebook, Twitter, Instagram, etc.), and study multiple ownership in the setting of *organizational computing* — medical records systems, documents sharing and co-authoring, business process support, etc. For instance, a patient, her treating clinicians and the hospital administration all share a privacy stake in a medical record. They co-own the record because they all want a say in the access control policy of the record. Again, colleagues from different departments who co-author a report share an interest in the access control of that report. As co-owners representing different departments, they may have different or even conflicting views on how the report shall be protected.

We propose in this work a framework for supporting multiple ownership in the family of Relationship-Based Access Control (ReBAC) models by Fong *et al.* [8, 10, 3, 22], through interactive policy negotiation with tool support. ReBAC is a general-purpose access control paradigm de-

SACMAT'16, June 05-08, 2016, Shanghai, China
© 2016 ACM. ISBN 978-1-4503-3802-8/16/06... $15.00
DOI: http://dx.doi.org/10.1145/2914642.2914652

signed for supporting organizational computing. It features a finer granularity of control over classical Role-Based Access Control (RBAC) models, and offers natural support for delegation of trust [8]. A first, large-scale implementation of ReBAC in an open-source medical records system was recently attempted [22]. We therefore ground the present work on ReBAC, as this forces us to confront the reality of fine-grained access control as well as trust delegation.

1.1 Rationale for Interactive Negotiation

A uniqueness of this work is the design and implementation of tool support for interactive negotiation of access control policies. We envision that co-owners engage in a conscious process of negotiating the access control policy of their co-owned objects. We fully acknowledge the importance of unsupervised conflict resolution schemes proposed in previous work, and we are in no way advocating interactive negotiation as a replacement for unsupervised conflict resolution. We, however, recognize the complementary role of interactive policy negotiation because of two reasons.

First, there is evidence that, in some circumstances, users feel the need to engage in policy negotiation. For example, the empirical study reported in [17] reveals that SNS users do negotiate boundary regulations. Even in the absence of much needed tool support, users find other methods to negotiate. For instance, they simply exchange emails to negotiate the suitability of a group photo before disclosing it. The authors of [17] advocate the need for supporting expectation discussion and privacy negotiation among co-owners *before* conflicts arise. The study reported in [2] also highlights the need for negotiation in photo sharing, and the fact that users make use of offline detours in the absence of tool-support for such negotiations. We believe that interactive negotiation empowers users to directly collaborate with one another. In many cases, conflicts occur because users are unaware of other co-owners' privacy preferences; otherwise, they display eagerness in accommodating the privacy preferences of other co-owners [17]. In collegial environments, such as those in organizational computing, interactive negotiation offers the opportunity for users to collaboratively arrive at a mutually agreeable policy.

Second, the accountability requirements of the application domain may demand the express consent of the co-owners in publishing information. In organizational settings such as a healthcare facility, in which co-owners may bear legal responsibilities for regulating information disclosure, conscious human consent in policy negotiation would be required. In addition, collaboration in organizational computing is usually highly structured, mirroring the structure of the organization. The number of co-owners are therefore much fewer than typical social computing applications. Interactive policy negotiation that reflects the accountability requirements of organizational computing is thus feasible.

Our position is that both unsupervised conflict resolution and interactive policy negotiation have their respective roles. Which approach to adopt must be determined on a case by case basis, depending on the application domain (social or organizational computing), nature of the co-ownership (number of co-owners), or accountability requirements (legal liability). In this work, we will study the less-explored design space of interactive negotiation, especially in the development of tools for supporting such negotiation.

1.2 Contributions

The concrete contributions of this work are the following:

1. An administrative model supporting multiple ownership is formulated for ReBAC (§3). Access control policies are specified in terms of graph patterns in order to facilitate policy negotiation and policy analysis. Administrative operations that require user consent and policy negotiation are explicitly identified.

2. A novel policy negotiation protocol is proposed for co-owners to arrive at and give consent to an access control policy (§4). Our design offers two unique features. First, structured revision of the policy under negotiation allows co-owners to express their privacy preferences through counteracting the policy components contributed by other co-owners. Second, the need for sharing is assessed against mechanically verified availability criteria. The two features jointly provide a balance of privacy and sharing.

3. Three formal criteria of availability (i.e., satisfiability, feasibility and resiliency) have been formulated for assessing negotiated policies (§6). These availability criteria are inspired by the analogous concepts recently proposed for workflow authorization systems [4, 28, 16, 5]. We show that all of the three criteria belong to the second level of the polynomial hierarchy [1, Chap. 5].

4. Focusing on the availability criterion known as policy satisfiability, we devise two decision procedures for assessing availability (§7). Rather than naively reducing policy satisfiability to Quantified Boolean Formula (QBF) satisfiability, our custom algorithms make use of a modern SAT solver to attack subproblems.

5. The performance of the two algorithms are evaluated in §8, in which we empirically justify the superiority of our custom algorithms over generic QBF solvers, compare the relative merits of the two algorithms, and demonstrate that their performance is adequate for mid-sized organizations of up to 100,000 users. To put this magnitude in perspective, Microsoft and Google employ 94,000 and 55,419 employees respectively.

2. RELATED WORK

The need for addressing the diverse privacy concerns of multiple privacy stakeholders has recently caught the attention of security researchers. The first work to address this problem is that of Squicciarini *et.al* [23]. Their work emphasizes the need to honour the privacy preferences of all co-owners. They used Mechanism Design (Clarke-Tax) and Game Theory in the setting of an auction to perform conflict resolution. Conflict resolution as proposed in this work is relatively complex for naive end-users. This shortcoming is addressed in their follow-up work [24], in which they apply majority-voting instead of the auction.

One of the early works which underlines the multiple ownership problem in online social networks is [26]. In this work, the privacy consequences of disregarding the co-owners' privacy preferences have been demonstrated by means of successful inference attacks.

In the seminal work of Hu and Ahn [12, 14], each co-owner submits her preferred privacy policy along with a number as how (s)he perceives the co-owned object to be sensitive. A conflict resolution mechanism is then employed to aggregate the preferred privacy policies and sensitivities of the co-owners into a single privacy policy. They are the first to make explicit the connection between policy composition (e.g., XACML) and conflict resolution mechanisms for multiple-ownership. In their follow-up work [13], they address the need for sharing, which is usually overlooked in the face of privacy. A quantitative scheme is then proposed to trade off between privacy and the need for sharing. In another follow-up work [15], they propose a game-theoretic analysis of their proposed model, showing there exist a Nash Equilibrium (NE) for multiple ownership problem.

An adaptive conflict resolution mechanism is proposed in [25]. This mechanism estimates if a user would concede based on her willingness to change action. Adaptiveness is captured in our work in the negotiation protocol (§4).

Mehregan and Fong make the important observation that multiple-ownership often arises "accidentally" when an object is composite, and when co-owners have privacy interests over various parts of the composite objects [21]. Therefore, resolving conflicting privacy preferences is genuinely needed only when indivisible objects are involved. We therefore focus on indivisible (atomic) objects in this paper.

Our approach is also comparable to [30], in which co-owners collaboratively author a privacy policy for a co-owned object, using a mechanism akin to a virtual whiteboard. Policy components come in two types: *weak* and *strong*. Weak policies are negotiable, and strong ones are not. This work is unique in prior literature in that it is the only one that involves negotiation among co-owners in coming up with a policy for the co-owned object. Our work is therefore comparable to this work. The drawback for [30] is that, when a strong policy is introduced, nobody would be able to edit/remove it except the co-owner who has contributed it. In our work, users can counteract restrictive atomic policies with permissive atomic policies (§4).

The ReBAC/MO model of §3 is a descendant of the line of ReBAC models of [8, 10, 3, 9]. Here we depart from [8, 10, 3, 9], which employs modal logic (and its extension, hybrid logic) for the specification of ReBAC policy. Instead, we revive the suggestion of [7] (see also [10, §4]) in using birooted graph patterns as the basis of policy specification. In both this work and that of [7], using graph patterns for policy specification facilitates policy analysis (in our case availability analyses). Our novelty includes (a) the identification of co-owners in atomic policies, (b) combination of privacy preferences of different co-owners, and (c) adoption of syntactic restrictions to facilitate policy negotiation and availability analyses.

The three availability criteria formulated in this work are inspired by the recent, exciting advancement of availability analyses in workflow authorization systems: satisfiability [4, 28, 5], resiliency [28], feasibility [16]. Compared to the analogous notions in the literature, our definitions are novel on three counts. First, they are defined to assess the availability of a resource in a ReBAC system, rather than the ease in which a workflow specification can be instantiated. Second, resiliency and feasibility are defined here via the notion of graph mutation. This is unique in comparison to workflow resiliency and feasibility, which are defined in terms of the departure of users. Third, the three notions of availability formulated here target the satisfaction of multiple-owners policies, whereas previous notions of availability attempt to satisfy security constraints in workflow specifications.

3. AN ADMINISTRATIVE MODEL OF MULTIPLE OWNERSHIP FOR REBAC

This section presents a ReBAC model that supports multiple ownership. §3.1 and §3.2 review notations previously defined in the ReBAC literature [7, 8, 10, 3]. §3.3 formalizes multiple-owners policies in terms of graph patterns. §3.4 presents a multiple-owners version of the ReBAC model, and highlights two prototypical administrative operations that are guarded by negotiation protocols.

3.1 Social Networks

A key component of the protection state for ReBAC is a social network [8, 10, 3]. Social networks are modelled as edge-labelled, directed graphs, in which vertices represents users, and edges represent interpersonal relationships. Edge labels denote the type of relationships that the edges signify (e.g., friend, parent, etc).

Definition 1 *Given a finite, non-empty set $\mathcal{L}$ of* **relation identifiers**, *a* **graph** G *is a pair* $\langle V, \{R_l\}_{l \in \mathcal{L}} \rangle$, *where V is the set of vertices, and R is an indexed family of binary relations over the vertex set, such that each $R_l \subseteq V \times V$ is a binary relation denoting the edges of type l.*

We write $V(G)$, $L(G)$ and $R_l(G)$ to denote respectively the vertex set (V), the label set ($\mathcal{L}$), and the type-l edge set (R_l) of G.

A graph G_1 is a **subgraph** of G_2 iff $V(G_1) \subseteq V(G_2)$, $L(G_1) \subseteq L(G_2)$, and $R_l(G_1) \subseteq R_l(G_2)$ for every $l \in L(G_1)$. In that case, we write $G_1 \subseteq G_2$. A bijective function $f : V(G_1) \to V(G_2)$ is a **graph isomorphism** iff $L(G_1) = L(G_2)$, and for every $l \in L(G_1)$, for every $u, v \in V(G_1)$, we have $(u, v) \in R_l(G_1) \Leftrightarrow (f(u), f(v)) \in R_l(G_2)$. In such a case, we write $G_1 \simeq_f G_2$. G_1 and G_2 are **isomorphic**, and we write $G_1 \simeq G_2$, if the above bijection f exists.

Given a finite, non-empty set $\mathcal{L}$ of edge labels, and a countably infinite universe $\mathcal{V}$ of vertices, we write $\mathcal{G}[\mathcal{V}, \mathcal{L}]$ to denote the set of all graphs G for which $V(G)$ is a finite subset of $\mathcal{V}$ and $L(G) \subseteq \mathcal{L}$.

3.2 Access Scenarios and Graph Patterns

Suppose G is the current social network. When a requester $v \in V(G)$ attempts to access an object owned by some user $u \in V(G)$, we have an **access scenario** characterized by these three components: G, u and v. The spirit of ReBAC is that this access scenario shall satisfy some graph-theoretic properties imposed by the access control policy in order for access to be granted. We model an access scenario by a **birooted graph** [7, 10], which is a graph plus the explicit identification of two vertices (not necessarily distinct).

Definition 2 *A* **birooted graph** BG *is a triple* $G_{(u,v)}$, *where G is a graph, and $u, v \in V(G)$ are called the* **roots** *of BG. More specifically, u and v are called the* **owner root** *and* **requester root** *respectively.*

In this work, access control policies are specified in terms of **graph patterns**, which are also modelled as birooted graphs. More specifically, a graph-theoretic property corresponds to whether a graph pattern is "*contained*" in the access scenario. This matching between a graph pattern and an access scenario is formalized by the notion of subgraph isomorphism between birooted graphs. Suppose $BG_1 = G_{1(u_1,v_1)}$ is a graph pattern, and $BG_2 = G_{2(u_2,v_2)}$ is an

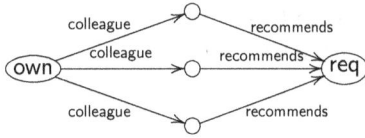

Figure 1: A birooted graph pattern that says "At least 3 colleagues of the owner recommend the requester." The owner and requester roots are labelled as own and req respectively.

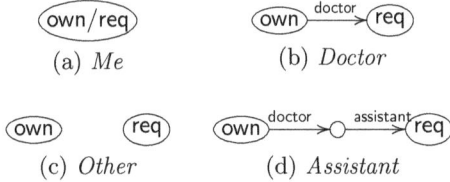

(a) *Me* (b) *Doctor*

(c) *Other* (d) *Assistant*

Figure 2: Four birooted graph patterns that are used for formulating policies in the clinic domain.

access scenario. BG_1 is a **(birooted) subgraph** of BG_2 iff $u_1 = u_2$, $v_1 = v_2$, and $G_1 \subseteq G_2$. Note that the two roots of a birooted subgraph must be identical to those of the birooted supergraph. A bijective function $f : V(G_1) \to V(G_2)$ is an **isomorphism** of BG_1 and BG_2 iff $f(u_1) = u_2$, $f(v_1) = v_2$, and $G_1 \simeq_f G_2$. We write $BG_1 \simeq BG_2$ iff such a bijection f exists. We write $BG_1 \lesssim BG_2$ iff there exists a birooted subgraph $BG_3 \subseteq BG_2$ such that $BG_1 \simeq BG_3$. That is, BG_1 is isomorphic to some subgraph of BG_2.

We write $\mathcal{B}[\mathcal{V}, \mathcal{L}]$ to denote the set of all birooted graphs $G_{(u,v)}$ for which $G \in \mathcal{G}[\mathcal{V}, \mathcal{L}]$. As a convention, we specify graph patterns using birooted graphs from $\mathcal{B}[\mathbb{N}, \mathcal{L}]$ ($\mathbb{N}$ is the natural number set).

Example 1 *Fig. 1 depicts a graph pattern asserting that the owner has at least three distinct colleagues who recommend the requester. Such a graph pattern can be used for expressing delegation of trust as well as level of trust.*

The next example illustrates how a policy can be specified by a disjunctive combination of graph patterns.

Example 2 *Consider a clinic domain, in which vertices are users, a* doctor *edge relates a patient to her family doctor, and an* assistant *edge relates a doctor to his assistant. The four graph patterns in Fig. 2 can serve as building blocks for specifying the policies below.*

- *"Only the owner can access." This policy is captured by the graph pattern Me in Fig. 2(a). The pattern requires that the owner is identical to the requester.*
- *"Either the owner or her family doctor can access." This policy demands a match between the access scenario and either one of the patterns Me or Doctor (Fig. 2(b)).*
- *"The owner, her family doctor, or the family doctor's assistant can access." This policy demands a match with one of the following patterns: Me, Doctor, and Assistant (Fig. 2(d)).*
- *"Everyone can access." The policy requires a match with either Me or Other (Fig. 2(c)). In short, access is granted if (a) the requester is the owner (Me), or (b) if the requester is not the owner (Other). That is, access is always granted.*

3.3 Policies and Authorization

In the original conception of ReBAC, an access control policy specifies how a legitimate accessor of a resource shall be related to the owner of that resource [8, 10, 3]. When we move to the context of multiple ownership, the notion of an access control policy shall be expanded: a policy specifies how a legitimate accessor shall be related to each of the co-owners. For example, co-owner u_1 demands that the accessor shares 5 common friends with u_1, but co-owner u_2 demands that the accessor be within a distance of 4 in the social network. The example underlines the compositional nature of access control policies when multiple owners are involved. We define here a simple language for specifying multiple-owner policies, by way of graph patterns. How policy negotiation is conducted among the owners to arrive at a policy that everyone can agree on is discussed in the next sections.

Fixing a universe $\mathcal{V}$ of vertices and a universe $\mathcal{PV}$ of legitimate graph patterns, the abstract syntax of a **policy** ϕ is defined as follows:

$$\phi ::= \alpha \mid \neg\phi \mid \phi \wedge \phi$$
$$\alpha, \beta ::= \mathsf{acc}(BG, u)$$

where each of α and β is called an **atomic policy**, which is composed of an **anchor** $u \in \mathcal{V}$ together with a graph pattern $BG \in \mathcal{PV}$ (u need not be a vertex in BG). We also define the usual derived form $\phi_1 \vee \phi_2 \equiv \neg(\neg\phi_1 \wedge \neg\phi_2)$. The intuitive meaning of an atomic policy $\mathsf{acc}(BG, u)$ is that owner u demands the requester to be related to u by a graph-theoretic relationship captured by the graph pattern BG. A policy is essentially a boolean combination of atomic policies.

The **anchor set** of policy ϕ, denoted by $anchors(\phi)$, is the set of all anchors appearing in the atomic policies of ϕ.

Authorization is defined in terms of the **satisfaction relation** ($\models$) between a graph G, a vertex $v \in V(G)$, and a policy ϕ for which $anchors(\phi) \subseteq V(G)$:

- $G, v \models \mathsf{acc}(BG, u)$ iff $BG \lesssim G_{(u,v)}$.
- $G, v \models \neg\phi$ iff it is not the case that $G, v \models \phi$.
- $G, v \models \phi_1 \wedge \phi_2$ iff $G, v \models \phi_1$ and $G, v \models \phi_2$.

Lastly, we write $\mathcal{P}[\mathcal{V}, \mathcal{PV}]$ to denote the set of all policies ϕ with anchors from $\mathcal{V}$ and graph patterns from $\mathcal{PV}$.

3.4 Putting It All Together

We define a **ReBAC model with multiple ownership (ReBAC/MO)**. The model is intentionally simplified for the purpose of highlighting only the essential elements.

Definition 3 (Scheme) *A **protection scheme** Σ is a tuple $\langle \mathcal{L}, \mathcal{U}, \mathcal{O}, \mathcal{PV} \rangle$, where $\mathcal{L}$ is a finite set of relation identifiers, $\mathcal{U}$ and $\mathcal{O}$ are countably infinite sets representing respectively the universes of **users** and **objects**, and $\mathcal{PV} \subseteq \mathcal{B}[\mathbb{N}, \mathcal{L}]$ is the **policy vocabulary**, which specifies the set of legitimate graph patterns that can be used for formulating access control policies.*

Definition 4 (State) *Given a protection scheme $\Sigma = \langle \mathcal{L}, \mathcal{U}, \mathcal{O}, \mathcal{PV} \rangle$, a **protection state** γ is a tuple $\langle U, O, G, \omega, \pi \rangle$, where $U \subseteq \mathcal{U}$ is a finite set of active users, $O \subseteq \mathcal{O}$ is a finite set of active objects, $G \in \mathcal{G}[\mathcal{U}, \mathcal{L}]$ is the current social network of the active users (i.e., $V(G) = U$), $\omega : O \to 2^U$ maps objects to their co-owners, and $\pi : O \to \mathcal{P}[U, \mathcal{PV}]$ maps objects to their access control policies. It is further required that $anchors(\pi(o)) \subseteq \omega(o)$ in order for γ to be well-formed.*

Definition 5 (Request) *Suppose $\gamma = \langle U, O, G, \omega, \pi \rangle$. An* **access request** *is characterized by a pair $(o, v) \in O \times U$. Request (o, v) is* **authorized** *in γ iff $G, v \models \pi(o)$.*

We outline here two prototypical administrative transitions. A fully specified system would offer more transitions (e.g., creation of users). These two prototypical transitions are singled out to highlight the need for different policy negotiation protocols.

Given a function $f : X \to Y$, we write $f[a \mapsto b]$ to denote the function $g : X \cup \{a\} \to Y \cup \{b\}$ for which $g(x) = b$ if $x = a$ and $g(x) = f(x)$ otherwise.

The first transition, $\mathsf{create}(o, U')$, creates a new object o with co-owners from user set U'. The following rule specifies when the transition is well-formed.

$$\frac{\begin{array}{cc} o \in \mathcal{O} \setminus O & \emptyset \subset U' \subseteq U \\ O' = O \cup \{o\} & \omega' = \omega[o \mapsto U'] \\ \pi' = \pi\left[o \mapsto \bigvee_{u \in U'} \mathsf{acc}(Me, u)\right] \end{array}}{\langle U, O, G, \omega, \pi \rangle \xrightarrow{\mathsf{create}(o, U')} \langle U, O', G, \omega', \pi' \rangle} \;(\textsc{Create})$$

Note that initially o is accessible only to users in U'.

The second transition, $\mathsf{release}(o, \phi)$, re-publishes the existing object o with the policy ϕ. Well-formedness of the transition is specified in the following rule.

$$\frac{\begin{array}{cc} o \in O & anchors(\phi) \subseteq \omega(o) \\ & \pi' = \pi[o \mapsto \phi] \end{array}}{\langle U, O, G, \omega, \pi \rangle \xrightarrow{\mathsf{release}(o, \phi)} \langle U, O, G, \omega, \pi' \rangle} \;(\textsc{Release})$$

While the rules above specify when a transition is well-formed, they do not articulate the protocols by which users sign up for co-ownership, and how they agree on a policy for a co-owned object. Such are the topics of the next section.

4. NEGOTIATION PROTOCOLS

The two administrative transitions, create and release, are supposed to be guarded by negotiation protocols that allow the co-owners to agree on the creation or publishing of objects. In particular, the two transitions are guarded respectively by two different protocols, simple consenting (§4.1) and policy negotiation (§4.2).

4.1 Simple Consenting

Facebook uses simple consenting in the befriending operation. When a user u befriends another user v, the system sends a befriending invitation v. If the latter gives consent, then a friendship relationship is recorded in the system. We call this protocol ***simple consenting***. In a similar vein, when an object is created in our model, all the co-owners are notified, and their consents are sought before the object creation process is complete.

Our model differs from Facebook on how the access control policy of a co-owned object is administrated. In Facebook, simple consenting is used only for forging co-ownership, but the access control policy of a co-owned object is not formulated collaboratively. When u_1 befriends u_2, the access control policy of the friendship relationship is not part of the consenting process. Once friendship has been forged, u_1 may unilaterally specify a policy ϕ_1 (for which $anchors(\phi_1) = \{u_1\}$), and u_2 may independently specify another policy ϕ_2

(again, $anchors(\phi_2) = \{u_2\}$). The friendship relationship is now visible to any requester who satisfies $\phi = \phi_1 \vee \phi_2$. This lack of collaboration allows a co-owner (u_1) to formulate a highly liberal policy (ϕ_1) without the consent of another co-owner (u_2), thereby compromising the privacy of the latter.

With this consideration, the create transition of our model initializes the policy $\pi(o)$ of a newly created object o to a highly restrictive default:

$$\bigvee_{u \in \omega(o)} \mathsf{acc}(Me, u) \tag{1}$$

When one or more co-owners of o attempt to update $\pi(o)$, they will have to perform the release operation, which is guarded by a policy negotiation protocol, in which all co-owners collaboratively work out an access control policy.

4.2 Policy Negotiation

The policy negotiation framework to be presented below is designed to allow co-owners to collaboratively arrive at an access control policy while balancing two considerations.

1. *Privacy preferences.* The co-owners want to make sure that only certain users may access the co-owned objects. The participatory nature of the negotiation process allows the co-owners to reflect their *subjective* privacy preferences in the final access control policy.

2. *Sharing needs.* An object is created because the co-owners desire to make it available to other users. The negotiation process allows each co-owners to state a desirable level of availability for the co-owned object. This specified level of availability will be used as an *objective* measure of policy quality.

The successful completion of the policy negotiation process for object o produces a ***settlement***, which is comprised of two components:

1. A ***settlement policy*** ϕ for which $anchors(\phi) \subseteq \omega(o)$, and all co-owners in $\omega(o)$ have expressed consent over the adoption of ϕ.

2. Every co-owner $u \in \omega(o)$ would have specified an ***availability criterion*** κ_u, and the system would have verified that the settlement policy ϕ satisfies κ_u for each owner u.

While the settlement policy expresses the privacy preferences of the co-owners, the availability criteria express their sharing needs.

The negotiation process proceeds in rounds. In each round, every owner u will be given a chance to contribute changes to the settlement policy ϕ in a controlled manner, as well as revising her availability criterion κ_u. Negotiation concludes successfully when the settlement policy ϕ is verified by the system to satisfy the availability criterion κ_u of every owner u. These availability criteria will be discarded once the negotiation concludes. Only the settlement policy is recorded.

Further details of the settlement policy and availability criteria are given in §4.2.1 and §4.2.2 respectively. Details of the negotiation protocol are given in §4.2.3.

4.2.1 Syntax of Settlement Policy

To facilitate the negotiation of policies and the verification of availability criteria, we constrain the syntax of an access control policy to the following form:

$$\phi = (\alpha_1 \vee \alpha_2 \vee \ldots \vee \alpha_m) \wedge (\neg\beta_1 \wedge \neg\beta_2 \wedge \ldots \wedge \neg\beta_n) \tag{2}$$

where α_i and β_j are atomic policies.

We define additional notations to facilitate discussion. We write $atom^+(\phi)$ and $atom^-(\phi)$ to denote respectively the atom sets $\{\alpha_1, \alpha_2, \ldots, \alpha_m\}$ and $\{\beta_1, \beta_2, \ldots, \beta_n\}$. We define the following notations for the set of positive (resp. negative) atoms that are anchored at user u.

$$atom^+(\phi, u) = \{\alpha \in atom^+(\phi) \mid u \in anchors(\alpha)\}$$
$$atom^-(\phi, u) = \{\beta \in atom^-(\phi) \mid u \in anchors(\beta)\}$$

We also write $pat^+(\phi, u)$ and $pat^-(\phi, u)$ to denote respectively the birooted graph sets $\{BG \mid \mathsf{acc}(BG, u) \in atom^+(\phi, u)\}$ and $\{BG \mid \mathsf{acc}(BG, u) \in atom^-(\phi, u)\}$. In short, $pat^+(\phi, u)$ is the set of positive graph patterns with u as the anchor, and $pat^-(\phi, u)$ is the analogue for negative graph patterns.

A comparison between the above syntactic form and the form of policies used in Facebook for controlling the visibility of a friendship relationship is in order. The four policies of Example 2 are all *positive policies* [7, 10]. This means each of them can be expressed as a disjunctive combination of finitely many graph patterns. It should be obvious to the reader that the four policies of Example 2 are but organizational variants of Facebook's standard policies: "only me," "friends," "friends of friends," and "everyone." This means Facebook's standard policies can also be represented by disjunctions of finitely many graph patterns. As discussed in §4.1, the policy that controls the visibility of the friendship relationship between users u and v has the form $\phi = \phi_u \vee \phi_v$, where each of ϕ_u and ϕ_v is a disjunction of atomic policies (because they are positive policies). Consequently, the access control policy of a friendship relationship in Facebook has the following form:

$$\phi = (\alpha_1 \vee \alpha_2 \vee \ldots \vee \alpha_m) \tag{3}$$

Two differences between our syntactic form, (2), and that of Facebook, (3), can be observed. First, our syntactic form allows negative graph patterns. A co-owner may counteract the positive graph patterns contributed by other co-owners through the specification of negative graph patterns. Second, the negotiation of policies of the above form is regulated by a policy negotiation protocol, while ϕ_u and ϕ_v are set unilaterally by u and v.

4.2.2 Availability Criteria

The sharing needs of a co-owner $u \in \omega(o)$ of a resource o is expressed in terms of an availability criterion κ_u. Intuitively, κ_u expresses how widely accessible u wants o to be. Co-owner u may choose to impose availability criterion κ_u on one of two formulas: (a) the settlement policy ϕ, or (b) the formula $\phi[u]$ defined as follows:

$$\phi[u] = \left(\bigvee_{\alpha \in atom^+(\phi, u)} \alpha \right) \wedge \left(\bigwedge_{\beta \in atom^-(\phi)} \neg \beta \right)$$

In short, $\phi[u]$ is obtained from the settlement policy ϕ by selecting *only* those positive atoms anchored at u, but including *all* the negative atoms. Intuitively, $\phi[u]$ specifies the legitimate accessors who are preferred by u. For brevity, we assume that an availability criterion is imposed on the settlement policy ϕ. The reader should keep in mind that in reality a co-owner may choose between ϕ or $\phi[u]$.

Three different families of availability criterion are proposed in this work. The first notion of availability is that of *satisfiability*, which requires that a resource be accessible by a specific number of users in the present protection state.

Example 3 (Satisfiability) *Object o shall be accessible by at least 35 users in the social network.*

Resiliency is a second family of availability criteria. Intuitively, resiliency mandates a level of availability even when the protection state is "slightly" perturbed by administrative actions. Resiliency is more demanding than satisfiability, in the sense that resiliency requires not only that a resource is accessible by some specific number of users in the present protection state, but also that the resource remains available as such when the protection state mutates. In the context of ReBAC, such mutations take the form of the introduction of new relationships (edges) or the dissolution of existing relationships. It is, however, unrealistic to expect that availability can be maintained against arbitrary mutation of the social network. Thus resiliency prescribes availability over a specific extent of mutation to the protection state.

Example 4 (Resiliency) *Even if Bob (one of the owner of resource o) were to acquire up to 10 additional patients (or lose up to 10 of my existing patients), object o shall remain accessible by at least 25 users.*

A third notion of availability, ***feasibility***, is a relaxation of satisfiability. A resource may not meet the requirement of satisfiability (accessible by a specific number of users), but it meets the demand of feasibility if the social network can be "repaired" to meet the requirement of satisfiability. Again, repairs are realized by edge addition or removal in the social network.

Example 5 (Feasibility) *I shall be able to make object o accessible by at least 50 users if the company hires no more than 10 additional members for my department (or fires no more than 10 existing colleagues).*

The formal definition of availability criteria and their mechanical verification are deferred to §6 and §7 respectively.

4.2.3 Protocol in Details

The negotiation of the access control policy of a co-owned object o proceeds in rounds. Throughout the process, the protocol maintains a policy ϕ as the candidate for $\pi(o)$, as well as an availability criterion κ_u for each co-owner $u \in \omega(o)$. The policy ϕ is always in the form of (2).

As mentioned before, ϕ is initialized to the default policy (1). The availability criterion κ_u of every co-owner u is initialized to 1-satisfiability (i.e., accessible to at least one user). The default policy trivially satisfies 1-satisfiability.

Round i proceeds according to the following steps:

1. **Notify.** Every co-owner $u \in \omega(o)$ is presented with the following: (i) the policy ϕ obtained in the previous round, including the positive and negative graph patterns ($pat^+(\phi, v)$ and $pat^-(\phi, v)$) of every co-owner v, (ii) the availability criterion κ_u adopted by co-owner u in the previous round, and (iii) a boolean flag indicating whether ϕ satisfies κ_u.

2. **Consent or Revise.** Each co-owner u will now be given an opportunity to take one of two options:
   (a) *Consent.* If κ_u is satisfied, u may choose to give consent to adopt ϕ as the policy of o.

(b) *Revise.* Otherwise, co-owner u may choose to revise (i) κ_u and/or (ii) the graph pattern sets $pat^+(\phi, u)$ and $pat^-(\phi, u)$. In short, co-owner u may only edit the atomic policies of ϕ for which u is an anchor.

The consent/revise step of different co-owners may be conducted concurrently.

3. **Verify.** If all co-owners give consent, then the protocol concludes successfully. Otherwise, at least one co-owner has revised either her availability criterion or her graph patterns. The system will now perform verification of the current policy ϕ against each of the availability criterion κ_u (see §6 for details). The result is reported to the co-owners in the next round.

5. AN EXAMPLE

The various features of our scheme are illustrated in the following example. A medical doctor $\mathcal{D}$ suspects that the unique conditions of her patient $\mathcal{P}$ are the symptoms of a new cardiovascular disease. $\mathcal{D}$ wants to share the medical record of $\mathcal{P}$ with two researchers, $\mathcal{CR}$ and $\mathcal{UR}$, who work in a pharmaceutical company and a university respectively. The following is a transcript of how they negotiate the access control policy ϕ of the co-owned medical record.

Round #1. In anticipation of referral, $\mathcal{D}$ adds a positive atom $\alpha_\mathcal{D}$ to ϕ, to grant access to those cardiologists belonging to the same health district as she does. $\mathcal{D}$ also imposes on $\phi[\mathcal{D}]$ a satisfiability requirement ($\kappa_\mathcal{D}$), demanding that at least two users (i.e., herself and a cardiologist) can access.

Company researcher $\mathcal{CR}$ contributes a positive atom $\alpha_{\mathcal{CR}}$, to grant access to all members of his research team. $\mathcal{CR}$ worries that 3 of his team members may leave the team due to personal reasons, and he anticipates that the research on the new disease needs at least a team of 5 researchers. $\mathcal{CR}$ then imposes $\kappa_{\mathcal{CR}}$, a resiliency requirement, on $\phi[\mathcal{CR}]$, demanding that at least 5 users (i.e., team members) can access even if the social network is changed by 3 edges (i.e., team members departing).

University researcher $\mathcal{UR}$ contributes a positive atom $\alpha_{\mathcal{UR}}$, to grant access to his graduate students. $\mathcal{UR}$ is expecting one new PhD student to join her research group in the upcoming Fall semester. By that time, she wants to make sure that at least herself and three of her PhD students can access the document. So $\kappa_{\mathcal{UR}}$ is set up to be a feasibility requirement, to be imposed on $\phi[\mathcal{UR}]$, demanding that there is a way to change 1 edge (i.e., the incoming student) in the social network so that 4 users (i.e., herself and 3 PhD students) have access.

$\mathcal{P}$ does not add any positive atom, nor does he alter the default availability criterion. Yet he does not want anyone associated with, or funded by, the insurance company $\mathcal{I}$ to see his record. So he introduces a negative atom $\beta_\mathcal{P}$ to deny access to such individuals.

It turns out that every cardiologist in the same health district as $\mathcal{D}$ is funded by insurer $\mathcal{I}$, and thus $\kappa_\mathcal{D}$ is violated by $\phi[\mathcal{D}]$. In addition, all but one of the PhD students of $\mathcal{UR}$ are funded by scholarships from $\mathcal{I}$, so $\kappa_{\mathcal{UR}}$ is violated by $\phi[\mathcal{UR}]$. A second round of negotiation is therefore needed.

Round #2. Noticing that $\alpha_\mathcal{D}$ is too restrictive, doctor $\mathcal{D}$ now revises $\alpha_\mathcal{D}$ to include cardiologists in both her own health district and neighboring health districts. Such a widening of access "counteracts" the limiting effect of $\beta_\mathcal{P}$.

University researcher $\mathcal{UR}$ figures that requiring the record to be accessible by 3 PhD students is probably too conservative. The project can be completed even if only two PhD students have access. So she revises $\kappa_{\mathcal{UR}}$ to a feasibility requirement, demanding that there is a way to change 1 edge in the social network so that 3 users have access (1 less than before). In short, $\mathcal{UR}$ "counteracts" the limiting effect of $\beta_\mathcal{P}$ by lowering her sharing expectation.

All the availability criteria check out, and negotiation concludes successfully.

6. AVAILABILITY CRITERIA

An important contribution of this work is the formulation of formal availability criteria as a means for expressing sharing needs, as well as the mechanical verification of such criteria to provide feedback to the negotiating co-owners. In this section, we formalize the three notions of availability in §4.2.2: satisfiability, resiliency and feasibility. While the spirit of these notions is inspired by their analogues in workflow authorization systems [4, 28, 16, 5], our technical formulation via graph mutation is a novel contribution.

In the following, a policy needs *not* be in the constrained form of (2). We do not anticipate that imposing restriction (2) affects our complexity results (Theorems 1, 2 and 3).

6.1 Satisfiability

The first notion of availability is that of *satisfiability*.
Problem: Satisfiability (MO-SAT)
Instance: a positive integer k, a graph G, a policy ϕ for which $anchors(\phi) \subseteq V(G)$
Question: Does there exist k distinct vertices $v \in V(G)$ for which $G, v \models \phi$?

Fixing the protection state (i.e., G), policy ϕ is said to be k-***satisfiable*** iff $\langle k, G, \phi \rangle \in$ MO-SAT. Intuitively, if a co-owner demands ϕ to be k-satisfiable, then there shall exists k potential requesters who are able to gain access in the current protection state. Obviously, a $(k + 1)$-satisfiable policy is also k-satisfiable.

Not only MO-SAT, but all the three availability criteria presented in this section belong to the second level of the polynomial hierarchy [1, Chap. 5].

Theorem 1 *MO-SAT is in Δ_2^P, and is both **NP**-hard and **coNP**-hard.*

See [20, Chap. 5, pp. 55–57] for a proof.

6.2 Feasibility

We need another notation before we can proceed: $d(G, G')$ is the *(edge) distance* between the two graphs G and G', which is defined to be $\Sigma_{l \in \mathcal{L}} |R_l(G) \, \Delta \, R_l(G')|$, where $S \, \Delta \, T$ is the symmetric difference of sets S and T.

Relaxing the definition of satisfiability gives rise to a second notion of availability — *feasibility*, which demands that the protection state can be "repaired" to render the policy k-satisfiable.
Problem: Feasibility (MO-FEA)
Instance: a non-negative integer δ, a positive integer k, a graph G, and a policy ϕ for which $anchors(\phi) \subseteq V(G)$
Question: Is there a graph G' for which $L(G') = L(G)$, $V(G') = V(G)$, and $d(G, G') \leq \delta$, such that there exists k distinct $v \in V(G')$ for which $G', v \models \phi$?

Obviously, we get back MO-SAT if $\delta = 0$. Fixing graph G, we say that ϕ is (δ, k)-***feasible*** iff $\langle \delta, k, G, \phi \rangle \in$ MO-FEA. Every k-satisfiable policy is (δ, k)-feasible.

Theorem 2 MO-Fea *is* Σ_2^p-*complete*.

A proof of the theorem is given in [20, Chap. 5, pp. 57–58].

6.3 Resiliency

Strengthening satisfiability yields the notion of **resiliency**, which demands that a policy remains k-satisfiable even if the protection state is mutated.

Problem: Resiliency (MO-Res)

Instance: a non-negative integer δ, a positive integer k, a graph G, and a policy ϕ for which $anchors(\phi) \subseteq V(G)$

Question: Is it the case that for every G' such that $L(G') = L(G)$ and $V(G') = V(G)$ and $d(G, G') \leq \delta$, there exists k distinct vertices $v \in V(G')$ for which $G', v \models \phi$?

Fixing G, we say that ϕ is (δ, k)-**resilient** iff $\langle \delta, k, G, \phi \rangle \in$ MO-Res. A (δ, k)-resilient policy is also k-satisfiable.

Theorem 3 MO-Res *is* Π_2^p-*complete*.

Consult [20, Chap. 5, pp. 59–60] for a proof.

7. VERIFYING AVAILABILITY

As the three availability criteria belong to the second level of the polynomial hierarchy, we do not expect that they can be solved in polynomial time. A natural starting point would be to reduce the problems to **Quantified Boolean Formula (QBF)** satisfiability, and then deploy a QBF solver to attack the problems [1, Chap. 5]. Experimental results suggest that this line of attack is not viable (§8.2). In this work, we focus on solving MO-Sat, since it belongs to Δ_2^p, and thus it has a higher degree of tractability. We defer to future work the exploration of more tractable subproblems of MO-Fea and MO-Res as well as their decision procedures.

As MO-Sat is both **NP**- and **coNP**-hard, it is not likely it belongs to **NP** [1, Chap. 2]. Consequently, we do not expect that we can reduce MO-Sat to the Boolean satisfiability (SAT) problem, and then employ a SAT solver to attack MO-Sat. Rather, we make use of a SAT solver as a *subroutine* for crafting two verifiers for MO-Sat. As MO-Sat $\in \Delta_2^p$, this is theoretically viable.

7.1 Reducing an Atomic Policy to SAT

The two MO-Sat algorithms to be examined in §7.2 both invoke a SAT solver for testing the satisfiability of atomic policies. We describe here a reduction of the satisfiability of atomic policies to SAT. This reduction will be used as a subroutine in the algorithms of §7.2.

We use Sat4j as our SAT solver [18]. Sat4J allows users to formulate not only regular clauses, but also what Wang and Li [28] call **Pseudo Boolean (PB)** constraints, which count the number of satisfied literals in a clause:

$$(l_1 \vee l_2 \vee \ldots \vee l_m)_{\leq k} \qquad (4)$$
$$(l_1 \vee l_2 \vee \ldots \vee l_m)_{= k} \qquad (5)$$

Specifically, (4) is satisfied if at most k of the literals are satisfied, and (5) is satisfied if exactly k literals are satisfied.

Algorithm 1, Reduce, reduces 1-satisfiability to SAT. Specifically, Reduce takes three parameters:

1. G is the social graph of the ReBAC protection state.
2. $acc(H_{(x,y)}, u)$ is the atomic policy for which 1-satisfiability is to be tested.
3. $\{Y_j\}_{j \in V(G)}$ is an indexed family of propositional variables, one for each vertex in G.

Algorithm 1: Reduce

input : G, $acc(H_{(x,y)}, u)$, $\{Y_j\}_{j \in V(G)}$
output: a CNF formula ϕ

1 Initialize ϕ to an empty set of clauses;
2 **foreach** $i \in V(H)$ **do**
3   **foreach** $j \in V(G)$ **do**
4   Create fresh propositional variable $X_{i,j}$;
5 **foreach** $i \in V(H)$ **do**
6    $\phi := \phi \wedge \left(\bigvee_{j \in V(G)} X_{i,j} \right)_{=1}$;
7 **foreach** $j \in V(G)$ **do**
8    $\phi := \phi \wedge \left(\bigvee_{i \in V(H)} X_{i,j} \right)_{\leq 1}$;
9 **foreach** $l \in L(H)$ **do**
10   **foreach** $i,j \in R_l(H)$ **do**
11   **foreach** $p \in V(G)$ **do**
12     $\phi := \phi \wedge \left(\neg X_{i,p} \vee \bigvee_{q \in \mathsf{neigh}^G(l,p)} X_{j,q} \right)$;
13 $\phi := \phi \wedge X_{x,u}$;
14 **foreach** $j \in V(G)$ **do**
15   $\phi := \phi \wedge (\neg X_{y,j} \vee Y_j) \wedge (X_{y,j} \vee \neg Y_j)$;
16 **return** ϕ;

The output of Algorithm 1 is a CNF formula ϕ, which contains, among other propositional variables generated within the algorithm, those variables Y_j's supplied by the caller. Formula ϕ is satisfiable iff there exists $v \in V(G)$ for which $H_{(x,y)} \lesssim G_{(u,v)}$. In addition, a satisfying assignment will turn Y_v to true, and all the other Y_j's to false. Having $\{Y_j\}_{j \in V(G)}$ as an input to the algorithm allows the caller to recover the identity of v with ease, and also makes it easy to embed ϕ in a larger SAT instance.

The returned formula ϕ tests if there exists a vertex $v \in V(G)$ as well as a birooted graph isomorphism f between $H_{(x,y)}$ and some subgraph of $G_{(u,v)}$. The mapping f is represented by the propositional variables $X_{i,j}$'s created on line 4. More specifically, $X_{i,j}$ is turned on iff f maps $i \in V(H)$ to $j \in V(G)$. Line 6 adds clauses to ensure that f is a function. Then on line 8, clauses are introduced to ensure that the f is injective. Function $\mathsf{neigh}^G(l,p)$ (read *neighbours*) used in line 12 is defined below:

Definition 6 $\mathsf{neigh}^G(l,p)$ *is a function with* $G \times L(G) \times V(G) \rightarrow 2^{V(G)}$ *signature and following definition:*

$$\mathsf{neigh}^G(l,p) = \{q \in V(G) \mid (p,q) \in R_l(G)\} \qquad (6)$$

Line 12 add clauses to ensure that adjacency is preserved by f. Line 13 ensures $f(x) = u$. The clauses added on line 15 ensure that $f(y)$ is identical to the selection of vertex indicated by the Y_j's.

The design of Algorithm 1 is comparable to the reduction of graph isomorphism to SAT reported in [27], with four differences. First, PB constraints have been employed in our reduction for ensuring that f is an injective function, where regular clauses are used in [27] for similar purposes. In our preliminary experiments, the use of PB constraints have significantly enhanced the performance of SAT solving. Second, adjacency preservation is only enforced in one direction in our algorithm (line 12), as we are testing subgraph isomorphism rather than graph isomorphism (as in [27]). Third, additional clauses are introduced to handle the mapping of roots in our algorithms (lines 13–15). Fourth,

Algorithm 2: VertexEnumerator

input : k, G, ϕ
output: A boolean value

1 **foreach** $j \in V(G)$ **do**
2   Create fresh propositional variable Y_j;
3 $vars := \{Y_j\}_{j \in V(G)}$;
4 $\psi := \left(\bigvee_{j \in V(G)} Y_j \right)_{=1}$;
5 $count := 0$;
6 **foreach** $v \in V(G)$ **do**
7   **foreach** *atomic policy* α *in* ϕ **do**
8      $\varphi_\alpha := (Y_v) \wedge \psi \wedge \mathsf{Reduce}(G, \alpha, vars)$;
9   apply $\mathsf{Sat4j}$ on φ_α to obtain truth value for α;
10   evaluate ϕ using truth values from line 9;
11   **if** ϕ *evaluates to true* **then**
12      $count := count + 1$;
13   **if** $count = k$ **then**
14   **return** *true*;
15 **return** *false*;

Algorithm 3: ModelEnumerator

input : k, G, ϕ
output: A boolean value

1 **foreach** $j \in V(G)$ **do**
2   Create fresh propositional variable Y_j;
3 $vars := \{Y_j\}_{j \in V(G)}$;
4 $\psi := \left(\bigvee_{j \in V(G)} Y_j \right)_{=1}$;
5 **foreach** $\alpha \in atom^+(\phi)$ **do**
6    $\varphi_\alpha := \mathsf{Reduce}(G, \alpha, vars)$;
7 $\varphi := \psi \wedge \mathsf{Disj}(\{\varphi_\alpha \mid \alpha \in atom^+(\phi)\})$;
8 $count := 0$;
9 invoke $\mathsf{Sat4j}$ to enumerate the models σ of φ;
10 **foreach** σ **do**
11   let v be such that $\sigma(Y_v) = true$;
12    $flag := true$;
13   **foreach** $\beta \in atom^-(\phi)$ **do**
14      $\varphi_\beta = (Y_v) \wedge \psi \wedge \mathsf{Reduce}(G, \beta, vars)$;
15   invoke $\mathsf{Sat4j}$ on φ_β to get truth value for β;
16   **if** β *is true* **then**
17        $flag := false$;
18   break;
19   **if** $flag$ **then**
20      $count := count + 1$;
21   **if** $count = k$ **then**
22   **return** *true*;
23   add the unit clause $(\neg Y_v)$ to φ;
24 **return** *false*;

---

according to theorem 4 the clauses added in line 12 have significantly better space complexity than the ones in [27].

Theorem 4 *Let m and n be the number of vertices for the graph patterns and the social graph, respectively. Suppose we fix the average degree of the vertices. The space complexity of the adjacency preservation clauses in Algorithm 1 (line 12) is $\Theta(m^2 n)$ and in [27] is $\Theta(m^2 n^2)$.*

A proof is given in [20, Chap. 6, p. 76].

7.2 Two MO-SAT **Verifiers**

We pointed out that checking MO-SAT by a QBF solver is inefficient (§8.2). Instead, we propose custom algorithms that invoke a SAT solver as a subroutine. As MO-SAT is in $\mathbf{\Delta_2^P}$, only polynomially many invocations are required.

Modern SAT solvers are highly optimized, and are better studied than QBF solvers. In this work we work with Sat4j [18], which is a SAT solver written in JAVA. According to its developers, Sat4j is only 3.25 times slower than its C++ counterpart. It has also been employed in the past for automating various analyses in Access Control [28].

We present below two algorithms for deciding MO-SAT. In both cases, the input is an MO-SAT instance (k, G, ϕ), and the output is a boolean decision. As we shall see, Sat4j is not only used as an oracle for deciding NP-complete subproblems, but also used in the second algorithm as a model enumerator for pruning the search space.

7.2.1 Vertex Enumerator

Our first algorithm is listed in Algorithm 2. This algorithm does not make any assumptions on the syntax of the input formula ϕ. The full syntax in §3.3 can be used.

Algorithm 2 iterates through each vertex v of the social graph G, and checks if v satisfies the policy ϕ (i.e., v can successfully access the resource guarded by ϕ), hence, the name VertexEnumerator. If k users are found to satisfy ϕ, then ϕ is k-satisfiable. To evaluate ϕ, each atomic policy in ϕ is evaluated independently, and their truth values are substituted into ϕ (line 10). To evaluate an atomic policy α, line 8 reduces α to a SAT instance (via a call to Reduce), and adds clauses to select v as the requester (and to deselect

other users). The resulting SAT instance is then solved by invoking Sat4j to obtain the truth value for α (line 9).

Algorithm 2 is basically a constructive proof that MO-SAT is in $\mathbf{\Delta_2^P}$. Its strength is generality: it works for all ϕ. Its weakness is that it examines every vertex of G without discretion, and thus leads to slower performance (§8).

7.2.2 Model Enumerator

Our second MO-SAT verifier is Algorithm 3, ModelEnumerator. This algorithm assumes that the input formula ϕ conforms to the constrained syntax of (2). This syntactic restriction is crucial to the design of the algorithm.

The design of Algorithm 3 is enabled by two features of modern SAT solvers, including Sat4j:

1. *Model enumeration.* The SAT solver does not only find one model (i.e., satisfying truth assignment) for the input CNF, but allows the caller to iterate through all models.

2. *Learned clauses.* During the enumeration of models, users may introduce additional clauses to the target formula, thereby eliminating certain models from subsequent enumeration.

The core idea of Algorithm 3 is to employ Sat4j to enumerate the models σ of $(\alpha_1 \vee \ldots \vee \alpha_m)$ (lines 9–10). Every such model identifies a v in G that can access so long as the negative atoms are ignored (line 11). The algorithm then invokes another instance of Sat4j to ensure that v does not satisfy any negative atom $\beta \in atom^-(\phi)$ (line 15). Once the model σ has been considered, a unit clause is introduced into ϕ to ensure that v is never considered again (line 23).

By employing $(\alpha_1 \vee \ldots \vee \alpha_m)$ to drive the process of identifying potential accessors, ModelEnumerator does not need to consider every vertex in G, this could lead to a performance advantage over VertexEnumerator. See §8.3 for an empirical comparison of the two algorithms.

The subroutine $\mathsf{Disj}(\{\varphi_1, \ldots, \varphi_k\})$ invoked on line 7 takes a set of CNF formulas $\varphi_1, \ldots, \varphi_k$ as input, and returns a CNF formula that is equivalent to $\varphi_1 \vee \ldots \vee \varphi_k$. We illustrate the construction in the case of $k = 2$. The general case is a straightforward extension. Suppose $\varphi_1 = \bigwedge_{i=1}^{m_1} C_i^1$ and $\varphi_2 = \bigwedge_{i=1}^{m_2} C_i^2$ are conjunctions of respectively m_1 and m_2 clauses. By introducing two additional propositional variables x^1 and x^2, one can construct a CNF formula φ that is equivalent to their disjunction $(\varphi_1 \vee \varphi_2)$:

$$\varphi = (x^1 \vee x^2)_{=1} \wedge \left(\bigwedge_{i=1}^{m_1} (\neg x^1 \vee C_i^1) \right) \wedge \left(\bigwedge_{i=1}^{m_2} (\neg x^2 \vee C_i^2) \right)$$

8. EXPERIMENTS AND RESULTS

This section reports three experiments we conducted for evaluating the performance of our MO-SAT algorithms. The first experiment (§8.2) compares the performance between Vertex Enumerator and two QBF solvers GhostQ and RAReQS. The second experiment (§8.3) compares the performance between Vertex Enumerator and Model Enumerator. The third (§8.4) demonstrates that the performance of Model Enumerator is adequate for mid-sized organizations.

8.1 Experimental Setup

Experiment Platform.
Our experiments are conducted using a machine with the following configurations.

Hardware: Intel® Xeon® CPU E5-1650 v3 @ 3.50GHz (6 cores); 64 GB RAM; 1 TB SSD.

Software: Operating System: Fedora release 20 (Heisenbug); Sat4j algorithms are programmed and run by Java™ SE Runtime Environment (build 1.8.0_05-b13).

Datasets.
All experiments are executed on synthetic datasets (including social networks and access control policies). We list the dataset generation parameters below.

- *Rep.*: number of times an experiment is repeated for a given set of parameters;
- k_u: number of requesters needed to satisfy policy (i.e., aiming for k_u-satisfiability);
- #$atom^+$: number of positive atoms (α) in policy (ϕ);
- #$atom^-$: number of negative atoms (β) in policy (ϕ);
- #V_{pat+}: number of vertices in the graph patterns of positive atoms (α);
- #V_{pat-}: number of vertices in the graph patterns of negative atoms (β);
- $Prob._G$: the edge probability by which social graph G is generated;
- $Prob._{pat}$: the edge probability by which graph patterns are generated;
- $AvgDeg._G$: the average degree of vertices (for outgoing edges) that we require social graph G to possess;
- $AvgDeg._{pat}$: the average degree of vertices (for outgoing edges) that we require the patterns to possess;
- $|\mathcal{L}|$: number of edge labels used in graphs and graph patterns.

We use Erdős-Rényi model [6] to generate the social graphs and graph patterns. In this model, an edge from any vertex

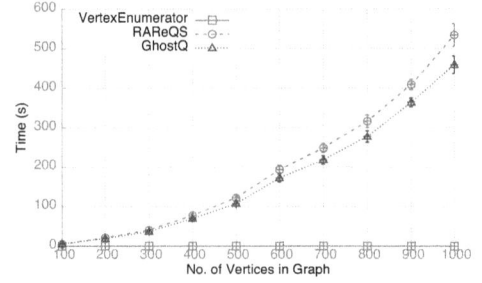

Figure 3: Vertex Enumerator versus QBF Solvers

u to any vertex v is set with a fixed probability, independent from other edges. We use this model to obtain randomness along with low deviation from average degrees of vertices.

There is also a validation phase after generating graph patterns. A graph pattern will be deemed "usable", if every edge in the graph pattern is connected to both roots. This guarantees the graph patterns represent **local policies** [7, 10]. "Unusable" graph patterns are discarded. Moreover, whenever an edge is being added, we choose its label uniformly at random from the available labels set.

We use the edge probability parameters ($Prob._G$ and $Prob._{pat}$) whenever we want the average degree of the vertices to grow proportionally to the size of graph. In other words, we keep the edge probability constant. On the other hand, whenever we want to keep the average outgoing edges degree of vertices constant, we use the average degree parameters ($AvgDeg._G$ and $AvgDeg._{pat}$).

In each round of experiment, we first create the dataset with the required parameters, and then all the algorithms are executed with the same dataset. Fairness in comparison is therefore guaranteed.

We consider 95% confidence interval in our experiments.

8.2 Vertex Enumerator vs QBF Solvers

This experiment compares the performance of Vertex Enumerator (Algorithm 2) against that of two non-clausal QBF solvers — GhostQ and RAReQS. In the latter cases, MO-SAT instances are first reduced to QBF satisfiability instances, and then the QBF solvers are invoked to solve them. We choose to work with non-clausal QBF solvers because converting the QBF encoding to CNF would increase the number of quantifier alternation of the resulting formulas, making the problem instances prohibitively challenging.

The experiment variable is the size of the social graph. The parameters for this experiment are as follows: • *Rep.*: 20; • k_u: 1; • #$atom^+$: 1; • #$atom^-$: 0; • #V_{pat+}: 5; • $Prob._G$: 0.1; • $Prob._{pat}$: 0.1; • $|\mathcal{L}|$: 1.

The average running time of the three solvers are plotted in Fig. 3. The performance of the QBF solvers are clearly inferior to VertexEnumerator. This confirms the need for custom MO-SAT algorithms.

8.3 Vertex Enumerator vs Model Enumerator

This experiment compares the performance of Vertex Enumerator (Algorithm 2) and Model Enumerator (Algorithm 3). The experiment is repeated for two different sizes of graph patterns in the positive atoms (α). The parameters for this experiment are listed below: • *Rep.*: 20; • k_u: 1; • #$atom^+$: 3; • #$atom^-$: 3; • #V_{pat+}: 5; • #V_{pat-}: 5; • $Prob._G$: 0.1; • $Prob._{pat}$: 0.1; • $|\mathcal{L}|$: 1; The size of social

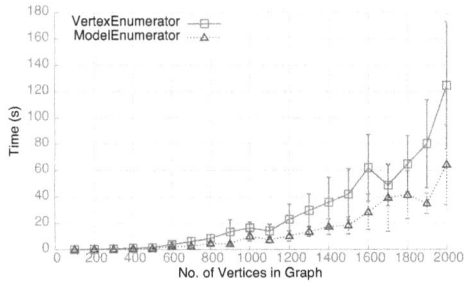

Figure 4: Vertex Enumerator versus Model Enumerator

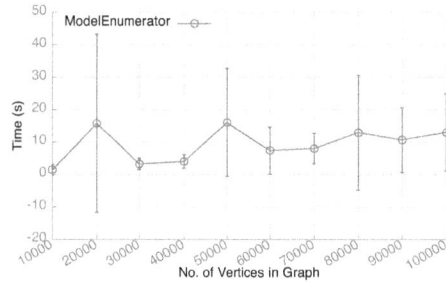

Figure 5: Model Enumerator with Large Social Graphs

graph is the variable of experiment, and we measure the performance of algorithms given different sizes of social graphs.

The average running times of the two algorithms are plotted in Fig. 4. Two observations can be made. First, Model Enumerator clearly out-performs Vertex Enumerator. This confirms our intuition that Model Enumerator is more selective in generating requester candidates than Vertex Enumerator. Second, the performance advantage of Model Enumerator widens as the size of social graph increases.

8.4 Large Social Graphs

This experiment evaluates if Model Enumerator is adequate for realistic social graphs for mid-sized organizations. The following are the parameters for this experiment: • $Rep.$: 20; • k_u: 1; • $\#atom^+$: 3; • $\#atom^-$: 3; • $\#V_{pat+}$: 5; • $\#V_{pat-}$: 5; • $AvgDeg._G$: 200; • $Prob._{pat}$: 0.5; • $|\mathcal{L}|$: 4;

In the previous two experiments, we employ only one edge label. That is done in order to make the problem instances challenging: edge labels provide useful information for the SAT solver. To make the social graphs more realistic in this third experiment, we follow [22] in adopting four edge labels. Moreover, we use more complex graph patterns by boosting the edge probabilities in graph pattern from 0.2 to 0.5. For realism, we also fix the average degree of vertices (outgoing edges) to two hundreds, instead of allowing it to grow proportionally to the size of the social graph (as in the previous two experiment). In an organizational setting, vertex degree is likely very stable.

We run Model Enumerator over social graphs of sizes 10,000 to 100,000 (increment 10,000). To put the scale in perspective, Microsoft and Google employ 94,000 and 55,419 employees, respectively. Fig. 5 depicts the average running times for Model Enumerator. Average problem solving times are within 50 seconds for social graphs of 100,000 vertices. This means that between successive rounds of policy negotiation, we can expect to have a delay of less than one minute for verifying availability criteria. This is well acceptable as Facebook-style consenting protocols (for befriending) work more in the style of email notification than instant messaging. Such performance indicates that our technology can be deployed comfortably in mid-sized organizations in the scale of, say, Microsoft or Google.

9. LIMITATIONS

A limitation of this work is that the following question remains open: What if the co-owners cannot settle on a policy in a timely fashion? This is known as termination or convergence guarantee in the literature. Convergence of collective access control decision is not a new topic, and is often conducted using Game Theory [15, 23].

One may be tempted to compare this work with Automated Trust Negotiation (ATN) [29, 31], and to expect that termination guarantees can be obtained in an analogous manner for this work. ATN is designed to enable the exchange of sensitive attributes among parties. These attributes are needed for authorizing access to a sensitive object in the paradigm of *Attribute-based Access Control*. The number of attributes each principal possesses is finite; an object's policy is fixed; each policy consists of only finitely many attributes. These settings guarantee termination.

In contrast, our interactive negotiation protocol is proposed for co-owners to collaboratively devise a ReBAC policy that satisfies their availability criteria. The atomic policies are comprised of graph patterns, and thus the space of atomic policies is infinite. Therefore, termination guarantee becomes nontrivial unless we introduce further restrictions on the space of atomic policies or on the refinement of the settlement policy in successive rounds.

10. CONCLUSION AND FUTURE WORK

We argued that interactive policy negotiation has an important role in supporting multiple ownership in organizational computing. We proposed a novel, tool-supported policy negotiation framework, in which policies under negotiation are assessed by formal availability criteria, including satisfiability, resiliency and feasibility. Although these availability criteria belong to the second level of the polynomial hierarchy, we designed and evaluated algorithms for deciding satisfiability, and showed that they provide adequate performance for mid-sized organizations.

We highlight three possible future works. The first is to formulate more tractable subproblems for feasibility and resiliency. A possible compromise is to aim for subproblems that reside in Δ_2^p. We have seen, in the case of MO-SAT, that such subproblems are quite amenable to the design of efficient algorithms based on modern SAT solvers.

A second future work concerns the generalization of the language for specifying multiple-owners policies. Currently, we use birooted graph patterns as the basis of the language. This constrains us to consider only binary relationships between the requester and one of the co-owners. In some cases, we may need to express relationships between the requester and multiple co-owners (e.g., the requester shall be a mutual friend of co-owners u_1 and u_2).

A third future work is to identify conditions under which the negotiation protocol is guaranteed to terminate. One possibility is to incorporate incentives into the negotiation protocol so as to promote collaboration among co-owners [15, 23]. Another way is to introduce syntactic restrictions on the refinement of settlement policy in successive rounds.

Acknowledgments

This work is supported in part by an NSERC Discovery Grant (RGPIN-2014-06611) and a Canada Research Chair (950-229712).

11. REFERENCES

[1] ARORA, S., AND BARAK, B. *Computational Complexity: A Modern Approach.* Cambridge University Press, 2009.

[2] BESMER, A., AND RICHTER LIPFORD, H. Moving beyond untagging: Photo privacy in a tagged world. In *Proceedings of CHI '10* (Atlanta, Georgia, USA, 2010), pp. 1563–1572.

[3] BRUNS, G., FONG, P. W. L., SIAHAAN, I., AND HUTH, M. Relationship-based access control: Its expression and enforcement through hybrid logic. In *Proceedings of CODASPY '12* (San Antonio, TX, USA, Feb. 2012).

[4] CRAMPTON, J. A reference monitor for workflow systems with constrained task execution. In *Proceedings of SACMAT '05* (Stockholm, Sweden, 2005), pp. 38–47.

[5] CRAMPTON, J., GUTIN, G., AND YEO, A. On the parameterized complexity and kernelization of the workflow satisfiability problem. *ACM TISSEC 16*, 1 (June 2013).

[6] ERDŐS, P., AND RÉNYI, A. On random graphs i. *Publication of the Mathematical Institute of the Hungarian Academy of Sciences 6* (1959), 290–297.

[7] FONG, P. W. L. Preventing Sybil attacks by privilege attenuation: A design principle for social network systems. In *Proceedings of IEEE S&P '11* (Oakland, CA, May 2011), pp. 263–278.

[8] FONG, P. W. L. Relationship-based access control: Protection model and policy language. In *Proceedings of CODASPY '11* (San Antonio, Texas, USA, Feb. 2011), pp. 191–202.

[9] FONG, P. W. L., MEHREGAN, P., AND KRISHNAN, R. Relational abstraction in community-based secure collaboration. In *ACM CCS '13* (Berlin, Germany, 2013), pp. 585–598.

[10] FONG, P. W. L., AND SIAHAAN, I. Relationship-based access control policies and their policy languages. In *Proceedings of SACMAT '11* (Innsbruck, Austria, June 2011), pp. 51–60.

[11] GRAHAM, G. S., AND DENNING, P. J. Protection: Principles and Practice. In *Proceedings of AFIPS '72 (Spring)* (Atlantic City, New Jersey, 1972), pp. 417–429.

[12] HU, H., AND AHN, G.-J. Multiparty authorization framework for data sharing in online social networks. In *Proceedings of DBSec '11* (Richmond, VA, USA, 2011), pp. 29–43.

[13] HU, H., AHN, G.-J., AND JORGENSEN, J. Detecting and resolving privacy conflicts for collaborative data sharing in online social networks. In *Proceedings of ACSAC'11* (Orlando, Florida, USA, 2011), pp. 103–112.

[14] HU, H., AHN, G.-J., AND JORGENSEN, J. Multiparty access control for online social networks: Model and mechanisms. *IEEE TKDE 25*, 7 (2013).

[15] HU, H., AHN, G.-J., ZHAO, Z., AND YANG, D. Game theoretic analysis of multiparty access control in online social networks. In *Proceedings of SACMAT '14* (London, Ontario, Canada, 2014), pp. 93–102.

[16] KHAN, A. A., AND FONG, P. W. L. Satisfiability and feasibility in a relationship-based workflow authorization model. In *Proceedings of ESORICS '12* (Pisa, Italy, Sept. 2012), pp. 109–126.

[17] LAMPINEN, A., LEHTINEN, V., LEHMUSKALLIO, A., AND TAMMINEN, S. We're in it together: Interpersonal management of disclosure in social network services. In *Proceedings of CHI '11* (Vancouver, BC, Canada, 2011), pp. 3217–3226.

[18] LE BERRE, D., AND PARRAIN, A. The sat4j library, release 2.2. *Journal on Satisfiability, Boolean Modeling and Computation 7* (2010), 59–64.

[19] LI, N., AND TRIPUNITARA, M. V. On Safety in Discretionary Access Control. In *Proceedings of IEEE S&P '05* (Oakland, CA, May 2005), pp. 96–109.

[20] MEHREGAN, P. *Multiple Ownership in Access Control.* PhD thesis, University of Calgary, March 2016.

[21] MEHREGAN, P., AND .FONG, P. W. L. Design patterns for multiple stakeholders in social computing. In *Proceedings DBSec '14*. July 2014, pp. 163–178.

[22] RIZVI, S. Z. R., FONG, P. W., CRAMPTON, J., AND SELLWOOD, J. Relationship-based access control for an open-source medical records system. In *Proceedings of SACMAT '15* (Vienna, Austria, 2015), pp. 113–124.

[23] SQUICCIARINI, A. C., SHEHAB, M., AND WEDE, J. Privacy Policies for Shared Content in Social Network Sites. *The VLDB Journal 19*, 6 (Dec. 2010), 777–796.

[24] SQUICCIARINI, A. C., XU, H., AND ZHANG, X. L. CoPE : Enabling collaborative privacy management in online social networks. *Journal of the American Society for Information Science 62*, 3 (2011), 521–534.

[25] SUCH, J. M., AND CRIADO, N. Adaptive conflict resolution mechanism for multi-party privacy management in social media. In *Proceedings of WPES '14* (Scottsdale, Arizona, USA, 2014), pp. 69–72.

[26] THOMAS, K., GRIER, C., AND NICOL, D. M. Unfriendly: Multi-party privacy risks in social networks. In *Proceedings of PETS '10* (Berlin, Germany, July 2010), pp. 236–252.

[27] TORÁN, J. On the resolution complexity of graph non-isomorphism. In *Proceedings of SAT'13* (Helsinki, Finland, July 2013), pp. 52–66.

[28] WANG, Q., AND LI, N. Satisfiability and resiliency in workflow authorization systems. *ACM TISSEC 13*, 4 (Dec. 2010).

[29] WINSBOROUGH, W. H., AND LI, N. Safety in automated trust negotiation. In *IEEE S&P '04* (Oakland, California, USA, May 2004), pp. 147–160.

[30] WISHART, R., CORAPI, D., MARINOVIC, S., AND SLOMAN, M. Collaborative privacy policy authoring in a social networking context. In *Proceedings of IEEE POLICY'10* (Fairfax, VA, July 2010), pp. 1–8.

[31] YU, T., WINSLETT, M., AND SEAMONS, K. E. Supporting structured credentials and sensitive policies through interoperable strategies for automated trust negotiation. *ACM TISSEC 6*, 1 (Feb. 2003), 1–42.

Automated Fault Localization of XACML Policies

Dianxiang Xu, Zhenyu Wang, Shuai Peng, Ning Shen
Department of Computer Science
Boise State University
Boise, ID 83725, USA
+1-208-426-5734
{dianxiangxu, zhenyuwang, shuaipeng, ningshen}@boisestate.edu

ABSTRACT

Access control policies in distributed systems, particularly implemented in the XACML standard language, are increasingly complex. Faults may exist in complex policies for various reasons such as misunderstanding of the access control requirements, omissions, and coding errors. These faults, if not removed before deployment, may lead to unauthorized accesses or denial of service. Manual localization of these faults, however, can be a challenging task. Inspired by spectrum-based fault localization for software debugging, this paper presents an approach for automatically localizing the fault(s) in a given XACML policy by exploring test coverage information of the policy elements. We investigate two test coverage criteria (i.e., reachability and firing) of policy elements and 14 scoring methods for ranking policy elements to determine the fault location(s). To evaluate the fault localization methods, we have used real-world policy files with different levels of complexity and a large number of policy mutants with one or two seeded faults. The experiment results show that the firing-based Naish2 and CBI-Inc methods are effective in fault localization of XACML policies.

CCS Concepts

• Security and privacy → Security services → Access control
• Security and privacy → Software and application security → Software security engineering.

Keywords

Access control; debugging, fault localization; XACML; testing.

1. INTRODUCTION

XACML (eXtensible Access Control Markup Language) [1] is an OASIS standard for specifying access control policies in the XML format. It supports a variety of data types and functions for defining access control rules as well as different combining algorithms for rule and policy composition. While such expressiveness is required of the specification of real-world policies, it raises challenges for quality assurance of access control policies. When an XACML policy is coded, faults can be introduced due to misunderstanding of the access control requirements, omissions, and coding errors. For example, various rule-related faults may exist in XACML policies, such as incorrect rule effect, incorrect rule target, and incorrect rule condition [2]-

SACMAT'16, June 5–8, 2016, Shanghai, China.
© 2016 ACM. ISBN 978-1-4503-3802-8/16/06 …$15.00.
DOI: http://dx.doi.org/10.1145/2914642.2914653

[6]. These faults, if not removed before deployment, may lead to serious security problems, such as unauthorized accesses and denial of service.

Several methods have been proposed to generate test inputs (i.e., access requests) for testing XACML policies in order to find potential faults [2]-[6]. A test fails if the actual response to the access request by the XACML policy under test is different from the expected response (called oracle value). This indicates that the XACML policy is faulty. However, the failure does not provide any information on where the fault is. Debugging of the policy is needed in order to locate and fix the fault. For complex XACML policies with a large number of access control rules, manual debugging can be a challenging task. Generally, we would need to walk through many policy elements in order to find out what has caused the failure.

This paper presents the first attempt to automatically localize faults of XACML policies that cause test failures. It is not concerned with how the faults will be fixed, though. Inspired by spectrum-based fault localization (SBFL) for software debugging [7]-[9], we exploit the test execution information of the policy elements in a given XACML policy to determine which policy element is faulty. Specifically, we introduce reachability-based and firing-based fault localization techniques with various scoring methods for ranking policy elements to predict the fault locations. A policy element is said to be reached by a test if it is evaluated during the test execution. A policy element is said to be fired by the test if it evaluates to true during the test execution. Our approach explores the correlation between reachability or firing of each policy element and the verdict (i.e., pass or fail) of each test execution.

We have implemented our approach based on Balana, an open source implementation of XACML 3.0 [10]. To evaluate the effectiveness of automated fault localization techniques, we have used real-world XACML policy files with different levels of complexity and a large number of policy mutants with seeded faults. Each mutant is a variation of the original policy with one or two injected faults. The main findings of the empirical studies are as follows: (1) For an individual scoring method, whether the firing-based fault localization technique is more accurate than the reachability-based fault localization technique depends on the scoring method. Nevertheless, the firing-based technique is more cost effective because the examination of a certain percentage of top-ranked policy elements usually reveals more faults than the reachability-based technique; (2) the firing-based Naish2 and CBI-Inc methods can accurately localize the fault(s) regardless of the policy size. They only require the examination of a few policy elements to reveal the fault(s). In other words, the faulty policy element is usually among a few top candidates that are suggested by the firing-based Naish2 and CBI-Inc methods. This is significantly better than the existing best-performing SBFL techniques for software debugging, which need to inspect more than 20% of the source code [7]. The other scoring methods are much less effective. They also depend on the policy size -- more policy elements need to be inspected for larger policies.

The rest of this paper is organized as follows. Section 2 introduces the main elements of XACML policies and a running example that will be used throughout the paper. Section 3 describes the reachability-based and firing-based fault localization techniques and the scoring methods. Section 4 presents empirical studies. Section 5 reviews related work. Section 6 concludes this paper.

2. XACML POLICIES

The main components of the XACML3.0 language model are rule, policy, and policy set [1]. An XACML policy or policy set defines the circumstances under which access to resources should be granted or denied. It responds to an access request with a decision such as permit or deny. As the most elementary unit of policy, a rule consists of a target, a condition, and an effect. The target is a logical expression that specifies the set of requests to which the rule is intended to apply. The condition is a Boolean expression that refine the applicability of the rule established by the target. A policy comprises a policy target, a rule-combining algorithm identifier, and a list of rules. A policy set consists of a policy set target, a policy-combining algorithm identifier, and a list of policies or policy sets. In XACML3.0, a rule, policy, or policy set may be associated with obligation expressions and advice expressions. This paper will not discuss obligation and advice because they are irrelevant to the work.

Figure 1 shows the relationships between the main elements of XACML3.0. The target of a rule, policy, or policy set is a conjunctive sequence of AnyOf clauses. Each AnyOf clause is disjunctive sequence of AllOf clauses, and each AllOf clause is a conjunctive sequence of match predicates. A match predicate compares attribute values in a request with the embedded attributes. Logical expressions for match predicates and rule conditions are usually defined on four categories of attributes: subject, resource, action, and environment. As XACML policies and policy sets are defined with respect to attributes, access requests are specified by attribute values.

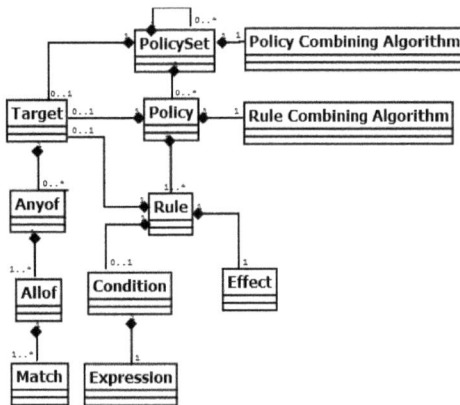

Figure 1. Main elements of XACML policies.

We use the policy in Figure 2 as a running example. The policy is named *KmarketBluePolicy* (line 2). The rule combining algorithm is deny-overrides (lines 3-5). The policy's target (lines 6-19) means *role=blue*, where *role* is an attribute in the subject category and both *role* and *blue* are strings. There are four rules: *total-amount* (line 20), *deny-liquor-medicine* (line 38), *max-drink-amount* (line 64), and *permit-rule* (line 92).

For illustration purposes, we describe the policy target and rules in plain text in Table 1. The policy target (denoted as *PT*) is *role=blue*. For rule *total-amount* (denoted as *R1*), its effect is deny, its target is *totalAmount>100*, and its condition is omitted. Its decision would be "deny" if *totalAmount>100* evaluates to true according to the given access request. Similarly, rule *deny-liquor-medicine* (*R2*) would result in a permit decision if *resource-id=Liquor ∨ resource-id=Medicine* evaluates to true. Rule *max-drink-amount* (*R3*) has both target and condition components. Its decision would be "deny" if both its target and condition evaluate to true (i.e., *resource-id=Drink ∧ amount>10*). Rule *permit-rule* (*R4*) has neither the target nor the condition. It results in a permit decision whenever it is applied.

Figure 2. A sample XACML policy.

Table 1. Main policy elements in the sample policy

Name	Target	Condition	Effect
PT	role=blue		
R1	totalAmount>100		deny
R2	resource-id="Liquor" ∨ resource-id="Medicine"		permit
R3	resource-id="Drink"	amount>10	deny
R4			permit

Given an access request, the decision of a policy not only depends on the policy target and the decisions of individual rules, but also the rule combining algorithm. In the above example, if the *total-amount* rule (*R1*) results in a deny decision (i.e., attribute *totalAmount*'s value is greater than 100 in the access request), then the policy's decision is deny because the rule combining algorithm is *deny-overrides*. In this case, other rules may not need to be evaluated. Generally, the purpose of a rule combining algorithm is to combine the decisions of individual rules into a single policy decision. Similarly, the decision of a policy depends on the policy set target, the decisions of individual policies, and the policy combining algorithm that combines the decisions of individual policies into a single decision of the policy set. In XACML 3.0, there are 11 rule combining and 12 policy combining algorithms (11 of them use the same names as respective rule combining algorithms). The most commonly used ones are *Deny-overrides*, *Permit-overrides*, *Deny-unless-permit*, *Permit-unless-deny*, *First-applicable*, and *Only-one-applicable*.

Note that a policy or policy set may yield one of the following six decisions: permit, deny, Not-Applicable, Indeterminate {D}, Indeterminate {P}, and Indeterminate {DP}. According to the XACML3.0 standard, Indeterminate {D}, Indeterminate {P}, and

Indeterminate {DP} will be a plain Indeterminate if it is the final decision returned by the Policy Decision Point (PDP). In our approach, an oracle value can be defined as Indeterminate {D}, Indeterminate {P}, or Indeterminate {DP}. In this case, a test passes only when the actual response is exactly the same as the oracle value. For example, a test fails if the oracle value is Indeterminate {D}, but the actual response is Indeterminate {P} or Indeterminate {DP}. In the experiment, however, responses produced by each subject policy are considered final decisions returned by the XACML engine. Thus, the set of access decisions for both oracle values and actual responses is {permit, deny, Not-Applicable, Indeterminate}.

3. AUTOMATED FAULT LOCALIZATION

3.1 Problem Formulation

The fault localization problem is defined as follows: given an XACML policy (or policy set) and a test suite with at least one test that fails when executed against the policy (or policy set), identify which element (e.g., policy, policy set target, and rule) of the policy (or policy set) is faulty. After the fault is identified, the policy developer can proceed to fix the fault. This paper is not concerned with how to fix the fault, though. Note that, if no test in the given test suite fails, the policy (or policy set) may not be faulty and thus fault localization makes no sense.

Table 2. A sample test suite

Test No	Input (attribute values in request)				Oracle Value
	role	resource-id	amount	totalAmount	
1	Blue	Drink	9	99	Permit
2	Blue	Drink	11	99	Deny
3	Blue	Liquor	9	99	Deny
4	Blue	Liquor	9	101	Deny
5	Blue	Drink	9	101	Deny

Table 2 is a test suite for the sample policy in Table 1. Each test input includes a value for each of the four attributes *role*, *resource-id*, *amount*, and *totalAmount*. When the tests are executed against the sample policy, test 3 reports a failure - the actual response to the access request is permit whereas the oracle value is deny. The failure is caused by the fault in *R2*, which should have a "deny" effect. The goal of our approach is to locate such a fault.

3.2 Our Approach

As shown in Figure 3, our approach first executes the test suite against the given XACML policy and builds a correlation between each policy element in the given policy and the execution of each test -- how each policy element is covered by each test (called test coverage criterion) and whether the test passes or fails (called test verdict). Then the correlation data is used to rank all policy elements with a certain scoring method. A policy element with a high suspicion score has a high probability of having fault(s). For simplicity, we first focus on faults in rules, policy targets, and policy set targets. Later we will discuss incorrect rule combining and policy combining algorithms.

3.2.1 Reachability-Based Fault Localization

Reachability-based fault localization is based on the correlation between whether each policy element is reached (i.e., evaluated) by each test and whether the test passes or fails. Table 3 shows the reachability information of the policy target and each rule in the sample policy when it is executed with the test suite in Table 2,

where 'x' means that the policy element in the given column is reached by the test in the given row. *PT* and *R1* were covered by all five tests; *R2* and *R4* were exercised by the first three tests; and *R3* was covered by the first two tests. The policy passes all tests except test 3. Test 3 is called a failed test, whereas the others are called passed tests.

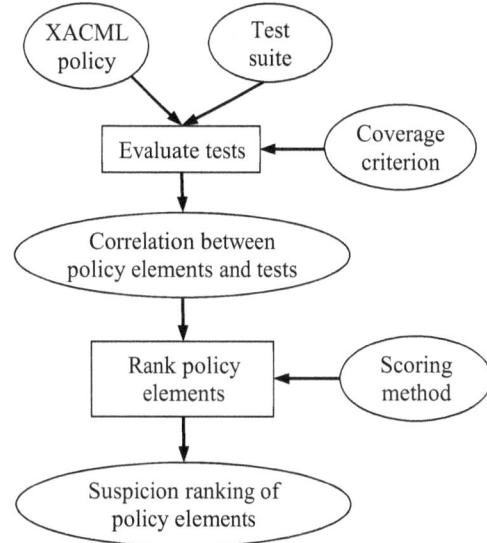

Figure 3. Architecture of fault localizer

Table 3. An example of reachability-based fault localization

Test No	Reachability of policy elements					Test Result
	PT	R1	R2	R3	R4	
1	x	x	x	x	x	Pass
2	x	x	x	x	x	Pass
3	x	x	x		x	Fail
4	x	x				Pass
5	x	x				Pass
$S_{jaccard}$	$\frac{1}{5}$	$\frac{1}{5}$	$\frac{1}{3}$	$\frac{0}{2}$	$\frac{1}{3}$	

We associate the following four variables with each policy element:

- a_{00}: number of passed tests in which the policy element was not **reached**,
- a_{01}: number of failed tests in which the policy element was not **reached**
- a_{10}: number of passed tests in which the policy element was **reached**
- a_{11}: number of failed tests in which the policy element was **reached**

For each policy element, the subscript i in a_{ij} refers to whether the policy element is reached ($i=1$) or not ($i=0$), whereas j is concerned with the number of passed tests ($j=0$) or failed tests ($j=1$).

We can calculate a suspicion score for each policy element by some formula (called scoring method) and then sort the scores of all policy elements to determine the most suspicious policy element that has the highest suspicion score. For example, the suspicion scores of the policy target and rules in Table 3 are 1/5,

1/5, 1/3, 0/2, and 1/3, respectively when the following Jaccard similarity coefficient formula (called Jaccard method) is applied:

$$S_{jaccard} = \frac{a_{11}}{a_{11}+a_{01}+a_{10}} \qquad (1)$$

As a result, the rankings of the policy elements are <[R2, R4], [PT, R1], R3>, where [R2, R4] means that R2 and R4 have the same score. They are considered as the most suspicious policy elements that contain the fault.

3.2.2 Firing-Based Fault Localization

Firing-based fault localization is based on the correlation between the evaluation result (firing) of each policy element by each test and whether the test passes or fails. A policy target is said to be fired by a test if it evaluates to true when the test is executed. A rule is said to be fired by a test if its target and condition both evaluate to true when the test is executed. For firing-based fault localization, a_{ij} for each policy element is defined as follows:

- a_{00} : number of passed tests in which the policy element was not **fired**
- a_{01}: number of failed tests in which the policy element was not **fired**
- a_{10}: number of passed tests in which the policy element was **fired**
- a_{11}: number of failed tests in which the policy element was **fired**

Table 4. An example of firing-based fault localization

Test No	Firing of policy elements					Test Result
	PT	R1	R2	R3	R4	
1	x				x	Pass
2	x			x		Pass
3	x		x		x	Fail
4	x	x				Pass
5	x	x				Pass
$S_{jaccard}$	$\frac{1}{5}$	$\frac{0}{3}$	$\frac{1}{1}$	$\frac{0}{2}$	$\frac{1}{2}$	

Table 4 shows the results of applying firing-based fault localization to the sample policy using the aforementioned Jaccard scoring method, where 'x' means that the policy element in the given column is fired by the test in the given row. PT is fired by every test, R1 is fired by passed tests 4 and 5, R2 is fired by test 3 (the only failed test), R3 is fired only by passed test 2, and R4 is fired by passed test 1 and failed test 3. The suspicion scores of the five policy elements are 1/5, 0/3, 1/1, 0/2, and 1/2, respectively. Their rankings are <R2, R4, PT, [R1, R3]>. R2 has the highest suspicion score. In this example, the result of firing-based fault localization is more accurate than that of reachability-based fault localization when the Jaccard scoring method is used.

3.2.3 Scoring Methods for Fault localization

Table 5 lists the 14 scoring methods that have been investigated in our work. They are selected from the commonly studied and/or best-performing spectrum-based methods for software fault localization [7]-[9].

Table 5. Scoring methods

Name	formula
Jaccard	$\frac{a_{11}}{a_{11}+a_{01}+a_{10}}$
Tarantula	$\frac{\frac{a_{11}}{a_{11}+a_{01}}}{\frac{a_{11}}{a_{11}+a_{01}}+\frac{a_{10}}{a_{10}+a_{00}}}$
Ochiai	$\frac{a_{11}}{\sqrt{(a_{11}+a_{01})(a_{11}+a_{10})}}$
Ochiai2	$\frac{a_{11}a_{00}}{\sqrt{(a_{11}+a_{10})(a_{00}+a_{01})(a_{11}+a_{01})(a_{00}+a_{10})}}$
CBI-Inc	$\frac{a_{11}}{a_{11}+a_{10}} - \frac{a_{11}+a_{01}}{a_{11}+a_{01}+a_{10}+a_{00}}$
Hamann	$\frac{a_{11}+a_{00}-a_{01}-a_{10}}{a_{11}+a_{01}+a_{10}+a_{00}}$
Simple Matching	$\frac{a_{11}+a_{00}}{a_{11}+a_{01}+a_{10}+a_{00}}$
Sokal	$\frac{2(a_{11}+a_{00})}{2(a_{11}+a_{00})+a_{01}+a_{10}}$
Naish2	$a_{11}-\frac{a_{10}}{a_{10}+a_{00}+1}$
Goodman	$\frac{2a_{11}-a_{01}-a_{10}}{2a_{11}+a_{01}+a_{10}}$
Sorensen Dice	$\frac{2a_{11}}{2a_{11}+a_{01}+a_{10}}$
Anderberg	$\frac{a_{11}}{a_{11}+2(a_{01}+a_{10})}$
Euclid	$\sqrt{a_{11}+a_{00}}$
Rogers Tanimoto	$\frac{a_{11}+a_{00}}{a_{11}+a_{00}+2(a_{01}+a_{10})}$

3.3 Implementation

We have implemented the fault localization approach in an open source tool[1] based on Balana, which is an open source implementation of XACML 3.0. For the empirical evaluation of the fault localization approach, we have also implemented test generators and mutant generators for XACML policies. A key to the implementation of the fault localization approach is to keep track of the execution of each policy element when a test suite is performed against a policy (i.e., the information in Table 3 and Table 4). Revising the source code of Balana is not a viable option because the implementation will not work for future versions of Balana unless the fault localization is re-implemented in the new versions. To solve this problem, we use aspect-oriented programming in AspectJ (an aspect-oriented extension to Java) to monitor the entry and exit points of policy execution and each point at which a policy element is evaluated. At these points, the monitoring aspect either creates a spreadsheet or records the evaluation results (e.g., firing of policy targets and rules) in the spreadsheet. As a runtime instrumentation mechanism, the aspect is a separate module from Balana and does not modify the source code of Balana. It is executed only when the fault localization function is enabled.

4. EMPRICAL STUDIES

The empirical studies aim at answering the following research questions:

> Q1. Which fault localization technique, reachability-based or firing-based, is better?

---

[1] https://github.com/dianxiangxu/XPA

140

Q2. Are there fault localization methods that can accurately localize faulty elements in XACML policies?

4.1 Experiment Setup

Because no faulty versions of real-world XACML policies are publically available, our experiment relies on mutants of XACML policies. Table 6 shows the list of XACML policies used in our experiment. They are collected from the literature. The number of lines of XML code (LOC) ranges from 227 to 12,803. The number of rules ranges from 12 to 640. Continue is an access control policy for a conference management system [12]; fedora is "an open source repository system for the management and dissemination of digital content"[2]; itrust is "a medical application that provides patients with a means to keep up with their medical history and records as well as communicate with their doctors"[3]. itrustX (X=5, 10) are expanded versions of itrust [13]. They have X times as many rules as itrust. We believe the sizes of the subject XACML policy files are a good representation of real-world applications because, for quality assurance and maintenance purposes, a very large policy is usually decomposed into a number of manageable XACML files.

Table 6. Subject policies, tests, and mutants

Policy	LOC	No. of rules	No. of tests	Single fault mutants	Two-fault mutants
continue	229	15	27	88	7,633
fedora	227	12	31	76	5,974
itrust	1,283	64	197	449	201,025
itrust5	6,403	320	983	2,241	N/A
itrust10	12,803	640	1,965	4,481	N/A

A mutant of an XACML policy is a variation of the policy with one or more fault(s) created by a mutation operator. Such mutation analysis a widely applied approach to the evaluation of software testing research. Program mutation has the following important hypotheses: (a) the mutants are based on actual fault models and are representative of real faults, (b) developers produce programs that are close to being correct (called the competent programmer hypothesis [14]), (c) test cases that are sufficient to detect simple faults (i.e., mutants) are also capable of detecting complex faults (i.e., higher order mutants or real faults). This is called the coupling effect hypothesis [15]. Experiments have confirmed that generated mutants are indeed similar to real faults for the purpose of evaluating testing techniques [16]. A recent empirical study that examined 357 real faults in 5 large, open-source programs using developer-written and automatically-generated tests has confirmed that a test suite's mutation score is correlated with its real fault detection rate [17]. We believe that the competent programmer hypothesis and the coupling effect hypothesis are also valid for mutation analysis of XACML policies. In addition, as discussed below, the mutants in our experiments are representative of real faults because mutation operators are defined over a comprehensive fault model of XACML policies (Table 7). For example, the running example in Section 2 is a mutant of a correct policy where the effect of *R2* is deny. This mutant can be generated from the correct policy by applying the CRE mutation operator to *R2*. Our experiment uses both single-fault mutants and two-fault mutants. A single fault

mutant is created by applying a mutation operator to a policy once. The fault location is the index of the mutated policy element (0 for a mutated policy target or the index of a mutated rule) in the policy. A two-fault mutant is created by applying a mutation operator to a single-fault mutant. The fault locations are the indices of the mutated policy elements. Table 6 only includes the single-fault and two-fault mutants that fail the given test suite of the corresponding policy such that fault localization is applicable. Equivalent mutants are excluded from the experiment. An equivalent mutant has the same behavior as the original policy - no failure would be reported when it is executed against the given test suite of the corresponding policy. Nevertheless, single fault equivalent mutants are used to generate two fault mutants, which may or may not be equivalent to the original policy. Note that the number of two-fault mutants grows quickly with the increase of policy size due to the combination of mutation operators. For example, itrust has only 64 rules, but there are 201,025 two-fault mutants used in the experiment. We were unable to complete the generation of two-fault mutants for itrust5 or itrust10 due to the limitations of memory and disk space.

Table 7. Mutation operators

Fault type	Mutation operator	
	Name	Meaning of Mutation
Incorrect policy target	PTT	set Policy Target True
	PTF	set Policy Target False
Incorrect rule effect	CRE	Change Rule Effect
Incorrect rule target	RTT	set Rule Target True
	RTF	set Rule Target False
	RPTE	Remove Parallel Target Element
Incorrect rule condition	RCT	set Rule Condition True
	RCF	set Rule Condition False
	ANF	Add Not Function in condition
	RNF	Remove Not Function in condition

To use mutants for the evaluation of fault localization, we need a test suite for each policy such that it can kill all non-equivalent mutants of the policy -- at least one test reports a failure when each mutant is executed against the test suite. If there is no failure when a mutant is tested, it would make no sense to apply fault localization to the mutant. So we generated the test suite for each policy by using the multi-condition/decision coverage (MC/DC) [18] for policy target, rule target, and rule condition. In MC/DC, a condition refers to a primitive Boolean valued expression that cannot be broken down into simpler Boolean expressions, whereas a decision is a Boolean-valued expression made up of conditions and logic operators. Thus, the policy target, rule target, and rule condition in XACML are all decisions that consist of one or more conditions. In addition to making a decision true and false at least once, a MC/DC test suite requires that: (1) every condition in a decision has taken on all possible outcomes at least once, and (2) each condition has been shown to independently affect the decision's outcome. For example, MC/DC of a conjunctive decision with n conditions (e.g., $c_1 \wedge ... \wedge c_n$) requires $n+1$ tests: one test that evaluates all conditions to true and one test that evaluate one condition to false and other conditions evaluate to true. Similarly, MC/DC of a disjunctive decision with n conditions (e.g., $c_1 \vee ... \vee c_n$) requires $n+1$ tests: one test that evaluates all conditions to false and one test that evaluate one condition to true and other conditions evaluate to false. The MC/DC test suites in our experiments killed all non-equivalent mutants created by the mutation operators in Table 7. Thus all the mutants are included in Table 6.

---

[2] http://www.fedora.info

[3] http://agile.csc.ncsu.edu/iTrust/wiki/doku.php?id=start

We execute each mutant against the test suite generated from the corresponding subject policy and apply each of the 14 scoring methods in Table 5 to both reachability-based and firing-based fault localization. Based on the rankings of suspicion scores, we collect the following data:

- Number of policy elements that should be examined in order to find the seeded fault(s). Consider the previous running example, where *R2* is the faulty rule. In the reachability-based fault localization using the Jaccard scoring method in Table 3, both *R2* and *R4* have the highest suspicious score. According the suspicion rankings, these two rules need to be examined in order to locate the fault. In the firing-based fault localization using the Jaccard scoring method in Table 4, *R2* has the highest suspicious score. The number of policy elements that need to be examined is 1. This fault localization result is accurate.

- Whether the mutated element is located successfully when we only examine a certain percentage (e.g., 5%, 10%, or 50%) of the top ranked elements. In the example of coverage-based fault localization using the Jaccard method in Table 3, we can locate the faulty element if we examine 50% of the top-ranked policy elements.

Furthermore, we sum up the results of all mutants for each subject policy to obtain the following evaluation metrics: (1) the average number of policy elements that need to be examined in order to locate the faulty elements in all mutants, and (2) the percentage of mutants for which the faulty element is revealed by examining a certain percentage of the top ranked policy elements.

4.2 Experiment Results

Now we present the experiment results according to the aforementioned evaluation metrics.

4.2.1 Single-Fault Mutants: Average Number of Policy Elements That Need to Be Examined

Table 8 shows the average number of policy elements that a reachability-based fault localization method needs to examine in order to find the seeded fault in each sing-fault mutant. The overall rankings of the scoring methods are consistent in all subject policies. If one scoring method has a lower or equal average number of policy elements than another method in the experiment of one policy, it is the same in the experiment of another policy. For example, CBI-Inc has outperformed Ochiai2 in the experiment of each subject policy. Six methods, Anderberg, Goodman, Jaccard, Ochiai, SorensenDice, and Tarrantula, have the same capability. Naish2 is slightly better for the continue and fedora policies. CBI-Inc and Ochiai2 are close to the above methods. An exception is fedora for which Ochiai2 is the best method. The above nine methods have performed much better than the remaining five methods Euclid, Hamann, RogersTanimoto, SimpleMatching, and Sokal, particularly for larger policies. These five are equally least effective.

Table 8. Reachability-based fault localization for single-fault mutants: average number of policy elements that need to be examined

Scoring method	Continue	fedora	itrust	itrust 5	intrust 10
Naish2	4.75	5.63	10.29	46.84	92.55
Anderberg Goodman Jaccard Ochiai Sorensen Dice Tarantula	4.80	5.70	10.29	46.84	92.55
CBI-Inc	5.10	5.71	10.43	46.98	92.70
Ochiai2	5.43	5.58	10.57	70.02	138.5
Euclid Hamann Rogers Tanimoto Simple Matching Sokal	7.32	7.20	27.96	137.7	274.8

Table 9 shows the average number of policy elements that each firing-based localization method needs to examine in order to find the fault in each single-fault mutant. The overall rankings of the scoring methods are consistent for all subject policies. Naish2 is the most accurate, and CBI-Inc is the second. Both are much more accurate than the other methods. They are followed by a group of five methods with the same capability: Euclid, Hamann, RogersTanimoto, SimpleMatching, and Sokal. They are also notably better than the remaining seven methods, among which five have the same capability.

Table 9. Firing-based fault localization for single-fault mutants: average number of policy elements that need to be examined

Scoring method	Continue	fedora	itrust	Itrust 5	intrust 10
Naish2	2.13	2.75	1.71	1.71	1.71
CBI-Inc	2.96	3.21	2.13	2.14	2.14
Euclid Hamann Rogers Tanimoto Simple Matching Sokal	4.32	3.09	10.13	44.14	86.71
Goodman	5.97	5.58	19.25	92.39	183.8
Anderberg Jaccard Ochiai Sorensen Dice Tarantula	6.48	6.05	19.53	92.67	184.1
Ochiai2	6.80	6.05	19.67	103.6	207.3

Comparing Table 8 with Table 9 results in preliminary answers to the research questions Q1 and Q2 with respect to single-fault mutants.

Answer to Q1: Whether the reachability-based fault localization technique or the firing-based fault localization technique is better depends on the scoring method. The firing-based technique is better for seven methods: Naish2, CBI-Inc, Euclid, Hamann, RogersTanimoto, SimpleMatching, and Sokal. It is the opposite for the other seven methods. Naish2 is the best in both reachability-based and firing-based localization. Except for Naish2 and CBI-Inc, the group of methods with a less average number of policy elements in the reachability-based fault localization has a greater average number of policy elements in the firing-based fault localization, and vice versa. The six most effective scoring methods (except Naish2) in Table 8 are among the least effective in Table 9. The five least effective scoring methods in Table 9 are only next to the two best methods (Naish2 and CBI-Inc) in Table 8.

Answer to Q2: The firing-based naish2 method is the most accurate. In the experiment of each subject policy, it only needs to examine one or two policy elements, regardless of the policy size. The firing-based CBI-Inc method is also very accurate. It only needs to examine two to three policy elements regardless of the policy size. Both of them are much better than the other firing-based methods, which require examination of more policy elements for larger policies. For all reachability-based methods, the average number of policy elements that need to be examined increases with the policy size.

4.2.2 Two-Fault Mutants: Average Number of Policy Elements That Need to Be Examined

Table 10 shows the average number of policy elements that a reachability-based fault localization method needs to examine in order to find both faults in each two-fault mutant. The overall rankings are consistent with that of single-fault mutant in Table 8.

Table 10. Reachability-based fault localization for two-fault mutants: average number of policy elements that need to be examined

Scoring method	continue	fedora	itrust
Anderberg			
Goodman			
Jaccard	6.62	6.48	18.83
Sorensen Dice			
Naish2	6.74	6.46	18.90
Ochiai	6.66	6.47	18.83
Tarantula	6.55	6.50	18.86
CBI-Inc	6.88	6.52	19.02
Ochiai2	7.16	6.51	19.38
Euclid			
Hamann			
Rogers Tanimoto	8.16	7.45	30.06
Simple Matching			
Sokal			

Table 11. Firing-based fault localization for two-fault mutants: average number of policy elements that need to be examined

Scoring method	continue	fedora	itrust
Naish2	4.62	4.14	6.54
CBI-Inc	4.76	4.06	6.82
Euclid			
Hamann			
Rogers Tanimoto	6.21	4.07	14.25
Simple Matching			
Sokal			
Goodman	8.20	6.9	23.46
Anderberg			
Jaccard			
Sorensen Dice	8.24	6.96	23.46
Ochiai	8.25	6.96	23.46
Tarantula	8.23	6.90	23.45
Ochiai2	8.51	6.89	23.56

Table 11 shows the average number of policy elements that a firing-based fault localization method needs to examine in order

to find both faults in each two-fault mutant. The overall rankings are consistent with that of single-fault mutant in Table 10.

Answer to Q1: for two-fault mutants, whether the firing-based technique or the reachability-based technique is better depends on the scoring method. This is consistent with the experiment of the single-fault mutants.

Answer to Q2: for two-fault mutants, the firing-based Naish2 and CBI-Inc methods are the most effective. They only need to examine a small number of policy elements regardless of the policy size. CBI-Inc is only slightly better than naish2 for the fedora policy.

For either question, the answers from single-fault mutants and two-fault mutants are consistent.

4.2.3 Percentage of Mutants with Successful Fault Localization When a Certain Percentage of Top-Ranked Policy Elements Are Examined

Another way to evaluate the effectiveness of a fault localization method is to measure the percentage of mutants whose faults are revealed when only a certain percentage of ranked policy elements are examined. For simplicity, here we only consider single-fault mutants. Table 12 presents the percentage of mutants whose faults are revealed when only top 10% of the ranked policy elements are examined in each reachability-based method. Here we do not consider the two small policies continue and fedora because 10% is not meaningful for them. The rankings of all methods are similar to those in Table 8 and Table 10. The group of top nine methods is much better than the remaining group of five methods.

Table 12. Percentage of mutants with successful reachability-based fault localization when only inspecting top 10% of the ranked policy elements

Scoring method	itrust	itrust5	itrust10
Anderberg			
Goodman			
Jaccard	73.72%	74.21%	74.25%
Naish2			
Ochiai			
Sorensen Dice			
Tarantula			
CBI-Inc	73.50%	74.16%	74.22%
Ochiai2	73.27%	61.22%	61.33%
Euclid			
Hamann			
Rogers Tanimoto	22.49%	22.89%	22.87%
Simple Matching			
Sokal			

Table 13. Percentage of mutants with successful firing-based fault localization when only inspecting top 10% of the ranked policy elements

Scoring method	itrust	itrust5	itrust10
Naish2	99.78%	99.96%	99.98%
CBI-Inc	99.11%	99.82%	99.91%
Euclid			
Hamann			
Rogers Tanimoto	86.41%	86.66%	86.68%
Simple Matching			
Sokal			
Goodman	71.49%	71.44%	71.43%
Anderberg			

Jaccard			
Ochiai	71.05%	71.35%	71.39%
Sorensen Dice			
Tarantula			
Ochiai2	70.82%	64.93%	64.87%

Table 13 shows the percentage of mutants whose faults are revealed when only top 10% of the ranked policy elements are examined in each firing-based method. The rankings of the methods are the same as those in Table 9 and Table 11. Except for the two best methods (Naish2 and CBI-Inc), the five least effective reachability-based methods in Table 8 (Euclid, Hamann, RogersTanimoto, SimpleMatching, and Sokal) become more effective firing-based methods in Table 9, and vice versa.

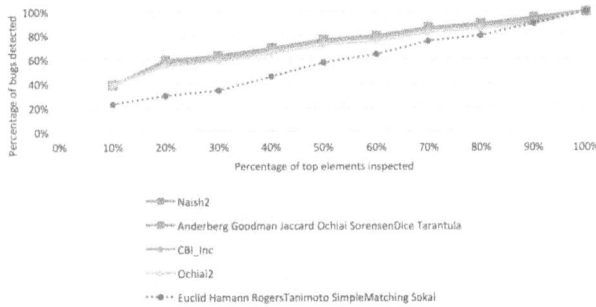

Figure 4. Percentage of top ranked policy elements inspected vs percentage of mutants with successful fault localization of the <u>reachability</u>-based methods for the <u>continue</u> policy

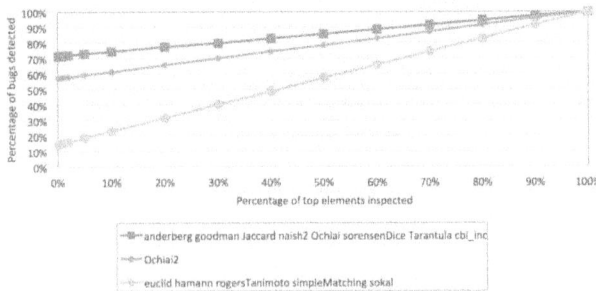

Figure 5. Percentage of top ranked policy elements inspected vs percentage of mutants with successful fault localization of the <u>reachability</u>-based methods for the <u>itrust10</u> policy

Figure 4 and Figure 5 show the correlation between the percentage of top ranked policy elements inspected and the percentage of mutants with successful fault localization for each reachability-based method with respect to continue (a small subject policy) and itrust10 (the largest subject policy), respectively. It is obvious that, for each reachability-based fault localization method, the percentage of mutants with successful fault localization increases with the increased percentage of top-ranked policy elements inspected (this is the case for all other policies). A reachability-based fault localization method usually requires the examination of the vast majority of the policy elements in order to reveal the vast majority of possible faults.

Figure 6 and Figure 7 show the correlation between the percentage of top ranked policy elements inspected and the percentage of mutants with successful fault localization for each firing-based method with respect to continue and itrust10, respectively. For a small range of policy element percentages (10-20% in Figure 5 and 0-1% in Figure 6), the percentage of mutants with successful firing-based fault localization increases as the

percentage of policy elements increases. Then, for a significant range of policy element percentages (up to 90% except for Naish2 and CBI-Inc, which have already revealed all faults), the percentage of mutants with successful firing-based fault localization remains unchanged even when the percentage of policy elements is increased. Comparisons between Figure 4 and Figure 6 and between Figure 5 and Figure 7 indicate that the firing-based technique is more cost-effective than the reachability-based technique.

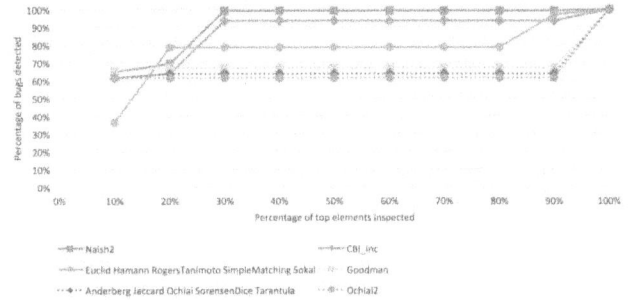

Figure 6. Percentage of top ranked policy elements inspected vs percentage of mutants with successful fault localization of the <u>firing-based</u> methods for the <u>continue</u> policy

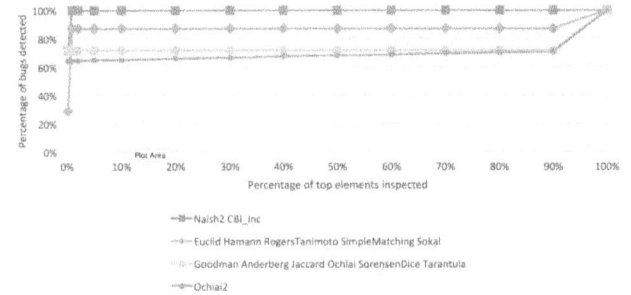

Figure 7. Percentage of top ranked policy elements inspected vs percentage of mutants with successful fault localization of the <u>firing-based</u> methods for the <u>itrust10</u> policy

4.3 Discussion

The previous sections have focused on policy (set) targets and rules as the main policy elements. Rule combining algorithms and policy combining algorithms are also important policy elements. The reachability-based and firing-based fault localization methods do not apply to combining algorithms because they always take effect. Nevertheless, incorrect combining algorithms can be easily localized as follows: we can change the given combining algorithm to a new combining algorithm and run the test suite. If the revised policy passes all tests, then the original combining algorithm can be considered incorrect. If not, we continue to try other combining algorithms. Our prior work offers another fault-based testing approach for detecting incorrect uses of combining algorithms [13]. In addition, an XACML policy may have such elements as obligation and advice. Obligation and advice, however, are primarily syntax sugar, not executable units. They are interpreted by the policy enforcement point, not the policy decision point or the XACML engine. Thus, the fault localization approach does not apply to obligation or advice.

The key finding of this work is that the firing-based Naish2 and CBI-inc methods are highly effective in localization of fault(s) in XACML policies. They only need to inspect a small number of policy elements. Although this work was inspired by SBFL techniques for software debugging, the results for XACML policies are much more encouraging. The best-performing SBFL methods for software debugging, including Naish2, need to examine more than 20% of the source code. This is far from practical for real-world software [7]. Consider a program with 50,000 lines of code. The suggestion on inspecting more than 10,000 lines of code is hardly useful. This paper shows that the firing-based Naish2 and CBI-Inc methods are accurate and practical for automated localization of faulty rules in XACML policies. They only require the examination of a few suggested rules even for policies with a large number of rules. An explanation for this is that XACML policies have a simpler structure than computer programs. Generally, a program involves such programming constructs as sequence, (nested) condition, (nested) loop, and multi-threading. An XACML policy consists of a sequence of rules, without explicit loop or multi-threading. Each rule bears similarity to a non-nested conditional statement. Nevertheless, the required uses of combining algorithms in XACML policies increase the complexity for policy semantics. They bear some similarity to the combination of conditional and return statements. Because of combining algorithms, each policy has a number of exit points. In brief, this work can be considered as a domain specific application of SBFL techniques. Accordingly, we hypothesize that SBFL can be a good candidate for fault localization of domain specific software that uses special programming constructs. Of course, this hypothesis needs to be validated through theoretical or empirical studies.

In the following, we discuss the main threats to validity:

Subject policies: due to the unavailability of real-world faulty XACML policies, the subject policies used this work are from the literature. They may not represent all XACML applications from the perspectives of rule structure, policy size, and combining algorithms. In particular, XACML 3.0 has predefined 11 rule-combining algorithms and 12 policy combining algorithms. Not all of them have been covered by the subject policies.

Policy mutants: the empirical studies in this paper rely on the use of policy mutants for evaluating the performance of fault localization. The mutants of subject policies are generated automatically by mutation operators. Each mutant has exactly one or two faults. Although the mutation operators provide a comprehensive coverage of fault types in XACML policies, the mutants may not represent all possible faults in real-world XACML policies.

Test suites: The tests in the empirical studies were generated automatically from the subject policies using MC/DC. An advantage is that these tests are able to kill all mutants so that all mutants can be included in the fault localization experiments. In reality, the fault localization task for an XACML policy may not have MC/DC tests available. It is yet unclear how test coverage and test suite size might affect the performance of fault localization.

Scoring methods: This paper has investigated 14 scoring methods. They are selected from the commonly studied and best-performing SBFL techniques. There are other scoring methods as well. While we have found that the firing-based Naish2 and CBI-Inc methods are very effective, the use of additional scoring methods may refine the answers to the research questions.

5. RELATED WORK

This paper is the first report on fault localization of XACML policies. Nevertheless, it bears some similarity to the debugging of security policies, especially firewall rules. It is also related to SBFL for program debugging.

Debugging of firewall policies has recently gained some attention. Marmorstein et al. proposed a technique for using failed tests to locate faulty rules in a small firewall policy with only several rules [14]. It does not identify faulty rules according to different fault types. Hwang et al. used failed tests to find the potential faulty rules based on structural coverage of firewall rules [20]. Only two types of faults, wrong decisions and wrong predicates, were considered. Chen et al. proposed an approach to automatic correction of five types of faulty firewall rules: wrong order, missing rules, wrong predicates, wrong decisions, and wrong extra rules [21]. Part of this approach converts the given firewall rules into a firewall decision diagram (FDD) as a compact representation for reasoning about faulty rules. This approach is not guaranteed to correct all faults [21]. Compared to firewall rules, XACML policies are much more complex for two main reasons. First, firewall rules are defined over a fixed set of network attributes and primarily specified in propositional logic. Rules in XACML policies are specified in first-order logic with various data types for user-defined attributes. The number and types of attributes in an XACML policy depend on the application. Because firewall rules have a small number of predefined attributes, FDD can be a compact representation of firewall rules for effective analysis. However, it is unlikely useful for the analysis of XACML policies. Second, XACML uses various combining algorithms for the composition of rules and policies. This increases the complexity of policy semantics. Rule and policy composition is not supported in the existing firewalls. In brief, the analysis of XACML policies is generally much more difficult than that of firewall policies.

In the past decade, various fault localization techniques have been proposed for program debugging, such as slice-based, spectrum-based (i.e., SBFL), statistics-based, machine learning-based, model-based methods [22]-[30]. This paper is primarily related to SBFL, which analyzes the differences in program spectra for passed and failed runs. A program spectrum is an execution profile that indicates which parts of a program are active during a run. SBFL entails identifying the part of the program whose activity correlates with the detection of errors. Because SBFL has a large body of literature, a comprehensive survey is beyond the scope of this paper.

Naish et al. [11] have compared a large collection of SBFL ranking metrics (i.e., scoring methods) and used a model to capture important features of the fault localization problem. They suggested eight new "optimal" metrics – two of which, Op (i.e., Naish2 in this paper) and CBI-Inc, are the best in this paper. Wang et al. [31] have proposed a search-based approach to composition of different SBFL metrics into an improved composite one. This was motivated by the observation that no single SBFL metric consistently outperforms others - a metric that is more accurate in localizing some bugs in some programs can perform worse while localizing other bugs in other programs. The search-based approach treats the composition of metrics as an optimization learning problem and uses genetic algorithm and simulated annealing to produce a near optimal composite metric. Lucia et al. [7] have also proposed a fusion fault localizer for composing SBFL metrics. It is based on the idea of data fusion, which aims at ranking the most relevant documents at the top positions by combining the ranking information from different retrieval systems. Different from [31] the fusion fault localizer does not need training dataset. It consists of three parts: score normalization, technique selection, and data fusion. Each step is beneficial for achieving improved metrics. The empirical evaluations show that fusion localizers can outperform the state-of-art SBFL metrics (Ochiai and Naish2) and a representative genetic programming method (GP13). In our experiments on fault localization of XACML policies, Naish2 and CBI-Inc are consistently better than the other metrics.

Abreu et al. [32] have developed BARINEL, a hybrid technique that combines the state-of-art SBFL and model-based fault localization techniques. While model-based techniques are inherently more accurate than SBFL, they are hardly applicable to large-scale programs due to their high computational complexity. BARINEL features a maximum likelihood estimation algorithm to compute the health factor of all components. It uses abstractions of program traces as in SBFL and a Bayesian reasoning as in model-based fault diagnosis. BARINEL outperforms those SBFL and model-based techniques with slightly higher costs than the SBFL techniques. Tang et al., [8] discussed SBFL techniques at both statement level and instruction level of code abstraction using an existing theoretical hierarchy of SBFL techniques. They show that this hierarchy is consistent across the two abstraction levels and that the same metrics can be more effective at the instruction level than at the statement level.

6. CONCLUSIONS

We have presented the approach to automated fault localization of XACML policies using various scoring formulas. Our experiment results show that the firing-based Naish2 and CBI-Inc methods are very effective in fault localization. For simplicity, this paper considers each rule as one policy element. In fact, our approach can treat the rule target and the rule condition of each rule as separate policy elements. When a rule is faulty, the fault localization method may further determine whether the fault lies in the rule target or the rule condition.

Our future work will study additional scoring formulas for fault localization and investigate how test coverage and test suite size would affect the accuracy of fault localization methods. In addition to MC/DC, for example, other coverage criteria can be defined for automated test generation from XACML policies, such as rule coverage and decision coverage. MC/DC tests are used in this paper because they can kill all policy mutants. It is worth investigating whether the fault localization methods such as Naish2 and CBI-Inc are still effective when the test suites for rule coverage and decision coverage are used. These test suites are typically smaller than the MC/DC test suite.

7. ACKNOWLEDGMENTS

This work was supported in part by US National Science Foundation (NSF) under grant 1359590.

8. REFERENCES

[1] OASIS. 2013. *eXtensible Access Control Markup Language (XACML) Version 3.0*, http://www.oasisopen.org/committees/xacml/.

[2] Bertolino, A., Daoudagh, S., Lonetti, F., and Marchetti. E. 2012. Automatic XACML requests generation for policy testing. In *Proc. of the Fifth IEEE International Conference on Software Testing, Verification and Validation (ICST)*, pp.842-849.

[3] Bertolino, A., Daoudagh, S., Lonetti, F., and Marchetti. E. 2012. The X-CREATE framework-A comparison of XACML policy testing strategies. In *Proc. of the 8th*

International Conference on Web Information Systems and Technologies (WEBIST). pp. 155-160.

[4] Li, Y.C., Li, Y., Wang, L.Z. and Chen, G. 2014. Automatic XACML requests generation for testing access control policies. In *Proc. of the 26th International Conf. on Software Engineering and Knowledge Engineering (SEKE'14)*, Vancouver. July 2014.

[5] Martin, E. and Xie. T. 2007. Automated test generation for access control policies via change-impact analysis. In *Proceedings of the Third International Workshop on Software Engineering for Secure Systems*. IEEE Computer Society, pp.5-11.

[6] Martin, E. and Xie. T. 2007. A fault model and mutation testing of access control policies. In *Proceedings of the 16th International Conference on World Wide Web*. ACM, pp.667-676.

[7] Lucia, Lo, D., Xia, X. 2014. Fusion fault localizers, In *Proc. of the 29th ACM/IEEE International Conference on Automated Software Engineering (ASE'14)*, pp.127-138, Västerås, September 2014.

[8] Tang, C.M., Chan, W.K., Yu, Y.T. 2014. Extending the theoretical fault localization effectiveness hierarchy with empirical results at different code abstraction levels. In Proc. *of the 38th Conference on Computer Software and Applications Conference (COMPSAC'14)*, pp. 161-170, Västerås, July 2014.

[9] Xie, X., Chen, T. Y., Kuo, F., and Xu, B. 2013. A theoretical analysis of the risk evaluation formulas for spectrum-based fault localization. *ACM Transactions on Software Engineering and Methodology (TOSEM)*, 22(4):31.

[10] Balana, 2012. *An Open Source XACML 3.0 Implementation*. http://xacmlinfo.org/2012/08/16/balana-the-open-source-xacml-3-0-implementation/, 2012.

[11] Naish, L., Lee, H.J., and Ramamohanarao. K. 2011. A model for spectra- based software diagnosis. *ACM Transactions on Software Engineering and Methodology*, 20(3): 11.

[12] Fisler, K., Krishnamurthi, S., Meyerovich, L.A. and Tschantz, M.C. 2005. Verification and change-impact analysis of access-control policies. In *Proc. of the 27th International Conference on Software Engineering (ICSE'05)*. pp. 196-205.

[13] Xu, D., Zhang, Y., Shen, N. 2015. Fault-based testing of combining algorithms in XACML3.0 policies, In *Proc. of the 27th International Conf. on Software Engineering and Knowledge Engineering (SEKE'15)*, Vancouver. July 2015.

[14] DeMillo, R.A., Lipton, R.J., and Sayward, F.G. 1978. Hints on test data selection: Help for the practical programmer. *IEEE Computer* no. 11, pp. 34-41.

[15] Offutt, A.J. 1992. Investigations of the software testing coupling effect. *ACM Trans. Software Eng. Methodology*, vol. 1, pp. 5-20, Jan. 1992.

[16] Andrews, J.H., Briand, L.C., and Labiche, Y. 2005. Is mutation an appropriate tool for testing experiments? In *Proc. 27th Int'l Conf. Software Eng (ICSE'05)*, pp. 402-411.

[17] Just, R., Jalali,D., Inozemtseva, L., Ernst, M.D., Holmes, R. and Fraser, G. 2014. Are mutants a valid substitute for real faults in software testing? In *Proc. of the Symposium on the*

Foundations of Software Engineering (FSE'14), Hong Kong, November 2014, pp. 654-665.

[18] *RTCA/DO-178B, Software Considerations in Airborne Systems and Equipment Certification*. RTCA, Inc., Washington, D. C., December 1992.

[19] Marmorstein, R., Kearns, P. 2007. Assisted firewall policy repair using examples and history. In *Proc. of USENIX Large Installation System Administration Conference (LISA)*, pp.1–11.

[20] Hwang, J., Xie, T., Chen, F., Liu, A.X. 2009. Fault localization for firewall policies, In *Proc. of IEEE International Symposium on Reliable Distributed Systems (SRDS)*. pp. 100–106.

[21] Chen, F., Liu, A. X. Liu, Hwang, J., Xie. T. 2012. First step towards automatic correction of firewall policy faults. *ACM Transactions on Autonomous and Adaptive Systems*, Vol. 7, No. 2, July 2012.

[22] Abreu, R., Zoeteweij, P., Golsteijn, R., van Gemund, A. J. C. 2009. A practical evaluation on spectrum-based fault localization. *The Journal of System and Software*, 82:1780–1792.

[23] Abreu, R., van Gemund, A. J.C. 2010. Diagnosing multiple intermittent failures using maximum likelihood estimation. *Artificial Intelligence* 174 (2010): 1481–1497.

[24] Briand, L. C., Labiche, Y., Liu, X. 2007. Using machine learning to support debugging with Tarantula, In *Proc. of the 18th IEEE International Symposium on Software Reliability (ISSRE'07)*, pp. 137-146, Trollhattan, Sweden, November 2007.

[25] Brun, Y., Ernst, M. D. 2004, Finding latent code errors via machine learning over program executions, In *Proc. of the*

26th International Conference on Software Engineering (ICSE'04), pp. 480- 490, Edinburgh, UK, May 2004.

[26] Jones, J.A., Harrold, M.J. 2005. Empirical evaluation of the Tarantula automatic fault-localization technique. In *Proc. of the IEEE/ACM International Conference on Automated Software Engineering (ASE'05)*, pp. 273–282.

[27] Santelices, R. Jones, J.A., Yu, Y., and Harrold, M.J. 2009. Lightweight fault-localization using multiple coverage types. In *Proc. of the International Conference on Software Engineering (ICSE'09)*, pp. 56–66.

[28] Wong, W. E., Shi, Y., Qi, Y., Golden, R. 2008. Using an RBF neural network to locate program bugs. *In Proc. of the 19th IEEE International Symposium on Software Reliability Engineering (ISSRE'08)*, pp. 27-38, Seattle, Washington, USA, November 2008.

[29] Wong, W. E., Debroy, V., Choi, B. 2010. A family of code coverage-based heuristics for effective fault localization. *The Journal of Systems and Software*, 83 (2010) 188–208.

[30] Xie, X., Chen, T.Y., Kuo, F.C., Xu, B. 2013. A theoretical analysis of the risk evaluation formulas for spectrum-based fault localization. *ACM Transactions on Software Engineering and Methodology*, 22(4).

[31] Wang, S., Lo, D., Jiang, L., Lucia, Lau, H. C. 2011. Search-based fault localization, In *Proc. of the 26th IEEE/ACM Int. Conf. on Automated Engineering (ASE'11)*, pp. 556–559.

[32] Abreu, R., Zoeteweij P., van Gemund, A. J.C. 2009. Spectrum-based multiple fault localization. In *Proc. of the IEEE/ACM International Conference on Automated Software Engineering (ASE'09)*, pp.88-99.

On Completeness in Languages for Attribute-Based Access Control

Jason Crampton
Royal Holloway University of London
Egham, TW20 0EX, United Kingdom
jason.crampton@rhul.ac.uk

Conrad Williams
Royal Holloway University of London
Egham, TW20 0EX, United Kingdom
conrad.williams.2010@live.rhul.ac.uk

ABSTRACT

Attribute-based access control (ABAC) has attracted considerable interest in recent years, resulting in an extensive literature on the subject, including the standardized XML-based language XACML. ABAC policies written in languages like XACML have a tree-like structure in which leaf nodes are associated with authorization decisions and non-leaf nodes are associated with decision-combining algorithms. In this paper, we consider the expressive power of the rule- and policy-combining algorithms defined by the XACML standard. In particular, we identify unexpected dependencies between the combining algorithms and demonstrate that there exist useful combining algorithms that cannot be expressed by any combination of XACML combining algorithms. We briefly discuss the decision operators defined in the PTaCL language, an abstract language for defining ABAC policies, and the advantages of replacing the XACML combining algorithms with the PTaCL operators. Following this, we review results in the literature on multi-valued logic and introduce the notion of canonically complete policy languages. We discuss important practical advantages of canonically complete policy languages, primarily in simplifying policy specification and providing efficiently enforceable policies. Finally, we propose a new policy authorization language PTaCL(E) which is canonically complete and show it is capable of expressing any arbitrary policy in a normal form and discuss the advantages of using PTaCL(E) over existing policy languages such as XACML and PTaCL.

CCS Concepts

•Security and privacy → Access control; Authorization; *Security requirements;* •Software and its engineering → Specialized application languages;

Keywords

XACML, PTaCL, decision operators, combining algorithms, functional completeness, canonical completeness

SACMAT'16, June 05-08, 2016, Shanghai, China
ⓒ 2016 ACM. ISBN 978-1-4503-3802-8/16/06. . . $15.00
DOI: http://dx.doi.org/10.1145/2914642.2914654

1. INTRODUCTION

One of the fundamental security services in computer systems is *access control*, which is a mechanism for constraining the interaction between (authenticated) users and protected resources. Generally, access control is implemented by an authorization service, which includes an *authorization decision function* for deciding whether a user request to access a resource (an "access request") should be permitted or not. In its simplest form an authorization decision function either returns an allow or deny decision.

A common method for specifying access control models and systems is through the use of *authorization policies*, where a user request for a resource is evaluated against a policy that defines which requests are authorized. Due to the increasing rise of collaboration between industry partners, there have been many proposed languages for the specification of authorization policies for "open" systems. This has prompted a move away from traditional means of using user identities for making authorization decisions. Instead, authorization decisions are made based on user and resource attributes, allowing greater flexibility as relationships between specific users and resources no longer need to be specified. The most widely used language of this type is XACML [10, 13]. However, XACML suffers from poorly defined and counterintuitive semantics [8, 11], and is inconsistent in its articulation of policy evaluation. PTaCL is a more formal language for specifying authorization policies [5], providing a concise syntax for policy targets and precise semantics for policy evaluation.

Typically, an authorization policy is defined by a target, a set of child policies and a decision-combining algorithm. The focus of this paper is on the way in which decisions (and hence authorization policies) are combined through the use of these decision-combining algorithms. The XACML standard specifies twelve rule- and policy-combining algorithms which are used to combine authorization decisions. In principle, customized combining algorithms can be written and deployed to supplement the twelve standardized algorithms. In contrast, PTaCL specifies only three policy operators for combining decisions, and all other policy operators can be represented in terms of these three operators. This is a powerful tool for policy authors as it allows them to design and implement new operators on an ad hoc basis. However, one drawback of PTaCL (and XACML and other similar languages) is that policies are defined by combining subpolicies. In other words, policy specification is performed in a bottom-up manner.

We believe there will be, perhaps many, situations where the policy writer knows what decision should be returned for each authorization request, but is unable to construct the desired policy using the operators provided by the policy language. As a simple example, suppose we have policies defined by the tables in Figure 1. Here we are assuming there are two sub-policies P_1 and P_2, whose targets partition the set of all authorization requests. The rows represent values that are returned by evaluating P_1, while the columns represent values that are returned by evaluating P_2. The values 0, 1 and $\perp$ represent the decisions "deny", "allow" and "not-applicable", respectively. Thus, if P_1 and P_2 evaluate to 0 and 1, respectively, the final result should be 0 if the policies are combined using $\oplus_1$ and $\perp$ if combined using $\oplus_2$.

$\oplus_1$	0	1	$\perp$
0	0	0	0
1	0	1	$\perp$
$\perp$	0	$\perp$	$\perp$

$\oplus_2$	0	1	$\perp$
0	0	$\perp$	0
1	$\perp$	1	$\perp$
$\perp$	0	$\perp$	$\perp$

Figure 1: Two combining operators for policies

PTaCL is known to be functionally complete, which means it is possible, in principle, to construct the policies $P_1 \oplus_1 P_2$ and $P_1 \oplus_2 P_2$ by combining copies of P_1 and P_2 using the PTaCL operators. It is also possible in XACML to define custom policy-combining algorithms to directly construct $\oplus_1$ and $\oplus_2$. However, it would be useful, both in theory and in terms of implementation, to develop an authorization language which is functionally complete, like PTaCL, and which enables a policy writer to write down any desired policy directly using the operators of the language. In propositional logic, for example, one can use the truth table for an arbitrary formula to write down a logically equivalent formula in disjunctive normal form. In short, in this paper we wish to develop a policy authorization language that has a "normal form" in which *any* desired policy can be expressed.

In order to do this, we apply concepts introduced by Jobe [6] in the study of multi-valued logics to the development of a policy language for attribute-based access control. We construct a new authorization language based on the operators in Jobe's 3-valued logic and show how arbitrary policies can easily be expressed in a normal form as a combination of Jobe's operators. In summary, the main contributions of this paper are:

- the identification of redundant XACML combining algorithms;

- a thorough investigation into how expressive the XACML combining algorithms are;

- an overview of how PTaCL operators can be used to construct arbitrary policy operators; and

- the specification of a new policy authorization language, PTaCL(E), based on Jobe's operators, which provides the means to express an arbitrary policy in a normal form.

The first part of this paper provides a comprehensive justification for the development of a new set of policy combining operators, while the second part introduces new operators chosen to address the shortcomings of existing

sets of operators. More specifically, in the following section we provide a brief introduction to tree-structured languages for attribute-based access control policies, including XACML and PTaCL, and notions of completeness for authorization languages. In Section 3, we show there is significant duplication and redundancy in the XACML rule- and policy-combining algorithms, in particular, we show only two XACML rule-combining algorithms are required to express all of the XACML rule-combining algorithms. We then conduct a detailed investigation into the expressiveness of these algorithms, demonstrating that XACML is not functionally complete. We briefly discuss the advantages of replacing the XACML combining algorithms with the PTaCL operators. Then, in Section 4, we review concepts of completeness and normal forms for 3-valued logics. In Section 5, we apply Jobe's results on multi-valued logics to develop a new language PTaCL(E) for specifying attribute-based access control policies. We introduce a new policy authorization language and a normal form for expressing policies in this language, and discuss some of the advantages of using this language. We conclude the paper with a summary of our contributions and suggest ideas for future work.

2. BACKGROUND AND RELATED WORK

In the context of attribute-based access control (ABAC), we assume there exists a set of attributes, each of which can take a range of values. An authorization request is specified in terms of attribute name-value pairs. Given a set of requests, an ABAC policy specifies whether each request is authorized or not.

Much of the research on ABAC policies assumes that policies are constructed from sub-policies. One sub-policy might, for example, specify that some subset of requests is allowed, while another sub-policy specifies that some subset of requests is denied. Defining policies in this way inevitably means that the sub-policies may "clash", so research in this area has focused on ways of resolving the conflicts that may arise when combining policies.

There are two broad approaches, which we may label as "policy algebras" [2, 14, 11, 12] and "tree-structured languages" [5, 13]. A policy algebra defines the semantics of a policy in terms of the sets of requests it allows and denies. Then sub-policies are combined by defining policy operators that are defined in terms of set operations (such as intersection, union and set difference) on the sets of allowed and denied requests. In contrast, a tree-structured language defines what decision to return for each sub-policy and then combines the decisions arising from the evaluation of sub-policies using decision-combining algorithms.

Of course, there are strong parallels between the two approaches, and it is often possible to define exact correspondences between policy operators and decision-combining algorithms. Nevertheless, the popularity and widespread use of XACML has led to more research on tree-structured languages in recent years (in comparison to policy algebras) [4, 5, 8, 13].

2.1 Tree-structured languages

Informally, we say a language is *tree-structured* if a policy is specified by a decision-combining algorithm and a set of child policies. A request is evaluated with respect to a policy by first computing a decision for each of the child policies and then combining those decisions using the decision-combining algorithm.

More formally, we assume the existence of a set of requests, defined in terms of attributes. Each policy specifies a target defining, in terms of attribute values, the set of requests to which a policy applies. A target t is evaluated with respect to a request q. We write $[\![t]\!](q) \in \{0_t, 1_t\}$ to indicate the result of evaluating target t with respect to request q, where

$$[\![t]\!](q) = \begin{cases} 1_t & \text{if the target is applicable,} \\ 0_t & \text{otherwise.} \end{cases}$$

We do not discuss here how target applicability is determined; the reader is referred to the literature for further details [5, 13].

We define a set of (authorization) decisions $D = \{0_a, 1_a, \perp_a\}$, representing "allow", "deny" and "not-applicable", respectively. Then an *atomic* policy has the form (t, d), where t is a target and d is a decision. We define the evaluation of an atomic policy (t, d) as

$$[\![(t,d)]\!](q) = \begin{cases} d & \text{if } [\![t]\!](q) = 1_t, \\ \perp_a & \text{otherwise.} \end{cases}$$

A policy may be represented as a triple $(t, A, \overline{p})$, where t is a target, A is a decision-combining algorithm and $\overline{p} = \langle p_1, \ldots, p_k \rangle$ is a tuple of policies. Then we define

$$[\![(t, A, \overline{p})]\!](q) = \begin{cases} A([\![p_1]\!](q), \ldots, [\![p_k]\!](q)) & \text{if } [\![t]\!](q) = 1_t, \\ \perp_a & \text{otherwise.} \end{cases}$$

Henceforth, we will confine our attention to authorization decisions, rather than target evaluation. Hence, we will simplify the notation and use $\{0, 1, \perp\}$ (that is, without the subscript) to denote the set of authorization decisions.

In general, a decision-combining algorithm may take an arbitrary number of inputs. It is convenient, in terms of formal exposition, to assume that a decision-combining algorithm is implemented using binary *decision operators*. (Thus, we would apply a binary decision operator $k - 1$ times to evaluate a call to a decision-combining algorithm with k inputs.)

Hence, we may visualize a policy as a binary tree, in which the atomic policies are leaves and non-leaf nodes are target-operator pairs. The policy P, for example

$$\Big(t_6, A_2, \big((t_5, A_1, ((t_1, d_1), (t_2, d_2), (t_3, d_3))), (t_4, d_4)\big)\Big)$$

may be represented by the binary tree depicted in Figure 2.

Then policy evaluation, from an algorithmic perspective, consists of assigning decisions to the leaf nodes, by determining whether the targets are applicable or not, and then combining the decisions using the decision operators, until a decision is obtained at the root node.

We say two policies p and p' are *equivalent*, denoted by $p \equiv p'$, if $[\![p]\!](q) = [\![p']\!](q)$ for all requests q. To simplify the notation, we will, henceforth, omit q when it is obvious from context. We will also make use of the following terminology [4] when describing decision operators.

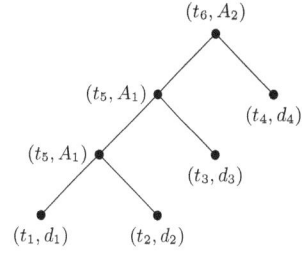

Figure 2: Policy tree

DEFINITION 1. *Let $\oplus : D \times D \to D$ be a decision operator. Then*

- $\oplus$ *is* commutative *if $d \oplus d' = d' \oplus d$ for all $d \in D$;*

- $\oplus$ *is* idempotent *if $d \oplus d = d$ for all $d \in D$, and* quasi-idempotent *if $d \oplus d = d$ for all $d \in \{0, 1\}$;*

- $\oplus$ *is* conclusive *if $d \oplus d' \in \{0, 1\}$ for all $d, d' \in D$, and* quasi-conclusive *if $d \oplus d' \in \{0, 1\}$ for all $d, d' \in \{0, 1\}$;*

- $\oplus$ *is a* $\cup$-operator *if $d \oplus \perp = d = \perp \oplus d$ for all $d \in D$;*

- $\oplus$ *is a* $\cap$-operator *if $d \oplus \perp = \perp = \perp \oplus d$ for all $d \in D$;*

- $\oplus$ *is* well-behaved *if it is either a $\cup$- or an $\cap$-operator.*

Any binary operator on the decision set $\{0, 1, \perp\}$ can be represented as a 3×3 array, as shown in Figure 3a. These decision tables correspond to the XACML rule-combining algorithms deny-overrides (do), permit-overrides (po), deny-unless-permit (dup), permit-unless-deny (pud), and first-applicable (fa) operators.

2.1.1 XACML

XACML [13] is the most commonly used authorization language for implementing attribute-based access control in the real world. An XACML rule corresponds to an atomic policy (as defined in the previous section), where the "effect" of the rule is the decision.[1] Similarly, an XACML *policy* may be represented as a triple $(t, A, \overline{r})$, where t is a target, A is a rule-combining algorithm and $\overline{r} = \langle r_1, \ldots, r_k \rangle$ is a tuple of rules. Thus an XACML policy is a non-leaf node in which all the child policies are leaf nodes (that is, rules). XACML also defines *policy sets*, which are triples of the form $(t, A, \overline{p})$, where $\overline{p} = \langle p_1, \ldots, p_k \rangle$ is a tuple of policies, t is a target, and A is a policy-combining algorithm. XACML policies and policy sets are evaluated in exactly the same way: (recursively) evaluate the "child" policies and then combine the decisions.

XACML 3.0 defines 11 rule-combining algorithms [13, Appendix C]. XACML defines ordered and unordered versions of most of the algorithms and also provides backward compatibility with previous versions of XACML. The decision tables for the ordered, unordered and legacy versions of do,

---

[1]In this paper we do not consider XACML "conditions", mostly because this notion is inadequately constrained in XACML 3.0. Indeed, a condition can be any boolean expression, including arbitrarily complex functions. In particular, the notion of condition makes the notion of target redundant, because any target can be expressed as a condition.

do	0	1	⊥
0	0	0	0
1	0	1	1
⊥	0	1	⊥

po	0	1	⊥
0	0	1	0
1	1	1	1
⊥	0	1	⊥

dup	0	1	⊥
0	0	1	0
1	1	1	1
⊥	0	1	0

pud	0	1	⊥
0	0	0	0
1	0	1	1
⊥	0	1	1

fa	0	1	⊥
0	0	0	0
1	1	1	1
⊥	0	1	⊥

(a) Decision tables

Operator	Idempotent	$\cup$-operator	Commutative	Conclusive	Quasi-conclusive
do, po	Yes	Yes	Yes	No	Yes
dup, pud	No	No	Yes	Yes	Yes
fa	Yes	Yes	No	No	Yes

(b) Properties

Figure 3: XACML rule-combining algorithms do, po, dup, pud and fa

po, dup and pud are identical for the decision set $\{0, 1, \perp\}$.[2] The one algorithm that is non-commutative (that is, the order of rule evaluation matters) is first-applicable (fa). Henceforth, we will treat the XACML rule-combining algorithms as decision-combining binary operators, as defined in Figure 3a. All five of the XACML decision operators in Figure 3a are $\cup$-operators (and thus well-behaved). Other properties of the XACML decision operators are summarized in Figure 3b.

All of the XACML rule-combining algorithms have associated policy-combining algorithms which have identical properties and produce the same decision tables[3]; the only difference is that they take decisions returned by the evaluation of policies (as opposed to rules) as input. Thus, the features and properties shown in Figure 3 also hold true for the XACML policy-combining algorithms. There is one additional policy-combining algorithm – only-one-applicable – which does not have an associated rule-combining algorithm. We do not consider this algorithm as it introduces a fourth, indeterminate, decision, and does not appear to be very useful.

2.1.2 PTaCL

PTaCL [5] is a tree-structured policy language intended to provide a generic framework for specifying target-based policy languages. Like XACML, it is defined (without indeterminacy) over a three-valued decision set, which makes it useful for comparisons with and analysis of XACML.

PTaCL defines two unary operators and one binary operator, whose decision tables are shown in Figure 4. The unary operators $\neg$ and $\sim$ simply modify the $\perp$ decision: the former switches the values of 0 and 1, leaving $\perp$ unchanged; the latter transforms $\perp$ to 0, leaving 0 and 1 unchanged. These operators are used to implement policy negation and deny-by-default policies, respectively. The binary operator $\wedge_{\mathrm{p}}$ corresponds to strong conjunction in the Kleene three-valued logic [7]. It returns 0 if at least one of the operands is 0, 1 if both operands are 1, and $\perp$ otherwise.

---

[2]There are some minor differences in the way in which the indeterminate value is handled. In this paper we do not consider indeterminacy further. To do so would complicate the exposition and we believe it is straightforward to extend our work to include indeterminate values using techniques proposed by Li *et al.* [8] (and since incorporated into XACML 3.0 [13]).

[3]For reference see Appendix C in the XACML standard [13].

$\wedge_{\mathrm{p}}$	0	1	⊥
0	0	0	0
1	0	1	⊥
⊥	0	⊥	⊥

d	$\neg d$	$\sim d$
0	1	0
1	0	1
⊥	⊥	0

(a) $\wedge_{\mathrm{p}}$ (b) $\neg$ and $\sim$

Figure 4: Decision operators in PTaCL

2.1.3 Policy representation

Tree-structured policies are evaluated in a bottom-up fashion and they must also be written in this bottom-up fashion: that is, by combining rules to form policies and policies to form policy sets. However, this may not be the most natural way of defining a policy. An administrator might simply wish to specify a decision for each of the possible outcomes arising from the evaluation of sub-policies $P_1, \ldots, P_n$. In particular, it would be natural to tabulate the possible decisions that can arise from the evaluation of $P_1, \ldots, P_n$, and for each row in the table, specify the value that P should take, as shown in Table 1 below. We may also view the decision tables in Figure 1 as two simple examples of a policy defined by the outcome of evaluating two sub-policies.

P_1	$\ldots$	P_n	P
0	$\cdots$	0	d_1
0	$\cdots$	1	d_2
0	$\cdots$	⊥	d_2
$\vdots$	$\cdots$	$\vdots$	$\vdots$

Table 1: A policy decision table

It is not at all obvious how we would represent such a policy by using $P_1, \ldots, P_n$ as rules and the standard rule-and/or policy-combining algorithms provided by XACML or PTaCL's decision operators. Moreover, as we will see in Section 3, XACML is not functionally complete, so it is possible to specify policies that cannot be represented in XACML at all (unless bespoke algorithms are written to cater for the policy).

2.2 Completeness properties

In an abstract sense, a policy may be thought of as some function from the set of requests to the set of authorization decisions. Table 1 is one possible representation of such a function. The expressivity of a policy language is a measure of the language's ability to represent an arbitrary function using the operators provided by the language. One of the contributions of this paper is to show that XACML is not functionally complete and to identify the limitations of XACML as a policy specification language.

Some languages [5] and policy algebras [12] are known to be *functionally complete*, in the sense that any arbitrary function can be expressed as a policy in the language or algebra. However, we believe that a practical policy specification language should also admit some kind of canonical representation of each policy, preferably a representation that is related to a policy's decision table. (Here we have in mind the correspondence between the truth table of an arbitrary Boolean function and its expression in disjunctive normal form.) Such a representation is likely to have significant benefits in terms of policy specification and request evaluation. A second contribution of this paper is to argue that PTaCL is unlikely to have a canonical representation for policies and to propose a set of decision-combining operators for a tree-structured language that does have a canonical representation.

3. XACML OPERATORS

In this section, we investigate what decision operators can be constructed using do, po, dup, pud and fa. In doing so, we characterize the expressive power of XACML policies. We first make the following remark:

REMARK 1. *Any operator constructed using* fa, po *and* do *will be an idempotent* $\cup$-*operator, since* $x \oplus \bot = \bot \oplus x = x$ *for* $\oplus \in \{fa, po, do\}$. *A corollary of this observation is that the operators* do, po *and* fa *are indistinguishable when one of the arguments is* $\bot$.

This seems somewhat counterintuitive, creates redundancy, and also suggests that combinations of XACML operators will tend to behave in similar ways. In the rest of this section, we confirm these observations.

3.1 Dependencies

Interestingly, despite the fact that do and po are commutative operators, it is possible to construct non-commutative operators by combining these two operators. Specifically, we have the following, somewhat unexpected, result, which asserts that the fa algorithm is redundant.

PROPOSITION 1. *For all rules* r *and* r',

$$r \text{ fa } r' \equiv r \text{ po } (r \text{ do } r').$$

PROOF. The proof follows by inspection of the decision table in Figure 5. $\square$

REMARK 2. *The ability to construct* fa *from* do *and* po *arises from the fact that* do *and* po *do not obey the identity* $x \oplus (y \otimes z) = (x \oplus y) \otimes (x \oplus z)$, *usually known as the distributive law. Specifically,*

$$0 \text{ po } (1 \text{ do } \bot) = 0 \text{ po } 1 = 1, \text{ whereas}$$
$$(0 \text{ po } 1) \text{ do } (0 \text{ po } \bot) = 1 \text{ do } 0 = 0;$$

d_1	d_2	d_1 do d_2	d_1 po $(d_1$ do $d_2)$	d_1 fa d_2
0	0	0	0	0
0	1	0	0	0
0	$\bot$	0	0	0
1	0	0	1	1
1	1	1	1	1
1	$\bot$	1	1	1
$\bot$	0	0	0	0
$\bot$	1	1	1	1
$\bot$	$\bot$	$\bot$	$\bot$	$\bot$

Figure 5: Encoding fa using do and po

and

$$1 \text{ do } (0 \text{ po } \bot) = 1 \text{ do } 0 = 0, \text{ whereas}$$
$$(1 \text{ do } 0) \text{ po } (1 \text{ do } \bot) = 0 \text{ po } 1 = 1.$$

We now show that dup and pud are also redundant. We first define the rules $\mathbf{1}$ and $\mathbf{0}$, where, for all requests q,

$$[\![\mathbf{1}]\!](q) = 1 \quad \text{and} \quad [\![\mathbf{0}]\!](q) = 0$$

Rule $\mathbf{1}$ may be realized in XACML by defining a rule such that the rule is applicable to every request and its effect is "permit"; rule $\mathbf{0}$ may be realized in an analogous way. We can then define the unary operators deny-by-default (dbd) and permit-by-default (pbd), where

$$dbd(r) \equiv (\mathbf{0} \text{ po } r) \quad \text{and} \quad pbd(r) \equiv (\mathbf{1} \text{ do } r).$$

Note that dbd and pbd may be viewed as unary operators on the decision set $\{0, 1, \bot\}$, where $dbd(x) = pbd(x) = x$ if $x \in \{0, 1\}$; $dbd(\bot) = 0$; and $pbd(\bot) = 1$. We can use dbd and pbd to construct pud and dup.

PROPOSITION 2. *For all rules* r *and* r',

$$r \text{ pud } r' \equiv pbd(r \text{ do } r') \quad \text{and} \quad r \text{ dup } r' \equiv dbd(r \text{ po } r').$$

PROOF. The proof for pud follows by inspection of the decision table in Figure 6. A similar decision table can be constructed for dup. $\square$

d_1	d_2	d_1 do d_2	pbd$(d_1$ do $d_2)$	d_1 pud d_2
0	0	0	0	0
0	1	1	0	0
0	$\bot$	1	0	0
1	0	0	0	0
1	1	1	1	1
1	$\bot$	1	1	1
$\bot$	0	0	0	0
$\bot$	1	1	1	1
$\bot$	$\bot$	$\bot$	1	1

Figure 6: Encoding pud using do and pbd

We have shown there is a significant amount of duplication and redundancy between the 11 XACML rule-combining algorithms. In particular, we have shown it is sufficient, for the purposes of constructing new decision operators, to consider the decision operators do and po, together with the constant rules $\mathbf{0}$ and $\mathbf{1}$, and the unary operators dbd and pbd.

3.2 Incompleteness

Any XACML policy set is constructed by combining XACML policies using policy-combining algorithms. The decision obtained by evaluating an XACML policy set is determined by the action of the policy-combining algorithm on decisions. Given the way in which policy evaluation works in XACML, this is equivalent to asking what functions we can build using $\{0, 1, \mathsf{dbd}, \mathsf{pbd}, \mathsf{do}, \mathsf{po}\}$. We have seen that do and po essentially act as logical AND and OR on the set $\{0, 1\}$; and we have seen that we can define two unary operators (dbd and pbd) for policies, which correspond to unary operators on $\{0, 1, \bot\}$.

There are two types of operators, likely to be useful in practice, that cannot be constructed using the XACML operators.

- A $\cap$-operator $\oplus$ has the property that $x \oplus \bot = \bot \oplus x = \bot$ for any $x \in \{0, 1, \bot\}$. In this context, we do not make a conclusive decision if at least one of the inputs is unknown. The operators do' and po' in Figure 7 are examples of this type of operator.

- The second type of operator has the property that a conclusive decision is returned whenever one is implied by at least one of the arguments. In this context, $\bot$ is interpreted as a value that could be either 0 or 1 but is not known at the time of evaluation. Thus $1 \mathsf{po} \bot = \bot \mathsf{po} 1 = 1$, since $1 \mathsf{po} x = x \mathsf{po} 1 = 1$ for any $x \in \{0, 1\}$; similarly $0 \mathsf{do} \bot = \bot \mathsf{do} 0 = 0$. The operators do'' and po'' in Figure 7 are examples of this type of operator. Note that do'' is equivalent to $\wedge_{\mathrm{p}}$ (the conjunction operator in PTaCL).

More formally, we have the following result.

PROPOSITION 3. *It is not possible to construct $\cap$-operators using the XACML operators.*

PROOF. The proof follows from the following observations: (i) all the binary XACML operators are $\cup$-operators; (ii) any combination of $\cup$-operators is itself a $\cup$-operator (since $x \oplus \bot = x$ for any $x \in \{0, 1, \bot\}$ and any $\cup$-operator $\oplus$); (iii) the two unary operators remove $\bot$; and (iv) $x \oplus \bot \neq \bot$ and $\bot \oplus x \neq \bot$ for any $x \in \{0, 1\}$ for any $\cup$-operator $\oplus$. Thus it is impossible to construct an operator in which $x \oplus \bot = \bot$. □

do'	0	1	$\bot$
0	0	0	$\bot$
1	0	1	$\bot$
$\bot$	$\bot$	$\bot$	$\bot$

do''	0	1	$\bot$
0	0	0	0
1	0	1	$\bot$
$\bot$	0	$\bot$	$\bot$

po'	0	1	$\bot$
0	0	1	$\bot$
1	1	1	$\bot$
$\bot$	$\bot$	$\bot$	$\bot$

po''	0	1	$\bot$
0	0	1	$\bot$
1	1	1	1
$\bot$	$\bot$	1	$\bot$

Figure 7: Commutative, idempotent operators that cannot be constructed using XACML operators

We have shown there is a significant amount of duplication and redundancy in the XACML rule-combining algorithms.

Specifically, only do and po are required to express all 11 combining algorithms. We have also shown that XACML is not functionally complete, and there are operators of practical relevance that cannot be constructed using the XACML operators.

In fact, there are only 22 binary quasi-idempotent operators that can be constructed from the XACML operators (of the 192 that are possible). These operators fall into one of four families: (i) six do operators; (ii) six po operators; (iii) five fa operators; and (iv) five la operators. Further details can be found in the appendix.

It is interesting to note that there is no way to negate policy decisions in XACML. Quite apart from the general incompleteness of XACML, the inability to negate decisions seems to be significant practical drawback to XACML, as negation is a useful unary policy operator in practice.

3.3 Using PTaCL operators

Crampton and Morisset showed that the three-valued logic expressed over the set $\{0, 1, \bot\}$ and defined by the operators $\wedge_{\mathrm{p}}, \neg$ and $\sim$ (Figure 4) is functionally complete. Essentially, they proved that the PTaCL operators could be used to construct the operators of a logic that was known to be functionally complete.

Given that PTaCL is functionally complete, there appears to be a good case for using the PTaCL operators in a language like XACML. The unary operator $\sim$ is already implicitly defined in XACML (as dbd), thus we only need to consider adding $\wedge_{\mathrm{p}}$ and $\neg$ to the minimal set of XACML combining algorithms $\{\mathsf{do}, \mathsf{po}\}$. (Recall $\mathsf{fa}, \mathsf{pud}$ and dup can be defined in terms of do and po.) It is easy to see that we cannot achieve functional completeness by adding just $\neg$ or just $\wedge_{\mathrm{p}}$ to the set of XACML operators. In the case of $\neg$, we would still be unable to construct $\cap$-operators, as there is still no operator that can change a conclusive decision into $\bot$. On the other hand, if we include $\wedge_{\mathrm{p}}$ but not $\neg$, we are unable to reverse the 0 and 1 decisions. In short, we must include both operators if we wish to make XACML functionally complete.

Given that PTaCL is functionally complete anyway, it seems pointless to provide po, as do (or any of the other 10 XACML operators). In particular, we can define the following operator

$$d \vee_{\mathrm{p}} d' \stackrel{\text{def}}{=} \neg((\neg d) \wedge_{\mathrm{p}} (\neg d')).$$

It is then possible to show that

$$d \mathsf{po} d' \equiv (d \vee_{\mathrm{p}} (\sim d')) \wedge_{\mathrm{p}} ((\sim d) \vee_{\mathrm{p}} d'), \text{ and}$$
$$d \mathsf{do} d' \equiv \neg((\neg d) \mathsf{po} (\neg d')).$$

In other words, there appears to be a good case, at least from the perspective of functional completeness, for defining only three policy operators in an ABAC language such as XACML: negation, deny-by-default, and a form of deny-overrides that only returns 1 when both arguments are 1.

It would be easy to write three custom XACML combining algorithms to implement the PTaCL operators. (The front-end of an XACML-based system could continue to expose specific algorithms (such as the usual deny-overrides and permit-overrides), if required by the application, but these can be compiled down into the three basic operators.) More complex policy-combining algorithms can be constructed, as required, from the three basic operators. However, it is still far from obvious how one would express an arbitrary policy decision table as a policy defined using the PTaCL operators.

4. CANONICAL COMPLETENESS IN MULTI-VALUED LOGICS

In this section, we introduce the theoretical foundations, based on results of Jobe [6], for developing an authorization language that is functionally complete and admits a simple normal form for policies, enabling the author of a policy to simply write down any desired policy from its decision table. We will use these foundations to propose a new set of policy operators for an ABAC language whose policies are evaluated in the same way as PTaCL and XACML.

4.1 Canonical suitability

Let L be a logic associated with a set V of m ordered values, $\{v_1, \ldots, v_m\}$, such that $v_1 < v_2 < \cdots < v_m$. Then L is *canonically suitable* if and only if there exist in L two formulas $\phi_{\max}$ and $\phi_{\min}$ of arity 2 such that $\phi_{\max}(x, y)$ returns $\max\{x, y\}$ and $\phi_{\min}(x, y)$ returns $\min\{x, y\}$.

EXAMPLE 1. *The 2-valued logic with values 0 and 1, and operators $\vee$ and $\neg$, representing disjunction and negation, respectively, is canonically suitable: $\phi_{\max}(x, y)$ is simply $x \vee y$, while $\phi_{\min}(x, y)$ is $\neg(\neg x \vee \neg y)$ (that is, conjunction).*

If a logic is canonically suitable, we will write $\phi_{\min}(x, y)$ and $\phi_{\max}(x, y)$ using infix binary operators: $x \curlywedge y$ and $x \curlyvee y$. For a 3-valued canonically suitable logic, with values $1, 2, 3$, the truth tables for $x \curlywedge y$ and $x \curlyvee y$ are shown in Figure 8.

x	y	$x \curlywedge y$	$x \curlyvee y$
3	3	3	3
3	2	2	3
3	1	1	3
2	3	2	3
2	2	2	2
2	1	1	2
1	3	1	3
1	2	1	2
1	1	1	1

Figure 8: Truth tables for $\curlywedge$ and $\curlyvee$ in a 3-valued canonically suitable logic

4.2 Selection operators and functional completeness

A formula containing n variables in an m-valued logic, is completely specified by a truth table containing n columns and m^n rows. However, not every truth table may be represented by a formula in a given logic. A logic is said to be *functionally complete* if for every positive integer n and every truth table containing n columns, there is a formula in the logic containing n variables whose evaluation corresponds to the truth table. We have seen that XACML is not functionally complete, while PTaCL is.

A *selection operator* $S_i^j(x_1, \ldots, x_n)$ is an n-ary operator whose truth table has value v_j ($1 \leqslant j \leqslant m$) in row i ($1 \leqslant i \leqslant m^n$), and v_1 in all other rows.[4] (Note that $S_i^j(x_1, \ldots, x_n)$ is

---

[4] Jobe called these *J-operators*; we prefer the more descriptive term "selection operator".

the same for all i.) Illustrative selection operators are shown in Figure 9 for a 3-valued logic with values $1, 2, 3$.

$S_2^2(x)$	$S_3^2(x)$		$S_2^3(x, y)$	$S_6^2(x, y)$
1	1		1	1
2	1		3	1
1	2		1	1
			1	1
			1	1
			1	2
			1	1
			1	1
			1	1

Figure 9: Selection operators $S_2^2(x)$, $S_3^2(x)$, $S_2^3(x, y)$, and $S_6^2(x, y)$

Given the truth table of function $f : V^n \to V$, we can write down an equivalent function in terms of selection operators. Specifically, let

$$I = \{(i, j) : \text{row } i \text{ in } f\text{'s truth table contains value } v_j > v_1\};$$

then $f(x_1, \ldots, x_n)$ is equivalent to

$$\bigcurlyvee_{(i,j) \in I} S_i^j(x_1, \ldots, x_n),$$

because, informally, the effect of this function is to take the maximum value in each row of a table comprising selection operators chosen specifically to produce the correct value in the ith row. Jobe established a number of results connecting the functional completeness of a logic with the unary selection operators. These results are summarized in the following theorem.

THEOREM 1 (JOBE [6, THEOREMS 1, 2; LEMMA 1]). *A logic L is functionally complete if and only if each unary selection operator is equivalent to some formula in L.*

The proofs of Jobe's results are by induction and constructive. Informally, if each unary selection operator is equivalent to some formula in L, then we can construct a formula (in L) for any selection operator; and if we can construct a formula for any selection operator, then we can construct a formula for an arbitrary truth table. More formally, we write $\phi_i^j(x_1, \ldots, x_n)$ to denote the formula (in L) whose truth table is that of the selection operator $S_i^j(x_1, \ldots, x_n)$. (Note that such a formula may not exist for a given logic.) Given $\phi_i^j(x)$ and $\phi_i^j(x_1, \ldots, x_n)$ for all i, j, we can construct $\phi_i^j(x_1, \ldots, x_{n+1})$. Specifically,

$$\phi_{(i-1)m+j}^k(x_1, \ldots, x_{n+1}) \equiv \phi_i^k(x_1, \ldots, x_n) \curlywedge \phi_j^k(x_{n+1}), \quad (1)$$

with $1 \leqslant k \leqslant m$, $1 \leqslant i \leqslant m^n$, and $1 \leqslant j \leqslant m$. (Note that $(i-1)m+j$ takes values from 1 to m^{n+1} inclusive, as required.)

To see the intuition behind this construction, consider the effect of calculating $S_i^k(x_1) \curlywedge S_j^k(x_2)$. We may construct an $m \times m$ table, with the rows indexed by the values in the truth table for $S_i^k(x_1)$ and the columns indexed by the values in the truth table for $S_j^k(x_2)$. The entry in the rth row and cth column (by definition of $\curlywedge$) is k if $r = i$ and $c = j$ and 1 otherwise. Writing out this two-dimensional table as a

155

truth table with a single column, we obtain the truth table for $S_{3(i-1)+j}^k$. Using $S_2^2(x)$ and $S_2^2(y)$ from Figure 9, for example, and computing $S_2^2 \curlywedge S_2^3$, we obtain the following table:

$\curlywedge$	1	1	2
1	1	1	1
2	1	1	2
1	1	1	1

which may be written out as a truth table with a single column, corresponding to $S_6^2(x,y)$, as expected (compare last column in Figure 9). More generally, in (1), $S_i^k(x_1, \ldots, x_n) \curlywedge S_j^k(x_{n+1})$ represents the construction of a table with m^n rows and m columns, with truth values indexed by the values in the truth table for $S_i^k(x_1, \ldots, x_n)$ and columns indexed by the truth table for $S_j^k(x_{n+1})$.

4.3 Normal form

The *normal form* of formula ϕ in a canonically suitable logic is a formula ϕ' that has the same truth table as ϕ and has the following properties:

- the only binary operators it contains are $\curlyvee$ and $\curlywedge$;

- it may contain arbitrary unary operators (defined in terms of the unary operators of the logic);

- no binary operator is included in the scope of a unary operator;

- no instance of $\curlyvee$ occurs in the scope of the $\curlywedge$ operator.

In other words, given a canonically suitable logic L containing unary operators $\sharp_1, \ldots, \sharp_\ell$, a formula in normal form has the form

$$\overset{r}{\underset{i=1}{\curlyvee}} \, \overset{s}{\underset{j=1}{\curlywedge}} \, \sharp_{i,j} x_{i,j}$$

where $\sharp_{i,j}$ is a unary operator defined by composing the unary operators in $\sharp_1, \ldots, \sharp_\ell$. In the usual 2-valued propositional logic with a single unary operator (negation) this corresponds to disjunctive normal form.

A canonically suitable logic is *canonically complete* if every unary selection operator can be expressed in normal form. It is known that there are canonically suitable 3-valued logics that are: (i) not functionally complete [6, 9]; and (ii) functionally complete but not canonically complete [6, Theorem 4].

Consider now the 3-valued logic E, whose operators $\wedge_e$, E_1 and E_2 are defined in Figure 10a. It is easy to establish that

$$x \curlywedge y \equiv x \wedge_e y \quad \text{and} \quad x \curlyvee y \equiv E_2(E_2(x) \wedge_e E_2(y)).$$

Thus E is canonically suitable [6, Theorem 6]. Henceforth, we will write $x \vee_e y$ to denote $E_2(E_2(x) \wedge_e E_2(y))$. The normal-form formulas for the unary selection operators are shown in Figure 10b. (Note that S_i^1 is the same for all i.) Thus E is functionally and canonically complete [6, Theorem 7].

5. A CANONICALLY COMPLETE LANGUAGE FOR ABAC POLICIES

We can immediately see that XACML is not canonically suitable, essentially because $\curlywedge$ must be a $\sqcap$-operator and

x	$E_1(x)$	$E_2(x)$		$\wedge_e$	3	2	1
3	3	1		3	3	2	1
2	1	2		2	2	2	1
1	2	3		1	1	1	1

(a) Operators

$S_i^1(x)$	$x \wedge_e E_1(x) \wedge_e E_2(x)$
$S_1^2(x)$	$E_1 E_2(x) \wedge_e E_1 E_2 E_1(x)$
$S_2^2(x)$	$x \wedge_e E_2(x)$
$S_3^2(x)$	$E_2 E_1(x) \wedge_e E_1(x)$
$S_1^3(x)$	$x \wedge_e E_1(x)$
$S_2^3(x)$	$E_2 E_1(x) \wedge_e E_1 E_2 E_1(x)$
$S_3^3(x)$	$E_1 E_2(x) \wedge_e E_2(x)$

(b) Normal forms for the unary selection operators

Figure 10: Jobe's logic E

such operators cannot be constructed using XACML combining algorithms (Proposition 3). (We have already seen that XACML is not functionally complete.)

While there is clearly an argument, based on functional completeness, for using PTaCL operators as the basis for a language to express ABAC policies, we still face the issue of actually expressing the desired policies in that language. It is all very well providing a set of functionally complete operators, but many policy authors may not be able to translate the desired policy into one using these operators.

The functional completeness of PTaCL implies that every unary selection operator has an equivalent formula in PTaCL. However, it is not clear that every unary selection operator has an equivalent formula in PTaCL *that is in normal form*.[5] Faced with this issue, we can adopt one of two approaches:

- We could try to determine whether each selection operator does indeed have an equivalent PTaCL formula that is in normal form, thus establishing that PTaCL is canonically complete.

- Alternatively, we can ask whether the PTaCL operators could be replaced with the operators from a logic that is known to be functionally and canonically complete.

We will adopt the latter approach, arguing that Jobe's logic E provides a suitable basis for a canonically complete language for ABAC policies. As well as obtaining functional and canonical completeness, we argue that the operators E_1 and E_2 have a natural interpretation in the context of access control.

---

[5]The fine-grained integration algebra (FIA) [12] is a functionally-complete policy algebra. The algebra defines two constants (one of which can be derived from the other), one unary operator and two binary operators. However, the emphasis on this work is very much on "integration" of multiple policies, rather than top-down specification of policies. Moreover, it is not clear how easily FIA can be integrated with standard XACML or whether it supports a normal form for policies.

The PTaCL(E) language, then, defines atomic policies and policies in exactly the same way as PTaCL. That is, an atomic policy has the form (t, d), where t is a target and $d \in \{0, 1, \bot\}$. We assume $0 < \bot < 1$, which corresponds with an intuitive understanding of the respective authorization decisions. Then a PTaCL(E) policy may be viewed as a formula in a propositional 3-valued logic, in which the variables correspond to atomic policies. A valuation on the variables is induced by the evaluation of a request, with atomic policy variable (t, d) evaluating to either $d \in \{0, 1\}$ or $\bot$, depending on whether the target is applicable or not (exactly as described in Section 2.1). In short, an atomic policy in PTaCL(E) is analogous to an XACML rule or an atomic PTaCL policy.

In the context of PTaCL(E), the values $1, 2, 3$ in Jobe's logic are translated into $0, \bot, 1$. The $\wedge_e$ operator is a form of deny-overrides and E_2 negates the two conclusive decisions. Specifically, the PTaCL(E) operators $\wedge_e$ and E_2 are equivalent to the PTaCL operators $\wedge_p$ and $\neg$, respectively. Note also that

$$E_1(x) \equiv (x \vee_p \bot) \wedge_p (\sim(x \vee_p \neg x)). \tag{2}$$

It is this equivalence, in fact, that Crampton and Morisset used to establish that PTaCL is functionally complete.[6]

The unary operator E_1 has the effect of flipping the values corresponding to 0 and $\bot$. Thus, we have

$$[\![E_1(t, 1)]\!](q) = \begin{cases} 1 & \text{if } [\![t]\!](q) = 1_t, \\ 0 & \text{otherwise.} \end{cases}$$

In other words, E_1 acts as a deny-by-default operator. Similarly

$$[\![E_2 E_1 E_2(t, 0)]\!](q) = \begin{cases} 0 & \text{if } [\![t]\!](q) = 1_t, \\ 1 & \text{otherwise.} \end{cases}$$

and $E_2 E_1 E_2$ acts as an allow-by-default (unary) operator.

The above observations suggest that Jobe's operators make an intuitively reasonable set of operators on which to base a 3-valued authorization language. Thus PTaCL(E) is functionally complete, its operators have intuitively reasonable interpretations, and it is canonically complete. We now illustrate why having a normal form may make it simpler to construct ABAC policies. Specifically, we represent the operator $\oplus_2$ from Figure 1 in normal form using Jobe's operators. To reiterate, it is impossible to represent $\oplus_2$ as any combination of XACML operators and it is difficult to see how to express $\oplus_2$ using the PTaCL operators (although it is theoretically possible to do so). We first represent the

operator as a truth table:

x	y	$x \oplus_2 y$
0	0	0
0	$\bot$	0
0	1	$\bot$
$\bot$	0	0
$\bot$	$\bot$	$\bot$
$\bot$	1	$\bot$
1	0	$\bot$
1	$\bot$	$\bot$
1	1	1

By first representing $\oplus_2$ as a truth table, it is easy to establish that it is equivalent to

$$S_3^\bot(x, y) \vee_e S_5^\bot(x, y) \vee_e S_6^\bot(x, y) \vee_e S_7^\bot(x, y) \vee_e S_8^\bot(x, y) \vee_e S_9^1(x, y).$$

Moreover:

$$S_3^\bot(x, y) \equiv S_1^\bot(x) \wedge_e S_3^\bot(y) \qquad S_5^\bot(x, y) \equiv S_2^\bot(x) \wedge_e S_2^\bot(y)$$
$$S_6^\bot(x, y) \equiv S_2^\bot(x) \wedge_e S_3^\bot(y) \qquad S_7^\bot(x, y) \equiv S_3^\bot(x) \wedge_e S_1^\bot(y)$$
$$S_8^\bot(x, y) \equiv S_3^\bot(x) \wedge_e S_2^\bot(y) \qquad S_9^1(x, y) \equiv S_3^1(x) \wedge_e S_3^1(y)$$
$$S_1^\bot(x) \equiv E_1 E_2(x) \wedge_e E_1 E_2 E_1(x) \qquad S_2^\bot(x) \equiv x \wedge_e E_2(x)$$
$$S_3^\bot(x) \equiv E_2 E_1(x) \wedge_e E_1(x) \qquad S_3^1(x) \equiv E_1 E_2(x) \wedge_e E_2(x)$$

Hence, we can derive a formula in normal form for $\oplus_2$.

Of course, one would not usually construct the normal form by hand, as we have done above. Indeed, it is easy to develop an algorithm that would construct the normal form of a policy from its decision table. Thus, we have identified the formal foundations for a policy authorization language in which we can automate the construction of a policy in normal form, given the decision table for that policy.

Moreover, since our language is a tree-structured language, having exactly the same operational semantics as XACML and PTaCL, we can implement Jobe's operators as (custom) XACML combining algorithms and then specify XACML policies using these operators. Thus we can readily obtain a functionally and canonically complete policy language, whose policies can be embedded in the rich framework for ABAC provided by XACML (in terms of its languages for representing targets and requests) and its enforcement architecture (in terms of the policy enforcement, policy decision and policy administration points).[7]

Using the structure and evaluation strategy for PTaCL policies and the operators $\wedge_e$, E_1 and E_2 makes it possible to define arbitrary policies and to represent them in normal form. We believe that this provides a number of advantages, in addition to those mentioned above, which we now briefly discuss. First, it is known that policy misconfigurations can be costly, both in terms of data leakage (when actions that should not be possible are authorized by the policy) and in terms of administration (when actions that should be possible are not authorized and the policy needs to be updated) [1]. We believe that the use of a canonically complete policy language is likely to make policy specification easier to understand for policy authors, thereby reducing the number of errors and policy misconfigurations. Future work will investigate whether this conjecture holds.

---

[6] It is easy to establish that the PTaCL formula $\sim x$ is equivalent to the PTaCL(E) formula $x \wedge_e E_1(x)$. In other words, it is far more straightforward to represent the PTaCL operators using the operators in Jobe's logic, rather than representing the operators in Jobe's logic using the PTaCL operators (compare equation (2)).

[7] This is contrast to proposals in the literature, which require the use of non-standard components, such as multi-terminal binary decision diagrams [12] or non-deterministic finite automata [8].

Second, policies in normal form may be more efficient to evaluate. Given a formula in a 3-valued logic expressed in normal form, any literal that evaluates to 0 causes the entire clause to evaluate to 0, while any clause evaluating to 1 means the entire formula evaluates to 1. We may also be able to apply some of the equivalences described by Jobe to minimize the size of a formula in normal form, thereby further reducing the effort required to evaluate it. We hope to investigate this idea further in future work.

6. CONCLUDING REMARKS

The use of attribute-based access control languages such as XACML continues to rise as the demand for collaboration between industry partners becomes increasingly important. Furthermore, the widespread distribution of users and resources prompts a move away from traditional identity based authorization languages. This paper focuses on the way in which decisions (and hence authorization policies) are combined in ABAC authorization languages.

We analyzed the XACML rule- and policy-combining algorithms and identified various shortcomings of these algorithms. First, there is significant duplication and redundancy in the combining algorithms, with only two of the specified algorithms (do and po) required to express all of the XACML combining algorithms. Second, the XACML operators are not functionally complete; indeed, there are many useful unary and binary operators that cannot be represented using the XACML operators. We noted that PTaCL is functionally complete and, in particular, allows us to construct the XACML operators.

However, we argued that the way in which PTaCL (and XACML) policies must be written because of the underlying structure of the language is not particularly helpful to policy authors. Accordingly, we introduced the PTaCL(E) language that is both functionally and canonically complete. We believe that PTaCL(E) has considerable advantages over languages like PTaCL and XACML, and policy algebras. In particular, it is possible to simply read off a policy from a decision table and thus automate the specification of a policy from a description that will be intuitive and easy for the policy author to construct. We believe that this should help reduce the number of errors and policy misconfigurations, and hope to confirm this conjecture in future work. Moreover, unlike other approaches to enhancing the expressive power XACML [8, 11, 12], our proposed policy language requires no modification to XACML or additional processing. All that is required is the implementation (as custom XACML rule- and policy-combining algorithms) of the three policy operators we defined in Section 5. Again, this is something we plan to do in future work.

In addition, Jobe identifies a number of equivalences (between formulas in the logic E) that may be applied to reduce the size of a normal-form formula in E. We plan to investigate the relevance of these equivalences to authorization policies in future work. Another natural extension for future work is to analyze methods for handling errors in policy evaluation [4] and see how these methods can be extended to our canonically complete language.

Acknowledgements

Conrad Williams is a student in the Centre for Doctoral Training in Cyber Security, supported by EPSRC award EP/K035584/1.

7. REFERENCES

[1] BAUER, L., GARRISS, S., AND REITER, M. K. Detecting and resolving policy misconfigurations in access-control systems. *ACM Trans. Inf. Syst. Secur. 14*, 1 (2011), 2.

[2] BONATTI, P. A., DI VIMERCATI, S. D. C., AND SAMARATI, P. An algebra for composing access control policies. *ACM Trans. Inf. Syst. Secur. 5*, 1 (2002), 1–35.

[3] CARMINATI, B., AND JOSHI, J., Eds. *SACMAT 2009, 14th ACM Symposium on Access Control Models and Technologies, Stresa, Italy, June 3-5, 2009, Proceedings* (2009), ACM.

[4] CRAMPTON, J., AND HUTH, M. An authorization framework resilient to policy evaluation failures. In *Computer Security - ESORICS 2010, 15th European Symposium on Research in Computer Security* (2010), D. Gritzalis, B. Preneel, and M. Theoharidou, Eds., vol. 6345 of *Lecture Notes in Computer Science*, Springer, pp. 472–487.

[5] CRAMPTON, J., AND MORISSET, C. PTaCL: A language for attribute-based access control in open systems. In *Principles of Security and Trust - First International Conference, POST 2012, Proceedings*, P. Degano and J. D. Guttman, Eds., vol. 7215 of *Lecture Notes in Computer Science*. Springer, 2012, pp. 390–409.

[6] JOBE, W. H. Functional completeness and canonical forms in many-valued logics. *The Journal of Symbolic Logic 27*, 04 (1962), 409–422.

[7] KLEENE, S. *Introduction to Metamathematics*. D. Van Nostrand, Princeton, NJ, 1950.

[8] LI, N., WANG, Q., QARDAJI, W. H., BERTINO, E., RAO, P., LOBO, J., AND LIN, D. Access control policy combining: theory meets practice. In Carminati and Joshi [3], pp. 135–144.

[9] ŁUKASIEWICZ, J. Philosophische Bemerkungen zu mehrwertigen Systemen des Aussagekalküls. *Comtes rendus des séances de la Société des Sciences et des Lettres de Varsovie Classe III*, vol. 23 (1930), 55–57.

[10] MOSES, T. eXtensible Access Control Markup Language (XACML) Version 2.0 OASIS Standard, 2005. http://docs.oasis-open.org/xacml/2.0/access-control-xacml-2.0-core-spec-os.pdf.

[11] NI, Q., BERTINO, E., AND LOBO, J. D-algebra for composing access control policy decisions. In *Proceedings of the 2009 ACM Symposium on Information, Computer and Communications Security* (2009), W. Li, W. Susilo, U. K. Tupakula, R. Safavi-Naini, and V. Varadharajan, Eds., ACM, pp. 298–309.

[12] RAO, P., LIN, D., BERTINO, E., LI, N., AND LOBO, J. An algebra for fine-grained integration of XACML policies. In Carminati and Joshi [3], pp. 63–72.

[13] RISSANEN, E. eXtensible Access Control Markup Language (XACML) Version 3.0 OASIS Standard, 2012. http://docs.oasis-open.org/xacml/3.0/xacml-3.0-core-os-en.html.

[14] WIJESEKERA, D., AND JAJODIA, S. A propositional policy algebra for access control. *ACM Trans. Inf. Syst. Secur. 6*, 2 (2003), 286–325.

APPENDIX

A. CONSTRUCTIBLE XACML BINARY OPERATORS

We now consider which binary operators can be constructed using the XACML operators. We will write $+$ and $-$ to denote pbd and dbd, respectively, in order to simplify the notation. There are four possible idempotent, $\sqcup$-operators that can be constructed using the XACML operators: for all $x \in D$, $x \oplus x$, $x \oplus \perp$ and $\perp \oplus x$ are pre-determined; only $0 \oplus 1$ and $1 \oplus 0$ may vary. These operators are do, po, fa and what we might call "last-applicable" (la).[8] We have $r_1 \,\mathsf{la}\, r_2 \equiv r_2 \,\mathsf{fa}\, r_1$, so we can construct each of these operators using the XACML operators. The commutative, idempotent $\sqcup$-operators are do and po.

We now consider operators having the general form $\diamond_1((\diamond_2 d_1) \oplus (\diamond_3 d_2))$ where $\diamond_1, \diamond_2, \diamond_3 \in \{-, +, \text{""}\}$ ("" is used to denote that the unary operator is omitted) and $\oplus \in \{\mathsf{do}, \mathsf{po}, \mathsf{fa}, \mathsf{la}\}$. If either $\diamond_2$ or $\diamond_3$ are $-$ or $+$, the application of $\diamond_1$ has no effect as the operator $(\diamond_2 d_1) \oplus (\diamond_3 d_2)$ will be conclusive (since $\diamond d \in \{0,1\}$ and $x \oplus \perp = \perp \oplus x = x$ for any $\oplus \in \{\mathsf{do}, \mathsf{po}, \mathsf{fa}, \mathsf{la}\}$ and any $x \in \{0,1\}$). This has the effect of limiting the number of possible operators of this form. The possible choices for $\diamond_1, \diamond_2, \diamond_3$ and $\oplus$ are tabulated in Table 2, which results in 44 quasi-idempotent operators.

$\diamond_1$	$\diamond_2$	$\diamond_3$	$\oplus$	Possible Ops
""	$+$	3	4	12
""	$-$	3	4	12
""	""	2	4	8
3	""	""	4	12

Table 2: Choices for $\diamond_1, \diamond_2, \diamond_3$ and $\oplus$

However, not all of these operators are unique, given the following equivalences between operators.

PROPOSITION 4. *For any $x, y \in \{0, 1, \perp\}$,*

$(-x) \,\mathsf{po}\, y = x \,\mathsf{po}\, (-y) = -(x \,\mathsf{po}\, y) = (-x) \,\mathsf{po}\, (-y)$;

$(+x) \,\mathsf{po}\, y = (+x) \,\mathsf{po}\, (-y)$;

$x \,\mathsf{po}\, (+y) = (-x) \,\mathsf{po}\, (+y)$;

$(+x) \,\mathsf{do}\, y = x \,\mathsf{do}\, (+y) = +(x \,\mathsf{do}\, y) = (+x) \,\mathsf{do}\, (+y)$;

$(-x) \,\mathsf{do}\, y = (-x) \,\mathsf{do}\, (+y)$;

$x \,\mathsf{do}\, (-y) = (+x) \,\mathsf{do}\, (-y)$.

These results follow by inspection of the relevant decision tables. The intuition behind the first three results is that $0 \,\mathsf{po}\, x = \perp \,\mathsf{po}\, x$ for all $x \in \{0, 1\}$; an analogous observation holds for the second three.

Then we can construct the following operators using do and different combinations of the unary operators $-$ and $+$:

$$x \,\mathsf{do}_0\, y \stackrel{\text{def}}{=} x \,\mathsf{do}\, y \qquad x \,\mathsf{do}_1\, y \stackrel{\text{def}}{=} (-x) \,\mathsf{do}\, (-y)$$

$$x \,\mathsf{do}_2\, y \stackrel{\text{def}}{=} (-x) \,\mathsf{do}\, y \qquad x \,\mathsf{do}_3\, y \stackrel{\text{def}}{=} x \,\mathsf{do}\, (-y)$$

$$x \,\mathsf{do}_4\, y \stackrel{\text{def}}{=} -(x \,\mathsf{do}\, y) \qquad x \,\mathsf{do}_5\, y \stackrel{\text{def}}{=} +(x \,\mathsf{do}\, y)$$

---

[8] Although fa (and hence la) is a redundant operator, we continue their use as a compact way of expressing operators (and later families of operators) instead of the lengthy expressions using do and po.

These operators comprise what we call the deny-overrides family of operators. These operators are all distinct and operate on $\{0, 1\}$ in exactly the same way as do. Moreover,

$$0 \,\mathsf{do}_i\, \perp = \perp \,\mathsf{do}_i\, 0 = 0$$

for all i. They differ in their effect on elements in $\{1, \perp\}$, as shown in Figure 11. Notice that do_5 is equivalent to three other operators (by Remark 4). Note that do_2 and do_3 are not commutative.

do_0	1	$\perp$
1	1	1
$\perp$	1	$\perp$

do_1	1	$\perp$
1	1	0
$\perp$	0	0

do_2	1	$\perp$
1	1	1
$\perp$	0	0

do_3	1	$\perp$
1	1	0
$\perp$	1	0

do_4	1	$\perp$
1	1	1
$\perp$	1	0

do_5	1	$\perp$
1	1	1
$\perp$	1	1

Figure 11: The family of deny-overrides operators

Analogously, we can define a family of six permit-overrides operators which act on $\{1, \perp\}$ in exactly the same way as the deny-overrides operators in Figure 11. Therefore, in total, we can construct six quasi-idempotent deny-overrides operators and six quasi-idempotent permit-overrides operators, of which one is idempotent and four are commutative.

In a similar manner we can identify the first-applicable and last-applicable families, consisting of operators obtained using fa and la respectively. We observe the following equivalences between operators.

PROPOSITION 5. *For any $x, y \in \{0, 1, \perp\}$, $\diamond \in \{-, +\}$,*

$(\diamond x) \,\mathsf{fa}\, y = (\diamond x) \,\mathsf{fa}\, (-y) = (\diamond x) \,\mathsf{fa}\, (+y)$;

$-(x \,\mathsf{fa}\, y) = x \,\mathsf{fa}\, (-y)$;

$+(x \,\mathsf{fa}\, y) = x \,\mathsf{fa}\, (+y)$;

$x \,\mathsf{la}\, (\diamond y) = (-x) \,\mathsf{la}\, (\diamond y) = (+x) \,\mathsf{la}\, (\diamond y)$;

$-(x \,\mathsf{la}\, y) = (-x) \,\mathsf{la}\, y$;

$+(x \,\mathsf{la}\, y) = (+x) \,\mathsf{fa}\, y$.

These results follow by inspection of the relevant decision tables. Unlike the deny-overrides and permit-overrides families, we obtain only five distinct operators for the first/last-applicable families. This is clear from the restrictions placed on the decision tables, and follows immediately from the equivalences in Remark 4. Thus, in total, the 44 possible operators actually represent 22 distinct binary operators. The 44 operators and their duplicate forms are tabulated in Table 3.

Thus far, we only considered operators having the form

$$\diamond_1((\diamond_2 d_1) \oplus (\diamond_3 d_2)).$$

It is not obvious that these are the only forms that yield new, distinct binary operators. These forms only contain single instances of each decision variable d_1 and d_2, which raises the question of whether new operators can be constructed from forms which contain multiple instances of d_1 and d_2. Recall the definition of fa ($x \,\mathsf{fa}\, y \equiv x \,\mathsf{po}\, (x \,\mathsf{do}\, y)$), which is constructed using more than one instance of x. We now investigate whether the inclusion of multiple instances of d_1 and d_2 yields any further operators.

Op	Construction	Alternative forms
do_0	x do y	
do_1	$(-x)$ do $(-y)$	
do_2	$(-x)$ do y	$(-x)$ do $(+y)$
do_3	x do $(-y)$	$(+x)$ do $(-y)$
do_4	$-(x$ do $y)$	
do_5	$+(x$ do $y)$	$(+x)$ do $(+y), (+x)$ do y, x do $(+y)$
po_0	x po y	
po_1	$(+x)$ po $(+y)$	
po_2	$(+x)$ po y	$(+x)$ po $(-y)$
po_3	x po $(+y)$	$(-x)$ po $(+y)$
po_4	$-(x$ po $y)$	
po_5	$+(x$ po $y)$	$(-x)$ po $(-y), (-x)$ do y, x do $(-y)$
fa_0	x fa y	
fa_1	$(-x)$ fa y	$(-x)$ fa $(-y), (-x)$ fa $(+y)$
fa_2	$(+x)$ fa y	$(+x)$ fa $(-y), (+x)$ fa $(+y)$
fa_3	$-(x$ fa $y)$	x fa $(-y)$
fa_4	$+(x$ fa $y)$	x fa $(+y)$
la_0	x la y	
la_1	x la $(-y)$	$(-x)$ la $(-y), (+x)$ la $(-y)$
la_2	x la $(+y)$	$(-x)$ la $(+y), (+x)$ la $(+y)$
la_3	$-(x$ la $y)$	$(-x)$ la y
la_4	$+(x$ la $y)$	$(+x)$ la y

Table 3: Operator constructions and alternative forms

To answer this question, we developed program with the aim of enumerating all constructible binary operators by brute force. The program works by generating all operators that can be created by combining other operators. The program generates all binary operators which have the general form $\diamond x \oplus \triangle y$ where $\diamond, \triangle \in \{-, +, ""\}$ and $\oplus \in \{do, po\}$. Note we omit fa and la from the set of binary operators, as these operators (being expressible in terms of do and po) will be generated automatically as we recursively create operators. We initialize the array variables $x = [0, 0, 0, 1, 1, 1, \bot, \bot, \bot]$ and $y = [0, 1, \bot, 0, 1, \bot, 0, 1, \bot]$. We store the decision table of a binary operator in a similar array variable. We generate the $3 \times 2 \times 3 = 18$ decision tables for operators of the form $\diamond x \oplus \triangle y$, of which 8 are duplicates. We remove the duplicates, storing the decision tables for the remaining 12 operators in an array. The process is repeated with each item in the array being reused as an input for x and y in the general form of a binary operator. This second iteration generates $12^2 \times 18 = 2592$ operators, of which 22 are distinct operators. We once again reuse these operators as inputs for x and y, yielding the the same 22 distinct operators. As no new operators are generated, the program terminates. The 22 operators discovered via exhaustive search correspond exactly to the operators we constructed above. The decision tables for these operators are listed in Figure 12.

do_0	0	1	$\bot$
0	0	0	0
1	0	1	1
$\bot$	0	1	$\bot$

do_1	0	1	$\bot$
0	0	0	0
1	0	1	0
$\bot$	0	0	0

do_2	0	1	$\bot$
0	0	0	0
1	0	1	1
$\bot$	0	0	0

do_3	0	1	$\bot$
0	0	0	0
1	0	1	0
$\bot$	0	1	0

do_4	0	1	$\bot$
0	0	0	0
1	0	1	1
$\bot$	0	1	0

do_5	0	1	$\bot$
0	0	0	0
1	0	1	1
$\bot$	0	1	1

(a) Deny-overrides family

po_0	0	1	$\bot$
0	0	1	0
1	1	1	1
$\bot$	0	1	$\bot$

po_1	0	1	$\bot$
0	0	1	1
1	1	1	1
$\bot$	1	1	1

po_2	0	1	$\bot$
0	0	1	0
1	1	1	1
$\bot$	1	1	1

po_3	0	1	$\bot$
0	0	1	1
1	1	1	1
$\bot$	0	1	1

po_4	0	1	$\bot$
0	0	1	0
1	1	1	1
$\bot$	0	1	0

po_5	0	1	$\bot$
0	0	1	0
1	1	1	1
$\bot$	0	1	1

(b) Permit-overrides family

fa_0	0	1	$\bot$
0	0	0	0
1	1	1	1
$\bot$	0	1	$\bot$

fa_1	0	1	$\bot$
0	0	0	0
1	1	1	1
$\bot$	0	0	0

fa_2	0	1	$\bot$
0	0	0	0
1	1	1	1
$\bot$	1	1	1

fa_3	0	1	$\bot$
0	0	0	0
1	1	1	1
$\bot$	0	1	0

fa_4	0	1	$\bot$
0	0	0	0
1	1	1	1
$\bot$	0	1	1

(c) First-applicable family

la_0	0	1	$\bot$
0	0	1	0
1	0	1	1
$\bot$	0	1	$\bot$

la_1	0	1	$\bot$
0	0	1	0
1	0	1	0
$\bot$	0	1	0

la_2	0	1	$\bot$
0	0	1	1
1	0	1	1
$\bot$	0	1	1

la_3	0	1	$\bot$
0	0	1	0
1	0	1	1
$\bot$	0	1	0

la_4	0	1	$\bot$
0	0	1	0
1	0	1	1
$\bot$	0	1	1

(d) Last-applicable family

Figure 12: Constructible Binary Operators in XACML

Extended ReBAC Administrative Models with Cascading Revocation and Provenance Support

Yuan Cheng
Institute for Cyber Security
Univ. of Texas at San Antonio
yuan@ycheng.org

Khalid Bijon
MosaixSoft
khalid@mosaixsoft.com

Ravi Sandhu
Institute for Cyber Security
Univ. of Texas at San Antonio
ravi.sandhu@utsa.edu

ABSTRACT

Relationship-based access control (ReBAC) has been widely studied and applied in the domain of online social networks, and has since been extended to domains beyond social. Using ReBAC itself to manage ReBAC also becomes a natural research frontier, where we have two ReBAC administrative models proposed recently by Rizvi et al. [30] and Stoller [33]. In this paper, we extend these two ReBAC administrative models in order to apply ReBAC beyond online social networks, particularly where edges can have dependencies with each other and authorization for certain administrative operations requires provenance information. Basically, our policy specifications adopt the concepts of enabling precondition and applicability preconditions from Rizvi et al. [30]. Then, we address several issues that need to be considered in order to properly execute operation effects, such as cascading revocation and integrity constraints on the relationship graph. With these extended features, we show that our administrative models can provide the administration capability of the MT-RBAC model originally designed for multi-tenant collaborative cloud systems [34].

Categories and Subject Descriptors

D.4.6 [**Operating Systems**]: Security and Protection—*Access controls*; K.6.5 [**Management of Computing and Information Systems**]: Security and Protection—*Unauthorized access*

Keywords

Access Control; Relationship; Administrative Model

1. INTRODUCTION

The rapid emergence of online social networks (OSNs) has led to emergence of several relationship-based access control (ReBAC) models in this domain, in both research and practice. In contrast with conventional access control, ReBAC determines access in terms of relationships among users and resources. Considerable research has been conducted on the extensions of ReBAC schemes in the context of OSNs [2, 6–9, 14, 16], offering users more fine-grained and expressive solutions than current commercial systems. In addition to social computing, Fong et al. proposed a series of ReBAC models that use modal logic as policy specifications and seek to apply ReBAC to general computing systems [2, 14, 16]. The RPPM model developed by Crampton et al. also intends to employ ReBAC to applications beyond social computing [11], with policy specifications similar to path expressions in Cheng et al.'s proposals for ReBAC [7, 8]. The name "RPPM" stands for "relationships, paths, and principal-matching".

Administration of ReBAC has to be carefully addressed, because a change of relationships may result in change of authorization. The dynamic and decentralized nature of OSNs, where ReBAC is mainly deployed so far, suggests a unified but decentralized solution to enforce administration in a scalable and efficient way. Following the prior success of using role-based access control (RBAC) to manage RBAC [10, 19, 21, 26, 31, 35], a natural direction for ReBAC adminstration would be using ReBAC itself to manage ReBAC.

Very recently we have seen proposals from researchers in this direction. Two groups of researchers extended the RPPM model by Crampton et al., and independently developed their models for ReBAC administration. The main contribution of Rizvi et al. [30] lies in the implementation of ReBAC in a medical record system, where administrative actions regarding relationship edges are addressed in terms of security preconditions and execution effects. Stoller's RPPM^2 model [33], on the other hand, focuses on policy specifications and provides a complete coverage of ReBAC administration, including changes on entities, edges, and policies.

In this paper we seek to extend the ReBAC administration models cited above, inspired by an application domain for ReBAC beyond those considered in the literature thus far. The concept of multi-tenancy is essential to cloud computing, where multiple customers are served virtual resources within a single, shared physical computing environment. In addition to isolating tenants from each other, cloud service providers have incorporated facilities for authorized cross-tenant interaction. Based on trust relations among tenants, a multi-tenant RBAC model, namely MT-RBAC, has recently been developed for this purpose. MT-RBAC has been defined in traditional RBAC terms in [34]. However, it can alternatively be viewed as a ReBAC model. MT-

SACMAT'16, June 05-08, 2016, Shanghai, China
© 2016 ACM. ISBN 978-1-4503-3802-8/16/06...$15.00
DOI: http://dx.doi.org/10.1145/2914642.2914655

RBAC features tenant trust relation, user-ownership, role-ownership, and object-ownership in addition to user-role assignments and permission-role assignments in the original RBAC model [13, 32]. These various relationships between users, roles, objects, and tenants can be cast as a relationship graph, analogous to the social graph in OSNs and thereby exploited for ReBAC authorization and administration.

A significant difference between the OSN domain wherein ReBAC emerged and more traditional IT (information technology) domains such as MT-RBAC is in the nature of integrity requirements for the relationship graph. Consider the familiar friend relationship in Facebook. Creation of a friend relation between, say Alice and Bob, often requires a prior friend-of-friend relation through some common third user, say Cathy [15]. However, once established the friend relationship between Alice and Bob will persist even if Cathy drops her friendship with either one or both of them. In MT-RBAC however the dependence of relationships on other relationships endures beyond the initial creation. To be concrete, a user u owned by tenant x can be assigned to a role r owned by tenant y only if tenant x trusts tenant y. This tenant-tenant trust is required not only when the u to r relationship is established but also subsequently. Therefore, if the tenant trust relationship is revoked at some later time there is an obligation to also revoke the u to r assignment. Depending on policy requirements this may entail a cascading revocation, which introduces subtleties in defining an appropriate ReBAC administration model. While cascading revocation has been extensively studied in the literature (e.g. [1,12,18]), to the best of our knowledge this paper is the first to incorporate this phenomenon in context of ReBAC.

In this piece of research, we develop a family of three administrative models for ReBAC. Our *first contribution* is the base model called AReBAC$_1$ that formally represents the administrative model proposed by Stoller [33]. It also augments the capability of Stoller's model by including consistency checking functionality to the administrative operations and adding support for pre-applicability conditions proposed in [30]. A pre-applicability condition seeks to preserve the integrity constraints of the relationship graph. Our *second contribution* is AReBAC$_2$ that extends AReBAC$_1$ to support cascading revocation. We propose a cascading revocation algorithm that is specifically designed for the context of ReBAC. We also conduct evaluation on the algorithm. Our *final contribution* is AReBAC$_3$ that offers additional ability to address authorization based on provenance information. To summarize, this work identifies and addresses some important issues in ReBAC administration, which the existing administrative models have not considered and, henceforth, promotes ReBAC administration beyond the conventional context of social computing. These models are inspired by considering administrative requirements for the MT-RBAC model. They are not intended as a replacement or generalization of MT-RBAC but rather proposed as a relation-based framework to explore ReBAC administrative issues. MT-RBAC is a rather novel ReBAC instance relative to current ReBAC literature, and brings to light significant administrative aspects which have not been recognized so far.

The paper is organized as follows. In the next section, we describe the motivating administrative issues inspired by MT-RBAC. Section 3 formally introduces AReBAC$_1$. Section 4 presents AReBAC$_2$ and AReBAC$_3$, and compares them

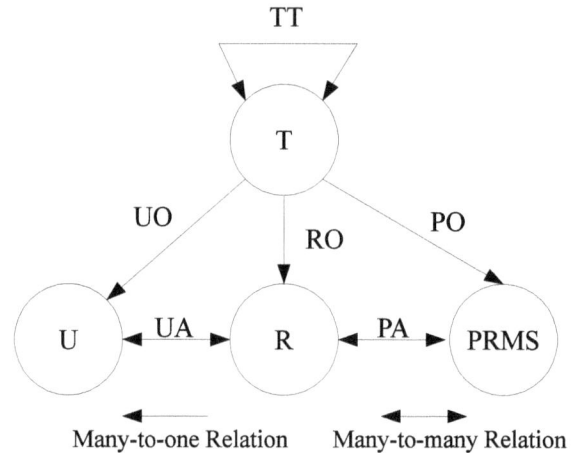

Figure 1: Multi-tenant RBAC model structure

with the prior work. This section also contains our proposed algorithm for cascading revocation. Section 5 analyzes performance of the algorithm. Section 6 reviews related work regarding ReBAC and administrative access control models. Section 7 gives our conclusions.

2. MOTIVATION

Administrative operations are more risky than regular operations. A properly designed administrative model needs to ensure that these operations are performed safely. It becomes an even more important requirement for decentralized systems as these operations can be done by regular users who may not possess the expertise as a system administrator does. Moreover, administrative operations must comply with the business logic of the system and the semantics of the data model. One such system is multi-tenancy authorization in cloud computing environment where dynamic trust relations among the tenants (organizations) drive their collaborations. The main challenge here is dynamic administration of user privileges that includes dynamic cascading revocation of user privileges and conflict resolution of the requested administrative operations from multiple tenants.

Recently, the MT-RBAC model [34] extends traditional role-based access control model to provide multi-tenancy authorization. MT-RBAC is defined in the traditional style of RBAC models. In this paper we recast it in the style of ReBAC models, which leads us to consider some administrative issues with respect to MT-RBAC which are not so convenient to formalize in the RBAC style formulation. Motivated by these considerations we extend the ReBAC administrative models proposed in [30, 33]. We show how to configure variations of MT-RBAC in these extended administrative models in a relatively straightforward manner.

MT-RBAC consists of four components as illustrated in Figure 1: tenants (T), users (U), roles (R) and permissions (PRMS). A tenant is a virtual partition of a cloud service. A user is an individual owned by a single tenant via user-ownership (UO) relation. Each tenant may own multiple users. Hence the UO relation is many-to-one, relating multiple users to one tenant. A role is a job function associated with a single tenant while a tenant may own multiple roles. Thereby, role-ownership (RO) is many-to-one. A permission is a specification of a privilege to an object in a tenant. A permission is denoted as a 3-tuple (privilege, tenant, object). For example, (read, Dev.E, /root/) represents a permission of reading the "/root/" path on tenant Dev.E. Every permission is associated with a single tenant, who can own multiple permissions. Therefore, permission-ownership (PO) is also many-to-one. User-role assignment (UA) and permission-role assignment (PA) relations connect users and permissions through roles. These are many-to-many relations.

Tenant-trust (TT) denotes a many-to-many trust relation between tenants. We use notation $\trianglelefteq$ to represent trust between two tenants so $T_A \trianglelefteq T_B$ means T_A (trustor) trusts T_B (trustee). The reflexive (but not transitive, symmetric or anti-symmetric) TT relation enables cross-tenant collaboration. If $T_A \trianglelefteq T_B$ then users of T_A can be assigned to T_B's roles by T_B, hence gaining permissions that are associated with T_B's roles. Note that due to reflexivity $T_A \trianglelefteq T_A$ always holds so intra-tenant assignment of T_A's users to T_A's roles is always allowed. The main objective of MT-RBAC is to enable cross-tenant assignment based on TT.

In MT-RBAC, along with the removal of a tenant entity, its correlated trust relations and authorization assignments should also be removed accordingly. Similarly, the revocation of a trust relation between two tenants should induce revocation of its correlated user-role assignments as well. This property is known as cascading revocation, however, the current MT-RBAC literature does not provide any mechanism to address it. Inspired by MT-RBAC we also recognize that edges and nodes in ReBAC systems can have dependency and correlation with each other, hence, cascading removal of nodes/edges is intrinsic to ReBAC. To make the administrative model comprehensive, we need to address the dependency issues adequately. The applicability check prior to the operation and the post-operation effects can accommodate the cascading revocation. It is more convenient to consider these issues in a ReBAC setting rather than in the traditional RBAC style of models.

Furthermore, in some settings for MT-RBAC, such relations can be added, altered or removed by multiple administrative users from different tenants, causing potential conflicts or unexpected results. To clarify the situation, the administrative model should offer the ability to distinguish administrative operations initiated by different users, or support additional data structures to record the provenance (history) of these operations. Again, some relations in MT-RBAC such as the user-ownership relation between users and tenants have to be many-to-one so each user has a unique owner tenant. Similarly for the tenant-role relationship. In general there are many global integrity constraints like these two examples, which need to be maintained before and after each administrative operation is conducted. These constraints specify the configurations of the data model for the relationship graph that are considered semantically correct. However, the integrity constraint check is often overlooked in ReBAC literature, since authorization in ReBAC mainly focuses on specifying path conditions that regulate the requesting subject. Specifically, the RPPM^2 model copes with the situations regarding adding an edge that already exists or removing an edge that does not exist, but these special cases are not further generalized in the policy language.

Motivated by these problems, we extend the existing administrative ReBAC models and propose a family of three

models that capture global integrity policy checks, cascading revocation, and multi-ownership conflict, respectively.

3. BACKGROUND

In this section, we first summarize the RPPM^2 [33] model. We then formally present our proposed core administrative model for ReBAC, namely AReBAC$_1$.

3.1 RPPM^2

In context of developing an administrative model for ReBAC, Stoller [33] proposed RPPM^2 (RPPM Modified), which extends the RPPM model proposed in [11]. Motivation and illustrative examples of these models are given in the respective papers. This paper introduces a family of administrative models, which basically extends the RPPM^2 model. We now describe the RPPM^2 model as follows.

System Model and System Instance. A system model comprises a set of types T, a set of relationship labels R, a set of symmetric relationship labels $S \subseteq R$ and a permissible relationship graph $G_{PR} = (V_{PR}, E_{PR})$, where $V_{PR} = T$ and $E_{PR} \subseteq T \times T \times R$. Given a system model (T, R, S, G_{PR}), a system instance is defined by a system graph $G = (V, E)$ and a type function $\tau: V \to T$, where V is the set of entities and $E \subseteq V \times V \times R$. G is well-formed if for each entity v in V, $\tau(v) \in T$, and for every edge $(v, v', r) \in E$, $(\tau(v), \tau(v'), r) \in E_{PR}$.

Request. A request req is in the form of $(s, op(v_1, \ldots, v_n))$, where s is the subject (i.e., an entity that requests for the operation), op is the operation, and the v_i are target entities on which the operation will perform.

Path Expression and Path Condition. Path expressions are defined recursively: $\diamond$ is a path expression; r is a path expression, for all $r \in R$; if π and π' are path expressions, then $\pi; \pi'$, $\pi+$, $\pi*$, and $\bar{\pi}$ are path expressions. A path condition in RPPM^2 has the form $e_1 \cdot \pi \cdot e_2$, where each e_i is an entity constant or a variable that belongs to V_{PR} of the permissible relationship graph $G_{PR} = (V_{PR}, E_{PR})$, and π is a path expression. A path condition $e_1 \cdot \pi \cdot e_2$ holds if there exists a substitution θ mapping the variables (if any) in the path condition to values such that the system graph contains a path from $e_1\theta$ to $e_2\theta$ that matches $\pi\theta$, where $t\theta$ denotes the result of applying substitution θ to term t.

Principal Matching. Principal matching replaces a path between two entities with a single principal name. The principal name is a shorthand for path expression. In RPPM^2, a name can be defined to represent multiple path expressions.

Authorization Rule and Authorization Policy. An authorization rule $\mathcal{R}$ is defined in the form (req, c, d), where req is a request, c is a conjunction of path conditions, and d is binary decision. A rule says that the decision d is true for request req if all conditions in c are satisfied. An authorization policy is a collection of authorization rules.

Defaults. A system-wide default decision can also be specified, which is used when no rules and no other defaults apply. We refer interested reader to [11, 33] for details.

Figure 2 shows the ReBAC configuration for MT-RBAC that we described in section 2. In this configuration, the set of types T contains tenant, user, role and permission. The set of relationship label R contains UO, RO, PO, UA and PA. Figure 2-A shows the permissible relationship graph. Suppose there is a rule $(read, c, d)$ in $\mathcal{R}$, where c is the condition defined as $user \cdot UA \cdot role \wedge role \cdot PA \cdot permission$.

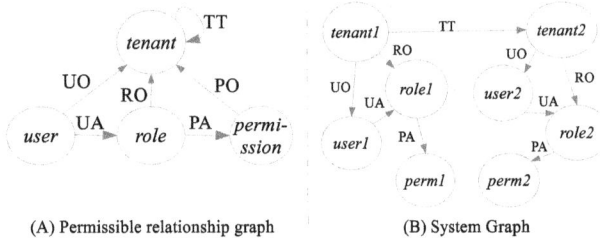

(A) Permissible relationship graph   (B) System Graph

Figure 2: ReBAC for MT-RBAC example

Now, given the system graph in Figure 2-B, if $user_1$ tries to access the permission $perm_1$, the value of d in the rule (*read*, *c*, *d*) is true.

3.2 AReBAC$_1$ Model

The administrative model proposed by Stoller [33] includes operations to add and delete entities, edges, and authorization rules, plus three administrative actions to set defaults. We only focus on administrative operations to add and delete edges. We now formally present AReBAC$_1$, which is the core model of our proposed family of administrative models. Basically, it summarizes these two operations as they are proposed in [33] with the extension of consistency policies and global integrity constraints. Consistency policies ensure that the system graph $G = (V, E)$ is always well-formed after allowing each administrative operation. The global integrity constraints are semantically equivalent to "applicability precondition" defined by Rizvi *et al.* [30] that constrain operations based on certain conditions for both primary and auxiliary participants. Note that, we augment this model for supporting cascading revocation of edges in the following section.

AReBAC$_1$ provides two operations called $\mathcal{A}dd$ and $\mathcal{R}M$ respectively to add and remove edges to a system graph $G = (V, E)$, where each operation is a function that takes as input the administrative entity that performs the operation, a relationship label and two entities between which the edge with given relationship label will be added/removed. Each operation also evaluates the consistency policy in order to keep G well-formed. Formally these two operations are defined as follows (the notation for defining these operations is similar to the notation of schema used in NIST RBAC [13]).

$\mathcal{A}dd(e_{admin}, e_1, e_2, r) \lhd$
$\quad e_{admin} \in V \wedge e_1 \in V \wedge e_2 \in V \wedge$
$\quad r \in R \wedge (\tau(e_1), \tau(e_2), r) \in E_{PR}$
$\qquad E' = E \cup \{<e_1, e_2, r>\} \rhd$

$\mathcal{R}M(e_{admin}, e_1, e_2, r) \lhd$
$\quad e_{admin} \in V \wedge (e_1, e_2, r) \in E$
$\qquad E' = E - \{<e_1, e_2, r>\} \rhd$

Here, a successful execution of an operation is allowed if the specified consistency policy is satisfied. Note that, e_{admin} is an entity, which we sometimes refer to as administrator. Besides she is authorized to perform an operation, an administrator is similar to other entities. For example, she may also have non-administrative permissions. In this system, the authorization of an administrator for an operation is regulated by a fixed set of positive policy rules $\mathcal{P}$. Each policy rule $p \in \mathcal{P}$ has the form $p = \mathsf{OP}(e_{admin}, e_1, e_2, r) \leftarrow \mathsf{enableC}(e_{admin}, e_1, e_2) \wedge \mathsf{preC}(e_1, e_2)$, where OP is $\mathcal{A}dd$ or

$\mathcal{R}M$. This represents that an administrator is authorized to request the operation if both predicates preC and $\mathsf{enableC}$ are satisfied. An $\mathsf{enableC}$ is an enabling precondition that specifies certain relationship between the administrator, e_{admin}, and two target entities, e_1 and e_2. An $\mathsf{enableC}$ can be specified as conjunction of multiple path conditions and verified with e_{admin}, e_1, e_2 and other necessary instances of the system graph. On the other hand, a preC specifies relations between two target entities disregarding the administrator who requests to perform the operations. Unlike $\mathsf{enableC}$, preC is not specified as path condition, rather it should be specified as hybrid logic formula as mentioned in [30]. In this paper, we do not aim to develop policy specification language for preC. Instead, we express them using simple set theory notation. Note that, in a policy rule $p \in \mathcal{P}$ one may also specify one or both predicates to be always true.

Table 1 shows examples of AReBAC$_1$ based on Figure 1. Example 1 shows an $\mathcal{A}dd$ operation for a tenant-trust (TT) edge where $tenant_1$ is the e_{admin} who wants to add the edge between $tenant_1$ and $tenant_2$. Note that, in order to authorize this operation only consistency check is necessary, hence, predicates $\mathsf{enableC}$ and preC are always true. In example 2, $tenant_1$ wants to remove a user-role (UA) edge between $user_1$ and $role_1$. Here, besides consistency condition, $\mathsf{enableC}$ ensures that both $user_1$ and $role_1$ belong to $tenant_1$. However, it does not require an applicability precondition, thereby preC is always true. Finally, in example 3, for adding a user-ownership (UO) between $tenant_2$ and $user_2$ no $\mathsf{enableC}$ is required. However, according to MT-RBAC, UO is one-to-many relation. Hence, it is necessary to check if $user_2$ already belongs to another tenant or not. A preC checks this global integrity constraint by checking if an edge (—, $user_2$, TT) already exists in G. Here, '—' represents all the tenants in the system. According to Figure 1 there exists no such edge and the request should be authorized.

4. ENHANCEMENT OF THE MODEL

In this section, we extend the AReBAC$_1$ model to facilitate cascading removal of edges and dynamic conflict resolution by provenance support.

4.1 AReBAC$_2$: Cascading Revocation

In ReBAC, creation of some edges might depend on the existence of another edge, whereby, dependent edges need to be removed at the time of removal of the dependency edge. We define this situation as cascading revocation of edges. Cascading revocation implies that the operation will trigger a series of recursive removal of edges on the graph in addition to the direct consequence of the operation. We augment the functionality of AReBAC$_1$ here in AReBAC$_2$ to support this cascading revocation.

AReBAC$_2$ augments the representation of each policy $p \in \mathcal{P}$ that regulates $\mathcal{R}M$ operations as follows.

$p = \mathcal{R}M(e_{admin}, e_1, e_2, r) \leftarrow \mathsf{enableC}(e_{admin}, e_1, e_2) \wedge \mathsf{preC}(e_1, e_2) : \mathcal{C}_{revoke}(e_1, e_2, r)$.

$\mathcal{C}_{revoke}(e_1, e_2, r)$ is a function that takes as input e_1, e_2 and r, and returns a set of edges that needs to be removed (possibly empty) when the policy p is used to authorize operation $\mathcal{R}M(e_{admin}, e_1, e_2, r)$. Note that, edges returned by the function are being removed without further authorization. In many systems, a cascading revocation is desired

164

Table 1: The Policies in AReBAC₁: An MT-RBAC Example

Description	Operation	Enabling Pre-Condition	Applicability Pre-Condition
1. Add tenant-trust edge	$\mathcal{A}dd$(tenant$_1$, tenant$_1$, tenant$_2$, TT)	True	True
2. Remove user-role assignment edge	$\mathcal{R}M$(tenant$_1$, user$_1$, role$_1$, UA)	$user \cdot UO \cdot tenant \wedge role \cdot RO \cdot tenant$	True
3. Add user-ownership edge	$\mathcal{A}dd$(tenant$_2$, tenant$_2$, user$_2$, UO)	True	$(—, \text{user}_2, \text{UO}) \notin E$

instead of a non-cascading one. For instance, in MT-RBAC, along with the removal of a tenant, its correlated trust relations, users, roles and permission assignments should be also removed. Again, when a tenant trust relation is revoked, the user-role assignments initiated by the trustee tenant also require to be consequently removed. Similar examples can be found in online social networks, health care systems, and database systems as well, where dependency of relationships exists.

Figure 3 illustrates two examples of the cascading revocation in MT-RBAC scenarios. Figure 3-A shows that the removal of a user-ownership (UO) edge between tenant$_1$ and user$_1$ also causes removal of user-role assignment (UA) edge between user$_1$ and role$_1$. In this case, $\mathcal{C}_{revoke}$ takes tenant$_1$, user$_1$ and UO as parameters and returns a set that contains a tuple (user$_1$, role$_1$, UA). Similarly, in Figure 3-B, when a revocation of a TT relation is issued, the correlated cross-tenant user-role assignments specified by the trustee are automatically removed. Here, $\mathcal{C}_{revoke}$ takes tenant$_1$, tenant$_2$ and TT as parameters and returns the set {(user$_1$, role$_2$, UA)}.

For a particular policy, a $\mathcal{C}_{revoke}$ may return zero to multiple edges that are revoked as a consequence of revocation of an edge. Note that, identification of such edges in an efficient way is a non-trivial process since a system graph can have thousands of edges with arbitrary cascading relations. One trivial solution is to maintain relations between each dependency and dependent edge pair in the system graph. When an administrator adds a new edge, the system will find the dependency edges for it and create a new relation. Later, if the dependency edge is removed, dependent edges for it will be retrieved from the maintained relations and removed accordingly. However, this process is not scalable in a large system. Toward this end, we develop a scalable solution for identifying dependent edges.

4.1.1 Dependent-Edge Discovery Algorithm

We discuss our developed procedure that dynamically discovers dependent edges. In this procedure, we maintain a function called $\Phi_{dependency}$ that maps an edge (e$_1$, e$_2$, *label*) to a tuple $\langle$ Path, R$_d$ $\rangle$. Note that, (e$_1$, e$_2$, *label*) is the dependency edge that will cause cascading removal of other edges from system graph G. Here, Path is an ordered set that contains relationship labels in order and R$_d$ is another set containing relationship labels where edges with these labels will be removed. Note that, Path can contain multiple instances of same relationship label. Algorithm 1 finds the dependent edges. Basically, it is based on a depth-first search algorithm, where, for a given dependency edge (e$_1$, e$_2$, *label*), it starts with a source e$_1$ (or possibly e$_2$) in G and recursively tries to reach destination node e$_2$ (or e$_1$). In order to reach e$_2$, it only visits edges according to the given

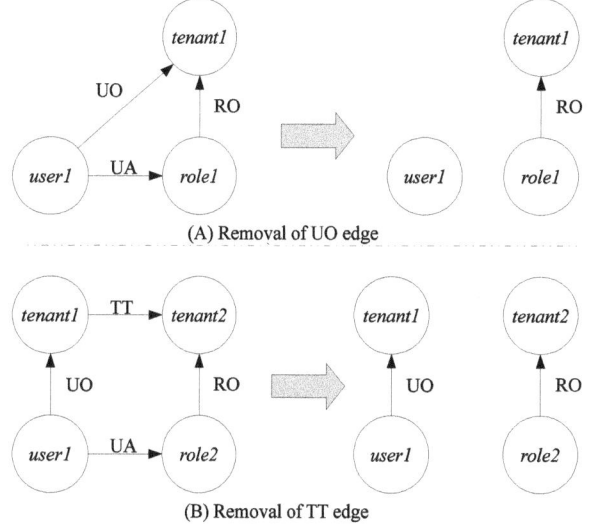

(A) Removal of UO edge

(B) Removal of TT edge

Figure 3: Cascading revocation during the removal of UO and TT edges

order of the labels in Path. Line 14 of the algorithm shows that a label called curE is picked from the top position of Path. Then, lines 16-17 ensures that the algorithm will only visit next node e$_i$ from node e$_s$, if the edge between e$_s$ and e$_i$ is labeled with curE. Line 18 further checks if the label is in R$_d$ and marks it as dependent edge by putting it in set T$_d$. Then, this scenario is recursively applied for e$_i$ with next top label in Path. Finally, if it reaches destination node e$_j$, lines 9-13 check if all the labels are used from Path, and then add the dependent edges from T$_d$ to E$_d$. Finally, the algorithm returns all the dependent edges in E$_d$ (line 7).

For the example given in Figure 3-B, $\Phi_{dependency}$ maps (tenant$_1$, tenant$_2$, TT) to the tuple $\langle$ Path$_1$, R$_{d_1}$ $\rangle$ where Path$_1$ = (UO, UA, RO) and R$_{d_1}$ = {UA}. Then, algorithm 1 takes as input tenant$_1$, tenant$_2$, Path$_1$, and R$_{d_1}$ and returns the set {(user$_1$, role$_2$, UA)}, which edges should also be removed. Note that a cascading revocation can be applied to all the dependent edges that the revokee (dependency) edge previously enabled and, recursively, all the dependents of the dependents of the revokee edge or entity. For simplicity, we only consider one-level of cascading revocation here.

4.1.2 Time Complexity of $\mathcal{C}_{revoke}$

In our proposed solution, the time complexity of $\mathcal{C}_{revoke}$ depends on the complexities of algorithm 1 and $\Phi_{dependency}$. $\Phi_{dependency}$ is a mapping function and the time complexity of it, to map an input edge to a tuple $\langle$ Path, R$_d$ $\rangle$, depends on the implementation choice. We implemented $\Phi_{dependency}$ as

Algorithm 1 Discover Dependent-Edge

Require: A source node e_s, a destination node e_d, an ordered set of relationship labels Path, a set of relationship labels R_d where edges with these labels are the dependent edges.
Ensure: Returns a set of edges E_d that will be removed.
1: $E_d := \emptyset$
2: Visited $:= \emptyset$
3: **if** $R_d = \emptyset$ *or* Path $= \emptyset$ **then**
4:     **return** E_d
5: **end if**
6: Find_Edges(e_s, e_d, Path, R_d, E_d, Visited, {})
7: **return** E_d
8: **procedure** FIND_EDGES(e_s,e_d,Path,R_d,E_d,Visited,T_d)
9:     **if** $e_s = e_d$ **then**
10:         **if** Path $= \emptyset$ **then**
11:             $E_d := E_d \cup T_d$
12:         **end if**
13:     **end if**
14:     curE $:=$ Path.top()
15:     Visited $:=$ Visited $\cup e_s$
16:     **for all** $e_i \in V$ **do**
17:         **if** $e_i \notin$ Visited *and* $\langle e_s, e_i, \text{curE} \rangle \in E$ **then**
18:             **if** curE $\in R_d$ **then**
19:                 $T_d := T_d \cup \langle e_s, e_i, \text{curE} \rangle$
20:             **end if**
21:             Find_Edges(e_i,e_d,Path-{curE},R_d,E_d,Visited, T_d)
22:             **if** $\langle e_s, e_i, \text{curE} \rangle \in T_d$ **then**
23:                 $T_d := T_d - \langle e_s, e_i, \text{curE} \rangle$
24:             **end if**
25:         **end if**
26:     **end for**
27:     Visited $=$ Visited $- e_s$
28: **end procedure**

HashMap, discussed in section 5, and its time complexity is $\mathcal{O}(1)$. Each execution of the algorithm 1 performs a depth-first search in the current system graph $G = (V, E)$. We assume that E is always represented as adjacency-list and, therefore, the time complexity of the algorithm is $\mathcal{O}(V + E)$. The overall time complexity of $\mathcal{C}_{revoke}$, to find the set of edges that needs to be removed due to dependency on a removed edge, is $\mathcal{O}(V + E)$.

4.2 AReBAC₃: Provenance Support

In ReBAC, relationships are utilized to make access decision. But it is likely the case that in a real world system, other forms of information and knowledge will also come into play together with relationships for achieving desirable access control objectives. There has recently been a surge of interest in harnessing provenance information to enable additional versatile control capabilities not available with conventional access control solutions [24, 28].

Provenance refers to the documentation of the history of a data item starting from its original sources to its current state. Provenance data can provide utilities such as pedigree information, query, usage tracking, versioning, data auditing, and error detection, etc. Among various kinds of provenance data and usage, we are particularly interested in causality dependencies that record the flow of transactions that occurred in the system, since they can provide us the foundation for building and delivering more expressive access control features.

The Open Provenance Model (OPM) [22] is a model of provenance that aims to capture the causality dependencies

between entities. It provides a foundation for expressing such dependencies, the provenance graph. A provenance graph is defined as a directed graph, whose nodes are artifacts, processes and agents, and whose edges are causal relationships between the aforementioned nodes. It can be computed from the transaction records of the system. An artifact is used to represent a state of a data object (e.g., an added edge or a removed edge). A process denotes an action or a series of actions performed on or caused by artifacts, and resulting in new artifacts (e.g., create or remove an edge). An agent corresponds to a user who executes the action (e.g., a tenant). There are five causal relationships defined in OPM: a process used an artifact; an artifact was generated by a process; a process was triggered by a process; an artifact was derived from an artifact; and a process was controlled by an agent. We adopt these causal relationships to represent dependencies among artifacts, processes and agents.

We build our provenance feature on top of OPM as the model enables us to capture and express the casuality dependencies. We name the provenance-assisted model, AReBAC₃.

Next, we present an exemplary usage of the provenance support in the multi-tenancy scenario mentioned earlier. In the previous MT-RBAC example, we assume that the user-ownership is one-to-many, which means a user is restricted to be owned by one single tenant. If many-to-many ownership is allowed, then a user can be assigned to multiple tenants, thus making the authorization assignments more complicated than before.

As shown in Figure 4, $user_1$ is owned by $tenant_1$ and $tenant_2$; meanwhile both $tenant_1$ and $tenant_2$ trust another tenant $tenant_3$. Due to the tenant trust with the owners, the trustee tenant $tenant_3$ is allowed to assign $user_1$ to one of its roles, say $role_1$. Later on when one of the tenants, say $tenant_2$, decides to revoke the tenant trust relation it previously initiated, we will have to consider whether to remove the UA relation between $user_1$ and $role_1$ or not.

There are many strategies to resolve conflicts among different administrators: permissions-take-precedence, denials-take-precedence, recency precedence, distance precedence, etc. This problem has been extensively studied in many domains in the past, and a detailed consideration is out of scope of this paper. We will leave it to the system architect to decide the conflict resolution policy. But first of all, we need to distinguish the two assignments from different tenants and then decide whether to remove them or not.

The RPPM² model offers relationship label with typed parameters. In our scenario, we can use typed parameters to distinguish edges assigned by different tenants. The user-role assignments become two separate edges ($user_1$, $role_1$, UA($tenant_1$)) and ($user_1$, $role_1$, UA($tenant_2$)). Revocation initiated by $tenant_2$ will only remove the edge ($user_1$, $role_1$, UA($tenant_2$)) and leave ($user_1$, $role_1$, UA($tenant_1$)) as it is.

An alternative way of distinguishing multiple ownerships is to incorporate provenance information to edges. We can capture the user-role assignment using the OPM provenance graph illustrated in Figure 5. The UO edge ($tenant_1$, $user_1$, UO) was generated by the process $create_1$ controlled by $tenant_1$. Similarly, we can express the causal relationships for edges ($tenant_3$, $role_1$, RO) and ($tenant_1$, $tenant_3$, TT). There are three "used" edges from the process $create_4$ to three artifacts generated in the prior processes. These artifacts are input objects used in the process $create_4$, indicating

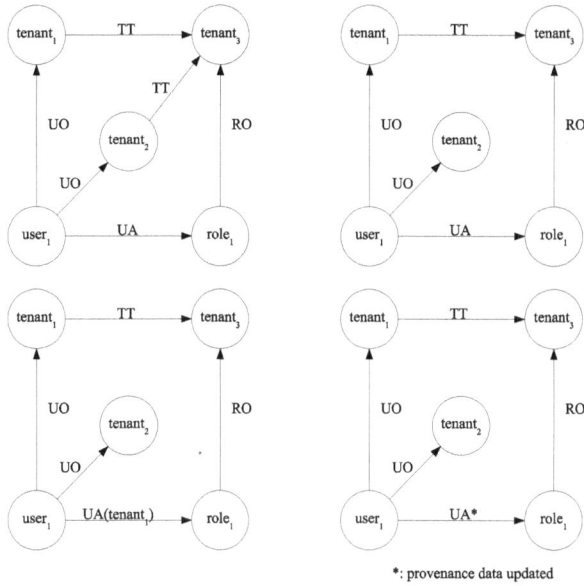

Figure 4: Two ways of distinguishing edges assigned by multiple administrators

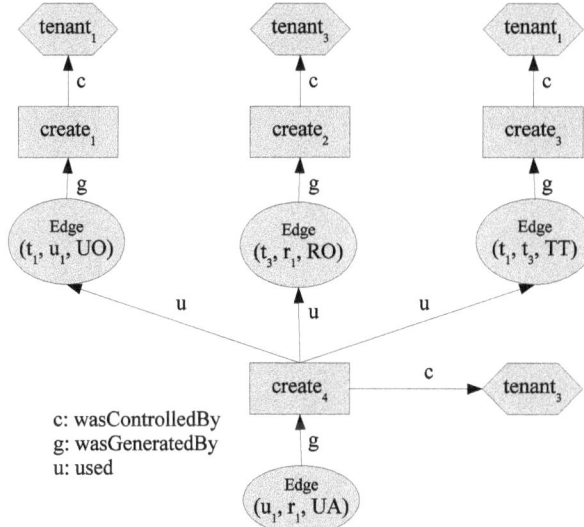

c: wasControlledBy
g: wasGeneratedBy
u: used

Figure 5: OPM provenance graph for adding UO edge

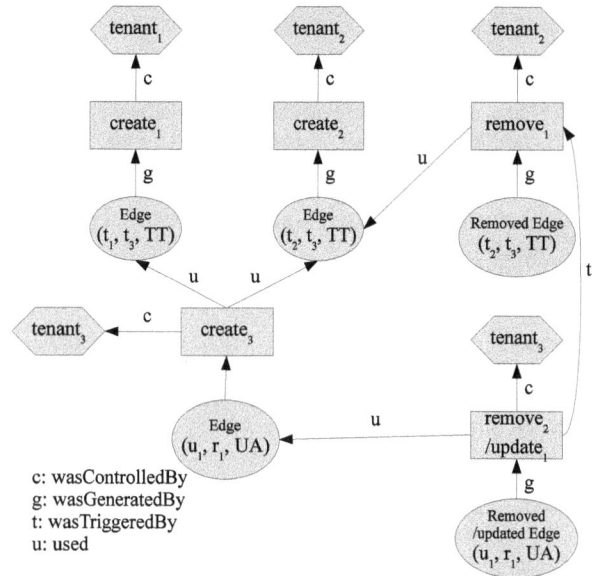

c: wasControlledBy
g: wasGeneratedBy
t: wasTriggeredBy
u: used

Figure 6: OPM provenance graph for removing UO edge

With the provenance data, we can keep track of the history of the relationship edges without creating multiple edge instances. The system is also able to get necessary information to remove or update dependant edges as a response to those changes that have been made in the system.

4.2.1 Discussion

The initial intention of introducing provenance information to ReBAC is to capture and express causality dependencies for assisting authorization decisions, such as resolving conflicts and ambiguity due to multiple ownerships. Therefore, we only need to model the provenance data and enable path queries on the provenance graph, which are independent from the formalization of the ReBAC language. We choose the Resource Description Framework (RDF) [20] data presentation to express the provenance data, as it naturally supports a directed graph structure. Standard RDF query languages, such as SPARQL [29], can be employed to query over provenance data stored in RDF triples. The provenance-assisted ReBAC model can be also extended to enable provenance-based access control [28], which means authorization decisions are made directly based on provenance information, in addition to relationships. In this case, we have to formalize provenance information in the existing ReBAC policy language. One possible way of such formalization can be achieved by extending the XACML language [23], as described in [3, 24, 25].

Querying over a provenance graph introduces additional computational overhead. The performance of such query depends on the shape of the provenance graph. As the system evolves, the provenance graph eventually grows in both width and depth. A performance study of a similar problem was conducted in [24]. However, the evaluation and optimization of the provenance graph query is beyond the scope of this paper. The nature of the provenance graph query indicates that, for the sole purpose of distinguishing multiple ownerships, the typed parameter approach in the RPPM^2 model is simpler and less costly. However, the provenance-

that a complete execution of the process create$_4$ requires the existence of these three edges. The "wasGeneratedBy" edge says that the process create$_4$ was required to generate the edge (user$_1$, role$_1$, UA).

The scenario depicted in Figure 4 can be captured in OPM provenance graph as well, as shown in Figure 6. Both edges (tenant$_1$, tenant$_3$, TT) and (tenant$_2$, tenant$_3$, TT) were used to generate the user-role assignment (user$_1$, role$_1$, UA) initiated by tenant$_3$. Depending on the conflict resolution strategy a system picks, the removal of the edge (tenant$_2$, tenant$_3$, TT) would trigger either the removal of the edge (user$_1$, role$_1$, UA) or an update on the UA edge (and its metadata). In either case, a new artifact would be generated by the triggered process to reflect the change.

based approach offers greater expressive power and richer information, which can be further utilized for many other purposes. Provenance-based access control is definitely among one of them. Multiple-level cascading revocation is another usage example that cannot be facilitated through typed parameter but can be realized via provenance information.

4.3 Comparison with Existing Administrative ReBAC Models

In [15], the proposed ReBAC model is designed to mimic the authorization process in Facebook-style OSNs. It models the communication protocol of friendship initiation and termination, and provides a discretionary policy administration based on resource ownership, which has limited expressive power compared with later proposals. The access control framework introduced by Carminati et al. features authorization, administrative and filtering policies in ontology-based representations [4]. However, this framework does not address administrative activities related to entities and relationships. Cheng et al.'s URRAC model proposes to arbitrate administrative activities using ReBAC, but it does not elaborate the details about administration [7]. These proposals are mostly targeted for OSN systems and are not applicable to general-purpose computing systems.

The RPPM^2 model [33] and the ReBAC implementation for OpenMRS [30] are two administrative ReBAC models appeared lately in literature. RPPM^2 is a comprehensive model that addresses administrative operations on entities, relationships as well as authorization policies. The main contribution of Rizvi et al.'s administrative model is on incorporating ReBAC in a production-scale system that originally uses RBAC. In particular, it mainly focuses on one type of administrative operations: adding or deleting relationship edges. In addition to regulating who can perform the operation, their hybrid logic-based policy language also captures the applicability of the operation, aiming to completely preserve the security constraints.

Our work follows the policy language defined in RPPM^2 and extends it to capture the issues we found in our use cases. Our models seek to preserve the global integrity constraints, address the cascading revocation as well as the multi-ownership issue. We also aim to apply ReBAC to applications beyond OSNs, thus using MT-RBAC, an access control model for collaborative cloud systems, for demonstration.

5. EVALUATION

The goal of the evaluation is to decide whether algorithm 1 can efficiently determine the set of dependent edges of a specific edge being removed. We implemented algorithm 1 using Java with version 1.8.0_60. The experiments are performed on an Intel Ci7 machine with 8 cores, 2.53 GHz and 16GB RAM, running Ubuntu 14.04.1 LTS (Trusty).

5.1 Implementation and Input Instance Generation

In our code, we represented $\Phi_{dependency}$, described in section 4, as java $HashMap$, where the key is the id of an edge and the value is the $CascadingElement$ object. A $CascadingElement$ has two variables: a java $Queue$ called $path$ and a java Set called $rSet$, which are the representation of Path and R_d of algorithm 1, respectively. Edges are

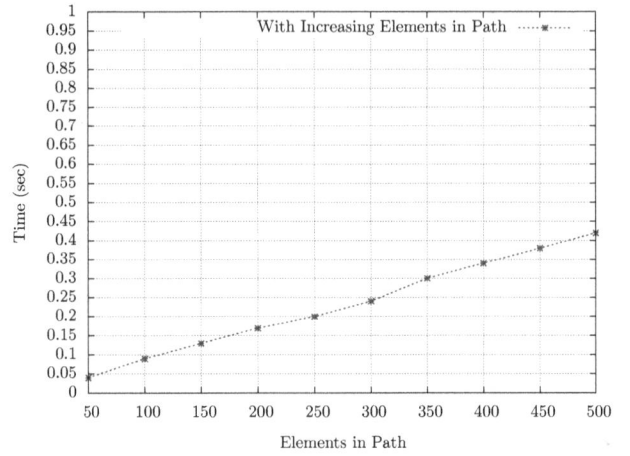

Figure 7: Dependent-Edge discover time for experiment 1

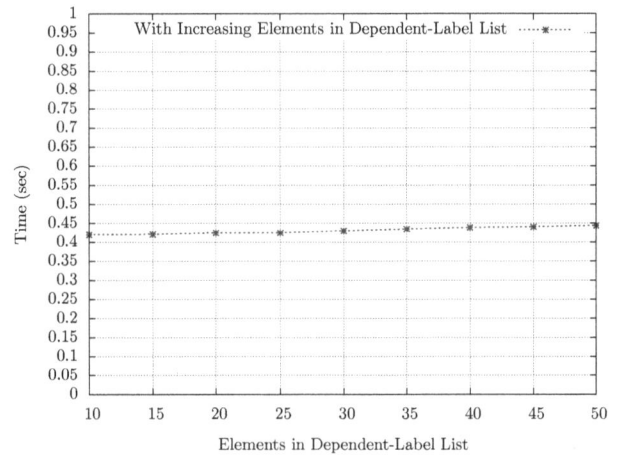

Figure 8: Dependent-Edge discover time for experiment 2

stored in a Set called E, where each edge is an object that has an id, id of node$_1$, id of node$_2$, and a label.

We synthetically generate problem instances for our evaluation. We believe the values of the different parameters are sufficient for a medium sized organization. We considered 100 types and 50 labels. Then we created the permissible relationship graph $G_{PR} = (V_{PR}, E_{PR})$, where $|E_{PR}| = 1000$. Based on G_{PR}, we created the well-formed system graph $G = (V, E)$, where the size of V equals to 10000, each type has 100 instance, and the size of E is 50000.

5.2 Evaluation Result

We populate $\Phi_{dependency}$ for 100 different edges. For each edge in $\Phi_{dependency}$, in the first experiment, we vary the size of $path$ from 50 to 500, where we ensure that there is at least one valid path in the graph in the order of edges in $path$. Note that, $path$ can contain same relationship label multiple times. However, each of them should be visited once and in the order it is specified. Also, for each element in $\Phi_{dependency}$, we fix the size of $rSet$ to 10. Then, for each element in $\Phi_{dependency}$, we execute the algorithm and record

168

the average time. We also repeat the whole process of first experiment for 15 times and record the average. From the results shown in Figure 7, we can see that for 50 elements in the *path*, the average time to discover the set is very minimal (< 0.05 sec); for 500 elements it is 0.415 sec. In the *second experiment*, we set the size of *path* to 500 elements and vary the size of *rSet* from 10 to 50. We record the average execution time of the algorithm. Similar to the first experiment, this experiment is also repeatedly conducted for 15 times and the average time is recorded. The results shown in Figure 8 indicate that time does not vary that much with an increase in the size of *rSet*. Since each new element in *path* increases one more round of recursion call, its impact on the running time of dependent-edge discovery is larger than that of the size of *rSet*.

6. RELATED WORKS

With the emergence and growth of OSNs over the last decade, new access control schemes have been called upon to address the issues that conventional access control approaches cannot properly address. In [5, 6], Carminati *et al.* developed a pioneering work for access control in OSNs, where authorization policies are specified in terms of type, depth and trust level of the relationships. This type of access control, namely relationship-based access control, exploits relationships between users and resources as the basis for authorization decision. Since the term was invented in [17], ReBAC has undergone considerable development.

In [15], Fong *et al.* formalized the privacy preservation mechanism in Facebook-style OSNs into a two-stage procedure. In addition to modeling the Facebook-style policy predicates, such as "only-me", "only-friends", "friends-of-friends", and "everyone", the model is capable of expressing some topology-based policies, including "degree of separation", "clique", and so on, which are not available in Facebook and other well-known OSN systems.

Modal logic and its extension, hybrid logic, have been used for expressing ReBAC policies in [2, 14, 16]. Fong *et al.* formulated a ReBAC model and introduced a modal logic language to compose complex relationship-based policies [14]. In a subsequent work, the modal logic proposed earlier was extended and improved with more expressive power [16]. In [2], the authors adopted a hybrid logic to achieve better efficiency and greater flexibility in policy specification. Pang *et al.* also adopted a hybrid logic approach to formulate access control policies in their model for OSNs, where public information is also exploited for regulating access [27].

Cheng *et al.* proposed a series of three ReBAC models for OSNs that utilize regular expression-based notations to specify policies. In [8], a sequence of relationship edge labels forms a path expression, which can be interpreted as regular expression. If there is a path between the access requester and the resource owner satisfying the path expression in the policy, the requested access is granted. A path-checking algorithm is used to determine the existence of such qualified path. The authors subsequently extended the model to incorporate resources and actions to social graph, and track relationships among users and resources in addition to relationships between users and users [7]. Since multiple policies may be applicable to single resource, conflict resolution policies were introduced to arbitrate authorization policies. In another subsequent work, the model proposed in [8] was extended to exploit attribute information of users and rela-

tionships for the purpose of access control, enabling a richer policy language [9].

Several attempts have been made to adopt ReBAC in domains beyond OSNs. The proposed work in [14] was aimed for general-purpose computing systems, with an example scenario of electronic health records. The RPPM model recently proposed by Crampton *et al.* is a variant of ReBAC model for general-purpose computing systems [11], where policies are expressed in terms of path conditions similar to path expressions in [8]. The RPPM model introduced authorization principals, which are analogous to roles in RBAC. In [33], the author developed the $RPPM^2$ model, a direct extension of RPPM, that addresses administrative operations in ReBAC. Rivzi *et al.*'s OpenMRS access control mechanism [30] also features an administrative model for ReBAC, addressing how to enable users to manage access control relationships safely. Our work in this paper is based on these two administrative models, building on the policy language in [33] and the design objectives identified in [30].

7. CONCLUSION

In this paper, we present a family of three administration ReBAC models based on the policy language offered in the RPPM and $RPPM^2$ models. Our models cover the administrative operations on edges. In addition to regulating who can perform administrative operations, we identify three problems that were rarely discussed in the literature of ReBAC: integrity constraints, cascading revocation, and multi-ownership of edges. We adopt and modify the concept of enabling precondition and applicability precondition from [30] to express path conditions and integrity constraints. The cascading revocation is achieved by using our proposed depth-first search-based algorithm, which discovers the dependent edges that need to be removed. An evaluation is conducted to show the effectiveness and efficiency of the algorithm. The multi-ownership of edges can be properly distinguished by typed parameters or provenance data incorporated in the models. We demonstrate that our ReBAC models are capable of expressing policies in MT-RBAC.

Still at its early stage, ReBAC administration will remain a new research frontier for some time to come. Towards the adoption of ReBAC in various other application domains, many new opportunities will be identified along this direction. We will investigate these problems and enrich the ReBAC models with greater flexibility and more expressive power. One of the possible directions for us is to extend our work to address policy administration, which is very critical with essential decentralized components for ReBAC systems.

Acknowledgments

This research is partially supported by NSF Grants CNS-1111925 and CNS-1423481.

8. REFERENCES

[1] E. Bertino, P. Samarati, and S. Jajodia. An extended authorization model for relational databases. *IEEE TKDE*, 9(1):85–101, 1997.

[2] G. Bruns, P. W. Fong, I. Siahaan, and M. Huth. Relationship-based access control: its expression and enforcement through hybrid logic. In *Proceedings of the second ACM CODASPY*, pages 117–124. ACM, 2012.

[3] T. Cadenhead, V. Khadilkar, M. Kantarcioglu, and B. Thuraisingham. A language for provenance access control. In *Proceedings of the first ACM CODASPY*, pages 133–144. ACM, 2011.

[4] B. Carminati, E. Ferrari, R. Heatherly, M. Kantarcioglu, and B. Thuraisingham. A semantic web based framework for social network access control. In *Proceedings of the 14th ACM SACMAT*, pages 177–186. ACM, 2009.

[5] B. Carminati, E. Ferrari, and A. Perego. Rule-based access control for social networks. In *OTM 2006 Workshops*, pages 1734–1744. Springer, 2006.

[6] B. Carminati, E. Ferrari, and A. Perego. Enforcing access control in web-based social networks. *ACM TISSEC*, 13(1):6, 2009.

[7] Y. Cheng, J. Park, and R. Sandhu. Relationship-based access control for online social networks: Beyond user-to-user relationships. In *PASSAT 2012*, pages 646–655. IEEE, 2012.

[8] Y. Cheng, J. Park, and R. Sandhu. A user-to-user relationship-based access control model for online social networks. In *DBSec XXVI*, pages 8–24. Springer, 2012.

[9] Y. Cheng, J. Park, and R. Sandhu. Attribute-aware relationship-based access control for online social networks. In *DBSec XXVIII*, pages 292–306. Springer, 2014.

[10] J. Crampton and G. Loizou. Administrative scope: A foundation for role-based administrative models. *ACM TISSEC*, 6(2):201–231, 2003.

[11] J. Crampton and J. Sellwood. Path conditions and principal matching: a new approach to access control. In *Proceedings of the 19th ACM SACMAT*, pages 187–198. ACM, 2014.

[12] R. Fagin. On an authorization mechanism. *ACM TODS*, 3(3):310–319, 1978.

[13] D. F. Ferraiolo, R. Sandhu, S. Gavrila, D. R. Kuhn, and R. Chandramouli. Proposed NIST standard for role-based access control. *ACM TISSEC*, 4(3):224–274, 2001.

[14] P. W. Fong. Relationship-based access control: protection model and policy language. In *Proceedings of the first ACM CODASPY*, pages 191–202. ACM, 2011.

[15] P. W. Fong, M. Anwar, and Z. Zhao. A privacy preservation model for Facebook-style social network systems. In *Computer Security–ESORICS 2009*, pages 303–320. Springer, 2009.

[16] P. W. Fong and I. Siahaan. Relationship-based access control policies and their policy languages. In *Proceedings of the 16th ACM SACMAT*, pages 51–60. ACM, 2011.

[17] C. Gates. Access control requirements for Web 2.0 security and privacy. In *Workshop on Web 2.0 Security & Privacy (W2SP)*, 2007.

[18] P. P. Griffiths and B. W. Wade. An authorization mechanism for a relational database system. *ACM TODS*, 1(3):242–255, 1976.

[19] W. Kuijper and V. Ermolaev. Sorting out role based access control. In *Proceedings of the 19th ACM SACMAT*, pages 63–74. ACM, 2014.

[20] O. Lassila and R. R. Swick. Resource description framework (RDF) model and syntax specification. 1999.

[21] N. Li and Z. Mao. Administration in role-based access control. In *Proceedings of the 2nd ACM AsiaCCS*, pages 127–138. ACM, 2007.

[22] L. Moreau, B. Clifford, J. Freire, J. Futrelle, Y. Gil, P. Groth, N. Kwasnikowska, S. Miles, P. Missier, J. Myers, et al. The open provenance model core specification (v1. 1). *Future generation computer systems*, 27(6):743–756, 2011.

[23] T. Moses et al. Extensible access control markup language (XACML) version 2.0. *Oasis Standard*, 200502, 2005.

[24] D. Nguyen, J. Park, and R. Sandhu. A provenance-based access control model for dynamic separation of duties. In *PST 2013*, pages 247–256. IEEE, 2013.

[25] Q. Ni, S. Xu, E. Bertino, R. Sandhu, and W. Han. An access control language for a general provenance model. In *Secure Data Management*, pages 68–88. Springer, 2009.

[26] S. Oh and R. Sandhu. A model for role administration using organization structure. In *Proceedings of the seventh ACM SACMAT*, pages 155–162. ACM, 2002.

[27] J. Pang and Y. Zhang. A new access control scheme for Facebook-style social networks. In *ARES 2014*, pages 1–10. IEEE Computer Society, 2014.

[28] J. Park, D. Nguyen, and R. Sandhu. A provenance-based access control model. In *PST 2012*, pages 137–144. IEEE, 2012.

[29] E. Prud'Hommeaux, A. Seaborne, et al. SPARQL query language for RDF. *W3C recommendation*, 15, 2008.

[30] S. Z. R. Rizvi, P. W. Fong, J. Crampton, and J. Sellwood. Relationship-based access control for an open-source medical records system. In *Proceedings of the 20th ACM SACMAT*, pages 113–124. ACM, 2015.

[31] R. Sandhu, V. Bhamidipati, and Q. Munawer. The ARBAC97 model for role-based administration of roles. *ACM TISSEC*, 2(1):105–135, 1999.

[32] R. S. Sandhu, E. J. Coyne, H. L. Feinstein, and C. E. Youman. Role-based access control models. *Computer*, 29(2):38–47, 1996.

[33] S. D. Stoller. An administrative model for relationship-based access control. In *DBSec XXIX*, pages 53–68. Springer, 2015.

[34] B. Tang, Q. Li, and R. Sandhu. A multi-tenant RBAC model for collaborative cloud services. In *PST 2013*, pages 229–238. IEEE, 2013.

[35] H. Wang and S. L. Osborn. An administrative model for role graphs. In *DBSec XVII*, pages 302–315. Springer, 2004.

Formal Comparison of an Attribute Based Access Control Language for RESTful Services with XACML

Marc Hüffmeyer
Hochschule Furtwangen
Robert-Gerwig-Platz 1
Furtwangen, Germany
huef@hs-furtwangen.de

Ulf Schreier
Hochschule Furtwangen
Robert-Gerwig-Platz 1
Furtwangen, Germany
schu@hs-furtwangen.de

ABSTRACT

This work introduces RestACL - an access control language for RESTful Services - and compares it with XACML using formal methods. XACML is a generic approach that targets Attribute Based Access Control (ABAC) in general. RestACL is founded on the ideas of the ABAC model, too, but utilizes the concepts of REST enabling a quicker evaluation of access requests. This work gives a brief introduction over the main ideas of RestACL and proves its evidence by giving transformation rules to translate security policies from RestACL to XACML and vice versa. The formalized transformation descriptions show the expressive strength of RestACL, because they demonstrate that any generic ABAC policy written in XACML can be expressed with RestACL, too. The correctness and completeness of RestACL can be proved with the transformation rules, too.

Keywords

REST, Attribute Based Access Control

1. INTRODUCTION

The architectural style called Representational State Transfer (REST) defines a set of concepts that can be used to build a scalable, distributed system [4, 11]. While the style is characterized by basic principles, the integration of access control models and mechanisms is not part of the concepts. Therefore, flexible and efficient access control models need to be found that enable privacy for such distributed systems. A great diversity of content types and content owners might be given in such systems and with this diversity also a lot of variations of security policies might ship. Therefore, an access control system for RESTful Services must be flexible in order to support rich variations of security policies.

Attribute Based Access Control (ABAC) is a promising candidate to become the access control model in a RESTful environment because it offers great flexibility. In consequence, one needs to find approaches that enable ABAC for RESTful Services. Systems implementing these approaches must be capable to evaluate access requests on a request base and handle frequently changes to the security policy in order not to break with the principles of REST. Therefore, such a system must be very efficient in terms of processing times in order not to become a bottleneck in the communication sequences between clients and servers.

This work introduces security mechanisms for RESTful Services that are build on top of the ABAC model and shows the correctness of the mechanisms by giving transformation rules that transform RestACL security policies into security policies written in a well-established ABAC standard named eXtensible Access Control Markup Language (XACML). The completeness of RestACL is shown by giving transformation rules for a transformation from XACML to RestACL. The existence of such transformation rules is the proof that the expressive strength of RestACL is equal to the expressive strength of XACML. Therefore, a formal analysis of XACML and RestACL is given on which the transformation rules are founded. Besides the transformation rules this work also provides formalizations about the semantics of XACML combining algorithm.

In section 2 we describe the foundations of this work. Section 3 introduces the mechanisms that can be applied to build an access control system for RESTful Services. We validate the approach using a formal comparison with XACML in section 4. Finally, we refer to related work in section 5.

2. FOUNDATIONS

This section introduces the core principles of REST and explains the main ideas of ABAC in more detail.

2.1 Representational State Transfer

Representational State Transfer (REST) defines constraints for distributed systems that enable high-performing, scalable systems [4]. The four most important constraints are *Resource Orientation*, the differentiation between *Resources and Representations*, a *Uniform Interface* to interact with resources and the concept of *Hypermedia As The Engine Of Application State (HATEOAS)* to achieve the goal of stateless communication. Details about these constraints are described in [4]. The Richardson Maturity Model can be used to determine the grade of how a system supports the concepts of a RESTful architecture [13]. The model categorizes a distributed system into one of four levels. The higher the level, the better the compliance of the constraints.

The RestACL language takes advantage of the *Resource Orientation* and *Uniform Interface* constraints. The idea

SACMAT'16, June 05-08, 2016, Shanghai, China

© 2016 ACM. ISBN 978-1-4503-3802-8/16/06. . . $15.00

DOI: http://dx.doi.org/10.1145/2914642.2914663

of *Resource Orientation* is that any entity of a RESTful application can be directly addressed. Therefore, any action that is executed in such a system points to exactly one resource using the address of that resource. Uniform Resource Identifiers URI are used for such purposes. The constraint of a *Uniform Interface* demands that interaction with any resource is done using the same finite set of methods. That means, there are no individual methods for resources or types of resources. Resources do not need to support the application of all of the interface methods. Therefore, resources can support a subset of methods of the interface. For example, the *Uniform Interface* might be defined through the underlying protocol such as HTTP. In that case, the methods of the interface are defined by the HTTP verbs like GET, POST, PUT and DELETE. A resource might support the application of a GET or a PUT request but not POST and DELETE requests.

2.2 Attribute Based Access Control

Attribute Based Access Control (ABAC) is a relatively new access control paradigm and is a promising candidate to be the dominating access control in the near future. ABAC is a suitable model that might enable the implementation of very flexible access control systems [12] because it offers a wide application context. The main idea of ABAC is that any property of an entity can be used to determine conditions of access control rules. For example, a subject may have a property *location*, a resource the property *privacy level* and a rule could restrict access in a manner that the conditions *subject's location is equal to Shanghai AND resource's privacy level is equal to secret AND access time is between 08:00 and 20:00*. The rule determines access depending on properties (attributes) of different entity types (subject, resource, environment). One can easily imagine that a system that enables ABAC systems ships with a great flexibility in specifying access control rules.

The eXtensible Access Control Markup Language (XACML [1]) is the most prominent example of a language that is build on top of the ABAC model. XACML allows the specification of access rules written in XML. XACML tries to address purely ABAC without any environmental restrictions. Therefore, it is a very generic solution.

3. RESTACL

RestACL is a policy language that enables resource protection for RESTful Services.

3.1 Architecture

Standardized *Clients* and *Servers* are well known components in RESTful environments. *Clients* use protocols such as HTTP to send uniform requests to *Servers* that provide a finite set of methods to access their resources. If a dedicated access control inspection must be performed, additional actions and components are required that execute this task. When a resource request from a *Client* arrives at the *Server* side, the *Server* must serve this request including the execution of access control logic. Before the *Server* can start processing a resource request, the access decision for that request must be determined otherwise an unauthorized access might be the result. Therefore, the *Server* must formulate an access request derived from the resource request and pass this access request to an *Access Control System*. The *Access Control System* computes the access decision based on attributes that are contained in the access request plus two additional information sources: *Domains* and *Policies*. While a *Domain* creates a mapping between resources and policies, the actual access control logic is described in policies located at a *Policy Repository*. Therefore, a *Server* in a RESTful environment has three interfaces to interact with the components of a RestACL system. The first interface allows to request access decisions from the *Access Control System*. The second interface enables the modification of the mapping between resources and policies and the third interface enables the modification of these policies. We already mentioned that an access request contains attributes that are used to determine the access decision. Therefore, a *Server* has to choose security relevant attributes and add it to the request. In addition, further relevant attributes can be collected from external attribute sources like Identity Providers. Therefore, the *Access Control System* might consult several *Attribute Providers* in the evaluation phase. Once the *Access Control System* has determined the access decision, the decision is returned back to the *Server* which has to enforce the decision by either processing or rejecting the initial resource request. A brief overview over the components is introduced in [6].

3.2 Resource-Policy Mapping

The design of RestACL was done accordingly to the REST constraints in order to optimally support the characteristics of such systems. Because a RestACL security policy is aligned to resources as described in section 3.3, an implementing system can create a mapping between resources and policies to accelerate decision making. When an access request arrives, the mapping from resources and their access methods to the policies that have to be applied is evaluated. That means, an access request must always contain the resource address and the access method. Otherwise the evaluation of the resource-policy mapping can not be performed. The utilization of mapping enables the quick identification of policies that have to be applied, because mapping ships with the benefit that only a small subset of the complete security policy has to be evaluated. Once the policies are identified using the references, the actual policies can be loaded from the *Policy Repository*. This approach reduces access request processing times down to a minimum and allows creating and storing large amounts of different policies without significantly affecting the processing times. The reason for reduced processing time is that the evaluation effort is reduced to the computation of an index plus the evaluation of only a small subset of policies. Experimental tests showed that the mapping concept decreases processing times in addition with decreased memory consumption [5].

The mapping approach also helps to reduce administration efforts and memory consumption. For example, a user might administer several photo resources. Typically, the same policies are applied to all of the photos. These policies can be written once and referred multiple times instead of rewriting it multiple times. Therefore, changes to larger amounts of resources can be applied in a fast way.

3.3 Language

This section introduces to the syntax of RestACL. Note that only a brief introduction to the syntax of *Domains* and *Policies* is given to understand the core principles of RestACL. A detailed description can be found in [6].

3.3.1 Domains

Resource orientation is the most important foundation of REST and enables a key-driven ABAC approach. A key-driven approach enables the utilization of efficient data structures such as hash tables to identify the *Policies* that have to be evaluated for an access request. Therefore, an access control system in a RESTful environment should be build resource oriented, too. This enables the creation of a mapping between application logic and access control logic. The *Domain* data structure describes this mapping. A *Domain* is build accordingly to the resource structure of the application. That means, the *Domain* contains nested *Resources* that are linked to so called *Access* elements. Each *Access* element targets one or more methods of the Uniform Interface of the RESTful application and maps resource requests using these methods to one or more *Policies*. This mapping concept can be used to heavily reduce the amount of potentially applicable *Policies* and therefore increases the whole systems efficiency dramatically. In addition, application developers and engineers of RESTful systems are very familiar with the concept of resource orientation and therefore can intuitively create access policies.

Listing 1 shows an example of a RestACL *Domain* written in JSON[1] syntax. The *Domain* administers access to a user list resource (identified by the /**users** path) as follows: access using the **GET** or **PUT** method is determined by policies **P1**, **P2** and **P3**. Multiple policies might be evaluated against an access request. In such a case, the applicable *Policy* with the highest priority determines the access decision. Access to a nested user resource (identified by the path /**users/1**) using the **DELETE** method is regulated in **P4**. **POST** access to a photo list resource (identified by the /**users/photos** path) is determined in **P5**.

```
1   {
2     "host" : "http://example.org",
3     "resources" : [{
4       "path" : "/users",
5       "access" : [{
6         "methods" : ["GET, PUT"],
7         "policies" : ["P1", "P2", "P3"]
8       }],
9       "resources" : [{
10        "path" : "/1",
11        "access" : [{
12          "methods" : ["DELETE"],
13          "policies" : ["P4"]
14        }]
15      }]
16    },{
17      "path" : "/photos",
18      "access" : [{
19        "methods" : ["POST"],
20        "policies" : ["P5"]
21      }]
22    }]
23  }
```

Listing 1: A RestACL Domain written in JSON

3.3.2 Policies

The actual access control logic is described using *Policies* that are designed to enable the implementation of the ABAC model. This offers the opportunity of creating rich variations of security policies that include a great diversity

[1] http://json.org/

of access conditions. Therefore, *Policies* declare *Conditions* based on attributes. For example, a real world requirement might be the restriction of access to a document with a **privacy level** equal to **secret** in a manner that only users with a **clearance** greater than **10** can perform **actions** like **read** or **modify**. One can see that the access regulation combines three *Conditions* and each *Condition* limits access to entities with dedicated attribute values. Therefore, a *Condition* has a *Function* that compares *Arguments*. *Arguments* either refer to attributes in a request or they are fixed *Values*. Attributes are demanded from an access request using a *Category* and a *Designator*. A demanded *Value* from an access request is compared to either a fixed *Value* or another *Value* demanded from the request. If the *Function* computes to true, the *Condition* matches and the *Policy* becomes applicable.

The language supports various combinations of logical expressions to concatenate *Conditions* using *CompositeConditions*. *CompositeConditions* have an *Operation* (e.g. *AND, OR, XOR, NOT*) that concatenates one or more *Conditions*. Listing 2 shows a *Policy* with a *CompositeCondition* that conjuncts two *Conditions*. The policy given in Listing 2 grants access to a **resource** with a **privacy level** of **secret** to **subjects** with a **clearance** greater to **10**. If the *Policy* is applicable, the *Effect* **Permit** is returned with a *Priority* of **1**. If another *Policy* is applicable to the request and has a higher priority than **1**, the *Effect* of this *Policy* will overwrite the *Effect* of *Policy* **P1**. Therefore, *Policies* should be evaluated in a decreasing order of their priorities to accelerate decision making.

```
1   {
2     "policies": [{
3       "id": "P1",
4       "effect": "Permit",
5       "priority": "1",
6       "compositeCondition": {
7         "operation": "AND",
8         "conditions": [{
9           "function": "greater",
10          "arguments": [{
11            "category": "subject",
12            "designator": "clearance"
13          },{
14            "value": "10"
15          }]
16        },{
17          "function": "equal",
18          "arguments": [{
19            "category": "resource",
20            "designator": "privacy"
21          },{
22            "value": "secret"
23          }]
24        }]
25      }
26    }]
27  }
```

Listing 2: A RestACL Policy with two conditions

4. FORMAL COMPARISON WITH XACML

In order to show the expressive potentials of RestACL, we compare it formally with XACML. We use XACML as object of comparison because it is established as the de facto standard for ABAC [2, 8]. Without loss of generality we focus on the core elements of XACML.

4.1 Formal Description of XACML

XACML uses *policy sets*, *policies* and *rules* to model access control. Each of these elements has a *target* that describes if the element is applicable to an access request. In Addition, policy sets and policies declare a *combining algorithm* that determines access decisions in case that multiple elements can be applied. Finally, rules declare an *effect*. Figure 1 shows an example of a XACML security policy in an abstract presentation avoiding less importing details and the longish XML syntax. The example policy grants **GET** access to a web resource to subjects named **Alice**.

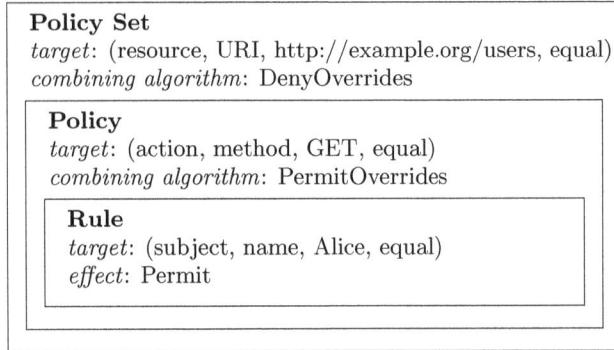

Policy Set
target: (resource, URI, http://example.org/users, equal)
combining algorithm: DenyOverrides

  Policy
  target: (action, method, GET, equal)
  combining algorithm: PermitOverrides

    Rule
    target: (subject, name, Alice, equal)
    effect: Permit

Figure 1: A XACML security policy protecting a web resource

Because we want to compare RestACL and XACML formally, we introduce the following abstract syntax:

Definition (Attribute): We define an attribute as a triple $a := (c, d, v)$ consisting of a category g, a designator d and a value v. Category, designator and value are all types like integers or character sequences. Further we define A as the set of attributes.

Definition (Attribute Condition): We define an attribute condition as a quadruple $ac := (c, d, f, v)$ consisting of a category c and a designator d to identify attributes plus a comparison function f that is used to compare the attributes value with another value v and. Further we define AC as the set of attribute conditions.

Definition (Target): We define $t := (ac_1 \circ ... \circ ac_n)$ as a XACML target with $ac_i \in AC$, $i \in 1, ..., n$ and $\circ$ representing a logical conjunction resp. disjunction. Further we define T as the set of targets.

Definition (Rule): We define $r := (t, e)$ as a XACML rule with $t \in T$ and e being the resulting effect with $e \in \{Permit, Deny\}$.

Definition (Policy): We define the triple $p := (R, t, l)$ as a XACML policy with R being a list of rules that are contained in p, $t \in T$ and l being a combining algorithm. A complete list of combining algorithms can be found in the XACML standardization documents [1].

Definition (Policy Set): We define $ps := (PS, P, t, l)$ as a XACML policy set with PS being the list of subordinated policy sets that are contained in ps. Further we define P as the list of policies that are contained in ps, $t \in T$ and l being a combining algorithm.

With theses definitions, the example shown in Figure 1 can be written as:

$$
\begin{aligned}
t_{ps_1} &= & ((resource, URI, equal, example.org/users)) \\
t_{p_1} &= & ((action, method, equal, GET)) \\
t_{r_1} &= & ((subject, name, equal, Alice)) \\
ps_1 &= & (\emptyset, \{p_1\}, t_{ps_1}, DenyOverrides) \\
p_1 &= & (\{r_1\}, t_{p_1}, PermitOverrides) \\
r_1 &= & (t_{r_1}, Permit)
\end{aligned}
$$

One can see that a rule becomes applicable to an access request if the target of the rule itself, the target of the policy and the targets of all superordinate policy sets are applicable to the request. For example r_1 becomes applicable to an access request if the targets t_{r_1}, t_{p_1} and t_{ps_1} are applicable to the request.

Definition (Target Path): We define $t'_r := \{t_r \wedge t_{p_r} \wedge t_{ps_{1_r}} \wedge ... \wedge t_{ps_{n_r}}\}$ as the set of targets that must be applicable for a XACML rule r to become applicable to an access request with t_r being the target of the rule r, t_{p_r} being the target of the policy p_r that contains r and $t_{ps_{1_r}}...t_{ps_{n_r}}$ being the targets of all superordinate policy sets of p_r.

XACML obligations, advices and rule conditions are out of the scope of this work. Obligations and advices are concepts that can be taken one by one to RestACL and therefore a closer analysis is not interesting. Rule conditions are a similar concept to targets of rules and can be expressed as RestACL conditions, too.

4.2 Formal Description of RestACL

We also want to describe RestACL in a more formal way. We use Greek letters to ease the differentiation to XACML.

Definition (Policy): We define a RestACL policy as triple $\rho := (\varepsilon, \pi, (ac_1 \circ ... \circ ac_n))$ with $\varepsilon \in \{Permit, Deny\}$ being an effect, $\pi \in \mathbb{N}$ being a priority and $\{ac_1, ..., ac_n\}$ being a set of attribute conditions analog to attribute conditions in XACML.

Definition (Access): We define a RestACL access as a pair $\alpha := (\{\mu_1, ...\mu_n\}, \{\rho_1, ..., \rho_m\})$ with μ_i being a method of the Uniform Interface, $i \in 1, ..., n$ and ρ_j being a policy, $j \in 1, ..., m$.

Definition (Resource): We define a RestACL resource as a triple $\sigma := (\phi, \{\alpha_1, ..., \alpha_n\}, \{\sigma'_1, ..., \sigma'_m\})$ with ϕ being the path of a resource (e.g. /users), α_i being access elements, $i \in 1...n$ and σ'_j being subresources of the resource σ, $j \in 1...m$

Definition (Domain): We define a RestACL domain as a pair $\varphi := (v, \{\sigma_1, ..., \sigma_n\})$ with v being the host for which the access control system is responsible and σ_i being resources in that domain, $i \in 1...n$.

With theses definitions, the example shown in Listing 1 can be written as:

$$
\begin{aligned}
\alpha_1 &= & (\{GET, PUT\}, \{P1, P2, P3\}) \\
\alpha_2 &= & (\{DELETE\}, \{P4\}) \\
\alpha_3 &= & (\{POST\}, \{P5\}) \\
\sigma_1 &= & (/1, \{\alpha_2\}, \emptyset) \\
\sigma_2 &= & (/users, \{\alpha_1\}, \sigma_1) \\
\sigma_3 &= & (/photos, \{\alpha_3\}, \emptyset) \\
\varphi &= & (example.org, \{\sigma_2, \sigma_3\})
\end{aligned}
$$

4.3 Transformation to XACML

In this section we describe how a security policy written in RestACL can be transformed into a XACML security policy. This transformation can be used as a convenient and practical way to describe the semantics of RestACL. As we saw in the previous sections, RestACL assigns access rights to individual resources and methods. Therefore, the first step is to create a root policy set in XACML that targets the host of the RestACL domain and then create subordinated policy sets for each resource. Because resource addresses are unique we can use $FirstApplicable$ as the combining algorithm for those policy sets. More precisely expressed for all resources σ_i that are covered by the domain φ we create a XACML policy set ps_{σ_i} as follows:

$$ps_{\sigma_i} := (\emptyset, P_{\sigma_i}, t_{ps_{\sigma_i}}, FirstApplicable)$$

P_{σ_i} is calculated in a second step. The target $t_{ps_{\sigma_i}}$ has exactly one attribute condition which can be written as:

$$t_{ps_{\sigma_i}} = ((resource, path, \phi_{\sigma_i}, equal))$$

For the domain φ we create a root XACML policy set ps_{root} as follows:

$$ps_{root} := (\cup_i ps_{\sigma_i}, \emptyset, t_{ps_{root}}, FirstApplicable)$$

Like before also the target $t_{ps_{root}}$ contains only one attribute condition:

$$t_{ps_{root}} = ((domain, host, v_\varphi, equal))$$

For example, the XACML policy sets for the user list given in Listing 1 can be written as:

$$
\begin{aligned}
t_{ps_{root}} &= ((resource, host, equal, example.org)) \\
t_{ps_{\sigma_1}} &= ((resource, path, equal, /users)) \\
ps_{root} &= (\cup_i ps_{\sigma_i}, \emptyset, t_{ps_{root}}, FirstApplicable) \\
ps_{\sigma_1} &= (\emptyset, P_{\sigma_1}, t_{ps_{\sigma_1}}, FirstApplicable)
\end{aligned}
$$

In the second step we need to convert the access elements of resources σ_i to XACML policies and add these policies to P_{σ_i}. Therefore we create a XACML policy for each method μ_i in every access element α_j as follows:

$$p_{i_{\alpha_j}} := (R_{i_{\alpha_j}}, t_{p_{i_{\alpha_j}}}, FirstApplicable)$$

The target of $p_{i_{\alpha_j}}$ has exactly one attribute condition in case of an access element that can be written as:

$$t_{p_{i_{\alpha_j}}} = ((action, method, \mu_{i_{\alpha_j}}, equal))$$

For example the XACML policies for the user list given in Listig 1 can be written as:

$$
\begin{aligned}
t_{p_{1_{\alpha_1}}} &= (action, method, equal, GET) \\
t_{p_{2_{\alpha_1}}} &= (action, method, equal, PUT) \\
p_{1_{\alpha_1}} &= (R_{1_{\alpha_1}}, t_{p_{1_{\alpha_1}}}, FirstApplicable) \\
p_{2_{\alpha_1}} &= (R_{2_{\alpha_1}}, t_{p_{2_{\alpha_1}}}, FirstApplicable)
\end{aligned}
$$

These policies are subordinated to the policy sets created in the first step. For our example that means:

$$P_{\sigma_1} = \{p_{1_{\alpha_1}}, p_{2_{\alpha_1}}\}$$

The third step is to create one XACML rule r_{ρ_i} for each RestACL policy ρ_i that is mentioned in the access elements α_j. We do this as follows:

$$r_{\rho_i} := ((a_{1_{\rho_i}} \circ ... \circ a_{n_{\rho_i}}), \varepsilon_{\rho_i})$$

The target for an XACML rule r_1 for the example RestACL policy shown in Listing 2 can be written as:

$$
\begin{aligned}
ac_{1_{P1}} &= (subject, clearance, greater, 10) \\
ac_{2_{P1}} &= (resource, privacylevel, equal, secret) \\
t_{r_1} &= ac_{1_{P1}} \wedge ac_{2_{P1}}
\end{aligned}
$$

The new XACML rules then are inserted into the policies in decreasing order of the priorities of their corresponding RestACL policy. For example if the policies for the user list mentioned in Figure 1 have the priorities $\pi_{\rho_{P1}} = 1, \pi_{\rho_{P2}} = 2$ then we can determine $R_{1_{\alpha_1}} = \{r_{P1}, r_{P2}\}$, $R_{2_{\alpha_1}} = \{r_{P1}, r_{P2}\}$.

4.4 Transformation to RestACL

In this section we describe how XACML policy sets, policies and rules for a RESTful API can be transformed into a RestACL security policy having a resource hierarchy and prioritized policies for each resource. We want to show that all XACML policies can be transformed to RestACL.

4.4.1 Mapping Rules

A request to a RESTful service must contain the address of the resource (the URI) and the method that is used to access the resource. Further we will refer to attribute conditions that address the resource address resp. the access method as a_{res} resp. a_{met}. To create a RestACL policy from an XACML rule, all attribute conditions contained in the target path t'_r become attribute conditions in the corresponding RestACL policy, except a_{res} and a_{met}. a_{met} is used to create an access element and a_{res} is used to map the access element into the resource hierarchy of a RestACL domain.

A formal way to describe this transformation is the following. For any rule r in the XACML security policy we create a mapped policy ρ_r in RestACL. Because the targets of a target path are logically conjuncted and logical conjunctions are commutative, we can write the target path of rule r as:

$$t'_r = ((ac_1 \circ ... \circ ac_n) \wedge ac_{res} \wedge ac_{met})$$

As a first step we construct t''_r as t'_r without a_{res} and a_{met}:

$$t''_r = (ac_1 \circ ... \circ ac_n)$$

Then we create a the policy ρ_r as follows:

$$\rho_r := (e_r, \pi_{\rho_r}, t''_r)$$

That means, the remaining attribute conditions in t''_r are mapped to the attribute conditions of the new policy ρ_r. The effect is mapped, too. The priority π_{ρ_r} is calculated in a separate step as described in the next section.

In a second step we create an access α_r for the RestACL domain description derived from a_{met} as follows:

$$\alpha_r := (\{\mu_1, ..., \mu_n\}_{a_{met}}, \{\rho_r\})$$

That means the values of the attribute condition a_{met} are mapped to a list of access methods. For example:

$$a_{met} = (action, method, POST, equal) \rightarrow \{POST\}_{a_{met}}$$

If the target path of the XACML rule does not describe any conditions about the access method (which is equivalent to a_{met} being a condition that is always met) we need to add all methods of the unified interface to the list of methods of α_r. Also the new policy ρ_r is added to the policy list of α_r.

In the third step the resource element σ_r that is associated with the attribute condition a_{res} needs to be identified within the RestACL domain. Therefore the resource address must be constructed from the path ϕ_σ of a resource σ, the path of all the superordinate resources and the host of the RestACL domain. If the resource address fulfills a_{res} then σ can be identifed as σ_r and the access element α_r is added to the access list of σ_r. If a_{res} covers several resources, multiple resource elements need to be identified and the access element α_r needs to be added to all these resource elements. If a_{res} does not state any condition about the resource address (which is equivalent to a_{res} being a condition that is always met) we need to add the access element α_r to all resources of the RestACL domain.

Using these three steps, the XACML example given in Figure 1 can be transformed as follows: The target path of the rule consists of three conditions: the target condition of the policy set, the target condition of the policy and the target condition of the rule. In the first step the condition of the policy set can be identified as ac_{res} and the condition of the policy as ac_{met}. Therefore we can construct $t''_{rule} = (ac_{rule}) = (subject, name, equal, alice)$. Because the rule declares the effect **permit**, we create a new RestACL policy $\rho_{rule} := (permit, \pi_{\rho_{rule}}, (subject, name, equal, alice))$. The priority $\pi_{\rho_{rule}}$ is calculated as described in section 4.2. In the second step we derive an access element from a_{met}. Because a_{met} only addresses the access method **GET** we construct the access element as: $\alpha_r := (GET, \{\rho_{rule}\})$. Finally, we create a resource element from a_{res} as follows: $\sigma := (http://www.example.org/users, \{\alpha_{rule}\}, \emptyset)$. This resource element is added to the domain.

4.4.2 Assigning Priorities

In a last step the priorities for the RestACL policies have to be calculated. Therefore we have to look at the XACML combining algorithm. Imagine a XACML policy with the combining algorithm *PermitOverrides* and several rules with different effects. It is obvious that the corresponding RestACL policies to XACML rules with the effect *Permit* must be higher prioritized than the rules with the effect *Deny*. In a similar way the prioritization can be done for the algorithm *DenyOverrides* and for the algorithm *FirstApplicable* priorities are assigned in a decreasing order. The algorithm *OnlyOneApplicable* acts the same as the algorithm *FirstApplicable* except that the evaluation is continued after the first applicable rule is found and an undetermined result is returned in case a second rule might be applicable.

We decided to not support such an algorithm because the priority concept is easy to understand and it would have a negative impact on the performance of the evaluation because all rules have to be evaluated for an access request. The semantics of the combining concept is very complex, hence the task of calculating priorities becomes challenging when multiple XACML policy sets and policies have different combining algorithms and multiple rules have different effects. The evaluation of XACML targets is done in a top-down fashion. But the decision making is then done in a bottom-up fashion. In order to determine a priority we need to determine combinations of applicable and non-applicable rules that force an effect to be passed up to the superordinated policy set and to become the final access decision.

Figure 2 shows a XACML policy graph with different combining algorithms and effects. According to the transforma-

tion described in section 4.4.1 this XACML security policy is transformed into four RestACL policies $\rho_{r_1}, ..., \rho_{r_4}$. The combining algorithm of p_1 indicates that the priority of ρ_{r_1} must be greater than the priority of ρ_{r_2}. Therefore we assign $\pi_{\rho_{r_1}} = 1$ and $\pi_{\rho_{r_2}} = 0$. From the combining algorithm of p_2 we can derive $\pi_{\rho_{r_3}} = 1$ and $\pi_{\rho_{r_4}} = 0$. From the combining algorithm of ps_1 we can derive two more priorities. First, we can derive that in case that r_1 is not applicable the priority of ρ_{r_2} has to be greater than the priority of ρ_{r_3}. Because r_1 must not be applicable in case that the effect is passed to ps_1, we need an additional policy that describes this behavior. The policy has to match the attribute conditions of t''_{r_2} and the negated attribute conditions of t_{r_1}. We note this new policy $\rho_{\overline{r_1}r_2}$ and assign the priority $\pi_{\rho_{\overline{r_1}r_2}} = 2$. The priority has to be greater because it is derived from a superordinated policy set of p_1. Second, we can derive that in case that r_3 is not applicable the priority of ρ_{r_4} has to be greater than the priority of ρ_{r_1}. Again we need a new policy that matches the attribute conditions of t''_{r_4} and the negated attribute conditions of t_{r_3} and assign the priority $\pi_{\rho_{\overline{r_3}r_4}} = 2$. Because the new policies are derived from ps_1 they have the dominating effect of ps_1 which is *Deny*. The dominating effect of *PermitOverrides* is *Permit*. In case *FirstApplicable* is the combining algorithm from which priorities are derived, no new policies need to be created. In that case the rules of the subordinated XACML policies resp. policy sets are prioritized in decreasing order with respect to the prioritization within a single policy resp. policy set.

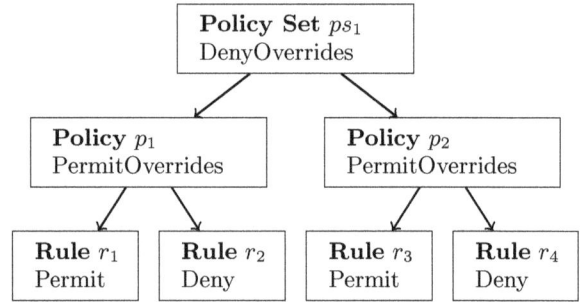

Figure 2: Different combining algorithms and effects

A formal way to describe the calculation of priorities is the following. We note effect *Permit* as P, the effect *Deny* as D, the combining algorithm *PermitOverrides* as PO, the combining algorithm *DenyOverrides* as DO and the combining algorithm *FirstApplicable* as FA. Initially all RestACL policies have the priority 0. We then assign the priorities depending on the combining algorithm of the XACML policy that contains r.

$$\forall r \in p : \pi_{\rho_r} = \begin{cases} 1 & \text{if } e_r = P \wedge l_{p_r} = PO \\ 1 & \text{if } e_r = D \wedge l_{p_r} = DO \\ pos_p^{-1}(r) & \text{if } l_{p_r} = FA \end{cases}$$

with $pos_p^{-1}(r)$ returning the position of r in inverse order. For example if a policy p contains 3 rules, $pos_p^{-1}(r)$ returns 2 for the first rule, 1 for the second and 0 for the third.

We then recursively create new RestACL policies and increase the priorities in a bottom-up fashion over the graph of XACML policy sets until the root node is reached. We define π_{max} as the highest priority within RestACL policies related to a XACML policy set ps at the beginning of the priority calculation for ps. We create new policies as follows:

$$\rho_{new} = \rho_{r_i \overline{r_j}...\overline{r_k}}$$

for all $r_j...r_k \in SUB_{ps}$ with SUB_{ps} being the set of rules in subordinated policies of ps. Additionally $r_j...r_k$ must be in the same subordinated policy or policy set as r_i. The RestACL policies need only be created if either (1) or (2) is met and (3) is met.

$$l_{ps} = PO \wedge e_{r_i} = P \wedge \forall e_x \in \{e_{r_j}, ..., e_{r_k}\} : e_x = D \quad (1)$$

$$l_{ps} = DO \wedge e_{r_i} = D \wedge \forall e_x \in \{e_{r_j}, ..., e_{r_k}\} : e_x = P \quad (2)$$

$$\forall \pi_{\rho_{r_x}} \in \{\pi_{\rho_{r_j}}, ..., \pi_{\rho_{r_k}}\} : \pi_{\rho_{r_x}} > \pi_{\rho_{r_i}} \quad (3)$$

Newly created RestACL policies get the priority $\pi_{\rho_{new}} = \pi_{max} + 1$.

If we have a look at our example again r_2 has the effect *Deny* and ps_1 the combining algorithm *DenyOverrides*. We now have to check all rules in the same branch of r_2 that have the effect *Permit*. If one or more of those rules prevent that r_2 determines the access decision, we have to create a new RestACL policiy that concatenates r_2 and those rules. In the example r_1 is in the same branch and prevents that r_2 determines the access decision. This is because the combining algorithm of p_1 states that the priority of r_1 must be higher than the priority of r_2. That means we have to create a new policy.

After new RestACL policies have been created we have to increase the priorities of all existing policies if necessary. This is done as follows:

$$\forall r \in ps : \pi_{\rho_r} = \begin{cases} \pi_{max} + 1 & \text{if (4)} \vee \text{(5)} \\ \pi_{\rho_r} + off_{ps}(r) & \text{if } l_{ps} = FA \end{cases}$$

$$l_{ps} = PO \wedge e_r = P \wedge \exists r' \in SUB_{ps} : e_{r'} = D \wedge \pi_{r'} \geq \pi_r \quad (4)$$

$$l_{ps} = DO \wedge e_r = D \wedge \exists r' \in SUB_{ps} : e_{r'} = P \wedge \pi_{r'} \geq \pi_r \quad (5)$$

That means, the priority has to be increased if the rule has the dominating effect of the policy set or if the combining algorithm of the policy set is *FirstApplicable*. In the first case the rule gets the priority $\pi_{max} + 1$ so that it becomes the highest prioritized rule in the policy set. In the second case the function $off_{ps}(r)$ is used to calculate an offset that is added to the priority of the corresponding policy. The offset equals to the number of rules that are contained in all policy sets and policies that are evaluated after the policy set or policy that contains r. For example if a first policy set contains 2 rules, a second contains 4 rules and a third contains 3 rules then the offset for the first policy set is 7, the offset for the second is 3 and the offset for the third is 0.

Because the priority calculation procedure is one fundamental step in the transformation operation, we want to give a detailed example to ease the understanding of the details of the procedure. Figure 3 shows a tree of XACML Policy Sets named ps_1, ps_2 and ps_3 containing the Policies p_1 to p_5. The Policies declare Rules r_1 to r_{10}.

Initially we set the priorities of all RestACL policies to 0. Depending on the combining algorithm and the effect of the XACML rules, we assign a priority of 1 to the corresponding RestACL policies. For example, the XACML Rule r_2 overrides the result of Rule r_1 and gets the priority of 1. If the combining algorithm is FirstApplicable, we assign priorities to corresponding RestACL policies in a decreasing order.

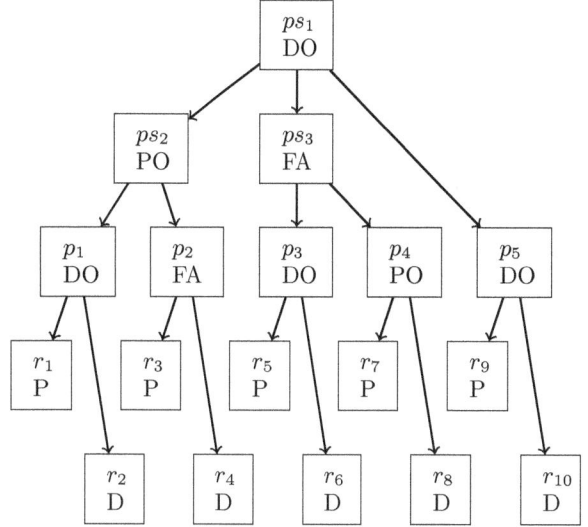

Figure 3: XACML combining algorithm and effects

$$\begin{aligned} p_1 &\Rightarrow & \pi_{\rho_{r_2}} &= 1 \\ p_2 &\Rightarrow & \pi_{\rho_{r_3}} &= 1 \\ p_3 &\Rightarrow & \pi_{\rho_{r_6}} &= 1 \\ p_4 &\Rightarrow & \pi_{\rho_{r_7}} &= 1 \\ p_5 &\Rightarrow & \pi_{\rho_{r_{10}}} &= 1 \end{aligned}$$

The next step is the calculation of priorities that are derived from the XACML policy sets. If we start with ps_2, we need to find all combinations of rules that pass the effect *Permit* up to ps_2 and assign their corresponding RestACL policies a higher priority if necessary. If we create new policies the priority of the new policy must be greater than the highest priority that has already be assigned related to ps_2.

$$ps_2 \Rightarrow \quad \pi_{\rho_{r_1 \overline{r_2}}} = 2$$

r_1 produces a *Permit* but only if r_2 is not applicable. If r_2 is applicable, p_1 will override the effect of r_1. Therefore, we need a new RestACL policy that has a higher priority than ρ_{r_2}. The effect of the new policy is *Permit* because r_1 has the effect *Permit*. In Addition, we can derive from ps_2 that the priority of ρ_{r_3} must be higher than the priority of ρ_{r_2}.

$$ps_2 \Rightarrow \quad \pi_{\rho_{r_3}} = 2$$

r_3 also produces a *Permit* regardless if r_4 is applicable or not. Therefore, ρ_{r_3} needs a higher priority than ρ_{r_2}.

Policy set ps_3 has the combining algoritm *FirstApplicable* and therefore no new RestACL policies need to be created but the existing policies must be ordered with respect to the subordinated policies. That means, the policies related to XACML rules contained in p_3 must have a higher priority than the policies related to rules contained in p_4. Therefore, we increase the priority of ρ_{r_6} and ρ_{r_5} with respect to the priorities they had before, what means $\pi_{\rho_{r_6}}$ must still be greater than $\pi_{\rho_{r_5}}$. Therefore, we add an offset of 2 to both priorities because the number of rules that are evaluated in the same branch regarding ps_3 after the rules of p_3 is 2.

$$\begin{aligned} p_3 &\Rightarrow & \pi_{\rho_{r_6}} &= 3 \\ p_4 &\Rightarrow & \pi_{\rho_{r_5}} &= 2 \end{aligned}$$

Finally, we have to derive priorities from ps_1. ps_1 has the combining algorithm *DenyOverrides* and therefore we have to identify the rule combinations that produce a *Deny*.

$$ps_1 \Rightarrow \quad \pi_{\rho_{r_2\overline{r_3}}} = 4$$

r_2 produces a *Deny* but only if r_3 is not applicable. The new policy $\rho_{r_2\overline{r_3}}$ has the effect *Deny*. The priority must be higher than any priority which has been assigned to policies related to ps_1. In the same way we can derive three more priorities leading to the final priorities shown in Table 3.

$$ps_1 \Rightarrow \quad \pi_{\rho_{r_4\overline{r_3}r_1}} = 4$$
$$ps_1 \Rightarrow \quad \pi_{\rho_{r_8\overline{r_5}r_7}} = 4$$
$$ps_1 \Rightarrow \quad \pi_{\rho_{r_{10}}} = 4$$

π	4	4	4	4	3	2
$\rho_{r_i\ldots r_j}$	$\rho_{r_{10}}$	$\rho_{r_2\overline{r_3}}$	$\rho_{r_4\overline{r_3}r_1}$	$\rho_{r_8\overline{r_5}r_7}$	ρ_{r_6}	ρ_{r_3}
ε	D	D	D	D	D	P

π	2	2	1	1	0	0	0	0
$\rho_{r_i\ldots r_j}$	ρ_{r_5}	$\rho_{r_1\overline{r_2}}$	ρ_{r_2}	ρ_{r_7}	ρ_{r_1}	ρ_{r_4}	ρ_{r_8}	ρ_{r_9}
ε	P	P	D	P	P	D	D	P

Table 1: Priority results of the transformation algorithm

5. RELATED WORK

An approach that covers the formalization of XACML is given in [9]. The approach provides an alternative syntax that should help software developers to ease the creation of security policies. In [10] an approach is shown that formalizes the reduction of access decisions for compositional security policies and access control systems. The approach investigates XACML combining algorithm in detail and provides solutions how different access decisions can be combined to one final decision that can be enforced. Our approach in contrast transforms any combining algorithm into a priority driven solution. The topic of compositional security policies is handled in [3], too. This work provides a language that splits target definition and policy composition into different areas. Our access control mechanism works similar, but with respect to the constraints defined by REST. While the aforementioned approaches formalize dedicated aspects of access control mechanisms, an approach described in [7] gives a formalized description of an attribute based access control model.

6. CONCLUSIONS

This work compares a language with a formally defined authorization model for RESTful Services with XACML providing formal evidence for the RestACL language. We showed that the language has a comparable expressive strength as XACML. The compositional approach of XACML uses nested policy sets and combining algorithms. The description of the transformation from XACML to RestACL in due consideration of the standard combining strategies conveys an impression of the complex semantics of XACML. As a consequence, it is a challenging and sophisticated task for system administrators and security engineers to define understandable and correct policy sets with XACML. Priorities are a meaningful alternative to XACML combining algorithm especially in environments with frequently changing security policies, because they enable a simple integration of new policies. The application of priorities and the mapping between resources and policies enables an efficient and scalable access control system for RESTful services. As mentioned in section 3.2, another parallel research contribution [5] provides practical evidence for RestACL by reporting experimental results of a prototype implementation.

7. REFERENCES

[1] Extensible Access Control Markup Language (XACML) Version 3.0. *Organization for the Advancement of Structured Information Standards (OASIS)*, 2013.

[2] N. Ammar, E. Bertino, Z. Malik, and A. Rezgui. XACML Policy Evaluation with Dynamic Context Handling. *IEEE Transactions on Knowledge and Data Engineering, Volume 27*, 2015.

[3] J. Crampton and C. Morisset. PTaCL: A Language for Attribute-Based Access Control in Open Systems. *POST '12 Proceedings of the First International Conference on Principles of Security and Trust*, 2012.

[4] T. R. Fielding. *Architectural Styles and the Design of Network-based Software Architectures*. University of California, Irvine, 2000.

[5] M. Hüffmeyer and U. Schreier. Analysis of an Access Control System for RESTful Services. *ICWE '16 - International Conference on Web Engineering*, 2016.

[6] M. Hüffmeyer and U. Schreier. RestACL - An Attribute Based Access Control Language for RESTful Services. *ABAC '16 - Proceedings of the 1st Workshop on Attribute Based Access Control*, 2016.

[7] X. Jin, R. Krishnan, and R. Sandhu. A Unified Attribute-Based Access Control Model Covering DAC, MAC and RBAC. *DBSec '12 - Proceedings of the 26th Annual Conference on Data and Applications Security and Privacy*, 2012.

[8] A. Liu, F. Chen, J. Hwang, and T. Xie. XEngine: A Fast and Scalable XACML Policy Evaluation Engine. *SIGMETRICS '08 - Proceedings of the 2008 ACM International Conference on Measurement and Modeling of Computer Systems*, 2008.

[9] M. Masi, R. Pugliese, and F. Tiezzi. Formalisation and Implementation of the XACML Access Control Mechanism. *ESSoS '12 Proceedings of the 4th Iinternational Conference on Engineering Secure Software and Systems*, 2012.

[10] C. Morisset and N. Zannone. Reduction of Access Control Decisions. *SACMAT '14 Proceedings of the 19th ACM Symposium on Access Control Models and Technologies*, 2014.

[11] L. Richardson and M. Amundsen. *RESTful Web APIs*. O'Reilly Media, 2013.

[12] R. Sandhu. The authorization leap from rights to attributes: maturation or chaos? *SACMAT '12 - Proceedings of the 17th ACM Symposium on Access Control Models and Technologies*, 2012.

[13] J. Webber, S. Parastatidis, and I. Robinson. *REST in Practice*. O'Reilly Media, 2010.

GemRBAC-DSL: a High-level Specification Language for Role-based Access Control Policies

Ameni Ben Fadhel, Domenico Bianculli, Lionel Briand
University of Luxembourg, Luxembourg, Luxembourg
{ameni.benfadhel,domenico.bianculli,lionel.briand}@uni.lu

ABSTRACT

A role-based access control (RBAC) policy restricts a user to perform operations based on her role within an organization. Several RBAC models have been proposed to represent different types of RBAC policies. However, the expressiveness of these models has not been matched by specification languages for RBAC policies. Indeed, existing policy specification languages do not support all the types of RBAC policies defined in the literature.

In this paper we aim to bridge the gap between highly-expressive RBAC models and policy specification languages, by presenting GEMRBAC-DSL, a new specification language designed on top of an existing, generalized conceptual model for RBAC. The language sports a syntax close to natural language, to encourage its adoption among practitioners. We also define semantic checks to detect conflicts and inconsistencies among the policies written in a GEMRBAC-DSL specification. We show how the semantics of GEMRBAC-DSL can be expressed in terms of an existing formalization of RBAC policies as OCL (Object Constraint Language) constraints on the corresponding RBAC conceptual model. This formalization paves the way to define a model-driven approach for the enforcement of policies written in GEMRBAC-DSL.

1. INTRODUCTION

In a role-based access control (RBAC) system, a user's request to access a resource or perform an operation is allowed or denied based on access control policies (also called authorization constraints) that take into account the role of the requester. Various types of RBAC policies have been proposed in the literature; in this paper, we refer to the policies classified in the taxonomy recently proposed in [7]. This taxonomy identifies eight types of RBAC policies: prerequisite [4,23], cardinality [2], precedence and dependency [24], role hierarchy [23], separation of duty (SoD) [3,25], binding of duty (BoD) [27], delegation and revocation [13,28], and contextual (both temporal and spatial) [10,19].

SACMAT '16, June 5–8, 2016, Shanghai, China.

© 2016 ACM. ISBN 978-1-4503-3802-8/16/06. . . $15.00

DOI: http://dx.doi.org/10.1145/2914642.2914656

Several RBAC models have been proposed to characterize the conceptual entities that are needed to represent these policies. The original, standardized RBAC96 model [23] supports only prerequisite, cardinality, role hierarchy, and simple SoD policies. Various extensions of this model have been defined to support additional policies. For example, support for delegation policies have been added in the models proposed in [13, 26, 28, 29]; the models introduced in [5, 9, 10, 19, 22] have added support for contextual policies. In our previous work [7] we proposed the GEMRBAC model, designed with the goal of integrating, in a coherent and comprehensive model, all the conceptual entities required to express the various types of RBAC polices proposed in the literature. We have also proposed the GEMRBAC+CTX model [8], which is an extension of the GEMRBAC model that adds support for richer and more expressive contextual policies.

On a par with the definition of complex and more expressive RBAC models, there is the problem of defining *policy specification languages* that are at least as expressive as the policies supported by the existing models. While RBAC models provide the fundamental concepts needed to formalize various types of RBAC policies, policy specification languages represent a means to express RBAC policies that can be used (for both policy definition and enforcement) in practice. One group of proposals to define such languages revolves around XACML [21], the OASIS standard for defining access control policy languages. Since XACML does not support RBAC models natively, it has been extended with profiles specific to RBAC [1,6]. Other types of RBAC policy languages are ontology-based [15,16] or logic-based [3,12,17] languages. The main problem of existing RBAC specification languages is that they do not support all the types of RBAC policies defined in the literature. For example, a simple delegation transfer policy like "any user with role r_1 can transfer her role to any user assigned to role r_2" cannot be expressed in any of the existing languages. Moreover, the semantics of some of these languages is not executable for the purpose of enforcing the policies specified with them. Furthermore, many of them are not designed to be used by practitioners.

These problems have practical implications, since the lack of expressive policy specification languages limits the adoption, among practitioners, of the more expressive RBAC models proposed in the literature. In turn, this situation makes practitioners use simple(r) RBAC models, resulting in systems underspecified from the point of view of access control. For example, the industrial partner for the research project in which this work has been carried out, is a provider of situational-aware information systems for emergency scenarios; given the criticality of such scenarios, highly-detailed role access control policies are an essential need for them. However, although our partner is aware of state-of-the-art proposals for expressive RBAC models, it could not adopt them in practice, because of the lack of a policy specification language as expressive as them. Besides the expressiveness, another requirement on the specification language stated by our partner is the possibility of interpreting the policies written in the language, with the purpose of automatically generating policy enforcement mechanisms.

In this paper we aim to bridge the gap between highly-expressive RBAC models and policy specification languages, by presenting GemRBAC-DSL, a new specification language for RBAC policies. The language has been designed to cover the various types of RBAC policies captured by the GemRBAC+CTX model. Being based on this model, the language is quite expressive (see Section 3 for a detailed comparison with the state-of-the-art). Moreover, GemRBAC-DSL sports a syntax close to natural language, to encourage its adoption among practitioners. Furthermore, we define semantic checks that can be run on a GemRBAC-DSL policy specification, to detect conflicting and inconsistent policy definitions (e.g., a conflict between two policies, one defining an SoD policy and another one defining a BoD policy *for the same set of permissions*). We have built an editor for the language based on the XText framework and the Eclipse platform, and integrated the semantics checks in it.

The GemRBAC+CTX model and its ancestor GemRBAC, which have inspired the design of GemRBAC-DSL, come with an operationalization of the semantics of the policies they support. This operationalization is defined following a model-driven approach, in which the semantics of each RBAC policy is expressed as an OCL (Object Constraint Language) constraint on the RBAC model. Since the expressiveness of GemRBAC-DSL is the same as that of the GemRBAC+CTX model, we define the semantics of GemRBAC-DSL by mapping the constructs of the language to the corresponding OCL constraints defined for the GemRBAC+CTX model in [7, 8]. This mapping allows users of GemRBAC-DSL to benefit from the model-driven approach for policy enforcement proposed in [7, 8]. Indeed, a policy written in GemRBAC-DSL can be enforced by evaluating the corresponding OCL constraint (as defined in the mapping) on an instance of the GemRBAC+CTX model obtained from the system in which the policy is being enforced. This model-driven approach for policy enforcement can be used both at design time and at run time and relies on standardized technologies, supported by industry-strength tools (such as Eclipse OCL [14]).

Summing up, the main contributions of the paper are: (a) the definition of the GemRBAC-DSL specification language for RBAC policies; (b) the definition of the semantic checks for a GemRBAC-DSL policy specification; (c) a publicly-available implementation of an editor to write policies in GemRBAC-DSL and check for potential conflicts and inconsistencies among them.

The rest of the paper is organized as follows. Section 2 illustrates a motivating example for this work. Section 3 discusses the state of the art. Section 4 presents the language, illustrating the syntax and providing examples for each type of policy. Section 5 defines the semantic checks

for policies expressed in GemRBAC-DSL. Section 6 provides a brief overview of the semantics of the language. Section 7 discusses the design trade-offs and the limitations of GemRBAC-DSL, as well as its adoption by our industrial partner. Section 8 concludes the paper and provides directions for future work.

2. MOTIVATING EXAMPLE

In this section we illustrate an example of RBAC policy specifications that motivates our work. The example represents a subset of a real-world case study, defined in collaboration with our industrial partner, a provider of situational-aware information systems for emergency scenarios. The case study deals with the specification of the RBAC policies for a Web application that provides information related to humanitarian missions, ranging from satellite images to highly-confidential data about refugees and casualties. For space and confidentiality reasons we consider a small, sanitized subset of the system, but provide a representative list of policies that covers exhaustively all the types of RBAC policies used in the policy specifications of the case study.

We consider a humanitarian mission taking place from February 12, 2016 to June 8, 2016 in a geographical area symbolically known as "*Zone1*", delimited by four segments with coordinates (longitude and latitude in decimal degrees, elevation in meters): (15:24:200)–(20:27:200), (20:27:200)–(17:27:200), (17:27:200)–(15:27:200), (15:27:200)–(15:24:200). The mission defines four roles (*admin, assistant, trainee, participant*), four permissions (*add_casualty, modify_casualty, delete_casualty, save_satellitePhoto*), four operations (*create, read, update, delete*). The access control policies for this mission are:

PL1: To acquire role *trainee*, a user must be assigned to role *participant*.

PL2: Role *assistant* cannot be assigned to more than three users.

PL3: Role *trainee* is enabled only if role *admin* is active. The latter cannot be deactivated if the role *trainee* is still active.

PL4: If a user acquires role *assistant*, she will also acquire all its junior roles.

PL5: A user can acquire either role *assistant* or *trainee*.

PL6: A user can activate roles *assistant* and *admin* at the same time, as long as she does not perform all the operations (*create, read, update, delete*) on the same object (of type "casualty record").

PL7: The operations allowed by permissions *add_casualty, modify_casualty*, and *delete_casualty* should be performed by users having the same role.

PL8: In case a user assigned to role *admin* is on leave, she has to delegate all the permissions associated with her role to another user that is assigned to role *assistant*. The delegation lasts for two weeks; during this period the delegator is still allowed to execute the permissions associated with the role she has delegated. Moreover, the delegated role can be further delegated (by a delegate), with a maximum delegation depth of 2.

PL9: The delegation regulated by policy PL8 can be revoked by any user assigned to role *admin*. The revocation will not affect the (further) delegations of role *admin* possibly performed by delegated users. Moreover, the revocation will only remove the affected

Table 1: Support of policies in RBAC languages

	Prq	RH	Card	Prec	SoD					BoD	Context		Deleg	Rev
					S	D	Obj	Op	His		T	L		
RCL2000 [3]	-	+	+	-	+	+	-	-	-	-	-	-	-	-
FORBAC [12]	+	-	-	-	-	-	-	-	-	-	+	+	-	-
Tower [17]	+	+	+	+	+	+	+	+	+	-	-	-	+/-	+/-
XACML [1,6]	+	+	+	-	+	+	-	-	-	-	+	+	GT	-
X-RBAC [18]	+	+	+	-	+	+	+	-	-	-	+	+	-	-
X-GTRBAC [11]	+	+	+	-	+	+	+	-	-	-	-	+	-	-
ROWLBAC [16]	+	+	+	-	+	+	+	-	-	-	-	-	GT	-
XACML+OWL [15]	+	+	+	+	+	+	+	+	+	-	-	-	-	-
RBAC-DSL [26]	+	+	+	+	+	+	+	+	+	-	-	-	GT	+

Legend. Prq: Prerequisite; RH: Role Hierarchy; Card: Cardinality; Prec: Precedence and Dependency; S: Static SoD; D: Dynamic SoD; Obj: Object-based DSoD; Op: Operational-based DSoD, His: History-based DSoD, Deleg: Delegation.

users from the delegated role *admin*, and will not impact the other roles possibly acquired through a role hierarchy (of the delegated role).

PL10: Role *participant* is enabled for the entire duration of the mission.

PL11: Role *admin* is enabled only in zone *Zone1*.

PL12: Role *trainee* is enabled at 100 meters from the boundary inside *Zone1*.

The policies above show that defining the access control requirements of our example requires to deal with several types of policies (see taxonomy in [7]): prerequisite (PL1), cardinality (PL2), precedence (PL3), role hierarchy (PL4), SoD (PL5, PL6), BoD (PL7), delegation (PL8), revocation (PL9), contextual (PL10–PL12). To express these policies security engineers need a policy specification language *expressive enough* to support all of them. In the next section we review existing RBAC specification languages in terms of the policy types they support.

3. STATE OF THE ART

One of the first policy languages proposed for RBAC is RCL2000 [3], which is a formal language based on first-order predicate logic and defined on top of the RBAC96 model. The language supports only role hierarchy and separation of duty policies. FORBAC [12] is also an extension of RBAC based on first-order logic. It adds support for attributes in policies and numeric constraints; both features enable the definition of more complex policies, like those containing contextual constraints. However, FORBAC does not support role hierarchy, delegation, cardinality, and separation of duty. Furthermore, a limitation shared both by RCL2000 and FORBAC is the difficulty of use by practitioners, since both languages require a strong mathematical background. Tower [17] is a high-level specification language for access control policies; it supports delegation and history-based SoD policies. However, delegation and revocation policies are defined only as administrative operations for role-to-user assignment, i.e., in terms of adding/removing a role to/from a user.

Another research stream considers XML-based languages, starting from the definition of XACML (eXtensible Access Control Markup Language) [21]. XACML is a language for access control, standardized by the OASIS community. The XACML standard provides not only the specification language for access control policies but also a reference enforcement architecture. XACML is a general-purpose language for expressing various types of access control models and policies; being general-purpose, it does not support RBAC natively (e.g., sessions are not supported). RBAC support can be added to XACML by means of profiles. The OASIS RBAC profile for XACML [6] supports only role hierarchy and static separation of duty policies. Another RBAC profile of XACML [1] supports separation of duty, delegation, and context-based policies. X-RBAC [18] is an XML-based specification language for RBAC policies in multi-domain environments where authorization policies are distributed over several domains. X-RBAC supports context-based, role hierarchy, cardinality and separation of duty policies. X-GTRBAC [11] is a language defined on top of the GTRBAC model [19] for specifying RBAC policies for heterogeneous and distributed enterprise resources. X-GTRBAC adds the concept of user's credentials to the GTRBAC model: users are grouped according to their credentials. X-GTRBAC supports cardinality, separation of duty, role hierarchy, and temporal policies.

Another language, conceptually similar to XACML, is xfACL (eXtensible Functional Language for Access Control) [20]. xfACL is a general-purpose access control language, which tries to combine the benefits of XACML and RBAC. It is based on the specification of attributes for entities involved in decisions (e.g., users, operations) and supports auxiliary policies to extend its expressiveness. The latter is also its main drawback, since support for each type of policy has to be manually added by means of an auxiliary function.

Other languages deal with the integration of ontologies to provide a semantic interpretation of access control policies across different, heterogenous organizations, and to support advanced access control policies. For instance, ROWLBAC [16] is an ontology-based language that combines OWL (Web Ontology Language) and RBAC properties. The language supports the specification of prerequisite, role hierarchy, SoD, and delegation policies. The XACML+OWL framework [15] combines OWL and XACML. Role hierarchy and separation of duty policies are specified using OWL, while the XACML engine is used to make decisions for user access requests. The interactions between the XACML engine and the OWL ontology are defined through semantic functions.

RBAC DSL [26] is a domain-specific language for RBAC based on UML diagrams and OCL constraints. The corresponding meta-model includes two levels: the *policy* level and the *user Access* Level. The first level defines the basic RBAC concepts: roles, resources, permissions and operations. At this level, SoD, cardinality, and role hierarchy policies are represented as UML attributes and associations. The second level defines the concepts of user, session, resource access, and snapshot (i.e., an instance of an RBAC model at a specific time point). A predecessor/ successor relation is defined for the concept of user, session and access to identify the individual users, sessions and accesses over time. At this level, authorization policies are defined as OCL constraints based on the information available in the policy level. RBAC DSL supports also delegation and revocation policies. However, as acknowledged also in [8], defining RBAC policies as OCL constraints can be difficult, since it requires a high level of knowledge and expertise with OCL, especially in our case in which OCL constraints tend to be rather complex to express RBAC policies.

Table 1 summarizes the support for the various types of RBAC policies in the policy specification languages discussed above. The types of policies used for the comparison have been taken from the taxonomy in [7] and reflect the ones we have observed in our industrial case study. We remark that the specification of some type of policies, such as context-based and delegation, depends not only on the language but also on the underlying model.

One can see that none of these languages is expressive enough to express all the policies presented in Section 2, related to our industrial case study. Moreover, the analysis has also shown that the majority of existing policy specification languages is based on some formalism (either first-order logic fragments, including OCL, or ontology languages based on description logic) that require a strong theoretical and mathematical background, which is rarely found among practitioners. Hence, we contend that there is a need for an expressive specification language for RBAC policies that can also be used by practitioners.

4. THE GEMRBAC-DSL LANGUAGE

The GEMRBAC-DSL policy specification language has been designed as a domain-specific language built on top of the GEMRBAC+CTX model. The choice of the underlying model for the language has been dictated by the need to support a large variety of RBAC policies, like the ones used for the specification of our industrial case study (see Section 2). Hence, the language inherits the expressiveness of the GEMRBAC+CTX model (see [7,8]).

The main goal during the design of the language has been to encourage its use among practitioners. Indeed, the language captures the main RBAC concepts that security analysts are familiar with and allows for their specification using a syntax close to natural language. Furthermore, the language design process has incorporated the feedback provided by the security analysts of our industrial partner, who have commented on the expressiveness and the clarity of the language. At the time of writing, the language is being introduced into the security development lifecycle of our partner, to support the top-down definition of access control policies and enforcement mechanisms.

4.1 Syntax

The syntax of GEMRBAC-DSL is shown in Fig. 1, using the Backus-Naur Form (BNF) notation: non-terminal symbols are enclosed in angle brackets; terminal symbols are enclosed in single quotes; (derivation) rules are denoted with the ::= symbol; alternatives within a rule are indicated using a vertical bar; a star stands for zero or more occurrences

$\langle RBAC\text{-}definition \rangle ::= \langle preamble \rangle \; \langle policies \rangle$

$\langle preamble \rangle ::= \langle users \rangle \; \langle roles \rangle \; \langle permissions \rangle \; \langle operations \rangle$
$\quad \langle role\text{-}hierarchy \rangle \; \langle permission\text{-}hierarchy \rangle \; \langle geofences \rangle$

$\langle users \rangle ::= \text{`users:'} \; \langle user \rangle \; (\text{`,'} \; \langle user \rangle)^* \; \text{`;'}$

$\langle roles \rangle ::= \text{`roles:'} \; \langle role \rangle \; (\text{`,'} \; \langle role \rangle)^* \; \text{`;'}$

$\langle permissions \rangle ::= \text{`permissions:'}$
$\quad \langle permission \rangle \; (\text{`,'} \; \langle permission \rangle)^* \; \text{`;'}$

$\langle operations \rangle ::= \text{`operations:'}$
$\quad \langle operation \rangle \; (\text{`,'} \; \langle operation \rangle)^* \; \text{`;'}$

$\langle id \rangle ::= (\text{`a'-`z'} \; | \; \text{`A'-`Z'} \; | \; \text{`0'-`9'})+$

$\langle user \rangle ::= \langle id \rangle$

$\langle role \rangle ::= \langle id \rangle$

$\langle permission \rangle ::= \langle id \rangle$

$\langle operation \rangle ::= \langle id \rangle$

$\langle role\text{-}hierarchy \rangle ::= \text{`role-hierarchy:'}$
$\quad (\langle rHierarchy \rangle \; (\text{`,'} \; \langle rHierarchy \rangle)^* \; | \; \text{`none'}) \; \text{`;'}$

$\langle permission\text{-}hierarchy \rangle ::= \text{`permission-hierarchy:'}$
$\quad (\langle pHierarchy \rangle \; (\text{`,'} \; \langle pHierarchy \rangle)^* \; | \; \text{`none'}) \; \text{`;'}$

$\langle rHierarchy \rangle ::= \langle role \rangle \; \text{`: \{'} \; \langle role \rangle \; (\text{`,'} \; \langle role \rangle)^* \; \text{`\}'}$

$\langle pHierarchy \rangle ::= \langle permission \rangle$
$\quad \text{`: \{'} \; \langle permission \rangle \; (\text{`,'} \; \langle permission \rangle)^* \; \text{`\}'}$

$\langle geofence \rangle ::= \text{`geofences:'} \; (\langle geofence \rangle \; (\text{`,'} \; \langle geofence \rangle)^*$
$\quad | \; \text{`none'}) \; \text{`;'}$

$\langle geofence \rangle ::= \langle id \rangle$

$\langle policies \rangle ::= \text{`policies:'} \; (\langle policy \rangle \text{`;'})+$

$\langle policy \rangle ::= \langle id \rangle \; \text{`:'} \; (\langle Prerequisite \rangle \; | \; \langle Cardinality \rangle$
$\quad | \; \langle PrecEnabling \rangle \; | \; \langle Hierarchy \rangle \; | \; \langle SSoD \rangle \; | \; \langle DSoD \rangle$
$\quad | \; \langle BoD \rangle \; | \; \langle Delegation \rangle \; | \; \langle Revocation \rangle \; | \; \langle ContextPolicy \rangle)$

Figure 1: Grammar of GemRBAC-DSL

of an element; a plus stands for one or more occurrences of an element; square brackets denote optional elements.

A GEMRBAC-DSL policy specification (captured by the start symbol $\langle RBAC\text{-}definition \rangle$) contains a $\langle preamble \rangle$ and a list of $\langle policies \rangle$. The $\langle preamble \rangle$ contains the declaration of the main entities that will be used in the rest of the specification[1]: the list of users $\langle users \rangle$, the list of roles $\langle roles \rangle$, the list of permissions $\langle permissions \rangle$, and the list of operations $\langle operations \rangle$. The $\langle preamble \rangle$ contains also the list $\langle role\text{-}hierarchy \rangle$ of role hierarchy relations, and the list $\langle permission\text{-}hierarchy \rangle$ of permission hierarchy relations. Within these lists, each hierarchy relation ($\langle rHierarchy \rangle$ for role hierarchy and $\langle pHierarchy \rangle$ for permission hierarchy) declares the parent (role or permission) followed by the list of its junior (roles or permissions, respectively). The absence of role (or permission) hierarchies is explicitly denoted with the keyword 'none'. The $\langle preamble \rangle$ ends with the list $\langle geofences \rangle$ of logical locations, i.e., symbolic abstractions that refer to real physical locations [8]. All the lists used in the $\langle preamble \rangle$ are comma-separated and contain alphanu-

---

[1]Notice that the assignments of users to roles, of permissions to roles, and of operations to permissions *are not* specified with GEMRBAC-DSL. We assume that these assignments are defined in the RBAC system on which the policies are going to be enforced.

meric identifiers. Finally, the list of policies ⟨*policies*⟩ contains the actual policy specifications, where each policy is composed by an identifier and by its body.

The following subsections illustrate each type of policy supported by GEMRBAC-DSL; for each policy, we include a short definition, the syntax, its explanation, and an example of specification based on the policies defined in Section 2.

4.2 Prerequisite policy

A prerequisite policy defines a precondition on a role or a permission assignment: to acquire a role (or a permission), a user must have been already assigned to another role (or permission) [4, 23]. The syntax for this policy is:

$$⟨Prerequisite⟩ := ⟨PrereqRole⟩ \mid ⟨PrereqPermission⟩ \quad (1)$$

$$⟨PrereqRole⟩ ::= \text{`assign-role'} ⟨role1⟩ \text{`prerequisite'} \quad (2)$$
$$⟨role2⟩$$

$$⟨PrereqPermission⟩ ::= \text{`assign-permission'} \quad (3)$$
$$⟨permission1⟩ \text{`prerequisite'} ⟨permission2⟩$$

The syntax uses keywords for defining a prerequisite policy either at the role (keyword 'assign-role' in rule 2) or at permission level (keyword 'assign-permission' in rule 3). In rule 2, ⟨*role2*⟩ corresponds to the precondition for the assignment of ⟨*role1*⟩. Similarly, in rule 3, ⟨*permission2*⟩ corresponds to the precondition for the assignment of ⟨*permission1*⟩. For example, the prerequisite policy on role assignment PL1 is expressed in GEMRBAC-DSL as:

```
PL1: assign-role trainee prerequisite
     participant;
```

4.3 Cardinality policy

A cardinality policy defines a bound on the cardinality of role activation and assignment relations [2]. Its syntax is:

$$⟨Cardinality⟩ ::= ⟨CardActivation⟩ \mid ⟨CardUser⟩ \quad (1)$$
$$\mid ⟨CardPermission⟩ \mid ⟨CardRoleToUser⟩$$
$$\mid ⟨CardRoleToPermission⟩$$

$$⟨CardActivation⟩ ::= \text{`maxActiveRoles ='} ⟨integer⟩ \quad (2)$$

$$⟨CardUser⟩ ::= \text{`maxUsers ='} ⟨integer⟩ \quad (3)$$
$$[\text{`only-for-role'} ⟨role⟩]$$

$$⟨CardPermission⟩ ::= \text{`maxPermissions ='} ⟨integer⟩ \quad (4)$$
$$[\text{`only-for-role'} ⟨role⟩]$$

$$⟨CardRoleToUser⟩ ::= \text{`maxRoles-User ='} ⟨integer⟩ \quad (5)$$
$$[\text{`only-for-user'} ⟨user⟩]$$

$$⟨CardRoleToPermission⟩ ::= \text{`maxRoles-Permission ='} \quad (6)$$
$$⟨integer⟩ [\text{`only-for-permission'} ⟨Permission⟩]$$

GEMRBAC-DSL supports five types of cardinality policies: maximum number of active roles within a session (rule 2), maximum number of users assigned to a role (rule 3), maximum number of permissions assigned to a role (rule 4), maximum number of roles assigned to a user (rule 5), maximum number of roles assigned to a permission (rule 6). In rules 2–6, ⟨*integer*⟩ represents the cardinality bound. In rules 3–6, if the optional element is omitted, it means that the bound will apply, respectively, to all roles (rules 3–4), all users (rule 5), all permissions (rule 6). For example, the cardinality policy on user-to-role assignment PL2 is expressed in GEMRBAC-DSL as:

```
PL2: maxUsers = 3 only-for-role assistant;
```

4.4 Precedence and dependency policies

A precedence policy establishes a precedence relationship between the enabling of a role and the activation of another one. A dependency policy restricts the deactivation of a role if another one is already active [24]. The syntax is:

$$⟨PrecEnabling⟩ ::= \text{`enable'} ⟨role1⟩ \text{` if active'} \quad (1)$$
$$⟨role2⟩ [\text{`,'} ⟨timeShift⟩] [\text{`deactivation-dependency'}]$$

$$⟨timeShift⟩ := \text{`after'} ⟨integer⟩ ⟨timeUnit⟩ \quad (2)$$

$$⟨timeUnit⟩ ::= \text{`second'} \mid \text{`minute'} \mid \text{`hour'} \mid \quad (3)$$
$$\text{`day'} \mid \text{`week'} \mid \text{`month'} \mid \text{`year'}$$

In rule 1, ⟨*role2*⟩ denotes the role whose activation has to precede the enabling of the role denoted by ⟨*role1*⟩. An optional ⟨*timeShift*⟩ can be specified to define the amount of time that has to pass between the role enabling and the role activation events (rules 2–3). The optional keyword 'deactivation-dependency' is used to express a dependency policy. For example, the precedence and dependency policy PL3 is expressed in GEMRBAC-DSL as:

```
PL3: enable trainee if active admin
     deactivation-dependency;
```

4.5 Role hierarchy policy

A hierarchy policy states that assigning a role r (respectively, a permission p) to a user u (respectively, a role s) implies assigning to u (respectively, s) also all the junior roles of r (respectively, the sub-permissions of p) [23]. Its syntax is defined as:

$$⟨Hierarchy⟩ ::= \text{`trigger-'} (⟨RoleHierarchy⟩ \quad (1)$$
$$\mid ⟨PermissionHierarchy⟩)$$

$$⟨RoleHierarchy⟩ ::= \text{`role-hierarchy'} ⟨role⟩ \quad (2)$$

$$⟨PermissionHierarchy⟩ ::= \text{`permission-hierarchy'} \quad (3)$$
$$⟨permission⟩$$

The syntax uses two different keywords for distinguishing between role hierarchy (rule 2) and permission hierarchy (rule 3). Notice that while the preamble of a GEMRBAC-DSL specification declares the role and permission hierarchy relations for the system, a security analyst has to explicitly define a role hierarchy policy (for a role or permission) to put the hierarchy relation(s) into effect. For example, the role hierarchy policy PL4 can be expressed as:

```
PL4: trigger-role-hierarchy assistant;
```

4.6 Separation of duty policy

A separation of duty (SoD) policy defines a mutual exclusion relation between users, roles, or permissions; mutually-exclusive entities involved in a SoD relation are called *conflicting*. SoD can be static or dynamic.

4.6.1 Static Separation of duty (SSoD)

An SSoD policy restricts the assignment of mutually exclusive roles, users, or permissions [2, 3]. Its syntax is:

$$⟨SSoD⟩ ::= ⟨SSoDCR⟩ \mid ⟨SSoDCU⟩ \mid ⟨SSoDCP⟩ \quad (1)$$

$$⟨SSoDCR⟩ ::= \text{`conflicting-roles-assignment'} ⟨role⟩ \quad (2)$$
$$(\text{`,'} ⟨role⟩)+ [\text{`on permission'} ⟨permission⟩]$$

$$⟨SSoDCU⟩ ::= \text{`conflicting-users-assignment'} ⟨user⟩ \quad (3)$$
$$(\text{`,'} ⟨user⟩)+ [\text{`on role'} ⟨role⟩]$$

$\langle SSoDCP \rangle$ ::= 'conflicting-roles-assignment'   (4)
$\langle permission \rangle$ (',' $\langle permission \rangle$)+ ['on role' $\langle role \rangle$]

SSoD policies can define conflicting roles (rule 2), conflicting users (rule 3), and conflicting permissions (rule 4). Rules 2–4 have an optional block that indicates that the SSoD policy is applied only when the roles are assigned to a specific permission (rule 2) and when the users (rule 3) or the permissions (rule 4) are assigned to a specific role. For example, the SSoD policy on conflicting roles PL5 is expressed in GEMRBAC-DSL as:

```
PL5: conflicting-roles-assignment assistant,
     trainee;
```

4.6.2 Dynamic Separation of duty (DSoD)

A DSoD policy allows the assignment of conflicting roles but forbids their activation in the same session [25]. GEMRBAC-DSL supports the specification of four types of DSoD: simple, object-based, operational-based, and history-based DSoD. We refer the reader to [7, 25] for more details about these types of policies. The syntax for DSoD policies is similar to the one for SSoD policies but uses different keywords:

$\langle DSoD \rangle$ ::= $\langle DSoDCU \rangle$ | $\langle DSoDCP \rangle$ | $\langle DSoDCR \rangle$ (1)

$\langle DSoDCU \rangle$ ::= 'conflicting-users-activation'   (2)
$\langle user \rangle$ (',' $\langle user \rangle$)+ ['on role' $\langle role \rangle$]

$\langle DSoDCP \rangle$ ::= 'conflicting-permissions-activation'(3)
$\langle permission \rangle$ (',' $\langle permission \rangle$)+ ['on role' $\langle role \rangle$]

$\langle DSoDCR \rangle$ ::= 'conflicting-roles-activation' $\langle role \rangle$(4)
(',' $\langle role \rangle$)+ ['depending-on-business-task-list'
$\langle operation \rangle$ (',' $\langle operation \rangle$)+] ['on-same-object']

The optional keyword 'on-same-object' in rule 4 is used to express an object-based DSoD policy. Similarly, the keyword 'depending-on-business-task-list' followed by a list of $\langle operation \rangle$s is used to specify an operational-based DSoD. A history-based DSoD is defined by combining these two keywords. For example, the history-based DSoD policy PL6 is expressed in GEMRBAC-DSL as:

```
PL6: conflicting-roles-activation assistant,
     admin depending-on-business-task-list
     create,read,update,delete on-same-object;
```

4.7 Binding of duty policy

A binding of duty (BoD) policy states that the operations of bounded permissions should be performed by the same role or subject [27]. Its syntax is:

$\langle BoD \rangle$ ::= 'bounded-permissions' $\langle permission \rangle$
(',' $\langle permission \rangle$)+ ('role-BoD' | 'subject-BoD')

The syntax distinguishes between a role- or a subject-based policy with the two keywords 'role-BoD' and 'subject-BoD'. The bounded permissions are specified as a list of $\langle permission \rangle$s. For instance, the role-based BoD policy PL7 is expressed in GEMRBAC-DSL as:

```
PL7: bounded-permissions add_casualty,
     modify_casualty, delete_casualty  role-BoD;
```

4.8 Delegation policy

A delegation policy allows a *delegator* (a user or any user assigned to a specific role) to delegate her role to *delegates* (the users or roles receiving the delegation). GEMRBAC-DSL adopts the concepts of delegation presented in [13, 28] and integrated into the GEMRBAC model [7], in which a delegation can be *single* or *multi-step*, *total* or *partial*, of type *grant* or *transfer*. A delegation of type *transfer* can be either *strong* or *weak*. Moreover, a *weak transfer* delegation can be of type *static* or *dynamic*. The syntax of a delegation policy is defined below:

$\langle Delegation \rangle$ ::= ('user ' $\langle user \rangle$ | 'role ' $\langle role \rangle$)   (1)
'can-delegate' $\langle role \rangle$ ('to users' $\langle user \rangle$ (',' $\langle user \rangle$)*
| 'to roles' $\langle role \rangle$ (',' $\langle role \rangle$)*) 'as'
('total' | 'partial with permissions ('
$\langle delegated\text{-}permissions \rangle$')') ','
('grant' [$\langle duration \rangle$] ('single' | 'multi-step' $\langle integer \rangle$)
| 'transfer' ('strong' | 'weak-static' | 'weak-dynamic'))

$\langle delegated\text{-}permissions \rangle$ ::= $\langle permission \rangle$ (2)
(',' $\langle permission \rangle$)*

$\langle duration \rangle$ ::= 'for' $\langle integer \rangle$ $\langle timeUnit \rangle$ (3)

In the syntax, keywords 'user' and 'role' are used to denote the delegator. The keyword 'can-delegate' denotes the $\langle role \rangle$ being delegated. The list of delegate $\langle user \rangle$s is denoted by the keyword 'to users'; similarly, the keyword 'to roles' denotes the list of delegate $\langle role \rangle$s. If the delegation is partial, the keyword 'partial-with-permissions' denotes the list of $\langle permission \rangle$s being delegated. In the case of a multi-step delegation, the syntax requires to indicate the $\langle integer \rangle$ corresponding to the maximum number of delegation steps allowed. If the delegation is of type grant, a duration (denoted with the keyword 'for', rule 3) can be optionally specified to indicate the amount of time after which the delegation is automatically revoked. For example, the delegation policy PL8 defines a delegation that is *multi-step* (with a maximum delegation depth of 2), *total* (because all the permissions of the delegated role have to be delegated), of type *grant* (because the delegator is still allowed to execute the permissions associated with the delegated role), with a *duration* of at most two weeks. This policy is expressed in GEMRBAC-DSL as:

```
PL8: role admin can-delegate admin to roles
     assistant as total, grant for 2 week,
     multistep 2;
```

4.9 Revocation policy

A revocation policy allows a user or a role to revoke a delegation. GEMRBAC-DSL supports the concept of revocation presented in [28] and integrated into the GEMRBAC model [7], in which a revocation can be *grant-dependent* or *grant-independent*, *strong* or *weak* and, *cascading* or *non-cascading*. Its syntax is defined as:

$\langle Revocation \rangle$ ::= ('user' $\langle user \rangle$ | 'role' $\langle role \rangle$ | 'delegator')
'can-revoke-delegation' $\langle id \rangle$
('from users' $\langle user \rangle$ (',' $\langle user \rangle$)* | 'from roles' $\langle role \rangle$
(',' $\langle role \rangle$)*)) 'as' ('strong' | 'weak') ','
('nonCascading' | 'cascading')

The syntax allows for specifying who can revoke a certain delegation; the keywords 'user' and 'role' denote, respectively, an explicit user or role, while the keyword 'delegator' implicitly refers to the user or role that originally performed the delegation. The delegation that is being revoked is referenced through its identifier, preceded by the keyword 'can-revoke-delegation'. The keyword 'from users' denotes the list of ⟨users⟩ from which the delegation is revoked; similarly, the keyword 'from roles' denotes the list of ⟨roles⟩ from which the delegation will be revoked. The additional keywords that come after the keyword 'as' indicate the type of revocation. For example, the revocation policy PL9 is defined as *weak* (because it will not impact the other roles possibly acquired through a role hierarchy) and as *non-cascading* (because it will not affect the further delegations performed along a delegation chain). This policy is expressed in GEMRBAC-DSL as:

```
PL9: role admin can-revoke-delegation PL8 from
     roles assistant as weak, nonCascading;
```

4.10 Contextual policy

A contextual policy allows (or disallows) a user to be a member of a role or to perform an operation according to her context, i.e., depending on the current time [19] and/or location [10]. The syntax for this policy is defined as follows:

$$\langle ContextPolicy \rangle ::= \langle RoleContextPolicy \rangle \qquad (1)$$
$$| \langle PermContextPolicy \rangle$$

$$\langle RoleContextPolicy \rangle ::= \text{‘role-context’} \qquad (2)$$
$$((\text{‘enable’} | \text{‘disable’}) \langle role \rangle$$
$$| ((\text{‘assign’} | \text{‘unassign’}) \langle role \rangle [\text{‘to user’} \langle user \rangle]))$$
$$[\text{‘only’}] \text{‘@’} \langle context \rangle$$

$$\langle PermContextPolicy \rangle ::= \text{‘permission-context’} \qquad (3)$$
$$((\text{‘enable’} | \text{‘disable’}) \langle permission \rangle$$
$$| ((\text{‘assign’} | \text{‘unassign’}) \langle permission \rangle$$
$$[\text{‘to role’} \langle role \rangle])) [\text{‘only’}] \text{‘@’} \langle context \rangle$$

$$\langle context \rangle ::= \langle temporal \rangle | \langle spatial \rangle \qquad (4)$$
$$| \langle spatioTemporal \rangle (\text{‘&&’} \langle spatioTemporal \rangle)^*$$

A contextual policy can be defined either at the role (rule 2) or at the permission level (rule 3). In rule 2 a security analyst can specify if a role should be enabled/disabled or if role should be assigned/unassigned (possibly to a specific user, as denoted by the optional keyword 'to user') in a specific ⟨context⟩. Rule 3 has a similar structure but it is used for specifying the enabling/disabling/assignment/unassignment of permissions. In both rules the optional keyword 'only' is used to specify that the role (or permission) referred in the policy should be enable/disabled/assigned/unassigned in any context different from the specified one. The context specification is preceded by the '@' symbol. As shown in rule 4, GEMRBAC-DSL supports temporal, spatial and spatio-temporal context specifications. Temporal and spatial policies will be illustrated in the next subsections, using the concepts of the GEMRBAC+CTX model introduced in [8]. Since spatio-temporal specifications can be seen as the conjunction of a temporal policy and a spatial one, we will omit their description for space reasons.

4.10.1 Policies with temporal context

The syntax for defining a temporal context is:

$$\langle temporal \rangle ::= \text{‘time’} (\langle absoluteTime \rangle | \langle relativeTime \rangle$$
$$| (\langle compositeTime \rangle (\text{‘&’} \langle compositeTime \rangle)^*)$$

$$\langle compositeTime \rangle ::= \langle absoluteTime \rangle \langle relativeTime \rangle$$

The type of temporal context supported by GEMRBAC-DSL corresponds to the one defined in [8], which distinguishes between absolute and relative time expressions. An absolute time expression refers to a concrete point or interval in the timeline; conversely, a relative time expression cannot be mapped directly to a concrete point or interval in the timeline. Furthermore, absolute time and relative expressions can also be composed. For space reasons, in this subsection we illustrate only the part of GEMRBAC-DSL that defines absolute time expressions; relative time expressions are illustrated in Appendix A. The syntax of an absolute time expression is:

$$\langle absoluteTime \rangle ::= \qquad (1)$$
$$(((\langle date \rangle [\text{‘at’} \langle hour \rangle]] | \text{‘(’} \langle date \rangle (\text{‘,’} \langle date \rangle)+\text{‘)’})$$
$$|(\text{‘starting from’} \langle date \rangle [\text{‘at’} \langle hour \rangle]$$
$$| \text{‘[’} \langle date \rangle \text{‘,’} \langle date \rangle \text{‘]’}$$
$$| \text{‘(’} \text{‘[’} \langle date \rangle \text{‘,’} \langle date \rangle \text{‘]’} (\text{‘,’} [\langle date \rangle \text{‘,’} \langle date \rangle \text{‘]’})+\text{‘)’})$$
$$[\langle periodicTime \rangle])$$

$$\langle periodicTime \rangle ::= \text{‘every’} [\langle integer \rangle] \langle timeUnit \rangle \qquad (2)$$

$$\langle date \rangle ::= \langle sDayOfMonth \rangle (\text{‘1’-‘9’})(\text{‘0’-‘9’})(\text{‘0’-‘9’})(\text{‘0’-‘9’})(3)$$

$$\langle sDayOfMonth \rangle ::= \langle integer \rangle \langle sMonth \rangle \qquad (4)$$

$$\langle sMonth \rangle ::= \text{‘Jan’} | \text{‘Feb’} | \text{‘Mar’} | \text{‘Apr’} | \text{‘May’} \qquad (5)$$
$$| \text{‘June’} | \text{‘July’} | \text{‘Aug’} | \text{‘Sept’} | \text{‘Oct’} | \text{‘Nov’} | \text{‘Dec’}$$

$$\langle hour \rangle ::= ((\text{‘0’-‘1’})(\text{‘0’-‘9’}) | (\text{‘2’})(\text{‘0’-‘3’})) \text{‘:’} \qquad (6)$$
$$(\text{‘0’-‘5’}) (\text{‘0’-‘9’}) \text{‘:’} (\text{‘0’-‘5’}) (\text{‘0’-‘9’})$$

An absolute time expression can have different forms. The simplest form is captured by ⟨date⟩, which is composed of a day of the month ⟨sDayOfMonth⟩ and a year (rule 4). An ⟨sDayOfMonth⟩ denotes a day, represented as an ⟨integer⟩, and a month, represented as an ⟨sMonth⟩. The latter corresponds to the abbreviation for a specific month (rule 6). A ⟨date⟩ can be optionally followed by the 'at' keyword and an ⟨hour⟩, to represent a specific hour during a day[2]. An absolute time expression can also correspond to a list of ⟨date⟩s enclosed in round brackets. Another type of absolute time expression is represented by intervals. An unbounded time interval is specified with a ⟨date⟩ prefixed by the keyword 'starting from'. A bounded time interval is represented as two ⟨date⟩s enclosed in square brackets. Lists of bounded intervals are enclosed in round brackets. Unbounded and bounded time intervals as well as lists of bounded time intervals can be followed by a periodicity expression (denoted with the keyword 'every', see rule 2), which specifies how often, during the selected interval(s), the action determined by the policy (e.g., enabling a role) should be in effect. For example, the role enabling policy PL10 can be expressed as:

```
PL10: role-context enable participant @time
      [12 Feb 2016, 8 Jun 2016];
```

4.10.2 Policies with spatial context

The syntax for defining a spatial context is:

$$\langle spatial \rangle ::= \text{‘location’} \langle location \rangle (\text{‘,’} \langle location \rangle)^* \qquad (1)$$

$$\langle location \rangle ::= [\text{relativeLocation}] (\text{‘physical’} \qquad (2)$$
$$\langle physicalLocation \rangle | \text{‘geofence’} \langle geofence \rangle)$$

---

[2]The current version of GEMRBAC-DSL does not support the concept of time zone.

$$\langle physicalLocation \rangle ::= \langle point \rangle \mid \langle polygon \rangle \mid \langle circle \rangle \qquad (3)$$
$$\mid \langle userPos \rangle$$

$$\langle point \rangle ::= \text{`(\texttt{lat}' } \langle float \rangle \text{': \texttt{long}' } \langle float \rangle \text{': \texttt{alt}' } \langle float \rangle \text{')'} \quad (4)$$

$$\langle userPos \rangle ::= \text{`\texttt{position}' } \langle user \rangle \qquad (5)$$

$$\langle circle \rangle ::= \text{`\texttt{center}' } \langle point \rangle \text{ `\texttt{radius}' } \langle float \rangle \langle locUnit \rangle \quad (6)$$

$$\langle polygon \rangle ::= \langle polyline \rangle \langle polyline \rangle \text{ (`,' } \langle polyline \rangle)+ \qquad (7)$$

$$\langle polyline \rangle ::= \text{`\texttt{line \{}' } \langle point \rangle \text{ `,' } \langle point \rangle \text{ `\}'} \qquad (8)$$

$$\langle relativeLocation \rangle ::= [\langle integer \rangle \langle locUnit \rangle] \langle direction \rangle \qquad (9)$$

$$\langle locUnit \rangle ::= \text{`\texttt{miles}' } \mid \text{`\texttt{meters}' } \mid \text{`\texttt{kilometers}'} \qquad (10)$$

$$\langle direction \rangle ::= \langle cardinalDir \rangle \mid \langle qualitativeDir \rangle \qquad (11)$$

$$\langle cardinalDirection \rangle ::= \text{(`\texttt{N}' } \mid \text{`\texttt{E}' } \mid \text{`\texttt{S}' } \mid \text{`\texttt{W}' } \mid \text{`\texttt{NE}' } \mid \text{`\texttt{SE}'} \quad (12)$$
$$\mid \text{`\texttt{SW}' } \mid \text{`\texttt{NW}'}) \mid \text{`\texttt{degree}' } \langle integer \rangle$$

$$\langle qualitativeDirection \rangle ::= \text{`\texttt{inside}' } \mid \text{`\texttt{outside}' } \mid \text{`\texttt{around}'} \quad (13)$$

The spatial context in GEMRBAC-DSL is represented as a set of locations. The concept of location is taken from [8]: it is a bounded area or a point in space. Reference [8] further classifies locations as physical (a precise position in a geometric space) and logical (a symbolic abstraction of one or many physical locations). Physical locations are denoted in GEMRBAC-DSL with the keyword '`physical`', while the keyword '`geofence`' denotes logical locations. Notice that the identifiers that can be used as logical locations are those declared in the preamble under the rule $\langle geofences \rangle$.

The simplest type of physical location is a $\langle point \rangle$, i.e., a set of geographic coordinates denoted with the keywords '`lat`', '`long`', and '`alt`', corresponding to latitude, longitude, and altitude (rule 4). Each coordinate is expressed as a floating-point number. The keyword '`position`' followed by a user id (rule 5) is used to define a location in terms of the coordinates of a user. Bounded physical locations can have the shape of a circle or of a polygon. A $\langle circle \rangle$ is denoted with a '`center`' and a '`radius`'; the latter is specified using units of length (see rules 6 and 10). A polygon is defined in terms of polylines, which are denoted with the keyword '`line`' and a start and an end $\langle point \rangle$ (rules 7–8). For example, the location-based policy on role enabling PL11 is expressed in GEMRBAC-DSL as:

```
PL11: role-context enable admin
         @location physical
line {(lat 15 : long 24 : alt 200),
      (lat 20 : long 27 : alt 200)},
line {(lat 20 : long 27 : alt 200),
      (lat 17 : long 27 : alt 200)},
line {(lat 17 : long 27 : alt 200),
      (lat 15 : long 27 : alt 200)},
line {(lat 15 : long 27 : alt 200),
      (lat 15 : long 24 : alt 200)};
```

As shown in rule 2, both physical and logical locations can be optionally prefixed by $\langle relativeLocation \rangle$, which represents a location defined with respect to another one. A $\langle relativeLocation \rangle$ is expressed with a $\langle direction \rangle$ and an optional distance expressed with a unit of length (rule 9). A direction of type $\langle cardinalDirection \rangle$ is denoted with symbols corresponding to cardinal and ordinal directions or with the degrees of rotation (denoted with the '`degree`' keyword followed by an integer) on a compass (rule 12). A direction of type $\langle qualitativeDirection \rangle$ represents a relative proximity to a location and is defined using the keywords '`inside`', '`outside`', or '`around`' (rule 13). For example, the contextual policy PL12, which contains a relative location, is expressed in GEMRBAC-DSL as:

```
PL12: role-context  enable trainee @location
       100 meters inside geofence Zone1;
```

5. SEMANTIC CHECKS

A security analyst can erroneously write policies that are inconsistent or conflicting. In the following paragraphs we describe all the possible conflicts that can be found in a GEMRBAC-DSL specification. We mainly focus on inter-policy conflicts, i.e., global conflicts between different policies. The Eclipse-based editor for GEMRBAC-DSL includes semantic checks for these conflicts, which are then reported to the user as errors or warnings.

Prerequisite role and SSoD on conflicting roles policies. Let PR be the set of roles involved in a prerequisite role policy, and SCR be the set of conflicting roles in a SSoDCR policy. If $PR \subseteq SCR$, the two policies are in conflict. The reason is that, while the prerequisite role policy requires the assignment of two roles to the same user (in a certain order), the SSoDCR policy prohibits this assignment. This situation can be avoided by not specifying prerequisite role policies and SSoDCR policies for the same subset of roles. This conflict is reported as an error. The conflict between the prerequisite permission policy and the SSoDCP one is defined in a similar way.

Prerequisite role and Role hierarchy policies. Let PR be the set of roles in a prerequisite role policy, and RH be the set $\{r\} \cup juniors(r)$ in a role hierarchy policy, where $junior()$ is a function that returns the junior roles of its argument. If $PR \subseteq RH$, the prerequisite role and the role hierarchy policies will require the assignment of the same subset of roles. Hence there is no need to define a prerequisite policy between a role and its parent role. This conflict is reported as a warning. The conflict between the prerequisite permission policy and the permission hierarchy one is defined similarly.

Cardinality (role-to-user assignment) and Role hierarchy policies. Let n be the number of juniors of role r in a role hierarchy policy, and $maxRoles$ be the maximum number of roles that can be assigned to a user, as specified by a cardinality policy. If $n \geq maxRoles$, the cardinality policy will be violated. This situation can be avoided by having $maxRoles$ greater than the number of juniors of any role. This conflict is reported as an error. The conflict between the cardinality (role-to-permission assignment) policy and the permission hierarchy one is defined similarly.

Cardinality (permission-to-role assignment) and Binding of duty policies. Let n be the number of bounded permissions in BoD policy, and $maxPerm$ be the maximum number of permissions that can be assigned to a role, as specified by a cardinality policy. If $n > maxPerm$, the cardinality policy will be violated, because the BoD policy will require a role to be assigned to more than $maxPerm$ permissions. This situation can be avoided by having $maxPerm$ be equal or greater than the number of bounded permissions in a BoD policy. This conflict is reported as an error.

Role hierarchy and SSoD on conflicting roles policies. Let RH be the set $\{r\} \cup juniors(r)$ in a role hierarchy policy, where $junior()$ is a function that returns the junior roles of its argument; let SCR be the set of conflicting roles in an SSoDCR policy. If $|RH \cap SCR| > 1$ the two policies are in conflict. Indeed, while the role hierarchy policy requires the assignment of a set of roles, the SSoDCR policy prohibits this assignment. To avoid this situation an SSoDCR policy should not contain a role and its junior(s) or, similarly, two juniors of the same role. This conflict is reported as an error. The conflict between the permission hierarchy policy and the SSoDCP one is defined similarly.

Role hierarchy and Context (role unassignment) policies. Let JRH be the set containing the juniors of role r. If a context policy on role un-assignment is specified for any role $s \in JRH$, the role hierarchy policy will be violated. Indeed, while the role hierarchy requires the assignment of a junior of role r, the role context policy can prohibit this assignment. This conflict is reported as an error. The conflict between the permission hierarchy and context-based (permission assignment) policies is defined similarly.

SSoD and DSoD on conflicting roles policies. Let SCR and DCR be the sets of, respectively, conflicting roles in an SSoDCR policy and a DSoDCR one. If $|SCR \cap DCR| > 1$, the assignment of at least two conflicting roles will be allowed by the DSoDCR policy but forbidden by the SSoDCR policy, generating an inconsistency in the system. This conflict is reported as a warning. The conflict between the SSoD and DSoD on conflicting users (or permission) policies is defined similarly. Notice that an SSoDCU policy and a DSoDCU one with the same list of users on different roles are not conflicting.

SSoD on conflicting permissions and Binding of duty policies. Let SCP be the set of conflicting permissions in an SSoDCP policy and let $PBoD$ be the set of bounded permissions in a BoD policy. If $|SCP \cap PBoD| > 1$, the two policies are in conflict. Indeed, while the SSoDCP restricts the assignment of at least two conflicting permissions, the BoD policy requires this assignment. To avoid this situation, an SSoDCP policy should not contain permissions that are used in a BoD policy. This conflict is reported as an error.

Delegation and SSoD on conflicting roles policies. Let SCR be the set of conflicting roles in an SSoDCR policy, r be the role being delegated, and $RECR$ be the set of roles that will receive the delegation in a delegation policy. If $(\{r\} \cup RECR) \subseteq SCR$, the two policies are in conflict. The reason is that, while the delegation policy allows the assignment of a set of roles to the same user, the SSoDCR policy prohibits this assignment. This conflict is reported as an error.

Additional checks. The editor also detects overlapping intervals in policies with temporal context, and circular dependencies for role hierarchy and precedence policies.

6. SEMANTICS

The GEMRBAC+CTX model (as well as its non-contextual ancestor GEMRBAC), which is the conceptual RBAC model on top of which GEMRBAC-DSL has been designed, comes with an operationalization of the semantics of the policies it supports. The operationalization follows a model-driven approach, by which the semantics of each RBAC policy is expressed as an OCL constraint on the RBAC model. Since the GEMRBAC+CTX model and GEMRBAC-DSL have the same expressiveness, we can define the semantics of GEMRBAC-DSL by mapping its constructs to the corresponding OCL constraints defined for the GEMRBAC+CTX model. In the rest of this section we sketch this mapping; we refer the reader to [7,8] for the details on the structure of the GEMRBAC+CTX model.

Each entity in the ⟨preamble⟩ of a GEMRBAC-DSL spec-

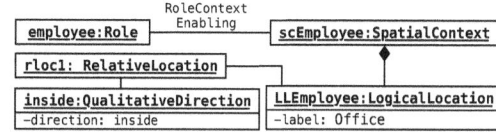

Figure 2: A fragment of an instance of the GemR-BAC+CTX model

ification corresponds to an instance of a UML class in the GEMRBAC+CTX model: users, roles, permissions, operations, and logical locations (⟨geofences⟩) are mapped to instances of the homonymous classes in GEMRBAC+CTX. Similarly, role and permission hierarchies correspond to the homonymous associations in the GEMRBAC+CTX model.

Each type of RBAC policy is mapped to the corresponding OCL constraint template defined in the GEMRBAC+CTX model; in each template the symbolic parameters are replaced with the actual entities used in the specification. For instance, the semantics of the object-based DSoD policy

```
objDSoD: conflicting-roles-activation author,
    reviewer on-same-object;
```

can be defined by the OCL invariant DSoD of the class Session (see [7], §7.5.2), by replacing the parameters r1 and r2 with roles author and reviewer.

Regarding contextual policies, the context to be assigned/enabled (as prescribed by the policy) is represented in the GEMRBAC+CTX model, as an association with the corresponding role/permission. For example, consider the policy

```
loc: role-context enable employee only
    @location inside office;
```

which enables role *employee* only inside the logical location denoted by the label "office". Figure 2 depicts an excerpt of an instance of the GEMRBAC+CTX model in which role employee is associated to a SpatialContext object that contains the object *LLEmployee* of type LogicalLocation, which denotes the location "office". This object is associated with object *rloc1* of type RelativeLocation, which contains a QualitativeDirection. The policy loc can be mapped to the OCL invariant relativeLocationRoleEnabling of class Session (see [8], §4.2), parametrized with role employee. A table describing the complete mapping of the GEMRBAC-DSL constructs to OCL constraints is available in Appendix B.

Expressing the semantics of GEMRBAC-DSL policies as OCL constraints on the GEMRBAC+CTX model enables the users of the language to benefit from the model-driven policy enforcement mechanisms described in [7,8]. Briefly, making an access decision for a policy can be reduced to checking the corresponding OCL constraint on a instance of the GEMRBAC+CTX model, which represents a snapshot of the system at a certain time.

7. DISCUSSION

Policy specification languages vs RBAC models. GEMRBAC-DSL is a domain-specific specification language, built on top of the GEMRBAC+CTX model, with the goal of providing a high-level specification language for the policies that can be defined using GEMRBAC+CTX. The constructs included in the language have been derived from the corresponding concepts defined in GEMRBAC+CTX. In this sense, GEMRBAC-DSL does not define new concepts related to RBAC; instead, it provides a practical way to express RBAC policies using the concepts provided by an expressive model like GEMRBAC+CTX. Although in our previous work [8] we reported on the use of OCL for the specification of RBAC policies based on GEMRBAC+CTX, we also mentioned the impracticality of such an approach and expressed the need for a higher-level specification language.

Adoption. GEMRBAC-DSL has been used by our industrial partner for the specification of the RBAC policies of a production-grade Web application. The adoption of GEMRBAC-DSL has allowed its engineers to easily specify all the policies for their system, including 19 new types of contextual policies. Despite the fact that some constructs of the language are non-trivial, the engineers were able to use GEMRBAC-DSL confidently after three half-day training sessions.

Tool Support. The GEMRBAC-DSL editor has been implemented as an Eclipse plugin. We used Xtext 2.8 to define the textual syntax and the semantic checks (illustrated in section 5) for the language. The editor is publicly available at `https://github.com/AmeniBF/GemRBAC-DSL.git`.

Limitations and Design Trade-offs. GEMRBAC-DSL can express *all and only* the types of policies supported by its underlying model, GEMRBAC+CTX. Since GEMRBAC+CTX is quite an expressive model, GEMRBAC-DSL includes many constructs that could have increased its level of complexity, hindering its adoption. Designing a simpler language would have implied providing limited support in terms of policy types, leading to partial fulfillment of our expressiveness requirements and a limited advance in terms of the state of the art. Hence, at the language design stage, we decided to pursue our expressiveness requirements, and to provide a syntax close to natural language to favor the adoption among practitioners and compensate (also by means of a rich editor) for the complexity of the language.

8. CONCLUSIONS AND FUTURE WORK

In this paper we presented GEMRBAC-DSL, a domain-specific language that facilitates the specification and consistency checking of policies based on highly-expressive RBAC models. GEMRBAC-DSL supports all types of policies captured by the GEMRBAC+CTX model, a comprehensive model encompassing all proposed types of policies. We have shown how the language can be used to specify the RBAC policies of an industrial application with complex, context-aware policies. The semantics of GEMRBAC-DSL has been defined with a mapping to an existing OCL formalization of the RBAC policies supported by GEMRBAC+CTX. This mapping paves the way for automating the enforcement of policies specifications written in GEMRBAC-DSL, using a model-driven approach.

As part of future work, we plan to extend GEMRBAC-DSL to support richer contextual policies, as well as administrative policies. We also plan to assess the usability of the language through user studies with practitioners.

Acknowledgments

The authors wish to thank Benjamin Hourte and his team from HITEC Luxembourg, as well as the anonymous referees for their valuable feedback. This work has been supported by the National Research Fund, Luxembourg (FN-R/P10/03) and by a grant by HITEC Luxembourg. Ameni Ben Fadhel is also supported by the Faculty of Science, Technology and Communication of the University of Luxembourg.

9. REFERENCES

[1] D. Abi Haidar, N. Cuppens-Boulahia, F. Cuppens, and H. Debar. An Extended RBAC Profile of XACML. In *Proc. of SWS 2006*, pages 13–22. ACM, 2006.

[2] G.-J. Ahn. Specification and Cassification of Role-based Authorization Policies. In *Proc. of WETICE 2003*, pages 202–207. IEEE, 2003.

[3] G.-J. Ahn and R. Sandhu. Role-based Authorization Constraints Specification. *ACM Trans. Inf. Syst. Secur.*, 3(4):207–226, Nov. 2000.

[4] G.-J. Ahn and M. Shin. Role-based authorization constraints specification using Object Constraint Language). In *Proc. of WETICE 2001*, pages 157–162. IEEE, 2001.

[5] S. Aich, S. Sural, and A. Majumdar. STARBAC: Spatiotemporal Role Based Access Control. In *Proc. of the OTM Conferences 2007*, volume 4804 of *LNCS*, pages 1567–1582. Springer, 2007.

[6] A. Anderson. XACML profile for role based access control (RBAC). *OASIS Access Control TC committee draft*, 1:13, 2004.

[7] A. Ben Fadhel, D. Bianculli, and L. Briand. A Comprehensive Modeling Framework for Role-based Access Control Policies. *Journal of Systems and Software*, 107:110–126, September 2015.

[8] A. Ben Fadhel, D. Bianculli, L. Briand, and B. Hourte. A Model-driven Approach to Representing and Checking RBAC Contextual Policies. In *Proc. of CODASPY2016*, pages 243–253. ACM, 2016.

[9] E. Bertino, P. A. Bonatti, and E. Ferrari. TRBAC: A Temporal Role-based Access Control Model. *ACM Trans. Inf. Syst. Secur.*, 4(3):191–233, Aug. 2001.

[10] E. Bertino, B. Catania, M. L. Damiani, and P. Perlasca. GEO-RBAC: A Spatially Aware RBAC. In *Proc. of SACMAT 2005*, pages 29–37. ACM, 2005.

[11] R. Bhatti, A. Ghafoor, E. Bertino, and J. B. D. Joshi. X-GTRBAC: An XML-based Policy Specification Framework and Architecture for Enterprise-wide Access Control. *ACM Trans. Inf. Syst. Secur.*, 8(2):187–227, May 2005.

[12] C. Cotrini, T. Weghorn, D. Basin, and M. Clavel. Analyzing first-order role based access control. In *Proc. of CSF2015*, pages 3–17. IEEE, July 2015.

[13] J. Crampton and H. Khambhammettu. Delegation in Role-based Access Control. *Int. J. Inf. Secur.*, 7(2):123–136, 2008.

[14] Eclipse. Eclipse OCL tools. `http://www.eclipse.org/modeling/mdt/?project=ocl`.

[15] R. Ferrini and E. Bertino. Supporting RBAC with XACML+OWL. In *Proc. of SACMAT 2009*, pages 145–154. ACM, 2009.

[16] T. Finin, A. Joshi, L. Kagal, J. Niu, R. Sandhu, W. Winsborough, and B. Thuraisingham. ROWLBAC: Representing Role Based Access Control in OWL. In *Proc. of SACMAT 2008*, pages 73–82. ACM, 2008.

[17] M. Hitchens and V. Varadharajan. Tower: A Language for Role Based Access Control. In *Proc. of*

POLICY 2001, volume 1995 of *LNCS*, pages 88–106. Springer, 2001.

[18] J. Joshi. Access-control language for multidomain environments. *Internet Computing, IEEE*, 8(6):40–50, Nov 2004.

[19] J. B. D. Joshi, E. Bertino, U. Latif, and A. Ghafoor. A Generalized Temporal Role-based Access Control Model. *IEEE Trans. Knowl. Data Eng.*, 17(1):4–23, January 2005.

[20] Q. Ni and E. Bertino. xfACL: An Extensible Functional Language for Access Control. In *Proc. of SACMAT 2011*, pages 61–72. ACM, 2011.

[21] OASIS. eXtensible Access Control Markup Language (XACML) Version 2.0, 2005.

[22] I. Ray and M. Toahchoodee. A Spatio-temporal Role-Based Access Control Model. In *Proc. of DBSec 2007*, volume 4602 of *LNCS*, pages 211–226. Springer, 2007.

[23] R. S. Sandhu, E. J. Coyne, H. L. Feinstein, and C. E. Youman. Role-based Access Control Models. *Computer*, 29(2):38–47, 1996.

[24] B. Shafiq, A. Masood, J. Joshi, and A. Ghafoor. A Role-based Access Control Policy Verification Framework for Real-time Systems. In *Proc. of WORDS 2005*, pages 13–20. IEEE, February 2005.

[25] R. T. Simon and M. E. Zurko. Separation of Duty in Role-based Environments. In *Proc. of CSFW 1997*, pages 183–194. IEEE, 1997.

[26] K. Sohr, M. Kuhlmann, M. Gogolla, H. Hu, and G.-J. Ahn. Comprehensive two-level analysis of role-based delegation and revocation policies with UML and OCL. *Inf. Softw. Technol.*, 54(12):1396 – 1417, 2012.

[27] M. Strembeck and J. Mendling. Modeling Process-related RBAC Models with Extended UML Activity Models. *Inf. Softw. Technol.*, 53(5):456–483, May 2011.

[28] L. Zhang, G.-J. Ahn, and B.-T. Chu. A Rule-based Framework for Role-based Delegation and Revocation. *ACM Trans. Inf. Syst. Secur.*, 6(3):404–441, 2003.

[29] Z. Zhang, J. Xiao, H. Li, and Y. Geng. An Extended Permission-based Delegation Authorization Model. In *Proc. of CSSE 2008*, volume 3, pages 696–699, December 2008.

APPENDIX

A. RELATIVE TIME EXPRESSION

A relative time expression is a time expression that cannot be mapped directly to a concrete point or interval in the timeline. The syntax of a relative time expression is:

$$\langle relativeTime \rangle ::= ((\langle iHour \rangle \ (\ `,\ ' \ \langle iHour \rangle))*)$$
$$| \ (\langle dayOfMonthH \rangle \ (`\text{and @ time}' \ \langle dayOfMonthH \rangle))*)$$
$$| \ (\langle dayOfWeekH \rangle \ (`\text{and @ time}' \ \langle dayOfWeekH \rangle))*)$$
$$| \ (\langle monthDayOfWeekH \rangle$$
$$(`\text{and @ time}' \ \langle monthDayOfWeekH \rangle))*))$$

A relative time expression can have different forms. The first form is as a list of hour intervals, which are intervals whose start and end points are hours; the syntax is:

$$\langle iHour \rangle ::= `\text{from}' \ \langle hour \rangle `\text{to}' \ \langle hour \rangle \qquad (1)$$
$$[(`\text{excluding}' \ (' \ \langle exHour \rangle \ (`,\ ' \ \langle exHour \rangle)* \ ')']$$

$$\langle exHour \rangle ::= `\text{from}' \ \langle hour \rangle `\text{to}' \ \langle hour \rangle \qquad (2)$$

Within the definition of an $\langle iHour \rangle$, one can also specify a list of hour intervals to be excluded, denoted with the keyword 'excluding' (rule 2).

A relative time expression can be also defined as a list of expressions starting with a day of month ($\langle dayOfMonthH \rangle$s). This expression corresponds to a day of month ($\langle dayOfMonth \rangle$) that optionally overlays an hour interval; its syntax is:

$$\langle dayOfMonthH \rangle ::= \langle dayOfMonth \rangle (`,\ ' \langle dayOfMonth \rangle)* \quad (1)$$
$$[(\langle iHour \rangle \ (\ `,\ ' \ \langle iHour \rangle)*)]$$

$$\langle dayOfMonth \rangle ::= \langle sDayOfMonth \rangle \ | \ \langle iDayOfMonth \rangle \qquad (2)$$

$$\langle iDayOfMonth \rangle ::= `\text{from}' \ \langle sDayOfMonth \rangle \ `\text{to}' \qquad (3)$$
$$\langle sDayOfMonth \rangle \ [`\text{excluding}' \ (' \ \langle exDayOfMonth \rangle$$
$$(`,\ ' \ \langle exDayOfMonth \rangle)* \ ')']$$

$$\langle exDayOfMonth \rangle ::= \langle sDayOfMonth \rangle | \langle exIDayOfMonth \rangle \ (4)$$

$$\langle exIDayOfMonth \rangle ::= `\text{from}' \ \langle sDayOfMonth \rangle \ `\text{to}' \qquad (5)$$
$$\langle sDayOfMonth \rangle$$

A day of month can correspond to a single day ($\langle sDayOfMonth \rangle$, see page 5) or an interval of days of month ($\langle iDayOfMonth \rangle$) (rule 2). The latter can also be defined to exclude a single day of month or an interval of days of month $\langle exIDayOfMonth \rangle$; notice that exclusion is not recursive.

A relative time expression can also have the form of a list of $\langle dayOfWeekH \rangle$s. The latter is a day of week that optionally overlays an hour interval; its syntax is:

$$\langle dayOfWeekH \rangle ::= \langle dayOfWeek \rangle \ (`,\ ' \ \langle dayOfWeek \rangle)* \qquad (1)$$
$$[\langle iHour \rangle \ (\ `,\ ' \ \langle iHour \rangle)*]$$

$$\langle dayOfWeek \rangle ::= \langle sDayOfWeek \rangle \ | \ \langle iDayOfWeek \rangle \qquad (2)$$

$$\langle sDayOfWeek \rangle ::= [[`\text{on}'] \ `\text{the}' \ \langle integer \rangle] \ (`\text{Monday}' \qquad (3)$$
$$| \ `\text{Tuesday}' \ | \ `\text{Wednesday}' \ | \ `\text{Thursday}' \ | \ `\text{Friday}' \ |$$
$$`\text{Saturday}' \ | \ `\text{Sunday}' \ )$$

$$\langle iDayOfWeek \rangle ::= `\text{from}' \ \langle sDayOfWeek \rangle \ `\text{to}' \qquad (4)$$
$$\langle sDayOfWeek \rangle \ [`\text{excluding}' \ (' \ \langle exDayOfWeek \rangle$$
$$(`,\ ' \ \langle exDayOfWeek \rangle)* \ ')']$$

$$\langle exDayOfWeek \rangle ::= \langle sDayOfWeek \rangle \ | \ \langle exIDayOfWeek \rangle \quad (5)$$

$$\langle exIDayOfWeek \rangle ::= `\text{from}' \ \langle sDayOfWeek \rangle \ `\text{to}' \qquad (6)$$
$$\langle sDayOfWeek \rangle$$

This syntax follows a pattern similar to the ones seen above.

A relative time expression can be also defined as a set of $\langle monthDayOfWeekH \rangle$s. The latter is a list of $\langle month \rangle$s that optionally overlays a $\langle dayOfMonthH \rangle$ or an $\langle iHour \rangle$. The syntax of $\langle monthDayOfWeekH \rangle$ is:

$$\langle monthDayOfWeekH \rangle ::= \langle month \rangle \ (`,\ ' \ \langle month \rangle)* \qquad (1)$$
$$[(`\#' \ \langle dayOfWeekH \rangle)+$$
$$|(\langle iHour \rangle \ (`,\ ' \ \langle iHour \rangle)*)]$$

$$\langle month \rangle ::= \langle sMonth \rangle \ | \ \langle iMonth \rangle \qquad (2)$$

$$\langle iMonth \rangle ::= `\text{from}' \ \langle sMonth \rangle \ `\text{to}' \ \langle sMonth \rangle \qquad (3)$$
$$[`\text{excluding}' \ (' \ \langle exMonth \rangle \ (`,\ ' \ \langle exMonth \rangle)* \ ')']$$

$$\langle exMonth \rangle ::= \langle sMonth \rangle \ | \ \langle exIMonth \rangle \qquad (4)$$

$$\langle exIMonth \rangle ::= `\text{from}' \ \langle sMonth \rangle \ `\text{to}' \ \langle sMonth \rangle \qquad (5)$$

Also this syntax follows the same structure of the previous definitions. Notice that in this case, the list of $\langle month \rangle$s can overlay either a list of $\langle iHour \rangle$s or a list of $\langle dayOfWeekH \rangle$s. An $\langle sDayOfWeek \rangle$ can contain an index (represented as an $\langle integer \rangle$), which refers to a specific occurrence of a day, as in "on the first Monday" (of a month).

B. MAPPING TO OCL CONSTRAINTS

Table 2 describes the mapping of each RBAC policy supported by GEMRBAC-DSL to its corresponding OCL constraint(s) defined on the GEMRBAC+CTX model. The first column indicates the type of policy and the corresponding grammar rule. The second column denotes the corresponding OCL constraints, whose full definition can be found in the reference indicated in the third column. The reference "web1" and "web2" are the websites `https://github.com/AmeniBF/GemRBAC-model` and urlhttps://github.com/AmeniBF/GemRBAC-CTX-model.git, respectively.

Table 2: Mapping of GemRBAC-DSL constructs to OCL constraints on the GemRBAC+CTX model

Type of policy	OCL constraint	ref
⟨*PrereqRole*⟩	`context User :: assignRole(r:Role): pre PreqRole`	[7]
⟨*PrereqPermission*⟩	`context Role :: assignPermission(p:Permission): pre PreqPermisssion`	[7]
⟨*CardActivation*⟩	`context Session inv Cardinality`	[7]
⟨*CardUser*⟩	`context User inv Cardinality`	[7]
⟨*CardPermission*⟩	This policy is expressed in a similar way as the previous one by replacing the context of User with the context of Permission.	[7]
⟨*CardRoletoUser*⟩	`context Role inv Cardinality`	[7]
⟨*CardRoletoPermission*⟩	This policy is expressed in a similar way as the previous one by replacing the instances of users with instances of permissions.	[7]
⟨*PrecEnabling*⟩	`context Session :: enableRole(r:Role): pre RoleEnablingPrecedence`	[7]
Dependency ⟨*PrecEnabling*⟩	`context Session :: deactivateRole(r:Role): pre RoleActivationDependency`	[7]
⟨*RoleHierarchy*⟩	`context User :: assignRole(r:Role): post RoleHierarchy`	[7]
⟨*PermissionHierarchy*⟩	`context Role :: assignPermission (p:Permission): post RoleHierarchy`	[7]
⟨*SSoDCU*⟩	`context Role inv SSoDCU`	[7]
⟨*SSoDCR*⟩	`context User inv SSoDCR` `context Role inv SSoDCP2`	[7]
⟨*SSoDCR*⟩	`context User inv SSoDCR` `context Role inv SSoDCP2`	[7]
⟨*SSoDCP*⟩	`context Role inv SSoDCP1`	[7]
⟨*DSoDCR*⟩	`context Session inv DSoD`	[7]
⟨*DSoDCU*⟩	`context Role inv DSoDCU`	web1
⟨*DSoDCP*⟩	`context Role inv DSoDCP`	web1
⟨*DSoDCR*⟩	`context Session :: performOperation(op:Operation, p:Permission, r:Role): pre ObjectDSOD`	[7]
⟨*DSoDCR*⟩	`context Session inv OperationalDSoD`	[7]
⟨*DSoDCR*⟩	`context Session :: performOperation(op:Operation, p:Permission, r:Role): pre HistoryDSOD`	[7]
Role-based ⟨*BoD*⟩	`context Session :: performOperation(op:Operation, p:Permission, r:Role) pre RoleBoD`	[7]
Subject-based ⟨*BoD*⟩	`context Session :: performOperation(op:Operation, p:Permission, r:Role) pre SubjectBoD`	[7]

⟨*Delegation*⟩	`context Delegation inv TotalDelegation`
	`context Delegation inv MultiStepDelegation`
	`context delegation inv PartialDelegation`
	`context Delegation inv StrongTransfer`
	`context Delegation inv StaticWeakTransfer`
	`context Delegation inv DynamicWeakTransfer`
	`context Delegation inv AutomaticRevocation`
		[7]

⟨*Revocation*⟩	`context Delegation :: revoke() pre RevacationDependency`
	`context Delegation :: revoke() post StrongRevocation`
	`context Delegation :: revoke() post CascadingRevocation`
		[7]

TPA with ⟨*absoluteTime*⟩	`context Session inv AbsoluteBTIRoleEnab`
	`context Permission inv AbsoluteBTIPermAssign`
	`context Role inv AbsoluteTPRoleAssign`
	`context Role inv AbsoluteUBIRoleAssign`
		[8]
		web2

TPA with ⟨*periodicTime*⟩	`context Role inv periodicUnboundTIRoleAssign`	[8]
TPA with ⟨*activeDuration*⟩	`context Session inv DurationAbsoluteBTIRoleEnab`	[8]
TPRInd ⟨*sDayOfWeek*⟩	`context Role inv indexRoleAssign`	[8]
TPRH <*iHour*>	`context Role inv RelativeHoursRoleAssign`	web2
TPRDM ⟨*dayOfMonthH*⟩	`context Role inv DayOfMonthHoursRoleAssign` `context Permission inv DayOfMonthHoursPermAssign`	web2
TPRDW ⟨*dayOfWeekH*⟩	`context Permission inv DayOfWeekHourPermAssign`	[8]
TPRMD ⟨*monthDayOfWeekH*⟩	`context Role inv MonthDayOfWeekHourRoleAssign`	web2
TPCT ⟨*compositeTime*⟩	This policy can be checked by a logical conjunction of two temporal policies: one with absolute time and one with relative time.	[8]
SPP ⟨*physicalLocation*⟩	`context Role inv physicalLocationRoleAssign`	[8]
SPL ⟨*geofence*⟩	This policy can be checked in a similar way as the previous one by replacing the instances of PhysicalLocation with instances of LogicalLocation.	[8]
SPR ⟨*relativeLocation*⟩	`context Session inv relativeLocationRoleEnabling`	[8]
SPT⟨*SpatioTemporal*⟩	This policy can be checked by a logical conjunction of the spatial and temporal policies.	[8]

Legend. TP: temporal policy; TPA: TP with absolute time; TPR: TP with relative time; TPRInd: TPR containing an index; TPRH: TPR of type hour interval; TPRDM: temporal policy with a relative time of type day of month that optionally overlays hours; TPRDW: TPR of type day of week that optionally overlays hours; TPRMD: TPR of type day of month that optionally overlays days of week (the days of week may optionally overlay hours); TPCT: TP with composite time; SP: spatial policy; SPP: SP with a physical location; SPL: SP with a logical location; SPR: SP with a relative location; SPT: spatio-temporal policy.

A Space-Efficient Data Structure for Fast Access Control in ECM Systems

Garfield Zhiping Wu[*]
The Third Research Institute
of the Ministry of Public Security
339 Bisheng Road
Shanghai, China
zhiping.wu@outlook.com

Frank Wm. Tompa
David R. Cheriton School of Computer Science
University of Waterloo
200 University Avenue West
Waterloo, ON Canada
fwtompa@uwaterloo.ca

ABSTRACT

An Enterprise Content Management (ECM) system must withstand many queries to its access control subsystem in order to check permissions in support of browsing-oriented operations. This leads us to choose a subject-oriented representation for access control (i.e., maintaining a permissions list for each subject). Additionally, if identifiers (OIDs) are assigned to objects in a breadth-first traversal of the object hierarchy, we will encounter many contiguous OIDs when browsing under one object (e.g., folder).

Based on these observations, we present a space-efficient data structure specifically tailored for representing permissions lists in ECM systems. In addition to achieving space efficiency, the operations to check, grant, or revoke a permission are very fast using our data structure. Furthermore, our design supports fast union and intersection of two or more permissions lists (determining the effective permissions inherited from several users' groups or the common permissions among sets of users). Finally, the data structure is scalable to support any increase in the number of objects and subjects.

We evaluate our design by comparing it against a compressed (WAH) bitmap-based representation and a hashing-based representation, using both synthetic and real-world data under both random and breadth-first OID numbering schemes.

CCS Concepts

•**Information systems** → **Data compression; Enterprise information systems;** Hashed file organization; •**Security and privacy** → **Access control;**

Keywords

ECM System; Compressed Bitmap; Permissions Lists

---

[*]Research conducted while at the University of Waterloo.

SACMAT'16, June 05-08, 2016, Shanghai, China

© 2016 ACM. ISBN 978-1-4503-3802-8/16/06. . . $15.00

DOI: http://dx.doi.org/10.1145/2914642.2914657

1. INTRODUCTION

Enterprise Content Management (ECM) systems have been widely used to manage an organization's digital contents. Examples of commercial ECM products include EMC's Documentum, IBM's Content Navigator, Microsoft's SharePoint, and OpenText's Content Suite. Although efficient access control is critical for a variety of data management applications, including ECM systems, previous work has focused on the design of models and not on efficient implementations. Meanwhile, the efficiency of access control can become a bottleneck for deployed ECM systems.

An ECM system stores information in whatever form it takes (including business records, documents, email, workflows, and web documents) and makes it available on demand to authorized users (including employees, customers, and business partners, whether based on their individual identities, roles, or memberships in groups). These are the *objects* and *subjects* that require access control. ECM systems typically employ a deeply nested permission inheritance hierarchy with many more subjects and objects than are found in a traditional operating system environment. Although an ECM system includes a search engine, most interactions are through a browsing interface. When a subject opens a *container object* (such as a folder, project, or mailbox), only those child objects for which the subject holds at least "view" permission are presented; thus the system has first to query the subject's permissions on all child objects before displaying a container's contents. In practice, such *browsing-oriented queries* impose the dominant requirement for access control once a user has been authenticated.

Because access control for a browsing-oriented operation involves one subject and many objects, a *subject-centric implementation* will be more efficient for ECM systems than using traditional access control lists (ACLs). In this approach, the system stores for each subject a *permissions list* containing all that subjects' explicit permissions. Furthermore, both space and time performance are improved by storing the children of any container object contiguously in each permissions list.

We present *Blocked and Ordered Permissions* (BOP), a simple data structure specifically optimized for ECM systems. Each permissions list is stored as a sequence of blocks, each of which contains an ordered list of permissions for objects on which the subject has been granted at least one permission. Our data structure is extremely space-efficient, making in-memory computing inexpensive in practice. Additionally, it is efficient when checking, granting or revoking a permission. Furthermore, it supports efficient union and intersection of two or more permissions lists so that deriving a subject's *effective* permissions list is fast, as is finding common permissions between several subjects. Finally, our data structure is able to scale to support significant increase in the number of subjects and objects.

We systematically evaluate BOP against representations based on hash tables (where each permissions list is a hash table with object identifiers as keys) and on compressed bitmaps (where bits in each permissions list are set to one when the subject has the corresponding permissions). We include both theoretical analyses and experimental results. Although hash tables outperform our data structure for isolated permission checks and updates (i.e., checking permissions on a single object or granting or revoking permissions on a single object), our evaluations shows that 1) BOP consumes the least space, 2) BOP is the most efficient data structure for browsing-oriented queries when objects within each container are clustered in the permissions lists, 3) BOP is faster for the union and intersection of permissions lists than the other two data structures.

The remainder of this paper is organized as follows. We review related work in Section 2. Section 3 presents our simple, yet novel, data structure, followed by Section 4 in which two alternative implementations are described. The performance evaluation is presented in Section 5. Finally, we summarize our work and discuss opportunities for further work in Section 6.

2. RELATED WORK

Our objective is to represent a (sparse) access control matrix [11]. There are many schemes for compressing a sparse matrix, such as using a dictionary of keys (DOK), list of lists (LIL), coordinate list (COO), compressed sparse row (CSR or CRS), and compressed sparse column (CSC or CCS)[7], variants of which are implemented in MTL4 [8]. Because a subject-centric representation will be more efficient in ECM systems, our task is to choose how to represent permissions lists as sparse rows.

A permissions list can be represented by a compressed bitmap. Database researchers have introduced many bitmap compression schemes, including the byte-aligned bitmap code (BBC) [3], PackBits (PAC) [4], hybrid run-length encoding (HRL) [12], and various word-based schemes [14], including word-aligned bitmap (WBC), pack word (PWC), and word-aligned hybrid run-length (WAH) codes. Among all these, WAH is fastest, at the cost of a little extra space, since modern CPUs access data by word [14]. Many compression schemes have been developed by researchers for storing postings lists in text search engines (lists of documents IDs for documents that include a given index term). The most commonly used schemes include (vbytes) [5], Simple-9 [1, 2], Simple-16 [16], and PForDelta [17]. These schemes are particularly effective when the document IDs are assigned in such a way that they are highly clustered in the postings lists. However, all such bitmap compression schemes, whether designed for use in databases or for postings lists, fail to support efficient update.

BOP, our proposed structure, was briefly described elsewhere to highlight its characteristics as a bitmap compression scheme [13].

3. BLOCKED & ORDERED PERMISSIONS

3.1 Object Identifiers and Permission Bits

To represent access control information in an ECM system, all subjects (users, roles, and groups) and all objects (files, directories, mail messages, etc.) are assigned numerical identifiers. Because we assume subject-centric permissions lists, the identifiers assigned to subjects are immaterial. However the assignment of object identifiers (OIDs) has a significant effect on performance: clustering of objects with similar permissions produces more compressible lists and clustering by object containers increases locality of reference for browsing-oriented queries.

The objects in an ECM system are hierarchically organized into folders and other object containers. Traversing this nested structure in breadth-first order, objects can be assigned sequential OIDs so that a browsing-oriented operation queries permissions on several objects with contiguous OIDs. Furthermore, there is a high correlation in ECM systems between the permissions granted on a container and on that container's contents; therefore storing permissions lists in OID order when objects are assigned sequential OIDs in breadth-first order leads to highly compressible structures.

We need to encode permissions to read an object's name, read its content, append to its content, alter its content, etc. Because the total number of permission types p in an ECM system is fixed and small, we use p bits to represent a subject's permissions on an object: if a subject has k permissions on an object, the corresponding k bits are set to 1 and the other $p - k$ bits for that object are set to 0. This corresponds to an access control matrix in which each cell contains p-bit data. The explicit permissions assigned to a subject are stored, and permission inheritance is handled at run time when necessary by searching multiple lists or finding the union of appropriate permissions lists. Figure 1 shows an example of an access control matrix for an ECM system: each column represents the permissions on an object, the header displays OIDs, each row represents a subject's permissions list, and each cell contains p *permission bits* corresponding to the p pre-defined permission types.

0	1	2	...
11111111111	00000000000	00000100100	...
00000000000	00000000000	00010000000	...
...	...	...	...

Figure 1: A simplified access control matrix

ECM systems will often support thousands of authorized users and contain millions of objects. Assuming 5000 subjects, 8 million objects, and 10 permission types, each permissions list would require 80 million bits yielding a requirement for 50 GB space to store the access control matrix. Clearly a more compact data structure is needed. In the remainder of this section, we describe our space-efficient permission representation.

3.2 Blocking

We first divide a permissions list into multiple blocks, each of which (logically) contains permissions for b objects. If a permission bit is not explicitly stored, it is assumed to have the value 0 (permission denied). Therefore, we do not store blocks in which no bit is set to 1, and as a result the number of physical blocks may be smaller than the number of logical blocks. Furthermore, we represent each block (as described in the next section) using a varying-sized representation. To locate a desired block within a permissions list efficiently, our data structure explicitly records the OID of the first object for each stored block, the *blocks' starts*, in a *block index*. Given an OID, the appropriate block can be quickly located (or determined to be absent, indicating that no permissions are granted on the corresponding object), and therefore for large blocks the search time for finding permissions for an object is dominated by the time to search within one block.

One benefit of using blocks is that we can choose each block's representation depending on its particular characteristics (i.e., its distribution of objects for which there are no permissions). A second advantage is to reduce the space required to represent an OID within a block. For a system with N objects, we need $\log N$ bits to represent an OID; however, with blocking, we need only $\log b$ bits to encode the offset from the beginning of a block. A final advantage of blocking is to reduce the cost of I/O when pure in-memory implementation is infeasible. Physical blocks can serve as our units of I/O, and we can store the indexes to all physical blocks in main memory. We are then able to read a specific block from disk instead of a whole permissions list. Because of locality of reference, most operations will check data in only one or two blocks, reducing the I/O cost significantly in the case of limited available main memory.

3.3   Representation within a Block

A straightforward way to represent a subject's permissions on all the objects assigned to a block is to materialize that block as an uncompressed bitmap corresponding to the concatenation of all the permission bits for its objects in OID order. In this case, the permissions for an object with OID i can be found at positions in the interval $[p * (i - s), p * (i - s) + p - 1]$, where s is the OID for the first object in the block, i.e., the block's start. Granting and revoking a subject's permission on an object involves setting the corresponding bit to 1 or 0, respectively.

Alternatively we can use zero-suppression to omit objects for which a subject has no permissions. That is, if a subject has no permissions on an object, that object's permission bits are not materialized in that subject's permissions list; otherwise, permissions on an object are represented by a pair representing (a) the relative OID with respect to the first object for the block and (b) the subject's permission bits for that object. Thus if a subject has one or more permissions on any object assigned to a block, that block is represented as a dictionary mapping rel-OIDs to permissions, where rel-OID is the object's relative OID. The simplest such dictionary is a list of (rel-OID,permissions) pairs, ordered by rel-OID to allow binary search. The permissions for an object with OID i can be found by searching the list for rel-OID $= i - s$: if it is found a permission can be read from the associated permission bits, and if not, permission is denied. Granting the first permission on an object requires insertion of a new pair, and granting of subsequent permissions requires setting a bit; similarly, revoking a permission involves clearing a bit, and if it is the last granted permission, deleting the (rel-OID,permissions) pair from the list.

As a specific illustration, let us return to our prototypical example with 5000 subjects, 8 million objects, and 10 permission types. If the number of objects per block b is chosen to be 100,000, then each object's permissions can be stored in 10 bits and storing the block as a bitmap requires 1 million bits, which covers 31,250 32-bit words. Since $\log b \approx 16.6$, a relative OID can be stored in 17 bits. Thus, a (rel-OID,permissions) pair requires 27 bits. Even if we wish to have every pair word-aligned, on a 32-bit machine we can store up to 31,250 pairs using less space than if we were to use an uncompressed bitmap. Thus, we save space whenever a subject has permissions on no more than 31.25% of the objects assigned to a block, and we choose instead to use an uncompressed bitmap for the block if the subject has permissions on more than 31.25% of the assigned objects. In our application, most permissions lists are quite sparse, since a subject typically has no permissions on most objects in a large enterprise.

3.4   Scalability

We consider scalability in three dimensions, including the increase in the number of subjects, objects and permission types. Our data structure can support all three dimensions quite well.

When a new subject is added into the system, we simply need to create an empty permissions list. Permission bits can be set as permissions are subsequently granted.

When a new object is created, the logical length of every permissions list grows; however, no physical operation is necessary until permissions on the newly created object are granted to a subject. If the number of objects is not a multiple of b, we simply assign a newly created object to the final block; otherwise we need to append a new entry to a permissions list's block index (i.e., create a new block) when the first permission on that object is granted to the corresponding subject. (It is also easy to support the deletion of objects by maintaining a bitmap in which the value corresponding to the position of a deleted object is 1; when a request is received, we first check whether an object has been deleted before searching a block.)

Our decision to pack each (rel-OID,permissions) pair into a word typically uses fewer bits than are available in the word. Although this wastes some space, there are at least two benefits. Most importantly, using a full word makes our scheme word-aligned, which makes the implementation easier and the processing faster [14]. Second, the spare bits can be used to accommodate additional permission types. For example, if a new permission type is introduced by the ECM system, we simply have to increase p by 1, and the previously unset bits in every pair will immediately represent that new permission as being denied to all subjects with no changes whatsoever to the list-encoded blocks. Of course, if the number of permissions increases beyond the number of unused bits in each packed word, the encoding scheme must be over-hauled to use longer words, choose smaller block size, or adopt more space-efficient compression or packing schemes. In practice, this situation only arises when there is a larger than unanticipated increase in the number of permission types in an ECM system after it is deployed, and this can be assumed to be quite rare.

Unfortunately, to accommodate an additional permission type, blocks represented as bitmaps need to be rewritten to include an extra 0-bit for every object, increasing the size of these bitmaps by b bits (e.g., using blocks of size 1,100,000 in place of blocks of size 1 million in our prototypical example).

Luckily, however, there are very few such blocks in practice, as almost all blocks are encoded using lists of pairs.

4. ALTERNATIVE IMPLEMENTATIONS

For the sake of comparison, in this section we describe two alternative approaches to implementing permissions lists. The first approach is based on hashing, and the second is based on compressed bitmaps using WAH.

4.1 Efficient Hash Table Implementation

A subject's permissions list can be represented by a hash table mapping OIDs to permission bits. Objects on which a subject has no permissions are not stored in the table. Because the number of entries in the table varies as a subject is granted permissions on more or fewer objects, we choose an implementation that accommodates dynamic growth. To this end, we allow the number of buckets in a hash table to be any power of 2.

We do not want an expensive-to-compute hash function in our application; so, for example, hash functions used in cryptography, such as MD5 or SHA1 [6], are inappropriate. Instead our hash function is simple (thus inexpensive to compute for any key), yet effective in randomizing the hash values of the keys [10]. Given an OID as key, we first multiply it by a large prime. We fetch the middle 24 bits of the product by dropping the 12 most significant bits and 28 least significant bits, producing a signature for the OID. Finally, we use the remainder after dividing this signature by the number of buckets in the hash table.

We choose *separate chaining* (Figure 2) as our collision resolution strategy [10], with short pointers in order to improve space efficiency. This is implemented as two arrays (see Figure 3). The first, Bucket Array, stores 32-bit pointers to the entries in the second array (Entry Array). Specifically, each pointer references the first entry of the linked list whose keys are hashed to the bucket. The Entry Array includes all materialized (OID,permissions) pairs, each with a pointer NEXT referencing the next entry on the linked list for its associated bucket. These are packed into 64-bit words for efficiency through word alignment. As a result, if we are to require 10 permission types, up to $2^{27} \approx 134$ million objects can be accommodated; with 16 permission types, up to $2^{24} \approx 16.8$ million objects can be accommodated.

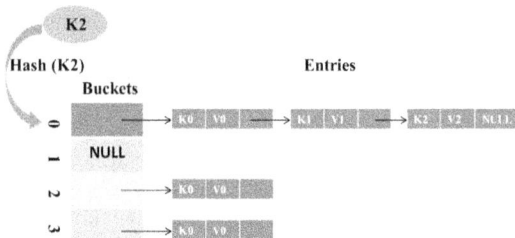

Figure 2: Permissions list as a hash table

For a given subject j, let M_j be the number of objects on which at least one permission has been granted. We then choose the number of buckets K to be $2^{\lfloor \log_2(M_j-1) \rfloor}$ so that collision lists have on average between 1 and 2 entries. For example, if $M = 100$, K is set to 64 and a bucket offset is represented by the last 6 bits of the OID's signature. If the

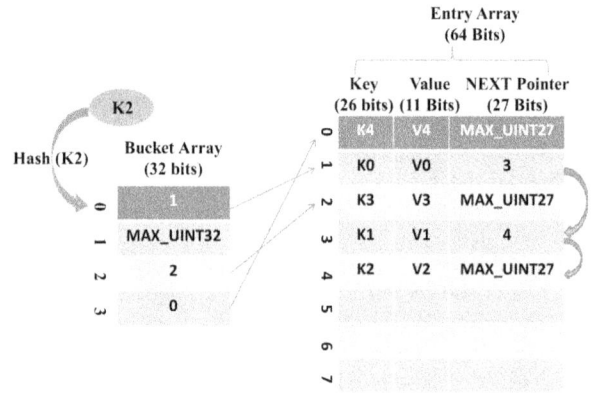

Figure 3: Implemented hash table example

number of buckets in the hash table doubles from K to $2K$ to accommodate more objects on a permissions list, one more bit of the signature is used as the hash address, and, for each bucket i, entries in that bucket can be simply re-assigned to bucket i or to bucket $i + K$ in the larger table. Similarly, pairs of buckets are simply merged if the hash table shrinks.

4.2 WAH Implementation

A permissions list in its literal interpretation is a bitmap. We can compress these permission bitmaps in order to get a space-efficient implementation and then carry out the necessary access control operations on the compressed bitmaps. For this purpose, we implemented a mainstream bitmap compression scheme called Word-Aligned Hybrid (WAH) [14].

WAH is a word-based scheme using two distinct encodings for words: fill words and literal words. It encodes a long run of contiguous 0s or 1s using run-length encoding (called a fill), and it represents a mixed-value word as an uncompressed bitmap. In any word, the most significant bit is used as a flag to distinguish a literal word from a fill word (0 for a literal word; 1 for a fill word). For a literal word, the next w-1 bits is used simply as a bitmap. For a fill word, the second most significant bit is called the fill bit which represents the value of the contiguous bits, and the rest of a fill word, interpreted as an integer v, encodes the length of the run r (the number of identical bits), where $r = (w - 1) \times v$ and w is the word size; for example, in a 32-bit implementation, 62 contiguous 0s may be encoded as 10000000000000000000000000000010. If the total length of the bitmap to encode is not a multiple of $w - 1$, a tail word encodes the last few bits of the bitmap (as a literal word). The final word in the encoding records how many bits are used in the tail word. For example, Figure 4 shows how a 128-bit bitmap is compressed using a 32-bit WAH [15].

128 bits	1, 20*0, 3*1, 79*0, 25*1				
31-bit groups	1, 20*0, 3*1, 7*0	62*0		10*0, 21*1	4*1
groups in hex	40000380	00000000	00000000	001FFFFF	0000000F
WAH (hex)	40000380	80000002	001FFFFF	0000000F	00000004

Figure 4: An example of WAH encoding [15]

Using WAH for a permissions list requires decoding the list to identify the ith permission for the jth object. Granting or revoking a permission requires that a bit change its value, and this might cause a fill word to be replaced by two or three words or allow two or three words to be collapsed into a single fill word.

5. PERFORMACE EVALUATION

This section compares the efficiency of BOP, hashing, and WAH when used to implement ECM permissions lists. We first describe the data we use for testing, including both real-world and synthetic data, and how this affects the parameter settings for each of our implementations. We then present and discuss the evaluation results for space consumption and execution speed. Because all permissions lists are stored in memory, no I/O is involved.

All experiments were performed on an AMD FX-6100 six-core 3.3Ghz Processor (8M L3, 6M L2 and 64K + 64K L1 caches) with 32GB main memory, running 64-bit Windows 7 Professional with single thread execution of code compiled using *gcc*.

5.1 Experimental Data

5.1.1 Real-world Data

The real-world dataset was provided by a mainstream ECM system vendor. In that vendor's system, there are 11 permission types, and therefore we assume $p = 11$ throughout our experiments.

The real-world dataset contains over 8 million objects and 6,053 active subjects. 892 of the subjects represent groups and the remaining 5,161 subjects represent individual users. A user can be a member of one or more groups, and a group can also be a member of one or more groups. The result is a subject hierarchy in which every subject other than the root is a direct member of the root subject. If a subject (whether an individual or a group) has any permission on an object, on average it has 5.96 permissions on that object, i.e., 54% of the possible permissions.

In an ECM system, every operation is always issued by a specific individual user, but permissions might be inherited. In response, the access control system must check the permissions lists of the issuer (a user) and all its ancestors. Thus it is important to determine how many permissions lists we have to check per operation in practice. In our specific dataset, the number of ancestors in the group hierarchy varies between 2 and 110 for the individual users. Figure 5 shows the percentages of individual users having a specified number of ancestors. The mean number of ancestors per user is 8.8, which means the system must check on average 9.8 permissions lists per operation.

5.1.2 Synthetic Data

In order to evaluate the implementation alternatives in a wider context, we also experiment with data for synthetic permissions lists. Nevertheless, we wish this data to maintain some real-world characteristics.

Each synthetic permissions list we generate contains 100M literal bits; for $p = 11$ this implies 9,090,909 logical objects. All permissions lists are sparse so that no blocks are stored in literal form. We first generate a permissions list in its literal form (a bitmap), and we then transform it to the BOP, hash table, and WAH formats for testing. A permissions list is generated by the following steps:

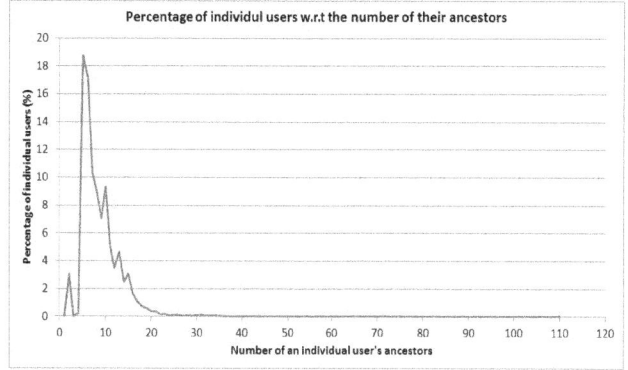

Figure 5: Percentage of individual users w.r.t the number of their ancestors

1. Pick a random[1] starting position s, where s is a multiple of 11;

2. Randomly set 60 % of the bits within the range specified by [s, s + 10];

3. Repeat 1 and 2 until 60,000 bits have been set.

4. Convert the literal bitmap to a BOP list, a hash table, and a WAH compressed bitmap

Unless otherwise stated, each experimental run (e.g., 500 permission checks) is performed on one list generated using these steps, and we report the average of five experimental runs (each applied to a newly generated list).

5.1.3 Implementation Settings

We choose parameter settings for each implementation to match the expected data.

For BOP, we need to choose how many objects b to assign to each block in each permissions list. Smaller values for b allow faster searching for an object's permissions within a block; however, binary search already mitigates that cost. On the other hand, having large blocks reduces the overhead when performing bitwise operations. We find that blocks around 1M bits in length yield a good compromise. Thus, since there are 11 permission types, b should be approximately 91,000 when designing for dense, bitmap-encoded blocks. On the other hand, sparse blocks store (relOID,permissions) pairs that need to be packed into words. If $b \approx 91,000$, we need $\log_2 91,000 = 16.5$ bits for storing a relative OID. We thus choose to use the 11 high-order bits in each 32-bit half-word for permissions and the 17 low-order bits for OID, packing two pairs into each 64-bit word and leaving 4 bits unused in each half-word. By using 17 bits, we can address up to 131,072 objects per block. With all this in mind, we choose $b = 95,296$ for our experiments, resulting in blocks of size 1,048,256 bits or 16,379 64-bit words. There are a few dense blocks in a small percentage of the permissions lists in the real-world ECM system; these are stored as uncompressed bitmaps.

As described in Section 4.1, our hash-based implementation uses the hash function

$$Hash(OID) = ((OID \times BigPrime) << 12 >> 40)\%K$$

---
[1] i.e., all valid values equally likely

195

where K is the number of buckets. Since a complete permissions list is stored as a single hash table, we need to be able to address any of the 8 million objects expected in the application; this requires at least 23 bits to store an OID. To make the Bucket Array and the Entry Array word-aligned, we use 32 bits for every pointer in the Bucket Array and 64 bits per entry in the Entry Array. Our implementation uses the high-order 26 bits for an OID, 11 middle bits for permissions, and the low-order 27 bits for a NEXT pointer, allowing for considerable expansion in the number of objects (or, with almost no code changes, for reassignment of bits to support more permissions).

The only implementation parameter for WAH is the choice of word size w, for which our implementation uses 64.

5.2 Storage Space

Before reporting the sizes of the data structures witnessed in the experiments, we examine the expected space requirements in general. It is straightforward to compare the space complexities between BOP and our hash table. BOP consumes 32 bits for each materialized unit of permission bits; assuming that there are M materialized units, we need $32 \times M$ bits in total. In addition, there are some pointers in the block index and other overhead, but this needs very little space. In contrast, our hash table needs 64 bits for each materialized entry; additionally, each element in the Bucket Array consumes 32 bits, and the number of elements in the Bucket array is over $1/2$ of M. Therefore, we need at least $64 \times M + 32 \times M/2 = 80 \times M$ bits in total (overhead data is again ignored). This indicates that our hash table consumes approximately 2.5 times the space compared to BOP.

The space used by WAH depends on the clustering of the M objects on which a subject has at least one permission, because this determines the extent to which fill words can be utilized. Assume for simplicity that a subject has at least one permission on m sequentially numbered objects and that there are M/m such clusters separated by at least enough other objects to require one fill word in the WAH encoding. The space required for WAH is then approximately $\frac{M}{m} \times (\lceil \frac{11m}{63} \rceil + 1)$ 64-bit words, which exceeds the space required by BOP whenever the average size of a cluster is smaller than 6. As we shall see next, the space required for WAH is, in fact, far greater in practice.

We measured the space required by BOP, hashing, and WAH to store a single synthetic permissions list (11.92 MB before compression) and to store all the permissions lists in our real-world ECM access control system (56.27 GB before compression). We implemented a buddy system [9] to manage dynamic storage allocation for BOP and for our hash table implementation; for WAH, we used a *vector* provided by C++ (always extending the size by half when needed).

Table 1: Comparison of sizes among BOP, hashing, and WAH implementations

	BOP	Hash Table	WAH
One synthetic permissions list	59.8 KB	163.8 KB	213.4 KB
Compression ratio* (synthetic)	204.1	74.5	57.2
All real-world permissions lists	0.36 GB	0.92 GB	1.1 GB
Compression ratio* (real-world)	156.3	61.2	51.2

* $\frac{|\text{uncompressed data}|}{|\text{compressed data}|}$

Therefore all implementations consume some unrequested, yet allocated, space; we do not include such space in our measure of space utilization. Table 1 shows that all three implementations have high compression ratios: they are much more space-efficient than storing literal bits, and BOP performs best. These results confirm our theoretical analysis showing that our hash table implementation consumes 2.5 times more space than BOP, but they also show that WAH uses much more space than we anticipated.

5.3 Execution Speed

We begin by examining the performance of individual operations and then consider the times required for executing several prototypical workloads.

Permission Checking.

We first test the time required to access a specific permission for a given object on a synthetic (subject's) permissions list. Specifically, we chose 50,000 to 500,000 individual permissions, (OID, permission type) pairs, and checked their values on a permissions list represented in each of the three implementations (Figure 6).

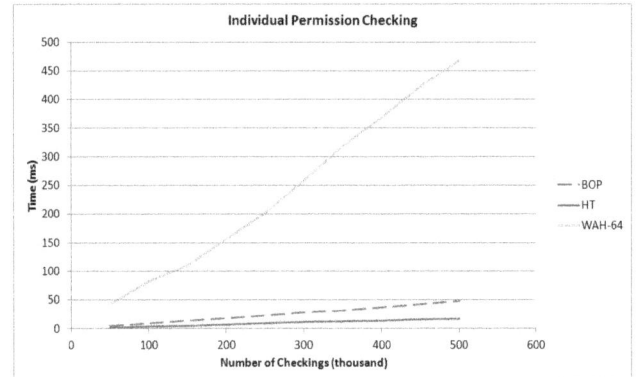

Figure 6: Experimental results for individual permission checking on the synthetic data

As expected, the time for all three implementations increases linearly as we increase the number of permissions to check. Using BOP takes 2.6 to 2.7 times longer than using hashing: the time complexity to search for an object using our hash table is $O(1)$ whereas BOP requires $O(1)$ for locating the block plus $O(\log n)$ for finding the object, where n is the number of materialized objects in the block.

However, BOP is approximately 10 times faster than WAH when applied to a synthetic bitmap. Instead of taking advantage of hashing, or the block index and binary search for efficient search, we have to interpret the WAH words one by one from the beginning of the compressed bitmap until we find the word containing the bit we are seeking. Obviously, this linear search with WAH is far more expensive than using either a hash table or BOP.

BOP, hashing, and WAH were then applied to our real-world data. We tested this operation 50,000 times, for each of which we randomly chose a subject and then checked the value of a randomly chosen (OID, permission type) pair (Table 2). We notice that using BOP now requires less than twice the time for hashing. However, the performance advantage of BOP over WAH is significantly amplified for the real-world data. There are two reasons. First, BOP is more space efficient, which results in less cache loading time. This is particularly important when there are 6,000 real-world permission lists instead of only a single synthetic list. In fact, the space efficiency factor also amplifies our hash table's performance advantage over WAH, but narrows the performance difference between BOP and using a hash table. Second, although the average density of the real-world permissions lists is close to the density of the synthetic ones, the densities of the real-world lists, in fact, vary widely, and this characteristic amplifies the performance advantage of binary search over linear search. Due to these two reasons, BOP is two orders of magnitude faster than WAH when applied to our real-world data.

Table 2: Time needed to check, grant, or revoke 50,000 random permissions on the real-world dataset (ms).

	BOP	Hash Table	WAH
Checking	18.6	10	1945
Granting	38.3	16.2	2629
Revocation	18.7	9.9	1987

Permission Granting.

For this experiment, we generate a subject's permissions list and then randomly grant 50,000 to 500,000 individual permissions to that subject. In so doing, we might grant a permission that had already been granted. This operation is similar to permission checking with the exception that a new permission word (for BOP), a new entry (for a hash table), or up to two additional WAH words may have to be inserted. Figure 7 shows the experimental results.

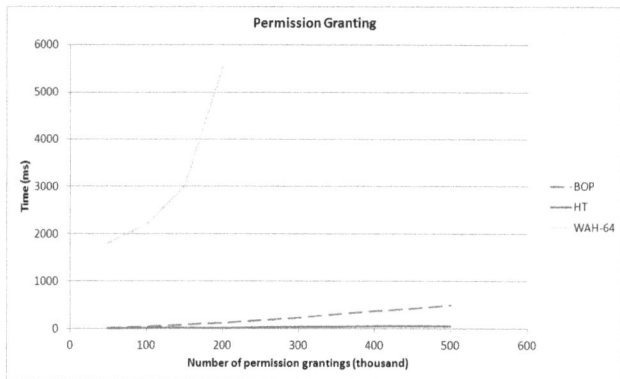

Figure 7: Experimental results for permission granting on the synthetic data

It is again more expensive to use BOP than a hash table for this operation. Besides requiring more searching time to locate an object (as for individual permission checking), BOP may need to insert a new permission word into the array holding the block or a brand new block on occasion, and this is more expensive than inserting a new entry into the hash table unless an extension is needed to enlarge the hash table. Furthermore, the cost for our hash table increases almost linearly as the number of permissions granted increases, whereas the cost for BOP increases super-linearly:

the arrays holding permission words become increasingly larger, and the time to insert an additional element into an array increases as the array gets larger (requiring more time to shift elements and to relocate the array when needed).

The cost for using WAH soars as more permissions are granted. This is due to the rapid increase in size of the compressed bitmap, and therefore both search and new WAH word insertion becomes ever slower.

Testing this operation on the real-world data produces the results shown in the second line of Table 2. Similar to checking individual permissions, the performance advantages of BOP or a hash table over WAH are considerable, and the performance difference between BOP and the hash table is relatively small.

Permission Revocation.

Figure 8 presents the results for permission revocation on a synthetic permissions list using BOP, a hash table, and WAH, and Table 2 includes the results for these tests on the real-world data. This operation is similar to the above two operations; thus it is not surprising that BOP is a little more expensive than using a hash table, and both BOP and our hash table significantly outperform WAH.

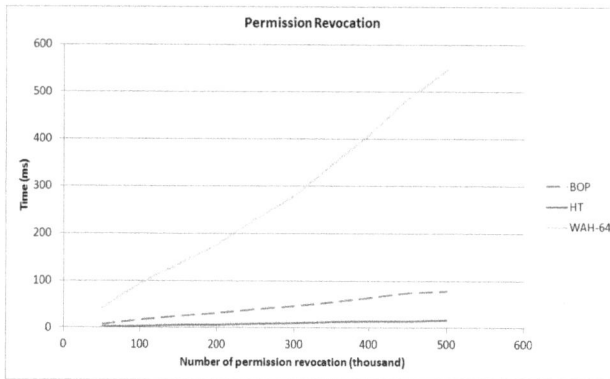

Figure 8: Experimental results for permission revocation on synthetic data

It is worth noting that after revoking a permission from a permissions list when using BOP, we may get a permission word containing no permissions, and we may even get an entire block with no permissions set. We implemented a garbage collection mechanism to reclaim such space. Specifically, if we get a permission word with no permissions on an object, we remove this word and shift the remaining elements in the array containing all permission words of the specific block (thus all unused words will always be at the tail of the array). This explains why permission revocation is slightly more expensive than individual permission checking when using BOP. However, we do not shrink the array size during this operation (therefore no array relocation), but we do completely remove a block that becomes empty after revocation.

We did not recycle garbage for our hash table, since it is costly to update all pointers referencing all entries shifted.

For WAH, after revoking a permission a word may become combinable with its neighbors. For example, suppose that we have a 0-fill followed by a literal word in which only one bit is set to 1. Revoking that permission results in a literal word in which every bit is 0, which can be combined with the adjacent 0-fill. However, for simplicity, we did not implement this since it requires array shift (and potentially allows the array to shrink). This wastes some space, but saves some time and explains why revoking a permission is only a little more expensive than checking a permission in our experiments.

Union of Permissions Lists.

We conducted two categories of experiments for this operation, one varying the number of lists involved in the union, and the other varying the number of objects on which there is at least one permission set.

For the first variant, we generate 100 permissions lists using the approach described in Section 5.1.2. We then perform 100 to 500 union operations, for each of which we randomly choose two of the generated permissions lists as input. Figure 9 shows that BOP is more efficient than the other two approaches: hashing taking approximately 5.2 times the time and WAH taking 6 times the time. For hashing, unlike the operations on individual permissions, we need to scan all the buckets in the smaller hash table and then insert each entry into an appropriate bucket in the larger one. As a result, our hash table barely outperforms WAH.

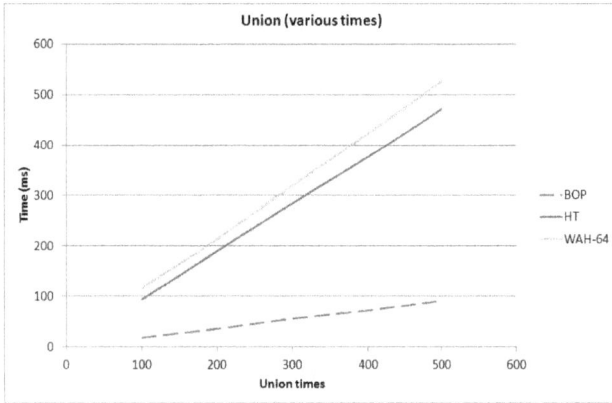

Figure 9: Union of k permissions lists

In the second category, we use a similar procedure to generate lists, but vary the number of objects from 900,000 to 9 million, fixing the density of permissions in step 3 so that 6% of all possible permissions are granted. The results are presented in Figure 10. It is interesting to notice that the cost for hashing increases faster for some settings than for others. In fact, this is not determined by the logical length but the total number of materialized entries. For each union, we first make a copy of the larger hash table. As we insert the entries from the smaller hash table into the copy of the larger one, we sometimes need to double the table size. For example, if we have two hash tables, each of which has 9 entries, the chance to require an extension is relatively small since the pre-allocated hash table is large enough as long as there are at least two buckets that merge (e.g., 16 entries after two merges); however, when both lists have 15 materialized entries, it is very likely that we need an extension, which causes the fluctuation of the slope of line for our hash table. For BOP, on the other hand, increasing the number of objects simply increases the number of blocks we need to merge, without making the blocks larger or denser on average.

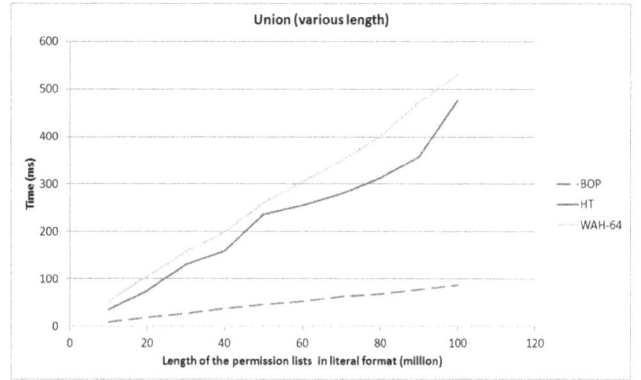

Figure 10: 500 unions between two permissions lists for various lengths and fixed density

For our real-world data, we repeatedly choose two random permissions lists and construct their union. Table 3 presents the time to compute 500 such unions using each of the implementations.

Table 3: Time needed for 500 unions or intersections using BOP, hashing, and WAH on the real-world data (ms)

	BOP	Hash Table	WAH
Union	72	190	368
Intersection	24	33	308

Intersection of Permissions Lists.

Figures 11 and 12 present similarly computed results for intersecting synthetic permissions lists. The results for real-world data are included in Table 3.

The performance advantages for intersection are very close to those for union, with two exceptions. First, intersection is faster than union using any of the implementations, because the result of an intersection will never contain more entries or granted permissions than the smaller participant. Second, the line for our hash table goes up more smoothly and the performance difference between our hash table and WAH is widened, since this operation requires no hash table extension and we did not implement table compression.

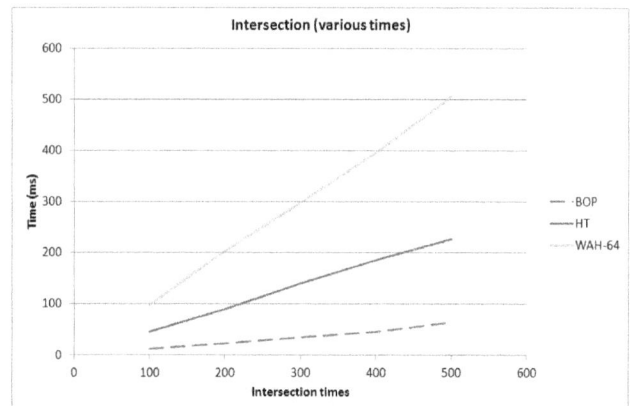

Figure 11: Intersection of k permissions lists

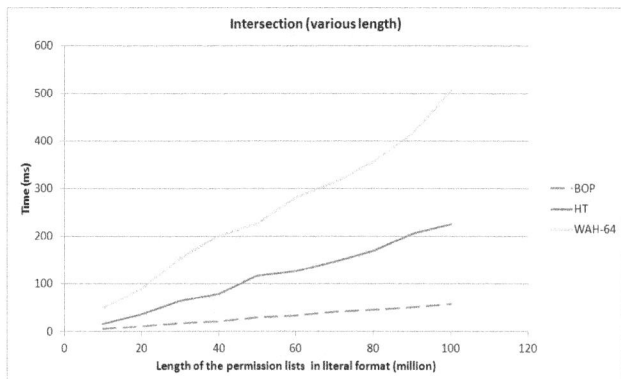

Figure 12: 500 intersections between two permissions lists for various lengths and fixed density

Browsing-oriented Querying.

Assuming that OIDs are assigned using a breadth-first traversal of the object hierarchy, a browsing-oriented query requires that we check multiple objects with contiguous OIDs. However, if some objects within a container (e.g., a folder) are deleted, then strict contiguity will be broken. Furthermore, if new objects are inserted into a container after other objects have been assigned OIDs, those objects will be assigned non-contiguous (essentially random) OIDs. We assume that only a small fraction of a container's objects are deleted or inserted after OID numbering. Checking permissions for a browsing-oriented operation can therefore be implemented as a search for the first object's permissions, followed by a sequential scan for most of the other objects' permissions, augmented by individual searches for objects with OIDs outside the (essentially) contiguous range.

Although checking an individual permission is extremely efficient with hashing, a major drawback of a hash table is that it is poor for iterating over the materialized entries in sorted order. Therefore, we support a browsing-oriented query by searching for each object individually when permissions lists are implemented using hashing.

Because searching for an object's permissions when using WAH is so much slower than when using BOP, it is obvious that WAH will be much less efficient than BOP for checking permissions for a list of contiguous objects. We therefore restrict our attention here to comparing BOP and hashing for browsing-oriented queries.

Figure 13 shows the results of our experiments for various lengths of contiguous OIDs (i.e., the number of OIDs to scan sequentially) and various numbers of out-of-order OIDs (i.e., the number of additional individual OIDs to check). All plots for BOP increase very slowly as the number of contiguous OIDs increases (corresponding to the number of objects in a container), and the cost almost doubles when the number of random OIDs doubles. This demonstrates that the cost of scanning sequentially is significantly less than the cost for finding a random OID in a permissions list when using BOP. In contrast, the cost when using hashing increases linearly with a far steeper slope as the number of objects to be checked in a query increases. (The number of random OIDs does not affect hash table performance since every OID is searched independently in any case.) When the percentage of random OIDs is small in a query (less

than approximately 10%), BOP is more efficient than a hash table. For example, the line BOP(3) shows that when 3 objects in a container encompassing 26 or more objects have been assigned out-of-order OIDs, BOP is more efficient than hashing.

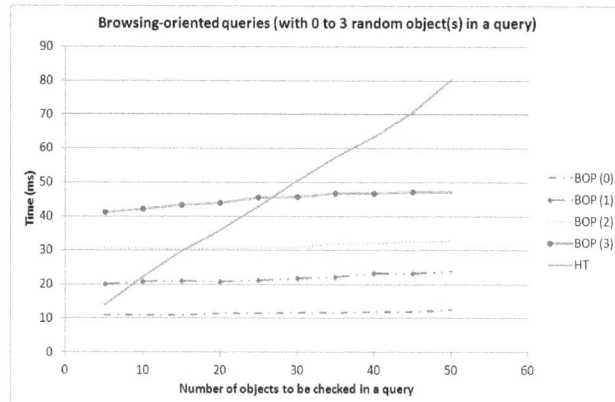

Figure 13: Experimental results for browsing-oriented queries on synthetic data. Lines labeled BOP(R) plot results for including R random OIDs.

In order to test this operation on the real-world data, we apply breadth-first numbering to all objects. We then re-assign random OIDs to $p\%$ of the objects, where p ranges from 0 to 10. (Note that the number of out-of-order OIDs per container is *not* constant.) We then measure the time to perform 50,000 random browsing-oriented queries. The results, displayed in Figure 14, show again that BOP is more efficient than hashing when the percentage of random OIDs is low.

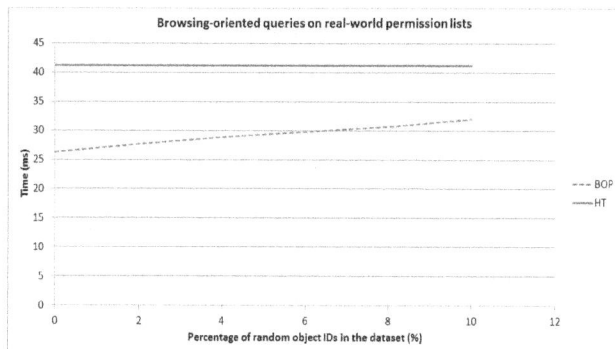

Figure 14: Experimental results for browsing-oriented queries on the real-world data.

Comprehensive Workloads.

Four prototypical workloads executed against the real-world ECM data round out our experimentation. In each one, 1) we include a variety of operations, 2) we incorporate the subject hierarchy to support permission inheritance, and 3) 10% of the objects are assigned random OIDs. Each of the four workloads includes 100,000 operations consisting of varying percentages of browsing-oriented queries, individual permission checking, permission granting, and permission revocation (Table 4). The first and third sets balance browsing and individual permissions checking, whereas the other two heavily favour browsing-oriented queries; the first and second sets include very little updating of permissions, whereas the other two include much heavier permission update loads.

Table 4: Query sets for comprehensive tests

	Browsing	Individual checking	Granting	Revoking
QS1	0.45	0.45	0.05	0.05
QS2	0.65	0.25	0.05	0.05
QS3	0.35	0.35	0.15	0.15
QS4	0.50	0.20	0.15	0.15

Table 5 presents the time to service these query sets. The first two query loads are more expensive to run because of the subject hierarchy (a browsing-oriented query or an individual permission query has to determine the *effective* permissions by searching, on average, 9.8 permissions lists, whereas granting or revoking a permission applies to only one permissions list). We find that BOP outperforms hashing for all four workloads: hashing is 5% slower for the first and third workloads, 7% slower for the second workload, and 9% slower for the fourth workload (which requires the fewest check, grant, and revoke operations on individual permissions). Thus, as expected, the performance advantage of BOP from quicker execution of browsing-oriented queries outweighs the performance advantage of hashing for checking, granting, and revoking individual permissions.

Table 5: Execution time for running comprehensive workloads (ms)

	BOP	Hash Table	Slowdown
QS1	1696	1778	5%
QS2	1801	1927	7%
QS3	1333	1397	5%
QS4	1398	1519	9%

6. CONCLUSIONS AND FURTHER WORK

In this paper, we surveyed the data and query characteristics of ECM systems' access control, observing that the most important characteristic is that there are many browsing-oriented queries in an ECM system. We then presented "blocked and ordered permissions" (BOP), a data structure specifically tailored to the browsing-oriented dominance of usage patterns in ECM systems. By comparing BOP against two alternative implementations, based on hashing and on WAH, we demonstrated that 1) BOP is much more space than either alternative, 2) BOP is much more time efficient than compressed bitmaps for both individual permission checking queries and browsing-oriented queries, and 3) when OIDs are assigned in conformance with the hierarchy of objects imposed by nested containers, BOP supports faster browsing-oriented queries as compared to a hash table. Through the comprehensive tests that contain realistic mixtures of operations and take the subject hierarchy into consideration, we found that BOP has the lowest overall cost.

The run-time performance advantage of BOP for browsing-oriented queries relies in part on most objects in a container being assigned sequential OIDs. As many more objects are inserted and deleted, this property deteriorates. Therefore to achieve good scalability, it is important that policies and mechanisms be developed to renumber objects when many components in a large container no longer have sequential OIDs. For highly dynamic systems, measuring the cost of OID renumbering may be important to understand how well BOP will perform in practice.

A second remaining challenge is to investigate the materialization of *effective permissions lists* in order to avoid the need to compute a subject's effective permissions for every operation at run time (by searching several explicit permissions lists or taking their union). However, if effective permissions lists are materialized, they need to be updated when changes are made to the explicit permissions lists (i.e., granting or revoking permissions) or to the subject hierarchy (i.e., updating group membership). The straightforward way is to refresh each potentially affected user's materialized permissions list completely (to re-compute the union of the explicit permission lists of the user and all its ancestor groups). However, there may be benefits to incorporating tailored algorithms for incrementally updating materialized effective permissions lists.

A final challenge is to explore how BOP can support negative permissions, such as explicit *deny* available in Share-Point 2013. The solution must support appropriate conflict resolution (when explicit or inheritable permissions include both "permit" and "deny") and fit into whatever strategy is adopted for materializing effective permissions lists.

7. ACKNOWLEDGMENTS

This research was supported by the NSERC Business Intelligence Network and by the University of Waterloo. Their support is highly appreciated. We also gratefully acknowledge the access control data and the insights provided by partner corporations outside the BIN network.

8. REFERENCES

[1] V. N. Anh and A. Moffat. Index compression using fixed binary codewords. In *Proc. 15th ACS Australasian Database Conf.*, pages 61–67, 2004.

[2] V. N. Anh and A. Moffat. Inverted index compression using word-aligned binary codes. *Inf. Retr.*, 8(1):151–166, 2005.

[3] G. Antoshenkov. Byte-aligned bitmap compression (poster abstract). In *Proc. 1995 IEEE Data Compression Conf.*, page 476, 1995.

[4] Apple Computer Inc. Understanding PackBits. http://devword.apple.com/technotes/tn/tn1023.html, 1996.

[5] W. Croft, D. Metzler, and T. Strohman. *Search Engines: Information Retrieval in Practice*. Addison Wesley, 2010.

[6] P. Gauravaram and L. R. Knudsen. Cryptographic hash functions. In *Handb. Inf. Commun. Secur.*, pages 59–79. 2010.

[7] G. Golub and C. Van Loan. *Matrix Computations*. Johns Hopkins Stud. Math. Sci. 2012.

[8] P. Gottschling and D. Lindbo. Generic compressed sparse matrix insertion: Algorithms and implementations in MTL4 and FEniCS. In *Proc. 8th ACM Workshop Parallel/High-Performance Object-Oriented Sci. Comp.*, pages 2:1–2:8, 2009.

[9] K. C. Knowlton. A fast storage allocator. *Commun. ACM*, 8(10):623–624, Oct. 1965.

[10] D. E. Knuth. *The Art of Computer Programming, Volume 3: Sorting and Searching.* Addison-Wesley, 1973.

[11] B. W. Lampson. Protection. In *Proc. 5th Princeton Conf. Inf. Sci. Sys.*, pages 437–443, 1971.

[12] M. Nelson and J.-L. Gailly. *The Data Compression Book (2nd ed.).* Wiley, 1996.

[13] G. Z. Wu and F. W. Tompa. Effective and efficient bitmaps for access control (summary). In *Proc. 2014 IEEE Data Compression Conf.*, page 433, 2014.

[14] K. Wu, E. J. Otoo, and A. Shoshani. A performance comparison of bitmap indexes. In *Proc. 2001 ACM Int. Conf. Inf. Knowl. Manag.*, pages 559–561, 2001.

[15] K. Wu, E. J. Otoo, A. Shoshani, and H. Nordbergi. Notes on design and implementation of compressed bit vectors. Technical Report LBNL/PUB-3161, Lawrence Berkeley Nat. Lab., 2001.

[16] J. Zhang, X. Long, and T. Suel. Performance of compressed inverted list caching in search engines. In *Proc. 17th ACM Int. Conf. World Wide Web*, pages 387–396, 2008.

[17] M. Zukowski, S. Héman, N. Nes, and P. A. Boncz. Super-scalar RAM-CPU cache compression. In *Proc. 22nd IEEE Int. Conf. Data Eng.*, pages 59–70, 2006.

Boosting GSHADE Capabilities: New Applications and Security in Malicious Setting *

Julien Bringer, Othmane El Omri†,
Constance Morel
Morpho, Issy-les-Moulineaux, France
surname.name@morpho.com

Hervé Chabanne
Télécom ParisTech, Paris, France
Morpho, Issy-les-Moulineaux, France
surname.name@morpho.com

ABSTRACT

The secure two-party computation (S2PC) protocols SHADE and GSHADE have been introduced by Bringer et al. in the last two years. The protocol GSHADE permits to compute different distances (Hamming, Euclidean, Mahalanobis) quite efficiently and is one of the most efficient compared to other S2PC methods. Thus this protocol can be used to efficiently compute one-to-many identification for several biometrics data (iris, face, fingerprint).

In this paper, we introduce two extensions of GSHADE. The first one enables us to evaluate new multiplicative functions. This way, we show how to apply GSHADE to a classical machine learning algorithm. The second one is a new proposal to secure GSHADE against malicious adversaries following the recent dual execution and cut-and-choose strategies. The additional cost is very small. By preserving the GSHADE's structure, our extensions are very efficient compared to other S2PC methods.

Keywords

GSHADE ; Secure Two-party Computation ; Semi-honest adversaries ; Malicious adversaries ; Biometrics

1. INTRODUCTION

An increasing amount of data are stored today by companies. They would like to keep this data private while securely performing analyses on data belonging to other parties. For instance in privacy-preserving biometric identification, a client has a fresh biometric acquisition and a server has a biometric database and they would like to determine whether the client is close to an element of the database without revealing anything else (e.g. the client fresh acquisition or the content of biometric database). One impor-

---

*This work has been partially funded by the French ANR projects BIOPRIV and SecuLar.

†Part of this work was done while Othmane El Omri was an intern at Morpho

SACMAT'16, June 05-08, 2016, Shanghai, China

© 2016 ACM. ISBN 978-1-4503-3802-8/16/06. . . $15.00

DOI: http://dx.doi.org/10.1145/2914642.2914658

tant cryptographic tool for data protection is Secure Two-party Computation (S2PC). This tool enables two parties to jointly evaluate a function over their inputs while preserving the privacy of their inputs. S2PC was introduced by Yao in 1982 [31] with the millionaire's problem. Plenty of S2PC protocols have been proposed so far, see for instance [6, 13, 27]. Numerous applications of S2PC exist such as secure machine learning (training between different databases or testing a new element) [3, 5, 30] or secure recommendation systems [11, 24].

Oblivious Transfer (OT) is the foundation of numerous S2PC protocols. This protocol first appeared in 1981 [27]. Here a Receiver inputs a bit b and a Sender inputs two elements (x_0, x_1). At the end of the protocol, the Receiver obtains x_b but has no information about x_{1-b} and the Sender obtains nothing. Based on OTs, two generic S2PC protocols - the Yao protocol [32] and the Goldreich-Micali-Wigderson (GMW) protocol [13] - are widely used in order to securely evaluate all Boolean circuits. An alternative generic S2PC protocol not based on OTs relies on the Homomorphic Encryption (HE) which permits to compute directly on encrypted data. Most efficient HE schemes can deal with only one operation with ciphertexts (e.g. [25] for additions) and although some recent HE schemes enable additions and multiplications [12]. They are still not the most practical S2PC protocols. SPDZ [10] is an interesting secure multiparty computation (SMC) protocol based on secret sharing and a somewhat homomorphic cryptosystem. This method has an efficient online phase and an expensive offline phase. For some decades, researchers have focused on improving the efficiency of these different protocols in order to solve real-world problems (e.g. Correlated OT [1], OT extension [16] for OTs; free XOR optimization [19], point and permute technique [22], garbled row reduction [21, 26], pipelined circuit evaluation [14] for Yao's garbled circuit). And some researchers have tried to build some S2PC specific protocols which evaluate only some functions but which are more efficient than generic protocols for the evaluation of these functions. For instance, the SHADE protocol [7] enables only the evaluation of Hamming distance. In 2014, SHADE has been generalized into GSHADE [6] in order to extend its evaluation function space to several metrics such as squared Euclidean distance, scalar product and squared Mahalanobis distance. SHADE and GSHADE are more efficient than generic S2PC protocols such as HE, Yao protocol and GMW protocol for the evaluation of these metrics.

More recently, researchers have focused on improving the security of S2PC protocols. Indeed, the first S2PC protocols are only secure against semi-honest adversaries where these adversaries follow the protocol but try to obtain as much information as possible from communications, but recent protocols try to be secure against malicious adversaries where the adversaries may deviate from the protocol in order to obtain more information. Several constructions based on zero-knowledge proofs [4, 13] or cut-and-choose construction [20] are known to protect against malicious adversaries but they are not efficient and thus can not be used in practice. For Yao's garbled circuit, an efficient method has been introduced [15]: a dual execution of the Yao protocol where the parties swap their roles between the two executions is followed by a secure equality test. This method is quite efficient because the two executions can be executed in parallel. Some attempts have been performed in order to secure SHADE in the malicious model. In [7], it is suggested to use additively homomorphic Committed OTs with zero knowledge proofs. Unfortunately, this new protocol is not sound because a malicious adversary may modify the output, which breaks correctness. Indeed [18, Section 5] presents a generic attack such that a malicious adversary can modify the Hamming distance result and pass the authentication with a $O(n)$ complexity where n is the input length. This can be fixed by adding some commitments and by modifying the zero-knowledge proofs (see [18, Sections 6 and 7]). To compute the Hamming distance between two n-bit vectors, the new secure protocol requires $3n$ commitments for the Client, n commitments for the Server, n zero-knowledge proofs, either n Committed Oblivious Transfers and n multiplications of ciphertexts if the Client obtains the output or n Verifiable Oblivious Transfers and $2n$ multiplications of ciphertexts if the Server obtains the output. Compared to the semi-honest SHADE protocol, this secure protocol from [18] is less efficient due to the numerous Committed and Verifiable Oblivious Transfers. In addition, this secure protocol cannot be extended to GSHADE protocol.

1.1 Our Contributions

This paper presents two extensions for the GSHADE protocol:

1. Adding new functionalities: GSHADE enables only to evaluate functions in the semi-honest model that can be expressed as $f(X, Y) = f_X(X) + f_Y(Y) + \sum_{i=1}^{n} f_i(x_i, Y)$ where $X = (x_1, ..., x_n) \in \{0, 1\}^n$ is the first party's input and Y is the second party's input. In this paper, we will suggest a new S2PC protocol based on GSHADE which permits to evaluate functions in the semi-honest model $f(X, Y) = f_X(X) \times f_Y(Y) \times \prod_{i=1}^{n} f_i(x_i, Y)$ where $X = (x_1, ..., x_n) \in \{0, 1\}^n$ is the first party's input and Y is the second party's input. This new protocol has a similar complexity as GSHADE (thus is as efficient). Moreover we show the usefulness of this extension on a secure machine learning application.

2. Security in the malicious model: GSHADE is only secure against semi-honest adversaries. In this paper, we will present two new efficient protocols based on GSHADE which are secure against malicious adversaries and which can evaluate functions

$$\begin{cases} f(X, Y) = \sum_{i=1}^{n} f_i(x_i, Y) = \sum_{i=1}^{n} f_i(y_i, X) \\ f(X, Y) = \prod_{i=1}^{n} f_i(x_i, Y) = \prod_{i=1}^{n} f_i(y_i, X) \end{cases}$$

where $X = (x_1, ..., x_n) \in \{0, 1\}^n$ is the first party's input and $Y = (y_1, ..., y_n) \in \{0, 1\}^n$ is the second party's input. Compared to GSHADE, the extra cost of these protocols is very small.

1.2 Notations

In the sequel, we will call GSHADE$_+$ the initial GSHADE protocol from [6] with the functions $f_+(X, Y) = f_X(X) + f_Y(Y) + \sum_{i=1}^{n} f_i(x_i, Y)$, GSHADE$_\times$ our first extension of GSHADE based on multiplications with the functions $f_\times(X, Y) = f_X(X) \times f_Y(Y) \times \prod_{i=1}^{n} f_i(x_i, Y)$, GSHADE$_\boxplus$ our extension of GSHADE$_+$ for malicious adversaries with the functions $f_\boxplus(X, Y) = \sum_{i=1}^{n} f_i(x_i, Y) = \sum_{i=1}^{n} f_i(y_i, X)$ and GSHADE$_\boxtimes$ our extension of GSHADE$_\times$ for malicious adversaries with the functions $f_\boxtimes(X, Y) = \prod_{i=1}^{n} f_i(x_i, Y) = \prod_{i=1}^{n} f_i(y_i, X)$.

In addition, κ denotes the security parameter. The notation $x \in_R S$ indicates that x is sampled uniformly at random from the finite set S. $[1, q]$ represents the set $\{1, 2, ..., q\}$. We write $(x_0, x_1) \xleftarrow{OT} b$ to represent an OT protocol with inputs (x_0, x_1) and b and the Receiver will obtain x_b. $a * b$ represents the entry-wise product $a * b = (a_1 \cdot b_1, ..., a_n \cdot b_n)$ where $a = (a_1, ..., a_n)$ and $b = (b_1, ..., b_n)$. $\bar{x}$ is the bit inversion of x: if x is a bit, then $\bar{x} = 1 - x$ and if $x = (x_1, ..., x_n)$ is a vector of bits, then $\bar{x} = (\bar{x_1}, ..., \bar{x_n}) = (1 - x_1, ..., 1 - x_n)$. In addition, $T = [t^1|...|t^\kappa] = [t_1|...|t_m]^T$ is a $m \times \kappa$ matrix where the i-th column is t^i and the j-th row is t_j.

1.3 Example Use Cases

In this section, we will give a non-exhaustive list of use cases where ours extensions can be applied.

Biometric access control.

In this use case, a building allows only the enrolled clients to enter. When a client would like to access the building, his biometric template is compared to all enrolled data. Since biometric data are sensitive, neither the client nor the building will learn information about biometric data of the other party. In the semi-honest model, the GSHADE$_+$ protocol is one of the most efficient protocol to respond this use case (see [6]). Unfortunately in the real world, most parties are malicious. Our GSHADE$_\boxplus$ extension secures the GSHADE$_+$ protocol against malicious adversaries with similar time performance.

Privacy-preserving clinical decision.

To improve healthcare, health professionals increasingly work with clinical decision support systems. Support Vector Machine (SVM) is a machine learning tool widely used by these systems to predict various diseases. The most common kernels used by SVM are the linear and Gaussian kernels. SVM with a linear kernel can be securely evaluated, in the semi-honest model, by GSHADE$_+$ protocol. In the same way, the Gaussian kernel can be securely evaluated by the GSHADE$_\times$ protocol. As biometric data, medical data are very sensitive. Thus, we need secured protocols against malicious adversaries : ours GSHADE$_\boxplus$ and GSHADE$_\boxtimes$ protocols satisfy these requirements.

1.4 Outlines

Firstly we introduce some security models and describe in details the two main protocols (OTs and GSHADE$_+$) which are the basis of our two extensions (see Section 2).

Then we present our two extensions of GSHADE: in Section 3 the extension to evaluate new functions $f_\times(X, Y) = f_X(X) \times f_Y(Y) \times \prod_{i=1}^{n} f_i(x_i, Y)$ and in Section 4 the extension which secures GSHADE in the malicious model. Finally, we compare GSHADE and its extensions to others S2PC protocols in Section 5. We conclude the paper in Section 6. In addition, in Appendix A, we show how to apply GSHADE$_\times$ to a classic machine learning algorithm: Support Vector Machine (SVM) with Radial Basis Function (RBF) kernel.

2. PRELIMINARIES

In this section, we introduce some security models for secure two-party computation and then we present in details two protocols which are essential for the understanding of our two GSHADE improvements.

2.1 Security Models

2.1.1 Security properties

There are two main requirements in S2PC:

- *Privacy/Security:* The protocol is *secure* if the parties learn their outputs and nothing else.

- *Correctness:* The protocol is *correct* if the parties obtain the correct outputs.

2.1.2 Adversarial behaviour

In S2PC, two main adversarial behaviours are considered:

- *Semi-honest* adversaries follow the protocol but try to obtain as much information as possible from their view of the protocol: inputs, outputs and all messages they received during the execution. This adversarial behaviour is also called *honest but curious* or *passive*.

- *Malicious* adversaries aim to obtain as much information as possible. To achieve his goal, a malicious adversary may follow his own strategy and deviate from the protocol, e.g. modify the sent messages/inputs, abort when he wants. This adversarial behaviour is also called *active*.

2.1.3 Security definitions

In malicious S2PC, the method to prove the privacy of the protocol consists in comparing the views of the protocol execution in two different worlds: the *real* world and the *ideal* world. In the *ideal* world, each party sends its own inputs to a third trusted party, this trusted party computes the outputs and then distributes the results to the parties. In contrast, there is no trusted party in the *real* world. A protocol is secure if when a probabilistic polynomial-time (PPT) adversary corrupted a party in the real world, the view distributions of this party in the real world and in the ideal world are indistinguishable.

We will prove the security of some constructions in the OT-hybrid model. In this model, the Oblivious Transfers are executed by a trusted party in the *real* world. Thus we prove that if the OTs used within our protocol are secure against semi-honest (resp. malicious) adversaries, then our protocol is secure in the semi-honest (resp. malicious) model. For the GSHADE$_\oplus$ and GSHADE$_\boxtimes$ protocols, we will prove the security of our constructions in the OT-hybrid and equality-test-hybrid model as in [15]. In this model, all Oblivious Transfers and equality tests are executed by a trusted party in the *real* world.

2.2 Oblivious Transfers

2.2.1 Oblivious Transfer protocol and its extensions

The Oblivious Transfer protocol first appeared in [27]. The main Oblivious Transfer used is the Naor Pinkas Oblivious Transfer [21, Section 3] (see Figure 1). It is a protocol between two parties: a Receiver and a Sender. The Receiver inputs a bit σ and the Sender inputs two vectors M_0, M_1. Finally, the Receiver obtains M_σ but obtains no information about $M_{1-\sigma}$ and the Sender obtains nothing (no information about σ). The protocol operates over a group $\mathbb{Z}_q$ of prime order with g a generator of this group such that the Computational Diffie-Hellman CDH problem is difficult. Moreover the function H is assumed to be a random oracle, e.g. a full domain-hash function. This protocol is secure against malicious adversaries thanks to these two assumptions: CDH problem and random oracle.

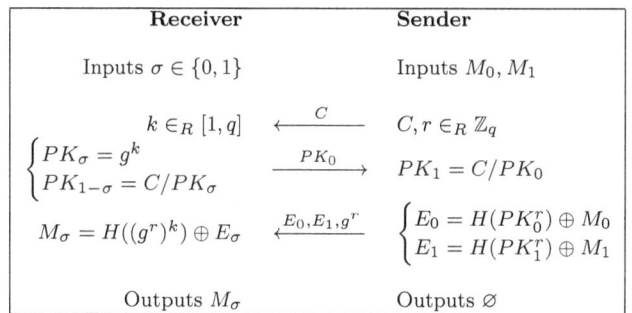

Receiver		Sender
Inputs $\sigma \in \{0,1\}$		Inputs M_0, M_1
$k \in_R [1, q]$	$\xleftarrow{\quad C \quad}$	$C, r \in_R \mathbb{Z}_q$
$\begin{cases} PK_\sigma = g^k \\ PK_{1-\sigma} = C/PK_\sigma \end{cases}$	$\xrightarrow{\quad PK_0 \quad}$	$PK_1 = C/PK_0$
$M_\sigma = H((g^r)^k) \oplus E_\sigma$	$\xleftarrow{E_0, E_1, g^r}$	$\begin{cases} E_0 = H(PK_0^r) \oplus M_0 \\ E_1 = H(PK_1^r) \oplus M_1 \end{cases}$
Outputs M_σ		Outputs $\varnothing$

Figure 1: Naor Pinkas Oblivious Transfer from [21, Section 3]

Oblivious Transfers are extensively used in secure two-party computation. In most cases, some thousands or millions Oblivious Transfers are required. Thus the Naor Pinkas Oblivious Transfer protocol (see Figure 1) is not sufficiently efficient in these use cases. A more efficient way to perform many Oblivious Transfers is the Oblivious Transfer extension which enables from few Oblivious Transfers (usually around $\kappa = 80$) and some symmetric cryptographic functions to evaluate a large number of Oblivious Transfers. The main OTs extension used is presented in Figure 2 (from [1, Protocol 52]). The Receiver inputs m bits $r_1, ..., r_m$ and the Sender inputs m pairs of vectors $\forall j \in [1, m], (x_j^0, x_j^1) \in (\{0, 1\}^\ell)^2$. At the end of the protocol, the Receiver obtains $\forall j \in [1, m], x_j^{r_j}$ and nothing else and the Sender obtains nothing. In this protocol, $H : \{0, 1\}^\kappa \to \{0, 1\}^\ell$ and $G : \{0, 1\}^\kappa \to \{0, 1\}^m$ are assumed to be random oracles. This protocol is secure in the semi-honest model.

The communications are often the bottleneck in protocols based on OTs. The Correlated OT extension has a lower communication complexity than generic OT extension. It was first introduced in [1, Section 5.4] for the Yao protocol where the Correlated function is a XOR. In the Yao protocol, $x_j^0 = k_j^0$ and $x_j^1 = k_j^0 \oplus \Delta$ where k_j^0 is a random value. In the last step of the OT extension protocol (see Figure 2), the Sender can set $k_j^0 = H(q_j)$ and send the single value $y_j = \Delta \oplus H(q_j) \oplus H(q_j \oplus s)$ instead of (y_j^0, y_j^1). The Receiver

	Receiver		Sender
Inputs	$r = (r_1, ..., r_m) \in \{0,1\}^m$		$\forall j \in [1, m], (x_j^0, x_j^1) \in \left(\{0,1\}^\ell\right)^2$
Random	$\forall i \in [1, \kappa], (k_i^0, k_i^1) \in_R \left(\{0,1\}^\kappa\right)^2$		$s = (s_1, ..., s_\kappa) \in_R \{0,1\}^\kappa$
Initial phase	$\forall i \in [1, \kappa], (k_i^0, k_i^1)$	$\xleftarrow{\text{OTs}}$	$\forall i \in [1, \kappa], s_i$ $\forall i \in [1, \kappa], k_i^{s_i}$
Extension	$\forall i \in [1, \kappa], t^i = G(k_i^0)$ notation $T = [t^1|...|t^\kappa] = [t_1|...|t_m]^T$		
	$\forall i \in [1, \kappa], u^i = t^i \oplus G(k_i^1) \oplus r$	$\xrightarrow{u^1, ..., u^\kappa}$	$q^i = (s_i . u^i) \oplus G(k_i^{s_i}) = (s_i . r) \oplus t^i$ notation $Q = [q^1|...|q^\kappa] = [q_1|...|q_m]^T$
	$\forall j \in [1, m], x_j^{r_j} = y_j^{r_j} \oplus H(t_j)$	$\xleftarrow{\forall j \in [1,m], (y_j^0, y_j^1)}$	$\forall j \in [1, m], \begin{cases} y_j^0 = x_j^0 \oplus H(q_j) \\ y_j^1 = x_j^1 \oplus H(q_j \oplus s) \end{cases}$

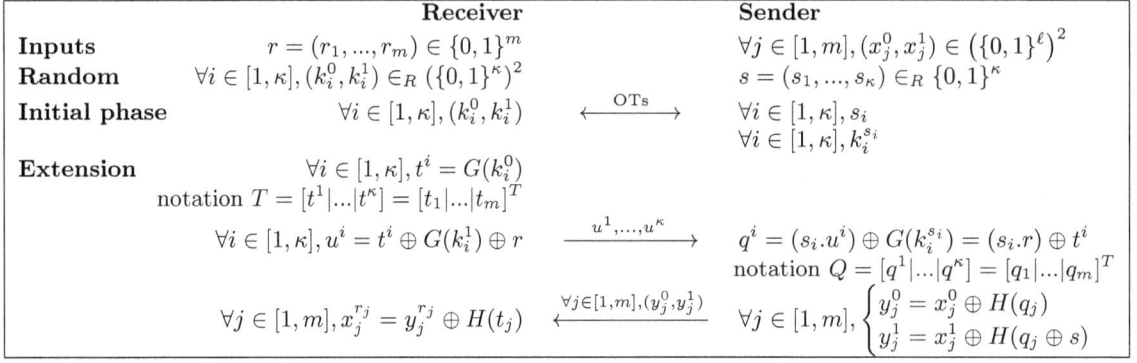

Figure 2: OTs extension from [1, Protocol 52]

outputs $H(t_j)$ if $r_j = 0$ and $y_j \oplus H(t_j)$ otherwise. Note that if $r_j = 0$, we have $t_j = q_j$ and thus $H(t_j) = k_j^0$. Otherwise, if $r_j = 1$, we have $H(t_j) = H(q_j \oplus s)$ and thus $y_j \oplus H(t_j) = \Delta \oplus H(q_j) = k_j^0 \oplus \Delta$.

2.2.2 Malicious attack against OTs extension

As explained in [2, 17, 23], the only cheating way for a malicious adversary is to not use the same r in each u^i computation. Let $\rho^1, ..., \rho^\kappa$ be the different r used by an adversary and $R = [\rho^1|...|\rho^\kappa] = [\rho_1|...|\rho_m]^T \in \{0,1\}^{m \times \kappa}$. Compared to the Figure 2, we have with a malicious Receiver:

$$\begin{cases} \forall i \in [1, \kappa], u^i = t^i \oplus G(k_i^1) \oplus \rho^i \\ \forall i \in [1, \kappa], q^i = (s_i . u^i) \oplus G(k_i^{s_i}) = (s_i . \rho^i) \oplus t^i \\ \forall j \in [1, m], q_j = (\rho_j * s) \oplus t_j \\ \forall j \in [1, m], q_j \oplus s = (\bar{\rho}_j * s) \oplus t_j \end{cases}$$

instead of:
$$\begin{cases} \forall i \in [1, \kappa], u^i = t^i \oplus G(k_i^1) \oplus r \\ \forall i \in [1, \kappa], q^i = (s_i . u^i) \oplus G(k_i^{s_i}) = (s_i . r) \oplus t^i \\ \forall j \in [1, m], q_j = (r_j . s) \oplus t_j \\ \forall j \in [1, m], q_j \oplus s = (\bar{r}_j . s) \oplus t_j \end{cases}$$

Assume that the adversary knows x_1^0. He can deduce at least one bit of s. For instance, the adversary chooses $\rho_1 = (1, 0, ..., 0)$. Thus we have $\rho_1 * s = (s_1, 0, ..., 0)$ and $H(q_1) = H(t_1 \oplus (s_1, 0, ..., 0))$. Then the adversary computes $H(t_1)$ and $H(t_1 \oplus (1, 0, ..., 0))$ and compares them to $y_1^0 \oplus x_1^0$ in order to infer from the comparisons the bit value s_1.

From some bit information on x_j^0, an adversary can deduce several bits of s. Let $e_1 = (1, 0, ..., 0)$, $e_2 = (0, 1, 0, ..., 0)$ and so on. Let $x_{|\{i_1, ..., i_k\}} = (x_{i_1}, ..., x_{i_k})$. Assume that an adversary knows $(x_j^0)_{|I}$ with $I \subset [1, \ell]$. If there exists a set $P = \{p_1, ..., p_k\} \subset [1, \kappa]$ such that the set

$$\left\{ H\left(t_j \bigoplus_{i=1}^k \lambda_i \cdot e_{p_i} \right)_{|I} \middle| (\lambda_1, ..., \lambda_k) \in \{0,1\}^k \right\}$$

contains no duplicate value, then the adversary can obtain $s_{|P}$ by choosing $\rho_j = \bigoplus_{j \in P} e_j$. Similar attacks are possible if the adversary has some information about x_j^1 (with $\bar{e}_j$ instead of e_j). If the adversary succeeds to deduce the whole s from some information on some x_j^i, then he can deduce all Sender's inputs $(x_j^0, x_j^1), \forall j \in [1, m]$.

Some protocols [2, 23] have been suggested to protect the OTs extension [1, Protocol 52] against malicious Receiver.

The main idea is to add some checks to verify that the Sender uses the same r in each u^i.

2.2.3 OTs extension security analysis with unknown inputs

In this section, we add assumptions to the OTs extension (see Figure 2) in order to secure this protocol against malicious adversaries. We assume that the Receiver has no information about the Sender's inputs which are uniformly and independently distributed over $\{0,1\}^\ell$ and the Oblivious Transfers in the initial phase are secure against malicious adversaries. Then we prove that the OTs extension protocol is secure against malicious adversaries if these assumptions are correct. Thus if the OT inputs are unknown and uniformly random, the OTs extension protocol is secure against malicious adversaries and is more efficient than more general malicious OTs protocols [2, 23]. In the GSHADE extension secure in the malicious model (see Section 4), we advise to use the OTs extension protocol instead of general malicious OTs protocols for efficiency reasons.

PROPOSITION 1. *In the OTs extension protocol from [1, Protocol 52] (see Figure 2), if the Sender's inputs are randomly and independently chosen in $\{0,1\}^\ell$, if the Receiver has no information about the Sender's inputs and if the OTs in the initial phase are secure in the malicious model, then this OTs extension protocol is secure against a malicious Receiver.*

PROOF. As the κ OTs in the initial phase are secure against malicious adversaries, we have only to demonstrate the indistinguishability between the real world and the ideal world in the extension phase.

Let A be a probabilistic polynomial-time PPT adversary controlling the Receiver in the real world. We describe a simulator S_A who simulates the view of A in the ideal world. S_A sends $r = (r_1, ..., r_m) \in \{0,1\}^m$ and $\forall i \in [1, \kappa], u^i = t^i \oplus G(k_i^1) \oplus r$ to the trusted party and obtains

$$\forall j \in [1, m], \begin{cases} y_j^0 = x_j^0 \oplus H(q_j) & \text{if } r_j = 0 \\ y_j^1 = x_j^1 \oplus H(q_j \oplus s) & \text{otherwise } (r_j = 1) \end{cases}$$

Then S_A picks randomly $a_j \in_R \{0,1\}^\ell, \forall j \in [1, m]$ and he builds pairs $(z_j^0, z_j^1), \forall j \in [1, m]$ such that if $r_j = 0$, then $z_j^0 = x_j^0 \oplus H(q_j)$ and $z_j^1 = a_j$, else $z_j^0 = a_j$ and $z_j^1 = x_j^1 \oplus H(q_j \oplus s)$. Finally S_A sends $(z_j^0, z_j^1), \forall j \in [1, m]$ to the adversary A and the adversary computes $x_j^{r_j} = z_j^{r_j} \oplus H(t_j)$.

In the real world, the malicious Receiver receives $\forall j \in [1,m]$, $\begin{cases} y_j^0 = x_j^0 \oplus H(q_j) \\ y_j^1 = x_j^1 \oplus H(q_j \oplus s) \end{cases}$ with $\begin{cases} q_j = (\rho_j * s) \oplus t_j \\ q_j \oplus s = (\bar{\rho}_j * s) \oplus t_j \end{cases}$

As s and $\forall j \in [1,m]$, (x_j^0, x_j^1) are random and initially unknown from the adversary A and as a_j are randomly picked over $\{0,1\}^\ell$ and as H and G are random oracles, the (y_j^0, y_j^1)'s distributions in the real world and in the simulated world are identically distributed (uniform distribution over $\mathbb{Z}_m^2$). Thus the Receiver's view in the real world and the simulated Receiver's view in the ideal world are indistinguishable. Moreover, the distribution in the ideal world only requires the knowledge of $x_j^{r_j}$ and does not require the knowledge of $x_j^{1-r_j}$. That proves full security against a malicious Receiver. $\square$

2.3 The original GSHADE Protocol

GSHADE$_+$ [6] is an efficient protocol secure in the semi-honest model to evaluate in S2PC all functions $f_+(X,Y) = f_X(X) + f_Y(Y) + \sum_{i=1}^n f_i(x_i, Y)$ where $X = (x_1, ..., x_n) \in \{0,1\}^n$ is the first party's input and Y is the second party's input. This protocol is only based on Oblivious Transfers (see Figure 3). Note that m is chosen such that the codomain of the evaluation function f is included into $\mathbb{Z}_m$. Several usual metrics can be evaluated with GSHADE$_+$ such as the Hamming distance, the squared Euclidean distance, the scalar product and the squared Mahalanobis distance. This protocol is secure in the semi-honest model. For a complete demonstration, see [6].

Client	**Server**
Inputs $X \in \{0,1\}^n$	Inputs Y
$\quad X = (x_1, ..., x_n)$	
	$\forall i \in [1,n], r_i \in_R \mathbb{Z}_m$
$x_i \xleftarrow{\text{OT}}$	$(r_i + f_i(0,Y), r_i + f_i(1,Y))$
$t_i = r_i + f_i(x_i, Y)$	
$T = f_X(X) + \sum_{i=1}^n t_i$	$R = -f_Y(Y) + \sum_{i=1}^n r_i$
Outputs T	Outputs R
such that $T - R = f_+(X,Y)$	

Figure 3: The GSHADE$_+$ protocol

2.3.1 Correlated OT extension optimization

The GSHADE$_+$ protocol is compatible with the Correlated OT extension as explained in [6]. First, we have to modify the Correlated OT extension for correlation functions $f_{\Delta_j}(x) = x + \Delta_j$. At the end of the OT extension protocol (see Figure 2), the Sender sends the single value $y_j = f_{\Delta_j}(H(q_j)) - H(q_j \oplus s)$ and the Receiver outputs $H(t_j)$ if $r_j = 0$ or $H(t_j) \oplus y_j$ if $r_j = 1$ (see Appendix A in [6]). Then the GSHADE$_+$ can be rewritten with Correlated OT extension. The correlation function is $f_{\Delta_i}(x) = x + \Delta_i$ where $\Delta_i = f_i(1,Y) - f_i(0,Y)$. In the Correlated OT, the Server outputs $\rho_i = H(q_i)$ and the Client outputs $\tau_i = \rho_i - f_i(0,Y) + f_i(x_i, Y)$. At the end of the GSHADE$_+$ protocol, the Server outputs $R = -f_Y(Y) + \sum_i (\rho_i - f_i(0,Y))$ and the Client outputs $T = f_X(X) + \sum_i \tau_i$. See Section 3.4 in [6] for more details on the Correlated OT extension in GSHADE$_+$ and its correctness and security proofs.

2.3.2 1-vs-N optimization

It is a GSHADE extension which enables to efficiently evaluate N functions $f(X, Y_1), ..., f(X, Y_N)$ where X is the Client's input and $Y_1, ..., Y_N$ are the Server's inputs. The main idea is to concatenate the partial masked results: $(r_i + f_i(0,Y), r_i + f_i(1,Y))$ is replaced by $(r_{1,i} + f_i(0,Y_1) \parallel ... \parallel r_{N,i} + f_i(0,Y_N), r_{1,i} + f_i(1,Y_1) \parallel ... \parallel r_{N,i} + f_i(1,Y_N))$.

3. MORE FUNCTIONALITIES IN THE SEMI-HONEST SETTING

Our first extension of GSHADE$_+$ aims to add some functionalities in order to be able to evaluate in the semi-honest model the functions

$$f_\times(X,Y) = f_X(X) \times f_Y(Y) \times \prod_{i=1}^n f_i(x_i, Y)$$

where $X = (x_1, ..., x_n) \in \{0,1\}^n$ is the Client's input and Y is the Server's input. This extension is compatible with the Correlated OT extension and the 1-vs-N optimization and has a complexity similar to the GSHADE$_+$ protocol. In Appendix A, we present how to classify in SMC some elements following a Support Vector Machines (SVM) classifier with a Radial Basis Function (RBF) kernel thanks to this GSHADE$_\times$ protocol.

3.1 Extension with Multiplicative Masks

The main idea is to replace the additions by multiplications. That requires also to replace the additive masks in the OTs by multiplicative masks. For security reasons, we would like that $r_i \times f_i(x_i, Y)$ be uniformly distributed over $\mathbb{Z}_m^*$. Thus we have to select m such that m is prime and the codomain of f is included into $\mathbb{Z}_m^*$ (this implies that $f_i(x_i, Y)$, $f_X(X)$ and $f_Y(Y)$ are never equal to zero).

In more details, all computations are performed into $\mathbb{Z}_m$. The Client inputs $X = (x_1, ..., x_n) \in \{0,1\}^n$ and the Server inputs Y. The Server prepares n random values $r_1, ..., r_n \in_R \mathbb{Z}_m^*$. Then the Client and the Server engage in OTs: the Client is the Receiver with input x_i and the Server is the Sender with input $(r_i \times f_i(0,Y), r_i \times f_i(1,Y))$. Thus the Client obtains $t_i = r_i \times f_i(x_i, Y)$. Then the Client computes $T = f_X(X) \times \prod_{i=1}^n t_i$ and the Server computes $R = (f_Y(Y))^{-1} \times \prod_{i=1}^n r_i$. Finally if the Client (resp. the Server) obtains the output, then the Server sends R to the Client (resp. the Client sends T to the Server) and the Client (resp. the Server) outputs $T \times R^{-1} = f_\times(X,Y)$. The Figure 4 presents this new protocol called GSHADE$_\times$.

The GSHADE$_\times$ protocol is compatible with OT extension, Correlated OT and the 1-vs-N optimization. These optimizations permit to obtain an efficient protocol with a complexity similar to the GSHADE$_+$ protocol complexity. The compatibility with OT extension and 1-vs-N optimization is obvious whereas the compatibility with Correlated OT needs a little work. The Table 1 presents the modifications to adapt Correlated OT from GSHADE$_+$ to our GSHADE$_\times$ protocol (we used the notations from [6, Section 3.4]). The main modifications consist to replace the additions by multiplications and the subtractions by multiplications by the inverse.

3.2 Security Analysis in the Semi-honest Model

PROPOSITION 2. *The GSHADE$_\times$ protocol is secure and correct in the semi-honest model with the OT-hybrid setting.*

Parameters	m is prime the codomain of $f_\times$ is included into $\mathbb{Z}_m^*$

Client	Server
Inputs $X \in \{0,1\}^n$ $X = (x_1, ..., x_n)$	Inputs Y
	$\forall i \in [1,n], r_i \in_R \mathbb{Z}_m^*$
$x_i \xleftrightarrow{\text{OT}} (r_i \cdot f_i(0,Y), r_i \cdot f_i(1,Y))$	
$t_i = r_i \cdot f_i(x_i, Y)$	
$T = f_X(X) \cdot \prod_{i=1}^n t_i$	$R = (f_Y(Y))^{-1} \cdot \prod_{i=1}^n r_i$
Outputs T	Outputs R
such that $T \cdot R^{-1} = f_\times(X,Y)$	

Figure 4: The GSHADE$_\times$ protocol

In GSHADE$_+$	In GSHADE$_\times$
$\Delta_i = f_i(1,Y) - f_i(0,Y)$	$\Delta_i = f_i(1,Y) \cdot (f_i(0,Y))^{-1}$
$f_{\Delta_i}(x) = x + \Delta_i$	$f_{\Delta_i}(x) = x \cdot \Delta_i$
$y_j = f_{\Delta_j}(H(q_j)) - H(q_j \oplus s)$	$y_j = f_{\Delta_j}(H(q_j)) \cdot (H(q_j \oplus s))^{-1}$
$\rho_i \in_R \mathbb{Z}_m$	$\rho_i \in_R \mathbb{Z}_m^*$
$\tau_i = \rho_i - f_i(0,Y) + f_i(x_i, Y)$	$\tau_i = \rho_i \cdot (f_i(0,Y))^{-1} \cdot f_i(x_i, Y)$
$T = f_X(X) + \sum_{i=1}^n \tau_i$	$T = f_X(X) \cdot \prod_{i=1}^n \tau_i$
$R = -f_Y(Y) + \sum_i \rho_i - f_i(0,Y)$	$R = (f_Y(Y))^{-1} \prod_i \rho_i (f_i(0,Y))^{-1}$

Table 1: Adaptation of the Correlated OT from the GSHADE$_+$ protocol to the GSHADE$_\times$ protocol

PROOF. *Correctness* To prove the correctness in the semi-honest model, we will detail the computations:

$$T \times R^{-1} = \left(f_X(X) \times \prod_{i=1}^n t_i \right) \times \left(f_Y(Y)^{-1} \times \prod_{i=1}^n r_i \right)^{-1}$$

$$= f_X(X) \times f_Y(Y) \times \prod_{i=1}^n (r_i \times f_i(x_i, Y)) \times r_i^{-1}$$

$$= f_X(X) \times f_Y(Y) \times \prod_{i=1}^n f_i(x_i, Y)$$

$$= f_\times(X, Y)$$

Privacy This security proof is similar to the proof of GSHADE$_+$. In this proof, we assume that our OTs are secure in the semi-honest model (OT-hybrid setting). As the OTs are secure in the semi-honest model and the Server receives no message except in the OTs, thus his view can be perfectly simulated and he cannot obtain information.

For a corrupted Client, we compare his view in the ideal world and in the real world. Let A be a PPT adversary controlling the Client in the real world. We describe a simulator S_A who simulates the view of A in the ideal world. S_A runs A on input X. S_A sends X to the trusted party and obtains $f_\times(X,Y)$. S_A picks n random values $t_1, ..., t_{n-1}, R \in_R \mathbb{Z}_m^*$ and computes $t_n = R \times f_\times(X,Y) \times \left(\prod_{i=1}^{n-1} t_i \right)^{-1}$. S_A sends the t_i's to the Client and sends R to the Server. Finally S_A outputs whatever the Client outputs.

In the real world, the malicious Client obtains $t_i = r_i \times f_i(x_i, Y)$ where r_i is randomly picked by the Server over $\mathbb{Z}_m^*$.

We can easily observe that the t_i's distributions in the real and ideal world are identically distributed (uniformly

distributed over $\mathbb{Z}_m^*$). Moreover the distribution in the ideal world requires only the knowledge of the final output. Thus this protocol is full secure against a semi-honest Client. □

3.3 Performance

As a reminder, the complexity of GSHADE$_+$ is $3n + 2nN\lceil \log m \rceil / o$ symmetric operations where o is the output size of the pseudo-random function G used in the OT extension, n is the Client's input size, the codomain of f is included into $\mathbb{Z}_m$ and N is the number of parallel executions (1-vs-N GSHADE$_+$ optimization). Our extension with multiplicative masks replaces additions by multiplications and adds two inversions (R^{-1} and $f_Y(Y)^{-1}$). Multiplications are negligible operations compared to symmetric operations. Thus when compared to GSHADE$_+$, the computation complexity of our extension adds only two inversions. To conclude the complexity of our extension GSHADE$_\times$ is similar to the complexity of the original GSHADE$_+$ protocol.

We implemented the GSHADE$_+$ and the GSHADE$_\times$ protocols. The similar runtimes for GSHADE$_+$ and GSHADE$_\times$ (see Table 2) confirm this complexity analysis. These experiments were done on two identical standard computers (Ubuntu 12.04 (VirtualBox), Intel Core i5 with 5GB RAM) connected via LAN. The measurements include the overall time spent included pre-computations. About the security parameters, we use κ OTs on κ bits in the OTs extension where $\kappa = 80$.

N	n	m	GSHADE$_+$	GSHADE$_\times$
1000	500	10 007	0.353s	0.369s
1000	500	100 003	0.411s	0.429s
1000	1000	10 007	0.672s	0.699s
1000	1000	100 003	0.791s	0.812s
5000	500	10 007	1.653s	1.715s
5000	500	100 003	1.946s	2.021s
5000	1000	10 007	3.288s	3.436s
5000	1000	100 003	3.875s	4.043s

Table 2: Runtimes for GSHADE$_+$ and GSHADE$_\times$

4. SECURITY AGAINST MALICIOUS ADVERSARIES

Our second GSHADE extension called GSHADE$_\boxplus$ aims to efficiently secure the GSHADE$_+$ protocol against malicious adversaries. For correctness reasons, we have to reduce the functions that can be evaluated with this protocol. In the malicious model, our function domain is $f_\boxplus(X,Y) = \sum_{i=1}^n f_i(x_i, Y) = \sum_{i=1}^n f_i(y_i, X)$ where $X = (x_1, ..., x_n) \in \{0,1\}^n$ is the Client's input and $Y = (y_1, ..., y_n) \in \{0,1\}^n$ is the Server's input. This function domain contains the Hamming distance and the scalar product. Similarly, we can secure GSHADE$_\times$ against malicious adversaries on the function space $f_\boxtimes(X,Y) = \prod_{i=1}^n f_i(x_i, Y) = \prod_{i=1}^n f_i(y_i, X)$ where $X = (x_1, ..., x_n) \in \{0,1\}^n$ is the Client's input and $Y = (y_1, ..., y_n) \in \{0,1\}^n$ is the Server's input. In this section, we will explain in details the GSHADE$_\boxplus$ and GSHADE$_\boxtimes$ protocols with their security and correctness proofs.

4.1 Extension in the Malicious Model

4.1.1 The GSHADE$_\boxplus$ protocol

Our main idea is to use the GSHADE$_+$ protocol [6] with a dual execution similar to [15]. A dual execution requires a symmetric function: $f(X,Y) = f_X(X) + f_Y(Y) + \sum_i f_i(x_i, Y)$ $= f_X(X) + f_Y(Y) + \sum_i f_i(y_i, X)$ where $x_i, y_i \in \{0,1\}$. In a dual execution, the two parties conduct two separate runs of the same protocol twice with the parties swapping roles and then they perform a security equality test. The two executions of the same protocol are independent, thus they may be executed in parallel. If the two parties have at least two cores each, the extra runtime of two executions (instead of one execution in the semi-honest model) will be very low. Figure 5 presents a high level view of a naive GSHADE$_+$ in dual execution.

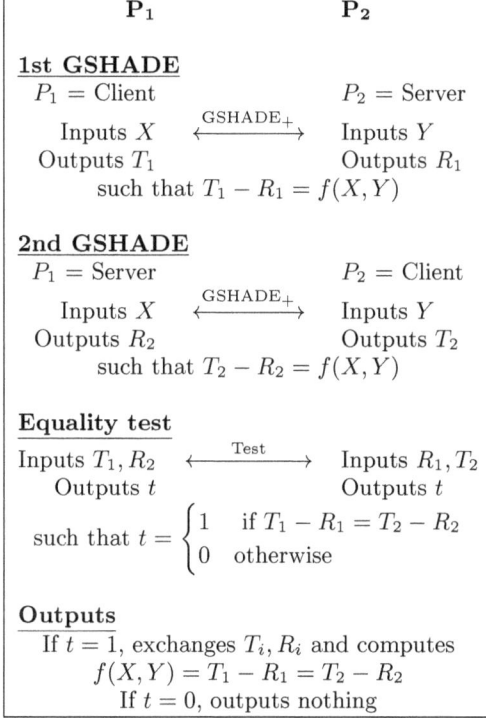

P$_1$ **P$_2$**

1st GSHADE

P_1 = Client P_2 = Server

Inputs X $\xleftrightarrow{\text{GSHADE}_+}$ Inputs Y

Outputs T_1 Outputs R_1

such that $T_1 - R_1 = f(X, Y)$

2nd GSHADE

P_1 = Server P_2 = Client

Inputs X $\xleftrightarrow{\text{GSHADE}_+}$ Inputs Y

Outputs R_2 Outputs T_2

such that $T_2 - R_2 = f(X, Y)$

Equality test

Inputs T_1, R_2 $\xleftrightarrow{\text{Test}}$ Inputs R_1, T_2

Outputs t Outputs t

such that $t = \begin{cases} 1 & \text{if } T_1 - R_1 = T_2 - R_2 \\ 0 & \text{otherwise} \end{cases}$

Outputs

If $t = 1$, exchanges T_i, R_i and computes

$f(X, Y) = T_1 - R_1 = T_2 - R_2$

If $t = 0$, outputs nothing

Figure 5: Naive GSHADE$_+$ in dual execution

Unfortunately this protocol (see Figure 5) is not yet correct because a malicious adversary can modify the result $f(X, Y)$. For instance, P_1 can use in the equality test the input $(T_1 + a, R_2 - a)$ instead of (T_1, R_2). That enables to keep the equality while modifying the output: now the output is equal to $f(X, Y) + a$. To avoid that, we will reduce the function domain to $f_{\boxplus}(X, Y) = \sum_i f_i(x_i, Y) = \sum_i f_i(y_i, X)$ because $f_X(X)$ and $f_Y(Y)$ are difficult to check. Moreover we will add a multiplicative mask, the OT inputs $(r_i + f_i(0, Y), r_i + f_i(1, Y))$ will be replaced by $(a(r_i + f_i(0, Y)), a(r_i + f_i(1, Y)))$ where a is an invertible element of $\mathbb{Z}_m$ picked randomly by the Server (the same for all i). m needs to be prime so that the $(a(r_i + f_i(0, Y)), a(r_i + f_i(1, Y)))$'s distribution is uniformly random over $\mathbb{Z}_m$.

In more details, all computations are performed into $\mathbb{Z}_m$ with m a prime such that the codomain of $f_{\boxplus}$ is included into $\mathbb{Z}_m$. The party P_1 inputs $X = (x_1, ..., x_n) \in \{0,1\}^n$ and the party P_2 inputs $Y = (y_1, ..., y_n) \in \{0,1\}^n$. Each party P_i prepares $n + 1$ random values $r_{1,i}, ..., r_{n,i} \in_R \mathbb{Z}_m$ and $a_i \in_R \mathbb{Z}_m^*$. In the first GSHADE, P_1 and P_2 engage in Oblivious Transfers where P_1 is the Receiver with input x_i and P_2 is the Sender with input $(a_1(r_{i,1} + f_i(0, Y)), a_1(r_{i,1} + f_i(1, Y)))$. Thus P_1 obtains $t_{i,1} = a_1(r_{i,1} + f_i(x_i, Y))$. Then P_1 com-

putes $T_1 = \sum_i t_{i,1}$ and P_2 computes $R_1 = a_1 \sum_i r_{i,1}$. In the second GSHADE, P_1 and P_2 swap their roles: P_1 obtains $R_2 = a_2 \sum_i r_{i,2}$ and P_2 obtains $T_2 = \sum_i t_{i,2} = \sum_i a_2(r_{i,2} + f_i(y_i, X))$. Then they perform a secure equality test. P_1 inputs T_1, R_2, a_2 et P_2 inputs R_1, T_2, a_1. The equality test outputs 1 if $(T_1 - R_1)a_2 = (T_2 - R_2)a_1$ and 0 otherwise. During this equality test, P_1 and P_2 learn only the output and nothing about the inputs of the other party. Finally if the equality test outputs 0, then the protocol aborts without any output. If P_1 obtains the output, then P_2 sends R_1, T_2, a_1 to P_1, P_1 checks $(T_1 - R_1)a_1^{-1} = (T_2 - R_2)a_2^{-1}$. If the equality is correct, then P_1 outputs $(T_1 - R_1)a_1^{-1}$, else P_1 aborts. The case P_2 obtains the output is similar. At the end of each GSHADE, if the Client obtains $t_{i,j} = 0, \forall i \in [1, n]$, then he aborts. The Figure 6 presents our new protocol in details.

4.1.2 The GSHADE$_{\boxtimes}$ protocol

Similarly to the GSHADE$_{\boxplus}$ protocol, the GSHADE$_{\boxtimes}$ protocol is based on a dual execution of the GSHADE$_\times$ protocol with a common exponentiation mask (instead of multiplicative). The Table 3 presents the modifications to adapt the GSHADE$_{\boxplus}$ protocol to the GSHADE$_{\boxtimes}$ protocol.

In GSHADE$_{\boxplus}$	In GSHADE$_{\boxtimes}$
$r_{i,j} \in_R \mathbb{Z}_m, a_j \in_R \mathbb{Z}_m^*$	$r_{i,j} \in_R \mathbb{Z}_m^*, a_j \in_R \mathbb{Z}_m^*$
$a_j(r_{i,j} + f_i(0, Y))$	$(r_{i,j} \cdot f_i(0, Y))^{a_j}$
$a_j(r_{i,j} + f_i(1, Y))$	$(r_{i,j} \cdot f_i(1, Y))^{a_j}$
$T_j - R_j = a_j \cdot f_{\boxplus}(X, Y)$	$T_j \cdot R_j^{-1} = (f_{\boxtimes}(X, Y))^{a_j}$
$(T_1 - R_1) \cdot a_2 = (T_2 - R_2) \cdot a_1$	$(T_1 \cdot R_1^{-1})^{a_2} = (T_2 \cdot R_2^{-1})^{a_1}$
$f_{\boxplus}(X, Y) = (T_1 - R_1)a_1^{-1}$	$f_{\boxtimes}(X, Y) = (T_1 \cdot R_1^{-1})^{1/a_1}$

Table 3: Adaptation of the GSHADE$_{\boxplus}$ protocol to the GSHADE$_{\boxtimes}$ protocol

4.2 Security Analysis

In our security analysis, we will assume that the OTs and the equality test (see Figure 5 in [15]) used in our protocol are secure in the malicious model (OT-hybrid and equality-test-hybrid settings). The OTs can be implemented with the OTs extension secure against malicious adversaries from [2] or with the OTs extension (see Figure 2) which is secure against malicious adversaries (cf. Proposition 1) if the Sender's inputs are uniformly random and unknown from the Receiver (which is the case in our protocol due to a and r_i). In our implementation (see Section 4.3), we will use the OTs extension presented in Figure 2 because that is more efficient than more general OTs extension secure against malicious adversaries such as [2].

PROPOSITION 3. *The GSHADE$_{\boxplus}$ (resp. GSHADE$_{\boxtimes}$) protocol is correct and secure with one-bit leakage in the malicious model with OT-hybrid and equality-test-hybrid settings.*

PROOF. We will only prove the security against a malicious P_1. The security against a malicious P_2 is similar because the two parties are symmetric.

Privacy During the 1st GSHADE, we will demonstrate the privacy in the real world. Let A be a PPT adversary controlling P_1 in the real world. We describe a simulator S_A who simulates the view of A in the ideal world. S_A sends X to the trusted party and obtains $f_{\boxplus}(X, Y)$ (resp. $f_{\boxtimes}(X, Y)$). Then S_A picks randomly $a_1 \in_R \mathbb{Z}_m^*$ and $t_{1,1}, ..., t_{n-1,1}, R_1 \in_R \mathbb{Z}_m$ (resp. $t_{1,1}, ..., t_{n-1,1}, R_1 \in_R \mathbb{Z}_m^*$) and computes $t_n =$

Parameters	m is prime the codomain of $f_\boxplus$ is included into $\mathbb{Z}_m$	
	Party 1	**Party 2**
Inputs	$X = (x_1, ..., x_n) \in \{0,1\}^n$	$Y = (y_1, ..., y_n) \in \{0,1\}^n$

1st GSHADE

Party 1 = Client

Party 2 = Server
$\forall i \in [1,n], r_{i,1} \in_R \mathbb{Z}_m, a_1 \in_R \mathbb{Z}_m^*$

$x_i \xleftarrow{\forall i \in [1,n], \text{ OT}} (a_1(r_{i,1} + f_i(0,Y)), a_1(r_{i,1} + f_i(1,Y)))$

$t_{i,1} = a_1(r_{i,1} + f_i(x_i, Y))$

Outputs $T_1 = \sum_i t_{i,1}$ ... Outputs $R_1 = a_1 \sum_i r_{i,1}$

such that $T_1 - R_1 = a_1 \cdot f_\boxplus(X,Y)$

2nd GSHADE

Party 1 = Server
$\forall i \in [1,n], r_{i,2} \in_R \mathbb{Z}_m, a_2 \in_R \mathbb{Z}_m^*$

Party 2 = Client

$(a_2(r_{i,2} + f_i(0,X)), a_2(r_{i,2} + f_i(1,X))) \xleftarrow{\forall i \in [1,n], \text{ OT}} y_i$

$t_{i,2} = a_2(r_{i,2} + f_i(y_i, X))$

Outputs $R_2 = a_2 \sum_i r_{i,2}$ ... Outputs $T_2 = \sum_i t_{i,2}$

such that $T_2 - R_2 = a_2 \cdot f_\boxplus(X,Y)$

Equality test

Inputs T_1, R_2, a_2 $\xleftarrow{\text{Test}}$ Inputs R_1, T_2, a_1

Outputs t ... Outputs t

such that $t = 1$ if $(T_1 - R_1)a_2 = (T_2 - R_2)a_1$ and $t = 0$ otherwise

Outputs

If $t = 1$, exchanges T_i, R_i, a_i in order to obtain $f_\boxplus(X,Y)$

$f_\boxplus(X,Y) = (T_1 - R_1)a_1^{-1} = (T_2 - R_2)a_2^{-1}$

If $t = 0$, outputs nothing

Figure 6: The GSHADE$_\boxplus$ protocol

$a_1 \times f_\boxplus(X,Y) + R_1 - \sum_{i=1}^{n-1} t_i$ (resp. $t_n = f_\boxplus(X,Y)^{a_1} \cdot R_1 \cdot \left(\prod_{i=1}^{n-1} t_i\right)^{-1}$). S_A sends $t_i, \forall i \in [1,n]$ to the adversary A and (a_1, R_1) to P_2. In the real world, the malicious P_1 receives $t_i = a_1(r_{i,1} + f_i(x_i, Y))$ (resp. $t_i = (r_{i,1} \cdot f_i(x_i, Y))^{a_1}$). It is easy to show that the t_i's distribution in the real world and in the ideal world are identically distributed (uniformly distributed over $\mathbb{Z}_m$ (resp. $\mathbb{Z}_m^*$)). Thus the P_1's views in the real world and in the ideal world are indistinguishable. We can notice that the t_i's distribution in the ideal world requires only the knowledge of $f_\boxplus(X,Y)$ (resp. $f_\boxtimes(X,Y)$) without knowledge of P_2's input. That ensures privacy against a malicious P_1.

During the 2nd GSHADE, P_1 only receives messages beyond the OTs. Since the OTs are secure against malicious adversaries, the malicious P_1 cannot obtain information during this 2nd GSHADE.

Finally, the equality test is secure against malicious adversaries. That means that a malicious P_1 will only obtain the output of the equality test without information about the P_2's inputs. Therefore only selective failure attack can be conducted on this protocol due to the public 1-bit result of the equality test. For instance, a malicious P_1 can test if $f_\boxplus(X,Y) = g(X,Y)$ (resp. $f_\boxtimes(X,Y) = g(X,Y)$) where g was chosen by P_1 by swapping f by g in the 2nd GSHADE execution. A malicious P_1 can learn no more than 1 bit.

In summary, during the overall protocol, a malicious P_1 obtains T_1 and t and chooses R_2 and a_2. These data reveal no information about P_2's input or $f(X,Y)$. Thus the GSHADE$_\boxplus$ (resp.GSHADE$_\boxtimes$) protocol is secure in the malicious model with OT hybrid and equality test settings.

Correctness In this part we will evaluate the probability that the protocol outputs a wrong result. We assume that P_1 is malicious and P_2 is semi-honest. We also assume that the OTs and the equality test are secure against malicious adversaries.

In our protocol, the final output is revealed if and only if the equality test succeeds. The inputs of the equality test are (T_1, R_2, a_2) for P_1 and (T_2, R_1, a_1) for P_2. A malicious P_1 can easily modify T_1, R_2, a_2, T_2 because T_1, R_2, a_2 are his own inputs in the equality test and T_2 is P_2's output in OTs where P_1 is the Sender (modification of P_1's inputs in the OTs during the 2nd GSHADE is easy for a malicious P_1). But he cannot modify the inputs R_1 and a_1 because these inputs are randomly chosen by P_2. Let T_1', R_2', a_2', T_2' be the new wrong inputs of the equality test. Let v the wrong result that P_1 would like to obtain. He can easily choose a_2', T_2', R_2' such that $(T_2' - R_2') \times a_2'^{-1} = v$ (resp. $(T_2' \cdot R_2'^{-1})^{1/a_2'} = v$). Then to succeed in the equality test, he has to choose T_1' (without knowledge about R_1 and a_1) such that $(T_1' - R_1) \times a_1^{-1} = v$ (resp. $(T_1' \cdot R_1^{-1})^{1/a_1} = v$). Only one value for T_1' over $\mathbb{Z}_m$ verify this equality: $T_1' = v \cdot a_1 + R_1$ (resp. $T_1' = v^{a_1} \cdot R_1$). As P_1 has no information about a_1 and R_1, he has a success probability of $1/m$. $\square$

4.3 Experimental performance

We implemented GSHADE$_\boxplus$ and GSHADE$_\boxtimes$ with the OTs extension [1]. Since the two GSHADE executions are independent, their executions can be overlapped by using two independent threads working in parallel. Table 4 shows the runtimes for the four GSHADE protocols: GSHADE$_+$,

GSHADE$_\times$, GSHADE$_\boxplus$ and GSHADE$_\boxtimes$. We observe that the extra cost due to the improvement of the security level (from semi-honest to malicious model) is low ($\approx 20\%$). That is due to the implementation of the two GSHADE executions in parallel with two threads in GSHADE$_\boxplus$ and GSHADE$_\boxtimes$.

n	GSHADE$_+$	GSHADE$_\times$	GSHADE$_\boxplus$	GSHADE$_\boxtimes$
1 000	0.050s	0.051s	0.062s	0.062s
5 000	0.061s	0.060s	0.072s	0.073s
10 000	0.075s	0.075s	0.088s	0.089s

Table 4: Runtimes for GSHADE and its extensions with $m = 1\,000\,003$

5. COMPARISON WITH RELATED WORK

In this section, we will compare the efficiency of the GSHADE protocol and its extensions to famous S2PC protocols (Yao [32], GMW [13], HE [12, 25]).

5.1 In the semi-honest model

The original GSHADE article [6] experimentally demonstrates that for classical metrics (e.g. Hamming distance, Euclidean distance) GSHADE$_+$ is more efficient than more traditional protocols (HE [12, 25], Yao [32] or GMW [13]). We recall this performances in Table 5.

Distances	DB size	S2PC	Time	Comm.
HD	320	Yao	42.9s	8.3MB
		GMW	0.5s	5.7MB
		GSHADE$_+$	0.3s	0.5MB
ED	1024	HE+Yao	1114.3s	17.5MB
		GSHADE$_+$	1.6s	13.8MB

Table 5: GSHADE$_+$'s performances from [6] (HD is an Hamming distance between two 900-bit vectors and ED is an Euclidean distance between two 640×8-bit vectors)

The Table 5 shows that GSHADE$_+$ protocol is really more efficient to evaluate f_+ functions than Yao or GMW protocol. Then, GSHADE$_\times$ has a similar complexity than GSHADE$_+$. In addition, the secure evaluation of $f_\times$ functions as a boolean circuit by Yao and GMW takes longer than f_+ because there are more AND gates to evaluate. All this prove that to evaluate $f_\times$ functions, GSHADE$_\times$ is more efficient than Yao or GMW. Moreover, GSHADE$_\times$ protocol can be way more proficient than HE in the evaluation of $f_\times$ (see in appendix Table 6).

5.2 In the malicious model

In the malicious model, the traditional protocols for SMC are cut-and-choose [20] and DualEx [15]. We will prove that to evaluate f_+ or $f_\times$ in S2PC, GSHADE$_\boxplus$ and GSHADE$_\boxtimes$ are more efficient than the cut-and-choose or the DualEx. The cut-and-choose construction secures the Yao protocol against malicious adversaries. To do that, the builder party creates many circuits and sends them to the evaluator party who will open some circuits to check that they are well built and evaluates the others. This method introduces significant overhead due to the number of circuits. The DualEx protocol is more efficient than the cut-and-choose construction to secure Yao protocol against malicious adversaries.

This protocol consists to conduct two independent runs of a Yao protocol and the parties swap their roles between the two executions. Ours GSHADE extensions in the malicious model are based on the same idea. Since GSHADE$_+$ and GSHADE$_\times$ are more efficient than Yao to evaluate f_+ and $f_\times$ functions, GSHADE$_\boxplus$ and GSHADE$_\boxtimes$ are more proficient than DualEx for these functions. Finally, we can also compare GSHADE$_\times$ and GSHADE$_\boxtimes$ to SPDZ [9, 10]. SPDZ on a single thread performed 7500 sequential multiplications per second on 32-bit integers during the online phase (see [9, Table 3]) and much more during the offline phase whereas our GSHADE$_\times$ and GSHADE$_\boxtimes$ protocols evaluated 10 000 sequential multiplications in 0.075s and 0.089s respectively on 20-bit integers without pre-computations (see Table 4). Noted that these results were measured on different machines (Intel Core i5 with 5GB RAM for GSHADE and Intel Core i7 with 4 GB RAM for SPDZ). Although not exactly on the same basis, this comparison underlines further the high efficiency of our proposals.

6. CONCLUSION

In the semi-honest model, GSHADE$_+$ is, to the best of our knowledge, the most efficient protocol for the S2PC evaluation of numerous metrics such as Hamming distance and scalar product. GSHADE$_+$ permits to evaluate functions which can be expressed as $f_+(X, Y) = f_X(X) + f_Y(Y) + \sum_i f_i(x_i, Y)$. Firstly we described GSHADE$_\times$ an extension of the GSHADE$_+$ application domain. By replacing the additions by multiplications, our extension enables to efficiently evaluate new functions which can be expressed as $f_\times(X, Y) = f_X(X) \times f_Y(Y) \times \prod_i f_i(x_i, Y)$. Moreover this extension is compatible with the OT extension, the Correlated OT and the 1-vs-N GSHADE optimization. In this way, we can efficiently classify an element held by a Client where the classifier parameters (SVM with RBF kernel) are kept secret and held by a Server. We believe that this extension would be useful in signal processing, data mining domains and biometric identification.

Moreover, we here describe GSHADE$_\boxplus$ and GSHADE$_\boxtimes$ two GSHADE extensions to secure GSHADE$_+$ and GSHADE$_\times$ against malicious adversaries. These extensions are based on a dual extension with some extra modifications in order to be fully secure. Our experiments prove that the extra cost due to this new security level is very small.

7. REFERENCES

[1] G. Asharov, Y. Lindell, T. Schneider, and M. Zohner. More efficient oblivious transfer and extensions for faster secure computation. In *ACM SIGSAC Conference on Computer and Communications Security, CCS'13*, 2013.

[2] G. Asharov, Y. Lindell, T. Schneider, and M. Zohner. More efficient oblivious transfer extensions with security for malicious adversaries. In *Advances in Cryptology - EUROCRYPT 2015 - 34th Annual International Conference on the Theory and Applications of Cryptographic Techniques*, 2015.

[3] S. Avidan, A. Elbaz, and T. Malkin. Privacy preserving pattern classification. In *Proceedings of the International Conference on Image Processing, ICIP*, 2008.

[4] F. Benhamouda, G. Couteau, D. Pointcheval, and H. Wee. Implicit zero-knowledge arguments and applications to the malicious setting. In *Advances in Cryptology - CRYPTO 2015 - 35th Annual Cryptology Conference*, 2015.

[5] R. Bost, R. A. Popa, S. Tu, and S. Goldwasser. Machine learning classification over encrypted data. In *22nd Annual Network and Distributed System Security Symposium, NDSS*, 2015.

[6] J. Bringer, H. Chabanne, M. Favre, A. Patey, T. Schneider, and M. Zohner. GSHADE: faster privacy-preserving distance computation and biometric identification. In *ACM Information Hiding and Multimedia Security Workshop, IH&MMSec*, 2014.

[7] J. Bringer, H. Chabanne, and A. Patey. SHADE: secure hamming distance computation from oblivious transfer. In *Financial Cryptography and Data Security - FC 2013 Workshops, USEC and WAHC*, 2013.

[8] C. Cortes and V. Vapnik. Support-vector networks. *Machine Learning*, 20(3), 1995.

[9] I. Damgård, M. Keller, E. Larraia, V. Pastro, P. Scholl, and N. P. Smart. Practical covertly secure MPC for dishonest majority - or: Breaking the SPDZ limits. In *Computer Security - ESORICS 2013 - 18th European Symposium on Research in Computer Security*, 2013.

[10] I. Damgård, V. Pastro, N. P. Smart, and S. Zakarias. Multiparty computation from somewhat homomorphic encryption. In *Advances in Cryptology - CRYPTO 2012 - 32nd Annual Cryptology Conference*, 2012.

[11] Z. Erkin, T. Veugen, and R. L. Lagendijk. Privacy-preserving recommender systems in dynamic environments. In *2013 IEEE International Workshop on Information Forensics and Security, WIFS*, 2013.

[12] C. Gentry. *A fully homomorphic encryption scheme*. PhD thesis, Stanford University, 2009.

[13] O. Goldreich, S. Micali, and A. Wigderson. How to play any mental game or A completeness theorem for protocols with honest majority. In *Proceedings of the 19th Annual ACM Symposium on Theory of Computing*, 1987.

[14] Y. Huang, D. Evans, J. Katz, and L. Malka. Faster secure two-party computation using garbled circuits. In *20th USENIX Security Symposium*, 2011.

[15] Y. Huang, J. Katz, and D. Evans. Quid-pro-quo-tocols: Strengthening semi-honest protocols with dual execution. In *IEEE Symposium on Security and Privacy, SP*, 2012.

[16] Y. Ishai, J. Kilian, K. Nissim, and E. Petrank. Extending oblivious transfers efficiently. In *Advances in Cryptology - CRYPTO 2003, 23rd Annual International Cryptology Conference*, 2003.

[17] M. Keller, E. Orsini, and P. Scholl. Actively secure OT extension with optimal overhead. *IACR Cryptology ePrint Archive*, 2015.

[18] M. S. Kiraz, Z. A. Genç, and S. Kardas. Security and efficiency analysis of the hamming distance computation protocol based on oblivious transfer. *IACR Cryptology ePrint Archive*, 2014.

[19] V. Kolesnikov and T. Schneider. Improved garbled circuit: Free XOR gates and applications. In *Automata, Languages and Programming, 35th International Colloquium, ICALP 2008, Part II - Track B: Logic, Semantics, and Theory of Programming & Track C: Security and Cryptography Foundations*, 2008.

[20] Y. Lindell and B. Pinkas. An efficient protocol for secure two-party computation in the presence of malicious adversaries. In *Advances in Cryptology - EUROCRYPT 2007, 26th Annual International Conference on the Theory and Applications of Cryptographic Techniques*, 2007.

[21] M. Naor and B. Pinkas. Efficient oblivious transfer protocols. In *Proceedings of the Twelfth Annual Symposium on Discrete Algorithms*, 2001.

[22] M. Naor, B. Pinkas, and R. Sumner. Privacy preserving auctions and mechanism design. In *EC*, 1999.

[23] J. B. Nielsen. Extending oblivious transfers efficiently - how to get robustness almost for free. *IACR Cryptology ePrint Archive*, 2007.

[24] V. Nikolaenko, S. Ioannidis, U. Weinsberg, M. Joye, N. Taft, and D. Boneh. Privacy-preserving matrix factorization. In *ACM SIGSAC Conference on Computer and Communications Security, CCS'13*, 2013.

[25] P. Paillier. Public-key cryptosystems based on composite degree residuosity classes. In *Advances in Cryptology - EUROCRYPT '99, International Conference on the Theory and Application of Cryptographic Techniques*, 1999.

[26] B. Pinkas, T. Schneider, N. P. Smart, and S. C. Williams. Secure two-party computation is practical. In *Advances in Cryptology - ASIACRYPT 2009, 15th International Conference on the Theory and Application of Cryptology and Information Security*, 2009.

[27] M. O. Rabin. How to exchange secrets with oblivious transfer. *Harvard University Technical Report 81*, 1981.

[28] Y. Rahulamathavan, S. Veluru, R. C. Phan, J. A. Chambers, and M. Rajarajan. Privacy-preserving clinical decision support system using gaussian kernel-based classification. *IEEE J. Biomedical and Health Informatics*, 18, 2014.

[29] M. Upmanyu, A. M. Namboodiri, K. Srinathan, and C. V. Jawahar. Blind authentication: a secure crypto-biometric verification protocol. *IEEE Transactions on Information Forensics and Security*, 2010.

[30] D. J. Wu, T. Feng, M. Naehrig, and K. E. Lauter. Privately evaluating decision trees and random forests. *IACR Cryptology ePrint Archive*, 2015.

[31] A. C. Yao. Protocols for secure computations (extended abstract). In *23rd Annual Symposium on Foundations of Computer Science*, 1982.

[32] A. C. Yao. How to generate and exchange secrets (extended abstract). In *27th Annual Symposium on Foundations of Computer Science*, 1986.

APPENDIX

A. MACHINE LEARNING USE CASE

A.1 Introduction

We would like to classify in SMC some elements following a Support Vector Machines (SVM) classifier with a Radial Basis Function (RBF) kernel [8]. The Server inputs the parameters of the classifier H which are b and $\forall i \in [1, N], \alpha_i, \gamma_i, y_i$ and the Client inputs an element x. Finally the Client obtains the classification of his input $H(x) = sign\left(b - \sum_{i=1}^{N} h_i(x)\right)$ where $h_i(x) = \alpha_i \cdot e^{-\gamma_i \|x - y_i\|_2^2}$ and no more information and the Server obtains nothing. The SVM protocol with a RBF kernel is for instance used for clinical decision [28].

A.2 Related Work on this Use Case

This use case has two main difficulties: it requires floating values whereas most S2PC protocols require integers and it evaluates a non linear function due to the exponentiation. Some articles [3, 28, 29] suggest methods to solve this use case. They all quantize values in order to compute on integers and justify the quantization by experimentations. In addition to compute $e^{f(x,y)}$, all these articles suggest to evaluate $f(x, y)$ in S2PC and to mask the output (one party obtain $f(x, y) + r$ and the other r where r is random). Then each party computes an exponentiation to obtain $e^{f(x,y)+r}$ and e^r respectively. Finally they combine their sharings to obtain the result $e^{f(x,y)} = e^{f(x,y)+r}/e^r$. For security reasons, $f(x, y) + r$ needs to be uniformly distributed over a finite space. That implies to work into $\mathbb{Z}_m$ (modulo m). Unfortunately the result will not be always correct because $e^{f(x,y)}$ might not be equal to $e^{[(f(x,y)+r) \mod m]}/e^r$. For instance, if $f(x, y) = m - 2$ and $r = 5$, then $e^{f(x,y)} = e^{m-2}$ and $e^{[(f(x,y)+r) \mod m]}/e^r = e^3/e^5$ are not equal. Thus the methods in these articles are either partially incorrect or not fully secure (if not computed on $\mathbb{Z}_m$).

A.3 Our solution with GSHADE$_\times$

This use case can efficiently and securely be solved with our GSHADE$_\times$ protocol. As previous method, we will quantize values in order to work on integers. With GSHADE$_\times$ we will securely evaluate $h(X, \alpha, \gamma, Y) = \alpha \cdot e^{-\gamma \|X - Y\|_2^2} = \left(\alpha \cdot e^{-\gamma \|Y\|_2^2}\right) \cdot \left(e^{-\gamma \|X\|_2^2}\right) \cdot \left(e^{2\gamma <X,Y>}\right)$ where X is the Client's input and (α, γ, Y) is the Server's input. Firstly we quantize $X = (X_1, ..., X_K)$ with $X_i \approx \sum_{j=1}^{\ell} 2^{j-1} x_{(i-1)\ell+j}$. Thus the quantization of X is equal to the $n = K \times \ell$-bit vector $(x_1, ..., x_n) \in \{0, 1\}^n$. Moreover the Client has to evaluate $\| X \|_2^2$ and to binarize the result $\| X \|_2^2 \approx \sum_{i=1}^{p} 2^{i-1} x_{n+i}$. In GSHADE$_\times$, the Client's input would be $X' = (x_1, ..., x_{n+p}) \in \{0, 1\}^{n+p}$ and the functions would be:

$$
\begin{cases}
f_X(X) = 1 \\
f_Y(Y) = \alpha \times e^{-\gamma \|Y\|_2^2} \\
\forall i \in [1, p], f_{K\ell+i}(x_{K\ell+i}, Y) = quant\left(e^{-\gamma 2^{i-1} x_{K\ell+i}}\right) \\
\forall (i, j) \in [1, K] \times [1, \ell], \\
\quad f_{(i-1)\ell+j}(x_{(i-1)\ell+j}, Y) = quant\left(e^{\gamma 2^j x_{(i-1)\ell+j} Y_i}\right)
\end{cases}
$$

where $quant(x)$ is an integer quantization of x (e.g. round to nearest). For more precise result, it is possible to multiply

each value by the element a (with $a > 1$) before performing $quant$. Hence the parties obtain a sharing of $a^n \times f(X, Y)$. Higher is a, more precise is the $quant$ function but higher is the computation complexity. Thus there is a trade-off between complexity and efficiency.

The GSHADE$_\times$ protocol is not sufficient to solve this use case but we can easily add a secure evaluation of a boolean circuit. The circuit has for inputs $T_1, ..., T_N, R_1^{-1}, ..., R_N^{-1}, b$ and outputs

$$
H(X) = \begin{cases}
1 & \text{if } \sum_{i=1}^{N}((R_i^{-1} \times T_i) \mod m) < b \\
0 & \text{otherwise}
\end{cases}
$$

This circuit contains only additions, multiplications and comparisons and so is very easy to build. The Figure 7 presents the complete solution. In this solution, the Client inputs X and the Server inputs b and $\forall i \in [1, N], \alpha_i, \gamma_i, Y_i$. Firstly we evaluate efficiently and securely $\forall i \in [1, N], h_i(X) = \alpha_i \cdot e^{-\gamma_i \|X - Y_i\|_2^2}$ thanks to GSHADE$_\times$. In these evaluations, we can benefit from the 1-vs-N GSHADE optimization because the Client's input is invariant. Then the Client obtains $H(X) = sign\left(b - \sum_{i=1}^{N} h_i(X)\right)$ from a secure boolean circuit evaluation. The circuit's inputs are $T_1, ..., T_N$ for the Client and $R_1^{-1}, ..., R_N^{-1}, b$ for the Server. The circuit evaluates $H(X) = \begin{cases} 1 & \text{if } \sum_{i=1}^{N}((R_i^{-1} \times T_i) \mod m) < b \\ 0 & \text{otherwise} \end{cases}$. Finally the Client obtains $H(X)$ and the Server obtains nothing.

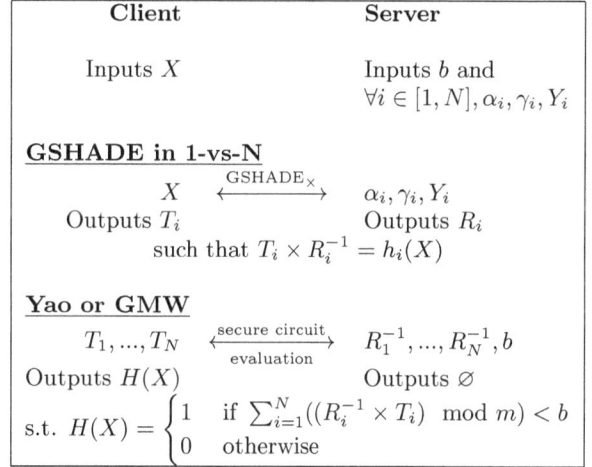

Client	**Server**
Inputs X	Inputs b and $\forall i \in [1, N], \alpha_i, \gamma_i, Y_i$

GSHADE in 1-vs-N

$X \xleftarrow{\text{GSHADE}_\times} \alpha_i, \gamma_i, Y_i$

Outputs T_i — Outputs R_i

such that $T_i \times R_i^{-1} = h_i(X)$

Yao or GMW

$T_1, ..., T_N \xleftarrow[\text{evaluation}]{\text{secure circuit}} R_1^{-1}, ..., R_N^{-1}, b$

Outputs $H(X)$ — Outputs $\varnothing$

s.t. $H(X) = \begin{cases} 1 & \text{if } \sum_{i=1}^{N}((R_i^{-1} \times T_i) \mod m) < b \\ 0 & \text{otherwise} \end{cases}$

Figure 7: Classification in S2PC of an element X following a SVM classifier with a RBF kernel

A.4 Performance

We implemented this solution based on GSHADE$\times$ and Yao. Then we testet it in the same context as experimentations from [28]. In the experimentations from [28], they use 205 support vectors for the WBC data set and 535 support vectors for the PID data set. In addition, the number of features for each sample in WBC and PID are 9 and 8 respectively and these features are between -10^4 and 10^4. Thus they multiply these features by 10^4 to work with integers. In our experimentations, we will quantify each feature on 15 bits. Thus we will have $n = 9 \cdot 15 = 135$ for WBC and $n = 8 \cdot 15 = 120$ for PID and N is equal to the number of support vectors. In addition, we choose the prime number $m = 1\,000\,003$ for the working field $\mathbb{Z}_m$.

Table 6 compares our runtimes with runtimes from [28]. Our experiments were done on two identical standard computers (Ubuntu 12.04 (VirtualBox), Intel Core i5 with 5GB RAM) connected via LAN. The measurements include the overall time spent included pre-computations. About the security parameters, we use κ OTs on κ bits in the OTs extension where $\kappa = 80$. We can observe a significant improvement with our GSHADE extension.

	$\text{GSHADE}_\times$ + Yao	HE from [28]
WBC	0.070+0.531=0.601s	41s
PID	0.102+1.385=1.487s	92s

Table 6: Runtimes for this machine learning use case

A Framework of Multi-Authority Attribute-Based Encryption with Outsourcing and Revocation

Sherman S. M. Chow
Department of Information Engineering
The Chinese University of Hong Kong
Sha Tin, N.T., Hong Kong
sherman@ie.cuhk.edu.hk

ABSTRACT

Attribute-based encryption (ABE) is a cryptographic tool for fine-grained data access control. For practical needs, an ABE scheme should support multiple authority and revocation. Furthermore, decryption should also be outsourced for higher efficiency. Researchers have been extending existing ABE schemes for these goals. Yet, the rationales are often hidden behind tailor-made number-theoretic constructions.

This paper proposes a framework for constructing multi-authority ABE schemes with attribute revocation and outsourced decryption, from any pairing-based single-authority ABE scheme which satisfies a set of properties we identified.

Keywords

multi-authority attribute-based encryption; pairing-based; outsourced decryption; revocation; design framework

1. INTRODUCTION

Access control appears in many aspects of our life, ranging from physical access to security gates at a building, to virtual access by a computer program to memory. There are various access control models, and correspondingly many cryptographic authentication protocols for enforcing access control. However, these traditional methods require the server which verifies the authentication to be honest, *i.e.*, granting access only when the authentication passed the access control policy. This implies that its administrator should be honest. Moreover, this server should be trusted to be free from any vulnerability, yet its online requirement to perform authentication makes it more susceptible to hacking.

1.1 Cryptographic Access Control

A better way is to enforce cryptographic access control, instead of the above software-based approach. Consider a confidential document which should only be revealed to some selected parties, we may employ encryption. Identity-based encryption (IBE) has been identified as a useful primitive.

Since the identities can be any arbitrary bit-strings, they can encode the access control policy, and only the one who should be granted access can get the decryption key corresponding to a particular policy. There are many extensions of the basic IBE notion for security and efficiency (*e.g.*, [2, 8]). Numerous applications of IBE in the context of access control have been proposed, such as supporting timed-release encryption (*e.g.*, [9]).

For IBE, decryption is only possible when the policy-string associated with the decryption key matches exactly with what was specified during encryption. In other words, it cannot support any fuzziness in the policy representation. Fuzzy IBE [25] is proposed to address this problem. As long as the strings are sufficiently close, decryption is still possible. A related concept is threshold policy, such that both the keys and the encryption are associated with different set of attributes. When the number of their overlapping elements exceeds a certain predefined threshold, decryption will be possible. A fuzzy IBE scheme with closeness defined upon a threshold is later generalized to attribute-based encryption (ABE) supporting threshold policy [11].

A distinctive feature of ABE is collusion-resistance. Consider using a trivial solution of double IBE encryption with respect to two policies involved in a conjunctive policy. Two colluding users can pull together their keys to decrypt something that none of them alone is entitled to[1].

Goyal *et al.* [11] formulated the idea of attribute-based encryption and classified it into ciphertext-policy ABE (CP-ABE) and key-policy ABE (KP-ABE). In CP-ABE [1, 28], ciphertexts are associated with access structures, and keys are labeled with attributes. Decryption is possible if and only if the key attribute set satisfies the access structure. KP-ABE [11] forms the reversed notion in which ciphertexts are associated with attribute set and keys are associated with access structures. Consider an untrusted-but-honest server model, such as in cloud storage systems, CP-ABE fit wells with application requiring access control of documents.

1.2 Applications of ABE

The policy supported by ABE constructions in the literature can be a tree of gates including AND, OR, t-out-of-n threshold, or even NOT gates. Recent ABE schemes support more generalized access structure in the form of monotone access structure, which can be represented by linear secret sharing [28]. Just like IBE, there is a trusted authority which issues attribute-based decryption keys to user. When com-

SACMAT'16, June 05-08, 2016, Shanghai, China

© 2016 ACM. ISBN 978-1-4503-3802-8/16/06. . . $15.00

DOI: http://dx.doi.org/10.1145/2914642.2914659

---

[1]Previous works which address the problem of access control, but without collusion resistance, are outside our scope.

pared with traditional public-key encryption, ABE is more efficient and flexible since one just needs to specify an access control formula instead of enumerating legitimate decryptors. Due to this level of *fine-grained access control*, ABE has found various applications, such as decentralized online social network (OSN) for ensuring privacy of the content to be shared over the network [15], or electronic healthcare system supporting patient privacy [20, 26]. In these scenarios, each OSN user or each patient takes the role of an authority respectively. Attributes are issued to the friends over the OSN, or healthcare personnel, for granting access of different kind of contents depending on the policy.

For a larger scale deployment of an ABE scheme, it may be unrealistic to assume the existence of a single authority to monitor all different domains of attributes. A *multiple authority* ABE scheme [4, 5, 17] allows distributing the job of issuing attributes over many attribute-authorities (AA's). For practical needs, just like other cryptosystems, an ABE scheme should support *revocation*. Furthermore, decryption can also be outsourced for higher efficiency [12]. However, revocation is a notoriously tricky issue in cryptosystem, and ABE is no exception. Moreover, splitting a single authority into multiple ones but preserving collusion-resistance is not an easy task. Finally, we need a better solution than simply leaking the decryption key for *outsourced decryption*.

1.3 Our Contributions

Researchers have been extending existing ABE schemes for the goals of multi-authority, attribute-level revocation, and outsourced decryption. Yet, the designs are mostly ad-hoc. While there are many ABE schemes being proposed in this decade, many ABE schemes with these extended features are not described with respect to the existing schemes. The rationales of the extensions are often hidden behind specific and tailor-made number-theoretic constructions [30, 29, 18, 20]. It becomes a laborious task to reverse engineer the constructions and assert their security. Unfortunately, some are later shown to be insecure [10, 14, 27, 22][2].

In this paper, we give a framework for constructing multi-authority ABE (MA-ABE) scheme with efficient decryption and revocation, from any single-authority ABE scheme which satisfies a set of properties we identified.

We do not claim that it is our contribution to achieve the aforementioned goals simultaneously, or to formulate a completely generic construction which automatically upgrades any ABE construction. However, we aim to give a blueprint which upgrades a class of ABE schemes, and possibly shed lights on how some of the constructions are extended from some others in the literature. To argue for the correctness and security of the resulting scheme, we still need to argue for some identified properties depending on the specific scheme we start with. Yet, we gain the benefits that the analysis can be simpler and modular since we do not need to consider the construction as a whole from scratch, but we can start with some specific structures of an existing scheme.

1.4 Key-Policy vs. Ciphertext-Policy MA-ABE

We chose to extend ciphertext-policy ABE instead of a key-policy one. If the policy is associated to a key, it is unclear which authority can determine the policy across different authorities. One of the first multi-authority ABE

schemes in the threshold setting [5] simply assumes a conjunction of *threshold clauses* where each clause is maintained by a specific authority.[3] For an ABE scheme to support more complicated policy, such as assigning different weights on the clauses managed by different authorities, probably more coordinations between the authorities are required. Either the weighting scheme is a result of communication between the authorities, or there is a "super-authority" with special overriding power and decides for all other authorities, which is against the original intention of powers separation.

1.5 Overview of Our Framework

We exploit the algebraic structures of pairing-based ABE constructions including different kinds of homomorphism. Our framework requires the underlying ABE schemes with keys and the ciphertexts which can be partitioned into two parts, namely, attribute-independent part, and attribute-dependent part. To support multi-authority extension in a generic manner, we require that the randomness contributed by a particular authority to be "carried over" to another authority. More precisely, the attribute-dependent part of the user key can still be generated with respect to the randomness introduced by other authorities, without revealing the random exponent, by requiring a two-round key generation process. The aim is to generate a key certifying attributes from multiple authorities, but with the same key structure as that of the underlying single-authority ABE scheme as if all the attributes are certified by a single authority.

We then use our multi-authority extension to realize outsourced decryption. Both extensions are described with respect to small universe ABE schemes (to be explained shortly), but they also apply on large-universe schemes. Yet, for attribute-level revocation, it only works for small-universe.

2. RELATED WORK

Since the first proposal of Sahai and Waters [25] and subsequent refinement by Goyal *et al.* [11], ABE attracted lots of attentions from researchers of different sub-fields on various aspects, *e.g.*, security, efficiency, functionality, modularity. A survey of the earlier ABE schemes can be found in [6].

Considering the workload issue and a single point of trust, single-authority ABE suffers from high risks. While in multi-authority ABE (MA-ABE) systems, attributes are independently managed by different authorities, and the corruption of one or more authorities would not influence the security of other authorities. Chase [4] proposes an MA-ABE solution, by still requiring the help of a central authority. Chase and Chow [5] removed the central authority, which resulted in a truly multi-authority ABE scheme. These schemes support threshold policy, which can be described as KP-ABE.

Multi-authority ABE schemes have been constructed using composite-order (bilinear) groups in the *random oracle model* (ROM) [17], and using prime-order groups but with proof relies also on generic group model [17]. These schemes

---

[2]Some of these schemes are omitted from the references.

[3]A few papers in the literature (*e.g.*, [17, 29]) mentioned that the scheme of Chase and Chow [5] is restricted to only "AND policy of a determined set of authorities", which should not be confused with "AND policy" in general since the AND gate happens at the authority level. The clause for the attributes managed by the same authority can be a threshold clause. As mentioned in two seminal papers [25, 4], a simple trick can be applied to adjust the threshold. One can also leave out a subset of authorities during encryption.

support an expressive kind of policies known as monotone span programs, but only over a *small universe* of attributes, which means that the size of the public parameter is linear in the number of supported attributes. For an ABE scheme which supports a *large universe*, any string can be used as an attribute, and these attributes are not necessarily pre-defined and enumerated during setup. Rouselakis and Waters [23] proposed a large universe multi-authority ABE scheme, also in the ROM. This scheme uses prime-order groups and hence is more efficient in general. Yet, a consequence is that the dual-system encryption framework basing on composite-order groups [17] cannot be applied. Instead, this scheme [23] is only proven secure in a static security model where both the challenge ciphertexts and key queries are issued before the parameters are published.

While these schemes form the foundation of later work, with their design rationale well-explained; they did not consider extra feature such as user revocation.

Revocation in ABE can be traced back to IBE revocation [2] where private keys are tied with expiration time and ciphertext are associated with creation time. Decryption is impossible if the expiration time of the key is earlier than the creation time of the ciphertext. Sahai *et al.* [24] designed a (single-authority) revocable-storage ABE system, with updatable dynamic credentials. The ciphertext can be self-updated, *i.e.*, without the intervention of any authority. While the self-update feature is attractive, the ciphertext size is large due to the tree-based revocation mechanism.

Apart from self-updatable encryption, there are other studies on revocable ABE, which may require data owner assistance [15] or proxy assistance [30, 15]. Some of these schemes only support user-level revocation. Since the possession of attributes defines users' access abilities, attribute-level revocation is more intuitive. Attribute-level revocation in MA-ABE can be realized by dynamically renewing ciphertext as well as the non-revoked users' keys when revocation happens [29, 20]. Instead of time-dependent revocation as discussed above, the revocable-ABE system can depend on a version key: a parameter embedded into ciphertexts and private keys. When revocation happens, the authority creates update messages for cloud server and non-revoked users. Also new keys (or new ciphertext) can be easily calculated from update messages and the old keys (or old ciphertext).

3. SYSTEM MODEL

We describe how different entities use the algorithms of an ABE system in realizing a multi-authority cryptographic access control system over cloud storage. Figure 1 depicts the major entities. It consists of a set of authorities and a cloud server with storage and computation ability. There are two kinds of users, namely, data uploader and data consumers. Any party can upload data (yet we can always incorporate external authentication mechanism to govern who can upload the data, *e.g.* [7]). Data consumers are characterized by different attributes, decided via external means (*e.g.*, an attributes list indexed by the data consumers' identities).

External to the ABE scheme, we assume the existence of a trusted certificate authority (CA) which certifies the identities of users. Note that for multi-authority ABE, the notion of global identifier is crucial to ensure collusion resistance [4]. This trusted CA is just a means to realize this

necessary condition[4]. In particular, this CA does not help in any algorithms of the ABE system except simply outputting certificates (different from [21]), and it lacks of the power of issuing decryption key nor decrypting any ciphertext.

3.1 Multi-Authority ABE

There are a number of attribute-authorities (AA's), which cooperatively setup and maintain the (MA-)ABE system. They first execute the Setup algorithm. The resulting public parameters param and the master public key mpk will be published. Each of them stores msk_i in secret. Correspondingly, the master public key mpk could be in the form of multiple mpk_i, one for each authority i.

Once the ABE system is setup, anyone can perform the encryption and upload the resulting ciphertext to the cloud. To do that, the data uploader first executes the Encap mechanism according to param and mpk with respect to the policy $\mathcal{P}$. Here, Encap is a key-encapsulation mechanism which outputs a ciphertext $\mathfrak{C}$ together with an encapsulated key $\mathfrak{K}$. The actual data will be encrypted by $\mathfrak{K}$ via symmetric-key encryption. Since it is the uploader who defined the access policy, and it is the authorities which grant the keys; the cloud server simply stores these ciphertexts in the data storage, and does not need to perform any access control.

Before the users can decrypt their first ciphertext, they need to talk to the AA's for getting the decryption key. Each of the AA's will issue keys to the user according the user identity certified by a CA. The identity can be used to determine the set of eligible attributes. For efficiency, each AA does not need to communicate with each other during the key issuing. After a user has interacted with all of the AA's, the keys from different AA's can be combined into a user attribute-based decryption key. This concludes the basic working mechanism of a multi-authority ABE scheme.

3.2 Outsourced Decryption

In the cloud computing settings, it is natural for the user to not only outsource the data storage but also the computation. In ABE, while still practically efficient, the decryption is usually the most computationally expensive task. In view of this, a user can outsource the decryption key to a *decryption mediator* performed by the cloud server. As usual, users want to minimize the trust on the cloud server, and hence the user should perform a (one-time) process such that only a blinded version of the decryption key is delegated to the mediator. The outsourcing thus includes three steps: (1) the data consumer (user) generates a blinded private key, and outsources it to the decryption mediator; (2) for every ciphertext, the user can request the decryption mediator to partially decrypt it by the outsourced key, which the mediator will reply with a partial decryption of the ciphertext to the user; (3) the user completes the full decryption of the ciphertext. In this way, as long as the first step is a one-time process, and the last step is efficient enough, the user can outsource most of the decryption computation to the cloud server which significantly reduces the decryption cost.

3.3 Revocation by Ciphertext and Key Updates

Considering dynamic credential in cloud storage, users' possession of a particular attribute can be dynamic. As in any other cryptographic schemes, revocation is a useful

---

[4]There can be privacy problem associated with having a CA to certify the global identifier of users, which is addressed [5].

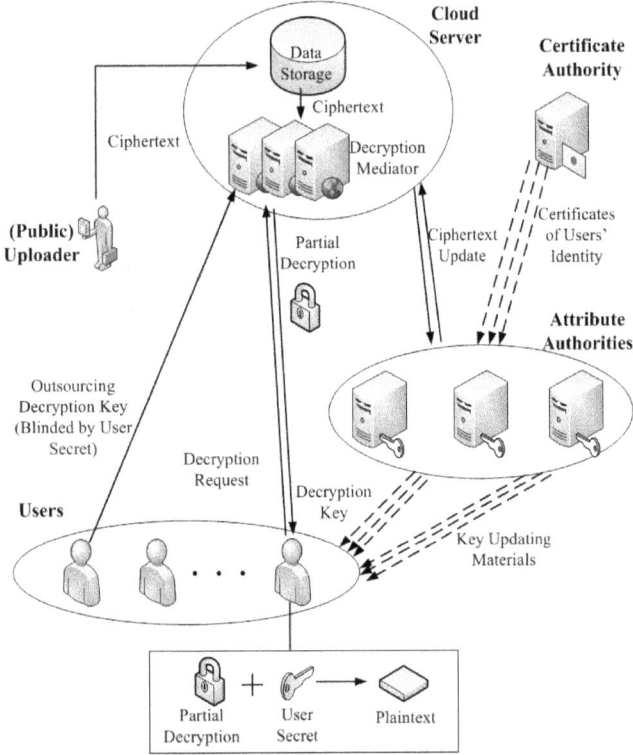

Figure 1: System Model

feature. For example, when a user reports a compromise of the decryption key, the whole key of this user should be revoked; or a user may be released from one of the duties and the corresponding attributes originally granted should be revoked. In this case, just like the access control policy, the revocation should also be fine-grained up to the attributes.

Fine-grained revocation is difficult to enforce especially for a multi-authority system due to the requirement of collusion-resistance. Some existing solutions only support revocation at the key-level instead of attribute-level, while some others require an online party to re-encrypt [30, 15] or partially decrypt for every ciphertext. Note that the partial decryption here is different from the outsourced decryption we discussed above. Revocation is for security concern and outsourced decryption is motivated by an efficiency concern.

Evolution of the "attribute-dependent key" is a way to support attribute-level revocation. It means that each AA can update a part of the master key which governs the attributes to its "next version" [30], via a *system-update* SU algorithm. After that, any existing ciphertexts should be updated, via a *ciphertext-update* CU algorithm. This update should not involve the decryption of the ciphertext for efficiency and security reasons. Yet, the update should probably be executed in a secure environment, and any old ciphertext should be securely deleted. To enforce revocation, only an updated decryption key can decrypt an updated ciphertext. Since the attribute-dependent keys for different domains of attributes are managed by the AA's independently, AA's are the parties to enforce the revocation. Via a *key-update* KU algorithm, AA's use the key-updating material to update the user decryption key if they are not revoked.

4. TECHNICAL PRELIMINARIES

This section gives a formal syntax of the suite of algorithms constituting an ABE scheme or an MA-ABE scheme. Then we present the necessary technical preliminaries for instantiating our framework, which include the relevant number theoretic primitives and cryptographic building blocks.

4.1 Syntax of ABE

In an MA-ABE scheme, each attribute authority handles a set of attributes, and all of these sets are disjoint.

Definition 1. *An N-authority ABE scheme consists of four algorithms:*

1. *Via* $(\mathsf{param}, \{(\mathsf{mpk}_k, \mathsf{msk}_k)\}_{k \in \{1, \dots N\}}) \overset{\$}{\leftarrow} \mathsf{Setup}(1^\lambda, N)$ *the randomized key generation algorithm takes as input a security parameter $\lambda \in \mathbb{N}$ and the number of authorities $N \in \mathbb{N}$, and outputs the system parameters param and N public/private key pairs $(\mathsf{mpk}_k, \mathsf{msk}_k)$, one for each attribute authority $k \in \{1, \dots N\}$.*

   For an ABE scheme with small universe, the list of attributes can also be an input of the Setup algorithm.

   For simplicity, we assume param and $\{\mathsf{mpk}_k\}_{k \in \{1, \dots N\}}$ are the implicit inputs of the rest of the algorithms.

2. *Via* $\mathsf{usk}_k[\mathsf{id}, \mathbb{A}_k] \overset{\$}{\leftarrow} \mathsf{KGen}(\mathsf{msk}_k, \mathbb{A}_k, \mathsf{id})$ *the attribute authority k uses its secret key msk_k to output a user (secret) decryption key corresponding to a set of attribute $\mathbb{A}_k$ for the user with identity id.*

3. *Via* $\langle \mathfrak{C}, \mathfrak{K} \rangle \overset{\$}{\leftarrow} \mathsf{Encap}(\{\mathsf{mpk}_k\}_{k \in \{1, \dots N\}}, \mathcal{P})$ *a sender creates a ciphertext and its encapsulated key $\mathfrak{K}$ under the policy $\mathcal{P}$.*

4. *Via* $\mathfrak{K} \leftarrow \mathsf{Decap}(\{\mathsf{usk}_k[\mathsf{id}, \mathbb{A}_k]\}_{k \in \{1, \dots N\}}, \mathfrak{C})$ *a user id who obtained from each authority k a sufficient set of decryption keys $\{\mathsf{usk}_k[\mathsf{id}, \mathbb{A}_k]\}$ decrypts $\mathfrak{C}$ to recover the encapsulated key $\mathfrak{K}$.*

4.1.1 Key Generation

Our framework considers KGen algorithm to be probabilistic, such that different users cannot mix-and-match their key components. This is similar to many MA-ABE schemes in the literature [4, 5, 23]. Nevertheless, we remark here that being probabilistic is only one of the ways to ensure collusion-resistance. As long as the user identity id is also one of the inputs, different users having different identities can get different keys for the same attribute even if KGen is deterministic. When colluding users share their attributes, the key component of user id_1 for a certain attribute will not be in the same format expected by the user id_2, and hence it does not work with the other key components of id_2. In this way, collusion-resistance is still possible, *e.g.*, [17].

4.1.2 Encapsulation

The key encapsulation algorithm Encap implicitly samples a session key $\mathfrak{K}$ uniformly at random. The corresponding decapsulation algorithm Decap will recover $\mathfrak{K}$ if the attributes in the key satisfy the policy specified as an input of Encap.

Both KGen and Encap are probabilistic. When describing how to extend an underlying ABE scheme in our framework, it is useful to make the randomness used by these algorithms explicit, which will be denoted by $\mathsf{KGen}(\mathsf{msk}_k, \mathbb{A}_k, \mathsf{id}; u)$ and $\mathsf{Encap}(\mathcal{P}; s)$ where u or s is the randomness, respectively.

218

4.1.3 Correctness and Security

Definition 2. *An N-authority ABE scheme satisfies correctness if for all $\lambda, N \in \mathbb{N}$ and all identities* id, *for all $\{\mathbb{A}_k\}$ and $\mathcal{P}$ such that $\mathcal{P}(\{\mathbb{A}_k\}_{k \in \{1, \dots N\}})$ returns true, we have*

$$\Pr[\mathsf{Decap}(\{\mathsf{KGen}(\mathsf{msk}_k, \mathbb{A}_k, \mathsf{id})\}_{k \in \{1, \dots N\}}, \mathfrak{C}) = \mathfrak{K} :$$

$$(\mathsf{param}, \{(\mathsf{mpk}_k, \mathsf{msk}_k)\}_{k \in \{1, \dots N\}}) \xleftarrow{\$} \mathsf{Setup}(1^\lambda, N);$$

$$\langle \mathfrak{C}, \mathfrak{K} \rangle \xleftarrow{\$} \mathsf{Encap}(\mathcal{P});] = 1$$

where the probability is taken over the random coins of all the algorithms in the expressions above.

We follow a common existing security definition for multi-authority ABE, which only allows static corruption model of authority [4, 5, 17, 23]. There are variations in the strength of the security model. For example, adaptive query of decryption keys [17] or static model which all decryption keys must be asked before the system parameter is published [23].

We remark that, while Chase and Chow [5] gave a security analysis with respect to $(N-2)$ authorities (similar to the underlying distributed pseudorandom function), it can be extended to allow static corruption of $(N-1)$ authorities by a specific argument.

4.2 Bilinear Groups and Other Notations

Definition 3 (BILINEAR GROUPS). *Let $\mathbb{G}_1$, $\mathbb{G}_2$, and $\mathbb{G}_T$ be three multiplicative cyclic groups all of order p. Suppose g_1 and g_2 are the generators of the base groups $\mathbb{G}_1$ and $\mathbb{G}_2$ respectively. A map $\hat{e} : \mathbb{G}_1 \times \mathbb{G}_2 \rightarrow \mathbb{G}_T$ is a pairing or a bilinear map if it satisfies the following properties:*

- (Bilinearity.) $\hat{e}(u^x, v^y) = \hat{e}(u, v)^{xy}$ *for all* $u \in \mathbb{G}_1$, $v \in \mathbb{G}_2$, *and* $x, y \in \mathbb{Z}_p$.

- (Non-degeneracy.) $\hat{e}(g_1, g_2) \neq 1$, *where 1 is the identity element in* $\mathbb{G}_T$.

- (Computability.) $\hat{e}(u, v)$ *can be computed in polynomial time for all* $u \in \mathbb{G}_1$ *and* $v \in \mathbb{G}_2$.

The order here is usually a prime number which is large (relative to the security parameter), but it can also be a product of a few large primes (*e.g.*, [21, 17]). Our framework can work in either case.

The bilinear groups context $(\mathbb{G}_1, \mathbb{G}_2, \mathbb{G}_T, g_1, g_2, p, \hat{e})$ will be used by any pairing-based ABE schemes. We overload the notation of param to refer to the groups description.

The pairing is symmetric when $\mathbb{G}_1 = \mathbb{G}_2$; otherwise, it is asymmetric. Group elements for asymmetric pairings are smaller, and the pairing is more efficient, when compared with the symmetric group at a fixed security level.

We assume that the isomorphism $\psi()$ from $\mathbb{G}_2$ to $\mathbb{G}_1$ is computable in polynomial time, but its inverse $\psi^{-1}()$ is not, *i.e.*, we are making the external Diffie-Hellman (XDH) assumption, which is for the pseudorandom function we use.

Assuming $\psi(g_2) = g_1$, where both g_1 and g_2 are the generators of the respective base groups given in param. To come up with a pair of random $\mathbb{G}_1$ and $\mathbb{G}_2$ element (h, h') such that $\psi(h') = h$, one may pick a random exponent $\beta \in \mathbb{Z}_p$, set $h = g_1^\beta$ and $h' = g_2^\beta$. We will use this notation to denote such a pair and also this procedure in our ABE instantiation.

For $r \in \mathbb{Z}_p$ and a set of group elements $\{g_i\}$, we write $\{g_i\}^r$ to refer to $\{g_i^r\}$.

Finally, we use $[i]$ to denote the set of integers from 1 to i.

4.3 Distributed Pseudorandom Functions

Pseudorandom functions (PRFs), informally, is a class of function family such that no polynomial-time adversary can distinguish between a randomly chosen function among this family and a truly random function (whose outputs are sampled uniformly and independently at random), with significant advantage relative to the security parameter. Each PRF takes a secret seed which also serves as an index to determine which function in the family to be used. We will use a set of distributed PRFs (DPRF) with outputs always multiply to the identity element on any input, as used in some existing multi-authority ABE schemes [5, 19].

Our framework expects the DPRF which takes an input of bit strings and outputs an element in group $\mathbb{G}_1$. In more details, looking ahead, there is a one-time setup cost among the AA's to setup this DPRF. Each pair of AA's, say, indexed by (j, k), shares a PRF seed $seed_{jk}$, say via a (non-interactive) key exchange. With these $O(N^2)$ PRFs in total, we set the PRF of the k-th AA, $F_k(\mathsf{id})$, to be a multiplication of $(N-1)$ basic PRFs on the same input id, each weighted by either 1 (for multiplication) or -1 (for division).

By choosing between multiplication and division accordingly, all these PRF values can cancel each other when $F_k(\mathsf{id})$ for different k are multiplied together. The final composite PRF is computed as $F_k(\mathsf{id}) = \prod_{j < k} \mathsf{prf}_{jk}(\mathsf{id}) / \prod_{j > k} \mathsf{prf}_{jk}(\mathsf{id})$, where $\mathsf{prf}_{jk}(\cdot)$ is the notation for a PRF which takes the secret seed shared by parties j and k. Informally, such a "product-of-PRF" construction still looks pseudorandom to any adversary controlling less than $(N-2)$ other authorities.

5. PARTITIONED ABE FROM PAIRINGS

Now we are ready to start the exposition of our framework of "upgrading" a single-authority ABE. Underlying our extensions for supporting multi-authority, attribute revocation, and outsourced decryption is the possibility of partitioning the master key and the ciphertext into two parts. One part is attribute-independent, and the other is attribute-dependent. This is a natural property in most existing schemes. Key partition will be one of the properties useful for our extension for multi-authority, which is also leveraged to support outsourced decryption. Ciphertext partition, together with other properties (in Section 7), will be useful for our extension to support attribute revocation.

5.1 Key Partition

The attribute-independent part of the master key corresponds to the authority-specific part of the key. Each authority manages a set of attributes, and correspondingly generates the attribute-dependent part of the master key.

For brevity of exposition, we abuse the term "key" to either refer to the public key and the corresponding private key collectively, or either one of them. Which one we mean should be clear from the context. For example, the key used to derive a ciphertext should be the public key, and the key used to derive a user secret key should be the private key.

We also abuse the notation of $\mathsf{KGen}()$ a bit to refer to the two conceptual sub-parts of

$$(\{L_k\}, \{K_i\}) \xleftarrow{\$} \mathsf{KGen}(\mathsf{gsk}, \{\mathsf{ask}_i\}, \mathbb{A}, \mathsf{id}; u)$$

as defined by the definition below.

Definition 4. *An ABE scheme is said to be having key partition if*

1. *(Partition of Master Keys:) The master key can be partitioned into two following parts.*

   (a) *An attribute-independent part:* gpk/gsk.

   (b) *An attribute-dependent part:* {apk$_i$/ask$_i$}.

2. *(Partition of User Secret Keys:) Each user secret key can be partitioned into two parts. Specifically,*

   (a) *An attribute-independent part* {L_k} *that is derived from* gsk, *i.e.,*

   $$\{L_k\} \xleftarrow{\$} \mathsf{KGen}(\mathsf{gsk}, \mathsf{id}; u),$$

   where u is the randomness used by KGen *and k is a counter which enumerates the terms in* {L_k} *according to the scheme.*

   (b) *An attribute-dependent part* {K_i} *that is derived from* {ask$_i$}, *i.e.,*

   $$\{K_i\} \xleftarrow{\$} \mathsf{KGen}(\{\mathsf{ask}_i\}, \mathbb{A}, \mathsf{id}),$$

   where i is a counter which enumerates the attributes.

5.2 Ciphertext Partition

For efficient revocation, we require the underlying ABE scheme to produce ciphertext featuring partition property similar to what we have defined for key partition.

Definition 5. *An ABE scheme is said to be having ciphertext partition if a ciphertext consists of the following components:*

1. *An attribute-dependent part* {D_i} *that is derived from* {apk$_i$}.

2. *An attribute-independent part[5]* {C_k} *that is derived from* gpk.

Since we partition all of the master public/private key, user secret key, and ciphertext into different components, for brevity we overload each function for referring to the part of the algorithm which processes the partitioned version, *i.e.*, taking part of the inputs and returning part of the outputs.

5.3 Pairing-Based Attribute-Based Encryption

Here we define a template for a pairing-based ABE scheme.

Definition 6. *In our framework, a pairing-based attribute-based encryption is defined to have the structures below.*

1. *We assume that there is a trusted initializer, which sets up the basic system parameters including the bilinear groups context* param[6].

2. *The attribute-independent part of master public key, gpk, is in $\mathbb{G}_T$, and that of the master secret key gsk is in $\mathbb{G}_1$. (It can be extended to be multiple elements.)*

3. *A user secret key is in the form of $(\{K_k\}, \{L_i\})$, all of them are $\mathbb{G}_1$ elements.*

4. *Each element in the set* {apk$_i$} *is a group $\mathbb{G}_2$ element, which is for encoding the attribute involved in the policy to be specified during encapsulation.*

5. *A ciphertext is in the form of $(\{C_k\}, \{D_i\})$, all of them are $\mathbb{G}_2$ elements.*

6. *(Pairing-Product Equation for Decryption:) The decryption algorithm recovers the encapsulated key by the equation $\prod \hat{e}(C_k, L_k) \prod \hat{e}(D_i, K_i)^{\omega_i}$, where ω_i can be derived from the ciphertext and the decryption key.*

It is natural for decryption to be relying on a pairing-product equation. Since, after all, the confidentiality provided by the ciphertext relies on a pairing-based assumption often related to the indistinguishability of a target group element from random. Thus, for an honest user, decryption should be done by pairing up the group elements from the private key with those group elements from the ciphertext. This also justifies the assumption that gpk is a $\mathbb{G}_T$ element.

There could be ABE schemes which are outside the above formulation, for example, having a $\mathbb{Z}_p$ element in the decryption key or a $\mathbb{G}_T$ element in the ciphertext.

6. MULTI-AUTHORITY DISTRIBUTION

With the above abstraction of partitionable ABE, we start with our first extension of turning a single-authority ABE scheme into a multi-authority ABE scheme. The high-level goal here is to create a user decryption key sharing the same structure as that of the underlying single-authority ABE, as if all the attributes are managed by a single authority.

The homomorphic structure of discrete-logarithm-based cryptosystems often makes the task of distributing the keys easier. For MA-ABE, we want to distribute the master keys, such that this distribution carries over to the user secret key (to be modelled by the homomorphic properties of user secret keys below) and the encapsulated key (to be modelled by the homomorphic property of encapsulated key below).

ABE should be collusion-resistant, such that any "mix-and-match" attacks across different user decryption keys cannot be successful as the key components from different colluding users are randomized in different ways. To ensure that, one way is to apply a pseudorandom function on the identity of the user which is supposed to be unique (and assumed to be certified by some means) [4, 5, 17]. For our extension, we use a DPRF as reviewed in Section 4.3.

Another complication is that, the user decryption key generation of the underlying single-authority ABE can be probabilistic. A reason is that the randomization can protect the master secret key, such that it cannot be recovered easily from the user decryption key. That means any random factor chosen by one authority cannot be simply passed to another authority. On the other hand, as discussed, collusion-resistance expects the decryption key from different authorities for the same user to be randomized (or if one resorts to the help of a random oracle [17, 23], it can just be user-specific instead of being randomized). The consequence is that, different authorities need to agree upon the same randomness whenever issuing keys to the same user.

These observations motivate an additional property in our framework, termed as inter-dependency of the user secret key. This property requires that the attribute-independent part of the user secret key can serve as a "carrier" for the randomness, such that the attribute-dependent part can still be generated with respect to the randomness chosen by the other authorities, without directly transferring any random coin used to create the attribute-independent part.

---

[5] While it is rare, this part can be absent from the ciphertext.
[6] Note that this is a common requirement in existing ABE schemes and even MA-ABE schemes [5, 17].

Definition 7. *An ABE scheme supports master key distribution/extension if it possesses of the following properties:*

1. *(Inter-dependency of the User Secret Key:) There exists a polynomial time algorithm* AGen *such that, for every* K_i *in the attribute-dependent part of the user secret key, it can be computed from* AGen *by taking the following two inputs, namely, the attribute-dependent part of the master secret key* ask_i, *and the attribute-independent part of the same user secret key* $\{L_k\}$, *i.e.,*

$$K_i \xleftarrow{\$} \mathsf{AGen}(\mathsf{ask}_i, \{L_k\}),$$

where $\langle\{K_i\}, \{L_k\}\rangle \xleftarrow{\$} \mathsf{KGen}(\mathsf{gsk}, \{\mathsf{ask}_i\}, \mathbb{A})$, $i \in \mathbb{A}$.

2. *(Homomorphic Properties of the User Secret Key:) For every* $\mathsf{gsk}, \mathsf{gsk}' \in \mathbb{G}_2$, $\{\mathsf{ask}_i\}$, *attribute sets* $\mathbb{A}$, $\mathsf{id} \in \mathcal{ID}$, *and randomness* u, u', *we have*

$$
\begin{aligned}
& \mathsf{KGen}((\mathsf{gsk}, \{\mathsf{ask}_i\}), \mathbb{A}, \mathsf{id}; u) \\
\cdot\ & \mathsf{KGen}((\mathsf{gsk}', \{\mathsf{ask}_i\}), \mathbb{A}, \mathsf{id}; u) \\
=\ & \mathsf{KGen}((\mathsf{gsk} \cdot \mathsf{gsk}', \{\mathsf{ask}_i\}), \mathbb{A}, \mathsf{id}; u), \\
and\quad & \mathsf{KGen}((\mathsf{gsk}, \{\mathsf{ask}_i\}), \mathbb{A}, \mathsf{id}; u) \\
\cdot\ & \mathsf{KGen}((\mathsf{gsk}, \{\mathsf{ask}_i\}), \mathbb{A}, \mathsf{id}; u') \\
=\ & \mathsf{KGen}((\mathsf{gsk}, \{\mathsf{ask}_i\}), \mathbb{A}, \mathsf{id}; u + u').
\end{aligned}
$$

3. *(Homomorphic Property of the Encapsulated Key:) For every* $\mathsf{gpk}, \mathsf{gpk}' \in \mathbb{G}_T$, *policy* $\mathcal{P}$, *and randomness* s, *if*

- $(\mathfrak{C}, \mathfrak{K}_0) \leftarrow \mathsf{Encap}(\mathsf{gpk}, \mathcal{P}; s)$,
- $(\mathfrak{C}, \mathfrak{K}_1) \leftarrow \mathsf{Encap}(\mathsf{gpk}', \mathcal{P}; s)$, *and*
- $(\mathfrak{C}, \mathfrak{K}) \leftarrow \mathsf{Encap}(\mathsf{gpk} \cdot \mathsf{gpk}', \mathcal{P}; s)$;

then $\mathfrak{K} = \mathfrak{K}_0 \cdot \mathfrak{K}_1$. *This implicitly requires that the encapsulated key* $\mathfrak{K}$, *is only dependent on the attribute-independent part of master key* gpk.

6.1 Construction

- Setup:

  1. Given the security parameter, the bilinear groups context param is established via the Setup algorithm of the underlying ABE.

  2. According to param, each authority j executes the master key generation part of Setup algorithm of the underlying ABE to obtain master public key $(\mathsf{gpk}_j, \{\mathsf{apk}_i\})$ and master private key $(\mathsf{gsk}_j, \{\mathsf{ask}_i\})$.

  3. The resulting gpk of our MA-ABE will be set to $\prod_j \mathsf{gpk}_j$.

  4. All authorities execute the setup stage of the distributed PRF [5] as described in Section 4.3. After this setup, each authority j obtains the secret seed to compute $F_j(\cdot)$, as defined in Section 4.3. Here, we utilize a set of DPRF's with $\mathbb{G}_1$ as its range. The instantiation of such DPRF under XDH assumption has also been previously used [5].

  5. Each authority also sets up a key pair for a secure signature scheme, such that any signature from one authority can be verified by another authority. For example, the public key for the signature scheme can be certified by the CA.

- KGen:

  1. For user id, each authority j uses its own gsk_j, and its own randomness u_j, to generate $\{L_{k,j}\}$, the attribute-independent part of usk, i.e.,

$$\{L_{k,j}\} \xleftarrow{\$} \mathsf{KGen}(\mathsf{gsk}, \mathsf{id}; u_j).$$

   For each group element in the above set, authority j blinds it with $F_j(\mathsf{id}\|k)$ where $\|$ denotes string-concatenation, i.e., $\{L_{k,j} \cdot F_j(\mathsf{id}\|k)\}$. Finally, it is signed and the signature is also sent to the user.

  2. In the second round of this protocol, the user has collected the set of $\{L_{k,j}\}$ for all $j \in [N]$.

   The user then combines the response from each authority and outputs $\{\prod_{j\in[N]} L_{k,j} \cdot F_j(\mathsf{id}\|k)\}$, which will result in set $\{L_k\}$ due to the DPRF. The user passes the set of $\{L_{k,j}\}$ for all $j \in [N]$ and the signatures collected to each authority.

  3. Upon successful verification of the signature, which means each authority j obtained an authenticated copy of $\{L_k\}$, it then uses the $\{\mathsf{ask}_i\}$ part of its own master secret key gsk_j to generate the attribute-dependent part of user key for each i, i.e.,

$$K_i \xleftarrow{\$} \mathsf{AGen}(\mathsf{ask}_i, \{L_k\}).$$

  4. The user then combines the response from each authority and outputs

$$\langle \{L_k\}, \cup_{j\in[N]}\{K_i\}\rangle.$$

- Encap and Decap remain the same.

6.2 Analysis

6.2.1 Correctness Analysis

- First, by the construction of DPRF, for each k we have

$$\prod_{j\in[N]} L_k \cdot F_j(\mathsf{id}\|k) = \prod_{j\in[N]} L_k.$$

- By construction, $\prod_{j\in[N]}(\mathsf{gpk}_j)$ is gpk. With the first homomorphic property of the user secret key, the role of $\prod_{j\in[N]} L_k$ with respect to gpk is similar to that of $L_{k,j}$ with respect to gpk_j for the jth copy of the single-authority ABE. A user thus recovers the attribute-independent part of user secret key with respect to gpk.

- Different authorities can use different randomness u_j in their key generation. The second homomorphic property of user secret key is crucial here, such that when the keys are multiplied together, $\sum u_j$ will play the role of the randomness as in the underlying ABE scheme.

- Now we turn our focus to the attribute-dependent part $\{K_i\}$, which will probably be determined by the random factor u. Yet, the $\{L_{k,j}\}$ component from each authority j will also have u_j embedded. With the inter-dependency of the user secret key, the set $\{L_{k,j}\}$ serves as useful material embedding information of $u = \sum_{j\in[N]} u_j$. By using the AGen algorithm, the $\{K_i\}$ parts can be created without learning $\{u_j\}$ explicitly.

6.2.2 Security Analysis

Intuitively, security follows from the DPRF-based security proof strategy [5] and a specific property which we require from the underlying ABE schemes for AGen. Namely, we require that the (part of the) key to be generated by the AGen algorithm can be simulated by the simulator for the security proof of the underlying scheme. While it seems that we cannot do a "clean" security reduction and need to look into the details of the underlying simulator, we expect that the use of DPRF can help us to ensure such a property.

It is often the case that, the simulator in the security proof for an ABE construction can return a correct key, as long as the key can be seen as chosen uniformly at random (recall that our formulation requires a probabilistic key generation algorithm). The constraint is that the exact choice of the randomness is unknown. In pairing-based constructions, such randomness is in the form of discrete logarithms, which is unknown to the simulator and cannot be revealed to the adversary. That is the reason our framework requires an additional AGen algorithm, which serves as a "carrier" of the randomness contributed by other authorities.

Our security reduction requires that, no matter what are the intermediate outputs (*i.e.*, the attribute-independent part $\{L_k\}$) from all the other corrupted authorities controlled by the adversary, we can still simulate the scheme.

The use of DPRF allows us to match with the key output by the underlying simulator by "adjusting" the term accordingly. Specifically, the required part of the key to be returned as an intermediate output can be obtained via dividing the key from the underlying simulator by the corresponding $(N-2)$ key components output by adversary. Such adjustment looks indistinguishable to the adversary due to the pseudorandomness of the DPRF.

For an adversary which corrupt $(N-1)$ of the authorities, in the static corruption model, we can set the remaining honest authority to be the one which executes the underlying single-authority ABE. The simulation can guess the correct choice of the honest authority with probability of $1/N$.

6.2.3 Stronger Security Model

For security against a stronger model, where the honest authority is not necessarily the last one to "complete" the user key generation, we need to leverage a universally composable commitment scheme [3] with an extra round of communication for key generation. The commitment key is generated as part of the system setup. The extra round occurs at the beginning, which requires each authority to commit to the attribute-independent part $\{L_k\}$, and send the commitment to the users instead. In the next round, the committed value $\{L_k\}$ is revealed. Upon successful verification, the user proceeds with the rest of the protocol as usual.

In the security proof, the simulator owns the trapdoors for equivocation and extraction. Even in this special mode, the commitment key is indistinguishable to the adversary due to the security of the commitment scheme. The rest is the usual trick which extracts the committed values from the authorities controlled by the adversary, adjusts the set $\{L_k\}$ accordingly, and uses the equivocation feature to explain the commitment for the case that it opens to "another" value which fits with the adjustment.

Due to the requirement of having AGen inside KGen to be dependent on the first-round output of all the authorities, the resulting KGen protocol requires more than one round. For security, concurrent execution should not be performed.

6.3 Discussion

While previous MA-ABE schemes have used the DPRF techniques [5, 19], our usage allows the attributes in a clause of the policy to be cross-authority; and without relying on the random oracle [17, 23].

One may consider our framework to be a generalization of the specific scheme proposed by Liu *et al.* [21]. However, their setting considers a set of "central authorities" which goes beyond the role of a typical certificate authority and needs to be involved in the user decryption key generation.

7. ATTRIBUTE-LEVEL REVOCATION

The key idea for enabling attribute revocation is that, the partition structure of the master key carries over to the user secret key and ciphertext, *i.e.*, both the user secret key and the ciphertext can also be partitioned into two parts. The first part is derived from the attribute-independent key and the second part is derived from the attribute-dependent key.

To revoke a certain attribute, we can update the corresponding attribute key by exponentiating it with a random factor. This change should be propagated to the ciphertexts associated with that attribute, and the user secret keys which we are not going to revoke. We just apply the random exponent for the update on the ciphertext, and apply the inverse of the same exponent to the secret key component. For decryption, the pairings pair-up a ciphertext component and a secret key component, so the decryption results remain the same for non-revoked users. This allows an updated ciphertext to be decryptable by an updated key.

Our attribute revocation extension only applies on ABE schemes with small universe of attributes, and can be seen as a generalization of an existing scheme [30].

7.1 ABE with Attribute-Level Revocation

We define the following ABE with partition for extension to support efficient attribute revocation.

Definition 8. *A pairing-based ABE scheme is said to be revocable if it possess of the following properties:*

1. *The scheme is ciphertext-partitionable (Definition 5).*

2. *(Homomorphic Property of Attribute-Dependent Part of the Ciphertext:) Suppose the ciphertext $\mathfrak{C}$ is generated by the encapsulation algorithm which takes the master key $(\mathsf{gpk}, \{\mathsf{apk}_i\})$ and a policy $\mathcal{P}$ as input, i.e.,*

$$\mathfrak{C} \xleftarrow{\$} \mathsf{Encap}((\mathsf{gpk}, \{\mathsf{apk}_i\}), \mathcal{P}),$$

if $\{D_i\}$ is the attribute-dependent part of $\mathfrak{C}$, then there is a (not necessarily proper) subset $\{D_{i,0}\}$ of $\{D_i\}$, such that for a random $r \in \mathbb{Z}_p$, $\{D_{i,0}\}^{1/r}$ follows the same distribution as the same subset of the attribute-dependent part of

$$\mathfrak{C}' \xleftarrow{\$} \mathsf{Encap}((\mathsf{gpk}, \{\mathsf{apk}_i\}^r), \mathcal{P}).$$

(We remark that one can generalize this definition to require $\{D_{i,0}\}^{f(r)}$ instead, where $f(r) := 1/r$, and replace it with other publicly computable function.)

3. (Public Randomizability of the Ciphertext:) There exists a probabilistic polynomial time algorithm Rand() *which takes in a ciphertext and outputs a randomized version of it following the same distribution as the output of* Encap, *but encapsulating the same key as the input ciphertext.*

7.2 Construction

We follow the framework implicitly defined in Section 3.3, which supplements an ABE scheme with three algorithms:

- To perform the system-update SU, for each attribute i, the authority controlling it picks a random element r_i from $\mathbb{Z}_p$, then, using the attribute-dependent component of the existing master key, computes $\mathsf{apk}_i^{r_i}$ as the attribute-dependent component of the new master public key. The corresponding attribute-dependent component of the new master secret key will be $\mathsf{ask}_i \cdot r_i$.

- To perform the key-update KU, if the user is entitled to have the same attribute i in the next time period, the K_i component will be updated to $K_i^{r_i}$.

- To perform the ciphertext-update CU, take the old ciphertext, re-randomize it by Rand(), then update the attribute-dependent component $\{D_i\}$ of the re-randomized ciphertext by setting those to $\{D_i^{1/r_i}\}$.

7.3 Analysis

Correctness of all the updates can be easily seen from all the homomorphic properties we require. Note that the update of the ciphertext is possible since we require every ciphertext to be accompanied by the policy. Correctness of decryption is ensured by the way we perform the updates of ciphertext and private key, the format of the decryption as a pairing product equation, and the bilinearity of the pairing function which makes the corresponding exponents from the ciphertext and the private key cancel each other.

Security analysis follows from a reductionist argument to the security of the underlying scheme. Note that we are considering a static corruption model. Our construction basically replicates the attribute set supported by the basic scheme into multiple copies, one supporting each time domain. It is easy to simulate the user secret key, given there are only polynomially many time periods. For challenge ciphertext, it is about truncating a long ciphertext to one which only contains the policy related to the challenge time period. By applying only the exponent $1/r_i$, with respect to the same attribute, parts of the ciphertext for different time period may be correlated. The public re-randomization procedure of the ciphertext breaks this possible correlation.

8. OUTSOURCED DECRYPTION

With our extension for multi-authority and revocation, outsourced decryption is readily available. Specifically, the user will take the role of the $(N+1)^{\mathrm{th}}$ authority, and delegate the part of the key from the N authorities to the mediator.

8.1 Construction

1. User randomly generates $(\mathsf{gpk}', \mathsf{gsk}')$ as in Setup.

2. User delegates to the mediator $\mathsf{usk}' = \langle \{L_k \cdot L_i'\}, \{K_i\} \rangle$ where $\mathsf{usk} = \langle \{L_k\}, \{K_i\} \rangle$ is the original decryption key, and $\{L_i'\} \xleftarrow{\$} \mathsf{KGen}(\mathsf{gsk}', \mathsf{id})$ will be kept as a secret.

3. Mediator decrypts $\mathfrak{C}$ by running $\mathfrak{K}' \leftarrow \mathsf{Decap}(\mathsf{usk}', \mathfrak{C})$. (Same as the last extension, we also expect a non-anonymous ABE scheme, in which the ciphertext is always appended with its associated policy.)

4. User computes $\frac{\mathfrak{K}'}{\prod \hat{e}(L_k', C_k)}$ to get the encapsulated key.

8.2 Analysis

Correctness is easy to see from the homomorphic property of the encapsulated key.

The user side computation is efficient. Most of the computations are outsourced since the user side decryption is as efficient as that of a single-authority ABE which "involves no attribute" at all, *i.e.*, only the attribute-independent part of the key for the last authority "run" by the user is used. Note that the number of pairing required is the number of elements in $\{L_k\}$. This is a scheme-specific parameter, and is independent of the number of attributes owned by the user, or the number of authorities. For example, the instantiation to be presented in the next section only requires two pairing operations (since the set only contains $\{L_0, L_1\}$). On the other hand, most pairing-based ABE constructions which support fine-grained access control policy often require a number of pairing operations which is linear in the number of attributes (except those restricted to conjunctive policy, which often allow ciphertext parts related to different attributes to be aggregated together).

Security follows from that of MA-ABE since we are conceptually introducing one more authority. Without the "last" authority, which is the user in this case, security preserves even if all the other authorities collude.

8.3 Discussion

The original work by Green *et al.* [12] on outsourcing the decryption of ABE ciphertexts extended two specific ABE constructions, one is from the collection of CP-ABE schemes by Waters [28] and another is the LSSS-generalization of the original KP-ABE scheme by Goyal *et al.* [11]. A major trick there is similar to what we did in the last section for updating the keys for a particular attribute. In more details, every term in the original decryption key will be exponentiated with the same random factor, and the result will be served as the outsourced key. The random factor will then be kept as the user-side secret for completing the decryption.

While this makes the user side decryption as efficient as a regular ElGamal decryption; the security proofs for both schemes need to be re-done from scratch [12]. Their basic constructions are proven in the selective model. It was mentioned [12] that the dual system encryption framework (*e.g.*, [17]) can be used for adaptively-secure extension. However, it was also acknowledged [12] that any security argument for such approach is difficult to be a black box reduction to the underlying scheme.

The idea of having an extra "default" authority can be seen as an abstraction of an existing idea of "default attribute" [18]. Yet, there are two important differences. First, the previous work [18] essentially assumes a setting which the trusted authority generates both the outsourced key and the user side secret (as far as the context of this paper is concerned). Moreover, only a specific construction was given [18]. Their construction conceptually splits the single authority into two for each decryption key generation. This approach requires proving the whole scheme from scratch.

9. PUTTING IT ALL TOGETHER

9.1 Sample Schemes within Our Framework

Our case study takes Waters efficient and expressive CP-ABE scheme [28]. We remark that all but one of the schemes there [28] can fit with our framework[7].

An adaptively-secure CP-ABE scheme based on composite order groups [16] has strong resemblance to a scheme in the work of Waters [28] as acknowledged by the authors [16]. This scheme [16] also fits with our framework. The resulting MA-ABE scheme naturally resembles to the specific MA-ABE scheme by Liu *et al.* [21], although in a different system model as discussed in Section 6.3.

Some schemes may satisfy one of our extensions but not the others. As an example, the threshold ABE scheme of Li *et al.* [18], which already support outsourced decryption, can be extended for attribute-level revocation.

- Setup:

  1. Pairing-groups parameterized by param are first chosen according to the security parameter λ.

  2. A group-$\mathbb{G}_1$ element g_1^a is randomly chosen. Note that the knowledge of $a \in \mathbb{Z}_p$ is never required in any step in any of the algorithms below, except in the form of g_2^a in KGen.

  3. The master key for authority j consists of:

     (a) An attribute-independent part:
         $\mathsf{gsk}_j = g_2^{\alpha_j}$ where $\alpha_j \in \mathbb{Z}_p$, $\mathsf{gpk}_j = \hat{e}(g_1, g_2)^{\alpha_j}$.

     (b) An attribute-dependent part: For each attribute i, $\mathsf{ask}_i = \beta_i$ where $\beta_i \in \mathbb{Z}_p$, $\mathsf{apk}_i = h_i = g_1^{\beta_i}$. We may also pre-compute $h_i' = g_2^{\beta_i}$ as part of the attribute secret key. Note that $h_i' = \psi^{-1}(h_i)$.

  The "partition of master keys" into gpk and $\{\mathsf{ask}_i\}$ has already been done. System-Update SU can be easily done too.

- Encap$(\mathsf{gpk}, \{\mathsf{apk}_i\}, \mathcal{P}; s)$: We first describe the original Encap algorithm of Waters-ABE.

  1. The policy is expressed in the form of an LSSS access structure $(\mathbb{M}, \rho)$. $\mathbb{M}$ is an $l \times n$ LSSS matrix and ρ maps each row of $\mathbb{M}$ to an attribute $\rho(x)$.

  2. This algorithm chooses a random vector $\vec{v} \in \mathbb{Z}_p^n$ denoted by $(s, v_2, \cdots, v_n)$, where s is a secret exponent used in encapsulated key $\mathfrak{K}$.

  3. For each row vector $\mathbb{M}_i$, this algorithm calculates $\lambda_i = \mathbb{M} \cdot \vec{v}$ and chooses random $t_i \xleftarrow{\$} \mathbb{Z}_p$.

  4. The ciphertext is
     $$\mathfrak{C} = \langle C_0 = g_1^s, \{D_{i,0} = g_1^{t_i}, D_{i,1} = g_1^{a\lambda_i} h_{\rho(i)}^{-t_i}\}_{\forall i \in [\ell]} \rangle$$
     and the encapsulated key is $\mathfrak{K}_j = \mathsf{gpk}_j^s$.

  To see how it fits with our framework:

  - Knowing the policy $(\mathbb{M}, \rho)$, it is easy to re-randomize the ciphertext by $\{D_{i,0} \cdot g_1^{t_i'}, D_{i,1} h_{\rho(i)}^{-t_i'}\}$ for $t_i' \in \mathbb{Z}_p$.

  - As we have already partitioned, C_0 is the attribute-independent part and $\{D_{i,0}, D_{i,1}\}$ is the attribute-dependent part.

  - For the homomorphic property of the attribute-dependent part, we only concern its subset which is just $D_{i,0}$. To see, when $\mathsf{apk}_i = h_i$ is exponentiated to $\mathsf{apk}_i' = \mathsf{apk}_i^r = h_i^r$. Keeping the same $D_{i,1}$ will implicitly change t_i to $t_i' = t_i/r$, *i.e.*,
    $$D_{i,1} = g_1^{a\lambda_i} h_i^{-t_i} = g_1^{a\lambda_i} (h_i^r)^{-t_i/r}.$$

    The attribute-dependent part $D_{i,0}$ can then be exponentiated with $1/r$ to obtain $D_{i,0}^{1/r} = g_1^{t_i/r} = g_1^{t_i'}$ to match with the t_i' in $D_{i,1}$. Note that it satisfies the distribution for a ciphertext w.r.t. $\mathsf{apk}_i' = \mathsf{apk}_i^r = h_i^r$.

    This also explains how ciphertext-update CU works.

  - The homomorphic property regarding the encapsulated key is easy to be seen.

- KGen: The key generation algorithm takes in the master secret key of an authority and a set of attribute keys of the authority; outputs $\mathsf{usk}_{\mathsf{id},j}$ defined by:
  $$\langle L_0 = \mathsf{gsk}_j \cdot g_2^{au_j} = g_2^{\alpha_j} g_2^{au_j}, L_1 = g_2^{u_j}, \{K_x = h_x'^{u_j}\} \rangle$$
  where $\{x\}$ is the set of attributes for user named id, and u_j is randomly chosen from $\mathbb{Z}_p$.

  To see how it fits with our framework:

  - As already partitioned, $\{L_0, L_1\}$ is the attribute-independent part, the set $\{K_x\}$ is the attribute-dependent part. With this structure, the key can be easily updated via the key-update KU.

  - For homomorphic properties of user secret key,
    $$
    \begin{aligned}
    L_{0,j} \cdot L_{0,k} &= (\mathsf{gsk}_j \cdot g_2^{au_j}) \cdot (\mathsf{gsk}_k \cdot g_2^{au_k}) \\
    &= (g_2^{\alpha_j} g_2^{au_j}) \cdot (g_2^{\alpha_k} g_2^{au_k}) \\
    &= g_2^{(\alpha_j + \alpha_k)} g_2^{a(u_j + u_k)}, \\
    L_{1,j} \cdot L_{1,k} &= g_2^{u_j} \cdot g_2^{u_k} = g_2^{(u_j + u_k)}, \\
    K_{x,j} \cdot K_{x,k} &= h_x'^{u_j} \cdot h_x'^{u_k} = h_x'^{(u_j + u_k)}.
    \end{aligned}
    $$

  - For inter-dependency, AGen outputs $L_1^{\beta_x} = g_2^{u_j \beta_x} = h_x'^{u_j} = K_x$.

- Decap: The decryption algorithm takes in a ciphertext encrypted under the access structure of $(\mathbb{M}, \rho)$, and a decryption key for the set $\mathbb{A}$.

  Let $\mathbb{I}$, be a subset of $\{1, 2, \cdots, \ell\}$ as defined by $\mathbb{I} = \{i : \rho(i) \in \mathbb{A}\}$. The algorithm computes constants $\omega_i \in \mathbb{Z}_p$ such that $\sum_{i \in \mathbb{I}} \omega_i \mathbb{M}_i = (1, 0, \cdots, 0)$, which is possible, and may not be unique, when $\mathbb{A}$ satisfies $(\mathbb{M}, \rho)$.

  Then it decrypts the ciphertext by recovering the encapsulated key as
  $$\mathfrak{K} = \frac{\hat{e}(C_0, L_0)}{\prod_{i \in \mathbb{I}} (\hat{e}(D_{i,1}, L_1) \hat{e}(D_{i,0}, K_{\rho(i)}))^{\omega_i}},$$

  which is obviously a pairing production equation.

---

[7]The remaining one can also be fitted if we further generalize our framework, which we decided not to, for better understanding of the essence by avoiding definitional clumsiness.

9.2 Our Instantiation

With reference to Section 9.1, we spell out how to instantiate our framework by using Waters CP-ABE [28].

- Setup: It follows directly from our framework and the Setup of the underlying ABE scheme. How $\{\mathsf{apk}_i/\mathsf{ask}_i\}$ can be updated also follows exactly as our framework.

- Encap: Different from the underlying Encap algorithm is that, for each attribute i, one needs to take the term $\mathsf{apk}_i = h_i$ from the master key of the corresponding AA's. The resulting ciphertext is

$$\mathfrak{C} = \langle C_0 = g_1^s, \{D_{i,0} = g_1^{t_i}, D_{i,1} = g_1^{a\lambda_i} h_{\rho(i)}^{-t_i}\}_{\forall i \in [\ell]}\rangle.$$

The encapsulated key is defined accordingly as:

$$\mathfrak{K} = \prod_j \hat{e}(g_1, g_2)^{\alpha_j s} = \hat{e}(g_1, g_2)^{\sum_j \alpha_j s} = \hat{e}(g_1, g_2)^{\alpha s}.$$

Both outputs are in the same format as the underlying ABE scheme. Re-randomization is easy and we omit Rand(). Update CU can be carried out by only updating the $\{D_{i,0}\}$ part as explained in the last subsection.

- KGen:

  1. User named id interacts with each authority j and obtains $\langle L_{0,j}, L_{1,j}\rangle$ which is defined by:

  $$L_{0,j} = F_j(\mathsf{id}\|0) \cdot \mathsf{gsk}_j \cdot g_2^{au_j} = F_j(\mathsf{id}\|0) \cdot g_2^{\alpha_j} g_2^{au_j}$$
  $$L_{1,j} = F_j(\mathsf{id}\|1) \cdot g_2^{u_j}.$$

  2. User id eventually obtains:

  $$\langle L_0 = \prod_{j \in [N]} L_{0,j} = g_2^{\alpha} g_2^{au}, L_1 = \prod_{j \in [N]} L_{1,j} = g_2^u\}\rangle.$$

  where $\alpha = \sum_{j \in [N]} \alpha_i$ and $u = \sum_{j \in [N]} u_j$.

  3. User id sends L_1 to each authority j and obtains

  $$\{K_x = L_1^{\beta_x} = g_2^{u\beta_x} = h_x'^u\},$$

  which computes the keys $\langle L_0, L_1, \{K_x\}\rangle$.

The involvement of signature is omitted here. Again, this is in the same format as the underlying ABE scheme. Key-update KU can be applied on $\{K_x\}$.

- Decap: With the same format of key and ciphertext, normal decryption is the same as the underlying Decap.

We do not repeat the details of outsourcing a decryption key and how to perform the corresponding partial decryption (which is the same as the Decap) and final decryption (which is just one pairing operation).

9.3 Security Analysis

Security follows from our generic framework. As mentioned, we need to argue that the key constructed from AGen algorithm can match with what is constructed by the simulator for proving the security of the underlying ABE scheme. The underlying simulator will output a key for a specific random exponent, say u^*. Note that we need to match with the random factor u in $L_1 = \prod_{j \in [1,N]} L_{1,j} = \prod_{j \in [1,N]} g_2^{u_j}$. To simulate the L_1 term, the authority of concern, say k^*, can set $u_{k^*} = g_2^{u^*} / \prod_{j \in [1,N] \setminus \{k^*\}} g_2^{u_j}$. For the L_0 term, it appears to require the knowledge of the discrete logarithm a.

However, this can be circumvented as explained in the analysis of our framework in Section 6.2.2. Specifically, the L_{0,k^*} component can be just a random group element, such that when all $L_{0,j}$'s are multiplied together, it will match with the key component L_0 returned by the underlying simulator.

10. EVALUATING A CRYPTOSYSTEM

We want to make two remarks regarding performance evaluation. While performance analysis on a prototype appear to be crucial to demonstrate the deployability in general, these analyses may not add much retention value for scientific use for cryptosystems which are neither sensitive to the system model (e.g., many rounds of interaction between possibly dynamic number of entities) nor to the input (e.g., the distribution of the plaintext to be encrypted). Specifically, for ABE, the interaction requires at most a constant number of rounds. Also, it is typical to use hybrid encryption such that ABE just encapsulates a symmetric-key, where the possibly large plaintext is encrypted by a fast symmetric-key encryption scheme. As a result, counting the number of operations almost directly suggests the computation time.

Another remark is that, the same cryptosystem design can always be instantiated with different security parameter, which should be chosen according to the tightness of the proof and the underlying assumption. As clearly demonstrated in the class of ABE schemes of Waters [28], apparently more efficient schemes can be built by making stronger assumptions. A stronger assumption means that it can be easier to solve the underlying hard problem, and hence the scheme should be instantiated with a larger security parameter. Doing so probably offset the efficiency gain of the newer design. Unfortunately, quite a few existing performance evaluations of cryptosystems, mostly from non-cryptography venues, did not take these into considerations. This renders the so-called performance analysis rather superficial.

To conclude, one should always consider the assumptions, no matter the performance evaluation is order analysis or benchmark. Evaluation should be done with security parameters chosen appropriately according to the assumptions.

11. CONCLUSION AND FUTURE WORK

We propose an abstraction of ABE which can be extended to support a set of nice features desirable for practical usage of ABE, namely, multi-authority extension, attribute-level revocation, and outsourced decryption. Instead of tailor-making a construction we define a set of properties which explains the correctness and security of our approach.

Our work opens an avenue of research in designing new extension frameworks for ABE. Specific goals include a new framework for features such as online/offline ABE [13]; or for the same set of features but with some requirements removed, for example, setting up the authorities in advance, or appending the access control policy to the ciphertext. We also note that for user-level revocation, sub-linear size of keying materials could be possible. However, for attribute-level revocation, how to reduce the key-update materials appears to be challenging, especially in the multi-authority setting. Another problem is to investigate if outsourced decryption for anonymous ABE can be done, in which the policy associated with the ciphertext remains unknown to any mediator.

Acknowledgement

The author would like to thank Hannes Hartenstein, Russell W. F. Lai, Ying-Kai Tang, and anonymous reviewers for their helpful comments which improve the paper.

Sherman Chow is supported by the Direct Grant (4055018) of the Chinese University of Hong Kong, Early Career Award and the Early Career Scheme (CUHK 439713), and General Research Funds (CUHK 14201914) of the Research Grants Council, University Grant Committee of Hong Kong.

12. REFERENCES

[1] J. Bethencourt, A. Sahai, and B. Waters. Ciphertext-Policy Attribute-Based Encryption. In *IEEE Security and Privacy*, pages 321–334, 2007.

[2] A. Boldyreva, V. Goyal, and V. Kumar. Identity-Based Encryption with Efficient Revocation. In *ACM Computer and Communications Security*, pages 417–426, 2008.

[3] R. Canetti and M. Fischlin. Universally Composable Commitments. In *CRYPTO*, pages 19–40, 2001.

[4] M. Chase. Multi-Authority Attribute Based Encryption. In *TCC*, pages 515–534, 2007.

[5] M. Chase and S. S. M. Chow. Improving Privacy and Security in Multi-Authority Attribute-Based Encryption. In *ACM Computer and Communications Security*, pages 121–130, 2009.

[6] S. S. M. Chow. *New Privacy-Preserving Architectures for Identity-/Attribute-Based Encryption*. PhD thesis, New York University, 2010.

[7] S. S. M. Chow, Y. J. He, L. C. K. Hui, and S.-M. Yiu. SPICE - Simple Privacy-Preserving Identity-Management for Cloud Environment. In *ACNS*, pages 526–543, 2012.

[8] S. S. M. Chow, J. K. Liu, and J. Zhou. Identity-Based Online/Offline Key Encapsulation and Encryption. In *ACM AsiaCCS*, pages 52–60, 2011.

[9] S. S. M. Chow, V. Roth, and E. G. Rieffel. General Certificateless Encryption and Timed-Release Encryption. In *Security and Cryptography for Networks (SCN)*, pages 126–143, 2008.

[10] A. Ge, J. Zhang, R. Zhang, C. Ma, and Z. Zhang. Security Analysis of a Privacy-Preserving Decentralized Key-Policy Attribute-Based Encryption Scheme. *IEEE Trans. Parallel Distrib. Syst.*, 24(11):2319–2321, 2013.

[11] V. Goyal, O. Pandey, A. Sahai, and B. Waters. Attribute-Based Encryption for Fine-Grained Access Control of Encrypted Data. In *ACM Computer and Communications Security*, pages 89–98, 2006.

[12] M. Green, S. Hohenberger, and B. Waters. Outsourcing the Decryption of ABE Ciphertexts. In *USENIX Security*, 2011.

[13] S. Hohenberger and B. Waters. Online/Offline Attribute-Based Encryption. In *Public-Key Cryptography (PKC)*, pages 293–310, 2014.

[14] J. Hong, K. Xue, and W. Li. Comments on "DAC-MACS: Effective Data Access Control for Multiauthority Cloud Storage Systems". *IEEE Trans. Information Forensics and Security*, 10(6):1315–1317, 2015.

[15] S. Jahid, P. Mittal, and N. Borisov. EASiER: Encryption-Based Access Control in Social Networks with Efficient Revocation. In *ACM AsiaCCS*, pages 411–415, 2011.

[16] A. B. Lewko, T. Okamoto, A. Sahai, K. Takashima, and B. Waters. Fully Secure Functional Encryption: Attribute-Based Encryption and (Hierarchical) Inner Product Encryption. In *EuroCrypt*, pages 62–91, 2010.

[17] A. B. Lewko and B. Waters. Decentralizing Attribute-Based Encryption. In *EuroCrypt*, pages 568–588, 2011.

[18] J. Li, X. Chen, J. Li, C. Jia, J. Ma, and W. Lou. Fine-Grained Access Control System Based on Outsourced Attribute-Based Encryption. In *ESORICS*, pages 592–609, 2013.

[19] J. Li, Q. Huang, X. Chen, S. S. M. Chow, D. S. Wong, and D. Xie. Multi-Authority Ciphertext-Policy Attribute-Based Encryption with Accountability. In *ACM AsiaCCS*, pages 386–390, 2011.

[20] M. Li, S. Yu, Y. Zheng, K. Ren, and W. Lou. Scalable and Secure Sharing of Personal Health Records in Cloud Computing Using Attribute-Based Encryption. *IEEE Trans. Parallel Distrib. Syst.*, 24(1):131–143, 2013.

[21] Z. Liu, Z. Cao, Q. Huang, D. S. Wong, and T. H. Yuen. Fully Secure Multi-authority Ciphertext-Policy Attribute-Based Encryption without Random Oracles. In *ESORICS*, 2011.

[22] H. Ma, R. Zhang, and W. Yuan. Comments on "Control Cloud Data Access Privilege and Anonymity with Fully Anonymous Attribute-Based Encryption". *IEEE Trans. Information Forensics and Security*, 11(4):866–867, 2016.

[23] Y. Rouselakis and B. Waters. Efficient Statically-Secure Large-Universe Multi-Authority Attribute-Based Encryption. In *Financial Cryptography and Data Security*, pages 315–332, 2015.

[24] A. Sahai, H. Seyalioglu, and B. Waters. Dynamic Credentials and Ciphertext Delegation for Attribute-Based Encryption. In *CRYPTO*, pages 199–217, 2012.

[25] A. Sahai and B. Waters. Fuzzy Identity-Based Encryption. In *EuroCrypt*, pages 457–473, 2005.

[26] Y. Tong, J. Sun, S. S. M. Chow, and P. Li. Cloud-Assisted Mobile-Access of Health Data With Privacy and Auditability. *IEEE J. Biomedical and Health Informatics*, 18(2):419–429, 2014.

[27] M. Wang, Z. Zhang, and C. Chen. Security Analysis of a Privacy-Preserving Decentralized Ciphertext-Policy Attribute-Based Encryption Scheme. *Concurrency and Computation: Practice and Experience*, 28(4):1237–1245, 2016.

[28] B. Waters. Ciphertext-Policy Attribute-Based Encryption: An Expressive, Efficient, and Provably Secure Realization. In *Public Key Cryptography*, pages 53–70, 2011.

[29] K. Yang, X. Jia, K. Ren, and B. Zhang. DAC-MACS: Effective Data Access Control for Multi-Authority Cloud Storage Systems. In *Infocom*. IEEE, 2013.

[30] S. Yu, C. Wang, K. Ren, and W. Lou. Attribute Based Data Sharing with Attribute Revocation. In *ACM AsiaCCS*, pages 261–270, 2010.

PolyStream: Cryptographically Enforced Access Controls for Outsourced Data Stream Processing

Cory Thoma, Adam J. Lee, Alexandros Labrinidis
Department of Computer Science
University of Pittsburgh
(corythoma, adamlee, labrinid)@cs.pitt.edu

ABSTRACT

With data becoming available in larger quantities and at higher rates, new data processing paradigms have been proposed to handle high-volume, fast-moving data. Data Stream Processing is one such paradigm wherein transient data streams flow through sets of continuous queries, only returning results when data is of interest to the querier. To avoid the large costs associated with maintaining the infrastructure required for processing these data streams, many companies will outsource their computation to third-party cloud services. This outsourcing, however, can lead to private data being accessed by parties that a data provider may not trust. The literature offers solutions to this confidentiality and access control problem but they have fallen short of providing a complete solution to these problems, due to either immense overheads or trust requirements placed on these third-party services.

To address these issues, we have developed *PolyStream*, an enhancement to existing data stream management systems that enables data providers to specify attribute-based access control policies that are cryptographically enforced while simultaneously allowing many types of in-network data processing. We detail the access control models and mechanisms used by PolyStream, and describe a novel use of security punctuations that enables flexible, online policy management and key distribution. We detail how queries are submitted and executed using an unmodified Data Stream Management System, and show through an extensive evaluation that PolyStream yields a 550x performance gain versus the state-of-the-art system StreamForce in CODASPY 2014, while providing greater functionality to the querier.

1. INTRODUCTION

With more devices connecting to the Internet, the amount and speed of data being generated is ever-increasing, and processing it is becoming progressively more challenging. Data is being generated by a more diverse set of instruments ranging from sensors embedded into natural environments to monitor earthquakes and tsunamis, to sensors embedded in the human body to monitor personal well-being, to an increasing array of sensors built into smartphones and other wearables, to social media which is constantly updating and evolving [20]. This increase in data quantity and diversity, coupled with the real time nature of most monitoring applications, has brought about the paradigm of Data Stream Processing.

In a streaming environment, queries are long-running and process transient data flowing through the system. Stream processing is especially well-suited for early detection of anomalous events and for long-term monitoring through the use of Data Stream Management Systems (DSMS). Streaming environments separate the *provider* of the data from the *consumer*, and often leverage third-party *computational nodes* for processing their continuous queries. Unlike traditional database systems, this separation leads to data sources having little control over *how* their data is handled or *who* has access to it. Given this separation of the data provider and the eventual data consumer, it becomes difficult to reason about how a data provider can protect their private data. For a system to guarantee the confidentiality of the provider's data once it has been emitted, it must provide an access control framework that allows a data provider to easily describe who has access to their data. To ensure data remains confidential, it should be encrypted to prevent unauthorized users from learning any information about the underlying data once it has left the data provider. To accommodate this encryption, there must be a protocol for an online key management system which can dictate who gets access and how they should be granted access. Furthermore, modern systems are ever-changing with users changing their preferences, leaving and entering the system, or changing their demand on the system. Over time, a data provider may wish to change their access control policies to match changes in the system or their personal preferences. To add a final complication to the problem of enforcing access controls over streaming data, modern systems often make use of outsourced third party systems to cheaply and easily manage their continuous queries. Adding access controls and encryption should not limit a data consumers ability to outsource computation or author meaningful and useful queries over data for which they have been granted access, nor should it greatly impact the performance of these queries either when outsourced or executed locally.

The current state-of-the-art system to solve this problem is Streamforce [5] and although it addresses many of the issues in enforcing access controls, it incurs prohibitive overheads, and limits the types of queries that can be issued to the system. A system like CryptDB [29] addresses a similar problem for outsourced databases but does not provide the dynamic online access control and key management protocol required for an ever-changing streaming environment.

To fully address these issues, we have designed the PolyStream framework, which considers data confidentiality and access controls as first-class citizens in distributed DSMSs (DDSMS) while supporting a wide range of query processing primitives and flexi-

SACMAT'16, June 05-08, 2016, Shanghai, China

© 2016 ACM. ISBN 978-1-4503-3802-8/16/06. . . $15.00

DOI: http://dx.doi.org/10.1145/2914642.2914660

ble key distribution and policy management. Unlike previous work in this space, PolyStream runs on top of an unmodified DDSMS platform; supports a wide range of attribute-based, user-specified cryptographic access controls; allows dynamic policy updates and online, in-stream key management; and enables queriers to submit arbitrary queries using a wide range of in-network processing options. More precisely, in developing PolyStream, we make the following *contributions*:

- *PolyStream allows users to cryptographically enforce access controls over streaming data and alter their policies in real time.* In PolyStream, access control is based upon a data consumer's cryptographically-certified attributes. PolyStream supports Attribute-Based Access Controls (specifically, a large fragment of ABAC$_\alpha$ [22]) and Attribute-Based Encryption (ABE) to enable data providers to write and enforce flexible access control policies over data at the column, tuple, or stream levels.

- *PolyStream provides a built-in scheme for distributing and managing cryptographic keys using ABAC.* PolyStream utilizes a modified version of Security Punctuations [25] (SPs) to enforce ABAC policies. SPs are typically used to allow data providers to communicate access control policies to the trusted servers on which users run queries over their streaming data. Prior work in the cryptographic DDSMS space has largely ignored the subject of key management and changes to policy by relying on separate offline systems to handle key and policy distribution. By contrast, PolyStream uses SPs to both communicate the policies protecting the contents of a given stream, as well as to provide a key distribution channel for decryption keys that are protected by Attribute-Based Encryption enforcement of ABAC policies. This enables a flexible, online key management and policy update infrastructure, even for stateful continuous queries.

- *PolyStream allows data consumers to submit a wide range of queries.* To the best of our knowledge, no streaming system has allowed in-network processing of arbitrary queries over protected data streams handled by an untrusted infrastructure. In systems supporting user-specified queries, the data processing servers are typically assumed to be trusted [3, 13, 14, 25, 26]. In systems processing data over untrusted infrastructure, cryptographic protections are enforced such that data consumers have only limited query processing abilities [5]. By contrast, PolyStream's key management infrastructure allows untrusted compute nodes to process equality, range, and aggregate queries, and also has limited support for in-network joins.

- *Finally, PolyStream functions as a stand-alone access control layer on top of an underlying DSMS.* PolyStream is not, itself, a DDSMS. Rather, it provides an access control service layer on top of another DDSMS. SPs are processed by PolyStream and are obtained via long-running selection queries on the underlying DDSMS. Queries are submitted via PolyStream, rewritten, and deployed using operations already available from the underlying DDSMS, thereby requiring no changes to the system.

We survey related work in Section 2, and describe our system and threat models in Section 3. Section 4 describes the design and implementation of PolyStream, which is then experimentally analyzed in Section 5. Finally, we present our conclusions and directions for future work in Section 6.

2. RELATED AND PRELIMINARY WORK

This section outlines the related work as well as the primitives necessary for understanding PolyStream.

2.1 Related Work

Many streaming systems have been proposed and studied to date. The most notable modern stream processing systems are the Aurora [2], its distributed version Borealis [1], and STREAM [9]. To protect the users of streaming systems from having their private data leaked or stolen, several access control techniques have been proposed. These techniques can be classified into two main categories: those that trust an outsourced third party to enforce access controls over their data, and those that do not.

FENCE [26] is a streaming access control system that trusts third parties to enforce access controls. Nehme et al. introduced the concept of a *Security Punctuation* for enforcing access control in steaming environments [25]. A Security Punctuation (SP) is a tuple inserted directly into a data stream that allows a data provider to send access control policies and updates to the stream processing server(s) where access controls are to be enforced.

Carminati et al. provide access control via enforcing Role Based Access Control (RBAC) and secure operators [13–15]. Operators are replaced with secure versions which determine whether a client can access a stream by referencing an RBAC policy. Their work assumes a trusted and honest server that enforces their access control policies. In [13], the authors extend this work to interface with any stream processing system through the use of query rewriting and middleware, as well as a wrapper to translate their queries into any language accepted by a DSMS.

Ng et al. [27] allow the data provider to author policies over their data. The system uses the principles of limited disclosure and limited collection to limit who can access and operate on data streams, requiring queries to be rewritten to match the level at which they can access the data. Their system requires changing the underlying DSMS and therefore is not globally applicable, and it also requires a trusted server to rewrite the queries.

Linder and Meier [24] focus on securing the Borealis Stream Engine [1]. They introduce a version of RBAC called owner-extended RBAC, or OxRBAC which operates over different levels of stream objects. OxRBAC allows for each object to have an owner, as well as allowing for rules and permissions. Owners are allowed to set RBAC policies over their objects, which the system will enforce. Objects include schemas, streams, queries, or systems. Users are limited to RBAC policies and must trust the server to enforce their policies as well as see their data in plain text.

Unlike the aforementioned work, Streamforce [5] does not trust the stream processing infrastructure to enforce access control and instead relies on cryptography. Streamforce assumes an untrusted, honest-but-curious DDSMS and utilizes Attribute-Based Encryption (ABE) to enforce access control. The data provider will encrypt their data based on what attributes they desire a potential data consumer to possess. Streamforce is able to enforce access control over encrypted data through the use of their main access structure, *views*. Views are submitted by the *data provider* to the (untrusted) server as a query and only those results are returned to the data consumer. The use of views in this system requires the data provider to be directly involved in the querying process, which has the consequence of limiting what a querier can do with the permissions they were given. Streamforce's use of ABE results in large decryption times depending on the number of attributes. In order to reduce the cost on the data consumer's end, Streamforce outsources decryption to the server [16, 17]. However, even with outsourced decryption, Streamforce reports up to 4,000x slowdown compared to an unmodified system due to their extensive use of ABE. Streamforce also requires the *data provider* to execute all aggregates locally, which may not be feasible since the provider may be a system of sensors, or simply a publish/subscribe system. Finally, Streamforce requires an offline key management solution which makes it hard to reason about key revocation and policy updates.

CryptDB [29] allows computation over encrypted data on an untrusted honest-but-curious relational DBMS. CryptDB's primary goal is not access control, but rather allowing computation over encrypted data stored on an untrusted third-party database system. Essentially, CryptDB offers protection from honest-but-curious database administrators through the use of encryption, but does not offer fine grained access controls over the data stored on the system, nor does it offer a key management mechanism since the data owner is in direct control of who can access their data and can change keys at will. CryptDB utilizes specialized encryption techniques for allowing queries to operate on untrusted servers over encrypted data. Specifically, CryptDB employs Deterministic, Order-Preserving, Homomorphic, Specialty Search, Random, and Join encryption techniques to enable many different queries to operate. CryptDB uses *onion* structures to store data, in which data is encrypted under multiple keys: the outer layer of the onion is the most secure, and successive layers provide more functionality (i.e., allow for queries to be executed), but may leak some data. The use of onions as tuples in a streaming system would lead to unnecessary encryptions and decryptions as not all encryption levels are required (cf. Section 5). MONOMI [32] extends CryptDB to allow the querier to also processes queries to provide a broader range of queries to the users.

2.2 Cryptographic Primitives

We now overview the basic encryption techniques that will be used in the coming sections. We use two main types of encryption: computation-enabling and attribute-based encryption.

2.2.1 Attribute-Based Encryption

Attribute-Based Encryption (ABE) is used to encrypt data such that only entities with the proper certified attributes can decrypt a given ciphertext. In an ABE system, an Attribute Authority (AA) holds a master key that can be used to generate decryption keys tied to an individual's attributes (e.g., *Professor* or *Orthopedist*). Encryption requires only public parameters released by the AA and a logical policy p in addition to the data to be encrypted, while decryption requires attribute-based decryption keys provided by the AA. The following functions comprise an ABE system:

- **GenABEMasterKey**(): Generates a master key MK.

- **GenABEPublicParamaters**(MK): Generates the public parameters pa_p needed for encryption.

- **GenABEDecryptionKey**(UA_{user}, MK): generates a decryption key k_d for *user* based on their set of attributes UA_{user}.

- **Enc**$_{ABE}$(pa_p, p, d): generates an ABE encrypted ciphertext c with the public parameters, a logical policy p, and the data d.

- **Dec**$_{ABE}$(p, k_d, c): recovers the data d using the ABE decryption key k_d, the policy p, and the ciphertext c.

Note that the first three functions are executed by the AA. On the other hand, **Enc**$_{ABE}$(pa_p, p, d) can be executed by any entity, as it relies only on public information, while **Dec**$_{ABE}$(p, k_d, c) can be executed by any entity with an ABE decryption key k_d.

2.2.2 Computation-Enabling Encryption

The computation-enabling encryption techniques allow a user to perform some sort of computation over the encrypted data and therefore allow for outsourced data to be processed without leaking plaintext data. However, each technique does leak some metadata about the underlying plaintext.

- *Random Encryption (RND)* uses a block cipher (e.g., AES in CBC mode) to encrypt fields so that no two fields are encrypted to the same value, and does not leak information regarding the correspondence of actual values. Ciphertexts are different even when RND is given the same input for any given value.

- *Deterministic Encryption (DET)* ensures that multiple encryptions of the same value result in the same ciphertext. DET is implemented using a standard cipher (e.g., AES) with some small alterations. Values less than 64 bits are padded, and any value greater than 128 bits is encrypted in CMC mode [18] since CBC mode leaks prefix equalities. This enables equality checking over encrypted values.

- *Order-Preserving Encryption (OPE)* enforces the relationship that $x < y$ iff $OPE(x) < OPE(y)$. The OPE scheme used in our system is adapted from Boldyreva et al. [11], where the authors present Order-Preserving Symmetric Encryption. This enables range queries over encrypted data, but only has IND-OCPA (indistinguishability under ordered chosen-plaintext attack) security and therefore can leak the ordering of tuples [12].

- *Homomorphic Encryption (HOM)* enforces the relationship that $HOM(x) * HOM(y) = HOM(x + y)$. This allows the execution of summation (and by extension average) queries on untrusted servers without leaking field data values or the summation value. PolyStream uses the Paillier [28] encryption scheme. This enables in-network aggregation of encrypted data without leaking individual data values, but comes at the cost of increasing the computational load of this aggregation. An adversary does learn a relationship for the sliding window, since the encrypted sum for the sliding window's worth of tuples is revealed. Note that a sliding window is simply the range of tuples used to generate a result (i.e. 3 minutes, 100 tuples) over the life of the stream.

As noted above, these four techniques make it possible for untrusted computational infrastructure to execute certain query processing functionalities over encrypted data. Deterministic, Order-Preserving, and Random cryptosystems are parameterized by a similar set of functions:

- **GenKey**$_{DET,OPE,RND}$(): Generates a symmetric key k corresponding to the technique used.

- **Enc**$_{DET,OPE,RND}$(k, d): Encrypts data d with key k.

- **Dec**$_{DET,OPE,RND}$(k, c): Decrypts ciphertext c with key k.

The Pallier homomorphic cryptosystem does not rely on a single key, but rather a pair of (public) encryption and (private) decryption parameters. For the purposes of this paper, we represent this functions parameterizing this cryptosystem as follows, and refer the reader to [28] for more information:

- **GenKey**$_{HOM}$(): Generates a encryption parameter pa_{HOM} and a private parameter pp_{HOM}.

- **Enc**$_{HOM}$(pa_{HOM}, d): Encrypts data d with key pa_{HOM}.

- **Dec**$_{HOM}$(pp_{HOM}, c): Decrypts ciphertext c with key pp_{HOM}.

3. SYSTEM AND THREAT MODEL

3.1 System Model

PolyStream provides an API that sits between end users (i.e., data providers and data consumers) and an underlying Distributed Data Stream Management System (DDSMS). No changes to the underlying DDSMS are required for PolyStream to work. Instead, PolyStream makes uses of common functions provided by all DDSMS. Specifically, DDSMSs provide the user with an *optimizeQuery* func-

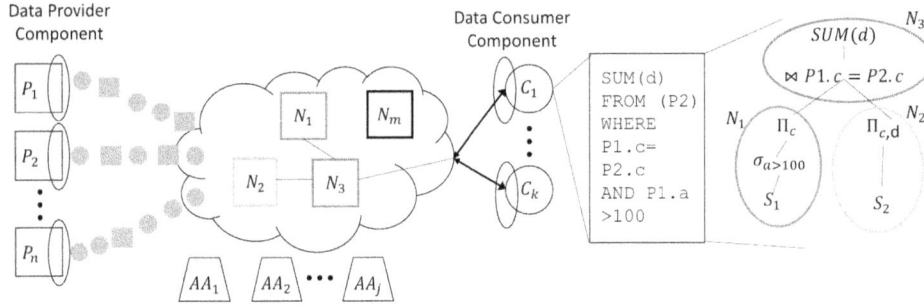

Figure 1: PolyStream system model. An example query is given and represented in the cloud. Node N_1 executes part of the query as represented by the dotted line, and similarly N_2 and N_3 are responsible only for what is represented in the execution tree depicting the query.

tion that takes a CQL query, verifies it, optimizes it, and returns a query plan, and a function *submitQuery* that places the query. DDSMSs also provide a *results* function that yields the result of a query. PolyStream provides functionality to support the three key players in a DDSMS, and one new component (cf., Figure 1):

- *Data Providers* (squares labeled "P_i") create and distribute data streams. Data providers do not necessarily trust all other parties in the DDSMS, which requires creating and updating access control policies for their streams. To aid data providers in creating policies, a trusted third-party *Attribute Authority* verifies the identities and attributes of other parties in the system.

- *Attribute Authorities* (trapezoids labeled "AA_i") verify and certify the attributes of system components. The scope of an AA may vary: while one AA may exist to certify the job titles or roles of employees within a company, others may certify attributes that cross-cut many organizations (e.g., ABET accredits many universities). One system can have many AAs, and individuals may choose which AAs they trust.

- *Compute & Route Nodes* (CRN, squares labeled "N_i") are tasked with executing queries on data streams. Data consumers place query operators on CRNs, which then process incoming tuples and produce output tuples that flow either to other CRNs or to the data consumer.

- *Data Consumers* (circles labeled "C_i") submit continuous queries. Depending on permissions, the query operators resulting from these queries are either submitted to CRNs via PolyStream or executed locally. Queries are submitted using a declarative language, such as CQL [7], and are optimized by the data consumer. PolyStream allows streaming operators to be spread across multiple CRNs with varying levels of trust.

A sample query is given in Figure 1. In this simple example, Data from P_1 and P_2 are combined from different machines running selection and projection operators. The results are joined and summed on a different node, and returned to the data consumer. PolyStream assumes that tuples arrive in order. This is easy to accomplish by utilizing sequence numbers from the data provider and enforcing that only the next tuple can be processed.

3.2 Threat Model

The main goal of PolyStream is to provide a mechanism that data providers can use to author and enforce access control policies over their own data streams. Access control policies are specified using Attribute-Based Access Controls (i.e., a fragment of $ABAC_\alpha$), and enforced using Attribute-Based Encryption (ABE). *Attribute Authorities* (AAs) are trusted to correctly issue attributes to entities within the system. There may be many AAs in the system, which can vary in the scope of attributes that they will certify. AAs

are the master secret key holders of the ABE system and, as such, are responsible for creating ABE decryption keys for the entities whose attributes they certify. AAs are also responsible for the revocation of attributes once a user's attributes have changed, which is outside the scope of this paper. The literature has explored attribute revocation [19, 21, 34] and interested readers are encouraged to explore further. *Data providers* are trusted by data consumers to correctly emit the data streams that they advertise. *Compute and Routing Nodes* (CRNs) may not be trusted by data providers; as such, data streams may be encrypted to hide information from these parties. Similarly, PolyStream avoids placing consumers' query operators on CRNs not trusted to execute these operators. CRNs are assumed to behave in the honest-but-curious model: they will not maliciously alter data that they process, but may attempt to infer information from the tuples that they process. *Data consumers* may or may not be trusted by data providers, who can make use of ABE to enforce ABAC policies protecting their data from unauthorized consumers. Finally, we assume that all entities can establish and communicate over pairwise private and authenticated channels (e.g., using SSL/TLS tunnels).

4. PolyStream

We now overview the PolyStream system. First, we introduce the access control framework that a data provider can use to describe and author policies. We then detail the online policy distribution and cryptographic key management channel used to communicate and enforce the access control policies. We also detail how data consumers' queries are handled in the PolyStream system.

4.1 Access Control Model and Mechanism

Given the dynamic nature of real-time data stream processing systems, data providers, data consumers, and compute and route nodes are likely to join and leave the system over time. This inhibits a data provider's ability to have a full understanding of every entity acting in the system. As such, PolyStream makes use of attribute-based policies to help data providers protect their sensitive data in a more generalizable manner.

Access Control Model. Attribute-based access controls allow a data provider to *describe* authorized consumers of their data, rather than listing them explicitly. PolyStream makes use of a large fragment of the $ABAC_\alpha$ [22] model. An $ABAC_\alpha$ system is comprised of the following state elements:

- Sets U, S, and O of users, subjects, and objects

- Sets UA, SA, and OA of user attributes, subject attributes, and object attributes

Furthermore, ABAC_α makes use of the following grammar for specifying policies:

$$p ::= \quad p \wedge p \quad | \quad p \vee p \quad | \quad (p) \quad | \quad \neg p \quad |$$
$$\text{set} \quad setcompare \quad \text{set} \quad | \quad \text{atomic} \in \text{set} \quad |$$
$$\text{atomic} \quad automiccompare \quad \text{atomic}$$
$$set ::= \quad set_{sa} \subseteq SA | set_{oa} \subseteq OA | set_{ua} \subseteq UA$$
$$setcompare ::= \quad \subset | \subseteq | \not\subseteq$$
$$atomic ::= \quad attribute \in SA | attribute \in OA | attribute \in UA$$
$$atomiccompare ::= \quad < | = | \leq$$
$$attribute ::= \quad < string >$$

In PolyStream, the set U is comprised of all entities acting in the system (i.e., data providers, consumers, and CRNs). The set O contains pairs (t, ℓ) containing all tuples t being processed by the underlying DDSMS (i.e., data fields or streams), and the access level ℓ at which they should be protected. PolyStream supports four such access levels, corresponding to the type of in-network processing that will be allowed: NONE (no in-network access), SJ (in-network selection and join), RNG (in-network range queries), and AGG (in-network aggregation). While there are no explicit subjects in PolyStream, queries issued by a data consumer can be given access to a limited set of the issuing user's attributes. As such, S is comprised of the long-running queries submitted by data consumers.

Data producers use the ABAC_α policy grammar to author protections over the data that they supply to the DDSMS. In this paper, we will use the shorthand $(q \wedge r) \vee s$ to express a policy of the form $(q \in UA \wedge r \in UA) \vee s \in UA)$, since all policies are written as constraints over the set UA of user attributes that must be possessed by an authorized data consumer (and thus by the query subject operating on their behalf). Note also that PolyStream does not make use of the atomic operators for $<$ and $\leq$, since our underlying ABE library supports only string attributes.

Enforcement Mechanism. Unlike most stream processing systems, in PolyStream, CRNs are not trusted to correctly enforce data provider access controls. As such, we enforce ABAC_α policies cryptographically by encrypting data prior to introducing it to the DDSMS. Recall that PolyStream supports four access permissions: NONE, SJ, RNG, and AGG. We now describe each in more details, and discuss how cryptography can assist in the enforcement of these permissions.

- **NONE**. This permission prevents all in-network processing. To enforce the NONE permission for a tuple t, we simply encrypt t using a randomized cryptosystem (e.g., AES in CBC mode) prior to transmission. That is, given a session key k, we transmit ciphertext $c = \mathbf{Enc}_{RND}(k.t)$ to the DDSMS. Intermediate CRNs cannot glean any information about the contents of this ciphertext, but authorized consumers can decrypt it upon receipt.

- **SJ**. This permission allows in-network selection and joins of streams sent by the same data producer. To enforce the SJ permission for a tuple t, we encrypt t using a deterministic cryptosystem (e.g., AES in CMC mode) prior to transmission. Given a session key k, we transmit the ciphertext $c = \mathbf{Enc}_{DET}(k.t)$ to the DDSMS. Since the same plaintext value will always encrypt to the same ciphertext value, untrusted CRNs can carry out selection on static values or join two streams whose join attributes are encrypted under the same key.

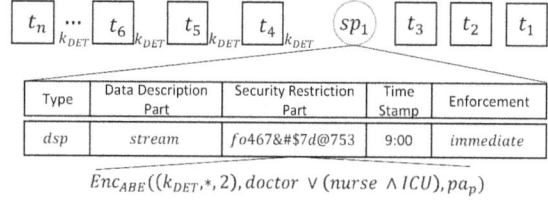

Figure 2: A typical Security Punctuation with an example use case.

- **RNG**. This permission allows in-network processing of range queries. To enforce the RNG permission for a tuple t, we use an order-preserving encryption scheme (e.g., [11]) and a session key k to transmit the ciphertext $c = \mathbf{Enc}_{OPE}(k, t)$ to the DDSMS. Given (encrypted) range bounds $l = \mathbf{Enc}_{OPE}(k, v_1)$ and $h = \mathbf{Enc}_{OPE}(k, v_2)$, an untrusted CRN can check whether $l \leq c \leq h$ without learning v_1, v_2, or t.

- **AGG**. This permission allows in-network processing of aggregate queries. Enforcement of the AGG permission uses an additively homomorphic cryptosystem (e.g., Pallier [28]) to enable in-network aggregation. Given tuples $t_1, t_2, \ldots, t_n$ and a public/private key pair $\langle k, k^{-1} \rangle$, we compute and transmit $c_1 = \mathbf{Enc}_{HOM}(k, t_1), c_2 = \mathbf{Enc}_{HOM}(k, t_2), \ldots, c_n = \mathbf{Enc}_{HOM}(k, t_n)$ to the DDSMS. An untrusted CRN can then compute $c_1 \times c_2 \times \ldots \times c_n = \mathbf{Enc}_{HOM}(k, s = t_1 + t_2 + \ldots + t_n)$ without learning s or any t_i.

Table 1 summarizes how each permission can be enforced cryptographically, as well as the DDSMS operations enabled by the permission. Note that PolyStream only supports encrypted joins on streams that are DET-encrypted under the same key. In principle, this likely means that joins are only possible over streams published by the same data producer. Supporting a richer variety of joins is left to future work.

Although the above constructions enable in-network processing, they do not enable attribute-based control of these access permissions. To cryptographically enforce ABAC_α policies over objects in PolyStream, we make use of attribute-based encryption to ensure that the session keys used above can only be recovered by authorized data consumers. In particular, consider an ABAC_α policy p authored over attributes issued by some authority AA_i whose public parameters are pa_i, and a session key k used to enforce one of the above four access permissions over some data tuple. In this case, the data producer can transmit $\mathbf{Enc}_{ABE}(pa_i, p, k)$ to authorized data consumers. Authorized consumers can then decrypt the session key k, which can be used to access protected data tuples. The exact mechanics of this policy distribution and key management process will be discussed next.

4.2 Policy Distribution

In a DDSMS, data providers do not control the paths taken by their data. As such, distributing, updating, and enforcing policies protecting that data take some effort, particularly if the infrastructure itself is only semi-trusted. Security Punctuations (SP) [25] address this issue by providing a mechanism for distributing policy along *with* data. A SP is simply a tuple injected into a provider's data stream (represented as a circle in Figure 2) that describes an access control policy over some set of protected data. For PolyStream, a SP dictates the ABE-enforced ABAC policy or policies protecting a stream to potential consumers. SPs are comprised of the five fields below (and the top box in Figure 2):

231

Permission	Scheme	Type of Queries	Supported operators	Information Gained by Adversary
NONE	RND	None	None	Nothing
SJ	DET	Equality	Equality Select, Project, Join, Count, Group By, Order by	Equality of attributes
RNG	OPE	Range	Equality Select, Range Select, Join, Count	A partial to full order of tuples
AGG	HOM	Summations	Aggregates over summations	Encrypted Sum for sliding window

Table 1: Summary of what types of queries and operators are supported by each encryption scheme, as well as what each scheme could reveal to a potential adversary.

- *Type*: Indicates that the SP originated from a data provider.

- *Data Description Part*: Indicates the schema fields (e.g., "heart rate") within a tuple that are protected by this policy. This may be as broad as an entire stream, or as specific as an individual field.

- *Security Restriction Part*: Describes the policy being enforced.

- *Timestamp*: The time at which the tuple was generated.

- *Enforcement*: Either *immediate* or *deferred*. Immediate enforcement applies the new policy to tuples in buffers, whereas deferred enforcement applies the new policy only to tuples timestamped after the SP.

While prior work has used SPs to distribute plaintext policies for enforcement by a trusted DDSMS, PolyStream makes use of SPs as a policy and key distribution mechanism, but relies on cryptography for policy enforcement. This means that while the *type*, *data description part*, *timestamp*, and *enforcement* fields are straightforward, the structure of the *security restriction part* (SRP) requires greater explanation. PolyStream uses the SRP field to transmit a tuple $\langle c, p \rangle$ where p is the ABAC$_\alpha$ policy protecting access to the fields listed in the data description part, and c is an ABE ciphertext generated by encrypting the following three pieces of information:

- *Access Type:* The type of in-network permission (i.e., NONE, SJ, RNG, or AGG) allowed by this policy

- *Index:* The position(s) of the data field(s) being protected by the policy, listed in the DDP.

- *Decryption Key:* The symmetric key k used to recover data protected at the NONE, SJ, or RNG levels, or the private key k^{-1} used to recover data protected at the AGG level.

Note that the above index information is needed due to the fact that a given stream may include several copies of a given schema field. For instance, if one policy on a stream grants AGG access to "heart rate" to some individuals while providing other individuals with SJ access, two copies of the "heart rate" field will be transmitted: one encrypted using Pallier (for AGG access) and one encrypted with AES in CMC mode (for SJ access).

Given an SP with an SRP containing the pair $\langle c, p \rangle$, a data consumer can inspect p to determine whether they possess the attributes needed to decrypt c. If so, decrypting c provides the data consumer with a description of the in-network processing allowed by the policy, the indexes upon which this processing can occur, and the (symmetric or private) key needed to decrypt result tuples. This is enough information to facilitate query planning (*Which queries can I run?*), operator placement (*How can I place physical operators for these queries in the CRN network?*), and results analysis (*How can I decrypt the results that I receive?*).

Key revocation in PolyStream is as simple as updating the access control policy (even the same one again) so that a new key is generated. A key is therefore revoked when a user no longer possesses the proper attributes to satisfy the ABAC policy to get the new key. Data providers can develop their own policy for updating and refreshing keys to satisfy their own needs. Key revocation does

not include the revocation of attributes. Attribute Authorities (AA) are responsible for the revocation of attributes so when a user loses possession of an attribute, a new ABE decryption key is issued. This could lead to a time where data consumers can have unauthorized accesses due to a loss of an attribute but still have the key from the last Security Punctuation. This can be protected against by data providers periodically updating the keys that they use to protect their streams, via the Security Punctuation mechanism described previously.

Algorithm 1 SubmitQuery

1: Submit query q to DSMS query Optimizer for Plan p
2: **for** Operation o in qurery q **do**
3:     **if** no entry in *schemaTable* **then**
4:       Return permission denied
5:     **else**
6:       retrieve Schema Key k from *schemaTable*
7:       Encrypt Attribute with k
8:       **if** o is Filter or Count **then**
9:         **if** Filtering on Equality AND *permissionTable* contains "SJ" **then**
10:           Encrypt value in o with key in *permissionTable*
11:         **else if** Filter on range AND *permissionTable* contains "RNG" **then**
12:           Encrypt value in o with key in *permissionTable*
13:         **else if** *permissionTable* contains "NONE" **then**
14:           Operator Executes Locally, exit
15:       **if** o is Sum **then**
16:         **if** *permissionTable* contains "AGG" **then**
17:           Change o to Multiplication
18:         **else**
19:           Operator Executes Locally, exit
20:       **if** o is Average **then**
21:         **if** *permissionTable* contains "AGG" **then**
22:           Create operations Count, SUM
23:           Create local operation Division for sum/count
24:         **else**
25:           Operator Executes Locally, exit
26:       **if** o is Join **then**
27:         **if** *permissionTable* contains "SJ" or "RNG" for the same provider **then**
28:           Encrypt value in o with key in *permissionTable*
29:         **else**
30:           Operator Executes Locally, exit
31:       **if** Other operator **then**
32:         Operator Executes Locally, exit
33: $submit(Q)$

4.3 Query Processing

This section overviews how a data consumer can submit and change queries based on policy updates from the data providers they are are interested in. When a data consumer authors a query, they submit it to PolyStream, which follows the steps outlined in Algorithm 1. Recall that PolyStream sits between an unmodified DDSMS and the data providers/consumers. First, PolyStream submits the query to the underlying DDSMS's query optimizer using the DDSMS's own *optimizeQuery* function, and receives back the generated query plan (in the form of a physical operator graph). Using this plan, PolyStream iterates through each operation of the

DP	location	*1*	9:00	IM.

DP	heartrate	*2*	9:00	IM.

DP	location	*3*	9:00	IM.

Schemas: S1: StreamId, Location, HeartRate, Timestamp
S2: StreamId, Location, Speed

1 $Enc_{ABE}((SJ, 2, k_{DET}), (serviceApp \land certifiedApp) \lor userApprovedApp, pa_p)$
2 $Enc_{ABE}((AGG, 3, k_{OPE}), (serviceApp \land certifiedApp) \lor doctor, pa_p)$
3 $Enc_{ABE}((SJ, 2, k_{DET}), (serviceApp \land certifiedApp) \lor certifiedMechanic, pa_p)$

```
1  SELECT s1.streamId, AVG(s1.heartRate) AS avht
2    FROM Stream1 as s1, Stream 2 as s2
3    WHERE s1.location = s2.location
4    AND s1.timestamp > 6:00am
5    AND s1.timestamp < 7:00pm
6    AND s2.speed < 30
7    EVERY 5 minutes, UPDATE 1 minute
```

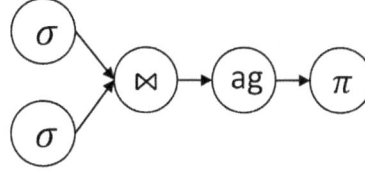

Figure 3: Motivating Example - RoadRageReducer App.

Algorithm 2 handleSecurityPunctuation

1: *SRP* = Security Restriction Part of *SP*
2: *DDP* = Data Description Part of *SP*
3: Have pa_{pr} ABE Decryption Key from AA
4: **if** pa_{pr} decrypts *SRP* **then**
5:    **for** Fields *f* in *DDP* **do**
6:       Associate *f* with permission *p* at index *i* from *SRP*

---

plan starting at the data source nodes in the graph (line 2) and determines where the operation must be placed.

Using data extracted from the SRP field of SPs received by the consumer from the data providers, PolyStream iteratively checks each operation to see if in-network processing has been enabled by the data provider (lines 8,15,20,26,31) and if access has been granted to the data consumer (lines 9,11,13,16,21,27). If so, this operation can be submitted to a CRN for in-network processing. If in-network processing is not possible, but the consumer has access to the field(s) being operated upon, the operator executes locally on the data consumer's device, where local decryption is possible (lines 14,19,25,30,32). We note that once *any* operator is placed on the data consumer's machine, all subsequent operations are placed on the data consumer's machine as well to avoid unnecessary network round trips. Once all operator placement decisions have been made, the query is submitted using the *submitQuery* function provided by the DDSMS and results are processed using the *results* function.

PolyStream provides a large number of operations that can be executed by CRNs over encrypted data, including operations that require multiple encrypted streams. For instance, a data consumer who is interested in aggregates over multiple encrypted streams can simply execute an aggregate separately over each encrypted stream and combine the results on their trusted machine once they are decrypted. A data consumer can also preform a join on two encrypted streams so long as they are encrypted with the same DET or OPE key. When the streams are encrypted under different keys, or processing on the CRN is otherwise not possible, PolyStream provides functionality similar to MONOMI [32] in that operations are executed on the data consumer's trusted machine after data is decrypted, so long as the data consumer possesses the proper decryption keys. Ultimately, this allows the consumer to issue *any* query for which they at least have decryption capabilities.

There exist alternative approaches to executing a multi-provider joins on the data consumer's trusted machine. One approach is for the data consumer to deploy a trusted node in the CRN network that simply decrypts multiple streams that are to be joined and re-encrypts each using a single symmetric key. This will allow later nodes in the CRN network to handle in-network joins, while minimizing the computational impact on the data consumer. Another

approach is to use proxy re-encryption to compute on data even when it is encrypted with different keys [33]. Proxy re-encryption will enable one stream to be joined with another simply by re-encrypting one (still in its encrypted form) so that it is encrypted form matches the other. These techniques are being considered in our ongoing work

Example. Consider the scenario presented in Figure 3 with a single data provider, a city commuter, who is producing two data streams. The first stream contains health and location data being produced by a fitness watch linked to a phone, while the second contains location and travel data from her car's on-board computer. Stream 1 is protected by SP_1, which enables in-network SJ processing on the Location field for entities satisfying the policy $p_1 = (serviceApp \land certifiedApp) \lor userApprovedApp$ to recover the resulting data. Stream 1 is also protected by SP_2 enabling in-network AGG processing on the HeartRate field for anyone satisfying $p_2 = (serviceApp \land certifiedApp) \lor doctor$. Stream 2 is protected by SP_3, which enables in-network SJ processing on the Location field for entities satisfying the policy $p_3 = (serviceApp \land certifiedApp) \lor certifiedMechanic$ to recover the resulting data.

A data consumer, a mobile app called RoadRageReducer (a certified service app), wishes to execute the query shown in Figure 3. This query determines if the commuter has road rage by checking whether they are in their car while their average heart rate is elevated. To reduce the overall workload of the query, only high traffic driving times at low speeds are considered. Optimizing this query using the underlying DDSMS produces the operator graph shown in Figure 3. Given the information recovered from SP_1, SP_2 and SP_3, each of these operators can be placed on the CRN network since (i) the initial selection operates over unprotected fields (Speed and Timestamp), (ii) the join combines both streams using the SJ protected Location field, (iii) the averaging operator aggregates over the AGG protected HeartRate field, and (iv) the only input to the projection operator is a field index. Once the query is processed and a result is returned, the RoadRageReducer app can then use its Paillier decryption key to decrypt the resulting average over the HeartRate field.

5. EXPERIMENTAL EVALUATION

Like many other confidentiality enforcement systems, PolyStream exposes a tradeoff between performance and confidentiality. To better understand this tradeoff, we examined many different configurations/workloads on an experimental system comprised of a cluster of 10 small instances on Amazon EC2, which implements PolyStream as described above. All network communications occur over SSL/TLS tunnels. We also compared PolyStream with the current state-of-the-art Streamforce [5].

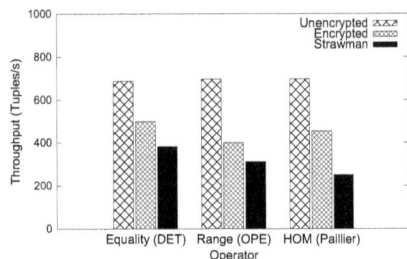

Figure 4: Throughput for each of the different operations supported for both unencrypted and encrypted streams.

5.1 Experimental Setup and Platform

Our system is built on top of the Storm distributed computing platform [30], as is the case for many other distributed DSMS prototypes/evaluations [4, 6]. Given that we do not use any functionality unique to Storm, we fully expect that PolyStream could be trivially ported to other distributed computing platforms like Spark Streaming [35] and Twitter Herron [23]. Storm provides a communication layer that guarantees tuple delivery. Storm accepts user-defined topologies that direct how components are networked. The main components of Storm are *spouts* and *bolts*. Spouts provide data to the system and therefore assume the role of data provider, and bolts compute on the data and take the role of data consumer or CRN. To better control experiments, a special scheduler was implemented to dictate which machines handled which components.

Tests were run on Amazon EC2 using small instances. All components were programmed in Java and packaged as JAR files. Each data consumer was assigned a set of attributes from a bolt *Central Authority*. One EC2 instance was devoted to controlling Storm's required libraries as well as assigning tasks and was not used in experimentation; leaving nine that were used as CRNs with data consumers on them. Data providers were generated from outside machines and fed into the cluster so that data generation would not alter the state and load of each machine. Tests involved between one and eight data providers; 1,000 and 8,000 tuples per second input rates; two and 20 data consumers; and two and eight CRNs. All CP-ABE functionality was provided by the Advanced Crypto Software Collection library [10], and the HOM key size was 1024 bytes.

5.2 Workload Description

For our experiments, we used simulated Twitter-like data from a workload generator which provided control over distribution and frequency of keywords as input data. This generator is capable of forming both text and numerical data. Values can be controlled in either a fine or course-grained fashion. Fine-grained control allows us to define a small dictionary and assign a distribution over the occurrence of each value in the dictionary. Course-grained support simply sets a desired amount of data and desired selectivities (as to control selectivity for windowed and one-shot queries). We chose not to the Linear Road [8] benchmark for two main reasons. First, adding encryption and policy changes to arbitrary values adds overheads to the actual benchmark and requires altering it, which could undermine the intentions behind the data and queries. Secondly, Linear Road requires compatibility with a traditional database system. In the PolyStream model, the database system may reside on the server (colocated with the data) which can leak data since it would be required to remain in plaintext. A system like CryptDB could be used in this regard, but that says nothing for the methods of PolyStream which focuses on data streams.

5.3 Overhead for Computation Functionality

To better understand the effect that each operator has on the overall throughput, we compared *unencrypted* versus *encrypted* processing using one encryption type. We also included a *Strawman* approach where all data is routed to the data consumer for processing under the RND encryption scheme.

Configuration One data provider with one stream distributed the data to a single CRN with a single data consumer. This data consumer posed one query to the stream corresponding to the given encryption scheme (e.g., DET encryption matched to equality select and OPE mapped to range queries). One field was encrypted for each operator. For equality queries, Range, and summation queries DET, OPE, and HOM were used, respectively.

Results (Figure 4 and Table 2) On average, deterministic encryption only incurs 12% overhead, whereas HOM decreases throughput by 49% on average. This large difference in HOM is attributed to its use of Homomorphic encryption, which involves costly homomorphic additions running on each CRN. We also evaluated a more secure scheme (implemented on the same system) in which RND encryption is used and all tuples are sent back to the data consumer for processing. This requires *every* tuple to be decrypted and the operation computed over the plaintext value. Since every tuple is encrypted, the overall cost of execution is hindered by the cost of decrypting each tuple before processing. The overhead incurred by each encryption scheme originates either from the encryption or the decryption phase of the algorithm. Table 2 shows exactly how much time is spent during each phase of encryption. Note that a summation for the HOM scheme itself takes on average .015ms, and the key size (modulus size) for HOM plays a significant role in its encryption and decryption time. It is also important to note that the system will always pay the encryption cost for every tuple, but may not pay the decryption cost for each tuple depending on the selectivities.

Takeaway Compared to an unmodified DSMS, PolyStream's overhead is a modest 28% in supporting access control on honest-but-curious CRNs. In contrast, the overhead of the state-of-the-art Streamforce [5] is 4,000x, according to the authors.

Mode	RND	OPE	DET	H-1024	H-2048	H-4096
Encrypt	8.2	13.1	12.5	18.1	70.2	151.8
Decrypt	8.2	13.2	12.3	12.9	21.6	36.5

Table 2: The encryption and decryption times (in ms) for each of the schemes used by our system (H-xxxx = HOM at that key size).

5.4 Effects on Latency per Encryption Type

To explore the perceived effect on waiting for a result based on an incoming tuple, this experiment compared the latency of PolyStream to that of the baseline Storm-based DDSMS without any encryption.

Configuration This experiment used only one EC2 small instance. One query was used to test each encryption type, and each query was simply a selection (i.e. on comparison) or addition wherein one addition or one comparison needed to be made. The input rate of tuples remained constant. Each query was tested five times with the average reported for 1,000 tuples per trial. Finally, experiments were carried out in succession with the same system setup and background. Results are reported in milliseconds (ms).

Results (Table 3) Table 3 shows the latencies for each type. The main differences between PolyStream and the baseline DSMS is in the decryption time on the data consumer. The actual computation on the CRN is roughly the same (with the exception of HOM) since

System	RND	OPE	DET	HOM
PolyStream	425	413	326	1,144
Baseline	356	357	308	485

Table 3: The latency (ms) of each encryption when used in a query.

Tuples/second	Encrypt	Decrypt	CP-ABE	Compute	Transmit	Idle
2,000	3.8	4.0	6.0	**41.2**	9.5	35.6
4,000	3.9	5.3	6.2	**61.7**	10.3	12.6
6,000	3.4	7.2	6.3	**69.0**	12.2	1.6
8,000	3.4	8.6	5.8	**76.2**	16.0	0.0

Table 4: The percentage of system time spent on a task based on the input rate. CP-ABE represents the time spent passing keys and managing attribute-based encryptions.

the operators are only comparing larger integers or strings. HOM, however, takes longer to compute since the integers are larger and require multiplication as opposed to simple summations. Note that the HOM latency is calculated as the arrival of the first tuple in a window until the time the resulting summation is outputted. For this experiment, the window size was five tuples.

Takeaway Summation or averaging queries incur larger delays due to the need for multiplying larger numbers (a costlier operation) to homomorphically sum tuples using the Paillier [28] scheme.

5.5 Total System Overview

Given that each encryption scheme yields an overhead, it is worth exploring exactly what percentage of system time is devoted to doing a given task. We consider six main tasks when examining where the system spends its time: encrypting, decrypting, attribute alterations (CP-ABE), computing, transmitting, and waiting.

Configuration The results are based on an hour-long simulation where over 40,000 tweets were generated, and 600 changes in policy were assigned. The worker nodes were in a wheel configuration (Figure 5) with each leaf sending data to a sink (a bolt which receives and deletes data) to emulate retransmission. We used a mixed query workload, consisting of equality, range, and summation queries (33% for each type). Since the workload depends largely on the input rate, results are given for different input rates. In the event that the machines became overwhelmed, a typical simple load shedding technique was used [31].

Results (Table 4) For all experiments, over 70% of the time was spent on computation or idling if the workload was light. The time spent on attribute alterations and the time spent encrypting stays relatively constant throughout the simulation. The system spends more time decrypting as the workload increases since more tuples are sent. The wait time of 0.0%, for the 8,000 tuples/sec case, indicated a system saturated with tuples and, as such, some tuples were dropped (4.9% of tuples).

Takeaway PolyStream spends on average 15-17% of the total time in encryption, decryption, and key management.

5.6 SP Frequency vs. Throughput

A change in policy can occur at any time. Next, we evaluate how the frequency of policy changes effects the overall latency.

Configuration We used two machines, each with two data consumers. The frequency of policy changes is determined by the frequency of inserting SPs into the stream. We compare against using ABE encryption for all tuples, similar to the state-of-the-art [5]. The number of attributes was fixed at five, with a mixed query

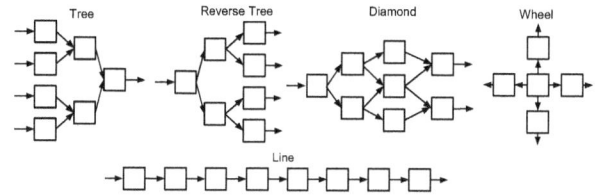

Figure 5: Configurations used to test how network topology affects PolyStream.

workload of equality, range, and summation queries (33% each).

Results (Figure 6a) Results are depicted in Figure 6a. Note that the per-tuple ABE uses outsourced decryption. These experiments show that PolyStream was better than per-tuple ABE for all cases except the degenerate case of one SP per data tuple. PolyStream performed well when changes in policy are infrequent. It is clear that PolyStream outperforms the state-of-the-art [5] in even the simple case of one policy update for every two tuples, while providing more flexibility in submitting queries.

Takeaway Given a ratio of 1/100 (data tuples to SPs), PolyStream outperforms Streamforce by over 40x.

5.7 Tuple vs. Punctuation Level ABE

The implementation of the current state-of-the-art, Streamforce [5], uses decryption outsourcing techniques from Green et al. [17] to outsource decryption of Attribute-Based Encryptions to the cloud. Through the use of a transformation key, the server (CRN) is able to aid in decryption by doing most of the decryption, leaving only a small decryption operation to the data consumer. For *every tuple* selected by the system, however, a full attribute-based decryption must be done, which is costly regardless of whether or not it is done on a server. This means the number of ABE decryptions in Streamforce is large when compared to PolyStream which only uses ABE for policy updates (SPs). To test the effects of outsourcing attribute-based decryption to the cloud, we implemented the scheme used by Streamforce to compare our key distribution approach with their attribute-based approach.

Configuration Streamforce used four different queries ranging from simple selections to summations. To compare their results with ours, the total decryption time is taken as the transformation time plus the decryption time performed on the data consumer. The total decryption time for PolyStream is simply the faster cryptographic scheme decryption time, which averages to 13.2 seconds, as mentioned above. Since PolyStream only uses ABE to share keys (i.e. only when a Security Punctuation is issued and processed), it does not pay the cost of ABE decryption on every tuple; instead, it only pays the cost once, as described above. One query was used, along with one stream on one machine. Note that the ABE decryption time depends on the number of attributes, so results are given for different numbers of attributes. Also, note that in this experiment the only comparison drawn between Streamforce and our work is Streamforce's use of ABE for each tuple. Streamforce relies on the data provider to do aggregates rather than the server, and the deterministic encryption and summations are the same as the ones used in PolyStream, so they were excluded.

Results (Figure 6d) Even with the smallest number of attributes, outsourced ABE is 4x slower than the PolyStream approach, and at one point it is nearly 550x slower depending on the number of attributes. These results are in line with initial results from Green et al. [17], which were on similar, yet better, hardware.

Takeaway By using ABE only for key management (i.e. not for every tuple), PolyStream incurs up to 550x less overhead per tuple than Streamforce.

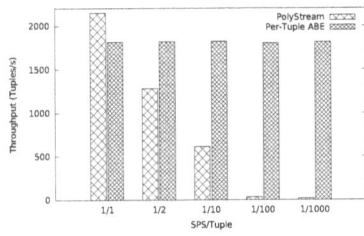

(a) Effect on average throughput by altering the frequency of Security Punctuations.

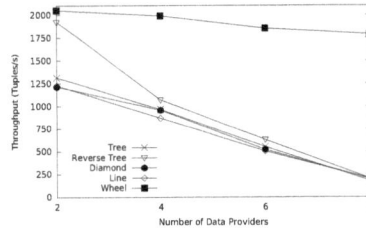

(b) Total throughput for increased load with selectivity .8, two clients per CRNs, and all encryption types used.

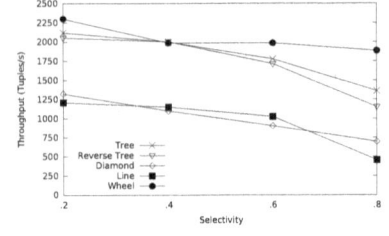

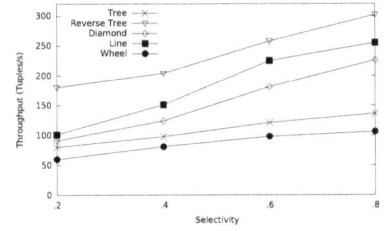

(c) Total throughput for increasing selectivity where there is one data source, two clients per CRN, with only DET used over selection queries.

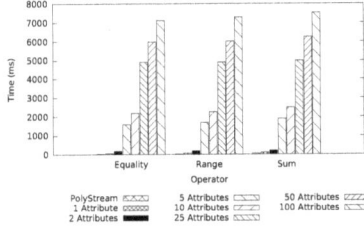

(d) Outsourced ABE decryption for different operators with different numbers of attributes. Note that PolyStream decryption are included as the first column per set.

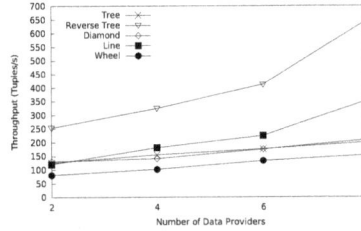

(e) Total latency for increased load with selectivity .8, two clients per CRNs, and all encryption types used.

(f) Total latency for increasing selectivity where there is one data source, two clients per CRN, with only DET used over selection queries.

Figure 6: Network Configuration, SPS frequencey, and Encryption Technique Effects on Throughput and Latency

5.8 Network Effect on Throughput & Latency

Configuration (Figure 5) Storm enables the user to describe the configuration of the network interconnecting the worker nodes. To better see how network connections affect the system, we tested five configurations with different input rates, data consumers, selectivities, and CRNs. These five configurations consisted of a tree, a reverse tree, a line, a diamond, and a wheel.

Throughput Results (Figures 6b, 6c) The first network experiment measured the throughput with respect to the workload. Each configuration had all of the worker nodes running. Figure 6b depicts the results. As the workload increases for each configuration, there is a corresponding drop in throughput. The wheel configuration is less affected as there is no single bottleneck whereas each other configuration has at least one bottleneck where multiple streams meet at a CRN. The throughput is not just a factor of the workload, it is also a factor of selectivity and the number of worker nodes. Only deterministic selection queries were used in this experiment. Figure 6c shows the effects of selectivity on throughput for each configuration. The results are similar to the increase in workload, but the trees have a higher throughput since they reduce the number of tuples at each stage due to changes in selectivity.

Latency Results (Figures 6e, 6f) Figure 6e shows that the reverse tree incurs the highest latency. Again, the output node becomes the bottleneck, causing delays to compound as the number of tuples increases. The wheel configuration preforms the best since there is no delay getting data consumers. Figure 6f shows the effects on latency when the selectivity of operatiors increases. Networks that reduce the number of CRNs as data flows tend to do worse as the workload increases. This verifies that PolyStream does not incur unnecessary overheads that would not appear otherwise.

Takeaway Network configurations have an impact on the latency and throughput of PolyStream since delays compound depending on the encryption types and selectivities.

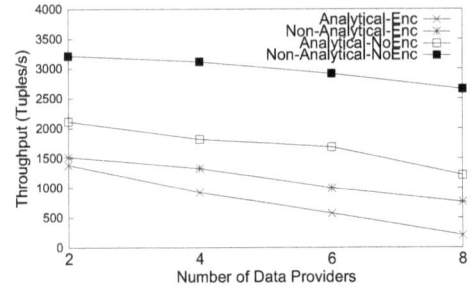

Figure 7: Effects of encrypted analytical workloads versus encrypted non-analytical workloads.

5.9 Overhead of Analytical Queries

Analytical queries can be more costly than regular queries when summation is involved. We explore these next.

Configuration For analytical queries, we used an equal mix of 100 range and summation queries. Range queries had a selectivity of 0.5. Ten queries were registered to each of ten data consumers who were assigned two per machine in a wheel pattern (see Figure 5). The same data was used for the non-analytical queries, but all query types were included to show how throughput was affected. Analytical queries were simply summations over a fixed window and filters over a fixed window, whereas non-analytical queries were equality filters and plain-text joins.

Results (Figure 7) Figure 7 shows the throughput for an analytical query-heavy workload and a non-analytical-query-heavy workload. Analytical queries must use the Paillier [28] encryption scheme, which requires large integer computations to be done on the server, resulting in the slowdown depicted in Figure 7.

Takeaway Analytical queries require multiplication of large numbers and will incur larger overheads than simpler queries.

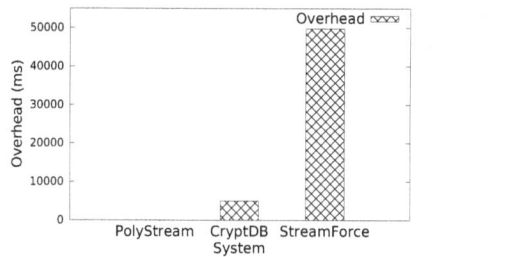

Figure 8: Comparisons between PolyStream, CryptDB (in a streaming environment), and Streamforce.

5.10 Encryption Overhead Comparisons

Configuration Here, we introduce CryptDB [29] as adapted for a streaming environment. CryptDB [29] and PolyStream utilize many of the same tools to accomplish their goals, although they were designed for very different system needs: CryptDB operates on traditional Database Management Systems, whereas PolyStream operates on DDSMSs. CryptDB's primary goal is not access control for all parties, but rather eliminating unwanted access by third-party storage systems by allowing computation over encrypted data on the untrusted third-party database. CryptDB utilizes specialized encryption techniques for allowing queries to operate on untrusted servers over encrypted data. Specifically, CryptDB employs Deterministic, Order-Preserving, Homomorphic, Specialty Search, Random, and Join encryption techniques to enable many different queries. Each technique leaks a different level of information (discussed in Section 4.3) but allows for different levels of functionality. These different techniques are structured in "Onions" in which the outer layer contains the most secure encryption technique. Removal of layers allows more functionality (i.e. going from RND to DET), but leaks some sensitive data.

When considered for use in a DDSMS, CryptDB encounters a few limitations. First, the data consumer no longer has control of the data source, meaning they do not control the encryption being used, or the accesses being given (including whether they themselves have access). This requires an online key management system as well as knowledge of what types of encryption are required for each potential data consumer, and an access control mechanism for different end users. In the system model described above, one data provider can have many data consumers digesting their data. Each data consumer may require a different level of encryption for processing.

We implemented a micro-benchmark to show the average overhead incurred by using onions in a streaming environment. This benchmark consisted of three onions (all those from CryptDB minus searches and joins) for a simple schema of four fields: Name, HeartRate, StepsTaken, and Glucose. Each field was onion-encrypted, resulting in 12 fields. Between 2 and 12 fields were chosen at random to be decrypted to a random level, for 10,000 tuples.

Results (Figure 8) The average overhead from decryption was 51.5ms per tuple for the stream adaptation of CryptDB. This means a DSMS that could handle 10,000 tuples per second would be reduced to 194 tuples per second, hindering the useful work being done by 98%, and causing an increase in encryption overhead of nearly 5,000%. These overheads and the need for an access control element limit the use of CryptDB in a streaming environment. PolyStream avoids these overheads by simply encrypting data at one level and by avoiding re-encryption. Also note that using CryptDB for a streaming application would cause greater overheads, due to a large number of insertions into the database and frequent query re-execution to

get up to the date results. Both of these overheads are not explored here.

In addition to these overheads, recall that the encryption overhead for Streamforce causes a 4,000x slowdown on an unaltered system (as claimed in [5]). Our experiments from Section 5.6 show that a workload with just 5 attributes would incur at least 49,000% overhead for every tuple. Note also that from Section 5.6, PolyStream with a relatively low policy update rate can incur as little as 12% overhead attributed to encryption, but will average roughly 56%. These overheads are displayed in Figure 8.

Takeaway PolyStream incurs very little overhead versus the closest related work.

6. CONCLUSION

Modern data streaming applications, which separate the source of data from its eventual consumer, make it difficult for data providers to author and enforce effective access controls. Access control frameworks for DDSMSs must allow data providers the ability to easily author policies, while supporting policy changes over time as the system evolves. To ensure data confidentiality from (potentially) untrusted third-party compute nodes, these policies should be enforced cryptographically, which requires an online key management system. A key challenge is enforcing these protections without incurring undue performance or utility degradation.

In this paper, we introduced PolyStream to address the above problems via cryptographically enforced access controls over streaming data. Through the use of various cryptographic schemes, PolyStream allows untrusted third-party infrastructure to compute on encrypted data, allowing in-network query processing and access control enforcement with minimal impact on system utility. PolyStream uses a combination of security punctuations, attribute-based encryption, and hybrid cryptography to enable flexible (ABAC) access control policy management and key distribution with minimal overheads. We have performed an extensive experimental evaluation on a real system (using Storm) and showed that PolyStream provides an excellent tradeoff between confidentiality and performance. Compared to the state-of-the-art, PolyStream performed up to 550x faster in our evaluation.

7. ACKNOWLEDGEMENTS

We would like to thank the anonymous reviewers and our paper shepherd, Sherman Chow, for their helpful and constructive feedback. This work was partially supported by the National Science Foundation under awards CNS-1228697, CAREER CNS-1253204, CAREER IIS-0746696, and OIA-1028162.

8. REFERENCES

[1] D. Abadi et al. The design of the borealis stream processing engine. In *CIDR*, 2005.

[2] D. J. Abadi, D. Carney, U. Çetintemel, M. Cherniack, C. Convey, S. Lee, M. Stonebraker, N. Tatbul, and S. Zdonik. Aurora: a new model and architecture for data stream management. *The VLDB Journal-The International Journal on Very Large Data Bases*, 12(2):120–139, 2003.

[3] R. Adaikkalavan and T. Perez. Secure shared continuous query processing. In *ACM SAC*, pages 1000–1005, 2011.

[4] T. Akidau, A. Balikov, K. Bekiroğlu, S. Chernyak, J. Haberman, R. Lax, S. McVeety, D. Mills, P. Nordstrom, and S. Whittle. Millwheel: fault-tolerant stream processing at internet scale. *Proceedings of the VLDB Endowment*, 6(11):1033–1044, 2013.

[5] D. T. T. Anh and A. Datta. Streamforce: outsourcing access control enforcement for stream data to the clouds. In *Proceedings of the 4th ACM conference on Data and application security and privacy*, pages 13–24, 2014.

[6] L. Aniello, R. Baldoni, and L. Querzoni. Adaptive online scheduling in storm. In *Proceedings of the 7th ACM DEBS*, pages 207–218. ACM, 2013.

[7] A. Arasu, S. Babu, and J. Widom. The cql continuous query language: semantic foundations and query execution. *The VLDB Journal—The International Journal on Very Large Data Bases*, 15(2):121–142, 2006.

[8] A. Arasu, M. Cherniack, E. Galvez, D. Maier, A. S. Maskey, E. Ryvkina, M. Stonebraker, and R. Tibbetts. Linear road: a stream data management benchmark. In *Proceedings of the Thirtieth international conference on Very large data bases-Volume 30*, pages 480–491. VLDB Endowment, 2004.

[9] S. Babu and J. Widom. Continuous queries over data streams. *ACM Sigmod Record*, 30(3):109–120, 2001.

[10] J. Benthencourt, A. Sahai, and B. Waters. Advanced crypto software collection: Ciphertext-policy attribute-based encryption. 2011.

[11] A. Boldyreva, N. Chenette, Y. Lee, and A. O'Neill. Order-preserving symmetric encryption. In *Eurocrypt*, pages 224–241. Springer, 2009.

[12] A. Boldyreva, N. Chenette, and A. O'Neill. Order-preserving encryption revisited: Improved security analysis and alternative solutions. In *Advances in Cryptology–CRYPTO 2011*, pages 578–595. Springer, 2011.

[13] B. Carminati, E. Ferrari, J. Cao, and K. L. Tan. A framework to enforce access control over data streams. *ACM Transactions on Information and System Security (TISSEC)*, 13(3):28, 2010.

[14] B. Carminati, E. Ferrari, and K. L. Tan. Enforcing access control over data streams. In *Proceedings of the 12th ACM symposium on Access control models and technologies*, pages 21–30, 2007.

[15] B. Carminati, E. Ferrari, and K. L. Tan. Specifying access control policies on data streams. In *Advances in Databases: Concepts, Systems and Applications*, pages 410–421. Springer, 2007.

[16] V. Goyal, O. Pandey, A. Sahai, and B. Waters. Attribute-based encryption for fine-grained access control of encrypted data. In *Proceedings of the 13th ACM conference on Computer and communications security*, pages 89–98, 2006.

[17] M. Green, S. Hohenberger, and B. Waters. Outsourcing the decryption of abe ciphertexts. In *USENIX Security Symposium*, 2011.

[18] S. Halevi and P. Rogaway. A tweakable enciphering mode. In *CRYPTO 2003*, pages 482–499. Springer, 2003.

[19] J. Hur and D. K. Noh. Attribute-based access control with efficient revocation in data outsourcing systems. *Parallel and Distributed Systems, IEEE Transactions on*, 22(7):1214–1221, 2011.

[20] H. V. Jagadish et al. Big data and its technical challenges. *Communications of the ACM*, 57(7):86–94, Jul 2014.

[21] S. Jahid, P. Mittal, and N. Borisov. Easier: Encryption-based access control in social networks with efficient revocation. In *Proceedings of the 6th ACM Symposium on Information,*

Computer and Communications Security, pages 411–415. ACM, 2011.

[22] X. Jin, R. Krishnan, and R. Sandhu. A unified attribute-based access control model covering dac, mac and rbac. In *Data and applications security and privacy XXVI*, pages 41–55. Springer, 2012.

[23] S. Kulkarni, N. Bhagat, M. Fu, V. Kedigehalli, C. Kellogg, S. Mittal, J. M. Patel, K. Ramasamy, and S. Taneja. Twitter heron: Stream processing at scale. In *Proceedings of the 2015 ACM SIGMOD International Conference on Management of Data*, pages 239–250. ACM, 2015.

[24] W. Lindner and J. Meier. Securing the borealis data stream engine. In *Database Engineering and Applications Symposium, 2006. IDEAS'06. 10th International*, pages 137–147. IEEE, 2006.

[25] R. Nehme, E. A. Rundensteiner, and E. Bertino. A security punctuation framework for enforcing access control on streaming data. In *IEEE 24th International Conference on Data Engineering (ICDE)*, pages 406–415, 2008.

[26] R. V. Nehme, H.-S. Lim, and E. Bertino. Fence: Continuous access control enforcement in dynamic data stream environments. In *Proceedings of the third ACM conference on Data and application security and privacy*, pages 243–254, 2013.

[27] W. S. Ng, H. Wu, W. Wu, S. Xiang, and K.-L. Tan. Privacy preservation in streaming data collection. In *Proceedings of the 2012 IEEE 18th International Conference on Parallel and Distributed Systems*, pages 810–815, 2012.

[28] P. Paillier. Public-key cryptosystems based on composite degree residuosity classes. In *Proc. of Eurocrypt*, pages 223–238, 1999.

[29] R. A. Popa, C. Redfield, N. Zeldovich, and H. Balakrishnan. Cryptdb: protecting confidentiality with encrypted query processing. In *Proceedings of the Twenty-Third ACM Symposium on Operating Systems Principles*, pages 85–100, 2011.

[30] StormProject. Storm: Distributed and fault-tolerant realtime computation. http://storm.incubator.apache.org/documentation/Home.html, 2014.

[31] N. Tatbul, U. Çetintemel, S. Zdonik, M. Cherniack, and M. Stonebraker. Load shedding in a data stream manager. In *Proceedings of the 29th international conference on Very large data bases-Volume 29*, pages 309–320, 2003.

[32] S. Tu, M. F. Kaashoek, S. Madden, and N. Zeldovich. Processing analytical queries over encrypted data. In *Proceedings of the 39th international conference on Very Large Data Bases*, pages 289–300, 2013.

[33] B. Wang, M. Li, S. S. Chow, and H. Li. A tale of two clouds: Computing on data encrypted under multiple keys. In *Communications and Network Security (CNS), 2014 IEEE Conference on*, pages 337–345. IEEE, 2014.

[34] S. Yu, C. Wang, K. Ren, and W. Lou. Attribute based data sharing with attribute revocation. In *Proceedings of the 5th ACM Symposium on Information, Computer and Communications Security*, pages 261–270. ACM, 2010.

[35] M. Zaharia, M. Chowdhury, M. J. Franklin, S. Shenker, and I. Stoica. Spark: cluster computing with working sets. In *Proceedings of the 2nd USENIX conference on Hot topics in cloud computing*, volume 10, page 10, 2010.

Author Index

www.ingramcontent.com/pod-product-compliance
Lightning Source LLC
Chambersburg PA
CBHW061406210326

41598CB00035B/6117